THE
LAST
AMERICANS
The Indian
in American
Culture

THE LAST AMERICANS

THE INDIAN IN AMERICAN CULTURE

William Brandon

McGRAW-HILL BOOK COMPANY

*New York   St. Louis   San Francisco   Düsseldorf
London   Mexico   Sydney   Toronto*

1 2 3 4 5 6 7 8 9 B P B P 7 9 8 7 6 5 4 3

Library of Congress Cataloging in Publication Data

Brandon, William
  The Last Americans

  Portions of this work were originally published
in 1961 under title The American Heritage Book of
Indians

    1. Indians.   I. Title.
E58.B814 1973   970.1   73-6956
ISBN 0-07-007201-9

Acknowledgments

Considerable portions of this book are revised from my text for *The American Heritage Book of Indians*, copyright © 1961 by the American Heritage Publishing Company; the introduction is adapted from "American Indians and American History," published in *The American West*, Spring 1965, American West Publishing Company, Palo Alto, California, copyright © 1965 by William Brandon; much of Chapter XVI is based on a series of articles, copyright © 1969, 1970, by *The Progressive* Magazine, Madison, Wisconsin (two trips back and forth across the country in connection with these articles were underwritten by a grant from the Stern Family Fund for Investigative Journalism); the postface appeared in somewhat different form in *Penthouse* Magazine for February 1973, copyright © 1973 by Penthouse International, Ltd. I take pleasure in acknowledging to all the above my grateful thanks for permission to revise and republish.

Individuals and institutions almost literally without number have been of endless help, without which, of course, no work of this kind would be possible at all. I could not thank them all singly without adding another volume to this already voluminous production; I thank them all collectively and most sincerely.

But I must add a special word of gratitude to my learned friends Wilbur R. Jacobs, Sherburne Friend Cook, and Ray A. Billington, each of whom read various pages of this manuscript and gave me excellent advice, some of which I even took; to Dr. Florence Hawley Ellis for permission to quote from her as yet unpublished manuscript on the historical relevancy of Pueblo creation myths; to Dr. George P. Hammond, Director Emeritus, and the staff of the Bancroft Library of Berkeley, California; to Dr. Carl S. Dentzel, Director, Ruth Christensen, Librarian, and the staff of the Southwest Museum, Highland Park, Los Angeles, California; and especially to Dr. James Thorpe, Director, Mary Isabel Fry, Registrar, and the staff of the Henry E. Huntington Library, San Marino, California, who have not only tolerated with excessive kindness my frequent presence there during so many years but have occasionally even acted as accessory to that situation by providing grants-in-aid.

William Brandon
Monterey, California

My children I do not know
if my singing
if my prayers
can reach the holy power

—*Pawnee, a prayer*

Contents

Introduction:
American Indians
and American History

The presence of the Indians in the history of western America, wrote James Bryce in 1887, has "done no more than give a touch of romance or a spice of danger to the exploration of some regions ... while over the rest of the country the unhappy aborigines have slunk silently away, scarcely even complaining of the robbery of lands and the violation of plighted faith."

In the early 1920s, as he approached the close of his teaching career, Frederick Jackson Turner summed up the presence of the Indians in the history of eastern America: "Between the beginning of the 17th century, when the West lay along the Atlantic coast, and 1850 when it had crossed the Mississippi ... the Indians had step by step, in successive wars, been defeated and removed. . . . Indians had influenced white development by this retardation of advance, compelling society to organize and consolidate in order to hold the frontier; training it in military discipline; determining the rate of advance, particularly at the points where the mountain barriers broke down. . . ."

Indians are traditionally viewed as natural features of the land, rather like mountains or rivers or buffalo or troublesome, if colorful, wild varmints, affecting American history only by at times impeding the civilizing progress of advancing settlers.

This traditional attitude remains overwhelmingly in evidence even though in recent years a great deal of important work has been done in local and regional Indian history, enhancing the value of basic historical contributions from earlier (and for the most part anthropological) writers such as George Bird Grinnell, J. P. Dunn, Frederick Webb Hodge, John R. Swanton, James Mooney, and others. Expert testimony of historians and anthropologists in connection with the hundreds of legal cases before the special commission for Indian claims that has been in operation since 1947 is piling up further raw material by the bale for tribal histories.

However, only a very few works have made any serious attempt to outline Indian history within the area of the United States or the entire continent, and any serious effect of Indians on American history in general has scarcely been considered. Several anthropological studies have been made of Indian influences on our culture but historians have not as yet given much shrift to any notion of effective Indian participation in our history.

Most of our history, wrote Bernard DeVoto, has been treated as if it were "a function solely of white culture—in spite of the fact that till well into the nineteenth century the Indians were one of the principal determinants of historical events. . . ." Disregarding Parkman's "great example," said DeVoto, "American historians have made shockingly little effort to understand the life, the societies, the cultures, the thinking, and the feeling of Indians, and disastrously little effort to understand how all these affected white men and their societies."

Parkman's example, though, is an example of the kind of befriending that leaves no need of enemies. His Indians are truly wild, they skulk, screech, slay with the mindless gluttony of weasels, and otherwise behave as barbarically as possible but they hardly ever (if not never) permit themselves to be seen behaving as reasonable men. A lone camper in the forest is ". . . no doubt an Indian, ambushed on the bank, watching to kill some passing enemy." Or the ferocious Iroquois are on conquest bent. "Yet it was not alone their homicidal fury that now impelled them to another war. Strange as it may seem, this war was in no small measure one of commercial advantage." Parkman summed up his judgment of Indians (in his Introduction to *The Jesuits in North America*): "It is obvious that the Indian mind has never seriously occupied itself with any of the higher themes of thought."

Parkman's persistent picture of the Indian as "man, wolf, and devil, all in one," has undoubtedly been of some consequence in rendering its subject historically ineffective. Painted savages who capered about in indecent clothes, ate nasty foods, and howled unintelligibly every time they came in sight, obviously could not have been of much more importance to the course of American history than so many grizzly bears.

But today we are not quite so confident of the self-evident superiority and manifest "progress" of our civilization. We are not even altogether confident as to who is savage and who is civilized. From the beginning of the present century anthropologists of rank have concerned themselves with the question of what is primitive and have found it very tough to answer.

A. L. Kroeber took stock of the aboriginal Australians, generally assumed to be the most primitive people available, and noted that from the point of view of a spiritual rather than a financial balance their culture was one of the most highly integrated in the world; he concluded that this marvelous integration may have been achieved rather in proportion to their voluntary renunciation of material possessions, "say somewhat on the principle of those who have riches hardly entering into the kingdom of God. But this leads us off from the question of primitiveness into something quite else. . . ." Franz Boas came to the conclusion that some of the more primitive people on earth, in the fullest sense of the word, might actually be found among aimless, valueless groups in our own modern civilized society: "Greater lack of cultural values than that found in the inner life of some strata of our modern population is hardly found anywhere."

It may be supposed at any rate that most of the people of the New World's ancient societies certainly thought of themselves as civilized. Certainly they made a conscious effort to try to live in the right way, toward what their society regarded as right and proper objectives. It would follow that in general their behavior was a product of the nature of their society, a deliberate behavior motivated by a conscious, deliberate point of view. Such peoples should be susceptible of full-scale consideration as responsible and effective agents of history.

There were a number of avenues by which the peculiarly Indian behavior of American Indians may have affected, directly or indirectly, the development of the United States and the history of the rest of the post-Columbian world. The introduction into the Old World of Indian medicines, such as quinine, or farm products, such as maize, white potatoes, chocolate, rubber, tomatoes, tobacco—in total well over half of all modern agricultural products—has been assessed time and again and need only be mentioned here. The same is true of the minor contributions of such items or complexes of items, as canoes, snowshoes, signaling systems, and the like. But there were other indirect effects of the Indian world that are extraordinarily interesting and have not been given the attention they surely merit. One was the effect of the Indian world on the changing European mind in the centuries after Columbus, most easily seen in the influence of the image of the American Indian on European notions of liberty.

From the beginning, Indians were reported to be beautifully free. Peter Martyr, the first historian of the New World, rhapsodized on the absence of deceit and pestiferous money in the Indian world, the absence of laws and quarreling judges, and even the absence of clothes, and concluded that Indians seemed to live in that golden world of which the ancients had spoken so much. This same passage appeared almost word for word in Montaigne's essay on the New World, in which he suggested the Indian world as an example of the ideal state dreamed of by Plato. The same passage then becomes Gonzalo's famous speech on the ideal commonwealth in Shakespeare's *Tempest*, written eight or nine years after the first appearance in English of Montaigne's essay.

Many travelers in the heart of America, the Indian world real before their eyes, echoed such sentiments year after year, generation after generation. These include observers of the most responsible sort, the missionary Du Tertre for a random example, writing from the Caribbean in the 1650s: ". . . they are all equal, without anyone recognizing any sort of superiority or any sort of servitude. . . . Neither is richer or poorer than his companion, and all unanimously limit their desires to that which is useful and precisely necessary, and are contemptuous of all other things, superfluous things, as not being worthy to be possessed. . . ." Or consider Father Charlevoix, the historian of New France, who wrote in 1721 of the Christian Hurons of Loretto: ". . . Savages, but they retain nothing of their Birth and Original but what is valuable; that is to say, the Simplicity and

Freedom of the first Age of the World. . . ." The missionary Lafitau in his incomparable work of ethnography first published in 1724 describes the "entire liberty" and yet beautiful dignity and "good sense" of the Iroquois. One might also include such unexpected frontier encomiums as that of Major Robert Rogers, writing of the Illinois and Missouri Indians of the 1750s: "These people of any upon earth seem blessed in this world: here is health and joy, peace and plenty: care and anxiety, ambition and the love of gold, and every uneasy passion, seem banished from this happy region. . . ."

Armchair travels to such happy lands became a literary convention in Europe. Wrote Geoffrey Atkinson, in 1920, of this body of literature, "Many travelers and missionaries had mentioned, even in the 16th century, the lack of private property among primitive peoples. Early writers had called attention to the generally happy condition of a primitive society founded upon equality and liberty. The cumulative force of such expressions in accounts of voyages published before 1700 would be a fascinating study."

Diderot summed up 250 years of such examples in an almost exact reiteration of the quoted theme from Peter Martyr, Montaigne, Shakespeare, et al.: "I am convinced that there cannot be true happiness for the human species except in a social state in which there is neither king nor magistrate nor priest nor laws nor thine nor mine nor property moveable nor real, nor vices nor virtues. . . ." Rousseau is of course the eighteenth-century climax of all this vectoring, the congealing of the Idea of the New World as liberty, equality, revolution against tyranny. He specifically credits Diderot's "counsels" as "most useful" and especially draws from Du Tertre, often word for word, but numerous other correspondents from the American Indian world of the preceding half dozen generations are audible in his perorations.

Rousseau was by no means alone in making a political symbol of the noble savage, the child of nature pure, unspoiled, and above all free (as Voltaire was by no means alone in occasionally choosing glorified Indians as heroes of plays and novels). How much Rousseau's thinking had to do with the overthrow of Europe's thrones or how much the image of the American Indian had to do with Rousseau's thinking are both eminently debatable, but the debate can only be concerned with the matter of degree. Both are undeniably present.

Present also was the Indian, real or trans-substantial, in other storms of egalitarianism that subsequently swept the world. Impressions of the Indian spirit were visible in the political societies of Revolutionary America that adopted Indian names and pseudo-Indian lodge-hall ritual. The most noteworthy of these was the Tammany Society, which devoted itself to the cause of popular liberty and federal union in the great post-Revolution contest as to what form of government the new United States should assume. The Tammany Society was a force in this struggle.

Another aspect of the Indian image was observed by Montaigne, who had talked to three Indians touring Europe and learned something of the common Indian custom of dividing a community into halves, or moieties, for ritualistic or administrative purposes. The three Indians told him they had noticed that in Europe there seemed to be two moieties consisting of the rich, "full gorged" with wealth, and the poor, starving "and bare with need and povertie." The Indian tourists not only marveled at this division, but marveled that the poor endured "such an injustice, and that they took not the others by the throte, or set fire on their house. . . ."

Columbus, returning from his first voyage, wrote of the Indians: "Nor have I been able to learn whether they held personal property, for it seemed to me that whatever one had, they all took shares of. . . . They are so ingenuous and free with all they have, that no one would believe it who has not seen it; of anything that they possess, if it be asked of them, they never say no; on the contrary, they invite you to share it and show as much love as if their hearts went with it. . . ." The negative Indian attitude toward private property and toward competition for gain was the subject of remark by countless witnesses, summed up in a concentrated understatement by Alexis de Tocqueville: "At the period when Europeans first came among them, the natives of North America were ignorant of the values of riches. . . ."

This phenomenon was so foreign to Europeans that they could not credit it even while they reported it. Indian societies socialist in character and governed, as a rule, by councils were described in terms of kingship and feudalism by the majority of authorities until a pioneer American anthropolgist, Lewis Henry Morgan, and Bandelier his prophet, exploded that point of view in the late nineteenth century. "All the grand terminology of the

Old World, created under despotic and monarchical institutions," Morgan wrote, ". . . to decorate particular men and classes of men, has been lavished . . . upon plain Indian sachems and war-chiefs, without perceiving that thereby the poor Indian was grievously wronged, for he had not invented such institutions nor formed such a society as these terms imply."

Morgan examined at length the rather propertyless Indian world in relation to modern materialistic civilization in the book that became his most influential if it was not his best—*Ancient Society.* His basic point therein, that primitive society is organized upon the basis of family ties whereas modern society is based upon property relationships, struck Karl Marx as an impressive corroboration of "the materialistic conception of history." The book was designated by Marx an important fundamental work and accordingly became a classic in socialist literature, and has circled the world in many translations. Soviet thinkers still endorse Morgan's views on social evolution, as was made clear during the VIIe Congrès International des Sciences Anthropologiques et Ethnologiques at Moscow in 1964, when a symposium devoted to Lewis Henry Morgan proved rather embarrassing to non-Soviet delegates, most of whom regard Morgan's evolutionary notions as hopelessly oversimplified and outmoded. The gist of these notions was stated by Friedrich Engels in a note to the English 1888 edition of the *Communist Manifesto,* emphasizing the classlessness of Indian society as revealed by Lewis Henry Morgan, whose "decisive discovery" led us to understand the true nature of the "gens." "With the dissolution of these primitive communities commenced the division of society into distinct classes, finally opposed . . . . "

Marx's notes on Morgan have been published in Russian, but he did not live to write the book he envisioned on Morgan's theories. Engels wrote it instead (*The Origin of the Family, Private Property, and the State*) and included yet another reading of Peter Martyr's Indian rhapsody: "No soldiers, no gendarmes or police, no nobles, kings, regents, prefects, or judges, no prisons, no lawsuits. . . . All are equal and free. . . ."

This vaunted Indian freedom may have been indeed only a persistent illusion, and certainly the testimony as to the alleged nobility of the unspoiled savage can be matched by testimony showing the unspoiled savage to be brutish, depraved, insensate, unclean, ill-mannered, impious, unregenerate in his addiction to his nasty foods and indecent clothes, and in every respect far from respectable. (Recall Mark Twain's reflections on the Gosiutes of the Utah deserts: ". . . the wretchedest type of mankind I have ever seen . . . I refer to the Goshoot Indians . . . indolent . . . prideless beggars . . . savages who, when asked if they have the common Indian belief in a Great Spirit show a something which almost amounts to emotion, thinking whisky is referred to . . . wherever one finds an Indian tribe he has only found Goshoots more or less modified by circumstances and surroundings—but Goshoots, after all. They deserve pity, poor creatures! and they can have mine—at this distance.")

But whether the freedom was illusory or not, the point is that the Indian *seemed* free, to European eyes, gloriously free, to the European soul shaped by centuries of toil and tyranny, and this impression operated profoundly on the process of history and on the development of America. Something in the peculiar character of the Indian world gave an impression of classlessness, of propertylessness, that in turn led to an impression, as H. H. Bancroft put it, of "humanity unrestrained . . . in the exercise of liberty absolute."

The basic difference between the Indian and European worlds may have been in the attitude toward property. The European way of life (with some notable exceptions) was basically one of individual competition for the acquisition of property, to the point that it would be more correct to describe white frontier expansionists as property- rather than land-hungry, to encompass the powerful forces of land and mineral speculation as well as the humble settlers content with small land-holdings.

The basic Indian attitude (also with some notable exceptions) seems to have leaned more often toward cooperation in the use of property in common, rather than competition to acquire private property. This would have helped create an appearance of classless freedom in Indian life, along with an apparent lack of striving and an emphasis on the non-material satisfactions that would result from a prevailing interest in matters other than work for profit. It might be said, in sum, that the Indian world was devoted to living while the European world was devoted to getting. This may be the essence of the Indian world and image.

This essence has been an incalculable force in American history, and was at the same time the structural weakness that made inevitable the collapse of the Indian world when it came into general conflict with a materialist civilization.

This essential difference has been a principal obstacle throughout the centuries, keeping the white and Indian worlds from direct communication, from direct understanding of each other. The word most often used by whites to describe Indians was "indolent." They would not work hard and thriftily because they simply were not sufficiently interested in acquiring property and nursing its increase—scandalous, but the Indian's gods were found at other altars. This essence of the Indian image, rendering the Indian incomprehensible but coloring him free, has wrought changes in the outlook of modern man while keeping the Indian himself, and his place in the historical process of such change, beyond the pale of understanding.

The effects of Indian participation in American history may appear wherever Indians have appeared, directly or indirectly.

The most striking direct participation is the assistance given by various Indian groups to embryonic colonies of Europeans. Massasoit and his Wampanoags were the salvation of the struggling colony of Plymouth, along with Tisquantum, who was called by Governor Bradford a "spetiall instrument sent of God for their good beyond their expectation" and by Sir Ferdinando Gorges one of "the meanes under God of putting on foote, and giving life to all our Plantations. . . ." The Wappinger people of Manhattan "preserved" the first Dutch traders "like the apple of their eye" and gave them "their Turkish beans and Turkish wheat" when the foreign invaders "sometimes had no victuals." At Jamestown Captain John Smith said of the neighboring Indians, with whom Captain Smith and his colonists had already fought, that "it pleased God (in our extremity) to move the Indians to bring us Corne, ere it was half ripe, to refresh us, when we rather expected . . . they would destroy us. . . ." Such was the weakness of the colony, said tough Captain Smith, "that had not the Indians fed us, we directly had starved. . . ." Indians taught the Jamestown people how to plant corn, and, after the strategic marriage of John Rolfe to Pocahontas, Indians taught the Englishmen how to raise tobacco. This gave the colony a cash crop and its first profit, and the appearance of the eagerly awaited profit entrained vast and enduring consequences for all English North America.

Commonly, in the earliest days of exploration and colonization, first arrivals were greeted with friendliness rather than with hostility: ". . . being of simple faith, the natives evinced for Collomba tenderness and friendship. . . ." reported a foreign agent at the Spanish court, sending out the first news of

Columbus' discovery. Jacques Cartier landed on an island in the St. Lawrence in 1535 and "met with five men, that were hunting of wild beasts, who as freely and familiarly came to our boats without any fear, as if we had ever been brought up together . . . one of them took our captain in his arms, and carried him on shore. . . ." Alvar Nuñez Cabeza de Vaca, traveling alone as a sea-shell peddler among Texas coast Indians who had probably never before seen a white man, this being circa 1529, wrote: "With my merchandise and trade I went into the interior as far as I pleased . . . Wherever I went I received fair treatment. . . ."

Accounts of early explorers furnish almost at random such passages as: "Food was placed before them, and, as the Illinois code of courtesy enjoined, their entertainers conveyed the morsels with their their own hands to the lips of these unenviable victims of their hospitality while others rubbed their feet with bear's grease. . . ."; or of the Arkansas: "I cannot tell you the civility and kindness we received from these barbarians. . . ."; or among the people of the Hasinai Confederacy: ". . . a tribe then powerful but long since extinct. Nothing could surpass the friendliness of their welcome. . . ."; or among the Sioux, where old men welcomed a stranger with caresses and tears. Alvar Nuñez Cabeza de Vaca also spoke of weeping in welcome: "They have a custom when they meet, or from time to time when they visit, of remaining half an hour before they speak, weeping, . . ."

Wrote Castañeda of the buffalo-hunting people of the plains he saw in 1541 who centuries later were to become the fearsome Apaches: "They are a gentle people, not cruel, faithful in their friendship. . . ." Said Raleigh's envoy Captain Barlow in 1584 of the Virginia people among whom ill-fated Roanoke was established the following year: ". . . most gentle, loving, faithful, void of all guile and treason, and such as live after the manner of the golden age. . . ."

The policy of the various Indian peoples, in these first meetings between two strange worlds, was obviously a vital factor in the success of colonies and exploration. When in these early relations the Indians became opposed to the foreigners, colonies or trading posts or missions could not as a rule survive. But since many colonies and trading posts and missions did survive and prosper, it seems probable that many Indian groups may indeed have welcomed the foreigners with more benevolence than belligerence, particularly during the crucial seasons of first meetings and first foundings.

The varying policy in this regard of the various Indian peoples could scarcely derive from any imposed outside control. Manipulation of the simple Indians by the Europeans has sometimes been stressed and may have been of moment now and then, but it seems unlikely that it could have been very often very weighty in the earlier centuries when the balance of power and consequent occasion for initiative was extravagantly on the side of the Indians. The weightiness of this factor is sometimes questionable even in later times, as in the interesting case of Pierre Vial, a champion frontiersman sent north from Santa Fe in 1805 in the employ of Spain to stir up the Plains Indians against Lewis and Clark. Vial couldn't get his own expedition out his own front door, so to speak, being stopped by hostile Indians (apparently Pawnees) at the Arkansas River. He tried again, in vain again, while the inexperienced Lewis and Clark were successfully passing through dozens of Indian nations all the way to the Pacific.

Other factors in early Indian behavior may have been, at one time or another, desire for trade or for knowledge of new things or fear of new things, domestic political conditions or relations with rival communities, the season of the year, the state of the corn crop, heavenly signs and portents, religious laws, any of the multifarious motives that bear on human conduct, especially on the group conduct in social and political actions. These factors and these political decisions were of import in our history and deserve thoroughgoing study, but the point is not simply this. The point is also that they all refer to other prevailing factors that must always be considered, the underlying attitudes and ways of life of the societies making up the Indian world, the attitudes and ideas that shaped the nature of those societies and the character of their people.

If there was a tendency for Indians to welcome foreign invaders with more benevolence than otherwise, this is important. At most it might indicate that the Europeans were invading what was in a sense a higher civilization. At least it is an indication of New World character that appears to deviate considerably from the more customary and familiar Old World character. The question of how much this peculiar Indian behavior had to do with the health and growth of the nursling colonies and their later careers of conquest takes on still more significance.

Africa was invaded for centuries by the same Europeans, but colonies their remained for the most part stunted enclaves walled in by rigid frontiers. Today the majority of those colonies have vanished and Africa is largely in the hands of its natives. Is it impossible to imagine a similar history for America if, among other changed circumstances, American Indians had behaved differently? Such a comparision, of course, convokes a very large cast of causes. The intention here is scarcely to claim that differences in the behavior of the natives played the sole or even necessarily a principle role in accounting for differences in the colonial histories of Africa and America. But it is the intention here to suggest that one of the identifiable roles may, on sufficient investigation, go to the peculiar character of the American Indian world.

When the Indian world was moved to resist, it could become a world most difficult to penetrate and conquer. Scattered bands of Apaches and their even more scattered allies declined to permit secure occupation of their country by foreigners for more than two centuries, enduring volumes of epic warfare and several earnest attempts at extermination by Europeans allied with other Indian nations. The Jibaros of Ecuador and Peru drove out Spanish colonists in the sixteenth century and have not accepted colonization of their country even yet. In the closing years of the seventeenth century French armies and allied Indians mounted repeated invasions that should have utterly smashed, but did not, the Five Nations Iroquois. In the middle years of the eighteenth century the French staged repeated full-scale campaigns against the Chickasaws and were repeatedly defeated. These two French failures played their part in the ultimate defeat of France in the New World. Some Indian conquests thought of as facile were, in actuality, not. The conquest of the Aztec state in Mexico required, even after the capture and death of Moctezuma, a year of desperate campaigning and embattled power diplomacy and the final bitterly fought months-long siege of Tenochtitlan, the Aztec Mexico City, surrounded by the Spaniards and their "numberless" Indian allies. The conquest of Peru required, even after the capture and death of the Inca, a long generation of tangled wars to end organized military resistance. The Spaniards were lavishly assisted in these wars by many Indian allies, but even so they came within an ace of total defeat in Manco Inca's great war raised against them in 1536.

Superior European tactics and arms notwithstanding, an intact Indian nation could be a formidable opponent to overthrow by force alone, even with the help of Indian allies. Without such Indian allies, invasions by blunt force were often if not usually disastrous. Such were the first large-scale invasions of Panama, which cost hundreds of Spanish lives and ended in utter defeat, until Vasco Nuñez de Balboa paved the way to victory with powerful Indian friends. In short, strictly military conquest in the New World was seldom easy, and seemed to have veritable need of Indian help to succeed at all.

If American conquest was this difficult, and since nevertheless it was accomplished, even against heavy numerical and logistical odds, the existence of factors other than the strictly military would certainly seem to be implied.

Presumptive among such factors, again, would be attitudes and ideas, fears and desires, foolishness and philosophies, founded upon the peculiar character of the Indian peoples.

The customary pattern of American conquest was for the initial penetration to be made by guile, diplomacy, or in response to open Indian invitation, as has been mentioned. Once pierced or broken, an Indian society, like any other, was naturally more inclined to fall to any sort of conquest. In most such conquests, Indians also played a part, sometimes a major part, as allies leagued with the conquerors.

Indian activity as auxiliaries of various European powers in their wars against each other was likewise of considerable magnitude in the multitude of North American conflicts, great and small, through the War of 1812. Indian activity as trade allies of various colonial powers was sometimes of decisive importance in the course of colonial affairs. It is unlikely that the position of organized Indian communities in these activities was always or even usually one of vassals under the control of their white associates. Too many events testify to the independence of Indian action.

The French were as a rule extraordinarily canny and persuasive in Indian dealings (". . . practice therein," urged Edmond Atkin in proposing to the British Lords of Trade his Indian policy of 1755, "the same little ingratiating Arts as the French do. . . ."), but the catastrophic war waged against them in 1729 by the Natchez, who had been sound friends, damaged the French severely in Louisiana. At about the same time, in the Great Lakes country, the French were seriously hurt by the Fox wars. The stubborn neutrality, and sometimes hostility, of the Five Nations Iroquois was a baffling problem to the French in

Canada for more than a century. French inability to solve this problem or to wipe the Iroquois out of the way had its effect, as previously mentioned, on the final fate of France in North America.

Spanish traders, missionaries, colonial officials, and soldiers had more experience with Indians than all other Europeans combined and much more permanent success than other Europeans in altering Indian manners and ways. And yet the Spanish world was rejected by not only the aforementioned Jibaros and Apaches but also by (among many others) the highly cultured Pawnees. The destruction of the Villasur expedition in 1720 by Pawnees was a blow to Spanish dominion of the Plains country east of the Rockies. The Yuman-speaking Quechan (then known as the Yumas) had been sound Spanish friends, but in 1781 (the year of the founding of Los Angeles) they destroyed Spanish farms and outposts that had been established at the "Yuma towns" on the Colorado River, and closed the overland trail to California, thereby rendering more remote and precarious than ever—and therefore a riper plum for eventual U.S. conquest—the struggling new California missions and settlements. Another overland route was not established for commercial caravans until 1830. The Apalachee people of Florida were famous fighters in the sixteenth-century days of the earliest Spanish explorers, but accepted, in fact are said to have requested, Spanish missionaries in the seventeenth century. After some fifteen years the Apalachees rebelled against mission rule, defeated a Spanish force sent to subdue them, and then reversed themselves "apparently through a counterrevolution in the tribe itself" and returned to the Spanish fold.

The Creeks generally refused Spanish overtures, although there were at times strong pro-Spanish factions in some of the Lower Creek towns. Together with allied Indians and, eventually, English slavers and traders from Carolina, the Creeks fought sporadically with the missionized Apalachee, and in a great raiding party of 1704, composed of fifty English volunteers and one thousand Creeks, destroyed the flourishing Apalachee missions, permanently impairing Spainish strength in the Southeast.

Creeks welcomed English colonists in Georgia and gave them every assistance. Creeks, Cherokees, Chickasaws, and some of the Choctaw towns gave alliance to the English on many occasions that were of value to the English and of pronounced effect on the history of the region. Iroquois partiality for the English at critical moments had its effect on the history of the Northeast. But Pontiac's partiality for the defeated French threw the West into a turmoil that was ultimately of heavy cost to the British and of some effect on the history of the American Revolution: William Christie MacLeod, in *The American Indian Frontier,* wrote that the "Indian policy of the Crown did more than anything else, to alienate the borderers from loyalty to the Crown, and led the frontiersmen to throw their weight on the side of sedition in the forthcoming struggle between constituted government and rebellion. . . . Turbulence on the border was continual from 1765 to 1775 when the torch of rebellion was lifted."

Delawares who had been dispossessed by fraudulent shenanigans between Pennsylvania and the Iroquois and land speculators became the hard core of the "French" Indians at Fort Duquesne who helped ruin Braddock in 1755. But other Delawares in Pennsylvania insisted on the risky peacemaking journey of the Moravian missionary Christian Post, in 1758, whose success with the quondam French Indians on the Ohio was such that Fort Duquesne fell to the English without a fight. Pennsylvania's inability to carry out the terms of Indian agreements made at this time no doubt contributed a glowing coal or so to Pontiac's war, as the British government's efforts to live up to agreements forced by Pontiac's war provided some sparks for sedition.

"American" Creeks and allied Yuchis and Cherokees bore a fair share of the fighting and the casualties against anti-American "Red Stick" Creeks in the Battle of Horseshoe Bend—the victory that first brought Andrew Jackson national recognition. The determined friendliness of the Northern Shoshonis and the Nez Perces for Americans from the time of Lewis and Clark to Chief Joseph's gentlemanly war seventy years later was of moment in the settlement of the Northwest; the results of this friendliness are easier to analyze than its origins.

Examples could be added ad infinitum. Many of these Indian actions simply will not fit any interpretation of Europeans dominating the policies and decisions of the Indians with whom they associated. Nor will the infinite variety of circumstances bear out easy notions of simple primitive diplomacy—of whites controlling Indian actions at one remove merely by overawing them with shows of force or winning their favor with trinkets and trade.

European tutelage in both warfare and trade is obvious in post-Columbian Indian history, but white efforts to influence Indian policies and decisions cannot be reckoned the dominant factors in most such decisions any more than France or Germany can be shown to have controlled historically the policies of each other or even of such lightweight colleagues as the Swiss Confederation.

We are accustomed to thinking of the Spanish and "their" Indians, the French and "their" Indians, and so on, but Indian nations doubtless thought of "their" European colonies and "their" European business connections and military allies in much the same way, and connived and intrigued to get the support of this or that European community for their own sovereign projects—projects certainly sovereign in their own plans and intentions, at least. Sir William Johnson, England's enormously successful superintendent of Indian affairs in the northern colonies, remarked that ". . . many mistakes arise here from erroneous accounts formerly made of Indians; that they have been represented as calling themselves subjects, although the very word would have startled them had it ever been pronounced by an interpreter. They desire to be considered as allies and friends, and such we may make them at a reasonable expense and thereby occupy our outposts and carry on trade in safety until, in a few years, we shall become so formidable throughout the country as to be able to protect ourselves and abate of that charge. . . ." Edmond Atkin, England's superintendent for Indian affairs in the southern colonies, wrote at about the same time, in the 1750s: "No people in the World understand and pursue their true National Interest, better than the Indians. . . . in their public Treaties no People on earth are more open, explicit, and Direct. Nor are they excelled by any in the observance of them." Atkin also recommends ". . . above all, to begin with building Forts in their hearts . . . after which we may build Forts wherever we please."

The shape of the Indians' own sovereign thoughts, to repeat, was drawn from the underlying attitudes and ways of life of the Indian world. These attitudes pervade Indian history. Indian attitudes toward war, for instance, naturally had a direct bearing on the outcome of various Indian wars. Most Indian societies appeared to look to matters other than war as the principal objectives of their organization, and in the midst of war could give fighting a back seat to religious ceremonies, or, like the classic Greeks, could be swayed in their battle strategy by omens; white communities were usually organized much more effectively for sustained war. War in the Old World definition seems, on the best evidence, to have been an almost unknown concept in the untouched Indian world of North America. There is little indication of whole countries being overrun by war. The raids that were called wars usually involved only a fraction of the available fighting men and those only briefly. Utterly defeated nations were assimilated rather than annihilated. Speaking of the Indian state most highly organized for warfare of any in North America—the Aztecs—Bandelier wrote: ". . . a military body doing permanent duty, [was] unknown to the Mexicans . . . only unarmed Indians met Cortés on his entrance to Mexico . . . no 'guard' came to Montezuma's rescue. . . ." Military forces based on Indian attitudes toward organization for war could not usually maintain strength in the field over a long period, thus a clear-cut Indian victory could only come from a clear-cut knockout; a decision on points would mean a negotiated truce, after which the Indian armies would melt away home, leaving the Europeans (with their permanent military establishments) to interpret and enforce the truce terms as they saw fit—this was quite often the upshot in Indian wars with Europeans.

Indian attitudes toward land ownership were of momentous effect on relations with Europeans. The control of specific territories by communities or families was a familiar concept to many Indian societies, but private ownership or private buying and selling of land was outside most Indians' experience. Above all, the common European ambition to own a landed personal estate as the most desired symbol of success was to most Indian people as incomprehensible as would have been an ambition to own the sky. The free and easy Indian land policies that were for centuries a central issue of Indian "troubles" are related to such basic attitudes. The United States Court of Claims, in an opinion of 1893 later sustained by the Supreme Court, stating that "Apart from the Indian tribes, communal property is with us a thing unknown. . . ." held that each member of the Indian community has an "absolute and complete" right of actual ownership. "Chiefs and headmen" have no authority to dispose of these rights, and even a majority of the tribe or community has no authority to sell the communal property, which would seem to constitute (said the Court), "taking away the property of the minority and disposing of it without their consent." The Court specifically remarked, of this matter so difficult for the Old World mind to grasp, "It is, indeed, not improbable that many of our troubles with the Indian tribes have sprung from the fact that our treaty-making commissioners and agents were ignorant of its nature, and of the fact that all Indian lands were communal property."

Indian influence on the movement of frontiers is another example of direct Indian participation in American historical processes. Very few if any frontiers, especially before 1800, were opened without the prior consent, if not the invitation, of at least some of the Indian peoples concerned. The Ohio River country of eastern Tennessee and parts of present West Virginia and Kentucky were largely uninhabited by the Indians, and regarded as an open domain, not under the dominion of any Indian nation, until shattered remnants of Delawares, Shawnees, Hurons, Kickapoos, and others drifted into the region during the eighteenth century. It is not surprising that this country became a political football for these Indian refugee groups and for powerful nations in the background such as the Six Nations Iroquois and the Cherokee. Indian political maneuvers carried out for Indian purposes and objectives were vital in opening this no man's land to white settlement—the earliest trans-Appalachian English settlements.

Once established, the white frontier became very much a force in itself, but even so continued for some time to depend rather more than less on Indian actions and decisions. The Kentucky Shawnees who were goaded into Lord Dunmore's War in 1774 were first abandoned to this fate by the Cherokee and by most of the Iroquois, an abandonment that permitted Lord Dunmore's high-handed course of action. The devious reasons behind these Indian decisions are perhaps as important to our history as Governor Dunmore's devious motives, but have received considerably less attention. The objection is customarily brought that materials are lacking for studying these or other Indian decisions, although, as mentioned earlier, new materials are appearing in ever-increasing amounts. But the need at this moment seems to be less for new materials than for a more serious approach to already extant materials. Existing materials of course include the mountainous literature of archaeology and ethnology; historians who would consider Indian participation in American history as the participation of reasonable and politic peoples worthy of serious attention would presumably wish to become fluent in anthropology just as scholars of ancient history study ancient languages. At present the anthropologists are doing most of the rapproching, with a growing interest in historical relevance, an interest at times reaching a degree that would have been regarded as downright frivolous only a few years ago.

The progress of North American frontiers, particularly in their earlier phases, was very possibly as much the result of Indian policies and attitudes as of white policies and pressures. Direct Indian influences gradually diminished, obviously, with each passing century, although areas of some importance still appear in the nineteenth century, as witness the aforesaid encounters with the Shoshoni and Nez Perce.

Direct white contact was not always the agency responsible for the shattering or transformation of Indian nations in the path of the white frontiers. A major aspect of the movement of frontiers was the purely Indian shock wave running ahead of the actual white frontiers, sometimes many years and many hundreds of miles ahead. Indian groups in contact with Europeans, stimulated by revolutionizing ideas and tools and weapons, hurled themselves into conflict or revolutionizing trade with other Indian groups who may never have seen white men. The resultant disruptions affected the subsequent movement of white frontiers. The earliest frontiers did not move in response to European settlement but as a result of the military or commercial aggressions of Indian nations who, in effect, had the bomb first—which is to say, who were in touch with Europeans. There were, in other words, two networks of frontiers, one strictly Indian, the other, often profoundly influenced by the kinetics of the first, European. The far-reaching conquests of the Iroquois and the farther reaching consequences therefrom are a familiar example of this Indian-versus-Indian frontier in operation.

Further, the Indian-versus-Indian frontier is amenable to still more delicate divisions, such as the horse frontier and the gun frontier, both traveling without benefit of white companionship. The horse frontier rolled across the West from New Mexico far in advance of most white traders and sometimes as much as a century and a half in advance of tangible white frontiers, reaching the Northern Shoshonis in the 1690s or even earlier. Shoshoni horsemen were terrorizing their earthbound

Blackfoot enemies by the 1730s. The gun frontier, moving from the east, reached the Great Plains at about the same time. The convulsions of these several Indian-versus-Indian frontiers sent reverberations rolling in all directions, changing in myriad ways the Indian world and thus affecting in myriad ways the setting and the course of American history—in areas where white men had never yet set foot. Obviously these frontiers moved only because Indians moved them, only Indians being present.

The whys and wherefores of the Indian actions are matters of many complexities. There were marked differences between the attitudes and behavior of intact Indian nations and the attitudes and behavior of scattered bands of broken nations. Very often it was the latter who represented the faceless "Indian tribes" in our frontier stereotypes—as in the conglomeration of refugees, migrants, and malcontents who made up the enemy Indians in Lord Dunmore's War, or the motley armies of displaced persons commanded by Pontiac. There were great differences also between the various Indian nations or groups, and great differences between the people of the same nation or group in different epochs.

A principal difficulty in treating Indian history in depth is its fragmentation. The task of examining each tribal group and each time-phase of each group and of conducting this investigation partly in such other languages as anthropology is forbidding. The Indian reality was of an astonishing diversity, a diversity that presents a constant problem in any wide-angle view of the American Indian. For example, there is a widespread notion that Indians never punished their children, which seems to have been true for many Indian groups. But Creeks and Aztecs, for two, were resounding exceptions. Tattooing, so common among Indians as to seem nearly universal, was never practiced by the Hopi or by the Aztecs or by the Yahgans at the tip of South America. The general impression that farming, among Indians, was woman's work is generally correct for the eastern woodlands of North America, but among the Pueblos and in the great agricultural states of Mexico men did most of the farm work. Some Indians were fierce and quarrelsome, some were more gentle and peaceable than Quakers, some were taciturn, some were jolly and voluble, some were wildly emotional, some were as reserved as well-brought-up Englishmen. These are only a few of the many, many significant differences among the various Indian peoples, countless differences variously reflected in the various Indian actions. Indian history is far from easy.

Fluctuations in the white point of view down through the centuries are also important. For a highly consequential example, Indians who had been for generations town-dwelling farmers, as were the majority of North American Indians, came to be characterized as raggle-taggle nomads, interested only in keeping their lands as "hunting grounds," which of course made it easier to justify seizure of the lands. Indians who had been thought of as first-class soldiers during the seventeenth and eighteenth centuries came to be pictured later as childlike primitives supposedly unable, for instance, even under circumstances that solved for a time the usual Indian problem of sustained organization and supply, to conduct a military siege of more than a few days—even though Pontiac's siege of Fort Pitt and Red Cloud's investiture of the Powder River road are among the longer sieges in all American history. Criteria of barbarism have rung through many changes; barbaric to the Victorian mind was the previously mentioned spared rod, resulting in the "unbridled and unruly children" that Parkman listed along with fleas and no privacy as among the chief annoyances of "savage" life. The nineteenth-century historian Henry M. Brackenridge, after a visit to the Missouri River Indians in 1811, wrote, "One thing I remarked as constituting the great difference between the savage and the civilized state, *their youth undergo no discipline. . . .*" (his italics). A missionary found the Opatas of the 1760s retained in the slough of heathenism by, among other things, a skepticism that made them say only, "Perhaps thou speakest truth," to any asserted fact they hadn't seen with their own eyes. "Until the ministering Father is able to banish this phase from his neophytes they cannot have the faith required by the infallible authority of God and Church. . . ."

There are innumerable other areas of possible Indian historical influence, some rather likely, some rather tenuous. The federation of the United Colonies of New England in 1643, for example, was the first union of English settlements in America, and came not only as a result of the Pequot war but possibly in some imitation of the many Indian confederacies—which appear to have been the typical supra-tribal states in aboriginal North America. The first formal intercolonial conference outside New England was held in 1684 at Albany, at the urging of the Iroquois and to meet with Iroquois spokesmen. The six most important colonies met in 1754 with the object of working out a plan of colonial union; these delegates also met in Albany, where for so many years by that time delegates from the several colonies had been gathering to meet with the Iroquois. The prevalent Indian institution of government by council (most Indian chiefs were inventions of Europeans) may have been one of the various factors contributing to the form of modern American republics.

Or the amalgam of tribal identity and corporate structure now appearing in some hypermodern Indian societies may foreshadow future forms of mainstream American society. Or, at the opposite end of the spectrum, effects of the subtlest sort may be ascertainable—scars on the American soul, perhaps—from acts of more or less open conspiracy and persecution, as in extremist anti-Indian policies carried out in Mississippi, Alabama, Georgia, and Texas. Or hitherto unexpected links may be discovered between the Indian image and modern views of art, philosophy, or morals. Or studies of Indian attitudes based on a prevailing interest in matters other than work for profit may have something to offer in visions of a future anticipating an immense technological unemployment. A modern economist writes, in speculating on this future: "What takes the place of wages in a workless society? . . . Does profit remain a useful standard of accounting in a propertyless society? . . . The wampum hoard that confers prestige in one culture becomes the potlatch of another. . . ." Or Indian studies may bear on the future in a different direction in the view of the late Benjamin Lee Whorf, whose analysis of Hopi languages led him to wonder if those American Indian languages which represent the world "not in the form of separate object-things (sky, hill, swamp, etc.)" but as a unity might not open "the way to possible new types of logical thought and new methods of perceiving the universe. . . ."

The important point is that the Indian world may really have been a genuine, influential civilization worth taking seriously in American history. It may really have been a civilization so firmly committed to its strange attitudes that it nourished its own conquerors and abetted its own conquest. It may really have been a civilization so incomprehensibly foreign to Europeans that Europeans could not recognize its existence even while in mortal embrace with it, somewhat as in the case of the "dark planets" imagined by Alfred North Whitehead that move on a scale of space and time so radically different from our own as to be undetectable to our sense and instruments. And finally it may have been a civilization affecting not only our past but still to affect our future.

Within this still-unexplored civilization, said Pierre Teilhard de Chardin, "some general and fundamental laws in human development are certainly hiding. . . ."

From the collision of this New World civilization with the Old, the modern world, and particularly modern America, was born. Without the Indian side of that story its history is only half written.

I
The Daybreak
People

In the first days of men the world was new, and it really was. It seems to be sober scientific fact that the world was veritably remade in the geologic era preceding the coming of man. Flowers appeared, and songbirds, and hardwood trees. The marsh and mud landscape over which the giant reptiles had crawled was transformed into mountains, lakes, streams, flower-strewn meadows, and forests that turned from green to golden with each passing summer. The earth was bejeweled with colors, grandeurs, and beauties great and small it had never known before. Into this setting mankind was born.

The half of this new-made Eden waiting in the Western Hemisphere remained untouched for hundreds of thousands of years, according to present evidence, while thousands of generations of the earliest ape men and men of the Old Stone Age roamed the other continents.

No race of these earliest men seems to have originated in the Americas. Fossil forms of anthropoid apes, or of the superapes which apparently set the stage for the emergence of man in Europe, Asia, and Africa, have never been found in the New World. No American skeletal remains of archaic human figures, no beastlike Australopitheci, no manlike Pithecanthropi, not even any all-but-modern Neanderthals, have yet been discovered. All the ancient human bones thus far brought to light in the Americas have been accepted by most experts as those of modern man in his present form, Homo sapiens.

Homo sapiens' precursors, the heavy-headed people of the Old Stone Age, are estimated to have begun fashioning their earliest fist-axes more than a million years ago. But the first appearance of Homo sapiens himself is usually estimated to date back less, and possibly considerably less, than 100,000 years ago.

At some unknown time and place after the development of Homo sapiens, the first forebears of the American Indians entered the still untouched New World.

The where and when of that entrance has excited a good deal of guesswork. In a more innocent age, when Archbishop Ussher's date for the creation of the earth (4004 B.C. at nine o'clock of a Friday morning) was still printed as a learned footnote in Bible margins, the American Indians were suspected of being Egyptians, Phoenicians, Greeks, Romans, Chinese, Japanese, Welsh, Irish, or descendants of the Lost Ten Tribes of Israel, or of having made their way to the Americas via a lost continent of Atlantis or a lost continent of Mu, or both.

It is now known that the American Indians are far more ancient than any of these candidates. Finds have been made proving the presence of man in America at the time of such Ice Age big game as camels, mammoths, giant ground sloths, and primitive horses—in other words during the last of the Pleistocene glaciations, the last great Ice Age, which drew to a close some 10,000 years ago. Even that remote data is being pushed back still farther into the past.

These dates can be given with a fair amount of assurance, long ago as they are, due to present techniques of radiocarbon dating, a system of archaeological dating that can sometimes provide almost calendar accuracy. This method was first developed using laboratory tests of organic substances to compute the residue of a radioactive isotope of carbon designated as carbon 14. Carbon 14 is present in fixed proportions in most living organisms, and disintegrates at a constant measurable rate after the death of its host. It thus acts as an atomic clock of sorts, pinpointing the age of the substance tested with a precision only limited by the exactness of the measurement. Other even more sensitive variations of this technique have been worked out, and the precision attained is quite remarkable, often within a margin of error of only a few hundred years out of many thousand.

These radiocarbon dates are not always infallible, but enough have accumulated, in conjunction with other archaeologic and geologic evidence, to place man unshakably in America well before 10,000 years ago, and probably before 20,000 years ago; certainly before the end of the last glacial period. Some eivdence even indicates dates of more than 30,000 years ago.

And the wind blows steadily toward a still more distant dawn. Blood-group studies of living Indians have recorded the purest O groups in the world, the purest B group in the world, and the only known populations entirely lacking A. In general American Indians are type O and distinctly separate from the A-groups of Asiatic Mongoloids who should have been presumably their most ancient neighbors. An eminent geographer concludes that the basic peopling of the Americas may have taken place "before the primordial blood streams of man became mingled."

One thing is obvious: if the American Indians can claim direct descent from those early people of 10,000 to 20,000 years ago, and some undoubtedly can, then they are the oldest known race on earth. There is no evidence of the identifiable appearance of any of the other modern races, Mongolian, white, or Negro, until much later.

Time is the tonic chord in the story of the Indian.

With this sort of antiquity, it is clear the first Indians must have arrived long before there were boats anywhere capable of ocean crossings. The only place of entry more or less accessible by land from the Old World was Alaska at Bering Strait, separated from northeastern Asia by less than sixty miles. Two steppingstone islands, the Diomedes, break the water distance into still shorter stages, the longest only twenty-five miles. At times, furthermore, the Strait is frozen over and can be crossed on the ice; at times in the geologic past it has been dry land—more often than has the Isthmus of Panama. Mongoloid characteristics of some Indians, implying an origin in later Asia, corroborate the proposition of a long-used Bering Strait entry, which is so universally agreed upon by present-day authorities that it is scarcely regarded as a theory any longer but as established fact.

But entrance via the North, before 10,000 years ago, collides with those Pleistocene glaciations which sheathed the shoulders of the earth in ice and may thereby have barred any migrations. Either the first people came between glaciations or a way must be found for them through the ice. Both are feasible.

There were four major Pleistocene glaciations, each enduring for many thousands of years, separated by interglacial periods that lasted even longer when the climate probably became much as it is today—we are supposedly living in one such interglacial period now. The last great glacial advance, known in America as the Wisconsin stage, is believed to have lasted some 60,000 years before its final retreat some 10,000 years ago; geologists nowadays divide this into five or six substages of heavy glaciation separated by "interstadial" periods of glacial ebb and warmer times, each of these divisions extending through thousands of years.

—The periods of glacial flow may have been distinguished by unimaginable rains and snows rather than unimaginable cold. The seas were lowered many feet by the volume of water turned into snow and ice, and the weight of the ice warped and buckled the crust of the land. Beaches and islands existed that are now ocean floor. At times during this glaciation Bering Strait may well have been a broad grass-grown plain—geologists suggest 26,000 to 28,000 years ago as the beginning of such a period, which lasted for perhaps 15,000 years.

These tremendous changes drove animals and plants from one part of the world to another, and where there were people they must have been driven also, even though so slowly they knew not that they moved. Each such tremendous change took many centuries if not millennia to come about, immemorial multitudes of generations to short-lived prehistoric men.

Most of Alaska was ice-free during the glacial periods—the glaciers did not spread from the North Pole but radiated in all directions from centers in the latitude of Hudson Bay. Most of Siberia was icebound, apparently, with the possible exception of occasional valleys and the farthest North.

Perhaps the first human beings to drift from Siberia into Alaska were thrust along by these conditions, ice slowly smothering Siberia behind them, Alaska's sweeping valleys imperceptibly filling up with refugee game ahead of them. Or perhaps they first came during an iceless interglacial period, following only the ineluctable gradient of time. Time, enough time, can herd along people unaided; it doesn't need an assist from discernible motives of man.

Movement southward from Alaska during stages of glacial

flows would have been limited. For some 7,000 years or so, after about 20,000 to 23,000 years ago, Canada generally was covered with plateaus of ice as much as 10,000 feet high. But there may still have remained a few possible routes. For a period of several thousand years, in the early middle of the Wisconsin, an ice-free corridor hundreds of miles wide ran along the eastern shadow of the Rockies all the way from the Arctic to the open country south of Canada. Several thousand years later another passage was open for a time through the Alberta-Saskatchewan plains east of the Rockies. Wanderers from Alaska could have reached them by way of the Alaskan north coast and the Mackenzie River valley—these areas were never glaciated. Several thousand years after that, in the last life of the Wisconsin, passable travel might have been managed via the Yukon and the Peace and the Liard River valleys of northwestern Canada.

The first passage mentioned appears to have been the only one open early enough to get the first man down into the continent in time to occupy the sites archaeologists are dating for him—if even that will do. If not, we will be forced to assume that the first American appeared some time in the long ice-free period known as the Sangamon interglacial that preceded the Wisconsin.

After that, any Ice Age routes later open could have been and probably were used by later peoples. The gradual populating of the Americas went on for a very long time and involved various groups of differing physical types. Mankind's dawdling and discursive march from Bering Strait to Tierra del Fuego may easily have taken, as a German geographer has calculated, something like 25,000 years.

Probably the view back through time to the childhood of man can only be seen in distortion. The world becomes a still picture when it was alive with motion, or it moves when it was as still as eternity.

The ice sheets of the glacial "movement" did not come and go as far as men living among them were concerned—they had always been there, the white lands beyond and beyond, and the tumbling cliffs of rotting ice along the edges, snarled with sodden vegetation; they were as permanent as mountains, and the countless lakes as permanent as the Great Lakes of today. The mammoths had not "migrated" from Asia with their mastodont ancestors—they had always been there, filling the forests with giant screams; the horses and camels were not "migrating" from

Asia but had always been there, racing in herds over the rain-swept tundra, and a man's mother's mother's mother could tell how they had always been there in her day.

There is no reason to suppose that men of such times were consciously undertaking great migrations; they were only living, and very likely this valley or that had always been home until eventually some families found themselves spending more time in the valley across the ridge, and that became in turn forever home.

"Anything seems possible that is not immediately necessary," wrote the philosopher J. H. Klaren, and the reverse is equally true; given enough time, anything is possible. Lands are remade, beasts become men, and men become strangers to their fathers.

The drift of the first population may have followed the Rockies and the Andes as principal north-south axes down into the two continents. From the eastern flanks of the Rockies people may have moved westward through South Pass to the Great Basin, eastward along the rivers leading to the Mississippi, westward around the southern heel of the Rockies to the pluvial lakes then watering what is now the desert of the lower Colorado, and on from this region to southern California, the Northwest Coast not being reached until much later.

In South America the hypothetical spread of the first population may have threaded down within the Andes from Venezuela to Bolivia, a center for subsequent penetration southward and eastward.

A few scholars have thought they detected linguistic, morphological, and ethnological relationships between certain South American Indians and Australian aborigines, and have wondered about prehistoric travel from Australia via the Antarctic. Since this would seem to have necessitated a champion ocean trip, most experts don't take the notion too seriously. The Aleutian Islands have been offered as another possible early "migration route," which it would seem they may have provided in times so long ago that the Chukchi-Bering platform connected some of the islands to the continental contour; but as islands requiring a fair amount of ocean travel they could only have served as a later travel route, much later, after the first capabilities of sea transport had been developed, long ages after the arrival of the earliest populations. Or so prevailing theory has it.

The coming of the people and the sagas of their ancient

wanderings are only matters for speculation after all. A figure stirs behind the mists across the river of time, nothing more. "The fogs of creation," goes a Zuñi legend, "the mists potent with growth."

But the story left in stone and bone is something else again. Wherever she came from, however she got there, a young woman died some 12,000 years ago or more in what is now west Texas near the New Mexico line at the site known as Midland; wind scoured the sand away from over her bones and they were found by an amateur archaeologist in 1953. And men lived in a cave near the southern tip of South America (Fell's Cave) some 8,000 or 10,000 years or so ago, as men lived in a cave at about the same time 4,000 miles away in Nevada (Gypsum Cave), in both cases seemingly butchering twenty-foot-long ground sloths that may have sometimes been kept penned up like cattle, and in both cases leaving behind stone tools and spearheads that were found in the bottom layers of successions of floor levels indicating thousands of years of occupancy. Stone points made by men of the same approximate epoch have been found at numerous places elsewhere on both continents.

Several thousand years earlier, at least 11,000 years ago or more, camel hunters cooked their meals beside Nevada lakes (Tule Springs), and people hunting mammoths on the shores of other Ice Age lakes near Clovis, New Mexico, left ivory spearheads as well as points of stone among the bones. Nearby in space but perhaps earlier still in time other people brought mammoth ivory into the New Mexico mountain cave (Sandia Cave) that was their home and left it there together with spear points and the bones of camels, mastodons, and the prehistoric American horses that have long been extinct. These things also were found in the lowest of several occupation levels. Many such dates (10,000 to 12,000 years ago) are now regarded as fairly certain in their general range, and those quoted above are on the conservative side.

The mammoth ivory found in the lowest level of Sandia Cave could have been several thousand years old, of course, when it was brought into the cave. Four samples of burned dwarf-mammoth bones from a "barbecue pit" on Santa Rosa Island off the California coast have produced radiocarbon dates of more than 30,000 years ago, but critics are not yet agreed that the barbecue was man-made, and not, for example, the result of a lightning fire.

Years ago, in 1870, deep-ditching work in the region of Tequixquiac, near Mexico City, uncovered a depth of forty feet a llama bone, from an extinct species, carved to represent the face of a wild pig or a coyote. A number of other artifacts and Pleistocene fossils have been found since in the same area, in two distinct geological formations, the younger dated at more than 11,000 years ago, the older far back in the middle of the Wisconsin glaciation. Near Malakoff, Texas, not far from Dallas, gravel-pit workers found three heavy disks of sandstone roughly carved into human faces, veritable men of stone peering out to us from across the past. The gravel pits, dated by geology to well before the close of the Wisconsin, also yielded bones of mammoths and Ice Age horses. Recent radiocarbon dates from South America seem to establish the presence of ancient man at a very early date in Venezuela (one being an age of more than 15,000 years given by tests made in 1969 to a projectile point found embedded in a mastodon bone), and at widely separated other South American localities more than 10,000 years ago. A distinctive assemblage of artifacts from the Cerro Chivateros in the lower Chillon valley in central coastal Peru is given an age of nearly 14,000 years, and a variety of bifacial implements found in Venezula, Peru, Chile, and Argentina are placed at more than 11,000 years of age.

In the spring of 1959, in the vicinity of a site known as Tetela, southeast of the City of Puebla, Mexico, four fragments of mammoth or mastodon bone were discovered on which were engraved feline heads, serpents, mastodons, and hunting scenes, all executed with an extraordinary artistic ability considering their probable antiquity. The belief at present, based on the geology of the site and the fossils found in association with these drawings, is that they may date back to mid-Wisconsin times or even earlier: mildest ages so far suggested range around 30,000 years.

The fragments of incised bone were found in two locations several miles apart, but in the same strata level. In 1967 artifacts perhaps even older were reported from the same place (the Valsequillo reservoir in the state of Puebla) and from not far away, at Tlapacoya in the state of Mexico, both under layers of volcanic ash apparently laid down some 20,000 to 40,000 years ago. Rough chipped-stone tools were turned up at both these sites but no projectile points of any kind, useful news for theorists who conjecture that the earliest New World people may have arrived before the development of any sort of stone points.

An international conference of archaeologists and geologists was held in 1970 in San Bernardino, California, to consider possible evidence in the nearby Calico Mountains that might indicate the presence of man at an extremely early date, perhaps in the long ice-free period before the beginning of the Wisconsin glaciation. The site, an alluvial fan at the root of the desert mountains, is unquestionably of considerable geologic age, but the presence of man is not yet admitted to be represented there. Should such presence eventually be established, it would place man in America more than 20,000 years ago by the lowest estimates at the Calico conference and possibly at some staggering date nearer 100,000 years ago, which would date back unnervingly near to the very birth of Homo sapiens.

And so the people came. They came before the domestication of the dog, long before the invention of the bow and arrow, possibly, as just mentioned above, before the use of any stone-tipped projectiles. They had fire, they roasted meat, worked stone, horn, bone, and probably wore skins—skeletons of the extinct great-horned bison killed some 10,000 years ago are missing the tail bones, which indicates that robes were taken. They made beads and used paint taken from a red iron oxide, and they drew pictures that are filled with exuberant action. And they were there. Scattered bands of new-made people watching through the interminable dawn of a new-made world, they were on hand when Niagara Falls came into being, and when Crater Lake in Oregon was exploded into existence.

"The Creator made the world—come and see it . . ." says a Pima prayer.

Inference may be a more hazardous game than pure speculation, but it might be inferred that at least some of the people practiced at least some of those rites thought to be nearly as old as humanity, rites practiced by Old World Neanderthalers 100,000 years ago and perhaps even by ape men of the earliest times, rites involving fire and thunder and lightning; or ceremonies involving physical demonstrations—dancing—of the entire family or band to show its wish to protect the individual member imperiled by such mysteries as birth, the rhythmic flow of woman's blood, and death. It might also be assumed that they lived with the world rather than in it, as much a part of the setting fashioned by nature around them as fingers are part of a hand, and it would follow as a matter of course that the beasts, trees, winds, and stars of that setting pondered and talked, aspired, feared, and desired as did anyone else. In fact, what was life but a conversation between all such beings of whom man was only one? Pan had a long childhood.

The impressive thing about this world is time. The people can be imagined, and their thoughts and ways, everything but those limitless reaches of time, time so much longer than all the centuries of written history, while men leaned on their spears and dreamed and nothing really changed at all.

Such divisions of that time as exist are marked off for us principally by the changing forms for spear points and dart points and, later, arrowheads. These, and other weapons and utensils, are usually in stone. Time has consumed, for the most part, relics in other materials. There are some scraps of basketry; fragments of fine twined work were found in Fort Rock Cave, Oregon, together with dozens of pairs of partly burned sandals made—and well made—of shredded sagebrush bark (the sandals produced a radiocarbon date of about 9,000 years); a few bits of wood, a number of pieces in horn and bone, and not much else as far as the earlier horizons are concerned.

The meager number of human bones from these times has a special explanation of its own: most of the experts, until recently, were not looking for them. They were looking instead for an American ape man, evidence that a separate branch of humanity might have originated in the New World. It used to be generally agreed (with a few noteworthy dissidents) that human beings could only have arrived a very few thousand years ago at the earliest, and therefore the relative age of their bones was unimportant. Skulls and human bones of supposed antiquity were examined, argued over, and judged on the basis of possible simian and other pre-Homo sapiens characteristics, and since no such characteristics were clearly established they were all discarded.

Nowadays some of them are being dusted off for another look, and the sites of their discovery re-explored. They range all the way from large finds of many burials to single bones, and geographically from South America through Mexico to Minnesota, and from Florida to California. Part of a skull found in Laguna, California, was knocking around among the experts for years until, in 1968, it turned up a radiocarbon age of more than 15,000 years, which, if correct, makes it the oldest New World human bone so far found. "Minnesota Man," who was really a young girl, and Mexico's Tepexpan Man, both subjects of angry controversy, are among several that claim guess dates in excess of 10,000 years (a recent study lists nineteen finds of "reasonably certain antiquity"). Preliminary reports give test dates of more than 20,000 years for the age of a skeleton found in 1972 near what was once the shoreline of a lake in what is now the Yuha Desert along the Californian-Mexican border. Texas' female "Midland Man," mentioned earlier, is commonly regarded as offering fairly sure proof of the cited age of 12,000 years, with even 20,000 years reasonably defendable.

Geologists have recently raised questions about the dating of the bottom level in Sandia Cave, which used to be placed in a range approaching 20,000 years ago, but the likelihood of more than 10,000 years of age at least remains unshaken. These early people left spear points of distinctive silhouette: one-shouldered, heavy, long (up to four inches), roughly bayonet-shaped. Points of this type have since been found elsewhere in the Southwest and claimed, although not to the satisfaction of some authorities, from other places as far apart as Alberta and Alabama.

The people who hunted mammoths on the shores of bygone lakes near Clovis, New Mexico, some 10,000 to 12,000 years ago, left stone spearheads of about the same size, but bullet-shaped and without the single shoulder, and grooved or "fluted" part way up the face. Clovis points have been found over the high plains of the Southwest together with bones of musk ox, mammoths, and the rest of the usual Pleistocene cast of characters, and other points of this type have turned up from the Texas Panhandle to the Atlantic coast, and from Florida to Nova Scotia. Several have been reported from Mexico and from the Alberta-Saskatchewan plains of Canada.

Many centuries later still, perhaps in the lower reaches of the area roundabout 10,000 years or so ago, the famous Folsom point came into use, developed from the fluted Clovis point. It is famous for having provided the first proof of existence of American Ice Age Man, with the discovery in 1927, near Folsom, New Mexico, of one such point embedded between the ribs of an Ice Age buffalo. A great number of Folsoms have since been found over a wide area, but centering in the High Plains region and remaining pretty much east of the Rockies. A light, beautifully made point, distinguished by a long groove or fluting running up each face, it is smaller than either the Clovis or Sandia. The Clovis and Folsom fluted points are distinctively American, possibly in specific response to the best ballistics for big-game hunting on the American plains—no similar points have yet been found elsewhere in the world.

The mammoth seems to have disappeared by this time, at any rate from the Southwest; the giant ground sloth, an emigrant from South America, had spread from coast to coast, but the commonest kill for Folsom man was the colossal antique bison, whose hornspread could measure up to six feet.

Assortments of implements in chipped stone and, occasionally, worked bone have been found with all these various points, as well as a few beads and pendants. At a Folsom site in northeastern Colorado (Lindenmeier) some mysterious bone disks decorated with tiny incised lines were discovered; there is a theory these might have been markers for a lunar count, or maybe even for a game of some kind. They look a little like poker chips.

With the Folsom people the last glacial period suffered its final decline and became the geological Present, which embraces the past 8,000 or 9,000 years.

By that time men had been in the New World for perhaps 20,000 years, to humor out all the current notions of earliest dates—and possibly more men than one would think from the foregoing list of scattered finds. One archaeologist reported in 1951 a survey of some 25,000 artifacts claimed to date from Wisconsin times, most of them in private collections, and commented on how many thousands of camp sites and artifacts must still lie buried in order for chance to have exposed such ancient remains in anything like such considerable numbers.

Several other "point industries" have been identified for the several thousand transitional years as the geological present took over from the glacial past. All these are considered more or less later than Folsom. Eden, Scottsbluff, and Cody are among the many site-names that have been bestowed on them, but there is a growing tendency for archaeologists to lump together several types under generic names derived from manufacturing techniques, such as Parallel-flaked points to cover all the above site-names, or from general locale, such as the term Plano to cover a very large variety of points dating between about 9,000 and 7,000 years ago distinctly identified with the Great Plains.

Some of the earliest New World "industries" are broadly

comparable to Old World techniques that appear to have been roughly contemporary, but specific relationships are few and none too solid.

An early date of much interest comes from the Great Lakes area in and about Wisconsin, where the people of the Old Copper Culture made lance points (some of them socketed) and a profusion of other articles from the copper native to the region. Before radiocarbon dating this culture was thought to date back 1,200 years or so, and even that was considered marvelously early. Since then, carbon 14 tests and other evidence have dated it back to something between 5,000 and 7,000 years ago, a very early time for use of metal anywhere in the world, and incidentally one of the earliest definite dates yet in hand for the presence of any people at all in the northeastern United States.

Another interesting early date comes from the site of a great bygone lake, given the posthumous name of Lake Cochise, in the now blazing desert country where Arizona, New Mexico, and Mexico meet. Here are signs of continuous habitation for many thousands of years by a people as ancient as the Folsom hunters, and yet quite different from them in their way of life. The chief items in all phases of this continuity are stones and pestles, described as "milling stones," obviously used for grinding or pounding some sort of food in the form of wild grains or seeds, and here again is an extremely early appearance anywhere in the world, for the oldest phase of the Cochise culture is dated at 9,000 years ago or more.

And still another comes from the maize found in a cave, Bat Cave, in western New Mexico. It is primitive maize, "pod corn," each kernel enclosed in a husk of its own (incidentally, it was also popcorn), but a hybridized form of the native wild corn and thus unquestionably cultivated by man (domesticated squash was grown along with it), and it is some 5,000 years old by carbon-validated dating. Presumably agriculture first began far to the south, in the regions that later produced high civilizations, and indeed tiny ears of pod corn have been found in central Mexico that were harvested more than 7,000 years ago, according to the stratum-date. These dates are truly venerable. Villages of outright farmers were still in the future, of course, but for comparison farming villages in the Old World are reckoned to have begun appearing only 7,000 or 8,000 years ago.

From end to end of the two Americas a people lived, many

differing groups of many diverse kinds of people, strangers to each other, unknown to one another éxcept at each little ripple of contact. The ripples transmitted ways of life and thought, sometimes with amazing fidelity and sometimes monstrously garbled, to the farthest ends of the inhabited land, and then rebounded with as much force as before. They started from nowhere and they never ended. They crossed and recrossed each other at all angles, and their patterns changed at each new voice.

A man might live out his life and never leave his valley, a family might never have seen foreigners as long as could be remembered, and the cycle of the years might never had been disturbed in their land that they knew bush by bush and that never changed, and yet life was in constant motion. New people crossed the sill of the world in the distant north, and still another ripple was added, and another and another and another, at every fear or joy or thought or hope encountered in its passage. Seen against a scale of centuries, the knots of people moved, merged, split, multiplied, died, appeared from every compass point.

We came from beneath the ground, the legends say, we came from the sunrise of the east, or the sunset of the west. We climbed up to the light from the bowels of our holy mountain, we climbed down from the sky by a ladder of arrows. At first there was only the god Coyote or Raven, Serpent or Jaguar, or the twins of origin, echo of cosmic duality. At first there was "only the calm water, the placid sea, alone and tranquil. Nothing existed," say the Mayas. At first there was only the sea, say also the seafaring Haida of the Northwest Coast.

In ancient times there were white men with long black beards, say people thousands of miles apart. A giant black man lives in the heavens, or the woods, or the mountains, and punishes those who do wrong. In ancient times women ruled, because they had the magic masks, or the magic flutes, but men spied on them and stole their magic away. In ancient times a beautiful girl had a lover who came each night but would not let her see who he was, so she painted her hands, or rubbed them in soot, and that night embraced her lover again, and the next day she saw the marks of her hands on the back of her brother. She ran from him in horror and he ran after her, so she turned herself into the sun and he turned himself into the moon, and he still appears at night looking for her, but she has always gone away; and the marks of her hands are still on his back. In the first days men despaired and lost their repose, so the Creator gave them the tobacco and they chewed it and gained their repose, but it only lasted a short time and they despaired and lost their repose again, so the Creator gave them women. Or this order was reversed in the myths which told of the tobacco plant's first appearance at the spot where a man and woman had lain to make love (the word for smoking tobacco among some people, the Creeks for example, was a word also used for sexual union).

All about them the world comprehended simply by being, and so did they. Of course there was meaning in the spring stars hanging in the silver branches of the spring forest, and the autumn stars hanging in the antlers of a tall silent beast, or the terror of a storm shouting in your ear, or the dread of hunger in black winter days.

With such comprehensions the American Indians came into existence, remarkably uniform genetically, infinitely diverse in look and manner. People of infinite differences and remarkable samenesses. Some feared the world and placated its ferocity, and some worshipped with praise its goodness. Some apologized to animals they killed, and others insulted them. Some feared the dead—not so much death as the dead, with their unnatural sightless eyes and their ghosts that sprang up in the dark—and fled from the dead in panic, even while weeping with grief, to abandon them where they died; others hung up the dead in a place of honor in the lodging and kept them there.

One insistent tone is present in all these varying examples, an awareness of the harmony of things that can be struck out of balance at any moment, even by a man's own actions. (By a knife or a stone I can bring the abnormality of death; by careful and right behavior can I keep my normal world free of such abnormalities as death and sickness?) If time is the tonic note in the story of the Indians, this theme of the world's precarious harmony is the dominant. It underlies one of the few traits that might be applied sweepingly to most American Indians, belief in a personally acquirable magic power. The widespread concept of ownership of land in common by a related group of people might be another such trait.

These attitudes appear to have been overwhelmed in emerging societies elsewhere in the world by other sets of notions drawn from other primitive world views, but they gained the ascendancy in America. Operated upon by untroubled time, they became distinctively Indian.

By the dawn of the geological Present (more often styled the Recent) the giant beasts of the Pleistocene were gone—or nearly; some animals once thought long extinct may have survived here and there until much later times. But the usual game, about 8,000 years ago, had become modern, from the guanaco to the buffalo to the caribou. Native American horses had gone over the hill to extinction. It was still long before the bow; men hunted or fought with spears, clubs, slings, bolas—cords weighted at the ends with stones, flung to whip around the animal's legs and trip it up—or, like the heroes of the *Iliad,* with boulders.

Except for scattered fragments of weapons and tools, basketry and mats, jewels of shell or bone, and some knowledge or reasonable inferences as to burial customs—naked in a pit or cremated, or the body tied huddled in a basket together with valuables, or the bones painted a bright red and laid out to point from the sunrise to the sunset—these people are as invisible today as the people of the long dawn before them.

Archaeology emphasizes weapon points, and later pottery, for the simple reason that these things offer a sequence of sorts and there's not much else in the way of concrete evidence to talk about anyway. But the making of the stone points could not have been a terribly important part of life for those people of so long ago; it certainly could not have taken up much of their time. Modern students have shown this by making very acceptable spear points and dart points, using the ancient flaking tools, in only a few minutes. Making them must have been as trivial a part of life as changing a tire or washing the car today. But otherwise the people are voiceless and vanished.

Projection of their shadows against the reality of how it must have been can only reveal further that they hunted or fished, built pitfalls and fish weirs, collected berries and nuts and grasses and roots that were good to eat, and that as a rule they did a great deal of moving. Even though a people stayed in a general area for thousands of years the usual life must have been one of frequent movement, following the seasons from the hills to the valleys, from the valleys to the hills. Exceptionally there may have been communities that stayed so close within favorite food-gathering areas as to become wholly sedentary. Although possibly this last is an unnecessarily refined point, turning on a notion of sedentariness rather too artificially limited. Some populations of Archaic peoples undoubtedly spent lives entailing less movement than the lives of sedentary urban commuters today. The association of certain peoples with certain regions over absolutely incredible lengths of time in the Archaic seems fairly well established. Seasonal fire-hunts, for example, are believed by some students to have continued for so long so regularly that they created the great plains of the American West; the Archaic-age people of the southeastern part of what is now the United States, including the "gracefully slender" peoples some archaeologists believe were distant ancestors of such Siouan-speaking modern groups as the Tutelo and Catawba, are thought to have fired the southern woods for so long that the Southern longleaf pine became dependent on this seasonal burning to reproduce—without its hot flash fire the tiny seeds could not have burst their shells and without the annual singeing off of the matted duff the rootlets could not reach the earth.

Still fainter shadows can be projected by speculation on the social intangibles of that seemingly endless and marvelously stable Archaic world. A number of experts caution against a notion of particularly "primitive" life in the Archaic or of necessarily sparse populations. On the contrary, the skillful use of all resources, of an optimum "forest efficiency" that did not disturb or destroy the "plant-animal-man-with-culture eco-system" may have developed, in passing through these enormous chasms of time, a way of life teeming with spiritual richness and genuine joys of fulfillment. There have even been hints that these people of the Archaic ages waited so long for new ideas (such as pottery and agriculture) and the resultant elaboration of their basic culture simply because they were content in their endless Eden and did not want to change. Heretical reflections threaten to follow, that change—we call it progress—might be a result not of "forward" social movement but of something wrong in the social animal: as it takes a sick oyster to spin a pearl.

There are some indications that those long Archaic times inclined to be peaceful, and a gradual change in this regard may identify at least one of the complex and subtle forces that conceivably might have sickened the strong and stable world of the Archaic until it was ready at last for "progress"—if there is anything to this intriguing line of thought.

Most present expert opinion sees the Archaic beginning to ring down its curtain someplace in the time between 2300 B.C.

and 1500 B.C. for most of North America, although the curtain took its own slow time in falling and for some areas, such as in the region of California, the Archaic remained in fairly full force into historic times.

Its close is customarily marked by the appearance of pottery, burial mounds, pipes and (wild) tobacco, and a few other items—otherwise there is no apparent basic change in the Archaic complex as modern Indian cultures appear built quite squarely upon it.

Someplace, a people who doubtless had gathered wild seeds as part or most of their food since time immemorial found among the plants they came back to each year one with delicious seeds that became (we shall assume) especially famous among them. Perhaps they encouraged its growth, possibly weeding or digging around it, eventually replanted seeds from its best stalks, and at length were no longer dealing with a wild plant but cultivating a domestic plant, a plant the botanists now call *Zea mays* and that cornbelt farmers call corn. The Bat Cave, New Mexico, instance, and sites in the state of Tamaulipas, northeastern Mexico, reveal the presence of corn, primitive but domesticated, at very early dates, 5,000 years ago or more; rock shelter sites in the state of Puebla in the heart of Mexico reveal corn as a primitive domesticate as much as 1,000 to 2,000 years earlier still; all bear out what nearly every student takes for granted, that agriculture first spread northward from beginnings somewhere in the south. An exhaustive report on this question was made in 1964, based on study of some 23,000 specimens of maize, concluding that the cultivation of corn had commenced 6,000 to 7,000 years ago in Mexico or nearby. The process of domestication must have taken many centuries.

The cultivation of gourds, beans, or squash may have preceded that of maize, and cultivation of different plants may have originated in different localities. Squash and pumpkins— harvested for their seeds—were present, and perhaps beginning to be cultivated, at various places in Mexico as early as 8,000 or 9,000 years ago. Beans and chili peppers and bottle gourds, these last possibly from points of origin in South America, were also plants tamed in the early stages of agriculture, as was tobacco. Evidently a little later came peanuts and sweet potatoes, both of these probably from South America, and perhaps later also, the Mexican staples of chocolate, tomatoes, and avocadoes.

Or the first plants worked with may have been still others,

possibly some that no longer appear in the seed catalogues, such as cattails, cultivated at an early date in South America for their roots. Wherever they began, those plants that proved themselves worth the work all spread, slowly but surely, along the ripples of contact from valley to valley, from people to people.

Crops imply staying more or less close at hand to take care of them. By 4,000 to 5,000 years ago there were permanent villages in Mexico and in the Guatemala region where the people raised both corn and cotton, and on the north coast of Peru where the people cultivated cattails, chili peppers, cotton, beans, although no corn for yet another thousand years or more. (The earliest tentative physical evidence for houses north of Mexico comes— outside the neat sphere of agriculture and pottery—from California, dating, if the evidence is correct, to at least 4,000 years ago.) The first appearance of pottery, by present information, was in the environs of 4,500 years ago at various widely separated spots: on the coast of Colombia in South America and the coasts of South Carolina and Georgia, or perhaps a shade earlier on the coast of Ecuador and perhaps a few centuries later on the Pacific coast of Mexico (at, among other places, the region of the modern Acapulco) and perhaps a few centuries later still in Panama. New finds can be expected more or less momentarily, for the earliest origin of pottery (of which more later) is currently a hot issue. Wherever it first originated in the New World, pottery began to appear rather soon in the young life of such new-forming (1700-800 B.C.) villages as El Arbolillo, Tlatilco, and Zacatenco in the Valley of Mexico, and with it little clay figurines—and the people are faceless no longer.

They come marching into view tattooed, hung with ornaments, wearing turbans or string hats, otherwise usually naked. Most of these figurines represent women with big hips, usually presumed to be the age-old goddess of increase. If I model a fertile woman and show it to the world, will not the world be fertile in response? For all their archaic rigidity and the helpless clumsiness of the bits of clay stuck on them for eyes and mouths they are as animate with locked-in life as the springtime they symbolize. Some, originating in new villages a bit to the south, in Puebla and Morelos, are graceful, seductive, and young. They dance and run, doe-eyed, with bewitching smiles and beguiling bodies; they wear earrings and their elaborately coiled hair is sometimes streaked red and white, as the thatched mud-and-stick houses of the people were painted. They became understandably popular and were traded to all the villages of the Valley during many years; for in the beginning the goddess of love and the Earth Mother were one.

Now occurs an interesting parallel. New ways of doing things came to the Valley of Mexico and to the north coast of Peru at about the same time, give or take a few hundred years. A popular religious cult appeared with these new ways, perhaps brought from some tropical lowland region: a "feline" in Peru, a jaguar in Mexico. This began happening some 3,000 years ago, and for the next 500 to 1,000 years the new styles, or the peoples, remained in mastery of the loops and whorls of evolving little worlds in Peru and Mexico.

There is no suggestion they were the same people, or that the new styles reached each of these areas at exactly the same time. They may have been centuries apart, and while a few hundred years are not much in gross archaeological guesswork they can be all-important in real history, as for example the small matter of only 400 years separating the high point of Athens from the high point of Rome.

The birthplace of these two styles is not yet pinned down (the search has been turning more and more to Central America); until it is, the early story of these little new worlds is rather like the story of early Greece (a contemporary) without Crete.

In Mexico, the strangers eventually became associated with the country later occupied by a people known as the Olmecs. Consequently, the early strangers have sometimes been called Olmecs too. Since 2,000 years separate them from the later, historic Olmecs, who are an entirely different people, this has given rise to much confusion in all accounts (such as this one) where both the early strangers and the later Olmecs of history must appear. To avoid this, the early people will be referred to here as the Ancient Olmecs. Whoever they were, they made essentially the same sorts of ornaments and pottery and figurines that had been made before them, but they did it a great deal better and they added their own particular designs. Their snarling jaguar's head or a peculiar "baby face" (maybe celebrating a custom of infant sacrifice), and a truly modern preoccupation with whatever was monstrous, deformed, disharmonic, appeared on all they touched.

And these people themselves come into view in their turn, fat little effeminate men with ornamentally deformed heads and ornamentally deformed teeth. They made some of the most charming of the seductive little figurines spoken of previously, some of them with two heads.

Through the years, through the centuries, they seemed to develop their most important centers in southern Veracruz, the rubber-producing country of Mexico. Archaeologists have worked out a succession of three important towns in this Ancient Olmec country, the best known being the middle one, the island town of La Venta, which dates from about 1,000 B.C. At La Venta (actually only a ceremonial center for the inhabitants of the surrounding country) multi-ton blocks of stone were carved into columns and monuments and especially into gigantic heads up to fourteen feet high, glorifying the typical fat-lipped "Olmec" baby face—the largest block of stone weighs an estimated fifty tons and must have been transported (perhaps rafted) at least sixty miles from its nearest source through the surrounding mangrove swamps. Turning from the monumental to the miniature the La Venta sculptors worked jade with wizard skill into jewel-like representations of their half-human jaguars, deformed people, bearded men, and other monstrosities.

Crude jade beads and jewels sometimes turn up in Mexican burials from the earliest times, but nothing comparable to the exquisite jade work of the Ancient Olmecs preceded their appearance—and nothing comparable has been done since. There is evidence that jade pieces executed by these consummate artists were treasured for centuries by neighboring peoples, as we preserve today the works of Rembrandt or Michelangelo. The Ancient Olmecs were more or less contemporary with the Chou Dynasty in China, which also saw the highest point of jade-working in Asia; naturally there has been speculation that there may have been some connection. The Ancient Olmec jade was jadeite, in general rather superior to the ancient Chinese jade, which was nephrite. Jade deposits have not yet been located in Mexico, but have been found in recent years in Guatemala.

In the region next door to the southeast, during about the same time as the flowering of the Ancient Olmec style, other maize-farming people were outgrowing the Ancient Olmec jaguar and baby-face cults to create a style of their own. In it they spring as resplendently to life as any people ever have in the art they left behind them. But they created more than a style; they created a civilization, one of the great civilizations of the ancient world. These were the Maya.

Nearly everything is known about the Maya (pronounced My-ah, being a Spanish spelling) that any earnest archaeologist could want to know. We can follow every step in the techniques involved in the building and adorning of their temples. We can unravel all the intricacies of their calendric calculations, which are quite impressive—their calendar in general use was one ten-thousandth of a day per year more accurate than is ours now. We know how they lived, loved, worked, talked, slept, worshiped, died. We know what they ate and how they cooked it, how they dressed and how they wore their hair.

We know nearly everything about them, really, except that we really don't know the Mayas at all. They present the most profound enigma in American history.

Why this should be so is a point of great interest. The Maya attained the highest civilization known in ancient America, and one of the highest known any place in the ancient world. They developed a genuine written language or a near thing to it— hieroglyphic ideographs; that is, conventionalized symbols standing for certain words, as in Chinese writing, or possibly to some extent (scholars disagree) phonetically representing syllables or sounds, as in the combinations of our own alphabet. Fragments of their written records remain and some numerical parts of them have been deciphered, although this is not much help in knowing the people—as if all we had of Greek literature were some disjointed scraps from farmers' almanacs.

And the people remain, two million or so who speak the various related Mayan dialects, and in many cases are so similar in appearance to the muscular, ugly, delicately posed little men on the temple walls that they could be the frescoes come to life.

Other people achieved less, left less, and in many cases have vanished altogether. Why, then, a Maya puzzle to outpuzzle all the rest? Because of the heights they reached and fell from.

The Maya practiced a primitive form of agriculture known to other primitive peoples all over the world since agriculture began: hacking down and burning trees and brush, planting a cornfield in the rough clearing, and slashing out a new such clearing a few seasons later. (Anthropologists call such a clearing a "milpa"—the Aztec for "cornfield.") In all the days of their greatness, this technology was never improved. This kind of farming, by its nature, operates against the growth of cities. Every man's home is his outlying jungle clearing, in contrast to the close communities fostered by such group undertakings as irrigation. Some specialists argue that one or two of the Maya ceremonial centers were truly urban communities, but for the most part house mounds in the vicinity of the centers are scattered about the surrounding countryside, revealing no particular pattern of urban density; and so the Maya, in the days of their greatness, never built cities, at least not in our sense of the word.

With no metals, they developed no metallurgy, no metal-working, no metal tools. With no draft animals (and probably no domestic animals of any kind except dogs), they developed no use of the wheel, although they used rollers on the *sacbeob* (artificial roads)—the raised causeways that ran from place to place and radiated into the countryside from the temple clusters. It was not easy to get from place to place in the Maya country; it still is not easy today. Although their world stretched from mountains to open savannas it had its glory in the lowland jungles.

There were social classes, and priests conducting a complex religion, but clear evidence cannot be found of any organized political government, centralized or local. The Maya never had an "empire" or anything approximating one, so far as has yet been determined.

In all these respects they differ from other early high civilizations in both the New World and the Old. They are the foremost exception to the apparent rules attending the birth of civilization.

They were painted savages, in the phrase of the good old (non-cosmetic) days, and throughout the ages of their greatness painted savages they remained. They tattooed their bodies and painted them red—priests were painted blue, warriors black and red, prisoners (captives) striped black and white. They occasionally filed their teeth. They distended their pierced ear lobes with barbaric ear plugs, and pierced the septum of the nose to insert carved "jewels," and in the later stages of their greatest age they wore artificial noses, in keeping with an ideal of high-nosed handsomeness. They flattened their foreheads, and made themselves, if they could, cross-eyed, cross-eyes being considered beautiful. They decorated themselves with feathers, breeding birds in aviaries for the most gorgeous plumes, and men wore brilliant little obsidian mirrors hanging in their hair.

But the Maya world was somewhat more: ". . . the multitude, the grandeur and the beauty of its buildings . . . for they are so many in number and so many are the parts of the country where they are found, and so well built are they of cut stone in their fashion, that it fills one with astonishment . . . that except to those who have seen them, it will seem to be jesting to tell about them . . ." So begins 400 years ago (with Bishop Diego de Landa's *Relación*) the testimony of awe—no other word will do—that has been repeated by students and artists ever since.

Their country extended over an area as large as modern Italy. Their Classic Age alone endured longer than the entire life of the Roman Empire from Julius Caesar to Romulus Augustulus—with which it was probably parallel in time. Their "cities," for want of a better term to describe their cathedral centers, numbered at least 116 great and small, for that many are already known as archaeological sites, and more, perhaps, wait to be discovered.

Besides the great temple-topped pyramids, various of the centers contained bridges, aqueducts, "palaces," reviewing stands, vapor baths, monumental stairways, ceremonial plazas for public spectacles, and astronomical observatories. Some of the more important "cities" were made up of numbers of building clusters around separate plazas, covering many acres or even extending for miles.

These buildings are genuinely impressive to a technicians' culture such as our own, and yet they take only second place among the Maya ruins left to us. Far and away in front are the records of their achievements in more abstract intellectual zones. The art, astronomy, and mathematics are world re-nowned. The literature, except for a few mangled scraps and tatters, is lost. It included history, science, the lives of great men, astronomy, astrology, prophecy, theology, ritual, legends and fables, "cures of diseases, and antiquities, and how to read and write with letters and characters with which they wrote," as Bishop Landa was told in the 1560s, and seemingly "certain songs in meter," and "farces . . . and comedies for the pleasure of the public."

"The original book, written long ago, existed, but its sight is hidden to the searcher and the thinker," wrote, in the sixteenth century, the compiler of the *Popol Vuh*, book of the highland Quiché Maya, striving from the depths of the long night to remember the long noon nine centuries before.

Another still more subtle accomplishment was discerned by Mayanists Sylvanus Griswold Morley and George W. Brainerd, who found the 600 years of the Classic Age marked by general tranquility, "a near absence of warfare," an absence of repressive government, and an absence of discernible strong rulers and who summed up by quoting Lord Moulton's remark that "the measure of civilization is the extent of man's obedience to the unenforceable." To which they added, ". . . the Maya must have measured high."

If all this sounds like a golden world, maybe it was. Or maybe it was not. Some other scholars have emphasized evidences of authoritarian priestly dynasties and stressed indications of occasional human sacrifice and warfare, illustrating that in the most detailed data there remains room for varying subjective interpretation.

The most reasonable suggestion seems to be that each of the great centers may have been a city-state unto itself, with as much difference between, say, the "city-states" of Copán and Tikal as between ancient Athens and Sparta.

An early Maya ceremonial center in Guatemala (Kaminaljuyu) dates by radiocarbon tests from 1182 B.C. (plus or minus 240), and Mayan agriculture may have first came into being some place nearby, much earlier, there on the flanks of the Central American Cordillera, a region of great beauty. (Linguistic specialists, studying structure and pattern in related languages, have succeeded in projecting shadowy forms of parent languages: thus a "Proto-Maya" parent language spoken in 2500 B.C. is believed to have contained words for "maize" and for "cotton cloth.")

The people of the Guatemalan mountains were the highland Maya, somewhat backward in the Classic Age in comparison with the lowland Maya, the typical Classic Maya, who expanded their way of art and life from the vicinity of Lake Peten in Guatemala to dominate all the rain-forest country of central Guatemala and adjacent areas of the Yucatan peninsula as well as, eventually, the dry brush country of northernmost Yucatan. The land of the Maya, excluding the Huasteca (a splinter group living far up the Gulf Coast, isolated from the main Maya world), crossed the borders of what are today Honduras, El Salvador, Guatemala, British Honduras, and the Mexican states of Quintana Roo, Yucatan, Campeche, Tabasco, and Chiapas.

How long it took the priests to work out their calendars and system of writing is anybody's guess. Their "Long Count" calendar started from a given point in the past, reckoned by modern scholars to be a century or so one side or the other of 3,000 B.C. This date may have historical meaning, like our B.C., or it may not, like Bishop Ussher's 4004. The beginnings of calendrics and of writing may have been borrowed from someone else (possibly those Ancient Olmecs, who, for that matter, may themselves have been a group of Proto-Mayas), as the Greeks took their alphabet from the Phoenicians. The basic calendar system was fully established long before Classic Maya times, and the earliest date so far found in the "Maya" Long Count system was not in fact found in Maya country at all but in the latest of the three important Ancient Olmec centers, the site known as Tres Zapotes, where the date, carved on a stone monument, or stela, equates, in the most generally accepted correlation, with 31 B.C. However, no other definite proof has yet been found of the Long Count calendar's existence in other typical Ancient Olmec centers, such as La Venta, so it is still an open question whether the Ancient Olmeca or the Maya were the original inventors.

In any case, all the essentials of great art and architecture, hieroglyphic writing and Long Count calendar, were established by the time a carved jade plaque now known as the Leyden Plate was inscribed with its date, probably at the great jungle center of Tikal, fifty miles north of Lake Peten, and by the time the earliest Maya stela so far discovered, the famous Stela 29, was dated in the Long Count, also at Tikal.

The Goodman-Martinez-Thompson (sometimes abbreviated to GMT) correlation of Maya dates gives the date for the Leyden Plate as A.D. 321, and the date on the Tikal Stela 29 as A.D. 292. A contending system, the Spinden correlation, reads these dates about 260 years earlier at this period.

Some radiocarbon tests seem to support the Spinden system for the early centuries of the Maya Classic Age, but more seem to support the GMT correlation, which has brought "sighs of relief" from the experts, as one Mayanist wrote in 1966, since most modern references are based on the GMT system. Nevertheless, the question is still unsettled; indeed it still remains, in the words of another authority, "the most vexing problem of Maya Lowland archaeology."

The period of the oldest dated Maya stela—circa A.D. 30 (Spinden) or circa A.D. 292 (GMT)—is generally regarded as the opening of the 600 years of the Maya Classic Age, although of course such early centers as Tikal had been more or less in operation during the long period of development called by archaeologists the Formative or Preclassic for many centuries before this time.

The calendar systems were corrected by startlingly accurate observations of the sun, moon, and Venus (*noh ek,* Great Star). They were noted down in a numbers system based on twenty (counting fingers and toes instead of only fingers, as in our system of tens) and using positional numbers and zero, two concepts unknown in Europe for another thousand years.

The *tzolkin,* or book of the days, a ceremonial round of 260 days in use all over ancient Mesoamerica, was the simplest unit of the various day counts; it may have originated in the annual coming and going of Venus, or it may have been based simply on the period between autumn and spring, the other 105 days of the year being devoted to the planting and growing season. It involved a series of twenty different day names revolving through an endlessly repeated number series of 1 to 13. Thus the same conjunctions of numbers and names were repeated in 13 x 20 or 260 days.

The solar calendar used nineteen named months (eighteen of twenty days each and one of five days) and turned through a cycle of fifty-two years between recurring conjunctions—in principle as if our calendar were arranged so that certain weekdays always fell on certain dates at regular intervals of so many years.

Further systems, a lunar calendar brought into a fixed relation with the day count (with an error of less than five minutes a year), and a Venus calendar meshing five Venus years of a mean 584 days each with eight solar years of 365 days each, were all more or less complex. They created whole galaxies of cycles, wheels within wheels, all turning like the perpetual works of an infinite clock, and the emphasis was always on that marvelous repetition of time. The dated stelae set up during the Classic Age commemorated various of these cycles, usually in the cycle of 7,200 days called a *katun.*

The most striking thing about the Maya achievements is that, as far as we can discern via our view of life, they were seldom of any practical use. The temples and the misnamed palaces, the "civic centers," as these collections of great buildings have been called, were magnificently nonutilitarian. If anyone lived in the "palaces" it was presumably for penance, for they must have been very uncomfortable; the buildings may have been monasteries of some sort.

The people lived in tiny houses of poles and thatch in their jungle hamlets, and while the calendars turned through their inexorable rounds the people made *maadz* (corn mush) and dangled bits of pitch between the baby's eyes to make him cross-eyed and trooped in to the ceremonies along the well-engineered, gun-barrel-straight roads, and the nobles nobled all day and raided each other on state occasions, and the priests gazed over their crossed sticks at the stars.

The temple ceremonies were for men only, women not allowed—with certain exceptions; but at the ceremonies in the plazas the people would have marked the time together, in communion with the brilliantly arrayed priests and the revered *halach uinic* (True Man), the chief priest, in ecstasy, probably, from the music and the dancing and the pageantry, the colors and the beauty, and the meaning of the ritual that marked another gesture in the tableau of good gods versus bad, another passing point on the holy calendar. As has been remarked of the ancient Egyptians, only the changeless was truly significant.

This entire world, with all its mathematical wonders, its art of life and its gods who assumed the forms of an old man or maize, bat or eagle, or a serpent with jaguar's teeth, was operated (so far as we can see) for the sole purpose of marking time.

And yet—the mathematical expertise, the achievements in art, the idealism in the remembered remnants of their literature, seem to insist the purpose must have been something more. Is it possible there could be mysteries in the passage of time outside the usual scope of even our modern computerized minds? A couple of the greatest noncomputerized minds of our era—philosopher Henri Bergson and Albert Einstein ("For us believing physicists, the distinction between past and present and future is an illusion")—have suggested there may well be.

Whatever might have been the conception at the core of the Maya preoccupation with time, it is lost to our understanding. Time has stopped for them and moved on for us (or if time is stationary they have turned one way from it and we another), and the people on the sculptured walls evade us utterly. They left no Aeschylus to tell us what they felt, no Heraclitus to tell us what they thought.

The fragments are only fragments, luminous with old light though they are. "Then there sprang up the five-leafed flower . . . the little flower . . ." from the *Chilam Balam* of Chumayel, the Book of the Prophet of Secrets, the Book of the Jaguar Priest, a post-Spanish collection of such fragments. "Then there sprang up the bouquet of the priest, the bouquet of the ruler, the bouquet of the captain; this was what the flower-king bore when he descended and nothing else, so they say. It was not bread that he bore . . ."

And, "He never arrives who travels an evil road . . ."

And, from the *Popol Vuh*: ". . . he who gives breath and thought . . . who watches over the happiness of the people, the happiness of the human race . . . who meditates on the goodness of all that exists in the sky, on the earth, in the lakes and in the sea . . ."

And a dawn prayer: "Look at us, hear us! . . . Heart of Heaven, Heart of Earth! Give us our descendants, our succession, as long as the sun shall move . . . Let it dawn, let the day come! . . . May the people have peace . . . may they be happy . . . give us good life . . . grandmother of the sun, grandmother of the light, let there be dawn . . . let the light come!"

Of course their annals are blank. Their prayers may have been heard and they may really have been a happy people, and happy people have no history, as everybody knows.

They built new temples, they dated new monuments, the people walked to the centers wearing their Sunday sandals, and the priests and the nobles read and wrote and studied; and time turned round and round, never changing.

They had no history until the Classic Age ended, when the central Maya, the people in the heart of the Maya country, abandoned their gleaming temple clusters and drifted away and out of the jungle, leaving no signs of war, invasion, or general unrest, and thus leaving the greatest mystery of all.

This was not the end of the Maya. We shall hear of them again. But it was the end of the great days, the long noon. The exodus from the Classic sites began in the seventh century A.D. (Spinden) or the ninth (GMT). A century or so later the towering pyramids and the lavishly decorated buildings (some buildings were left half-finished) were all but deserted. No one knows why. Apparently the few residents who stayed on for several generations after the marvelous machinery stopped tried, here and there, to keep alive the cult of the monumental stelae, reverently resetting broken fragments—but sometimes, in their helpless ignorance, placing the ancient inscriptions upside down.

The two foremost puzzles of the Maya civilization concern their form of government and the abandonment of the scores of communities that composed their most important city-states.

But these are only different views of the same face, of the total enigma that is the Maya Classic Age, primitive, wise, poetic, placid, the unique example in the history of the world of a people lost in thought.

"Go and read it and you will understand . . ." says the Jaguar Priest. But we can't. It's gone.

II
Cities
of Gods

The Maya (as previously noted) were not necessarily the first people in America to build pyramids and crown them with temples. Their art in carved wood and stone, stucco modeling and painting, is considered by general consent to include the finest such work in the New World and some of the finest anywhere, but they may not have been the first among their neighbors to practice it. The corbeled vault distinctive to their architecture, some of the aspects of their written language, and possibly their use of zero, seem to have been exclusively their own; but they may not necessarily have been the first to use the principles of their famous calendar mathematics. Somewhat as in the case of the Ancient Olmecs, they did many of the same things that were done by others around them, only better. They were far from being alone in the growing world of their time, and ideas are no respecters of state lines. All the middle zone of the Americas, from central Mexico south to Bolivia and Peru, was spawning varicolored little towns and cities. Corn-farming, and the revolution in living that went with it—new gods, new wealth, new ways, new worries—had spread far beyond this sophisticated heartland.

54

A people who may possibly have included descendants of long-ago émigrés from someplace in that heartland were established in scattered villages in the Ohio Valley, far up in North America, and making pottery and building enormous burial mounds, hundreds of years before the beginning of the Maya Classic Age. Also, centuries before the first dated Maya monuments, corn was under cultivation among the already ancient Cochise people in the adjoining southerly corners of what is now Arizona and New Mexico, and not long afterward was being grown by the incipient villagers of the Southwest we call the Basketmakers, ancestors of the modern Pueblo Indians. The potato, as much of a civilizer in South America as maize, was coming into use in the Andes region, and manioc, the third great South American staple, was cultivated still earlier. Tobacco was nearly everywhere.

While everywhere beyond the belts of little slashed-out planted fields, everywhere throughout the boundless areas surrounding these few frontiers, the wandering tribes, untouched, lived as they always had.

"The people of the wood," the Maya poets called them in the *Popol Vuh*. "There are generations in the world, there are country people, whose faces we do not see, who have no homes, they only wander through the small and large woodlands . . ."

Some of these people then living in the Grand Canyon of Arizona were making tiny figurines, while the Maya were building temples—figurines of little deer fashioned from twigs, with twig spears run through them: if this unnatural phenomenon is modeled and inserted in the world, might not the world produce it in response? (Archaeologists first discovered these, incidentally, for sale at a roadside curio stand in Arizona; they are more than 3,000 years old.)

Trading in more than ideas went on between the towns and cities—trading in everything from slaves to kitchenware. Articles of commerce found their way from town to town and covered, sometimes, astonishing distances.

West along the Gulf Coast from the Maya country were the fat-faced Ancient Olmecs and their old, faded city of La Venta. A possibly related people, known to us as Totonacs, may have built Tajin, the next town of importance up the coast, a town of a great pyramid and many temples.

Inland, in the southern highlands, a profusion of towns and cities were inhabited by a profusion of peoples as yet far from clear to modern students, from the Zapotecs in their brilliantly painted mountain-top cities in the Oaxaca area to the great religious center of Cholula, in the present state of Puebla, for centuries evidently the capital, the cultural capital at least, of the Mixtec people. The Zapotecs traded their elaborate incense burners far and wide and their country may have been the birthplace of the god Xipe, god of springtime, in whose honor the priest danced in the skin of a flayed sacrifical victim. At Cholula the immense sacred pyramid was enlarged by successive additions until it eventually exceeded in volume Egypt's Pyramid of Cheops. A mural of butterfly gods decorated a room inside it, together with a painting of Quetzalcoatl who, as the Plumed Serpent, God of the Morning, the Bearded Man, Lord of Life, Lord of the Wind, Bringer of Civilization, and in countless other guises, was known to all these differing peoples from the earliest times.

As far as present comprehension comprehends, these urban glories reached their apex in the Valley of Mexico, a high land-locked basin, wrinkled with networks of little valleys and ringed by smoking volcanoes, set in the southeastern end of the vast plateau that is mid-Mexico. Here in this "Valley" at an altitude of nearly a mile and a half were numerous towns and villages and cities, most of them congregated around the great salt lake, Lake Texcoco, and its fresh-water feeder lagoons, sizable lakes in themselves.

The Classic Age in central Mexico was in some certain respects uncultivated and immature compared to the same period of the Mayas, but its works made up in dimension what they lacked in elegance. From the Pyramid of the Moon to the Temple of Quetzalcoatl, Teotihuacan, the great city of the Valley of Mexico's Classic Age, was a solid procession of majestic public buildings and religious barracks, decorated with the serpents, beasts, and feathered men of heaven, dominated in the center by the tremendous Pyramid of the Sun. A paved area more than three miles long and nearly two miles wide was occupied by these structures and their plazas, parks, and avenues—and by what were evidently closely packed houses, leading to the current view that Teotihuacan was no empty ceremonial center but a genuine city in the modern urban sense, with a population of perhaps 50,000 or even more. The drought-ridden countryside roundabout has also led some scholars to the conclusion that large scale irrigation must have been practiced, to sustain so many city-dwellers, although definite evidence has not yet been found of irrigation canals at so early a period in the Valley of Mexico. In any case the organization required to create and operate such a vast city certainly must have made of it a place of worship famous throughout all the land, to which the faithful must have thronged from many miles around, joining the black-robed priests in celebrating the mysteries that kept the world in balance—rain and fire, planting and harvesting, and the endless, mystical renewal of the holy days of the calendar.

Varying forms of the typical Mesoamerican calendar systems—including most of the Maya calendrics except for the Mayan long-count—were in use among all the sprouting cities of Mexico, the calendar that swallowed itself, like the two-headed serpent, every 260 days and every 52 years, spinning out the revelation that everything comes to an end and yet is reborn, everything changes and yet remains the same, only the circle, revolving forever, remains unchanged.

The sacrifice of human beings, dogs, birds, flowers, anything that lived, was an act in recognition and sustenance of this eternal process. The notion of sacrifice to appease angry gods is Mesopotamian, not Mesoamerican. Angry gods are shepherds' gods, living in the lightning, and the Indians kept no flocks. The gods of Teotihuacan were in the sunlight that buttered the Valley and brought growth, and in the stars that hung like volleys of javelins in the sharp brittle air and never failed in the ceaseless repetition of their flight. The American gods were hungry, not angry, hungry for the destruction of living things that was the bass-drum beat of the rhythm of life, the death that brought new life. Without constant death the life of the gods grew weak, for was not death the ultimate objective of life, and thus its food? The Teotihuacanos, in common with many other people before and since, ate the god to achieve divine communion, in ritual cannibalistic feasts.

The influence of magnificent Teotihuacan—in architecture, pottery, in its gods—can be traced for century after century over all middle Mexico and even into the heart of the Maya country some seven hundred miles to the south, until about A.D. 600 when began the generations of invasion or revolution that continued until the great city was destroyed.

But before that final ending Teotihuacan was twice rebuilt, lower rooms filled in and buildings covered with cut stone and adobe to provide platforms for new and larger buildings. Tem-

ples were customarily enlarged or rebuilt at the close of each
fifty-two-year "century," but these reconstructions apparently
indicated something more, very possibly clean-sweep changes of
political administration. Religion and politics were so entwined
as to be one and the same thing; when the party of the old gods
was overthrown the party of the new gods raised new temples as
well as a new society, and probably fed the new gods with any
priests of the defeated opposition who could be chased down
and caught. Such changes may or may not have meant invasion
of new people; perhaps more likely a shift in alignment of
powerful families or clans. Sometimes they may have reflected a
climax of discontent among the more numerous poor relations
—i.e., a revolt of the masses.

The old gods, however, never really disappeared. Tlaloc, the
Rain God, who was defeated at Teotihuacan, had the teeth of the
long-ago Ancient Olmec jaguar, and with new added attributes
he reappeared in the front rank of the pantheon. Quetzalcoatl,
whose ornately sculptured temple was completely covered over
and turned into the foundation for new construction, remained
nevertheless a star actor in the march of the following centuries.
The old gods melted into the new. The new gods became other
faces for the old. The gods of good and the gods of evil, locked
in their eternal embrace of combat were all, conceivably, only
opposing manifestations of the same beings—even of the same
single being, in some current scholarly opinion.

In the centuries following A.D. 600 turmoil became epidemic
among the city-states of central and southern Mexico, and the
Classic Age was pulled to pieces. It was during this time that
Cholula of the great pyramid fully emerged as a holy city, caught
the fallen metropolitan mantle of Teotihuacan so to speak, or so
some present readings of the archaeological records appear to
indicate. But it also seems that the Mixtec people, if clinging
to their center at Cholula, were pivoted still further southward to
come in conflict with the Zapotecan peoples of Oaxaca. It may
have been due to some such pressure that the Zapotec people
abandoned their mountain-top city of Monte Alban—many
generations later Mixtecs were using the then-ghost town of
Monte Alban as a cemetery, and some of the richest treasures of
ancient Mexico have been found there in their tombs. Descendants of the Ancient Olmecs and their relatives the Totonacs (if
they were indeed relatives) left their Vera Cruz coast and raged
inland into the mountains of Puebla and Oaxaca, adding to the
disturbances among the Mixtecan and Zapotecan peoples there.

A number of towns and cities throughout the civilized regions of central Mexico were abandoned, as the Maya were abandoning their jungle temples at about the same time. (If the GMT correlation of the Maya long-count calendar is followed, the wave of collapse appeared first in central Mexico and later—a couple of centuries or so later—among the Maya; the Spinden correlation brings the decline in both areas closer to simultaneity.) It seems a little easier to find reasons for the break-up outside the Maya borders, but still, the war-making migrations that appear to have been one immediate cause must have been in turn set afoot by something, some prodigious motivations. Whatever these may have been, famine, disease, or signs and portents in the priest-watched skies, they—or at any rate the dislocations they set in motion—went on for centuries.

The people of the woods who crowded down from the north to attack Mexico's cities during this age of chaos may have been driven by the general fever of unrest or may have been the germ of its beginning. This, though, would not explain the preceding and following centuries of comparative stability. But no doubt unrest was endemic among the wild tribes, especially during the difficult process of splitting and dividing whenever they grew so large as to be unwieldy units for their way of life. Probably these divisions were seldom peaceful. Probably the exiles went forth in anger. Certainly they went forth in grief, condemned as they were to separation and banishment.

Long afterward, a thousand years afterward, the grandson of the last "king" in the Valley of Mexico compiled a set of annals from the records then still existing in books of picture-writing. Fable, myth, and legend mingle in them, evoking all the more movingly the distant shadows. Listen to the saga of the Toltecs, a nation of barbarians who have dwelt for ages in "the country toward what is now called California, in the Southern Sea" (that is to say, Mexico's Pacific coast), who have sent Mosquito to stab the sun in the rump and keep him moving when he stopped, who have learned the calendar (strayed into the magnetic field of civilization and absorbed its beginnings), have suffered earthquakes and eclipses, and who now have been split by civil war.

The defeated rebels, driven away, sojourned for eight years in this place, three years in that, made slow, dragging marches of only 200 or 300 miles "because of their great multitude" to new countries for new sojourns of four years, five years, and again marched on, always toward the east, stopped among islands on a seacoast for five years, crossed arms of the sea in "boats and canoes." They left families to populate this land or that and traveled on. They calculated the end of one fifty-two-year cycle since they had commenced the civil war that ended in their expulsion, and at the end of a second cycle they were still moving on, stopping for seven years here, eight years there. After 122 years, and a series of thirteen temporary homelands, "they marched on, and founded . . . the city of Tula, which they were six years building."

The chant echoes from across that still river of time, perhaps truly the voice of the people of the wood moving so arduously into the light.

It may have been sometime in the eighth or ninth century A.D. that a final overwhelming horde of foreigners streamed into the Valley of Mexico, possibly Toltecs allied with the Otomi, residents of the northern end of the Mesa Central, the country just above the center of civilization around Lake Texcoco. It is believed these may have been the people who at last looted and burned and utterly destroyed once-splendid Teotihuacan— somebody did. Bands of Teotihuanaco refugees fled as far as Guatemala, others to a brother city west across Lake Texcoco, and others may have sold their skills (or spent them in slavery) to help the Toltecs build their capital city, Tula, north of the lake—which (unlike earlier cities) was built on a defensive height, reflecting the temper of the times.

The Otomi, or most of them, appear to have returned later to their own homeland to the north. The Toltecs stayed to found the first real empire in the New World.

By the middle of the tenth century they had extended their conquests as far as the heart of the Maya country, in Guatemala and northern Yucatan. The somewhat disorganized Mayas were reorganized and endured a long Indian-summer renaissance under Toltec domination, faithfully reflecting Toltec art and thought at such Yucatan Maya cities as the eloquent Chichen Itza and the rather dispirited Mayapan.

It would please our taste for sequence, maybe, to think of the Toltecs as uncultured conquerors with the artistic sensibilities of rich used-car dealers, but this doesn't seem to have been the case. Mexican tradition has remembered the Toltecs as the Master Architects, the brilliant innovators, the ideal expression of the Mexican genius. For centuries after the Toltec empire had vanished, ruling families from Yucatan to Texcoco insisted on claiming Toltec descent. And a modern archaeologist writes of a

Toltec temple pyramid: ". . . far better proportioned and more richly decorated than anything that came later, and far more delicate than any of the massive monuments of Teotihuacan."

The scholars and the diggers have revealed a great deal of the New World's tangled past, the least known and therefore the most intriguing of ancient histories, but there are so many things that are not yet understood and possibly never will be. The pattern is hopelessly elusive. It changes with each shifting wind that stirs the ashes. But here and there a coal is glowing yet, alive with a memory still warm to the touch. These bring the excitement of reality even though the cleverest of the specialists may be unsure—precisely the cleverest are the least sure—as to their exact place in the pattern. Such are the Maya and such are the people we call the Toltecs. Their magic still shines in the dark of the past, the Maya with grace and profuse reflection, the Toltecs with grace and profuse power.

Tradition says the Toltecs introduced idolatry and human sacrifice to the Maya. Tradition says they brought to Mexico the black god Tezcatlipoca, Lord of the Sky, the North, and the Night, to war with the white Quetzalcoatl, the Morning Star. Tradition says they introduced the sacred ball game, at which whole populaces, kings and commoners alike, bet and won and lost everything from their lip-jewels to their lives. Tradition says that in the time of the Toltec ruler Iztaccaltzin a gracious lady of blessed memory named Xochitl (the commonest Nahua girl's name, meaning Flower) invented *octli,* a booze made from the maguey plant, today called pulque and still the drink of the country.

But human sacrifice had been known before, although it may be not so commonly, among the Mayas as elsewhere in Middle America. No one can guess how long ago the practice began of sending dead souls to help the sun in his war against the stars, and feeding the rain with blood. What more could devotion offer, and who wouldn't be glad to go? "Quickly slay me, trample me with thy feet! . . . May my body come to rest!" in the words of an ancient Mexican prayer. And Tezcatlipoca, whose symbol was a jaguar skin (and the jaguar of the Ancient Olmecs had arrived two thousand years before), had been fighting the sun on temple walls for hundreds of years before Toltec times. And surely some of the ball courts in various cities were pre-Toltec; the origin of the Mexican ball game, in which players, without using their hands, tried to knock a solid rubber ball through the goal of a vertical ring set in the wall of the ball court, is believed to be very ancient indeed. The game was surrounded by ceremonies that were evidently of a sacred character. Ball-game terminology (as in the verse from a Nahuatl hymn: "He plays the ball game the servant of marvelous skill he plays at ball/ Youths make yourselves equal in the ball court to your forebears") could express the most solemn religious connotations.

And if the Maya wine called *balche,* so much used in religious ritual, had not wafted its idea northward to Mexico proper in times long before it would be surprising.

Tradition says the Toltecs' most glorious leader, Topiltzin, being born on the day called in the calendar Ce Acatl (One Reed) was given its name, after their custom, and since he was educated as a priest of Quetzalcoatl he therefore was given the god's name too, as was the custom, so that he was called in full Ce Acatl Topiltzin Quetzalcoatl. He was Hamlet in a feather crown: his wicked uncle, Lord of the Water Palace, murdered his father and stole the kingdom, and when Ce Acatl Topiltzin Quetzalcoatl reached manhood he killed his uncle on the Hill of the Star (where the New Fire ceremony opened each fifty-two-year "century") and took the kingdom back. He was a ruler of unparalleled goodness and wisdom.

But now tradition dissolves the priest into the godhead and says the vengeful god Tezcatlipoca appeared on earth and drove Ce Acatl Topiltzin Quetzalcoatl from Tula to Cholula and then to Yucatan, and that as he passed through all these places "he was regarded as a saint. He taught them by his words and by his works the road of virtue . . . After having taught . . . he departed by the way he had come, that is to say, to the East, and . . . told them that in time to come, in the year of Ce Acatl, he would return, and that his doctrine would be received . . ." So says Ixtlilxochitl, the previously mentioned (Spanish-educated) grandson of the last "king" of the Valley of Mexico.

Other chroniclers say Topiltzin Quetzalcoatl burned himself in a funeral fire and his heart leapt into the sky as the morning star; or his heart became a comet; or the smoke from his pyre became green-feathered quetzal-birds; or his heart went into the underworld for four days and returned as the morning star; or he parted the sea and walked away through it; or he sailed away on a raft made of snakes. He says, in the translation of the Nahuatl manuscript known as the Florentine Codex, "I am called hence.

The sun hath called me." Quetzalcoatl, Feathered Serpent, translated into the Maya language is Kukulcan, who was worshipped thereafter in the Maya country as a powerful god—he came to live, says legend, in both Chichen Itza and Mayapan.

Quetzalcoatl taught and left behind him, they say, all the arts of peace, from metalworking to feather-working, from writing to weaving. He tried to abolish human sacrifice in Tula, and limit worship to the burning of copal (resin) as incense, and the sacrifice of flowers and butterflies; but as Kukulcan he demanded human sacrifice at Chichen Itza.

Possibly all this contradictory clamor of tradition is based on bits of truth. The Toltecs seem to have brought a burst of energy, new ideas or a reformation of old ideas, new learning or a wider spread of old learning, in short a blazing rekindling of the old cultural fires all but snuffed out in the collapse of the Classic Age. Every flying spark would have set off a different conflagration, blown this way and that by different many-sided winds, leaving different memories in different places. These may very well have spread the religion of both white Quetzalcoatl and black Tezcatlipoca.

The Toltecs' greatest figure may very well have been Topiltzin. His time is variously ascribed to the ninth or tenth centuries, which puts him fairly well in the company of Charlemagne, Harun al-Rashid of the Arabian Nights, and Alfred the Great—maybe there was something in the air.

Metalworking clearly was introduced during this period (about A.D. 900)—at last the sun could burst forth in the splendor of gold, "excrement of the gods"—and trade was enormously expanded. Cargoes of everything from macaw feathers and jaguar skins to drinking tubes and chewing gum traveled the roads in the tumpline packs (back packs held by a band passed around the forehead) of merchants and their slaves.

Certain areas exported products—salt, rubber, dogs fattened for the table, cacao for the delicious foaming chocolate so much in demand that cacao beans were used for currency. Other regions worked up manufacturing specialties—yarn, embroidered cotton cloth for mantles, loincloths, skirts, hair-ribbons; warclubs with inset sword-blade edges of obsidian; rope, carved jade and turquoise, flutes and tobacco pipes of clay, pottery, paper, paints and dyes.

Some trade went by sea—the Maya imported at this time the famed Orange pottery from Vera Cruz, that had to be freighted more than 600 miles by seagoing canoe. The Maya dugouts, crewed by as many as twenty-five paddlers, carried for trade such building materials as lime, clay, and the metal-hard sapodilla wood, as well as corn and vanilla, wax and honey, stone cutlery from razors to hatchets, and chiefly (so wrote an early European explorer) "draperies and different articles of spun cotton in brilliant colors."

By circa A.D. 1000 the growing of corn and the other crops that followed (or sometimes preceded) it, such as squash and beans, and its accompanying art, the making of pottery, had seeped and trickled here and there throughout nearly all North America where the climate permitted, except the far west coast. The descendants of the Cochise people built ball courts for the sacred game in the Arizona desert, where their irrigation ditches had by this time already been carrying water for perhaps 200 years; and in the cottonwood canyons of the rainbow country where New Mexico, Arizona, Utah, and Colorado join, the Golden Age of the Pueblos was dawning (live parrots were brought here in trade, carried at least 1,200 miles from the markets of Mexico).

A corridor of maize-farming people extended from this Arizona-New Mexico outpost down the eastern slope of the Sierra Madre to the northwestern frontier of the Mexican civilization of the south, this frontier falling in the western marches of the land of the Zacatecas, nearly as far above the Valley of Mexico as the Maya country was below it. Pyramids, columns, and masonry buildings were constructed during Toltec times in these northwest frontier regions.

Apparently another corridor, a sea lane, reached across the Gulf of Mexico to the Mississippi, and a long list of trade items, some markedly Mayanesque in style, went from hand to hand through what seems to have been a grand network of prosperous little nations in and about the Mississippi valley. Many of these people built earthwork walls and mounds, as burial monuments, ceremonial designs, or embryonic temple platforms.

The ripples of contact carried ideas, customs, fragments of holy ceremony, to the most distant peoples of the woods as well as to settled farmers—and brought back new ideas in return.

The bow and arrow was working its way down from the North, and in the northern forests moccasins were replacing bark sandals. A sporty small-caliber weapon, the blowgun, shooting little clay bullets to knock down birds and small game, had appeared in Classic Teotihuacan. But the universal arms in A.D. 1000 were still the mace, knife, spear, and spear-thrower.

Worked gold came to the Mayas from Panama and Costa Rica, presumably drifting northward from Peru and Colombia, where metallurgy had developed long before this time. Gold objects (beautifully made) from Colombia have been dated as early as 457 (plus or minus 150) B.C., and evidence of metallurgy found in Peru dates from about the same period. The Maya never became metalworkers, but the Mexican city-states beyond them developed guilds of goldsmiths and silversmiths and poured forth lavish art in precious metals, such as the Mixtec treasure found at Monte Alban that, in the words of a specialist, "ranks with the greatest works of art of all time." In casting gold and silver, Mexican metalsmiths used an investment compound of clay and powdered charcoal that could be carved for cores, superior in this sense to modern compounds that become too brittle for carving—thus modern cores have to be mold-made, a technique used by the ancient Mexicans rather for cheap mass-produced objects.

In this matter of metalworking, as in so many other respects, parallels with the Andean region of South America, evidences of some kind of tenuous communication or counterpoint of influence, would appear to be obvious.

Each of these two separate centers of high civilization— Mexico and the South American Andes—practiced intensive farming, understood irrigation, shared some of the same basic crops, shared in their early ages even some identical pottery styles as well as the similar jaguar-feline cults; each built ceremonial centers and then towns and cities, temple mounds and step-pyramids; each organized society into classes dominated by priests and then by priest-politicians or priest-warriors, and so on through an impressive inventory, including such details as Chichen-Itza-style spindle whorls in Ecuador and the use in common of roller-seals made of clay.

On the other hand, there are equally impressive time-lags and differences to be found between the South American and the Mexican high civilizations.

Metallurgy w s known in the Andean region a thousand years before it reached Mexican America. If there was any contact to speak of, what ook so long? The widespread calendar of Mexican America never reached the Andes at all. Of course it is possible the Andeans would not have been particularly interested in the marvelous sacred calendar. The differences between the two civilizations of South America and Mexico seem to have been in some respects much deeper and subtler than the similarities, as shall be seen.

Since the clearest resemblances between these two areas of high civilization fall in an early period and since the differences grow more pronounced as time goes on, some experts have been tempted to the conclusion that both developed from a more or less common source and then grew apart. Other experts are inclined to take a cool view of anything approaching twinship, explaining the broad similarities as the natural result of similar levels of culture.

It is worth repeating that those levels of culture in South America and Mexico were not necessarily synchronized in time. It does appear that most of the specific parallels between them may stem from a single period in each area, the time of the feline cult on the Peruvian coast and the Ancient Olmec jaguar cultists in Mexico, but whether one of these cults preceded the other, or they overlapped or were contemporaneous, the evidence sayeth not, at least not clearly enough for this sort of detailed speculation. Before and after this period any communication between the two worlds was doubtless indirect, haphazard, and hazy in the extreme. Maize reaching Peru at this time, after thousands of years of cultivation in the Mexico area, and after at least more than a thousand years of a maizeless agriculture in Peru, certainly argues against any common source in the veriest beginnings. A basic difference in crops—root crops (such as potatoes) predominating in South America, grain crops (such as corn) predominating in North America—argues likewise.

Agriculture in Peru, at the time of the feline cultists (roughly the thousand years preceding the Christian era), had squash, gourds, beans, cotton, and manioc to work with, as well as newly introduced corn, peanuts, and avocados. The llama may have been domesticated at this time. Weaving was known. Primitive metalwork in sheet gold is reported, "among the earliest—if not the earliest—major examples of decorated metal working in the New World" (with a likely date as early as 800 B.C.), and, at the highest point of the florescence of this long period, exquisite gold ornaments of an "artistic quality and design not later surpassed . . ." The Peruvian north coast and the adjacent highlands were apparently dotted with villages, more or less independent of each other, with here and there religious centers

consisting of temple platforms and buildings of massive construction faced with dressed stone. Such a center was Chavin de
Huantar, the type site of the age, located in a little valley near a
little river, the Marañón—deceptively modest tail end of the
Amazon.

During these many generations of this thousand years the
fundamental principles of architecture, irrigation, and terracing
were developed that remained essentially unchanged through all
later Andean civilizations. The use of fertilizer (guano) was
learned. Farming by digging-stick and hoe was established,
never to change—the plow was unknown in the New World.
Basic ceramic techniques were fixed, never to change—the
potter's wheel never came into general New World use.

Then, after its thousand years or so, from circa 1000 B.C. to
circa A.D. 1, the Chavin style vanished. Revolution? Invasion?
The same people remain (and even the recurring fashion of little
conical hats). Possibly it was nothing more than too many
centuries of singing the same hymns. The feline god sank from
sight, and a half dozen or so "regional" styles of life laboriously
built their way into view, to shine forth here and there during the
following thousand years (circa A.D. 1-1000) in the various
flowerings of the Andean Classic Age.

The remains of this period, intricate mountainside terracing,
systems of irrigation canals running for miles, flood-fields pat-
terned with ridges for high-yield cultivation, somewhat similar in
principle to the chinampas or "floating islands" of central
Mexico, wide roads, monumental fortresses and ceremonial
centers, terraced houses of stone and adobe and underground
stone-paneled galleries, skilled work in precious metals—but
above all the pottery and the weaving—have been buried under
so many superlatives that their creators have for the most part
lost real-life identity, like the citizens of Renaissance Florence.

An exception is the case of the north coast people from the
Moche, Viru, and neighboring valleys, known as the Mochica
people, the makers of the Mochica pottery that reproduces with
portrait-and-caricature realism every detail of their lives, from
childbirth (women delivered on their knees) to sexual extrava-
ganzas, war, and the resplendent songs and dances of religion.
Helmeted warriors lope home carrying trophy heads, captives
are sacrificed by being hurled from cliffs, impersonal execution-
ers cut off a convict's lips, but strange and savage genres are
only part of the program. These are, in effect, thousands of

motion-pictures modeled in ceramics with a rambunctious virtuosity that seizes on everything in life, and many scenes picture familiar, everyday subjects as recognizable to us as a TV comedy—a good deal more recognizable, in fact, since they do not have television's primmer restrictions. Comedy, incidentally, was given high billing, which ought to be considered indicative of something.

The uncanny plastic skill and a certain taste for the maimed and the monstrous hint faintly and no doubt wrongly at an echo of the Ancient Olmec mind, dead these many lifetimes, but a feline returns to their pantheon, nevertheless, after an absence of centuries, in the cat fangs and whiskers of their monster-god, Ai apaec. They may have had a sort of writing system, ideographs indented in lima beans.

The textiles made by the Paracas and Nazca people of the Peruvian south coast represent, in the opinion of connoisseurs, the greatest textile art ever produced anywhere. They were woven from cotton and the wool of llamas, alpacas, and vicuñas into every sort of cloth from gauze and lace to brocade and tapestry, in every sort of color—archaeologists have classified as many as one hundred and ninety hues in seven color ranges. Apparently the finest were made as clothing for the dead, who were wrapped in huge mummy bundles of dazzling linens and richly embroidered brocades.

And in the Nazca deserts giant geometric and animalistic figures were etched on the earth, figures so huge some have only been noticeable since the advent of air travel. Sidereal surveys? Messages meant for the eye of the sun?

Over the Andean regions in general people took to wearing noseplugs and lip plugs in addition to the usual distending earrings and skull deformation, and possibly body-consciousness accounted for an extraordinary practice of the time—cutting baseball-sized holes in their skulls. This trepanning (it's not taken lightly by a modern surgeon) was fairly common, and examples of later bone growth around the edges of the cuts demonstrate that patients usually survived.

Medicine, surgical, herbalist, and magical, was well advanced. The white and sweet potato, quinoa, pineapple, and various other plants had been added to the fields; llamas, alpacas, ducks, and guinea pigs were raised. Coca had come into use, mixed—in the worldwide way of masticatories—with a touch of lime or ashes to release the narcotic. A beer, *chicha,* was fermented from corn or fruit. The permanent central Andean costume had evolved—loincloths, waist bands, knee-length shirts, various sorts of little hats, headbands, or turbans (Mochica aristocrats wore splendrous headdresses, with much gold). Balsa boats, large and small, traveled the oceans and lakes. The bladed club and spear-thrower ("estolica" in Mochica) were still the standard weapons. Feather masks and musical instruments from tambourines to coiled trumpets were used in the dances.

Everything, in fact, had been created that the Andean world was to have, except really widespread conquest and empire.

This came along in due course, in the final centuries of the first millennium A.D., creeping down in an almost all-enveloping tide from the central Andes. The capital and center may have been the city of Huari, although this first empire period is customarily called Tiahuanaco, after a city on skyhigh Lake Titicaca. Under whatever name, before A.D. 1000 most of the little nations from Nazca in the south to Moche in the north were united in following its style.

At about this same time, in the mountain valley of Cuzco midway between Tiahuanaco and Huari, a backwoods tribe of Quechua-speaking people who called themselves the people of the Inca were living in rough-stone villages, making bone tools, and, it may be, singing to the sunlit highlands the so-called Inca hymn:

> O Viracocha! Lord of the universe,
> Let it not be
> That I should tire,
> That I should die.

"Who this race were, and whence they came," wrote William Hickling Prescott in his *Conquest of Peru,* "may afford a tempting theme for inquiry to the speculative antiquarian. But it is a land of darkness that lies far beyond the domain of history."

The origin of the Incas is of course no more mysterious than the origin of any of the scores of other Andean tribes—well over a hundred have been identified; there were many more. Here as everywhere else on the two continents the knots of people had moved, merged, split, multiplied, appeared and disappeared from every compass point for untold thousands of years before history first caught them in its lens.

But extend the question, as Prescott intended, to inquire into the origin of this whole remarkable Andean civilization, or extend it even further, to inquire into the development of the entire civilization of all the New World: as has been seen, the general outlines of this development show slow growth and accretion over immense periods of time.

The developing civilization of the Andes had witnessed Tiahuanacan warriors, coeval with iron-gauntleted Crusaders in the Old World, marching past stone felines of Chavin that were already as ancient, to them, as Cleopatra is now to us. It had seen the cat-cult priests of the Chavin period, coeval with the Druid priest-rulers of England, invoking blessings upon farm fields that were already more ancient, to them, than the Crusaders are now to us.

There doesn't seem to be any scoring here for the sudden trombones of unexpected mysteries.

But for centuries there has been no lack of speculative antiquarians presenting evidence to prove that the civilizations of Peru or Mexico were brought to the New World more or less ready-made from some Old World point of origin.

Exhaustive efforts have been made to establish an Egyptian origin for New World civilization, or to show that civilization was transported to the New World by sailors of Alexander the Great, or that the civilization of the Incas was the creation of the troops of the "Grand Khan Kublai." And indeed a learned French traveler saw in 1746 in Canada "nine hundred leagues to the west of Montreal, a tablet of stone fixed in a sculptured pillar" on which was (so he led himself to believe) a Tartar inscription. The Spanish historians Oviedo and Gomara, among others, decided on the authority of no less than Aristotle that the Indians were Carthaginians, Aristotle having related that some Carthaginians were storm-driven to an unknown island. Another Spanish scholar, Vanegas, supporting their theory, showed that both the Carthaginians and the Americans "practiced picture-writing, both venerated fire and water, wore skins of animals, pierced the ears, ate dogs, drank to excess, telegraphed by means of fires on hills, wore all their finery on going to war, poisoned their arrows, beat drums and shouted in battle." However, the Spanish historian Acosta, after nine years study in Peru, was able to demonstrate that America was the Ophir of Solomon. The early-nineteenth century scholar, Edward King, Viscount Kingsborough, spent his life, his fortune, and his sacred honor (he died in debtors' prison) proving that the

Mexican civilization was built by the Hebrews, and Lord Kingsborough was withal only one of many who filled great volumes with endless Aztec-Holy Land parallels (circumcision, for example) that had a most persuasive ring to Bible-conscious Victorian ears.

All unanswered questions and apparent parallels—and there are many—spur on such speculation. Anthropologists noticed long ago fairly lengthy lists of correspondences between New World and Old World culture traits, ranging from similarities in certain folktales to similarities in such occasional items as various games or widespread addiction to gambling, ritual "giveaways" of food and property, specific fire-making techniques, blowguns, scattered use of wooden pillows, stilts, plaited fans, and so on through some dozens of items. Some of these were doubtless part of the universal baggage of Paleolithic man, some were probably incidental imports (or exports), some were probably independent convergences or coincidences. Most, regarded as elements of culture growth, seemed to be trivial—with the exception of pottery, evidently first introduced among North American Woodland peoples during late Archaic times via Siberia, Bering Strait, Alaska and points southeastward, although some early occurrences are suspected of being independent developments born from previous stone bowls. Recent ponderings of earliest North American pottery have come up with transatlantic introduction as more acceptable than trans-Siberian, alleging striking resemblances to Neolithic ware in north Russia and Scandinavia. But in any case no one has proposed such hypothetical contacts with primitive north Europe as transmission points for a ready-mixed high culture.

However, more exciting possibilities appeared with botanical studies published some twenty-five years ago that offered genetic evidence seemingly showing prehistoric New World cotton to be a cross between Asiatic cotton and American wild cotton. The sensational prospect therefore arose of cotton-clad plant-breeders from Asia appearing on the bleak north Peruvian coast some 5000 years ago (place and time of the earliest archaeological appearance of this cotton, at a primitive pre-pottery site known as Huaca Prieta). Here, then, were perhaps the superior civilization-bringers so long longed for by the more persistently romantic of Europe's speculative antiquarians, and intensified attention was turned anew toward Asiatic contacts.

Later botanical studies, though, published within the last ten years, have cast considerable doubt on the Asiatic cotton-crossing notion, offering genetic evidence that New World cotton was very likely all-American after all in its origins. But by this time theorists had already ransacked Asia searching for still further connections or parallels between its ancient civilizations and the ancient civilizations of the New World.

They have found many, almost as many as had previously been found proving a connection with the Hebrews. None seem to be very weighty additions to the lists of parallels already familiar to anthropologists, except, again, pottery, this time in South America. Very early pottery found on the coast of Ecuador bears striking resemblance, in the opinion of most experts, to an early pottery of Japan. Radiocarbon dates go back as far as 3000 B.C. for this earliest Ecuadorian pottery, known as Valdivia, giving it a good claim for being the earliest pottery yet discovered in the New World, from one to several centuries older than other finds on the Caribbean and Atlantic coasts. These other finds, however, are of distinctly different typology and obviously of distinctly separate origins. It would seem, therefore, that the possibility of ceramic introduction from Neolithic Japan might merely be added to the previous possibilities from north Europe and Siberia. But the idea of transpacific contact at such an early period has again engendered considerable excitement, and new digging up and down the Pacific coast is going on apace.

Some archaeologists are inclined to give serious consideration also to arguments that New World metallurgical techniques derived from some outside stimulus—if not, they represent the one and only independent invention of metallurgy in all the world. Its earliest presence in the New World, as has been mentioned, is in Peru during the first millennium B.C. But the exquisite, unsurpassable work that appeared so early, as was also previously mentioned, poses a sore mystery, as does the extraordinary fact that platinum was worked in pre-Columbian Ecuador and Colombia, by a process usually thought to be a strictly modern method of working high-melting-point metals, and is the first known application anywhere of this basic principle, called nowadays powder metallurgy. Maybe metallurgy was introduced via contacts with Mount Olympus.

The ultimate origins of the various early New World pottery complexes and the ultimate origin of New World metallurgy are still open questions and are likely to remain so for at least some time to come. But this primitive pre-agricultural pottery, wherever its origins, scarely carried with it a determination of the shape the great New World civilization would assume. In the words of a recent authority, even proven "remote Asiatic origin" could only have little effect "on the integrity of Nuclear American civilizations." Metallurgy could have had even less effect on the Maya world, where it never appeared at all, or Mexico in general, where it appeared only toward the end of Classic times, when the form and structure of the Mesoamerican world had been firmly fixed for centuries.

The vast majority of the claimed Asian influences put forward in recent years have been art motifs, some of which seem to have merit as possible actual resemblances and some of which do not, but all are proclaimed with considerable zeal and all are adduced to "prove" once more the creation by the Old World of New World civilizations. One leading proponent offers a speculative theory arguing in some detail how various Asian societies may have transported these civilizations across the Pacific piece by piece in a rather regular traffic of transpacific sailings continuing for more than two thousand years and barely ending, circa A.D. 1200, in time to make way for Columbus.

The zeal and fervency, sometimes in fact reaching vociferousness, of some of the proponents of the Old World as father of the New is of particular interest in itself. The center of this faith has remained in Europe down through the centuries—American scholars in general have never bought much of it—and so a comparatively distant acquaintance with the New World civilizations may have been added to a residue of European ethnocentricism at bottom emotional. But of more immediate weight, apparently, is the principle of the universality—in effect the unity—of world history which became popular in Germany in the nineteenth century and still carries some weight in German historical theory. This concept of world history can of course not survive if the aboriginal New World maintains its position as a major isolate. Hence the determined, if not at times desperate, efforts to achieve what the European theorists frankly designate the desired "breakthrough."

But the civilizations of the Old World were based on sown cereals, the plow, the cow (or the goat or the pig), and the wheel. Is it to be supposed that the generations of technicans sent to America left all those behind and brought countless cargoes of art motifs instead? And obviously none of them, on the return voyages, bothered to carry back the New World products that after Columbus took the Old by storm: potatoes, tomatoes, corn, chocolate, all the list of more than one hundred crops that now make up three-fifths of the world's agricultural items. Of all these products, only a half dozen or less seem to have occurred in both the Old and New Worlds in pre-Columbian times: coconuts, calabashes, sweet potatoes, and maybe peanuts are the most likely candidates for this rare honor.

It does seem unlikely that transpacific merchant ships plied much of a pre-Columbian trade. It also seems unlikely that all the reported parallels are derivations. Art motifs and generalized culture traits can be made to prove anything, as the wildly divergent previous theories of this sort demonstrate. It is also unlikely that of the actual derivations all derived in one direction—it is only reasonable to suppose that some at least originated in America and went the other way.

The whole argument is a sterile, Bacon-wrote-Shakespeare kind of thing, and a pity because the study of ancient America is so often sidetracked into this controversy and away from consideration of the American contributions themselves.

For the important point is that the American high cultures differ basically from those of the Old World, as they differ also from each other.

Clearly pre-Columbian contacts with Old World civilizations can have been of no great significance in the direction taken by the development of the American civilizations, or those basic differences would scarcely have remained basic.

Undoubtedly there were such occasional contacts, transoceanic, even transpacific. There were myriad years for them to be made in, and any craft, no matter how primitive, once launched on the bosomy deep can conceivably be carried to very strange and faraway places indeed. Probably some of the earliest contacts by sea came by way of the Aleutian Islands. Some scholars have also suggested an ancient passage by sea between Australia and the tail of South America, via Antarctica.

Appearances of Norsemen on the eastern coast of North America unquestionably took place. At about the same epoch (after the tenth century A.D.), with the beginning of settlement on the nearer Polynesian islands, some trips back and forth (with a bow to *Kon-Tiki*) certainly occurred. There were indubitable later contacts between Asia and the Northwest Coast; some of the results re-echoed to Hawaii and thence the far western Pacific, back to the doorstep of Asia, to create scholarly confusion today. There are a number of recorded instances of Chinese junks and Japanese fishing vessels driven ashore on the Northwest Coast; there must have been many more during the previous unrecorded centuries—but except for the Northwest Coast, chances would have been better for accidental crossings from South or Middle America to Asia rather than the other way around. The sixteenth-century Spanish, champions of their day when it came to voyaging, tried for thirty-seven disastrous years before they were able to make their way eastward across the Pacific to Mexico. Chance trips to and from Africa would have been more probable still.

Phoenicians, Egyptians, Greeks, Chinese, Britons, Irish, how many wandering boatloads or lunatic marooners stumbled ashore on this land as strange as the moon in time incredibly long ago? If the greatest epics were unsung, here they are.

And there is plenty of matter (other than metallurgy) for mystery in the marvelous fabric of New World cultures. There are the Negroid characteristics some see, or imagine, in the Ancient Olmecs, or the bands of white Indians, such as the highland Chachapoya of the Inca Empire, famous fighters. There is the sometimes white, sometimes bearded, sometimes bald Quetzalcoatl, much too ancient, alas, to be a Viking, as the old favorite theory had it. There are the black-boned, black-fleshed Araucanian chickens that lay blue eggs, and might be pre-Columbian, and might be related to the Silkies, a breed of Africa and Asia. There are the resemblances between Asiatic parcheesi (pachiti) and the Middle American game of patolli. And the resemblances some see, or imagine, between certain written ideographs from the pre-Inca Andes and the so-called"rongo-rongo writing," or Easter Island script, from 2,000 miles out in the Pacific and in use as late as the mid-nineteenth century.

Some culture elements must have been exchanged to be sure, and it is interesting to guess what they may have been. None could have been fundamentally important in the formation of New World civilizations, for the reasons previously noted; some alleged resemblances turn out on closer examination to be quite doubtful; most root back to the primitive Ice Age soil out of which both the Old World and the New World grew.

But the Old World civilizations turned one direction and the New World another. Besides the basic differences already noted—the plow, the cow, the wheel, sown grains (to which could be added an all but endless list of other highly practical items, from iron and the keel and the chimney to stringed musical instruments)—prevailing patterns of Old World civilizations included kingship and inherited personal wealth, private property particularly in landed estates, individual competition for acquisition of wealth at the expense of one's neighbor, this leading to an individual spiritual and intellectual freedom, but also leading to veritable war and military conquest.

New World civilizations exhibit these various aspects, so fundamental to the Old World, as exceptions rather than the rule. Communities were usually under the rule of councils, a true kingship pattern being exceptional. Much property, and particularly land, was usually held communally. Individual competition for individual acquisition of wealth at the expense of one's neighbors was uncommon. As a consequence individual spiritual and intellectual freedom was not customary; spiritual and intellectual activity was pursued, rather, in group participation. Belonging, as has been said elsewhere in this volume, was more important than belongings. One believed, felt, strived, rather as a member of a group than as a solitary individual, in comparison to a typical subject of Old World societies.

The basic unit of social construction in the New World was kinship—family relationship. The basic unit of social construction in the Old World was property relationship.

The great reigning motive of life in the New World civilizations was always religious—from the earliest archaeological reconstructions to the arrival of the Europeans religion appears to have been the principal and almost the only key to the organization of society, religious behavior the chief force everywhere, from the wildest people of the woods to the most dazzling Maya cities.

The great reigning motive of life in the Old World was acquisition of wealth, property, business, the commerce of individual gain and individual ambition, leading to (as noted) the ultimate business triumph of true military conquest, and in this wordly welter religion was only one of many forces. Business assumed so large a role so early that Pindar, in seeking to illustrate how much he loved his homeland, said, "I will put your interests even before business."

A society must be the product of its total time, not merely of this or that hypothetical instant of culture-contact. Every impulse that enters or goes out from it, crosses over it or clashes with it, develops within it or is rejected by it, the thoughts that are not thought as well as the thoughts that become ideas, all must contribute to any society's complex pattern, a pattern infinitely too intricate for glib dismemberment into similarities of art motifs or furniture styles. In the New World patterns were formed that were elaborately distinctive from those formed in the Old World, and distinctively Indian.

An impulse went forth (in the latter centuries of the first millennium A.D.) from the sprawling Andean city of Huari (if not from Tiahuanaco) that unified to some degree the people of the central Andes for the first time since the collapse of the ancient cat cult nearly one thousand years before. Nobody is sure this was a war-won unification; maybe everyone simply liked doing things the Tiahuanaco way.

Whatever it was it fell apart, after a century or two or three, and the half dozen different Andean regions returned to an independence that took the shape of building large cities, more terraced farmlands, more irrigation systems, more roads and bridges and walls, and conquering each other. The Mochica bounced back as the center of the little Chimu empire in the north, that stretched for 600 miles along the coast. Scattered villages surrounding ceremonial centers seem to have been the more usual pattern until Tiahuanaco times, which introduced a style of planned enclosures, walled cities that were truly cities although Tiahuanaco itself was apparently less an inhabited city than the site of a great ceremonial shrine. Such cities reached their highest point along the Chimu coast; in the inland mountains the old custom of separate ceremonial centers and separate mountain-top fortresses continued even until later times, the great center of Cuzco, for example, being separated by fields from its surrounding villages.

During this period, variously called Chimu or Fusion or, by one leading authority, the epoch of the City Builders, more goods of all kinds were made, and very skillfully, but the masterpieces of old, of the great Mochica ware, of the Nazca and Paracas weaving, of all the arts which poured forth in Florescent times centuries before, were never again approached. The making of bronze was developed, restricted to the inland high-mountain country of Bolivian tin—a mighty feat of leap-frogging if introduced by sea. Much more gold and silver was worked; in Ecuador even the fishhooks were of gold. The fashion for featherwork boomed. Priest-politicians ruled, seemingly, and classes were divided into priests and farmers, warrior aristocrats and artisan workers.

The Incas in their Cuzco valley were one of the many little states only trying to survive in the political atmosphere of devious alliances, treachery, ambitious conspiracy, and sudden death. They had done well at it: Cuzco was one of the few central Andean towns that had not been absorbed into the Tiahuanaco sphere.

Viracocha Inca, eighth in a line of insignificant local chiefs claiming direct descent from the legendary Manco Capac, son of the Sun, played for a long time a wily game of balancing powerful neighbors against each other, but eventually artful diplomacy and astute political marriages were not enough—the city-state of Chanca to the northwest sent invading armies, and Viracocha fled with the heir apparent, Inca Urcon, to a mountain fort, abandoning his city.

In the high Andes, everything is larger than life. You could drop an ordinary mountain in any chasm, Baron Alexander von Humboldt said, and lose it there. The country cries out for Wagnerian music, and gods in the shape of heroes. At this moment it got one.

Yupanqui, a son of Viracocha, refused to run, led Cuzco in a hopeless defense, and at the critical moment the stones of the battlefield became warriors, so they say, and fought for the outnumbered Incas. The city was saved; the Chanca were utterly defeated.

When Viracocha died he was given a priest-ruler's usual deification (his women and servants would dance ceremonially at the funeral dance until they were ceremonially drunk on the ceremonial wine, when they would joyously surrender themselves to the strangler so they might accompany their lord; living servant-women would be assigned in perpetuity beside his mummy bundle to whisk the flies away), but Yupanqui casually set Inca Urcon aside and took for himself the strip of braid that was the Inca crown. He also took a new name, Pachacuti ("Cataclysm"), by which he was known forever afterward.

This was in the year 1438 (or thereabouts); during the next fifty-five years Pachacuti Inca Yupanqui and his son, Topa Inca, by a process of adroit propaganda, diplomatic maneuvering, power politics, and the persuasive matter of eight major military campaigns, built and organized the Inca empire, extending for over two thousand miles from north to south and ruling over an estimated six million subjects (other estimates have run from three and a half million to thirty-two million). The population of England at about the same time was some four million.

It has been mentioned that the ideological differences between the Andes and Mexico ran deep. The Maya and the Mexicans were Greeks, the Incas were Romans, as many writers have remarked. The Maya dreamed, the Mexicans worshipped, the Incas built.

The things the Incas built were copied from the older civilizations that they conquered. In their cities, fortresses, roads, terraces, temples, they did only what had been done before by the people around them, but a great deal more of it. The ornamentation, the woven fabrics, the work in gold they pursued so avidly as a symbol of the Sun, all were adopted from their predecessors. In general none of their art approached in quality the best work of earlier times, although in quantity it was truly inspired.

The Incas were almost alone in the New World in achieving true war and true military conquest, conquest in which conquered lands were permanently occupied, conquered peoples were permanently organized into the world of their new masters. This world was built on the social group called the *ayllu*, a community of families living together who may or may not have been interrelated, working land which was owned in common, and which was redistributed in family lots each year to provide for rotation of crops and equal opportunity. Certain fields were cultivated for the support of the political and religious apparatus, and taxes were paid by such labor; there was no money. There were a number of royal *ayllus*, eleven at the time of the first Spanish records; the emperor, the "Inca" (the word meant "Lord"), was chosen from among the male members of these special groups (there were probably some five hundred or so such individuals at the time of the Spanish invasion). Once maneuvered into the top job the ruler was an absolute ruler whose people were virtually his slaves, but on the other hand he was obligated, at least in theory, to care for his people's needs and keep them contented. This was carried out by an immense and highly organized bureaucracy that extended from imperial, territorial, and provincial levels down to ward-heelers responsible for ten families (who reported to bosses responsible for fifty, who reported to bosses responsible for one hundred, and so on up). The territorial governors and the heads of the four great quarters into which the entire empire was divided formed a council of state advisory to the Inca. But the Inca's word was law, as was every subordinate's word all the way down the line.

Totalitarian political organization may have been the Incas' own invention. They naturalized trustworthy subject peoples as honorary citizens of the Inca nation and settled them among untrustworthy peoples, or resettled untrustworthy peoples where they could be more easily controlled. Regimentation of all aspects of public life and even some aspects of private life and thought reached such Orwellian heights as attempts to obliterate pre-Inca history. The amazing Inca vigor was directed not toward timeless dreams or ageless gods but toward the fabrication of an Inca past and the creation of an Inca future.

Occasional human sacrifice, especially of children, existed among the Incas, and for that matter they also sometimes made the skull of a fallen enemy leader into a cup, in the age-old trophy of total vanquishment, or sewed his skin up as a drum. "Our Inca will conquer you and make you a drum," Inca ambassadors warned the chief men of hostile peoples. More commonly still a state prisoner or an important criminal was disposed of privately, in the Cuzco dungeons furnished with snakes and wild beasts. Religion was of first importance, and certainly the Incas were divine (springing from the Sun) but they had no interest in the intellectual game of a complex world-devouring theogony. Public death as a daily bread for the gods was by no means their ultimate purpose of being; they had more practical things to do.

Their most reverent moment came with the simple offering of a chalice of wine to the Sun by the emperor. Religion was rich with rites, administered by innumerable priests and priestesses housed in innumerable temples and convents; every act of life was adorned with religious ceremony, each day at sunrise priests cried out to the Sun to remember that we are thy children, and in the great public ceremonies before the gold-sheeted Temple of the Sun each step of the glittering dance, each drumbeat and each note of a flute, was exactly prescribed. And yet in essence religion was comparatively simple: one worshipped creator Viracocha (who had made the world, taught all goodness and virtue, and then walked away on the water across the Pacific), the Sun, the Thunder, and observed the sacredness of the huacas—holy things, holy places, such as the tombs and the mummified bodies of ancestors (usually, for ordinary families, the mummy bundles of dead grandfathers), the extremely sacred bodies of dead emperors, the miraculous stones of Pachacuti's first battlefield. The Mayas sang:

> The red wild bees are in the east. A large red
> blossom is their cup
> The white wild bees are in the north
> The black wild bees are in the west
> The yellow wild bees are in the south

And to many American Indians, before and since, the Four Directions, or Five or Six, counting up-and-down as either one or two, have been the very cornerstones of religious structure—the symmetry of a universe in tune. But while the practical Incas administered their country in four political quarters, a division established by Pachacuti in 1460, they recognized in their religion only east and west: the rising and setting of the sun.

The Inca world of elegant gentlemen taking snuff, of engineers and sorcerers and busy city streets and the greatest collection of art in gold and silver the world has ever known, with everything meticulously organized from the careful education of the flawless girls chosen to be priestesses, imperial concubines, or sacrificial victims, down to the orderly rows of psalm-chanting farmers digging their fields in unison, brought nothing really new to Andean civilization except this rigid totalitarian organization. (Aristocracy by family relationships it took from the preceding Chimu, who regarded aristocrats and commoners as the product of two different creations.)

It touched, the Inca world, only erratically the numerous peoples beyond its boundaries, so far as present study—which is pretty erratic here too—has shown.

Southward the Calchaqui, of northwestern Argentina, part of the larger nation called the Diaguita, were farmers and town dwellers similar in many ways to the North American Pueblo Indians. Eastern neighbors of the Diaguita were the Guaicuruan hunters of the Chaco region, some of whom, notably the Abipon, developed striking parallels to the hunting tribes of the North American plains.

Farther south still, in central Chile, the Araucanians, farmers and llama herdsmen and extraordinarily fond of freedom, lived in family villages, worked gold, grew the same crops (they may have been the first to domesticate the potato), but were otherwise thoroughly unlike the class-conscious, temple-building central Andeans and gave the Incas as little shrift as possible.

Below them only people of the wood roamed the storm-swept bush of Patagonia—some of them living in the same cave that had been the home of giant-sloth hunters eight or ten thousand years before. And some of them, incidentally—the towering Tehuelche of eastern Patagonia—were the tallest of all Indians and some of the tallest people in the world.

Except in a few rather isolated instances Andean ways, and the Incas, seem not to have penetrated very deeply into the entire continent east of the Andes. In the Amazon rain-forest the common staff of life was flour made from the bitter manioc (modern tapioca comes from its root), from which the poison had to be extracted by a tricky process worthy of a chemical laboratory. Fish were drugged; tobacco was rolled into cigars; signal drums sounded in the night; and God was most often made manifest in masks and skirts of shredded bark.

Here was (and still is) the New World epicenter of the ceremonial use of narcotics; the Jibaro people of the upper river forests (in the easterly reaches of modern Ecuador and Peru) drink *maikoa,* a datura, at boys' puberty rites and before going on a raid to capture their famous trophy heads; in the course of the lengthy and complex ceremonies associated with the "shrinking" of the trophy head, or *tsantsa,* a narcotic called *natema (Banisteria caapi)* is drunk, to bring visions believed to foretell the future. Among the Zaparo, traditional Jibaro ene-mies, along the interior borders of present Colombia and south-ern Venezuela, a powerful infusion of tobacco is drunk as well as various other drugs, but above all *ayahuasca* (a Quechua word meaning vine of death or vine of dreams), a violent narcotic taken by men only (so they say).

Many Amazonian people knew that if a father did not take to his hammock and rest for a certain number of days after childbirth the baby would die. Here in uproariously stinking river villages lived the most jovially uninhibited cannibals on earth; some of the many bands of Tupian people bred their women to captives of war and raised the resultant children like veal calves for butchering.

To the north of the Inca empire, in what is now Colombia, Ecuador, Venezuela, and the southeasterly states of Central America, were various barbaric chiefdoms and petty priest-ruled states, the best known being the extensive domain of the

Chibcha, centering in Colombia. Some of these had histories of more or less high culture as old as any in the Andes or Mexico, and with more archaeological work in the future may assume a larger share of the record than they are given at present; especially that troubling origin-point of New World metallurgy may be found here. Extravagant human sacrifice and a few other Mexican customs appeared in the northwesterly marches, but most of the people were clearly South American (Chibchan the commonest language) all the way to the southern Maya frontier in the region of the Ulua River in Honduras.

The islands of the Caribbean had been populated mainly by Arawak village people from South America—but some of them had learned the ceremonial ball game of Mexico—gentle, kindly, ridiculously inept at war. During Inca times or thereabouts raids and invasions began from a ferociously warlike set of cannibals along the South American coast, the Caribs, who gave their name to the sea as well as the word cannibal to the English language; the raids continued for generations, great sport to the Caribs.

Erratically, some Andean ways migrated during the centuries across the Gulf of Mexico to the melting pot at the mouth of the Mississippi; and even the farming people far to the north who were later called the Sioux, and who might have been descendants of people building temple-mound communities in the Mississippi valley centuries before the Incas rose to power, used the word "wakan" (identical in sound with the Inca word "huaca") for something holy, sacred, supernaturally inspired.

III

Nations
of the Sun

In Mexico drought, famine, and wars of the gods, which is to say revolution and foreign attacks, had long ago caved in the Toltec empire. Tula (". . . a very large city, and truly a marvel . . . A great many powerful and wise men lived there . . .") had fallen in the year 1168, some say, and that same year is one of the traditional dates for the beginning of new barbarian migrations from the north, migrations of various tribes collectively called the Chichimecs (Dog People), tough, brutal, hungry, and armed with bows and arrows.

They pushed their way into the Valley of Mexico, probably over a period of many years, seized, sacked, and destroyed everything in sight, and emerged toward the end of the thirteenth century as rulers (usually claiming Toltec lineage) of some of the various city-states rebuilt, bigger and richer with gods than ever, about the great salt lake, Lake Texcoco.

They were a fiercely pious people and brought a tremendous increase in the pattern of human sacrifice and wars instigated at least partially for the purpose of capturing prisoners as sacrificial victims. They were also a supple people, and within a very few generations had become as aggressively cultured as they once had been savage—grand patrons of the arts, swooning esthetically over tastefully arranged bouquets and manipulating feather fans with a fine aristocratic grace. If they were not already Nahua-speaking people (some spoke Otomi or Pamé) they became so, and forgot the tongue of their uncouth grandfathers.

However, they did not lose their muscles. Besides the wars customary to ducal states jostling for gain, power, dominance, there were the hungry gods and that constant need for prisoners to feed to them: warriors and priests remained the elite castes. For several centuries, ever since the establishment of the Tolteca, warriors had vied with the priests—previously the unrivaled culture heroes—for space on the wall and column-carvings, with the warriors always gaining, an obvious reflection of the way the world was trending. "Then the man dexterous in arms . . . such honor he won that no one anywhere might be adorned [like him] . . ." says the Florentine Codex. And the ascetic priests praying in the mountains sawed skewers and cords through their own tongues, lips, ears, hands, genitals, to pour out their own blood in a thousand midnight fountains for the gods. One drew blood as penance from the part of the body that had sinned; one wore magic charms at ears, nose, and lips—in a hole pierced below the lower lip for the "lip plug"—so sin and sickness could not enter there.

Curiously, bows and arrows, after conquering the cities, largely gave way (except for the use of fire-arrows in sieges) to the old standard arms of spear and spear-thrower and battle-ax, and of these it is the obsidian-bladed club that is most often pictured in the codices. It is hard to take prisoners with long-distance bows and arrows, of course, which may have been the reason.

Wars were battles royal, hand-to-hand; you either disarmed your opponent and made him surrender or beat him unconscious and then dragged him away. Battles were gorgeously costumed affairs, men in headdresses and shirts of yellow parrot feathers, sprays of costly quetzal feathers set off with gold, whole squadrons uniformed in jaguar skins or golden hoods with feather horns, carrying shields decorated with golden disks, butterflies, and serpents, wearing embroidered sandals with thongs of orange leather. And they raised a gorgeous din as well, with the two-toned drums, conch-shell trumpets, shrill clay whistles, screams full voiced (so heaven could hear, and slyly designed besides to shock and terrify the enemy) calling on God for help and witness. The priests led the way to combat, carrying the gods, and then chanted promises of paradise and blew encouragement with piercing trumpet blasts while they waited with ready obsidian knives for the first prisoners to be dragged out from the battle for sacrifice on the spot, to be yanked spread-eagle on their backs, their chests slashed open, their hearts torn out and triumphantly raised ". . . there toward where the sun came forth . . ." Decision gained, the victorious troops charged into the defeated town, burning the temple, butchering and capturing the noncombatants, until finally they deigned to listen to the losing leaders' supplications for peace and promises of tribute.

These were not, to be sure, the constant pleasures of all. While every able-bodied man was subject, if need be, to soldiering, the best of the warriors tended to become more and more an exclusively military class. Farmers, stonemasons, featherworkers, goldsmiths, silversmiths, singers, musicians, worked at their work as they always had. But even the everyday world was full of spectacle, excitement, terror, and joy, so why resent a famous warrior's glory? He didn't get there without sweat either; and for that matter anyone, with courage and a lucky birthday and the help of the gods, could become a ranking warrior or a priest. And anyway, tortillas were yellow as sunlight or white as snow, green chocolate was tender, delicious, and foaming, and the girls, with their beautiful teeth and their blue-dyed hair, were always pretty.

The art of the featherworkers is gone, except for a rare time-tattered example, but the art in stone and gold and silver can still speak to us with passion, enthusiasm, and a dedication terrible in its intensity. Good work is hard work, usually, in art. They produced some wonderfully good work.

To the west of Lake Texcoco the city of Azcapotzalco, ruled by the Tepanecs, grew in dominions.

To the east of the lake the great city Texcoco, seat of the Acolhuas, had seventy towns paying it tribute.

To the south, where Lake Texcoco joined the freshwater Lake Xochimilco, the Culhuas at Culhuacan grew in power.

The Culhuas employed as mercenaries a landless tribe of spearmen, the Mexica, who had a heavy date with the future. They took a first step toward it when, wishing on a certain occasion to flatter the Culhua chief of council with the highest honor they could think of, they sacrificed his daughter and invited the ruler to watch the solemn climax of a priest dancing in the girl's skin. To their amazement the chief was enraged, caused the individuals responsible to be sacrificed or enslaved, and drove the rest of the Mexica people into exile. The dismayed fugitives founded a town on a miserable little group of islands in the lake, partway between Culhuacan and Azcapotzalco; they called their shantytown Tenochtitlan, which may have meant Place of the Cactus in the Rock or maybe Place of the Hard-as-Rock Cactus or maybe was named after Tenoch, a revered elder, as the name Mexica may have been taken in honor of a former leader named Mecitli. The founding of Tenochtitlan took place, according to the traditional date, in 1325; other dates have been suggested ranging from 1280 to 1362.

Such is one of the stories given by the chroniclers relating the establishment of the Mexica city. Another version has it that the Mexica were being held in slavery in Culhuacan, and escaped to their island hideout. On one point though most of the chronicles are in agreement—only yesterday the Mexica were the rankest of nobodies: ". . . nowhere were they welcomed . . . they were told, 'Who are these uncouth people?' . . . they could settle nowhere . . ."

Installed on their mudcaked islands the beggarly Mexica split into two rival factions, one of which founded a neighboring island town called Tlatelolco and became, some say, auxiliaries of the Tepanecs at Azcapotzalco—at any rate, Tezozomoc, tlatoque (supreme chief-of-council) of Azcapotzalco is said to have given them one of his own sons as governor. The faction at Tenochtitlan received as governor a grandson of the tlatoque of Culhuacan, presumably indicating an alliance with their quondam masters, the Culhuas. But when, some time later, Culhuacan was destroyed by the voracious conqueror Tezozomoc, the victory was followed by signal favors granted to the people of Tenochtitlan, possibly hinting that their alliance with Culhuacan may have contained a dash of perfidy and possibly helping to explain why, although the twin cities continued to live together and grow, Tenochtitlan grew faster. Tezozomoc even condescended to give his daughter in marriage to Huitzilhuitl II, its chief (who being the son of the Culhua governor was of course better born than the low-brow Mexica); and Tenochtitlan thereupon assumed identity as a full-fledged city-state and flourished to become Tezozomoc's stoutest and most worthy vassal, and the Mexica people there began calling themselves Tenochcas, after the name of their proud new city.

With the constant help of the Tenochcas, Tezozomoc extended his conquests for many miles beyond the Valley. Each new expansion of power tightened his rivalry with the only remaining other great Valley power, Texcoco, across the lake.

At last, in the year 1416, when Tezozomoc was in his nineties and had to be wrapped in down and cotton and carried in a basket, he raised the curtain on the big war and sent his troops of Azcapotzalco against Texcoco. Huitzilhuitl and his Tenochca Mexicas gave good service among the armies of subject warriors; Tezozomoc conducted the campaign with relentless craft; Texcoco was besieged, invaded, and finally taken. Its tlatoque, Ixtlilxochitl, tried to escape from the conquered city with his son Nezahualcoyotl (Hungry Coyote). The father was caught and died under the spears and battle-axes of Tezozomoc's soldiers. But the son escaped, to become Mexico's most resplendent legend.

He hid in the forests and the mountains, or in disguise in friendly cities; he wrote poetry, studied philosophy, discovered a personal religious faith in an Unknown God to whom sacrifice should not be made but only prayers; he was absolutely valorous, completely skilled in arms; he never did wrong, he always did right.

The followers who flocked to his secret standard (under the green oak greenwood tree) were loyal unto death; when he was once captured and put in a wooden cage to await execution a guard released him and died in his place. The incredibly aged Tezozomoc—he was now past a hundred years—could conquer the world but was powerless against the destiny of Nezahualcoyotl. A dozen times, according to the stories, Hungry Coyote miraculously eluded capture and certain death when Tezozomoc all but had him in his grasp.

"The goods of this life, its glories and its riches, are but lent to us . . . Yet the remembrance of the just shall not pass away from the nations . . ." so sang, more or less, the poet Nezahualcoyotl . . . while the armed men of Tezozomoc went from house to house in vanquished Texcoco slaying out of hand all children who mistakenly answered "Nezahualcoyotl" when asked who was their tlatoque.

And Tenochtitlan, become strong and formidable and putting on airs, perhaps began to seem less a vassal than a rival to great

Azcapotzalco, for it appears that two opposing factions now came to grips in the ruling council of Azcapotzalco, one no longer trusting the Mexica, one—headed by ancient Tezozomoc —still warmly trustful. When Huitzilhuitl II of Tenochtitlan died, the Tenochca elders and chief priests and warriors elected his son Chimalpopoca (Tezozomoc's favorite grandson) as their new leader. But the anti-Tenochca party at Azcapotzalco decreed that Chimalpopoca must die and Tenochtitlan be subjugated and fully incorporated into the Tepanec state. It is said that his dispair over this decision finally killed old Tezozomoc, at the age of 106, finding himself at the end more powerless than ever at his all-powerful capital of Azcapotzalco.

Chimalpopoca was duly murdered (by stranglers in the night, some stories say), and Tezozomoc's successor as tlatoque among the Tepanecs, Maxtla, as implacably hostile toward the Mexica as Demosthenes against Philip—and evidently for the same reason, fear of a growing power—insisted on either total surrender or total war. The Mexica, urged on by a young (twenty-nine-year-old) councilor named Tlacaelel, reluctantly and, one gathers, fearfully chose war.

But they elected a new leader, the famous Itzcoatl, and formed an alliance with the exiled Nezahualcoyotl. Armies of the faithful sprang up from Texcoco to follow Hungry Coyote. A third member joined the alliance, the strategically situated town of Tlacopan, which provided a beachhead for fleets of canoes sent across the lake from Texcoco. Maxtla was defeated and his city of Azcapotzalco taken by storm, although it took seven years—until 1434—for the gradual conquest of all the Tepanec towns, as far afield as Cuernavaca.

Nezahualcoyotl returned in triumph as the rightful tlatoque of Texcoco, married a hundred wives, built a matchless palace at his summer place of Texcotzingo, and lived a long life of matchless wisdom and probity. So they say.

And Tenochtitlan, the island shantytown of a century before, suddenly found itself (with Texcoco) one of the two chief cities of the entire country.

As the Mexica people of Tenochtitlan had risen in power and eminence, they had given themselves a suitable family history, and taken as their own a suitable god, Huitzilopochtli, "omen of evil . . . creator of war." (Teoyaotlatohuehuitzilopochtli, "Divine Lord of War, Great Huitzilopochtli," to give him his formal epithet.)

They had originally come from some place in the northwest of Mexico, a place they called in their legends Aztlan, and so they called themselves the People of Aztlan, or Aztecs.

Their god had told them to wander until they came to a cactus growing from a rock, on which an eagle would be perched, holding in his beak a serpent—the symbol of water and abundance; this promised land had been found, cactus, eagle, snake and all, exactly as predicted, at the site of Tenochtitlan. (The first Incas had been given a golden staff by the Sun and told they would find their promised land where the staff should enter the ground—which had been at the site of Cuzco.)

Huitzilopochtli had also told the Aztecs they were his chosen people and would rule the world. Together with Texcoco, and with Tlacopan for a junior partner in a continuing triple alliance, they proceeded to do so, as far as their known world of Mexico was concerned. Their conquests multiplied, extending far to the north and south. Tribute and captives poured into the city, and Tenochtitlan exploded in size.

The sister city of Tlatelolco became a commercial center, famed for its market, and in a bitter interborough war in the 1470s was at last taken over by the Tenochcas and absorbed into Tenochtitlan. This may have represented a final victory for Tlacaelel, who according to some accounts had by then served as the principal administrator of the Tenochca state for more than forty years, during the rule of three "kings" or chiefs-of-men and the initial great expansion of Aztec influence. (Among his other achievements, it is recorded that Tlacaelel led a purely scientific expedition to the north searching piously but in vain for Aztlan, the Aztecs' original home.)

Now the island foundations of the city were enlarged, for the use of houses and buildings and for the enormously productive *chinampa* agriculture, still practiced today among the "floating gardens" of Xochimilco. Swampland was reclaimed, blocks of new temples were raised, a three-mile-long aqueduct (double-barreled so its channels could be closed alternately for cleaning) was built to bring fresh water from the mainland, and a second had to be built soon afterward. A thousand people, so they say, were employed each day in washing down the streets. There were in the city 60,000 hearths, so most contemporary records seem to say, or an estimated 300,000 white-mantled people, although one recent study on population density is inclined to reduce that figure. (The population of London at the same epoch was 120,000.)

Texcoco became the artistic and intellectual capital of the Valley, but Tenochtitlan became the center of power and wealth for all Mexico. By constant intrigue as well as by constant war, the Aztecs gradually assumed leadership over Texcoco; Tlacopan was gradually forgotten as any kind of partner at all. After the death of Nezahualcoyotl in 1472—he left a reported sixty songs—the Aztec ascendancy grew still more pronounced.

Sometime in the 1470s, in Peru, another renowned leader died—Pachacuti; he also, incidentally, is credited with the authorship of many poems and psalms, including his own death song:

> I was born like a lily in the garden
> And so also was I brought up
> As my age came, I have grown up
> And, as I had to die, so I dried up
> And I died.

Pachacuti's son Topa Inca had been in command of military matters for some years while Pachacuti concerned himself with organizing administration; now Topa Inca campaigned to the south, whereas he and his father had previously driven toward the north. He marched his mace-men and peltists (who carried their slings wound like headbands in their hair) down into Chile, across the Atacama desert where rain has never been recorded, into the frontier zone of the country of the Araucanians, and set up, for all time, the southern boundary-markers of the empire on the banks of the River Maule, at what is now the modern town of Constitución. He spent his later years perfecting the Inca machinery of rule over this giant country, something more than eighty-five provinces (probably more than one hundred), far and away the largest political state yet known in the New World, and in the last year of his reign could see this creation trouble-free, perfectly functioning, magnificently complete.

This was in the year 1492.

The Aztecs conquered from sea to sea, from the Gulf Coast to the Pacific. They ran into setbacks with the Tarascans to the west, murderous bowmen who walloped them with a resounding defeat, and they were never able to crush the Tlaxcalans to the east, who used squadrons of Otomi archers as auxiliaries, although they surrounded Tlaxcala with satellite Aztec states that left its independence isolated and precarious, and its people deprived of the luxuries of commerce. Or Tlaxcala had been deliberately left unconquered, say some of the chroniclers, to serve as a nearby training (and captive-catching) ground for Tenochca warriors: a policy attributed to Tlacaelel.

Nearly all the rest of Mexico below Tampico and Guadalajara paid Aztec tribute—more or less, with frequent defections requiring frequent reconquests.

The Aztecs established no political empire in the Inca or Roman sense; they never thought of fighting wars for keeps in the modern sense. War remained at least partly a captive-catching game, its most notable feature the delayed-action battlefield casualties, the captured victims who played out their death roles later in ostentatious temple ceremonies rather than in the anonymous immediacy of battle. Occasionally some portion of conquered lands was placed under direct Aztec dominion, but in general defeated states were looted and then, in effect, left alone—as long as they continued to furnish the often heavy tribute assigned and recognize Aztec political hegemony.

Some peoples, theoretically subjugated, were in such a constant state of revolt that their names became almost synonymous among the Aztecs with the terms for captives, slaves, sacrificial victims—such were the Huastecs (the northern cousins of the Maya) and the Totonacs (the relatives, if they were, of the Olmecs), both in the Vera Cruz region along the Gulf Coast. This area had first been conquered in 1462, the year also of a memorable earthquake.

Even so, there were still not enough wars to furnish enough prisoners to feed the gods with sacrifice, and so artificial wars, Wars of the Flowers they were called, were instituted between neighboring states for the sole purpose of capturing victims from each other. These battles were formally arranged, each side fought until enough prisoners had been taken to satisfy the gods, and all parted friends, with no hard feelings. So they say.

It will bear repeating that the Aztecs did not introduce human sacrifice into Mexico. It had existed, at least to some degree, from the earliest times. They simply did the same things that had always been done but, according to all accounts, much bigger and better.

Anyone or any group, a war captain or a trade guild, the merchants' association or someone ill with an itch, needing the intercession of a god, bought a slave and on the god's feast day had him (or her—goddesses, naturally, were fed with women and girls) ceremonially bathed and slain. The priests at the many temples needed slaves (or captives—all captives of war were slaves, although all slaves were not captives; one might sell himself or a family might sell its children into bondage and possible sacrifice, and many did when times were hard) for the established, official temple rites. Military organizations needed victims for their established religious observances. In the case of the Aztecs, the state needed slaves constantly for the state God, Huitzilopochtli, who fought each day against the darkness of the night: without blood and human hearts the very order of the world would fail.

Each of the eighteen twenty-day months of the year had its ceremonies and sacrifices. Hearts were torn out for Huitzilopochtli, and then, at Tenochtitlan, the heads of the victims were impaled on the towering skull-rack in the central plaza. Captive warriors were given mock weapons and led by their celebrated keeper Old Wolf ("he in whose care lay the captives, as if they had become his sons") to be tied to the gladiator's stone and killed in a pretense of combat by warriors armed with real weapons, and then the priests danced with the heads of the captives ("And Old Wolf wept at this; he wept for his sons who had died"). Priests danced wrapped in the skins of victims, "stained, dripping, gleaming" with blood, "so that they terrified those whom they followed," in honor of Xipe Totec. Victims were lashed up as targets and shot full of arrows and darts so their dripping blood would fertilize the earth; children were sacrificed to the rain god, Tlaloc; victims were burned alive to celebrate the August heat of harvest. In the ceremony of the Volador four men costumed as macaws swung down by ropes from a high platform, whirling round and round a tall pole to which the ropes were attached; at the top, perhaps a hundred feet up, a fifth celebrant danced on a tiny platform that turned as the ropes of the flyers unwound. This may have been a calendar ceremony illustrating the years turning through the fifty-two-year "century," although it has been suggested that this rite was (and still is, in the Totonac and Huastec villages where it is still performed) a survival of a precipitation sacrifice, since the dancer at the top of the pole sometimes fell. Crowds danced and sang hilariously around the slave girl dressed as the Earth Mother, laughing and joking to conceal from her her fate, and the young war captive chosen to represent Tezcatlipoca lived a full year as the god, amidst every comfort, pleasure, and delight, and at the end of the year climbed the temple pyramid, breaking at each step a flute symbolic of his joyous incarnation, to meet his death on the sacrificial stone at the summit.

The deep-voiced drum, the huehuetl, throbbed like an enormous pulse, and the people celebrated, "jostling, howling, roaring. They made the dust rise; they caused the ground to smoke. Like people possessed, they stamped upon the earth."

The Aztecs were full of contradictions: arrogant and yet prizing humility, implacable and yet emotionally tender and affectionate, and like the ancient Greeks devoted equally to law, order, and loot. A boisterous, ebullient, but intensely earnest people, with an absolute certainty of the superiority of their way of life, they were well organized, technically and psychologically, for the mastery of the less zealous world around them.

Tizoc, supreme chief of council of Tenochtitlan from 1479 to 1486, was poisoned by the clan councils (it is said) because he was weak in war, for all that he performed the devout service—the chief of council was also one of the two supreme chief priests—of having a gigantic block of stone dragged to the city where it was carved into a monstrous bowl for burning human hearts.

Ahuitzotl, his brother and successor, left a more satisfactory trail of terror up and down the land, conquering forty-five provinces. Together with Nezahualpilli, son of Nezahualcoyotl and tlatoque of Texcoco, he campaigned for two years in Oaxaca to gather a fitting mass of captives for the dedication of the new temple to Huitzilopochtli. Twenty thousand people were sacrificed on this occasion, so they say—or so some say; others say 80,000 (but more about this later).

Ahuitzotl gave his niece to Nezahualpilli for wife, but this act of solidarity did not work out well; she not only took lovers with royal abandon in the court of Texcoco, but had statues made of them and worshipped them as her gods. Nezahualpilli, a true son of the just and austere Nezahualcoyotl, had her publicly judged, condemned, and executed in 1498. Her brother Moctezuma II (the familiar Montezuma of history, his name being Moctecuçuma in Nahua, usually rendered Moctezuma in modern Mexico, "Angry Lord" in English), who became the ruler of Tenochtitlan five years later, never forgave him, and after several years of strained relations took cold revenge by allowing the Texcocan force to be wiped out when the ostensible allies were attacking (unsuccessfully, again) the Tlaxcalans. When Nezahualpilli died in 1516, Moctezuma named his successor, as if Texcoco were a subject state instead of an equal ally; an opposing candidate raised a party of revolt, and the alliance was, at last, totally broken.

But by this time there were other even graver matters weighing on Moctezuma's mind. A temple burst into flame without cause and burned to the ground. In a school for musicians, a ceiling beam sang a prophecy of national doom. A temple was struck by lightning out of a clear sky. The waters of the lake suddenly rose up in a flood and destroyed some of the city's houses. A comet fell in broad daylight, in sunlight. In the year 1511 a column of fire appeared by night in the east, piercing the heavens; the people watched in terror, striking their mouths with their hands, "all were frightened; all waited in dread." It appeared each night for four years. Cihuacoatl, Serpent Woman, the Earth Goddess who wailed in the night streets to tell mothers when their children were to die, was heard weeping at night, crying out, "My beloved sons, whither shall I take you?" A marvelous bird was brought to Moctezuma, an ash-gray crane with a mirror in its head, and in the mirror could be seen people "coming massed, coming as conquerors, coming in war panoply. Deer bore them upon their backs." Moctezuma summoned his soothsayers and wise men, but the bird vanished before their eyes.

The New Fire ceremonies were held in 1507—the critical rites celebrating the end of a fifty-two-year cycle in the sacred calendar. Temples were enlarged or rebuilt, old debts were paid, injuries forgiven, enmities reconciled. Sins were confessed (at any rate by those too old to sin anymore) to the goddess Tlazoteotl, Eater of Filth. On the night of the New Fire all old fires were put out, and until midnight demons were free and the world hung in delicate balance—pregnant women were locked in windowless rooms so they could not be changed into animals, and children were kept forcibly awake so the demons could not eat them in their beds. The priests knew the world had been destroyed four times before, and would be destroyed again—this time by fire—in a divine rhythm that was ultimately inescapable, although it might be delayed by correct action. It would happen on such a night as this, when the New Fire would refuse to respond to the priests' control. But at midnight the fire priests succeeded in kindling the New Fire on the Hill of the Star and raced with it along the miles of causeway to the city, and rejoicing burst forth over all the land. The sun would rise again, the world would continue; all would go on as before.

Cristoforo Colombo (Italian), Cristóbal Colón (Spanish), Christopher Columbus (Anglicized Latin), Christ-bearing Dove (as we would literally translate his name if it were Indian), wrote in his first report, while on his way home from his first voyage of discovery across the unknown western sea: "The lands . . . are all most beautiful . . . and full of trees of a thousand kinds, so lofty that they seem to reach the sky. And some of them were in flower, some in fruit, some in another stage according to their kind. And the nightingale was singing, and other birds of a thousand sorts, in the month of November . . . The people of this island, and of all the others that I have found and seen . . . all go naked, men and women . . . they are artless and generous with what they have, to such a degree as no one would believe but he who had seen it. Of anything they have, if it be asked for, they never say no, but do rather invite the person to accept it, and show as much lovingness as though they would give their hearts . . . they believed very firmly that I, with these ships and crew, came from the sky; and in such opinion they received me at every place where I landed, after they had lost their terror. And this comes not because they are ignorant; on the contrary, they are men of very subtle wit, who navigate all those seas, and who give a marvellously good account of everything . . . And as soon as I arrived in the Indies, in the first island that I found, I took some of them by force, to the intent that they should learn and give me information of what there was in those parts. And so it was, that very soon they understood and we them, what by speech or what by signs . . . To this day I carry them who are still of the opinion that I came from heaven, from much conversation which they have had with me. And they were the first to proclaim it wherever I arrived; and the others went running from house to house and to the neighboring villages, with loud cries of 'Come! Come to see the people from heaven!' . . ."

Learned opinion favors Watling's Island in the Bahamas for the scene of the first landing, October 12; Columbus named the place San Salvador. Then, doubtless with the help of Arawak guides, he went to Cuba and then to Santo Domingo, which he named Española, where the *Santa Maria* was wrecked, and where he left a few dozen of his men to establish and hold a little fort, La Navidad. He sailed away to return to Europe on January 4, 1493, taking with him his six Indian interpreters, and returned to the Caribbean the following autumn with seventeen ships and fifteen hundred more people from heaven, most of them coming as colonists. He also brought horses, twenty stallions and mares surviving from thirty-four he had shipped aboard at the start of the voyage out.

Other islands in the Antilles were explored, a town was founded on Española and later moved to the south coast of the island (and called Santo Domingo) when gold was discovered there.

Christ-bearing Dove attacked the cannibal Caribs wherever they were found—a cargo of 600 of them were sent to Spain to be sold as slaves in 1498—but he did his best to enforce just treatment of the guileless and defenseless Tainos, as the Arawak island people called themselves. Two days after first encountering them on that October day in 1492 he had noted in his journal that "These poeple are very unskilled in arms . . . with fifty men they could all be subjected and made to do all that one wished . . ." But he had also written, "I knew that they were a people who could better be freed and converted to our Holy Faith by love than by force . . . they remained so much our friends that it was a marvel . . ."

But the Spanish settlers needed laborers for their plantations and mines, and the Indians were uninterested in work; the priests also protested that the Indians couldn't be taught and converted unless they were forced into congregations. More settlers came, two hundred more in 1498, twenty-five hundred in 1502, one to two thousand a year thereafter. It became necessary, of course, to congregate the Indians in villages under Spanish jurisdiction and see that they stayed congregated, and worked and worshipped properly.

Some of the Tainos tried to rebel, more fled to the hills and other islands and the mainland, more still died in the epidemics of the strange new diseases that had come with the people from heaven. By 1513 there were seventeen chartered towns in Española, and 14,000 Tainos left out of an estimated original several million on the island.

And the invaders, hunting cannibals and other native peoples classified as hostile who could legally be made slaves, as well as following the incessant rumors of gold, were penetrating the other islands of the Caribbean, the coasts of Florida and South America, and Panama—where 1,500 Spanish settlers arrived in 1514 to reinforce a colony founded some five years before.

The first Indian children fathered by the people from heaven grew to manhood. The survivors, if there were any, of the first naked islanders who had ventured down to the beach to approach the hairy, shining strangers became old men, and their stories had long ago lost all their wonderful savor. Christ-bearing Dove, white-haired and bumbling among important newcomers who refused to obey him, sailed away for the last time. Some of the Tainos may have heard that he died a year or so later. They may have been too busy dying themselves, and running and hiding, to care.

Spanish shipyards came into being, and horse and cattle ranches to supply the settlers with livestock. Throughout these years the Spanish never heard, except in dream-sequence Indian tales describing golden cities in a gilded cloudland, of the Aztec and Inca empires.

But in the year 1511 a Spanish ship, bound from Darien in Panama to Santo Domingo, struck a reef and sank in the Caribbean. Survivors reached the east coast of Yucatan where, ragged and starving, they were found by coastal Indians. Some were killed and ceremonially eaten, others died in slavery; eventually only two were left, two men named Aguilar and Guerrero, enslaved to Maya chieftains.

At about the same time, far up the Nahua coast of Mexico, a little girl named Malinal was stolen and sold into slavery. That this could happen is evidenced by the stringent Aztec laws against such kidnapers; but some say the little girl's father, chief and governor of the town of Paynala, had recently died, and her mother, remarried, had Malinal secretly sold to make secure the position of her new children. In any case, Malinal was owned by some people in Xicalingo, who in turn sold her to someone in Tabasco, on the frontier of the Maya country, in southeastern Mexico.

In the Maya country the ancient life of grandly marking time, the ancient cycles of solemn raptures, had ended long ago. If it is to be assumed the Toltecs had taught them the arts of pride and war, the Mayas had learned exceedingly well. The cowering Maya warriors of the eleventh-century sculptures had become, by the sixteenth century, some of the harshest fighters in the New World.

The sacred center of Chichen Itza and the city of Maya-pan—one of the few definite Mayan cities, in that it was an urban community rather than only a ceremonial center for scattered milpas—were no more, devastated and abandoned after centuries of intrigue and counter-intrigue, treachery, murder for power, and civil war.

The family of the Itzas (who claimed Toltec decent) had been driven with its followers back into the jungles to Guatemala, to the Lake Peten region where the classic Maya world had centered a thousand years before. Mayapan, long ruled by the Cocom family, had been destroyed in the middle 1400s, and all the Cocoms murdered except one son, who had been absent on a trading trip to Honduras at the time. The little Mayapan confederacy broke up into many quarreling city-states (at least eighteen), and the surviving Cocom, with what was left of his people, established a new city and carried on a smoldering cold war against the Xiu family, destroyers of Mayapan.

The Xiu claimed Toltec descent and had their name, a Nahuatl word meaning "fire" to prove it; on the other hand the name may be a Mexicanization of the Maya word "ciu" meaning "lord." After all but annihilating the Cocoms, the Xiu leaders and their supporters abandoned their old capital of Uxmal and built a new city at Mani ("It is passed"). Truly so, and the gods knew it; in 1464 a hurricane smashed Yucatan, in 1480 a pestilence decimated the people, and in the 1490s furious war became so general that the dead in the towns outnumbered the living.

In 1516 a terrible new pestilence swept over Yucatan, a disease never known before, with "great pustules that rotted the body," and the people died so quickly from it that the Maya named it "the easy death." It was apparently smallpox, passed along on ripples of contact from Panama, perhaps, where a wildfire epidemic had followed the arrival of the colonists in 1514. It came like the first trumpet call announcing the people from heaven, for the next year a Spanish ship from Cuba hunting slaves touched on the Yucatan coast, not far from where the slave-girl Malinal was living.

The Maya people there were unimpressed by the first white men they had ever seen, and drove the Spaniards away in a hot fight, in spite of gunfire. But the Spanish leader heard of cities and saw gold; he died of his arrow wounds not long after getting back to Cuba, but the next year four more Spanish ships came to cruise along the Yucatecan coast. Again they were driven away, but again, a few months later, the Spanish returned, this time with eleven ships and five hundred men. They also brought sixteen horses. Warriors gathered from Maya towns along the coast and fought "face to face, most valiantly," and kept on fighting off and on for three days, until the Spanish were able to disembark their horses and field a little troop of barely over a dozen mounted lancers. The Indians, who had never seen horses before, fled in terror, and this time the Spanish stayed.

The new Spanish captain, a young man named Hernando Cortes, had heard of bearded men in the Maya towns and gotten a message through to Aguilar and ransomed him from his seven years of slavery. The other surviving Spaniard had become a Maya and would not leave. ("Brother Aguilar, I am married and have three children and the Indians look upon me as a Cacique and captain in wartime—You go and God be with you, but I have my face tattooed and my ears pierced, what would the Spaniards say should they see me in this guise?" so reported Bernal Diaz del Castillo, a twenty-seven-year-old soldier with Cortes.) And among other gifts of tribute the now-subdued people of the Maya coast gave to Cortes their choicest girls, and among these the slave-girl Malinal.

Malinal had grown up to be not only pretty but bright ("good looking and intelligent and without embarrassment," said Bernal Diaz). She spoke Nahuatl as a birthright tongue, and in Tabasco she had learned the border Maya dialect known as Chontal, and also, possibly from merchants visiting the household where she lived, Maya proper, as spoken throughout Yucatan. She could talk to Aguilar in Yucatecan Maya, and Aguilar could then translate into Castilian for Cortes.

The Spanish called her, after she was baptized, Marina. She proved herself such a brilliant and valuable girl Friday that some historians are almost tempted to think of her as the real conqueror of Mexico.

". . . and thus God," wrote Bishop Landa some forty years later, "provided Cortes with good and faithful interpreters, by means of whom he came to have intimate knowledge of the affairs of Mexico, of which Marina knew much . . ." Landa's modern editor adds, "God also provided Cortes with a mistress . . . she lived with Cortes and bore him a son." (Cortes at first allotted her to one of his lieutenants, but before long took her for himself.)

It was in March, 1519, that the people of Tabasco gave the Lady Marina (as Bernal Diaz always speaks of her) to the strangers, and this was in the shadowland country at the far frontier of the Aztec confederacy. That confederacy was a land larger in extent than all Spain, filled with towns and cities that astonished the Spaniards who in a generation in the New World had not yet seen anything more than villages of thatched huts. Estimates of the population have run from three to twelve million, with the best recent guesses, based on Aztec tribute-rolls, hovering close to ten million. (Spain at the time had a population of four and a half million.) And these were no timorous Arawaks or unorganized Caribs; city after city could produce ranked and trained armies of thousands, war-loving soldiers whose courage and tenacity were never belittled by anyone who had fought them—they went to church to death daily. Even on the remote Tabasco coast the great city of Tenochtitlan, sometimes called Mexico after the Aztecs' other name, the Mexica, was famous, the center of the world, and the omnipotent Moctezuma, who ruled there, was obeyed to the ends of the earth.

But by the end of the year the Spanish expedition, by then only some four hundred men, held Moctezuma prisoner in the center of the city of Mexico, and through him commanded all the country.

The Spanish had superior weapons—but not that much superior. The quilted cotton armor of the Mexicans was superior, in fact, to the Spanish steel breastplates—and the Spaniards were quick to change. No more sudden decisions were won by the sight and sound of horses or cannon.

The important point is that thoughout the first march on Mexico, after they were joined by Malinal, the Spanish were forced to fight in only one instance—where only their immensely superior tactics saved their lives. Otherwise, the road of their first penetration into the country—the perilous interval while they were still without important allies and and could have been wiped out a dozen times over—was paved by a string of diplomatic victories as remarkable as so many straight passes at dice.

On the Veracruz coast, where the little Spanish army sailed from Tabasco, Cortes played a double game, first with the fat Totonacs, who lived there, encouraging them to rebel against their Aztec oppressors; and then with the Aztec ambassadors from Moctezuma, convincing them that he was on their side against the treacherous Totonacs. The Totonacs gave him workmen, food, and warriors; Moctezuma sent a solid gold disk as large as a cart wheel, carved to represent the sun and a larger silver disk carved to represent the moon, and a helmet full of grains of gold, and one hundred bearers loaded with other gifts of richly embroidered mantles, gold ornaments, crests of feathers, and declarations of friendship, and a polite refusal to permit the mysterious strangers to visit the city of Mexico.

But the refusal was evasive and half-hearted; for who, indeed, were the bearded white men?

Quetzalcoatl, the bearded white god (born, it will be remembered, in a year of Ce Acatl), had said, so the legends recorded, that in another year of Ce Acatl he would return from the sunrise to reclaim his kingdom, and by a coincidence out of grand opera the year 1519 was another year of Ce Acatl in the Aztec calendar. Was it possible?

It is reasonable that Malinal, fully aware of this stage setting of prophecy, would have intimated that truly it was very possible, when she talked for Cortes to the chief men of cities and to the chief priests of temples—the long haired ones, the Nahua annals call them, their ears shredded from acts of penance and their waist-long hair matted with the blood of sacrifices.

Everywhere the troubled people flocked to the temples, and at each town the strangers entered they found sacrificed bodies on the altars, hearts before the idols, and the temple walls desperately splashed with blood. (One of the most memorable things about the temples, not surprisingly, was their overpowering stockyard smell.)

Deftly juggling friendly Totonac allies and uncertain Aztec ambassadors, and with flowery expressions of the sincerest respect sent ahead to the great prince Moctezuma, the Spaniards marched inland for Mexico City.

The one instance of fighting was found in the independent city-state of Tlaxcala, where stubborn armies threw themselves against the strangers in a running engagement that went on for days. Javelins fell as thick as straw on a threshing-floor (said the Spaniards), and the Tlaxcalans and their Otomi archers, far from panicking at the explosion of gunpowder, drowned its noise with their shrill whistles and threw dust in the air while they rushed the dead and wounded away, so no one could see what damage the little cannons might have done. They killed a mare, a good and handy mare belonging to Pedro de Moron, and almost captured her rider. Three times, by day and by night, the Spaniards only survived by the hottest of sword work while holding their ranks exactly intact. ("We dared not charge them, unless we charged all together, lest they should break up our formation.") Repeatedly Cortes requested peaceful passage through their country, and repeatedly the Tlaxcalans responded with attacks of redoubled fury and, if we are to believe the communiqués, in enormous numbers. The gifts Cortes sent, including "a fluffy red Flemish hat, such as was then worn," were sacrificed on the Tlaxcalan altars, and the Tlaxcalan war leader, Xicotencatl, insolently presented the head of Pedro de Moron's mare "on the point of his lance" to the Tlaxcalan Senate.

Bernal Diaz credits Doña Marina with wringing victory out of this equivocal and exceedingly dangerous situation—several of the Spaniards had been killed, a faction was for retreating to the coast, and "all of us were wounded and sick"—by discovering so readily the plans of enemy war-councils that the Tlaxcalans might have been pardoned for deciding the strangers were genuine wizards, and by then delivering with unfailing valor ("although she had heard every day how the Indians were going to kill us and eat our flesh with chili") arguments of a most telling mixture of threat and persuasion to the Tlaxcalan envoys. The problem for the Tlaxcalans seems to have been to decide if the strangers were pro- or anti-Aztec: Cortes ingratiatingly presented himself as anti, but he was traveling with Indian allies from the coast who were Aztec subjects, and the Tlaxcalans had learned through a century of bitter conflict to trust nothing that smacked even faintly of Aztec brewing; obviously the sort of problem Marina's fluent explanations might well have helped solve.

Once decided on friendship the Tlaxcalans remained the firmest of allies, and the march was continued with an extra added ball to keep in the air—a large Tlaxcalan detachment trailing along, implacable enemies of the Aztecs and all their subject states.

At the ancient metropolis Cholula, of the great pyramid, and very much an Aztec subject state, Cortes tactfully encamped the Tlaxcalans outside the city, juggled exchanges of friendship again with the Aztec ambassadors, discovered a plot against him in the city, and arranged instead for the Tlaxcalans to rush into the town at a prearranged signal and join the Spaniards in a massacre to punish the Cholulans' planned treachery. The surprise massacre—and accompanying looting—went off elegantly, except that Cortes had a hard time getting the Tlaxcalans to stop, once he thought the punishment had gone far enough. Cortes reported 3,000 of the city's inhabitants killed; others say 6,000 or more.

Evidently there really was a plot against the strangers on the part of a faction in the city—"(for it is a large city and they have parties and factions among themselves)"—and agents sent by Moctezuma, all of whom were profoundly disconcerted by the strangers' ability to read their most secret thoughts, which is to say by the alertness of the Spaniards' intelligence service, which is to say the Lady Marina.

Cortes, through Malinal, blandly forgave everyone concerned, assured the Aztec ambassadors that he knew Moctezuma could have had no hand in such an ungentlemanly plot, even succeeded in representing himself to the Cholulans as their protector agains the Tlaxcalans—henceforward to be friends with one another—and marched on to the capital, the city of Mexico, Tenochtitlan.

There is no way of telling, of course, whether the extraordinarily effective cunning and guile displayed all the way along this march was due to the devious genius of Cortes or of the Lady Marina. Cortes, as he proved often enough in other situations, was one of the great non-losers of all time. Regardless of the odds or setbacks he seemingly could not lose, and until he tangled with lawyers he never did. Perhaps one reason was that he knew how to make true use of such loyal confederates as the Lady Marina. A modern historian writes, "Had it not been for her devotion to Cortes and his various and sundry captains, she could well have caused the destruction of the small Spanish army . . . Most great captains in history found their defeat in the arms of a tender morsel—not so Cortes, he conquered Malinche and thus the New World." The Nahua people called her Malinche, or so it sounded to Spanish ears (her supposed Nahua name of Malinal may have been only the Nahua pronunciation of Marina—where Cristo became Quilisto—and Malinche could have been made by a suffix of some form of cihuatl, "lady"). Cortes was known to the Nahua people by the name Malinche's Captain or, for short, also as Malinche. Marina is given much importance in the Spanish chronicles, and it is even more striking that, in such Indian chronicles as the *Lienzo* (picture history) of Tlaxcala, Marina not only appears in every important scene but is customarily drawn larger than any of the other actors, including Cortes.

All the wonders the Spaniards had seen had not prepared them for the numerous cities around Lake Texcoco, the towers and temples rising out of the waters of the lake, the long straight causeways eight paces wide jammed with welcoming crowds, the dignitaries tall with the dazzling plumes of the scarlet spoonbill, hung with jewels of gold and jade and pearls, sent to greet them, and finally the capital, the city of Mexico; the soldiers asked each other if they were dreaming, "... for it is," Cortes wrote, "the most beautiful city in the world."

No doubt the strangers were of equal interest to the Aztec public, with their curious weapons and dress, the one black man among them, a slave owned by Juan Sedeño, the richest soldier in the company; the tired and scarred but caparisoned horses (there were thirteen or fourteen left) and one six-months-old foal, it being Juan Sedeño's mare, naturally, that had foaled; the two greyhounds; the loads of mysterious baggage borne by Indian servants from among all the allies they had so far made—Totonacs, Tlaxcalans (who had given Malinal alone three hundred handmaidens, so some say), Cholulans, as well as a half dozen foreign Indian servants brought from Cuba.

Moctezuma himself was carried out in his litter to meet them; all the people bowed their heads so as not to affront the chief-of-men by looking into his face; his priests fumigated Cortes with incense and presented him; and Moctezuma quartered the strangers and all their people in an immense house, with courtyards and many rooms and with walls of sculptured stone, the palace, so they gathered, of his father Axayacatl, the conqueror of Tenochtitlan's twin city of Tlatelolco fifty years before.

After a week or so of polite visits back and forth, during which Moctezuma showed the strangers his city, his temples, the Tlatelolco market place greater than Rome's, so said the soldiers who had served in Italy, Cortes came calling one day with a handful of men and the Lady Marina, and took Moctezuma prisoner. This was accomplished with no more than a flimsy pretext and "smooth speeches"; it took Malinal an hour or two of smooth speeches—coupled with the most courteous of threats—to convince Moctezuma it would be best for him to come along quietly. He went with the Spaniards to their quarters and remained from then on in their custody, although treated with the greatest respect, accompanied by his household, and free to carry on each day the business of state.

The pretext for this action involved news of an attack, purportedly at Moctezuma's orders, on soldiers of a garrison Cortes had left at Veracruz; the immediate reason, however, was that the Spaniards were beginning to feel seriously uneasy, so few as they were in this great and warlike city, and a hostage of such quality was their best and boldest security; the basic reason, of course, was that they had come on conquest and it was high time to set about it.

Moctezuma swore fealty to the strangers' Don Carlos, King of Spain, and at the suggestion of Cortes got together a princely present for the lord across the sea—his family's heirlooms, and what he could raise from his empire; gold, Cortes wrote, such as no monarch in Europe possessed. The Aztecs regarded gold as of small value except when transformed by the goldsmith's art; jade was the precious stone. The Spanish preferred gold, and they liked it in the raw; they had most of the worked pieces melted into ingots. Scholars disagree on the total value— Prescott made it some six million nineteenth-century dollars, exclusive of silver, carved ornaments, and some of the delicately worked gold figures left unbroken.

Only the royal fifth was set aside for the lord across the sea; the rest was divided, with many angry rows, among the company of the people from heaven. The Spanish captains had their shares made into heavy chains of gold, and wore them wound around their doubleted shoulders.

The war was still to come, but the conquest was accomplished. From the moment of the magic touch of so much gold so tamely taken the strangers were masters and could never believe otherwise; these sumptuous people in their glorious cities were only Indians after all.

This whole unbelievable interlude, four hundred Spaniards coolly taking over a capital that could (and eventually did) raise an army of many thousands of fanatically determined warriors, has troubled historians ever since. Moctezuma had but to lift a finger, in the good old prose of Prescott, and the little band of strangers would be stormed under and destroyed.

Maybe the smooth speeches of young Malinal really were enchantment. Maybe Moctezuma did believe the strangers were gods; maybe he reasoned that only gods would have their audacity. He seems to have been hopelessly uncertain, anxious to get the strangers to go away, but anxious not to anger them. It is possible that he did not quite realize a conquest was going on. Who knows the proper protocol for visitors from outer space?

And so months passed, and in the spring of 1520 a new Spanish army—a much bigger one—landed at Veracruz. This was a force of 1,400 men under the command of a red-bearded bully boy named Panfilo de Narvaez, come not to help but

hijack; Narvaez had emerged from high-level political maneuvering back in Cuba, whose high-level politicians would have
liked a share of the Aztec treasure, with authority to make
Cortes his captive, dead or alive, and assume command of
Cortes' people.

Cortes sent emissaries loaded with gold to talk to various of
Narvaez' captains, arranged for a couple of thousand mountain
Chinantecs to meet him at the coast as allies (he had his own
men armed and trained with long Chinantec lances, as an
improvement over Spanish arms for fighting horsemen from the
ground, and then with 250 or so of his men—266 including the
drummer and fifer, says Bernal Diaz—went to deal with these
interloping people from heaven.

He left Pedro de Alvarado in charge in the city, where a
highly touchy situation had developed: the Aztec priests were
beginning to urge death or expulsion for the strangers. Moctezuma's scientists were reporting, in effect, that the visitors from
outer space were radioactive and would melt the country's
marrow.

Alvarado was blonde and handsome (the Aztecs called him
Tonatiuh, "Sun God"), chatty, edgy, covetous, and vicious.
Apparently with some shaky idea of terrorizing the Aztecs by a
repetition of the Cholula massacre, and maybe with some idea of
a repetition of the Cholula looting, he ordered an insane attack
on the people dancing at the feast of Huitzilopochtli, and the
city, shocked and enraged, burst into violence.

Cortes returned, having whipped Narvaez handily—Narvaez
lost an eye in the battle—and bribed or persuaded most of his
fine big army into changing sides, and found a full-scale war in
preparation in the city of Mexico. He forced Moctezuma to try
to calm his subjects (And the great Moctezuma said with grief:
"What more does Malinche want from me?"), and Moctezuma
was killed in the attempt, some say by the infuriated Aztecs,
some say by the desperate Spaniards.

The strangers had to fight their way out of the city and make
for the safety of Tlaxcala. Cortes escaped, with Marina, but of
his handsome new army—the 1,000 or so additional recruits
from Narvaez' forces and his 400 veterans—more than 800 were
killed in the fighting, drowned in the canals by the weight of gold
they were trying to carry, or captured and sacrificed. The gods
ate well on this midsummer Noche Triste, Cortes' Night of
Sorrow.

It took a year to gather armies of Indian allies and return to attack Tenochtitlan again. The real war was fought during this time, a war for empire between the Aztecs and the invaders, a war of intrigue, deals, and ruthless force where needed, carried out in a land torn from end to end not only by dissension but by disease: the first smallpox epidemic of record swept over Mexico in 1520, set off, says Bernal Diaz, by "a black man whom Narvaez brought covered with smallpox." This, though, was evidently the still-running wave of the great epidemic reported from Panama in 1514, from Yucatan in 1516, from Española in 1518-19, and no doubt found many more entrances than only one into Mexico in 1520. The Indians had no immunity whatsoever to this first hot breath of civilization and, worse, their custom of frequent bathing (the unwashed Spaniards knew that had to be unhealthy) constantly fanned the spread of the disease.

In the marshaling of power, Tlaxcala and the Totonac towns and the anti-Aztec factions in many subject-states, including Texcoco (Moctezuma's vengeance for his sister turned out to be costly), threw in enthusiastically with the Spanish. States loyal to the Aztecs were put to fire and sword by Cortes and his insurgent allies, and their populations were branded on the face and sold as slaves. Captured Spaniards were sacrificed in the temples; sometimes their faces were skinned (with the beards) for trophies to give to the gods. The heads of horses as well appeared on the skull-rack in Tenochtitlan. Cortes' policy with prisoners of war was to free them, if there was any chance of making peace with their people; if not, he had their hands cut off and sent them home.

It was a long and bitter war, but the strangers pulled away more and more of the confederacy, and the Aztecs could never trap and destroy them—there was always Tlaxcala for refuge; and eventually it became clear that the invaders had won and the Aztecs had lost. When at length the strangers came back in massive strength to besiege the capital the issue could not be in doubt.

The attack on the city was mounted from Texcoco, where the anti-Aztec leader, Ixtlilxochitl II, helped work out the same sort of operation that his grandfather Nezahualcoyotl had used with the Aztecs against the then capital of Azcapotzalco—heavy attacks by water and encirclement by land. The pincers closed and the island city was held under siege until fresh water and food became more precious than jade. Hundreds of thousands of allied warriors ("an infinite number," Cortes wrote) were supporting the Spanish.

But seemingly inexhaustible squadrons of Aztec spearmen fought like demons, from house to house, from temple to temple, along the canals that were the city's streets. Cuauhtemoc, a nephew of Moctezuma and the new Aztec leader, had told his soldiers they would either be victorious or die fighting. They did, almost to a man—in the usual hyperbolic sense of the term. Losses of Aztecs and their allies in the city were put by Cortes at 117,000; survivors, excluding women and children, at 30,000. Losses of the Texcoco troops were estimated at 30,000.

"It was useless to tell them," Cortes reported, "that we would not raise the siege, and that the launches would not cease to fight them on the water, nor that we had already destroyed the people of Matalcingo and Malinalco, and that there was no one left in the land to bring them succour, and that there was nowhere whence they could procure maize, meat, fruit, water, or other necessaries, for the more we repeated this to them the less faintheartedness they showed. On the contrary, both in fighting and in stratagems we found them more undaunted than ever."

The battle lasted eighty-five days, and ended on the 13th of August, 1521, when the last few defenders in the northeast corner of the city were cut down.

"All through the Colonial era, and even up to now," writes a modern archaeologist, "the northern district of Mexico [City] has found favor neither as a residential quarter nor as a business center. Today there are railroad yards and slums where the Aztec civilization bled to death. The ghosts of its heroic defenders still haunt the place."

Nothing in all that has been written about the Aztecs tells as much about them as one of their songs, a hymn, that runs:

> We only came to sleep
> We only came to dream
> It is not true, no, it is not true
> That we came to live on the earth
> We are changed into the grass of springtime
> Our hearts will grow green again
> And they will open their petals
> But our body is like a rose tree:
> It puts forth flowers and then withers.

In Peru at about the same time, sometime in the early 1520s, barbarians crossed the Andes from the east and raided the border provinces of the Inca empire. They came from the wild bush country across the mountains called the Chaco, a Quechua word meaning hunting ground. They were the Guarani, bowmen and cannibals. This was not their first plundering appearance on the Inca frontiers nor their last—Huayna Capac, the Inca, son of Topa Inca, built three fortresses to guard against them. But on this invasion they were accompanied by a few white men, shipwrecked survivors from an exploring fleet commanded by Juan de Solis, chief pilot of Spain. In 1515 and 1516 Solis had sailed down the east coast of South America as far south as the Rio de la Plata, where he had been killed and (it was said) eaten by the inhabitants. Consequently the Europeans with the Guarani must have spent the intervening five or ten years wandering the length and breadth of interior South America, from the region of the present Buenos Aires to Peru, some of it country that is virtually unexplored yet today.

One of these Europeans, and the only name we have from among them, was Alejo Garcia, a Portuguese. Along with what may have been one of the most imposing lists of firsts in all exploration, he was the first European of record to see the wealth and civilization of the Incas. His name might be more than a footnote to history except that his Guarani friends killed him on the way back east.

The importance of this invasion to the Incas is in the sudden pestilence that followed it (maybe there was no connection, or maybe the Guarani and their guests had been carrying it wherever they went, or maybe this too was a rolling wave of the great smallpox plague sent forth from Panama in 1514, taking a dozen years to roll its way to the highlands of the Andes). For during the epidemic Huayna Capac died, so quickly and unexpectedly that he did not have time to make the usual formal announcement of his successor. He meant his son Huascar to succeed him, and Huascar was invested with the office at Cuzco by the high priest. But Huayna Capac happened to die at Quito in the north, where he had a separate wife and a son by her named Atahuallpa. Atahuallpa assumed the governorship of Quito and the northernmost regions of the empire (the northerly regions of modern Ecuador) and command of the army that had been with Huayna Capac when he died.

The two leaders of that army, Quisquis and Challcuchima,

gave Atahuallpa their complete loyalty. They were the empire's foremost generals, and their seasoned troops by far the empire's best. In the civil war that followed, and lasted for five years, Quisquis and Challcuchima won a solid string of victories, ending in a decisive triumph north of Cuzco. Huascar was taken prisoner, his forces scattered, his lieutenants executed.

Huayna Capac died in 1527. In the same year word came of strange beings (perhaps gods, perhaps Viracocha returning?) at the far northern outposts of the empire. The Viracochas went away, but five years later they returned. Atahuallpa was at the town of Cajamarca in the north central highlands when he received the great news of the final victory over Huascar and, at the same time, a visit from the Viracochas. The Viracochas (164 Spaniards, 62 horses) were led by a hard-eyed old soldier named Francisco Pizarro, who sent his brother Hernando and a young captain named Hernando de Soto to invite Atahuallpa to visit the Viracochas' quarters. The next day, November 16, 1532, Atahuallpa came in his litter accompanied by several thousand warriors. The Viracochas (who had been planning this expedition in search of the fabled Birú for years, and meanwhile listening attentively to tales of the way Cortes did things in Mexico) met him with a prepared ambush, blew his soldiers to pieces with cannon, rode down the remnants with cavalry, and took Atahuallpa prisoner.

The story of the conquest of Peru contains no psychological mysteries, no subtle and beautiful heroines, no heroics, and above all no heroes. It is a simple tale of unrelieved double-dealing and violent crime. Francisco Pizarro, illiterate, sixty-one years old, with a lifetime of blood on his hands, was a plain man with uncomplicated notions: blunt treachery, suspicious self-interest, and a sword-thrust for persuasion.

With the sacred person of the Inca as hostage the Spanish were immune from attack, and Atahuallpa was now ordered to produce a ransom. Gold was gathered (in the process the gold sheathing was torn off the Temple of the Sun at Cuzco and such objects of art were brought as a golden ear of corn sheathed in silver leaves with a tassel of silver threads) that amounted to a treasure considerably more than twice as large as Moctezuma's—Baron Humboldt made it twenty million nineteenth-century dollars.

Among the Inca people there was some feeling that the Viracochas may have appeared and seized Atahuallpa in answer to the prayers of Huascar, who was still the prisoner of Atahuallpa's generals and still claiming to be the true Inca. When the captive Huascar managed to get into communication with Pizarro, the captive Atahuallpa smuggled out orders to his generals to put him to death. Tradition says Huascar was drowned by his jailors. A few months later, in August, 1533, the gigantic ransom having been collected, melted down, and distributed among the enraptured Viracochas, Pizarro had Atahuallpa publicly strangled.

And again a conquest was completed, although the war was still to come. In this case it was a savage, stubborn war that lasted forty years in the Inca empire itself, and three hundred years longer in the border country to the south. In the wild Chaco and Montaña to the east (where the first of the Viracochas appeared and disappeared, and where tribes still exist who have scarcely seen white men), it hasn't been completed yet.

IV

People
of Peace

Columbus's great discovery had burst upon a Europe in full flower of Renaissance, and nothing would ever be the same again. But more to the point, it had burst upon a Spain in the first flower of nationhood, at the precise moment that Spain, newly united under Isabella of Castile and Ferdinand of Aragon, completed its seven centuries of reconquering the country from the Moors. The fall of Granada, marking the end of that 700 years of troubled enchantment where ceaseless war had seemed the natural order of life, came in 1492.

The first objective of Ferdinand and Isabella was to unify their raw, jangling, quarrelsome domains under the strict rule of an absolute monarchy. They made efforts to expel the Moors and the Jews, and among the many councils they established for various special tasks was the Council of the Inquisition. They extended royal sway over towns and castles with the help of their secret police and seized for the crown the grand commandership of the powerful orders of knights. They followed what were then, in the hour of Europe's birth of nations, the newest and most modern ideas: one nation, one speech, one God, one king; and they created a rigid dictatorship in which the

king's word cut through any law and the king's hand covered
every thread of the national existence.

The contract for his first voyage made Columbus governor-
general of any new lands he might add to the Spanish crown, and
gave him a cut (ten per cent) of any net profits from trade or
precious metals. With the establishment of the colonies in the
New World a foreign trade office was set up in Seville and later
placed under the supervision of a royal Council of the Indies.
Through this council the crown controlled—and closely—all
colonial matters; until her death in 1504 the "crown" meant
Isabella alone, for she alone had title to the Indies operation.
Multitudes of laws were placed on the books dealing with the
welfare of overseas trade, exploration, mining, church, colonists, and Indians. (One of the earliest, instigated by a well-
meaning Isabella years before any smallpox epidemics, was a
law to prohibit Indians from taking so many baths, as bound to
be injurious to their health.)

The governor distributed conquered lands to colonists, and,
after the institution of the *encomienda* system in 1503, villages of
Indians were "commended" to the care and protection of an
encomendero, who could exact their labor, but as free men
(technically) and for pay (technically). This resulted, in most
cases, in virtual slavery. Encomenderos commonly spoke of
owning their Indians; Cortes raised money by mortgaging his
encomienda of Indians in Cuba when, being a young man long on
promise but short on cash, he was appointed to lead the
expedition to Mexico.

Bartolomé de Las Casas, the first priest ordained in the New
World and son of a veteran of Columbus' first voyage, thundered
against the practice, but it persisted. The encomenderos enjoyed
being feudal lords; the Council of the Indies continued to hope
abuses could be corrected; all agreed it was certainly vicious and
absolutely destructive of the Indians; but it was certainly
convenient for the Spaniards.

Las Casas received his baptism of fire when Cuba was
"reduced" by blood and terror. He tried in vain to stop the
carnage, and at last was impelled to call down on reducer Panfilo
de Narvaez a wrathful, wholesouled, and formal curse. (One of
Columbus's gentle Tainos, being burned at the stake, refused
baptism for fear that in heaven he would find more Christians
there.) From this time on Las Casas raged through the New
World, and back and forth to Spain, swinging a propaganda

sword of truly archangelical proportions on behalf of oppressed Indians.

Expedition after expedition received the royal commission and sailed forth, first from Española, then from Cuba. One after another hurled itself against Panama, in search of its storied gold and pearls and Southern Sea, only to be shattered by yellow fever and the poisoned arrows of the people of the little chiefdoms there, who were frequently friendly at first but customarily alienated in short order by slaving, murder, torture, and extortion.

A number of questionable notions are widely held in regard to the early Spanish conquests, one being that the Spaniards merely walked in and took possession, frightening the simple Americans into fits of submission by their horses and godly cannon. As has been seen in the case of Mexico and Peru, it seldom worked that way. It was true that the Indian inferiority in offensive weapons and especially in tactics was enormous; in many cases the Spaniards (well-armored) were up against nothing more serious than rock-throwing mobs. It was also true that the strangers often gained a foothold with the help of a peaceful or even hospitable welcome. But the opening of hostilities could still bring man-sized fighting in which the Spaniards could lose as well as win. Plenty did.

The Spanish soldier was considered (after the Swiss) the best of his time, as the Spanish horse, sprung from the breedy Barbs and Arabs of the Moors, was the toast of Europe. Ingrown chivalry reached its most rococo luxuriance among the Spanish knights but so far it had only made them unbelievably vain and valiant: lean, fanatical El Grecos not yet distorted into Don Quixotes. They habitually tackled matters that required more guts than sense, and more greed than either—they raised their war cry "Santiago!" (St. James!) in the face of any odds, if the smell of gold was in the offing. Above all, they were bounteously equipped with grand gestures—Cortes literally burned his boats behind him on the beach at Veracruz when he started inland to Mexico City, so there could be no turning back, and hanged a couple of men and cut off the feet of another who conspired to return to Cuba.

The driving forces of hot new nationalism, zealous religious solidarity, and capable armed strength under direct central authority eventually gorged Spain on fat New World pickings, but it was far from easy. The *Conquistadores* earned their name.

(The chief expansionist power in Europe at the time, the Ottoman Turks, conquered and held more territory in Europe—fighting Europeans—during the first century after the discovery of America than the Spanish, with all their early conquests, managed to take in the same period from the Indians of the New World.)

But with all their boldness, it is of significance that those Conquistadores who won usually did so with some Indian help. As a rule those who lost, such as the leaders of the first two formal expeditions to Panama, who met utter disaster and left hundreds of Spaniards dead in the jungles and sand dunes, had none.

And so Vasco Nuñez de Balboa, a destitute ex-colonist from Española, too poor to outfit himself as a proper Conquistador (it was an expensive line of work), stowed away in a barrel on a ship bound for Panama, there successfully romanced the daughter of Careta, cacique of Coiba, made friends with Panciaco, son of Comogre, cacique of Comogra, and with God's grace and such allies became a leader of men and fought his way to the Pacific.

And now expeditions went forth from Panama as a base, from Mexico, and later from Peru, and from every little foothold in between, like hungry wolves plunging into a giant carcass in search of the richest mouthfuls. The royal permission to explore continued to provide the explorers with a percentage of profits and governor-generalships of new lands found—powerful incentives for rapidly expanding exploration. But the geography of territory assigned was necessarily vague, leading to contest, intrigue, and conflict between rival would-be conquerors. And so when the expeditions bumped against each other they fought or sued or preferred charges before the king. Superior courts, the *Audiencias,* were set up in the New World to unsnarl such imbroglios.

Expeditions sent north from Panama by the governor there met and fought with expeditions sent south from Mexico by Cortes, and prospective Conquistadors from Española who had wangled new royal permissions met and fought with both. One of the faithful comrades in Balboa's wild surmise was Francisco Pizarro; when five years later a new governor of Panama had Balboa arrested and beheaded as a too-dangerous rival, faithful old Pizarro made the arrest.

The first to enter the country of a chief named Nicaragua

brought back more than 30,000 recorded baptisms and gold trinkets and pearls in the amount of more than $100,000. In the next five years at least four more expeditions plundered up and down the Costa Rica-Nicaragua-Honduras region, usually accompanied by thousands of Indian allies happy to help the mighty strangers destroy their traditional enemies beyond the mountains.

The destroyed peoples were branded and sold as slaves; the usual ultimate fate of the allies was to be granted in encomiendas, although important men among them might be rewarded with fiefs of their own, to help hold their people in line. More commonly, persons of consequence sooner or later found themselves in the hands of the torture squad, for the Spaniards operated on the European model, knowing no other. In Europe the velveteened burghers of a submitted town were as a matter of course given a touch of torture to make them cough up the last of their silver spoons. You got at the real marrow of truth by cracking joints. Were these people of the Indies any different, didn't they too have joints to pull apart?

A few of the Spaniards, not many, had the wit to perceive that these people of the Indies were indeed different and that truly they treasured raw gold no more than clay, as Panciaco once contemptuously remarked to Balboa.

In Mexico, christened New Spain, the Spaniards laid out a new city on the site of Tenochtitlan—crushed Aztec gods were used in the foundation of the Cathedral of Saint Francis. Cuauhtemoc, the last Aztec leader, who had been captured alive, was put to the torture to make him reveal the rest of the Aztec treasure; but there wasn't any left. (Cortes later had to answer for this indignity to a royal person in a formal trial before the royal Council.)

The people of Tlaxcala, as a reward for their faithful services, were specifically exempted from being distributed in encomiendas. Cortes wrote the king that he had wished to avoid the system altogether in New Spain, but that the Spaniards could not exist without it. The Council of the Indies, less and less encomienda-minded, decided they would have to exist without it and revoked the encomiendas, but the colonists, as usual, found ways to get around the Council's ruling.

In theory grants to Spaniards were given an appearance of legality, either by being made from lands not under Indian use, or by being obtained by one means or another from Indian "lords." Many such "lords" and "kings" were maintained in their supposed offices by Spanish support, and a number of them, such as Ixtlilxochitl of Texcoco, were officially ennobled and became grandees of Spain.

The Spanish made a fundamental error in equating the society of the Aztecs and other nations of Mexico with European feudalism, somewhat like equating the Athens of Pericles with the France of Louis XIV. Until recent years they were excoriated for this by anthropologists, who generally preferred to equate the Aztecs with the Iroquois or Pueblos, which is rather like equating the Athens of Pericles with North Danville, Vermont. At present there seems to be a swing back again toward equation with, if not the France of Louis XIV, at least the authoritarian organization of an IBM or General Motors.

The Aztecs—to use them as a paradigm of the various Mexican peoples—founded their social and political organization on (what was probably) a kin-group known as the *calpulli* (plural *calpullec*). More than sixty such groups made up the city of Tenochtitlan. The calpulli, says a recent authority, was "a fundamental structural unit . . . basic pattern on which all larger social groupings were based." All larger organizations, towns, cities, city-states, and "empires," were "growths from this pattern." A calpulli may have contained several hundred or even several thousand persons, and might be divided into still smaller territorial units called *tequitanos*, perhaps specific extended families or clans. In Tenochtitlan at least several of the calpullec maintained plazas and markets of their own and elected local officials for themselves roughly corresponding to our county clerk, treasurer, sheriff, deacon, and so on, although the correspondence is pretty rough, since the same person might hold widely varying posts at the same time. The Spaniards for example found themselves calling the same official "captain of the guard" and "abbot." The functions of the calpulli were economic as well as political and social, educational as well as religious.

Each calpulli elected a *tlatoani*, or "speaker," for membership in the presiding council of the entire city. This council in turn chose four executives for the four quarters of the state, into which the several dozens of calpullec were organized. In Tlaxcala this council of four seemed to rule jointly (there were even dividing walls between the four quarters of the city), which accounts for the Spaniards usually referring to Tlaxcala as a republic. (They were thinking of the Republic of Venice, not a republic as we think of it today.)

In Tenochtitlan a supreme ruler, *tlacatecuhtli*, chief-of-men or chief-of-warriors, or also known as *hueytlatoani*, revered speaker, was chosen by the supreme council from among these four executives. This was an office similar to what has usually been called that of tlatoque in this text, using a title (and a rather less thorny one to our eyes) apparently common to some of the other cities around Lake Texcoco.

This top job was for life, and was always filled from the same family or at any rate from the same patri-clan, which readily explains why the Spaniards referred to such rulers as kings. Primogeniture was not followed, and the election appears to have been really an election (". . . they cast votes for . . . brave warriors . . . who knew not wine . . . the prudent, able, wise . . . who spoke well and were obedient, benevolent, discreet, and intelligent. . . .") but otherwise the tlacatecuhtli, by any other name, was a right royal figure, even indeed a sacred, a godly figure.

The nub of the Spanish error was not in calling the elected tlacatecuhtli a king—after all, their own Charles I, grandson of Ferdinand and Isabella, had just become Emperor Charles V of the Holy Roman Empire by election—but in assuming the tlacatecuhtli enjoyed absolute one-man rule as a real king should, in calling the councilors, elected representatives of their calpullec, "nobles" and assuming they possessed individually all the hereditary rights and privileges, particularly in property, that the title implied to the title-worshiping Spanish mind, and in assuming as a matter of course the private ownership of property, particularly land.

As we have seen in the case of the great Tezozomoc, powerless in the midst of all his mighty power, or Moctezuma, slain out of hand by his people when he tried to urge them to a different course of action, the apparent ruler, godlike figure though he might be, was far from being any absolute monarch. It appears that as long as his gestures were perfectly proper, as long as he remained non-controversial so to speak, the illusion of absolute rule might prevail, but clearly a major policy conflict could reveal him for what he evidently was, a symbol only symbolizing authority, possessing none of his own beyond that of any elder with the right to speak in council. The propriety of his acts seems to have been determined by their religious correctness. As a recent authority has put it, religion "intervened" in areas we would regard as remote from its bailiwick; religion controlled commerce, politics, and war, and religion expressed the purpose of the state, the purpose of education, the purpose of life. Everything, even conquest with all its pleasures, was subordinated to religion.

This situation we have mentioned before and will see again in these pages. The Inca world seems to have come close to breaking out of the crystal shell of religion—the state, power, real war, real conquest, almost if not quite springing into the free and terrible existence in and of themselves so familiar in our own world, ancient and modern. This tendency provides one measure of the profound differences between the Inca and Mexican worlds. And yet across all its gulf of difference Inca organization, with its ayllu corresponding to the calpulli, its council of state presided over by the regents of the four quarters (the Inca name for the empire was the Land of the Four Quarters), strikes note after note of sameness with the Mexican city-state, as well as with numerous other examples of American Indian political organization.

The Aztec tlacatecuhtli, the "emperor" as the Spaniards called him, fulfilled important priestly functions, it may be rather as representative or even as the personification of Quetzalcoatl. Another person of political importance, sometimes designated as second in rank in the city, represented the goddess Cihuacoatl, Serpent Woman, the earth goddess. The great minister Tlacaelel held this post during much of his public life. Together these two leaders embodied the concept of dualism that appears again and again as one of the basic ideas in American Indian thought. They were the dualism of state and religion, the dualism of the things of the spirit (Quetzelcoatl) and the things of the earth (Cihuacoatl). They were, in the view of some students, representative of the dual government, the government outside the walls and the government inside the walls, so commonly met with in American Indian political structure. For the world outside the walls the tlacatecuhtli seemed to personify the totality of the city-state; for the world inside the walls the Cihuacoatl was the very model of real workaday authority. In actual authority both were without doubt principally dependent on the consent of the council, and all that entailed of clan and family intrigue, ward politics, factional logrolling, and especially of theological dexterity.

The problem of ownership has always provided great difficulties in our understanding of the Indian world. This is especially true with the Aztecs, one of the most highly stratified and in our sense of the word the wealthiest Indian group in North America. But with a few exceptions land belonged to the calpulli, which apportioned its use to member families. The same fundamental situation existed among the Incas, as we have seen, and in fact was as universal throughout the New World as the concept of private property in the Old.

On occasion lands, sometimes in areas of recent conquest, seem to have been bestowed on particularly noteworthy persons by the Aztec leadership—Tlacaelel was said to have bestowed such grants. These may have been special tracts set off for the purpose of raising tribute, the crops to be gathered for the grantee or perhaps for his family or calpulli. There seems to have been no question of ownership European style, with the right to convey to any individual—in or out of the family, clan, or tribe—the owner might choose. Or perhaps such grants are reflected among the later Maya in the perquisites of a class exhibiting some evidence of inherited rank, possibly descendants of Mexican conquerors centuries before, who simply held a preferred position in regard to the apportionment of the communal lands. Whatever its exact nature, this special use of land was exceptional; normally lands were held in common, a fact "rendered certain enough to be accepted as probably characteristic of Mexican society," in the words of a classic study.

It is possible that among the Aztecs, as among the Inca, the use of certain luxury items—such as in gold, silver, jade, featherwork—was limited to specific honored groups. It is conceivable that the "emperor" held custody of treasures—predominantly religious works of art—in his position as the living embodiment of the godhead, similar perhaps to such religious treasures as the treasure of this or that European church or cathedral or religious chapter. In any case there is no indication they were owned as treasure in the European sense—treasured up as wealth, spendable for goods and services.

A special conception of ownership—that we cannot own things, no matter how desirable they may be—is visible at the very foundation of ancient Mexican thought. It is the constant theme, as has previously been mentioned, of the finest poetry. (We can own only our own soul, the quality of our behavior, "the remembrance of a good act.") The description by Nahua priests of one of the principal religious observances, the sacrifice of the matchless (captive) youth who had spent a year as the personification of the god Tezcatlipoca and who climbed alone the pyramid to his death casting aside at each step the gorgeous and enjoyable possessions he has (temporarily) owned during the year of his godly role—the description concludes with the words: "For says the god himself/ Tezcatlipoca/ No one takes with him into death/ the good things of life."

The point is ownership precisely, and its unreality, its ephemeral quality. It is a strain not unknown in the West—Book II of Boethius' *De Consolatione Philosophia* makes much of the point that "we cannot lose external goods because we never really had them. . . . The beauty of fields or gems is theirs, not ours." And the theme of *carpe diem* delighted dangerous Rome ("put out the wine and the dice," says Virgil, or at any rate a poet some claim is Virgil, "and perish who thinks of tomorrow"), but a minor strain, a philosopher's game.

But in ancient Mexico, the basic idea.

The youth chosen to impersonate Tezcatlipoca was dressed and adorned in the greatest magnificence (Moctezuma himself adorned the young man, arrayed him as the god), taught to converse with the greatest grace; he went where he pleased attended by his servants and his beautiful women, and everywhere he was honored, before him the people bowed and kissed with reverence the earth. Someone who didn't know might have mistaken him for the "emperor" himself; wherein, very possibly, lay the whole idea: the daily statement, before the eyes of all, of a philosophy incarnate.

The ownership of things in common had been noticed from the first by Europeans. Columbus wrote, "Nor have I been able to learn whether they held personal property, for it seemed to me that whatever one had, they all took shares of. . . ." Even the simmering pepper pot, Columbus noted, seemed to be free to any neighbor who wanted to fill a gourd, even—to his amazement— in starving times.

But it struck too deep a root of difference to be grasped. Europeans simply could not comprehend it. Likewise, the people of the New World were hopelessly bewildered by the European's spirit of competition for personal gain; for as says a recent analysis of the Aztec state: "Social structure on all levels lent itself to cooperative labor. . . ."

Much more was at issue here than a difference of abstract

ideologies. Ramifications ran through every tissue of life. These two world views, each never dreaming of the other's existence, had really created two totally different worlds.

On the one hand the communal outlook produced attitudes toward cooperation and group identity that were reflected in some measure in every gesture of Indian existence, from practical jokery to religion. On the other hand the ingrained custom of personal acquisition at the expense of one's neighbors, of striving in constant competition against each other, colored every aspect of European life and thought.

In ancient Mexico, "freedom of thought, individual liberty, personal fortunes, were non-existent," wrote one of the most penetrating of modern archaeologists, but ". . . an Aztec would have been horrified at the naked isolation of an individual's life in our Western world." Or as it is put in another recent study, "A great deal of symbiosis in all kinds of cultural activity obtained between segments of the population, giving the city-state much integration and stability . . ."

But a symbiosis quite beyond conquistadorial perception, and since the only thing to be done with the incomprehensible is to pretend it does not exist, the Spaniards blithely designated council members "nobles" and owners of "estates," dealt with them as landed aristocrats, called on them to furnish feudal tribute and service from their peasants, and married their daughters, from whom descended some of the first families of a later Spain as well as of a later Mexico.

The Spanish gave deeper thought to what they could see of Aztec religion, especially after the missionaries arrived and the whipping and burning of the so often "sullen" natives became the commonest topic of official correspondence.

The famous Aztec sacrifices have fascinated one and all to the exclusion, nearly, of the rest of Aztec history. The offering up of human lives—even their first-born sons—in the belief that this gravest of transactions would keep the shaky world upright and maintain their cherished way of life is again something inconceivable to our higher civilization, even though we fight wars today for precisely the same reason, offering up everybody's first-born sons. The automobile and its enormous toll in traffic deaths and injuries is possibly a still more apt comparison; anyone seriously suggesting that we abolish this custom of human sacrifice by abolishing the god, the automobile, would surely be regarded as out of his mind, and all our highest priests—economists and social scientists—can easily explain that on the motor industry (with, alas, its thousands of unavoidable sacrifices) depends our cherished way of life.

Concrete facts and figures concerning the Aztec sacrifices are suspect, having been composed or interpreted after the Conquest by converts who may have been eager to please their new holy men. For example, the recorded 20,000 victims at the previously mentioned dedication of Huitzilopochtli's temple: several post-Conquest chroniclers give the number of victims all the way from 20,000 to 80,000. All agree that the victims stood in long lines, extending far out on the causeways, that the two sponsoring kings themselves tore out the hearts of the first two victims, and that two teams of priests then took over, relieved by other teams when they tired. Some say the work took one day, others that it required up to four days, from sunrise to sunset.

Now the feast of Huitzilopochtli occurred in May, when the days between sunrise and sunset are about twelve hours. So we picture the four sacrificial assistants seizing a victim, throwing him on his back and holding him down on the convex altar stone, while the fifth man of the team gouges into his chest at the fork of the rib cage with an obsidian knife, finds the heart, saws and tears it loose, offers it to the sun, and deposits it in the Stone of Tizoc. The body is then dragged away and hurled down the temple steps, and the next victim is seized.

Even allowing for the most practiced efficiency on all hands, it is hard to imagine this being accomplished in less time than, say, one minute per victim. At that rate two teams could conceivably finish off 120 victims an hour, or 1,440 in a twelve-hour day, or 5,760 for the outside limit of four days.

Racing each other for the fattest mouthfuls, the people from heaven coursed the seas and the shores, the mountains and valleys. Another Mexico, another Peru, might be just beyond— the pagans always said so. Mines of gold or silver might be anywhere; or spices or pearls; and there were sure to be slaves for the taking, and souls to be saved for Christ.

The Huastecs, on the old northeastern frontier of the Aztec country, beat back a Spanish attack from the sea, were swamped by an invasion of 40,000 allied warriors under the leadership of Cortes, rose again against the strangers when Cortes turned to fight and defeat a new rival Spanish intrusion from the sea. An officer of Cortes subdued them in a manner recalling Aztec days—he rounded up 400 of the principal men and sacrificed them to the new gods by hanging.

Tangaxoan, a chief among the heretofore never-conquered Tarascans to the west, was one of the many local caciques from all over Mexico who visited Cortes, made submission, was appointed a Spanish satrap, and gave the strangers a center in his territory. But many other Tarascans refused satellite status, and their country long remained a fighting frontier. A leader of the Otomis to the north was commissioned a captain-general of Spain by Charles V, made a Knight of the Order of Santiago, given the Christian name of Nicolás de San Luis, and with the help of another noted Otomi satrap, Fernando de Tapia, held the northern frontier for Spain for thirty years.

The Maya gave up hard, with wars and repeated invasions that went on for years. At one time five different Spanish adventurers were stalking each other in the highland Maya country—Cortes, as usual, came out the winner. Pedro de Alvarado, the febrile young Sun God, marched to Guatemala with 400 Spaniards and 20,000 Mexican allies and taught the obstinate Mayas a lesson by catching and hanging their women; babies were in turn hanged to their mothers' feet. Alvarado had recently married a bride from faithful Tlaxcala and proved how little interest he and his men had in the Maya women by picking out the most beautiful unmarried girls to be left scrupulously unraped while they were hanged or thrown to the packs of fighting dogs to be eaten alive.

Cortes, when he marched to Honduras himself to settle matters, found himself involved in one of the great epics of Central American exploration just getting there through the jungle. He took along Cuauhtemoc, his captive Aztec king; crushed though the Aztecs were he seems to have been wary of Cuauhtemoc, and when he so much as took a walk beyond his garden walls would demand that Cuauhtemoc come along to stay under his watchful eye. On this Maya campaign Cortes' nerve broke and he had Cuauhtemoc executed, charging rumors of a conspiracy. Bernal Diaz was skeptical, and wrote that the killing "was thought wrong by all of us who were along on that journey." Recently discovered documents, though, lend some support to the likelihood that Cortes acted under the necessity of a real and urgent crisis.

Cuauhtemoc's widow, the fair Tecuichpo, his cousin and a daughter of Moctezuma, later became the wife of a prominent

Spaniard, Don Thoan Cano, and mothered an illustrious Spanish family. On this same trip, Cortes married off the Lady Marina to Don Juan Xamarillo, one of his captains, and, so they say, she lived happily ever after.

Among the Mayas, the Xiu family frequently made alliance with the Spaniards, giving aid that is regarded as a principal factor in the eventual establishment of Spanish authority. Most of the other Maya groups kept up an incessant guerrilla warfare that by 1536, after more than ten years of fighting against two major invasions, succeeded in driving—for a time—the last Spaniard out of Yucatan. During the following interval of comparative peace, the Xiu people made a pilgrimage to the old abandoned center of Chichen Itza—the sacred pool there, scene of human sacrifice in the days of Toltec rule, was still regarded as a holy place. The Xiu had to pass through Cocom territory on the way, and the Cocoms had not forgotten the destruction of their city Mayapan and nearly all the Cocom family at the hands of the Xiu a hundred years before. According to the stories, the Xiu dignitaries were invited to a banquet at the Cocom town of Otzmal, where in the course of the festivities Cocom warriors treacherously killed them all.

This act was, in effect, the final phrase of the long Maya history. The gods repaid it in kind with further calamities—plagues of locusts, famine, uncontrolled civil war. When the Spanish again invaded five years later, there was no strength left for resistance.

The last shreds of the Maya civilization went with their books: ". . . as they contained nothing but superstition and lies of the devil, we burned them all, which the Indians regretted to an amazing degree and which caused them great anguish," wrote Bishop Landa from Yucatan. ("With rivers of tears we mourned our sacred writings among the delicate flowers of sorrow," wrote the unknown poet of the Book of Chilam Balam of Tizimin.)

Bishop Landa's zeal in torturing idolaters brought scandal, investigation, churchly rows, and left a persistent touch of sullenness in the air. The subjugation of some scattered Maya groups went on for generations longer—the important Itzas of Lake Peten, who had fled there long before at the fall of their city Chichen Itza, held out for another century and a half, and the Lacandon Maya of the Chiapas forests have held out into our own day. But the grandeur was gone, and the Maya renown. They sank into the anonymity of "Indians."

With the conquest of Mexico and Peru the carcass of the hemisphere had lost its liver and lights. But the magnitude of early Spanish penetration is more evident in its extent of contact than of conquest. Early conquest was limited and insecure, but by the middle 1530s, when men who had sailed with Columbus were still living, the Spanish had already established contact with by far the largest population blocs in the New World.

Estimates of the total hemispherical population before white invasion scatter all the way from eight or nine million to nearly one hundred million. A few years ago middle-of-the-road guesses assigned seven million or so for South America and another seven million or so for Mexico, the West Indies, and Central America, but these figures are in process of being revised dramatically upward. Projections calculated from recent and detailed studies of Aztec and Spanish tribute rolls go as high as some twenty-five million for the pre-Spanish population of Mexico alone—reduced by disease and other disasters to between only one and two million by the middle 1600s.

Most experts agree that whatever the hypothetical population of the hemisphere may have totaled, three-fourths or more of it was concentrated in the Mexican and Andean areas, the chief targets of early Spanish activity. In the enormous fringe area that was North America north of Mexico, population estimates allow a far smaller total than that concentrated in the high-culture areas below the present Mexican border, and yet here too present estimates are under serious debate. Arguments are being pressed for figures up to several times as high as the one to two million souls rather generally accepted twenty years ago for all the present United States, Canada, and Alaska; now a figure of from two to four million seems more acceptable, with possibilities of twice that or even rather more being suggested.

But though Spanish penetration had reached the heaviest populations, the total body of the New World's nations had only been scratched. The number of separate tribes, bands, groups, then inhabiting the Americas is all but immeasurable; estimates here really run wild.

The most conservative guesses put the number of mutually unintelligible languages in North America north of Mexico at about 200, with about 350 more for Mexico and the rest of Mesoamerica, and perhaps 1,450 for South America to make a round total for the hemisphere of some 2,000.

But linguistic diversity is a poor scale for counting separate groups of people. Some peoples might be very closely related in everything except language—as are the speakers of various provincial languages in modern France; or many completely independent societies widely differing culturally and racially might speak the same language—as in the varieties of English-speaking people over the world today.

In the time of the mid-1530s the great majority of the New World's nations and tribes had received no inkling of collision with another world. In North America north of Mexico very few of the many villages, tribes, chiefdoms, confederacies, had heard of the people from heaven, and fewer still had seen any. Time went on as it always had.

Time is invisible unless we see it in relation to something in motion—a river standing still while life comes and goes on its banks. We tick off the life to measure the time, and a man stops the clock when he dies—we don't think of Shelley as older than George Bernard Shaw. There are not many other places on earth, perhaps none, where time in this sense, uninterrupted time, had gone on as long as it had in certain areas of what is now the Southwest of the United States.

The Papagos and Pimas, close cousins, speaking dialects of the same language, the Papagos dwelling in the southern Arizona deserts and the Pimas in the nearby semiarid river valleys, are descendants of an earlier people who had lived in the same country in basically the same way, never catastrophically disturbed, for at least more than 9,000 years. Such at least seems to some archaeologists probable, judging from what appear to be continuously related sequences of artifacts stretching across this giant reach of time. While every conquering Ozymandias in all history rose and fell and was forgotten, these people, peaceful people, grinders of meal and singers of songs, endured, as natural as mountains.

They seem to have sprung from the western branch of the Cochise ancients, embryonic farmers living along the banks of lakes and streams that then existed in their country, left over from the Ice Age, among cottonwoods and hickory trees and such roaming beasts as dire wolves and mammoths (which apparently lingered on a little longer here than elsewhere). Thousands of years later, the lakes and Ice Age animals long since vanished, the nearest hickories seven hundred miles away, their land a yellow desert of salt bush, mesquite, scarce water and rare rivers, and tall dust devils rising each noon to dance, they appear as a farming people who have been given the name Hohokam—a Pima word meaning "those who have gone."

While the Maya Classic Age flourished and withered, while the Toltecs came and went and the Aztecs rose to eminence, these people planted their corn and pumpkins, hunted the little desert deer, and squeezed some sort of use out of nearly every wild plant on their sundazzled horizon, They had many things familiar to the belt of farming villages that ran all the way south to the Valley of Mexico and beyond, all the way to Central America—little clay figurines (sometimes turbaned, and with earrings, and often, of course, ripe and female), a snake and bird as the commonest religious motif, mirrors made of flakes of iron pyrite set like mosaic work in stone plaques, ball courts (after about A.D. 500) and the rubber balls to go with them, and the jingling copper dance bells that were traded so widely from Central America and Mexico. Around A.D. 1000 someone among the Hohokam seems to have developed a process of etching, using a weak acid possibly made from fermented cactus juice (the fruit of the saguaro, source of their ceremonial wine) to etch designs on seashells that had come by trade from the Pacific. After a century or two the practice ceased; it may have been a single family's magic secret. It is the first known use of etching in the world.

The Hohokam who lived in the river valleys, their center in the region where the Gila meets the Salt, the neighborhood of present-day Phoenix, built miles of irrigation canals, tremendous undertakings comparable to the city building in the Valley of Mexico not only in their construction but in their constant maintenance. Scholars and modern farmers (and modern politicians) argue about how many thousand acres were under irrigation, but single ditches, some as large as twenty-five feet wide and fifteen feet deep, have been surveyed that ran as far as sixteen miles, and one network alone along the Salt River totaled 150 miles. The irrigation systems were well under way by A.D. 700 and reached their maximum size six or seven hundred years later. The first Europeans to see them naturally but wrongly supposed they had watered large cities; a Spanish priest wrote more than two hundred years ago of "a very large canal, still open for the distance of some two leagues (six miles) . . . it appears to have supplied a city with water, and irrigated many leagues of the rich country of those beautiful plains."

A reflection of the great civilizations far to the south is the occasional occurrence of rather rudimentary (at the most about ten feet high) mounds, evidently meant as platforms for temples; one recently excavated near Gila Bend, Arizona, offers a hint of its purpose in the presence nearby of a large cremation area, containing burned human bones and offerings of dance bells and the points of darts or arrows. But some things the Hohokam had not at all in common with the mighty world of far-off Mexico— these were a resolute democracy and peaceableness, an almost aggressive non-aggressiveness.

There was no division into classes, in spite of the organized labor the canals must have demanded, involving close coopera- tion among numbers of villages. Each family lived in the same sort of earth-and-pole house built over a dropped living-room floor, and even the house of the most respected elder, the house of the most holy priest who lived with august dream beings and gods, the "house, enveloped in white winds and white clouds, into which we went to perform our ceremonies" (in a later Pima description), was only somewhat larger than the others, if different at all. The manner of government might have survived in the Papago council of four from whom was chosen one, the best and wisest, to be the principal leader—we seem to have heard of this before; but the spirit that made this government work is best revealed in a line from a Pima children's tale, a line expressing, in fact, a spirit typical of aboriginal America, from the disciplined Aztecs to the wild Tupian cannibals: "I . . . went to consult a man of authority, to whom a boy should not have had the temerity to go. . . ."

There are few indications of war and fewer of aggressiveness in the archaeological record of the Hohokam people, and while there is a sharp decline in their material culture after about A.D. 1400 the later Pimas and Papagos seem to have retained much of the same spirit, a spirit of quietness and peace. When eventually habitual war did come to Pimeria and the people discovered a knack for it and fought well and hard, like beasts of prey, like raptorial birds, so say their songs, a successful warrior returning (bringing the four hairs from his enemy's head that customarily served them as scalp or trophy) had to undergo the sixteen-day cure for insanity. Many Indian societies required purification ceremonies for warriors who had killed, but not usually quite this purifying. Ceremonial war speeches of the Pimas collected in 1900 by Frank Russell all close with the ritual phrase: "You may think this over, my relatives. The taking of life brings serious thoughts of the waste; the celebration of victory may become unpleasantly riotous."

Studious individuals with their gaze fixed on the past sooner or later go a little nutty; every now and then someone springs up shouting he has found the secret of it all. Today, when historians and archaeologists work with biologists, geophysicists, agronomists, chemists, the whole palette of the solemn sciences, and when the comparative advantages of solid carbon or gas sample methods in radiocarbon dating, or the beautifully esoteric mechanics of submarine geology, have become as meet for discussion as pottery sequences or Etruscan inscriptions, the secret of it all seems much nearer. The intricate wizardry in the darkened laboratories, the awe-inspiring formulae in the physicists' notebooks, can only reveal Truth, can't they? But it is really very difficult to fit scientific theories of human behavior around ancient fears that the celebration of victory may become unpleasantly riotous. For the real stumbling block is that these attitudes of peace and quiet may be very ancient indeed, as ancient as any attitudes of savagery.

There has been a tendency for a long while to associate the most ancient instincts with the most savage, the underlying idea being that that all men are ferocious by nature but that some (like us) have been steadily moving upward from their savage beginnings when they brained each other daily. There is, in addition, a current fashion of extracting structures of natural (and therefore unavoidable) Fascist human behavior from the behavior of apes or ants, positing thereby an instinct for mayhem, especially in connection with some notion of "territoriality," as the deepest bias of all life.

But the history of Indian America is riddled with instances of inexplicable (to us) pacifism, and with instances of the willing surrender of territory or seemingly any other possessions—even lives—merely when asked. We have seen this with the peaceful Arawaks who died by the millions after welcoming Columbus with such open hearts to Española. Their general lack of resistance to outrage—any outrage no matter how outrageous—leaves our best experts utterly bewildered: "*Although* peaceful and lethargic, they possessed considerable intelligence and were quite emotional," says one of the best, with my italics.

The peaceful Arawaks and the savage Caribs, who preyed upon them, both of a reasonably equal "primitiveness" in their material culture, might be supposed to represent survivals of equally ancient attitudes. For an extreme example of instinctive pacifism and meek surrender of territory—even to the ultimate territory of life itself—the Arawakan Chané of the eastern slope of the Andes were dominated, enslaved, eventually destroyed as a separate entity by bands of Guarani, all without any evidence of fighting back; an early Spanish explorer reported 400 Guarani ruling a herd of 5,000 Chané, another band of 350 Guarani "owning" 4,000 Chané, regularly rounding up a few to butcher and eat.

The peaceful people of the Southwest (although far from being this peaceful, and by no means particularly "primitive") could trace their pedigree of non-aggressiveness back to a very early root, surely one of the deepest roots of their being. Maybe the sons of Abel have always been with us too.

Northeast of the Hohokam country was the land of another peaceful people, known to us by the name the Navahos gave them when speaking of the ruins of their long-ago towns: the Anasazi, "Ancient Ones." Their early center was in the high, broken country where the four corners of New Mexico, Colorado, Utah, and Arizona come together: red-rock canyons and sagebrush flats, grasslands in the rolling foothills, juniper ridges and pine-clothed mountains.

The earliest Anasazi are called the Basketmakers, from the many examples of their extraordinary basketwork that have been found—some of them watertight for cooking vessels (hot rocks were tossed in until the mush boiled). They too lived in houses built over a dug-down floor until, about the seventh or eighth century A.D., they began building their houses entirely above ground, of log and adobe mortar and then of stone. At about the same time, they acquired the art of making pottery, the cultivation of cotton and beans to add to their crops of corn and squash, and slowly changed their way of life. The first introduction of pottery may have come across the plains from the southeast, from the lower Mississippi Valley, rather than from the south, from Mexico. Clans—a mother and her married daughters and their families—joined their houses together in a single structure of a number of rooms, and finally a whole village dwelt in the same many-roomed, multistoried building.

The pit houses remained as religious centers for the men, subterranean chambers, usually circular, entered from the roof, with paintings of gods around the walls and the mystical hole in the floor, the *sipapu*, to remind the devout of the birth of their first ancestors from the belly of the earth. These chapels are known today as kivas, from their Hopi name, and we call the modern descendants of the Anasazi the Pueblo Indians.

It was for a long time believed that the Basketmakers and the Pueblos were separate races, representing two distinct "migrations," since the early Anasazi, the Basketmakers, seemed to be a long-headed people, and the later Anasazi, the Pueblos, a relatively roundheaded people. It has since been found that in Europe as well as America most people's heads have been getting rounder down through the centuries, for reasons still unknown; it was also discovered that the later Anasazi had picked up the fashion of skull deformation, flattening the backs of their heads by strapping infants to cradle boards, which made their skulls look rounder than they were naturally. It is now generally agreed that the Basketmakers were direct ancestors of the Pueblos, although there were many other intermixtures.

Seen in close focus, a given Anasazi "pueblo" (Spanish "town") was a right little, tight little, closed little world, and years passed, sometimes a great many, while the people sang up the corn, called the rain with puffs of pipe smoke and clouds of eagle down, danced together with their mother the Earth, worked together, laughed together, gradually became grandparents and died and watched with their mountain-mahogany faces through the unchanging masks of the dancing gods while their grandchildren gradually became grandparents—and nothing interrupted, nothing penetrated, nothing interfered.

House timbers from a single site in the Canyon de Chelly, now part of the Navaho country in Arizona, give tree-ring dates from A.D. 348 to A.D. 1284. Dates from the Mesa Verde, Colorado, complex of cliff pueblos, cave villages, and pueblos built in the open cover a thousand years, A.D. 300 to A.D. 1273. The mesa-top pueblo of Acoma, New Mexico, has been continuously occupied for more than 600 years to date. The Hopi are believed to have lived on or about their same three mesas in Arizona for 1,500 years or more, and their modern villages of Old Oraibi, Shungopovi, and possibly Walpi have been continuously inhabited for at least some 800 years.

But seen from a long view, the Anasazis moved, merged, split, built and abandoned towns, appeared and disappeared from every compass point. Strangers entered, and sometimes learned Anasazi ways and themselves became Anasazi—and sometimes did not. In an early Anasazi burial there is a foreigner wearing moccasins, centuries before moccasins replaced the Anasazi sandals, and his body had been cut in two and then sewed together again; did the Basketmakers wonder what he was made of? But the Anasazi world seems to have offered a happier way of life than most of its neighbors knew and so it expanded willy-nilly, naturalizing many varied groups of people.

Non-aggressive though this expansion generally appears to be, there must have been contentions, with each other as well as with wandering people of the wood such as the Utes of the Colorado Rockies; the communal buildings were sometimes made as defendable as fortresses. But the more usual motive that put people in motion seems to have been the death of old fields through drought or erosion—or other natural catastrophes such as a volcano eruption (it left a scar now called Sunset Crater near Flagstaff, Arizona) circa A.D. 1066 that sent a pre-Pueblo people fleeing from their surrounding homes; when they came back years later to fields now fertile with volcanic ash, Puebloan and Hohokam people came with them.

The square-shouldered figures of Basketmaker petroglyphs (pictures on rocks) range over a wide area. The Pan of the later Pueblos, a humpbacked ithyphallic love god usually shown leeringly playing a seductive flute, journeys into newer pastures green. By the time of the Classic Age of the Great Pueblos (*ca.* 1100-1300) the way of life of the Pueblo world had grown offshoots and tendrils that reached from Nevada to Texas. These people spoke different tongues in different villages and were in no sense a single "tribe." They were related only in that they all followed a remarkably similar way of living.

The art and architecture of this way of living came to its finest hour in the time of the Great Pueblos. In the canyon of the Chaco River (northwestern New Mexico) are the ruins of at least a dozen giant community houses. The best known of these, Pueblo Bonito, rose to five terraced stories, had more than 800 rooms and could have housed well over 1,000 inhabitants, and, like a medieval cathedral, was 150 years building, from the year 919 to 1067 (by tree-ring dates).

The people made feather cloth and colored cotton cloth (high-style sashes, masterfully designed, have been found in burial caves where they had kept like new in the dry air of the Southwest), beautifully decorated pottery (although the finest, true works of great art, come from a distinctly separate early culture known as Mogollon, a people who lived in the Mogollon mountains of southwestern New Mexico), and magnificent jewelry, particularly of turquoise, some necklaces containing thousands of worked stones.

Judging from the many ceremonial kivas and dance courts religion must have been a constant occupation, which is one of a number of indications that the congregations regarded it as fun as well as sacred duty. Constant sacred duty tends to become onerous, hence the usual necessity of high-powered high priests to keep enforcing it. But among the Pueblos as among the Hohokam democracy ruled and there were no distinguishable high priests—distinguishable, that is, by any upperclass attributes. The highest-ranking theocrats were simple farmers like everybody else.

Toward the end of the thirteenth century the Pueblo world began to shrink in upon itself. The people drifted away from the great pueblos until many were left abandoned.

Tree rings tell of a long and murderous drought, a period of twenty-three almost utterly rainless years (1276-1299). This would seem to have been enough in itself to have filled the land with the dispossessed.

It is also possible that wolf packs of the immigrants who were to become the Apaches and Navahos began to push their way in from the north at about that time, twanging their new and improved weapon, the sinew-backed bow (as against the flimsier oak or skunkwood bow of the Pueblos) with a new and improved arrow-release (arrow held between first and middle fingers, pull on string with fingers) that pulled three times the power of the less sophisticated release (arrow held between thumb and first finger, pull on the arrow) then apparently in general use in the Southwest.

For whatever reasons, times were hard and troubled here and there in the Pueblo country, and burned villages here and there and mutilated unburied bodies were left to prove it. The desertion of many of the great communal dwellings has led to theories from some archaeologists that perhaps they simply grew too large for the local-option Pueblo democracy, and the Pueblo people chose to stick with neighborhood rule and small towns. And yet even larger towns appeared in the following centuries—Zuñi in western New Mexico and, the biggest of all, Pecos at the farthest eastern frontier of New Mexico.

A Puebloan population in the Tonto Basin of Arizona pulled up stakes and moved gradually southward until eventually, during the thirteenth century, they began moving in with the Hohokam along the Salt and Gila rivers. There was no invasion, no fighting, no conquest physical or spiritual on either side. They lived mingled together for several generations, probably about a century, and each people followed its own customs—the Pueblos made tobacco pipes (the Hohokam smoked ceremonial cigarettes); the Hohokam got drunk once a year on their cactus juice, welcoming the green sun of summer (the Pueblos didn't drink); the Pueblos buried their dead (the Hohokam practiced cremation). Kitchenware and houses remained pretty much in their separate styles, which were considerably separate, with the single exception that in both cases house entrances faced the east, as did the house entrances of many other right-thinking Americans everywhere. Otherwise the houses of these Puebloans—the Casa Grande ruin in Arizona is an example, described in 1764 as "of four stories which are still standing; its ceiling is of the beams of cedar . . . the walls of a material very solid, which appears to be the best of mortar. . . ."—were a far cry from the humble Hohokam dwellings.

About the year 1400 these Puebloan people by then resident so long among the Hohokam began moving on again, maybe south into what is now Mexico, maybe northeast to the Zuñi towns of western New Mexico, ending an instance of tolerance between strangers that has left archaeologists bedazzled, not to say bemused. The Hohokam people stayed where they were, eventually to become the Pimas and Papagos of today.

For the Pueblo world in general the center of things shifted a little southward, from the present New Mexico-Colorado line to the pueblos in the region of the upper Rio Grande River in New Mexico and scattered villages in the same latitude westward among the deserts and mesas into Arizona and eastward to the headwaters of the Pecos.

In the reeds along the rivers, in the willows on the creeks, in the dust-veiled, red-streaked canyons, the still wind of time never died. In their heaped-up, earth-colored towns the Pueblos prospered, diverse and yet identical. Some said one name and some another, "Posoge," "Tséna," "Pajo," "Paslápaane," for the Big River, the Rio Grande, or "mowa," "piki," "hewe," for the paper-thin cornbread everybody made; everybody also made the sweetened dumplings—blue cornmeal mixed with ashes, sweetened by mouthfuls of chewed stale bread—that the old men traditionally filched from the pot, spearing them with splinters, as quickly as they cooked.

Among some, the people were divided into two birthright groups, the Summer People and the Winter People, each group taking turns at running the town for half a year. Among others, the head of a certain society automatically became the town leader. Among most, men grew the corn and women ground it, and among some the husband owned the house but among more the wife owned the house and everything in it, including the corn as soon as it was brought in from the field, and a man belonged more to his mother's house than to his wife's, and was more the preceptor of his sister's children than his own. Among some, membership in the various societies whose important activities filled the days was inherited; among others, one could choose what religious, war-making, hunting, medical, or social clubs he might wish to join. Some wore cotton clothes and some, living too high in snow country to raise cotton, wore buckskin.

But the Milky Way was to all, with different words, the Backbone of the World, and all knew, under whatever names, the Corn Maidens, and the powerful gods, the kachinas, who had granted men the right to wear masks and represent them in dances of prayer. Most also knew the koshare, gods of sunshine and laughter and instruments of discipline by public ridicule, who had granted the same privilege of remembering them in masks when they had gone away long ago to their homes in the east. To most, in common with many other people all over the Americas, the first gods on earth had been two brothers, and men of authority were still called elder brother (the Aztec term for an army colonel).

All knew the fragility of the world's harmony and the danger of throwing it out of key by wickedness, ignorance, or accident. Evil magicians did so on purpose, and when one was caught (you could usually tell them by their harsh and aggressive nature; they also gave themselves away by such acts as peering in through a window at night), he might be hung by the thumbs until he died or his shoulders were crippled for life.

There were beasts, trees, snakes, birds, mountains, stars, of super-natural power, and a right way of living in concert with them, from presenting a newborn baby to the sun to the wealth of pageantry surrounding the growing of the varicolored corn. Some of these rituals were complex and the formal property of specified organizations of priests, but some were not, such as cleaning up the pueblo for the arrival of the harvest (so "the corn will be glad we bring it in"). Anyone could pray anywhere, as long as it was done the heedful way, with a good heart, and votive offerings were also optional (a feathered prayer stick from a man, generally, a sprinkle of cornmeal from a woman).

The first rule of this living, above all, was everything in moderation; nothing too much. None of the ecstatic religious visions of the Mexican eaters of the narcotic peyote or the narcotic mushroom, the *teonancatl,* although a powerful narcotic, datura (Jimson weed), grew at hand. This was sometimes used as an anesthetic at Zuñi for putting a patient to sleep while the director of a curing society set a broken leg or, with an agate scalpel, cut out a tumor, but even then it was usually only given to women or children; men did not need such nonsense. The Pueblos knew and used at least seventy medicinal plants, some restricted by secret power-invoking evil-averting ritual, some free to all—in moderation, and if used with a good heart. Plants too were living beings; one talked to them, and if the words were genuine the plants talked back.

There was none of the furtive, self-conscious fear of sex so important to many other peoples, Indian and otherwise—he's a likeable fellow, he's always in trouble over women; so ran a common, casual phrase in some pueblos. Puberty, menstruation, even childbirth, were not ringed around with supernatural terrors. There was little dread of the dead, or the dramatic, hysterical grief so common among many other peoples, Indian and otherwise. Grief was kept deep but decently within, and the most beautiful of pottery was broken in the grave. There was none of the ascetic self-torture, the gashes, the blood, the wild saintly suffering so important to many other deeply religious peoples. The body was purified for certain rituals by induced vomiting, as among many Indians, but a yucca-suds shampoo was more usual. There was little of the dour, haughty exterior associated with such warrior people as the Aztecs; most of the Pueblos liked a man who, as the saying still has it, talked easy and talked lots.

No excesses; industry, sobriety. But the women were expected to make a social bee of the never-ending community work of grinding corn, and the right way of doing things also demanded a man at the door of the grinding room, playing the grinding song on a flute.

Each gesture of living was an obeisance to living the right way, in unison with each other and with the past and with the rest of the living world, an acceptance of living, a reverence for living—in moderation. The Pueblos made a divinity of living, in moderation.

"I'm for the power of men . . . I strive toward joy," says the Politician to the Poet in Jean Giono's *Que Ma Joie Demeure.*

"I'm against the power of men . . . and I've found joy," says the Poet to the Politician. "It's all around us, as inexhaustible as the air . . . if instead of hounding it we accept it. . . ."

He might have been talking Hopi.

On a day in May in the year 1539 foreigners appeared at Hawikuh, the westernmost of the Zuñi towns; they were Indians from the land of the parrot traders to the south, probably Cahita-speaking people from Sinaloa, some three hundred of them; but they were led by a man who was a new thing to Pueblo eyes, a man who was black. He was Estevanico (Stevie), a Negro from the west coast of Morocco, a Spanish slave, and (for the European history books) the discoverer of New Mexico. He was a veteran at meeting strange Indians, but whatever it was he did at Hawikuh, it was not the right thing.

Some say, with a Zane Grey ring, that the medicine rattle he carried was recognized by the Zuñis as having been made by a people who were their "traditional enemies." Some, leaning more to the adult Western, say the Aristotelian epistemologists of the Zuñi council were affronted by the black man's doubly fantastic claim that a white man was coming along three days behind him. Some say Estevanico made piratical demands of girls and turquoise. Perhaps some of Estevanico's Indian bearers happened to reveal that he represented a people who would come bringing war.

Whatever it was, the Zuñis, after a long deliberation, took up their bows and killed him. Panicked fugitives from among Estevanico's Mexican Indians fled with the news to the party of the white man three days down the back trail, a Franciscan friar, who sprinted back for Mexico "with his gown gathered up to his waist." But in midsummer of the next year, when the corn was just beginning to ear, a terrifying army appeared from the south that contained not only white men, along with more Indians from Mexico, but hundreds of weird and gigantic beasts that were horses and mules.

The Zuñis collected at Hawikuh the warriors from all their six or seven towns, sent the women, children, and old people of Hawikuh to hideouts, probably high on the top of Corn Mountain, their sacred mesa, and telegraphed each movement of the approaching strangers with smoke signals from town to town. When the strangers arrived at Hawikuh, the Zuñis were unbendingly defiant. The Spaniards begged them repeatedly to submit without fighting, while the Zuñis came up to the very heels of their horses to shoot arrows at them and try to drive them away, until at last the "Santiago!" was raised and the town was stormed.

The Spanish leader, Don Francisco Vasquez de Coronado, was battered with so many rocks hurled down on his gilded helmet that he was knocked unconscious and carried from the field "as one dead," but the taking of the town was only the work of an hour.

An even larger army, the main force of the Coronado expedition, came up from the south in September, with more horses and mules and even odder animals—pigs, sheep, goats, cattle, and white women and children. The whole horde moved on to the pueblos of the Rio Grande for the winter.

The reports of the expedition list seventy to eighty pueblos, containing a total (at a broad guess, probably low) of some 20,000 to 30,000 people, stretching from the Hopi towns in the west, almost as far west as the Grand Canyon country, to metropolitan Pecos (with its five plazas and sixteen kivas) on the edge of the great plains to the east; and from Taos in the north to the Piro towns in the south, in the region of the present Socorro, New Mexico. The Zuñis spoke their own language, the Hopis a Shoshonean tongue, and the other towns a variety of languages gathered into two general groups, the Keres group and the Tano (including Tewa, Tiwa, Towa, Piro, and Tano) group, which does not mean—far from it—that all the speakers of each group could converse with each other, any more than an Englishman can talk Dutch.

But they were the same people by their way of life, as the Spaniards immediately realized, and what one of Coronado's private soldiers (Pedro de Castañeda) wrote of Zuñi he meant for all: "They do not have chiefs as in New Spain, but are ruled by a council of the oldest men. They have priests, who preach to them, whom they call *papas*. (The Zuñi word for 'elder brothers.') These are the elders . . . They tell them how they are to live, and I believe that they give certain commandments for them to keep, for there is no drunkenness among them nor sodomy nor sacrifices, neither do they eat human flesh nor steal, but they are usually at work. . . ."

During the winter of 1540-1541 they were usually at work for the Spaniards, who took their food, blankets, women, and houses, and when the people resisted took their lives by sword, fire, and rope—although with real regret. It comes through rather clearly that in spite of their disappointment at not finding riches, the Spaniards genuinely liked these brave and modest little people and were impressed by them. Coronado earnestly did his utmost to avoid violence. But why wouldn't they submit? Unfortunately the Pueblos didn't have any history of submission. They didn't know how. Even the quiet Hopis insisted on a fight.

The Hopis' name, by the way, is their own word for themselves, from Hopitu, "peaceful ones"—most names Indian people used for themselves simply mean people, or people of such and such a place, as Englishmen means men of England, but the names by which we have come to know them are seldom their own. The Zuñi name for themselves, for example, is Áshiwi, "the flesh," while Zuñi is a garble of the name the Keresan-speakers called them: Sunyitsi, meaning unknown. The Zuñi called the Keres people "drinkers of the dew," one of the few examples of poetic names. The Tewa Pueblo people got their name from a Keres word meaning "moccasins," which might provide a hint as to the order of their coming to the Southwest (or as to their taking up first a new style?). Papago means "bean people" (a chief crop), but Pima is a nonsense name bestowed by Spanish missionaries because the Pimas answered Spanish questions with it; it means "no" ("I don't know"). The Pima name for themselves is A-a-tam or O-o-tam (cognate Hohokam), "the people."

In the summer of 1541 Francisco Vasquez Coronado led his army eastward on the great plains looking for cities of gold and found only Indians living in grass houses; he returned discouraged for another winter, and in the spring of 1542 all the strangers trailed away and went back to Mexico except for a couple of small missionary parties that stayed, one at Pecos (consisting of "a very saintly lay brother," a young slave, and a flock of sheep) and one that returned to the people far out on the plains, in the country the Spaniards called Quivira, this a sizable operation under the command of the only ordained priest then with the expedition, with two Indian "donados" (lay brothers) from Zapotlán, a Portuguese soldier-gardener, a black freedman with wife and children, and the party equipped with sheep, mules, and a horse. This, doubtless the first Christian mission regularly established in what is now the United States, came to grief in rather short order with the death of the priest at the hands of unknown natives. The Portuguese gardener, Andrés do Campo, accompanied by the two donados, made it to Mexico after an epic journey of several years; he arrived "longhaired and his beard hanging in braids." The report naturally got about that the lay brother and his servant left at Pecos had also been martyred, but nothing definite of them was ever learned. It was forty years before any Spaniards returned (1581), and then only a tiny party of Franciscan friars and a few soldiers from the mining frontier in what is now Chihuahua; two more friars stayed among the Rio Grande pueblos with a few Mexican Indian assistants, expecting martyrdom, which they received, probably as soon as they tried to interfere with the dances of prayer. A pious merchant came up with a small group the following year to find how they were faring and learned they had been slain, but also found several Christian Indians who had come up from Mexico with Francisco Vasquez Coronado forty years before and had lived among the Pueblos ever since, and who told great tales of great riches they had heard about; so in the following years a few more small bands of the white strangers appeared, mining-camp toughs for the most part, hanging Indians right and left along their way in approved mining-camp style, and Spanish soldiers sometimes came in pursuit of them and took them away. But in 1598 a whole population suddenly arrived, 400 men, women, and children, 7,000 head of stock, more than eighty ox-carts, "carretas" (that is, more than eighty started; sixty-one got through). The land of the Pueblos was being colonized.

Only the desert pueblo of Acoma, seemingly impregnable on the summit of its steep-walled mesa, made any serious resistance; when some of the strangers tried to take blankets and food they were shot down with arrows. Other Spaniards came and fought their way up to the town, impregnable or not, killed the warriors in their kivas, and took 500 women and children back to the Rio Grande for trial. The few men over twenty-five years of age who had been captured were sentenced to the loss of one foot and "personal service" for twenty years; women, and children above the age of twelve were given only the twenty years slavery; children under twelve were put in the care of the priests. Two Hopis who happened to be visiting Acoma at the time were sent home with their right hands cut off, as a warning. The Spanish governor, Don Juan de Oñate, was later (fifteen years later) fined and stripped of his honors and titles by a Spanish court for these forbidden acts of violence, among other charges.

Oñate, son of one of the richest of the fabulously rich Zacatecas mine-owners, and with a wife who was descended from both Moctezuma and Cortes, colonized the new province at his own expense, in the usual way of such affairs, and lost his shirt. The country was too poor. There was no gold or silver, and not even enough corn and cotton to feed and clothe the colonists—regular supply caravans had to be sent from New Spain (Mexico), at the public charge. The tribute from the pueblos—a yard of cloth or leather and a bushel of corn a year from each house seems to have been standard, although firewood was a common substitute—helped the colonists survive but was far from enough to turn a profit. The whole project would have been called off after a few years, except that the priests had by then (so they said) baptized thousands of Pueblos, and insisted that these new converts could not be abandoned. This was a reflection of religious politics; testimony at Oñate's trial gave the total of a few score baptisms only, of women and children in the Spanish service (". . . the reason why no more had been baptized was that the friars were not interested as they believed the land was poor and that it would not be maintained permanently. . . ."). But there was sudden news of thousands of baptisms, indicating either a sign from on high or a basic shift in policy here below, resulting in a new royal order retaining New Mexico in the Spanish Empire after all. Conflict between churchly orders or individuals played a role of occasional weight in empire matters.

Succeeding governors, who bought the office and had to get their money back somehow, made desperate attempts to squeeze more return out of the Pueblos. The priests, outraged by the stubbornness of the Pueblos in clinging to their "devil-worshiping" dances, took increasingly stringent measures against them. The Pueblos, outraged by the public whippings (occasionally fatal) of their most respected elder brothers, now and then martyred a few more priests.

After fifty years of enduring, the Pueblos joined with their ancient enemies the Apaches (who were, of course, subject to a continual open season of outright slave raids, being unsettled infidels) and tried to raise a fight against the Spaniards. It was beaten down before it got started. Twenty years later disasters struck in clusters—there was a year of death-dealing famine, and the next year a sweeping plague, and the next year a furious onslaught of the Apaches, who "totally sacked" the entire province; and two years later, officials in Mexico stopped sending the supply caravans. The year after that a new governor, determined to put an end to the complaints of the priests, hauled forty-seven Pueblo "medicine-men" into custody, hanged three of them, and kept the others imprisoned in Santa Fe.

One of these was an elder brother named Popé, from the Tewa pueblo called by the Spaniards San Juan. He was released after several years, filled with bitterness over the punishments he had received, and went into hiding in Taos, where in the summer of 1680 he organized a real rebellion. Concerted action was very hard to achieve, due to the fairly strict Pueblo adherence to the unanimity rule—if the council of a given pueblo did not agree unanimously on the point at issue, no action was taken. ("We are in one nest," runs a Tiwa saying.) But this time all the towns except those farthest down the Rio Grande—Isleta and the Piro villages—joined in, and this one worked.

Priests were murdered in their missions and their bodies piled on the altars. Families were slain in outlying haciendas. Santa Fe was held under siege for days, until the Spaniards broke out and fled down the river.

The Pueblos attacked "with shamelessness and daring" reported the governor, and of the total Spanish population of 2,500 or so in the province, nearly a fifth were wiped out. The rest, leaving their possessions and their homes of almost a century, made their way south along the blast-furnace desert trail the muleteers called Dead Man's Road, and didn't stop until they reached El Paso del Norte, the present El Paso, Texas. The governor summed up, with infinite sadness, the Pueblo situation: "Today they are very happy without religious or Spaniards."

And the celebration of victory became unpleasantly riotous. Not only churches, church furniture, and Spanish houses were burned, but pigs, sheep, anything living or dead that had been brought by the Metal People (Tewa for Spaniards). Popé, the Spaniards learned, "saw to it that they [the Indians] at once erected and rebuilt their houses of idolatry which they call estufas [kivas], and made very ugly masks in imitation of the devil in order to dance the dance of the cacina . . . " The Indians said, so the Spaniards were told, that "God, the father of the Spaniards, and Santa Maria, their mother, were dead." Popé ordered that nothing should ever again be used that the Spaniards had brought, including the plants they had introduced—watermelons, chilis, onions, peaches, wheat—but here he went too far for people who saw God in every flower and knew plants by their first names (generic words for tree, plant, bush, are often lacking in Pueblo languages); the Pueblos "obeyed in everything except with regard to the seeds."

Popé was carried away by his success, and became, or tried to become, a dictator, demanding obedience from all, seizing whatever caught his eye, and ordering instant execution of any opponents. War broke out between the towns, Taos and Pecos and the Keres pueblos remaining loyal to Popé, the other river pueblos insurgent against him. He was deposed (although later restored to power, eight years after the rebellion, shortly before his death).

But long before that, reaction had set in. The excesses, the civil wars, the bewildering despotism of a leader preaching freedom, were followed by repeated Spanish attempts at reconquest—four in eight years, and for a final nightmare touch the plague returned. Many people went away to the wild mountain canyons of the north, in the region of the present Colorado line, and hid out for years with Apaches and Utes, while thinking serious thoughts of the waste. Others went west to the country of other "traditional enemies," the Navahos. A couple of Rio Grande villages moved all the way west to settle among the Hopi—one (Hano, settled *ca.* 1700) is there yet. The Hopis moved their villages to the tops of their mesas, and the Zuñis moved up to their sacred fortress-mesa, the gorgeously colored Corn Mountain that stands like a red and white banner in the desert, and stayed there for some ten years.

Twelve years after the revolt, in 1692, the Spaniards at last returned in sufficient force for a reconquest. It took four years of sporadic but sometimes heavy and brutal fighting. Some of the Hopis were now mounted "on good horses" and offered a show of force, "giving fearful yells," when the Spaniards approached their mesas but were pacified when the Spanish commander, Don Diego de Vargas Zapata Lujan Ponze de Leon, told them "I did not come to do them any injury nor ask them for anything. . . ." Eight years later, though, in 1700, a mission was reestablished in the Hopi town of Awatobi; it was destroyed almost immediately, and the town around it for good measure, by the people of the other Hopi towns, after which the stubborn Hopis were left alone.

And when at last the people of the Rio Grande pueblos

rebuilt their towns—most of them in new sites—they locked the years of war away and never, as a people, returned to them.

But neither, even yet, did they submit. The dances and the old ways continued, in secret in the kivas if necessary. Nevertheless, Spanish rule was never again as muscular as before the revolt. For Spain by then was a different Spain.

V

The Empire
of the Indies

Spain, a nation on the move, met Zuñi, a nation that wasn't going anywhere, and conquered it with an almost casual "Santiago!" in a few minutes of a hot July desert afternoon. Zuñi wasn't going anywhere because Zuñi, in Zuñi's opinion, was already there. But Spain was on its way to building the greatest empire, as we say, that the world had ever known.

It was built of Indians—without the Indians there would be no Indies, said the Conquistadores, who were bristling believers in the power of men—and in this monstrous, sprawling edifice, burnished with blood and crowned with a cross of solid gold, the trifling conquest of Zuñi was surely one of the most insignificant of architectural details.

At the time of Zuñi's fall to Francisco Vasquez Coronado (1540), the Chibcha people of the Andean plateaux at the topmost shoulder of South America (present Colombia) had met the conquistador Quesada and been vanquished after two years of war in a grade A conquest to rank with the invasion of Mexico or Peru. The confederacies of what is now Venezuela had experienced colonization and exploitation by agents of the Augsburg banking house of the Welsers—Charles V had given the Welsers, to whom he was in debt at the time, hunting rights in that area, the only major deviation from the early Spanish policy of Spaniards only. The Welser adventure is remarkably confused, everyone from priests to freebooters seems to have bought a piece of the show, but it was clear enough as far as the Venezuelans were concerned, since it scored in the aggregate one of the finest achievements in the history of the New World for heartless and wholesale enslavement, mass murder, torture, and general rapine. The Welser concession was revoked after some twenty years.

Peru was the scene of large-scale fighting for a generation, collaborationist Quechua troops serving with the Spanish (there seems to have been some class-war feeling involved, the serf population tending to swing to the Spaniards as bringers of liberty from Inca rule) against the neo-Inca Manco, a youthful brother of the murdered Huascar, who almost turned the trick of equaling his great-grandfather Pachacuti—but not quite. He held the Spaniards under extended siege in Cuzco, his peltists fired the city with white-hot projectiles, but the gods were gone. This time the stones of the battlefield remained merely stones. The new Viracochas ultimately prevailed.

In 1538 the honest old soldier Francisco Pizarro and one of his original (supposedly equal) partners, Diego de Almagro, turned to fighting each other over the spoils of Peru, Almagro being defeated and executed. Almagristas assassinated Pizarro a couple of years later and set up Almagro's son as leader, who was defeated and executed by a royal governor sent out from Spain.

In the north, at Quito, lieutenants of the murdered Atahuallpa had led a war against one of Pizarro's lieutenants, known as Belalcázar, who had bought out Almagro for the privilege of looting to the north, who had previously bought out Cortes' golden boy Pedro de Alvarado, who had come down from Guatemala with 500 followers to horn in. Above them in Colombia the famous Welser advance man Nikolaus Federmann collided with Quesada, and while they argued jurisdiction Belalcázar fought his way up from Peru and joined in—all three went back to Spain to clamor before the king.

In all these turmoils Indian auxiliaries furnished the main bodies of soldiery, and Indian cities and towns the battlefields, and Indian possessions or Indians themselves the objectives— one of the bitterest issues of the civil wars and rebellions was the right of holding encomiendas and exacting forced personal service, which the conquistadors indignantly refused to give up even if it meant defying king and council. And above all, Indians remained the symbols: the son of Inca Manco, Sayri Tupac, was given a little court and a pension as long as he appeared safely tamed, but after his death his younger brother, Tupac Amaru, excited the fears of a nervous new viceroy and in 1571 the last of the Incas was publicly beheaded in the square of Cuzco.

One of Francisco Pizarro's brothers, Gonzalo, led a disastrous expedition across the Andes to the upper Amazon, looking for a reported Land of Cinnamon. The countless river tribes of the lower Amazon were treated to a glimpse of the people from heaven when one of Gonzalo's lieutenants, Francisco Orellana, succeeded in a wildly surrealistic journey through the Amazon rain forests all the way to the Atlantic (1541). Eight years later another Spanish explorer, Benavente, spent some time among the Jibaros of the upper Amazon forests and may have been the first to examine the shrunken heads they kept as trophies. More than a trophy, the famous Jibaro "shrunken head"—actually the skin of a head (human or animal, sloth or jaguar preferred), contracted by heat to about the size and hardness of a baseball—was and is fetish, status symbol, and a most sacred and powerful relic. The magical ceremonies surrounding its preparation and purification required weeks; the quest for it came close to being a respectable man's reason for being in Jibaro society. Eight years after Benavente's exploration the Jibaro country was granted in encomiendas; the landlords who came so innocently to take possession didn't stay long; the last of those lucky enough to escape were gone before 1600.

From Peru the conquistador Pedro de Valdivia made his way south across the deserts to the pleasant farmlands of the Araucanians, in present Chile. He had the gold from his plunder—there wasn't much—made into stirrups and scabbards so horsemen could transport it to Peru. A half dozen of his men started (in 1541) with this richest equipage cavaliers had ever boasted but were cut off by Araucanians on the way, who took the golden trappings back and left only two of the cavaliers alive. The Araucanians killed Valdivia himself a dozen years later and made his skull into a cup.

The New World's lure of riches came to mean silver as much as gold after 1545, when two Peruvian Indians (legend gives their names as Gualca and Guanca) made the first silver strike on the tall sugarloaf mountain known as Potosi. The immense yield of the Potosi mines brought the king's fifth alone to 3,000 pesos daily in the early years—and those in the know said that in spite of official watchfulness not a third of the silver taken out was registered. Forests of beehive-shaped native smelting-ovens sprang up on the surrounding hillsides, and files of Indian laborers toiled up the long rawhide ladders in the shafts, each with a fifty-pound pack of ore on his shoulders, the leader with a candle tied to his thumb; there was a resting place every 140 feet. The Indians worked under varying degrees of servitude, commonest being the mitayos working out the *mit'a*, or tribal labor tax, a neat custom carried over intact from Inca times. But Indians could and did own claims, and some grew rich; since they were prohibited by law from wearing Spanish dress, the Indian section of the boom town of Potosi produced native Andean costumes as rich as any the Incas had ever known, and even slave-laborers (those with a gift for theft) could pay the Potosi prices of $21.00 for a pound of sweets or $350.00 for an arroba of wine. And the universal beggar's cry all over the Spanish New World became "No tengo Potosi!" ("I have no Potosi!").

In northern Mexico the infamous Nuño de Guzmán, bent on conquest toward the north, in Sinaloa, led 10,000 Indian allies in a two-year career (1529-1531) of unmitigated atrocities, for which he was later imprisoned. Another result of this campaign was the so-called Mixton war of 1541, in which Guzmán's ex-victims (or more accurately the survivors therefrom) rose against the Spanish, killed priests, prospectors, and encomenderos, and destroyed crops and cattle. They dug in near Guadalajara and fought off the ubiquitous Alvarado, who happened to arrive from Guatemala in time to participate and lose his life in this war. The revolt was finally put down by the viceroy, with 450 Spanish troops and 30,000 Indian allies.

In 1548 the Zacatecas silver mines of northern Mexico were opened; unbelievably rich, they made their four proprietors (one of whom was the father of Don Juan de Oñate) the richest men in America of their day. More mines were found, rushes of prospectors overran new country so that the frontier strode northward in seven-league boots and ranches and towns came into being, seemingly overnight—by the 1560s the area around Querétaro, 120 miles north of Mexico City, was sending thousands of head of cattle south to market on yearly trail drives, and by 1586 one of the Zacatecas bonanza kings branded 33,000 head on his ranch in what is now Durango, some 600 miles northwest of Mexico City, and even so was not the biggest operator of his region.

Indians were sold to slavery in the mines or reduced to serfdom on the vast estates of the conquerors, and in the incessant search beyond the frontier for fresh supplies of slaves still new country was explored, still new mines discovered, the process exploding its way along as naturally as the wind and the rain.

The progress of such a storm front was of course furiously turbulent. Desperate fighting ran before and followed after; supply trains and cattle drives now and then included armored wagons elaborated into rolling fortresses. Indian states were laid waste in "a crusade of fire and steel, of death and enslavement" and whole populations were smashed into scattered bands of fugitive guerrillas. As one consequence history for years thought of northwestern Mexico as containing only "nomadic tribes," although today archaeology gives us indications of high civilization all the way to the modern states of Zacatecas and Durango, with tombs and ruins still offering up pre-Columbian art objects of the highest order.

The Indian world was violently remade by these convulsions of growth in the brand-new Spanish empire, and the growth, once triggered into being by genes of greed and piety, continued in something very like spontaneous reaction, as blind as pulsing blood. Had the Zacatecas frontier leaped north to the Pueblo country, as it might well have done if the reports of Francisco Vázquez Coronado had been favorable rather than otherwise, the Pueblos too might have been obliterated as independent and identifiable societies. And it was precisely during the following decades of respite that the Spanish government, urged on by growing criticism at home and abroad, took the most extreme measures in New World history to try to safeguard newly subjected Indians from enslavement and wanton destruction. Reforms were terribly slow, enforcement being so difficult, but efforts were pressed with dogged persistence so that by the end of the century, when Oñate brought colonists to the Pueblo country, survival chances for Indian groups enmeshed in the frontier were really somewhat better.

But blind reaction also played its part in the reconquest of New Mexico, twelve years after the Pueblo revolt of 1680, which was prompted more by the story of the Sierra Azul than by any political (either churchly or stately) strategizing, the Sierra Azul being a quicksilver mine someplace in the Hopi country (so they said), a mine so rich that little pools of liquid mercury just stood here and there over the ground, waiting for somebody to use it. The mines of New Spain were always in need of quicksilver, to reduce the silver ores, and the legend of the Sierra Azul remained for a long time one of the brightest of the Spanish frontier's many golden dreams.

But who could say dreams when the reality of riches lay everywhere in this New World, for all to see? Peru was producing two-thirds of the whole world's precious metals by 1600, and the New World has produced by far the largest share of the world's silver ever since. Peru itself was for years nothing but one of those golden dreams, the fabled Birú, until the swords of Almagro and Pizarro cut it open to the light of day. Who wouldn't dare the barbarous nations to find another Peru, another Mexico, another Potosi? To find the Land of Bimini, the Land of Cibola or Cali or Quivira or El Dorado or the marvelous realm of the White King, or the Golden Temple of Dabaiba?

And even if these were only mirages forever retreating behind the ranges, there were the lesser treasures men actually found from day to day, so common they weren't worth reporting (the king would never miss his fifth): even in tombs, as in the Colombian Andes, country of the Treasure of Quimbaya and the long, long tradition of working gold, where "they energetically put all hands to work at disinterring the dead, opening the sepulchres. . . . They found them so rich that they took out thirty thousand pesos, twenty thousand, twelve thousand, six thousand, and down to fifty, the least find. . . ."

In 1528 a certain Captain Francisco César, with Sebastian Cabot at the Rio de la Plata in South America, came back from a scouting trip of some weeks up the Paraná River to report tales of a land of great wealth to the west—he may have gotten near enough the Andes to have heard of the Incas. In 1540 the flagship of an ill-starred expedition sent down to the foot of South America to colonize Patagonia capsized in the strait— presumably many of the 150 men aboard reached the nearby shore. Indian stories began to drift up to Peru of a land some place down in the mysterious south populated by white people, and these stories mingled with the old report of Captain Francisco César, which had lost everything but his magic name.

And the Land of the Caesars came into being: ". . . a city,

commonly called the city of the Caesars . . ." Rich, of course. Could there be a mysterious land in the New World that wasn't rich? ". . . beautiful church buildings . . . Indians for their service . . . many mines of gold and silver . . . ranches of many cattle . . . farms, where they gather an abundant harvest of grains and vegetables . . . cedars, poplars, orange trees, oaks, and palms, with an abundance of very delicious fruit. . . . The climate is the best of all the Indies, so healthful and cool that people die of sheer old age. Unknown here are the diseases of other places; all that is lacking is Spaniards to settle and exploit the great wealth. . . ."

Who wouldn't go searching for it? And expeditions did go, at least a half dozen from 1540 to 1600; the city of Córdoba in present Argentina was founded (1573) as a base for, among other urgent needs, Caesar-searchers. In 1604 the governor of Buenos Aires led the largest expedition in Spain's colonial history—800 men—hunting the city of the Caesars. Some fifteen years later his son-in-law (and grandson of another noted Césarista) inherited the quest, and led still another expedition.

". . . inland from Chile, toward the Strait . . . a nation called the Caesars. . . ."

With such rich dreams and the grace of God, and in one tremendous generation of incredibly widespread war-making— always remembering the massive support of native American auxiliaries—the Spanish turned their first contacts into solid conquests over vast areas in South and Central America, Mexico, and the Caribbean. The probing contacts northward, into the great unknown continent above Mexico and Cuba, were, unless they should turn up another Mexico, another Peru, minor elements in that grand design. By the time of the fall of disappointingly minor Zuñi, other probes, far to the east, were reaching up into the northward mainland, into the country the Spanish knew as the Floridas.

The first Spanish slavers there met on the coast of the Carolinas a "gentle, kindly, hospitable" people they called the Chicoreans—the first two shipmasters to meet them traded for the few gold trinkets they had, then invited as many on board as their ships would hold, then invited them to inspect the interiors of the vessels below-decks, then closed the hatches on them and sailed away. One ship foundered but the other made it back to Santo Domingo and sold the cargo to work in the mines. A rich man of Santo Domingo, named Ayllón, owner of a slaving fleet, wangled a commission as *adelantado* (explorer, colonizer, and potential governor) of the Floridas, and in 1526 took a would-be colony to the Carolina coast to look into the source of the gold trinkets. (The source was probably storm-wrecked Spanish treasure ships cast up on the beaches.) The Chicoreans were hospitable as ever, and according to one account invited a number of Ayllón's people to one of their principal villages and there gently slew them all. The rest of the colony, after a struggling year or two, collapsed.

The red-bearded Panfilo de Narvaez, now a one-eyed bully boy, next got permission for a crack at the Floridas and landed on the Gulf Coast, near Tampa Bay, with some four hundred men and forty-two skeletal horses, to begin a saga of unrelieved calamities, both for the Spaniards and everyone they met.

Gulf Coast villages had also been visited by slavers for several years and were not inclined to be overly friendly, and without interpreters Narvaez could not persuade them with soft speeches. When he finally made friends with the people around Tampa Bay and coaxed their chief and his family into the Spanish camp, he had the chief's nose cut off and his mother torn apart by dogs. He then tried to explore along the coast, hoping to travel westward to Mexico, and ran into the country of what Henry Rowe Schoolcraft a hundred and some years ago called the athletic Apalachee, at that time the most famous fighters in those parts. The expedition took to a fleet of home-made boats; all were wrecked on the coast of Texas, and four miserable survivors spent nearly seven years traveling across Texas, Coahuila, Chihuahua, and Sonora to reach (in 1536) the frontier of New Spain in Sinaloa.

One of these four was the "bearded Negro" Estevanico (later to find his fate at Zuñi), another was his Spanish master; another was Alvar Nuñez Cabeza de Vaca, middle-aged treasurer of the expedition, who emerges as one of the most remarkable of the invaders the New World had yet seen, being, it seems, quite without guile and ingenuously addicted to honesty, decency, and faith in his fellow man.

All four were enslaved by wandering peoples of the Texas coast and shared, season after season, a poverty-stricken life of moving from the land of the pecan groves to the land of the prickly pears and back again and starving in between. During the starving times the famished people scrabbled for anything they could get, bark, bugs, dung, bones, or whatever could be bitten into, including on occasion each other. Wild was the rejoicing when by good fortune a deer was surrounded, driven into the ocean, caught, and clubbed.

Nuñez and his companions, after sundry adventures, became practicing physicians, at which Nuñez particularly became famous. He says simply, and with unquestionable sincerity, that he prayed over sick people and they got well—even a man thought dead being brought back to life.

In the end Nuñez and his three fellow-travelers were passed from band to band in a blaze of glory and reached the Mexican frontier accompanied by hundreds of faithful followers, whom Nuñez then had to save, at considerable effort, from enslavement by the welcoming Spaniards.

The stories the four men had heard of the wonderfully wealthy Pueblos (they seemed wonderfully wealthy, by report, to the underprivileged Muruam Indians of the Texas coast) and especially of the wonderfully rich Zuñi towns (the Seven Cities of Cibola) were responsible not only for the Coronado expedition to New Mexico but also for another entry via the Floridas—a well-equipped army led by Hernando de Soto, Pizarro's dashing young captain of horse in Peru, and financed by de Soto's cut of the ransom of the Inca. From 1539 to 1542 this invasion force, led on by constant reports of riches just beyond, marched and fought its way from Tampa Bay to the mountains of North Carolina and westward across the Mississippi as far as present Oklahoma. Not surprisingly de Soto found more war than peace in Narvaez' legacy, and the venture was as much a total financial loss as the Coronado expedition.

But in spite of blind alleys, setbacks, internecine feuds and hollow dreams, the Spanish empire laboriously persisted in constructing its unpredictable new world from the world of Indians.

The people thus constructed were seldom grateful for their destiny. Their gods and homes were shattered, and from an enjoyment of living they were turned to working for it. They lost their subtle, mystic pride and forgot their very names, so that they called themselves by the mocking Spanish names of Big Ears or Short Hairs. They died in massive numbers from measles, smallpox, cholera, and tuberculosis, from starvation, incredible overwork, from desperation, from sheer horror at inhumanities they could not believe even while they were happening. They died drunk, they died insane, they died by their own hands; they died, they said, because their souls were stolen. They vanished in such numbers that African blacks could not be shipped in fast enough to take their places. Their children were born dead, from syphilis; or their women, rotted with syphilis, became unable to bear children at all.

And so they went mad and rebelled and fought, fought and rebelled, escaped and fought, murdered and burned, and the *Indios bravos*, the wild Indians, filled with dread, became only wilder still.

Wrote the French essayist Montaigne, in the 1570s: "So many goodly cities ransacked and razed; so many nations destroyed or made desolate; so infinite millions of harmless people of all sexes, status, and ages, massacred, ravaged, and put to the sword; and the richest, the fairest, the best part of the world topsy-turvied, ruined, and defaced for the traffic of pearls and peppers! Oh, mechanical victories, oh, base conquest!"

There were outraged Spanish consciences, quite a few of them among the Conquistadors themselves. Cortes, in his will, questioned the right of Indian slavery. Some old Conquistadors not only inveighed against the oppressions of the defeated peoples but rhapsodized over the civilizations they had helped destroy, where everything was "so administered that everyone had enough, . . ." where "there was not a single thief, vicious or lazy man," as said in his deathbed statement the last surviving Conquistador in 1589, speaking of the Inca empire. But those who really got something done about saving the Indian population from destruction were such men as the friar Bartolomé de Las Casas, or Julián Garcés, Bishop of Tlaxcala, or, in Spain, the eminent theologian and master of laws, Francisco de Vitoria. There were many such. They were as much the Spain of the time as the Pizarros and Guzmáns, and they were still more, when all was said and done, the spirit that formed the new world of the Spanish Indies.

One was Fray Bernadino de Minaya, who was with Pizarro in Peru (although as unauthorized personnel): ". . . when some Indians were sent to Panama to be sold as slaves . . . I notified Pizarro of Your Majesty's law against enslaving Indians even when they were the aggressors. He proclaimed the law but at the same time stopped giving me and my companions mainte- nance . . ."

The whole matter of Indian slavery in all its aspects was a hot issue at the time in the Council of the Indies, and Cardinal

Loaysa of that Council, being informed that some Indians had thought the Ave Maria was something to eat, decided they were not capable of learning the Holy Faith ("no more than parrots") and so could be enslaved at will. Brother Bernadino begged his way to Spain, saw the puissant Cardinal but could not change his mind, upon which Brother Bernadino set his jaw and begged his way to Rome to see the Pope. ". . . although merely a poor friar, I should not fear to oppose a cardinal on this matter . . ."

He saw the Pope (Paul III) and the bull *Sublimis deus* of 1537 resulted, accompanied by various papal briefs outlawing Indian slavery in any form. Unfortunately Brother Bernadino sent the glorious news direct to the Indies instead of through channels (the Royal Council), and a major international incident ensued; Charles V, feeling his sovereignty impugned, forced the Pope to call back the briefs, and had Brother Bernardino Minaya tossed into prison to reflect on diplomatic procedures while the affair was being settled—it took a couple of years. But *Sublimis deus* still stood.

Las Casas' monument, the *New Laws* for the Indies, was unveiled to the New World in 1544. They provided for the gradual abolition of encomiendas, at which the Spanish pioneers in Peru staged a full-scale revolt, under Gonzalo Pizarro, who defeated and killed the viceroy, and, among other rampages, raided the royal treasury at the silver mines of Potosi—one of his lieutenants took 1,500 llama loads of silver bars in a single raid. But the king's long arm bore him down, and after four wild years Gonzalo was captured and executed.

The abolition of encomiendas simply could not be enforced and was delayed another half century, and Las Casas kept on battling until he died (he "has twenty-seven or thirty-seven Indian carriers with him—I do not remember the exact number —and the greatest part of what they were carrying was accusations and writings against the Spaniards, and other rubbish . . ." wrote an angry opponent, the friar Motolinia, in 1555, when Las Casas was eighty-one years old). In 1550, the year in which Spain reached her "zenith of glory," the king and the Council of the Indies ordered that all further conquests and explorations should be halted while the justice of warring against and enslaving Indians was debated. The debate took place in Valladolid, before a panel of jurists and theologians, between Las Casas and the great champion of the propriety of Christian conquest, Juan Ginés de Sepúlveda. The specific point of debate: "How can conquests, discoveries, and settlements be made to accord with justice and reason?" was subordinated to argument over the best way to spread the faith (by force or otherwise) and over the Aristotelian point that some are born to be slaves, Sepúlveda arguing that this last applied to the rude and infidel Indians. The subject was in effect racism, and the great debate is in effect still going on, but the basic point established by Las Casas and the many others of the time who espoused his point of view that "mankind is one, and all men are alike in that which concerns their creation and all natural things, and no one is born enlightened . . ." and that "the law of nations and natural law apply to Christian and gentile alike, and to all people of any sect, law, condition, or color without any distinction whatsoever . . ." and that, in short, "all the peoples of the world are men . . ." became the basis of modern international law, holding that treaties must be honored even between peoples of opposing faith and customs.

Slowly but inexorably reform won the day. Indian slaves in Mexican mines—160,000 of them—were to some degree actually, not only technically, freed from forced labor in 1551, and a special court for protection of Indian rights was established in Mexico the following year. Juan de Zumárraga, bishop of Mexico and lifelong friend of Las Casas, had already started schools for Indian boys and girls and produced books written specifically for Indians (incidentally bringing the first printing press to America). Encomiendas, revoked, restored, reverted, regranted, the subject of furious lobbying, were in the end not made perpetual (a final victory for Las Casas). Encomiendas, being built of Indians, died when the Indians died, and many had become empty title to the ownership of corpses, but there were always new-found Indians to parcel out in new encomiendas. Now the mission (often accompanied by a presidio with troops, just in case) began to take the place of encomiendas in frontier organization. In Paraguay the Jesuits built, from the bravest of *Indios bravos*, a network of missions so prosperous and successful it became a glittering working model of a well-oiled, machine-tooled theocratic state.

The Conquistadors had been obliged by law (technically) to read a rather lengthy legal document to any Indians before making war on them—it explained the growth of humanity since Adam and Eve, the supremacy of the Pope, who had given the New World to the King of Spain, and ended by requiring the

Indians to submit to said king. In the middle 1500s this was changed to a friendly, downright genial proclamation of greeting, rather as from one monarch to another, from the King of Spain to the "kings and republics of the mid-way and western lands." The new *New Laws* of 1573—reflecting much of Las Casas' position in the great debate of 1550—stated that even the word "conquest" was not to be used; the word from now on was to be "pacification," in order not to furnish any possible color or cause for aggravation to the Indians.

There were still 4,000 encomenderos left in the two Americas in 1574, out of some 32,000 Spaniards then settled with their families in the New World. There were about 1,500,000 male Indian taxpayers recorded in the Spanish colonies, representing a population of perhaps 5,000,000 left from the original populations of eighty years before. These original populations have been estimated by modern scholars at some 7,000,000 to some 80,000,000 souls in the areas of Spanish conquest, with present opinion favoring the higher levels of this range. While some probably small part of this stupendous population drop, this "tremendous demographic fact," may be attributed to flight out of the white man's reach—an occasional complaint of the authorities—most of it clearly came from disease, raging epidemics of smallpox and measles and other such Old World favors visited upon the totally non-immune New World peoples, "one of the great catastrophes in the history of the human race." Pillage and enslavement, with attendant malnutrition, exposure, overwork, and psychological devastation played at least some role in addition to disease, even allowing for what is now seen as gross exaggeration in the "black legend" of Spanish mistreatment of the Americans, and it would be very wrong to assume this role was entirely ended with the enlightened new laws of 1573. There was a touch of truth in the old Spanish saying, "Obedesco, pero no cumplo" (I obey but I do not comply), and in the words of an ironic professor at the University of Mexico in the sixteenth century, Bartolomé de Albornoz, who remarked that although there were now 400 defenders for every Indian, they continued to be enslaved, bought and sold.

Trials of Conquistadors accused rightly or wrongly of atrocities against Indians became almost standard procedure, as increasingly rigorous laws prohibited any punishment of Indians, even for refusing to become Christians—leaving a single loophole for punishment of those who "hindered the teaching" of Christianity, a clause much used by missionaries in commending troublesome elder brothers to the lash or the gallows.

Indian wars and outbreaks continued, and many of them. For more than two hundred years there was a major uprising about every ten years in the mine-and-mission frontier of northern Mexico, from Sinaloa and Sonora to the Pima country. Nor were such disorders confined to the frontiers. Profitable silk culture, introduced into Mexico by Cortes, was killed not only by the rapid decline of the labor force from pestilence, but by the demand of officials for higher and higher quotas from their villages of Indians until, in the 1580s, Indian workmen destroyed their mulberry trees, wrecking the whole costly silkworm industry that had taken so long to build up. In the capital itself the "tumultos" that were to give Mexico City such a riot-spangled history frequently had their origin among the most downtrodden, the most malnourished, the most oppressed of all the miserable urban poor, the Indios. In a fairly real sense, Latin America has been in a constant state of revolution from its beginning.

But an uneasy balance was at length achieved that made possible the comparatively stable colonial centuries, and that ultimately left traces of a Spanish stamp on the vast majority (ninety per cent, at a moderate guess) of all surviving Indians who were to be much touched by any European culture.

From the first, as has been seen, outbreaks of Indian rebellion had been put down with the help, often substantial, of Indian allies. But by the end of the sixteenth century the Spaniards were beginning to find a new and even more urgent use for Indian alliances—as buffers against other European encroachment in the New World. This consideration was to become an increasingly important part of Indian policy as time went on, not only for the Spanish but for the other European encroachers as well.

Portugal, formally if reluctantly given a bite of the Indies by treaty with Spain, had ceased to be a threat for the time being, with the union of the two kingdoms in 1581. But France and England, Spain's blood enemies, and Holland, just breaking free of Spanish subjection, were interloping with growing insolence.

Francis of France, noted for his wit as well as his women, had mentioned that he would like to see the will by which Adam had divided the world between Spain and Portugal: this while admiring part of Moctezuma's treasure, which had been intercepted by a French privateer on its way to Spain from Cortes.

Thereafter France had taken a piquant interest in the Americas from Canada to Rio de Janeiro, and French Huguenots in the 1560s were building Fort Caroline in the Carolinas to overlook the passing Spanish plate fleets, and finding, so they said, ". . . the natives . . . very kind to them out of hatred to the Spaniards . . ."

Spain had just failed in still another attempt to colonize Florida, even though the colonists had been instructed to "settle and by good example, with good works and presents, to bring the natives to a knowledge of our Holy Faith and Catholic truth." But now a do-or-die Spanish effort founded St. Augustine, massacred the French colony at Fort Caroline, and installed a Spanish garrison. A private French vengeance party returned a couple of years later and with Indian help massacred the Spanish garrison, hanging those who surrendered, but by then, at last, the Spaniards were firmly settled in St. Augustine.

The Spanish governor, Menéndez de Avilés, a renowned naval officer, negotiated an alliance with Florida's most powerful nation, the Calusa, by marrying the sister of their chief, Carlos, equally renowned in his world. Missions and presidios were planted up the Atlantic coast as far as South Carolina, and inland to western Georgia.

Sometime about 1560 an Indian youth had been taken to Mexico from the coastal region the Spaniards called Axacan. He was given the Christian name of Don Luis de Velasco (the name of Mexico's great viceroy of the time) and was sent to Spain for a European education. In 1570 a party of Spanish Jesuits returned with him to Axacan to establish a mission. Luis de Velasco went home to his village of Chiskiac, where he was the nephew of one of the leading men and should have been able to get friendly support for the missionaries; but it didn't work out that way. Perhaps the Chiskiac people were scandalized at Don Luis' European ways. Anyway they got him into proper clothes forthwith, and were thenceforth suspicious and resentful of the priests, who were finally massacred, putting a stop to the mission before it really got started. The Chiskiacs became part of the strong and influential Powhatan Confederacy; some thirty-five years later the English were established among them and named the country roundabout Virginia, the first families of which might now have somewhat different names if it hadn't been for young Don Luis' hose and doublet. The Chiskiac country was along the York River in present York County, Virginia, and marked the point of farthest north in the Spanish struggle to create an Indian bulwark on the Atlantic coast against other Europeans.

As already intimated, a gaze fixed on the past becomes more and more untrustworthy (eventually even reporting that there is no past at all, only a boundless present), but one thing it does sometimes seem to see is that the seeds of greatness, as we call it, are also the seeds of self-destruction. The forces of hot new nationalism under total central authority, crusading religious passion, and the lure of quick riches that hewed out Spain's vast empire became the forces of its ruin.

The hot new nationalism, kept sealed in a vacuum of Spaniards only, cooled to stagnation. Central authority grew hard and rigid, and changed from a whip to a bar—nothing could be done without royal permission; every detail had to be reported, at officious length, through endless official channels. Oñate was kept marking time for several years, his army of colonists already assembled, while the king decided whether or not to let him colonize New Mexico. Alvar Nuñez Cabeza de Vaca, made governor of Buenos Aires and Asunción in present Argentina-Paraguay, tried to protect the Indians and thus gained the enmity of the local slavers; it was the royal pleasure to throw both Nuñez and his principal opponents in prison, not being certain which side had the right of it.

Ecclesiastical zeal, solidly ensconced and grown unrecognizably fat, devoted itself to a chronic war with the miners and ranchers (and between rival religious orders) over Indian jurisdiction—it became customary for each faction to blame the other for every Indian upheaval, often with justice, and the spectacle of priests inciting Indians to murder settlers and settlers inciting Indians to murder priests was not unknown. Each courted the Indians with one eye and winked at subterfuge slavery with the other.

The king poured the wealth of the Indies into European adventures, and crusading religious passion put Spain in the forefront of the war against the Reformation. The gold and silver that poured in from across the sea brought wild inflation with it—five per cent a year in Andalusia all through the sixteenth century, blighting small business and sinking the Spanish masses into a poverty they have never gotten out of since. The rich grew richer, with estates more and more enormous, and the church grew until one-third of the country's eight million people were in some manner of religious employment, and the nation sustained

nine thousand monasteries. But the national exchequer collapsed under the weight: Spain repudiated its debts three times
during the sixteenth century, the last time, in 1596, abrogating a
debt of fourteen and a half million ducats owed to European
money-lenders and leaving the state with ruined credit.

The Spanish knights were no longer chivalric, eagle-eyed El
Grecos but Velasquez dwarfs, with tragic, noble faces and
helpless, stunted arms.

And throughout the generations, from one century to the
next, still more Spanish expeditions toiled hither and thither
beside lost pampas streams "haunted by flamingoes and Magel-
lanic swans" and through the howling winds of Patagonia,
inquiring of the towering Tehuelche the way to the City of the
Caesars.

In 1559 the new Spanish king, Philip II, severely pious,
attended in person, along with an audience of some 200,000, an
auto-da-fé at Valladolid, at which ten heretics were strangled
and two burned alive. But the new king was also so severe in his
repression of the slave trade that he opened up bright new fields
for the enterprising English, one of whom, John Hawkins,
numbered Queen Elizabeth herself among his backers on his
illicit slave-run in 1564 from Africa to the West Indies. He
successfully brought and sold four hundred blacks, and the
queen made sixty per cent on her investment.

VI

King of
the World

Rivals shouldered their way into the New World, and Spain, gorged, awkward with fat, could not hold them off.

The Spaniards centered in Florida, the English above them on the Atlantic coast, English and French pirates and later colonies below them on heretofore unoccupied West Indian islands, and by the beginning of the eighteenth century the French were west of them, toward the mouth of the Mississippi, a wedge driven between Spanish Florida and Spanish Mexico.

The American nations caught in the middle of these European advances took sides, often with gusto, for most of these people of the Southeast were lovers of fighting.

Some of them were also people with a long and notable history.

By present evidence, villages that practiced at least some agriculture began to appear here and there in the Mississippi Valley two thousand years ago or more. Communities of scattered hamlets that built burial mounds existed for a thousand years before that time, and fiber-tempered pottery (point of origin unknown) occurred in the Southeast still another thousand years previously, or as early as 2,000 B.C.

An elaborate society gradually came into being based on this triple alliance of burial mounds, pottery, and some agriculture along with the main business of hunting—an elaborate world that appears to have had its focal point toward the north, in the valley of the Ohio, and its main interest (so far as we can tell now) in stylish funerals. Archaeologists have identified two distinctly different cultures within this general frame of time and manner, one, somewhat earlier, called Adena after the name of one of its sites in southern Ohio, and the other, overlapping Adena in both time and place, known as Hopewell, also after a site in southern Ohio.

The Adena people appear to have differed physically from their neighborhood predecessors and from the Hopewell people. Some think they may have been culture-bringers from someplace; they certainly brought a new sophistication to their Ohio Valley homeland. The Hopewell way of things, perhaps involving a confederacy of different peoples, later spread far beyond this heartland, down the Mississippi and throughout a region reaching from the Gulf to Wisconsin, from New York to Kansas. The Hopewell people built great burial mounds and extensive earthwork systems—sometimes enclosing as much as a hundred acres—in their riverside towns or ceremonial centers, traded for raw materials (pipestone, seashells, obsidian, metals) all over eastern North America from the Rockies to the Atlantic, and made objects of art of a high order in everything from wood and mica to copper, to leave for posterity in their rich and splendid burials. According to radiocarbon dates the Hopewell world reached its finest development a very long time ago indeed—in the centuries from about 300 or 400 B.C. to about A.D. 300 or 400.

At a later time a new and somewhat different order of things came into being toward the south, centering along the Mississippi from the present Cairo to the delta. This consisted of little city-states, stockaded towns and villages built beside streams and bayous around ceremonial centers that featured flat-topped temple pyramids made of earth, sometimes quite large—seventy or eighty or even a hundred feet high, and covering large areas; and "the sides so upright," as a traveler wrote of one in 1790, "that the cattle cannot get upon it to feed."

This Temple Mound tradition (usually called Mississippian nowadays by the archaeologists) flourished for many centuries, reaching a peak of operation from about A.D. 1300 to 1500, and was still in business to some extent, although possibly rather on a remnant basis, when the first Europeans appeared in the Southeast. The great center of Cahokia, just across the Mississippi from modern St. Louis, may have ruled its stretch of the river for nearly a thousand years.

The thatched houses sometimes resembled Mexican houses, the pyramids resemble the pyramids of Mesoamerica and were topped by wooden temples in the manner of the earlier Maya, and were built in successive layers, probably at periodic renewal ceremonies, as in Mesoamerica; an eternal fire was kept burning in the temple, as in Mexico, and was renewed at a new-fire ceremony—although once a year, at least in the later times we know about, rather than every fifty-two years, as in Mexico.

Sacrifice of war captives was an enthusiastic community activity—occasionally the victim was tied spread-eagled in a wooden frame, much as in the ancient Mexican arrow-shooting sacrifice.

There are so many points in common, even to some specific pottery styles, with the Maya and other early civilizations of Mexico and Central America and even of South America that there must have been contacts.

It does not seem likely that the scattered gangs of emaciated indigents feeding among the cactus flats of Texas, as described by their sometime slave and physician Alvar Nuñez Cabeza de Vaca, would have handed on the torch of learning from Mexico by way of the Gulf Coast. So it would seem the connections must have been by sea, across the Gulf, possibly from the Yucatan peninsula, possibly from Toltec ports along the Mexican east coast.

At the fullest development of this Temple Mound society, "the most vigorous, the most impressive" of aboriginal societies in the area of the eastern United States, influences that were clearly Mesoamerican operated upon prototypes that were clearly local (some extending back to Hopewell times) to produce the extraordinarily rich trappings of what is known as the Southern Cult, a renewal ceremony very likely, an emotional religion, that captivated nearly all the area of the Southeast. Skulls and bones, weeping eyes, feathered serpents, cat-man gods abounded, and cryptic mystic symbols of an eye in the palm of a hand, a swastika in a star.

Here as elsewhere populations had entered and vanished, merged and divided; only more so. Probably more than any place else north of Mexico, the lower Mississippi and environs had been a maelstrom of those ripples of contact. The loose Burial Mound confederacy, and the even looser Temple Mound confederacy or confederacies—if confederacies they were—were composed of tangled multiplicities of peoples, of varying customs and cultures, speaking different languages. The buzzard symbol of the Southern Cult spread its wings over a medley of nations from the numerous Caddo people west of the Mississippi, on the shore of the great plains, to the villagers of Georgia—probably ancestors of some of the later Creeks—who built the mound town of Etowah and crammed its graves with spectacular Southern Cult ornaments.

In a general sense, all were hoe farmers growing the same crops; fishermen using the same tackle; hunters coursing the same piney woods, cypress swamps, and canebrakes and gaudy hardwood ridges where bears started up and ran like rolling drums. Buffalo as well as deer were hunted on the Mississippi bluffs, and along the rivers a fearsome game was the "crocodile . . . it squashes people with its murdering tooth," as an erudite traveler reported (the line is a quote, more or less, from Ariosto). All rode the winding rivers in similar models of dugout canoes or poled the swamps with the same cane raft. All boiled corn soup and hominy from the same recipes, and took the same extras and delicacies from the larder of wild nut trees and berry bushes. The village systems were more or less alike: a large town of perhaps 200 or 300 cabins, usually palisaded and moated for defense, serving as a center for a number of smaller outlying communities.

But the deepest underlying unity seems to have been one of a passionate and somewhat mystic endeavor. Living was on a high note. Death was the great crescendo. This traced back to an antiquity so remote that it was in another world (the world of the first elder and younger brother, or the first mother—made pregnant by a snake—who gave birth to the first life and the first death).

A story told by the Alabama people (who helped the Mobile people and their famous leader Tuscaloosa engage Hernando de Soto's army, on October 18, 1540, in one of the largest Indian battles ever fought in the area of the present United States) deals with a familiar Indian theme, people descending from heaven "in a canoe singing and laughing," and a man on earth who catches and marries a girl from among them. But later she and their children sail back up to heaven, "singing and laughing, continually singing." In the Alabama ending to the story, the husband tries to follow in another canoe: "He went on for a while, singing, but looked down to the ground. Then he fell back and was killed."

There is a definite feeling that in later times the meaning of this music of passion and aspiration had been forgotten, and that it was only followed because it had always been followed. Or, rather, that the theme was in a stage of change, modulating to a new key, as it must have done many times before down the years.

But the order of living remained: the great midsummer renewal festival, requiring purification from the celebrated "black drink"—the purifying emetic of the Southeast, taken, says an early account, "until the blood comes"—and from physics that sometimes left the purified crippled from violent convulsions, and featuring the mass ball game in which arms and legs and sometimes necks were fractured; the engrossing game of sliding sticks and stones called *chenco* (English traders called it chunkey), on which wild bets were made; the taboos heaped on sex, which was charged with many perils (according to some reports, Creek women had to run and hide in a swamp, entirely alone and unattended, at time of childbirth); and the heart-springing excitement of battle and raid.

And there was the dramatic torture-sacrifice of captured enemy warriors, as good as a play. It is hard to escape an impression that simply the entertainment involved had become the main force behind the ritual torture of captives of war; with certain exceptions, religious significance is either absent or disguised out of recognition by the time European observers arrive.

In any case, this was no world of contentment but a world in search of rapture and excitement; this was no land for people of moderation.

When, in the seventeenth century, the Spanish, French, and English established the battlefronts of empire in the Southeast, the largest and most powerful Indian group was a loose confederation of some fifty towns (perhaps 30,000 people all told) in the area of present Georgia and Alabama dominated by a nucleus of associated tribes known as the Muskogee. Early English traders from South Carolina first met citizens of this confederacy living along a river the English called Ocheese Creek (now Ocmulgee River) and spoke of them as the Indians of the Creek, the Creek Indians, by which name all the members of the confederacy have been known ever since.

Composed of a number of different peoples and fragments of many earlier groups, most of them related but some utter aliens (a half-dozen languages were spoken within it), the Creek confederacy was divided into two principal parts, the Upper Towns, and in theory below them on the rivers, the Lower Towns, a division reflecting the widespread Indian arrangement of double government. The Summer and Winter people of the Pueblos became in the Southeast (and quite a few places elsewhere) the Peace and War people. Among the Creeks the Upper Towns (again only in theory, since in practice these matters got mixed up) were primarily the Peace Towns, the White Towns, controlling important civil ceremonies such as the *puskita* (the *bosquito*, the *busk*), the eight-day festival of the first corn, when new fire was made, grudges were forgiven, plazas were swept and sprinkled with new sand, and in general life was scrubbed, shined, and started afresh on another year. The principal chief of the confederacy was supposed to be chosen from a White Clan. The Lower Towns were the Red Towns, consecrated to ceremonies of war, and the elders of the council, the Beloved Men, were supposed to choose the confederacy's battle chief, the Great Warrior, from a Red Clan.

West of the Creeks were the people whose road to their landing place on the Father of Waters, the road known later as the Old Chickasaw Trail, first led English traders to the Mississippi. This traditional Chickasaw river port, more than 150 miles west of their central villages, was on the site of modern Memphis. Below the Chickasaw toward the Gulf Coast the most important nation was that of the Choctaw, who gave their name to a lingua franca used thereabouts in trade, the Choctaw Jargon—also called, depending on where one was trading at the moment, the Chickasaw Jargon or the Mobile Jargon, these languages all being much alike.

The Choctaw, Chickasaw, most of the Creeks, in fact most of the people over all this southern country from the Mississippi River eastward to the Atlantic, spoke languages related to various divisions of the Muskogee language family. But, to repeat, related languages did not necessarily mean related people. The Choctaw and Chickasaw, for example, with very similar languages, were considerably less similar physically and in their natures: the Chickasaw far-ranging, quarrelsome, aggressive; the Choctaw close-mouthed farmers inclined to stay home and tend their gardens, which, in the rich bottom lands of southern Mississippi and Alabama, were some of the best in North America—the two were, of course, bitter enemies.

In this Southeastern sea of Muskogian tongues there were islands of Siouan speech (notably the Biloxi) and Algonkian (notably bands of Shawnee). Up the Atlantic coast in North Carolina were the Iroquoian Tuscarora people, and north of the Creeks were the Cherokee, most populous single tribe in all the area (20,000 souls in sixty villages) speaking variant (the most variant known) Iroquoian dialects.

As noted, linguistic relationships are often purely technical morphological connections charted by linguistic anthropologists—they were or were not recognized as relationships by the Indians involved, depending on the circumstances. Speakers of English might or might not feel a kinship to speakers of German, a very closely related language—the two have probably not been separate languages as long as Cherokee has been separate from Iroquois—but it is doubtful that English-speakers would feel any relationship with, say, peoples who speak Hindustani or Kurdish, which are nevertheless in a technical sense distantly related to English, somewhat as a Muskogian tongue of one division might be related to a language of another Muskogian division.

The main Siouan frontier of the seventeenth century, zigzagging northward up the west bank of the Mississippi, might be said to have begun in the south with the Quapaws (the name means "downstream people"). Their territory lay generally westward of the Chickasaw country, most of it across the Mississippi, centering around the mouth of the Arkansas. Below the western range of the Quapaws, over an immense region with its heart in present east Texas, were the principal Caddo confederacies.

The lower Mississippi, from the Yazoo to the delta, was controlled by a series of little riverine states, small in area compared with their surrounding neighbors but not necessarily always weaker in population or influence, the best known of these being the famous Natchez.

The Natchez (the spelling is old French, apparently meant to indicate a pronunciation something like Natchay) occupied nine or more villages, most of them on the east side of the present city of Natchez, and at the end of the seventeenth century may have numbered approximately 4,000 in total population, including two villages of refugee foreigners they had taken under their wing (the Grigra and the Tiou; the Tiou, at least, were refugees from Chickasaw aggression). This, as single "tribes" north of Mexico go, is a considerable size: twice as numerous as the Quapaws, almost equal to the Chickasaws, a fourth as large as the Choctaws, who almost equalled the Cherokees in number.

It should be mentioned again that these estimates of early population figures are only guesses, somewhat as if we might guess the population of various foreign places after a summer in Europe, and estimates expecially untrustworthy as an indication of the pre-Columbian state of things. Even the earliest reports of European explorers and colonists may not reflect pre-Columbian conditions, since disruptions and epidemics may well have preceded the first appearance of any people from heaven, sometimes by many years.

Three great outbreaks of pestilence ravaged the villages collected around the Spanish missions in Florida during the seventeenth century (1613, 1649, and 1672) and there was no reason for the contagion to confine itself to Christian Indians.

Thus the population of 420 estimated for the Biloxi in 1699 may easily be less than earlier numbers, and the 214 given by a report of 1715 for the Apalachicola, a leading people among the Lower Creeks, one of the original organizers of the Creek Confederacy, known to the Muskogee as the ancients of the country, may be, as it might seem from this impressive history, nothing more than a shadow of former strength.

The Natchez told a story of a great sickness in which "multitudes of people" died, lasting four years, and reducing them from a great nation of 50 towns, stretching fifteen days' journey in one direction and twelve days' journey in the other, an unheard-of disaster caused, they said, by an unfaithful temple guardian who had let the sacred fire go out.

In any event the celebrity of the Natchez is out of proportion to their size and importance, but comes from their position as a preeminent, if perhaps not typical, example of a Temple Mound state surviving into modern times.

They were ruled by a king, a descendant of the sun and called the Great Sun. Every deference was shown him, and his power over his individual subjects, their lives, labor, and property, was absolute and despotic; although in political decisions involving the nation as a whole the Great Sun in turn was controlled by the council of respected old men.

His residence, in the principal village, was a large cabin

(forty-five by twenty-five feet) built on a long, flat-topped mound (some eight or ten feet high). Nearby on a similar mound was another large cabin, decorated with two carved birds perched at each end of the roof. This was the temple, in which two guardians watched the eternal fire, and in which were the sacred bones of previous Great Suns. No one but the Great Sun, who was high priest as well as king, and the few appointed temple officials, were permitted to enter the temple—whether its forbidding sanctity came primarily from the fire within it or from the bones interred there is uncertain; experts disagree.

The relatives of the Great Sun (with the exception of his children) were Little Suns; his mother or sister was the principal woman Sun and chose the successor, from among her sons or brothers, when the Great Sun died. The Great Sun appointed the two war chiefs of the nation, the two masters of ceremony for the public rites in the plaza before the temple, and other important functionaries, from among the Little Suns, all of whom were given slavish respect by the rest of the people.

Below the Suns in importance was a class of Nobles, and below the Nobles a class called Honored Men (to which anyone could aspire by distinction in war or piety), and lowest of all were the commoners, the masses, treated like dirt by the aristocrats, say the early accounts, and referred to as Stinkers (*Miche-Miche-Quipy* in the Natchez tongue, rendered in French as "Puant"), although the term was not used in the presence of the Stinkers themselves, as it offended them.

Suns could not intermarry—all Suns, male and female, including the Great Sun, had to take their wives or husbands from among the Stinkers. The children of male Suns were only Nobles, who again were obliged by law to marry Stinkers, and the children of male Nobles were reduced one more grade to Honored Men or Women, who also had to marry Stinkers. The children of Honored Men were Stinkers. Descent holding in the female line, the children of female Suns were Suns, the children of female Nobles were Nobles, the children of Honored Women were Honored People. The children of two Stinker parents were of course absolute Stinkers.

This Gulliveresque system is unique, although its basis, descent through the mother, was and is very common among "primitive" societies all over the world.

Female Suns, naturally, must have held a decisive behind-the-scenes power, as well as living the life of a maiden's dream—at any rate the dream of a maiden of the gallant court of

Louis XV, whose Louisiana subjects recorded most of this; there would be a temptation to think their powdered wigs were getting in their eyes except that five reasonably dependable contemporary accounts all agree in essential facts. Anyway, the Stinker husband of a woman Sun had to stand in her presence like a servant, shout his praise of her every remark, was not allowed to eat with her, and if he displeased her, particularly by any infidelity, she could "have his head cut off in an instant." Privilege of rank permitted her, of course, as many lovers as she pleased. She could also, if the whim struck her, have her base-born husband thrown out at a snap of her fingers, and pick another Stinker in his place.

And yet this was a warrior state and the situation in the usual Natchez home was that the husband "alone commands." Old men were held in such respect that "they are regarded as judges. Their counsels are judgments."

The Natchez may have been the people spoken of in a chronicle of the Hernando de Soto expedition as worshipers of the sun, to whom de Soto sent word that he was the Sun's younger brother. They replied that if he would dry up the Mississippi they would accept his credentials. Possibly they joined other Mississippians in merrily chasing the Spaniards down the river. But it was not until a century and a half later that their old life was definitively interrupted by Europeans who came to stay, when the French founded the colony of Louisiana, first established at Biloxi (1699) and then on Mobile Bay (1702).

The Natchez had seen Frenchmen occasionally for several years previously, leathern strangers who came floating down the river in canoes beautifully fashioned of bark, marvelously swift—the first of these (of record) had been a band led by a fretful trader named Robert Cavalier, Sieur de La Salle, an overnight guest with the Natchez in March, 1682.

Now French missionaries began appearing and newcomers not only from Canada but direct from France, seamen in great boots, soldiers in steel breastplates, clerks from counting houses, farmers from Gascony—and three Carolina Englishmen came by way of the Chickasaws, already stout English allies, to visit the Natchez villages of White Apple, the Hickories, Grigra, and Tiou. The French would enslave the Natchez in their own country, the English traders said, and furthermore French guns and hatchets and knives were not as good as the English, and furthermore the English would trade for a lower price in pelts.

The Englishmen fled back to the Chickasaws when a French

trading post was opened at the Great Village of the Natchez in 1713. But some of the Natchez (from the villages of White Apple, the Hickories, and Grigra) murdered several Frenchmen and brief hostilities followed—armed parleys rather than a war—resulting in the execution of six village war chiefs, and delivery by the Natchez of the heads of three others: their heads, not their scalps, the French governor specified, "in order to recognize them by their tattoo marks." Another result was a garrisoned French stockade, Fort Rosalie, established in the Natchez country.

These first French colonies had been a business venture on the part of a rich French merchant who had obtained sole exploitation rights for all North America from the Illinois to the Gulf, from the Carolinas to New Mexico, but could not make his investment pay.

In 1717 a promoter took over his grant on speculation, formed a company that was given total power over this land and anyone in it, ransacked jails and hospitals or kidnaped people from the streets for colonists, sent out shiploads of black slaves to implement tobacco farming, exacted taxes from Indians of buckskins and bear oil, and in general went at things in a vigorous, businesslike way.

Agents of this company obtained large tracts among the Natchez towns for plantations, the region became the most flourishing department of the Louisiana culture, and seemingly every Frenchman there who knew how to write recorded his observations on the remarkable Natchez—who are given more space in the literature of the period than all the other fourteen Indian states of the lower Mississippi put together.

The Natchez girls received much attention, due to their custom of extreme licentiousness before marriage and (Woman Suns presumably excepted) their extreme virtuousness afterward, just the opposite of the European ideal of feminine behavior.

Natchez warriors are seen again and again, heads flattened to a mitred point, hair cut in whatever bizarre fashion the wearer likes—shaved on one side, left long on the other, or trimmed to a single scalp lock, or tonsured like a priest's. They stroll the plaza, tattooed (tattoos were, so to speak, war medals) from face to ankle, negligently waving fans, or recline on their mats while the women work the fields.

Homosexuals appear, male concubines as one French observer calls them, men who wear their hair woman-style, long and braided, wear skirts instead of loin cloths, and work with the women. Many Indian societies gave transvestites some recognition, ranging from an embarrassed tolerance to a sort of priestly distinction—although Maya tradition is reported to say they had never heard of homosexuality before the Toltecs came, and the Aztecs and Incas punished it severely by law; Inca soldiers, about to make war on a notoriously homosexual nation, joked about the danger of rape. Sodomy was one of the common charges brought by early Spanish priests to justify annihilation of various stubborn peoples; Las Casas claimed the reports were exaggerated for propaganda purposes, as the stories of Central American caciques who kept "hundreds" of effeminate men in "harems" might seem to indicate. But in general the whole Indian attitude toward what Europeans regarded as obscenity seemed shameless and arrantly sinful to European eyes and ears, and still does—even in our own time scholarly recorders of Indian folk tales have made a plentiful use of Latin paragraphs to veil the (to them) dirty passages. Conversely, many Indians found European attitudes (such as not isolating women during menstruation) not only grossly obscene but so wicked as to be terrifying.

The sensational torture scenes were painted by all. Male captives of war were brought back to dance and sing before the temple and then were scalped and lashed up naked in the wooden frames to be tortured and burned. Etiquette demanded that the victim sing his death song as long as life remained, and some, says Le Page du Pratz, the best of the Natchez reporters, "have been seen to suffer and sing continually during three days and three nights . . ." Captive women and children had their hair cut short, badge of slavery, and were put to work pounding corn. As among most Indians, it was also possible for captives to be adopted into the nation, and even attain later eminence.

But it was the un-Indianlike kingship and caste system that made the Natchez remarkable to their French neighbors, who saw in hereditary aristocracy the surest proof that civilization's gentle step had once trod these woodlands rude, sometime or other. When it came to the Great Sun, his Louis Quinze admirers were downright charmed.

There were dissenters. The first French governor wrote of the Great Sun of his day (1700): "He appeared to me the most absolute savage I had seen, as beggarly . . . as his subjects." But other witnesses sing panegyrics on the reverences of his subjects, his absolute authority, and his kingly demeanor. "When he gives the leavings (of his dinner) to his brothers or any of his relatives, he pushes the dishes to them with his feet." "The submissiveness of the savages to their chief, who commands them with the most despotic power, is extreme . . . if he demands the life of any one of them he comes himself to present his head."

Wearing his crown of swan feathers tasseled in scarlet, the Great Sun was carried in a litter to the festival of the new corn; his platform bed of state was furnished with a goose-feather bolster and heaped with the richest buffalo robes and bearskins, and he was wakened in the mornings by the most distinguished old men, who saluted him with respectful cries and bows that he didn't deign to notice (a royal levée, to the life).

And "these people blindly obey the least wish of their great chief . . . for whatever labors he commands them to execute, they are forbidden to exact any wages. The French, who are often in need of hunters or of rowers for their long voyages, never apply to anyone but the great chief . . . "

This last hints at a practical charm in addition to the regal romance of it all. One suspects the Natchez warriors did not spend too much time reclining on their mats after the French appeared.

This may have been a factor, along with constant English-Chickasaw agitation, for the fairly clear emergence of two political parties among the Natchez: pro-French and anti-French. There may have been some tendency for certain classes to cleave to one party or the other. The Great Sun and his brother, war chief of the nation, whose name was Tattooed Serpent, and their mother, the principal woman Sun, whose name was Tattooed Arm, were all strongly pro-French. The majority of the higher aristocracy seems to have followed them in pro-French leanings. The clearest division was among the villages (of which only six seemed to exist after 1713): the Great Village and the Flour Village were pro-French centers, while the Hickories, White Apple, and the immigrant districts of the Grigra and Tiou seem to have been hotbeds of anti-French feeling, although here again some of the chiefs of these seditious villages, Suns all, appear to have maintained a sturdy pro-French loyalty as long as possible.

In the autumn of 1722 a young sergeant of the Fort Rosalie garrison had an argument with an aged Natchez warrior over a debt, "threatened to give the old man a cudgeling," at which the old man, riled, said they might see who was the stronger. "At this defiance, the soldier, crying 'murder,' summoned the guard to his assistance." The old man, walking toward his village "at an ordinary gait" was shot in the back. He died the next day of the wound. The commandant of Fort Rosalie reprimanded the young sergeant.

Some White Apple men a few nights later (drunk, the Tattooed Serpent said) shot and wounded one of the directors of the plantation (called "the concession of St. Catherine," giving the name it still bears to the creek running through the Natchez towns) neighboring their village, and killed and scalped a French soldier.

A detachment of troops was immediately sent up the river from the recently founded capital of New Orleans. Tattooed Serpent managed to make peace, and forced the villages of White Apple, the Hickories, and the Grigra to pay an indemnity to the French troops.

Not long afterward resentful individuals from these villages killed some cattle on the concession of St. Catherine and this time a larger army, with Choctaw and Tunica allies, came up from New Orleans, the French after vengeance for the murdered cows, the Choctaw and Tunica along for incidental plunder. Again Tattooed Serpent made every effort for peace, but the French commander, this time the governor himself, was bent on blood, although he at length agreed to spare the Great Village and the Flour Village.

The expedition marched by stealth against White Apple, but on the way they came in sight of three Natchez women pounding hominy in front of a lone cabin, and since the governor had inspired his troops, among whom were many New Orleans volunteers, by promising that they could keep as slaves any females they could catch, the whole army stormed the three women and the cabin with such an uproar and fusillade that the White Apple people were alerted and abandoned their village.

Thereafter the army found only empty villages to burn, although by chance an old woman was encountered, "who was perhaps more than one hundred years old, since her hair was entirely white, a very rare thing among these savages. . . . The general . . . after having questioned her . . . abandoned her on the spot, as a useless incumbrance, to the discretion of a little slave he had, who took her scalp and killed her."

The Choctaws and Tunicas managed to scare up four women

and one man during several tiresome days of marching, and the governor, who wanted "blood worthy of being shed," summoned Tattooed Serpent and told him they were going to destroy the Great Village and the Flour Village after all, since they couldn't find anyone at home elsewhere. Tattooed Serpent, "who was really a friend of the French, made no other reply than to ask for peace."

The governor finally granted it, on condition that the head of the chief of White Apple be delivered to him. This was a Sun of great distinction named Old Hair, particularly respected by all the nation, and, very probably, the bulwark of the hard-pressed pro-French party in White Apple. Being a Sun, he was supposed to be exempt from capital punishment for any reason whatsoever, which made the request rather like asking the Pope to serve up the head of a cardinal.

But Tattooed Serpent submitted, and after two days for the necessary ceremonies and leavetakings brought the head of Old Hair. The governor, rather as an afterthought, also demanded and got the head of a free black man who had come to live with the Natchez—"It was justly feared that he would teach them the manner of attack and defense, and for that reason it was of the utmost importance . . . to get rid of him."

Sometime later a malefactor from Tiou cut the tail off a planter's mare (a trophy as good as a scalp). Tattooed Serpent bought peace this time with a tribute of corn from all the nation, "more than sufficient to pay an entire regiment of cavalry."

Tattooed Serpent died in 1725. The whole nation (and quite a few of his friends among the French) wept, for he was much beloved. His two wives, his chancellor, doctor, principal servant, pipe bearer, and various other followers, went joyously to the funeral rites, at which they were drugged and then, with their heads concealed in skin bags, strangled.

Several other volunteers insisted on being strangled to go along, one of them a Noble woman, a great beauty, a particular friend of Tattooed Serpent, and "intimate only with distinguished Frenchmen." The French called her La Glorieuse.

A Stinker couple sacrificed their child and threw its body under the feet of the pall-bearers (a means of being raised to Honored rank), and the Great Sun himself, wildly grieving, had to be restrained from suicide.

One cashiered warrior marked for sacrifice didn't want to go, and Tattooed Serpent's favorite wife sent him away: ". . . it is not good that you come with us and that your heart remain behind you on the earth." To French friends who begged her not to die, she said "with a smiling air": "Do not grieve. We will be friends for a much longer time in the country of the spirits than in this, because one does not die there again . . . Men do not make war there any more, because they make only one nation. I am going and leave my children without any father or mother. When you see them, Frenchmen, remember that you have loved the father and that you ought not to repulse the children of the one who has always been the true friend of the French." She was, it will be remembered, from the class of Stinkers.

The Great Sun died three years later, in 1728. The succeeding Great Sun was young and less effective. The old queen-mother, Tattooed Arm, was left alone as the mainstay of French support. The White Apple chief who had taken the place of Old Hair was hotly anti-French, and of growing influence. Pro-English Chickasaws, according to an English account, won the Natchez to their side in the year of the Great Sun's death: "But as the Indians are slow in their councils on things of great importance, though equally close and intent, it was the following year before they could put their grand scheme in execution."

For a final argument there came now as commandant at Natchez an unbelievably villainous ass (all accounts agree) named Chépart (also given as d'Etcheparre and Echepare), who tyrannized over everyone in sight, French as well as Indian. The best plantation land being taken up, he commandeered the Great Village itself for his plantation, and ordered the youthful Great Sun to move his people away instantly. He granted a delay until harvest time (the first corn having just sprouted), on consideration of a sufficient rental paid in fowls, bear's oil, corn and pelts—but at first frost (the year was 1729) the people would be gone or he'd haul the Great Sun down to New Orleans in irons.

The old men met in secret councils. There could be no other decision than war. Messages were sent to some of the Choctaw, who agreed to join in and attack New Orleans. Tattooed Arm, in desperation, tried to warn the Sieur Chépart—he paid no attention to her messengers except to have them jailed.

At the first frost of 1729 the Natchez attacked the French everywhere in their country, killed more than two hundred and made prisoners of several hundred women, children, and blacks. Natchez warriors refused to touch the Sieur Chépart with their weapons, but had a Stinker beat him to death with a stick.

The Choctaws played a double game and sided with the French, so this was, of course, the end. Even so it was a long time coming, and required two full-scale comic-opera invasions from New Orleans, some savage fighting here and there, and a grand display of power politics up and down the river as each side tried to line up allies. In town after town the red-painted war posts were set up and hung with red feathers, red arrows, and red tomahawks, and, after furious vomiting, warriors danced and struck the post (with their red-painted war clubs, with all their might) to signify their enlistment, and war chiefs anxiously consulted their dreams for guidance and good augur. The Yazoo Indians murdered the French among them, and one of them dressed himself in the clothes of their slain missionary to go to the Natchez and announce allegiance; the French secured the home front by sending black slaves to exterminate thirty inoffensive Chaouachas, the nearest Indians to New Orleans.

But the defection of the Choctaws had been decisive, even though only the western villages of the colossal Choctaw nation were involved in the conspiracy and double cross—the Choctaw also were divided into two parties, pro-English in the east, pro-French in the west. These internal politics undoubtedly played their part in the devious course of Choctaw policy.

Eventually, after more than a year of maneuvering, the French managed to persuade a few dozen Natchez warriors and several hundred women and children to surrender. These included most of the leaders of the aristocratic pro-French party. Tattooed Arm refused to come along, but it is reasonable to suppose the children of Tattooed Serpent were among them. The French commander picked out a few men and women for public burning and sold the rest, including the Great Sun and his family, as slaves in Santo Domingo.

For a long while afterward bands of implacable Natchez harassed French voyageurs along the river, but the largest groups went into exile and established towns among the Chickasaw, Creeks, and Cherokee, where they acquired some reputation as mystics, possibly because of their antique religion.

In its small way the story of the Natchez is the story of the whole Southeast, where the three great Christian nations on the move, France, Spain and England, all collided, boldly determined to fight to the last Indian.

VII

War in
the Forest

From the time of the Old Copper people on the shores of
Lake Superior until the appearance of pottery along the upper
Mississippi was perhaps four thousand years. From the time of
the appearance of pottery until the flourishing mid-point of the
great confederacy (as it seemed to be) of the Hopewell city-
states was another thousand years or somewhat more. From the
Hopewell high point until the general invasion of Europeans
along the Atlantic coast was another fifteen hundred years or a
bit more.

Beside the lakes and rivers, in the occasional park lands and
in the long reaches of unbroken forest of the Northeast, a people
lived, multitongued, of great diversities and many samenesses,
who at the Europeans' arrival still traveled the worn paths of all
these accumulated ages.

They hunted with the skill of Neolithics, and the Deer, Bear,
Wolf, and Turtle were their brothers. They used wild plants with
the magic incantations and racial memories of peoples who had
gathered seeds, nuts, and berries in this country for so long
before any knowledge of farming had appeared. Trade networks
moved obsidian from the Rockies to Ohio, tobacco from Vir-

ginia to the St. Lawrence, copper from the present Canadian border to North Carolina, flint and salt and pipestone everywhere. The political structure was the confederacy, a nucleus of associated bands in hegemony over other bands and fragments of bands, related or not, ex-enemies or ex-allies, ancient or recent acquaintances; immigration into the tribe was as a rule open to all.

They sought guidance in the supernatural dreams of the solitary hunter, and in the united prayers of farmers. They raided each other for loot, glory, revenge, trophy heads or the skins thereof, or for captives to sacrifice or adopt to take the place of lost relatives. Indian "war" north of Mexico in prewhite times was customarily a private activity triggered by the death of a relative at the hands of foreigners—the concept of national war was apparently unknown. Sometimes captive-killing was embroidered with tattered vestiges of sacrificial ceremony, including occasional ritual cannibalism, and often with frenzied excesses of public torture. Here and there over the spruce and fir of northern woods appeared Quetzalcoatl, disguised as the Morning Star.

Various gods were worshipped that were the same under the skin, from the solemn Master of Breath, the supreme being, to the deity straight out of a cartoon pantheon, the Great Rabbit, who went skipping about setting a chaotic world to rights (right by his wild lights), playing jokes (the funniest being the dirtiest by European standards), and getting himself into (and always out of) terrible trouble. The Great Rabbit's home in the North was among the people around the Great Lakes, but he reappears again and again elsewhere in the continent, sometimes as a rabbit and sometimes in other disguises (Coyote, Old Man, Raccoon, and many more); he is, in fact, the Trickster God known around the world, one of the universal inventions of the human mind.

Slash-and-burn cornfields were cultivated as far north as the climate permitted. Nearly all these forest-dwelling people were confirmed townsmen, although a few groups spent much time wandering and only touched base at a village during certain seasons. Many lived in long barrackslike multifamily houses, some in huts of pole-and-wattle "much like the wild Irish," as a New Englander of the 1620s observed.

Some reckoned descent by the father, some by the mother; some organized society into clans that claimed descent from the spirit of an animal, Bear, perhaps, or Beaver, some into special societies formed for a specific purpose such as war or healing.

Some, notably the Huron, north and east of Lake Ontario, practiced elaborate mass-burial ceremonies, when the collected bones of the deaths of ten or twelve years were formally interred together with mountains of rich funeral gifts, from furs to beautifully worked tools and arms.

The Southern ball game, with racquets, was played: French traders called the racquet, and the game as well, *la crosse.* An East Coast innovation introduced in the centuries following the decline of the Hopewell world was in wide use: seashells strung on strings or beaded into belts, used almost like money, and exchanged between nations at diplomatic councils as guarantees of earnest intentions: English traders called it wampum, after an Algonquian word, wampompeag.

These Northeastern people enter our history to the cries of woodland battle. "The place where they fought was of great advantage to the savages, by means of the thick trees, behind which the savages through their nimbleness, defended themselves, and so offended our men with their arrows, that our men being some of them hurt, retired fighting to the water side where their boat lay, with which they fled towards Hatorask . . ." says an account from the year 1586, of a little engagement near the short-lived colony of Roanoke, in Virginia.

Or, in a description of Indians fighting Indians published in 1634 by the trustworthy William Wood, a Plymouth settler, the Mohawks come "running, and fiercely crying out, *Hadree Hadree succomee succomee* we come we come to sucke your blood, not fearing the feathered shafts of the strong-armed bow-men, but like unruly headstrong stallions beate them down with their right hand Tamahaukes, and left hand Javelins . . . Tamahaukes be staves of two foote and a halfe long, and a knob at one end as round and bigge as a football . . . one blow or thrust with these strange weapons, will not neede a second to hasten death, from a Mohackes arme. . . ."

The Indian story gives an impression of being writ larger in war whoops in the neighborhood of the English colonies along the Atlantic coast than elsewhere in the invaded hemisphere.

It is important to realize that this is a distorted impression. The Indians of the Northeast were, most of them, warlike peoples, but no more so than many others Europeans had met, and less so than some. Their wars were of critical importance and cataclysmic dimension for all parties concerned but they were fewer and smaller, even so, than the wars in a number of other areas of European colonization. The subtler turmoils of peace were of equal or greater importance, and there were more of them.

Not only is it a distorted view as regards the nature of the considerable Indian participation in American colonial history, but also in regard to Indian life in the region before European contact.

Will Wood's foregoing picture of charging Mohawks has been often quoted; another line in his 1634 survey hasn't received so much attention: ". . . But to leave their warres, and to speak of their games in which they are more delighted and better experienced. . . ." Speaking of a New England tribe he remarked, "Take these *Indians* in their own trimme and naturall disposition, and they be reported to be wise, lofty-spirited, constant in friendship to one another. . . ." Thomas Morton, the merry trader of Merry Mount, Massachusetts, who probably knew the Indians of New England as intimately as any Englishman of his time, wrote of their festivals in the 1620s when "they exercise themselves in gaminge, and playing of juglinge trickes, and all manner of Revelles, which they are delighted in, that it is admirable to behould, what pastime they use, of severall kinds, every one striving to surpasse the other, after this manner they spend their time. . . ."

In the untouched Indian world, even among peoples of dreaded warlike reputation, there was a great deal more peace than war. War in the Old World definition was virtually unknown, and only approached by such highly organized states as those of the Aztecs and, particularly, the Incas. There is very little indication of whole countries being overrun by war. A meeting between strangers was more likely to be peaceful, even open and hospitable, than warlike. The raids that were called wars usually involved only a fraction of the available fighting men and those only briefly. Utterly defeated nations were assimilated rather than annihilated.

All this was to change somewhat under European tutelage but the point is that the life lived by these woodland people in their stockaded bark-built towns, while it had its sudden storms of terror and violence, was by no means one of constant strife.

It was a life filled with discomfort, excitement, pageantry, color, emotion and uneasiness anent gods, ghosts, and goblins. It was made up of play taken seriously, and duties stylized into solemnity. But above all it was pervaded with the magical sense of rightness that inevitably settles on people who have lived a very long time in a very old house, and in this respect life was underlain by a certain serenity.

The nations inhabiting the Northeast at about the time of the first European landings were for the most part divided among three large language stocks: Algonquian, Iroquoian, and Siouan.

What had been so long ago the Old Copper country, from Lake Michigan to Lake Superior and environs, was now the Wild Rice country, where on the countless lakes and northern marshes, under a sky alive with waterfowls, people thrust their canoes and rafts, harvesting the rice. Judging from the reports of early European explorers this region was teeming with a surprisingly heavy population, the most important groups being the Siouan Winnebago, in the region of Lake Winnebago and Green Bay; the Kickapoo, Sauk, Menominee, and Foxes west and north of them, the Ojibwa west and north beyond, on the shores of Lake Superior, these people speaking Algonquian languages; and various towns of the Siouan Dakota in the Wisconsin woods stretching westward to the Mississippi.

The Ojibwa made up one of the largest nations north of Mexico, with a wild-guess population of 25,000 or more—very probably more. The last syllable of Ojibwa is pronounced "way"; the name refers to the peculiar puckered seam of their moccasins; Europeans garbled it into Chippeway and stuck to it so persistently that many Ojibwas today call themselves Chippewa; but some Ojibwas today prefer another more ancient name for themselves, Anishinabeg or Anishinaubag, meaning "we people." North of the Ojibwa an almost identical people known as the Cree controlled the enormous spruce-fir country that ran all the way up to Hudson Bay. At the eastern end of Lake Superior, at the present Sault Ste. Marie, the Ojibwa joined with the Ottawa and Potawatomi in a loose confederacy known to white traders as the Three Fires. In the traditions of all three of these tribes they were originally one, and that not too many centuries ago.

The Ohio Valley, that had been the heart of the Hopewell burial-mound commonwealth some hundreds of years before, had apparently become surprisingly sparse in population since that time. The Miami confederacy of Indiana and environs (one of their villages was called Chicago, meaning "Skunk Place") and the perhaps somewhat more populous Illinois confederacy to their west were not large in numbers, at any rate in historic times. These people too were of Algonquian speech. The Erie to their east, below Lake Erie, spoke an Iroquoian tongue.

Strongholds of Shawnee towns were south of the Miami (the name means "Southerners") and extended to the hills of the Chickasaws and the Great Smoky Mountains of the Cherokees, with their traditional center in the Cumberland Valley in present Tennessee, but the Shawnee appear to have been nearly everywhere throughout the Middle West and Middle South at various times. They were very closely related, in language, style, and race with the Sauk and Foxes, the Kickapoo, and with other Algonquian peoples on the Atlantic coast.

A sizable area embracing parts of present Kentucky, southern Ohio, and West Virginia was so thinly settled portions of it were regarded as practically uninhabited, a sort of no man's land, a hunting ground and battlefield open to all. At least such seems to have been the case at the moment of the first European look. Since this was for so long the very epicenter of the ancient, thriving, town-dotted Hopewell world some small riddle seems to be afoot, beyond those mists of time that hang like fogs of a frosty Indian Summer over the beautiful Ohio.

Tidewater Virginia and adjacent beaches and backwoods, scene of some of the earliest European exploration and settlement along the Atlantic coast, was the home of a union of Algonquian-speaking nations called the Powhatan (accent on last syllable) Confederacy. The name means Falls of the River and was specifically applied to the falls of the James River (present Richmond). The "king" whose home village was located there was called by the English colonists after the name of his town, and is in our folklore as King Powhatan. His real name was Wahunsonacock. In accordance with a widespread Indian usage his real name was as much his own discreet private property as is a movie star's real name today; the evil-intentioned, by pronouncing one's real name, could gain a handhold on one's soul; thus one was more customarily addressed by a title, Brother, Uncle, Warrior—as we might say Senator or General—or by a nickname.

The giant Powhatan Confederacy numbered some 200 villages and included quite a few separate tribes or little states, each ruled (so it seemed to the English) by a minor "king," known as a werowance—said to mean "rich man." "The great king Powhatan hath devided his countrey into many provinces or shiers (as yt were), and over every one placed a severall absolute weroance or comaunder . . . and his petty weroances, in all, may be in number about three or fower and thirty, all which have theire precincts and bowndes . . ." wrote William Strachey, Gent., First Secretary of the Colony of Virginia.

It appears that the patriarchal Powhatan (at least sixty years old when the English first met him) had constructed this confederacy almost from scratch during his own lifetime. Early reports of several other confederacies indicate they were in process of being created by conquest and diplomacy—or dying from dissension—at the instant of European arrival. Since archaeological evidence hints at previous confederacies throughout much of the long past, it might be assumed that the centuries had seen a slow but incessant rise and fall, alignment and realignment, of such unions large and small, and that the confederacy was the normal American pattern. This could be a natural concomitant, perhaps, of the previously mentioned deep-rooted Indian tendency toward cooperation rather than competition.

Some, at least, of the confederated provinces paid tribute to Powhatan, but quite a bit of autonomy was apparently enjoyed by the several werowances or the councils of oligarchs that the English also mention as ruling the destinies of various tribes. This or that village could and did separately make war on the English settlers while the confederacy was nominally at peace—Strachey, speaking of a "weroancqua, or queene," of one of the confederacy's towns, says, "Howbeyt, her towne we burnt, and killed some of her people, herself miscarieng with small shott in pursuit in the woods in winter 1610, for a treacherous massacre which she practized upon fourteen of our men. . . ." Similar incidents are far from uncommon in the early history of the Virginia colony.

Howbeit, peaceful coexistence was the general rule during the ghastly early years of the Virginia colony, when the settlers died in batches in the miasmic Jamestown swamps (of the first 900 colonists landed during the first three years, 1607 to 1610, only 150 were still alive in 1610) and old Powhatan could have stamped it out or left it to starve with the greatest of ease—as easily as, it may be from only a slightly different turn of Indian politics, Roanoke had been weeded out only twenty years before, only a hundred and some miles down this same coast. In fact, the 150 miserable Jamestown survivors were in process of abandoning the colony, and were actually aboard ship to depart when a vessel arrived with reinforcements and supplies.

There was distrust and blundering on each side in this meeting of worlds so disparate, quarrels between Indians and the German, Irish, French, Polish, and English artisans and would-be gentry who made up the colonists, and there was deliberate trouble stirred up by the Spaniards to the south— Spanish embassies to the Powhatans in 1609 are blamed for Indian attacks on Jamestown in 1610, and might have been responsible for the treacherous massacre practiced by the above-mentioned "weroancqua." Other such Spanish embassies followed.

But peace, even though ill-policed, persisted. There were two immediate reasons for this: the directors of the joint-stock company in London that owned and operated the Virginia colony voted, as the most profitable and least expensive course, to conciliate Powhatan as an independent sovereign rather than make war upon him as a savage—and sent him a copper crown to wear; and Powhatan himself earnestly desired peace, with an eye on the benefits of English trade.

He said to Captain John Smith, so Captain Smith reported: "Why should you take by force from us that which you can obtain by love? Why should you destroy us who have provided you with food? . . . I am not so simple as not to know that it is better to eat good meat, be well, and sleep quietly with my women and children, to laugh and be merry with the English, and being their friend, to have copper hatchets and whatever else I want. . . ."

No king, but a kingly figure—"such majesty as he expresseth," marveled Strachey—Powhatan kept the peace.

The first settlers sometimes obtained Indian help by force or cajolery, but also, wrote Captain John Smith: ". . . it pleased God (in our extremity) to move the Indians to bring us Corne, ere it was halfe ripe, to refresh us, when we rather expected they would destroy us. . . . [and later] . . . the Indians brought us great store both of Corne and bread ready made. . . ."

But still later, when the shoe was on the other foot and the colonists had corn to sell to some starving Indian villages near Jamestown, the English governor traded 400 bushels for "a mortgage on their whole countries."

It was impossible, of course, for businessmen not to feel

contempt for such people, and once again a conquest was completed, in effect, although the war was still to come.

Peace was badly strained during the troubles of 1609-1610 (a little army of colonists seized and held for a while Powhatan's own village at the Falls of the James and its 300 acres of cornfields and gardens, as being simpler than building a new town and clearing fields of their own, and wished to tax the Powhatans for the privilege). Tranquility of a sort was restored by the tyrannical acting-governor Sir Thomas Dale (1611-1616), who saved the colony by working colonists under the lash, burning captured runaways at the stake, and kidnaping and holding as hostage Powhatan's beloved daughter Pocahontas.

Pocahontas (a nickname meaning something like "Frisky"— her real name was Matowaka) is the most famous woman in early American history, and justly so, judging by subsequent events. "Blessed Pocahontas, the great King's daughter of Virginia, oft saved my life," wrote Captain John Smith, never a man to mince sonorities; and apparently she oft saved the colony as well, being "much at our fort," and a great friend of the English, supplying their wants and filling their jars with corn. "She, under God, was the instrument to preserve this colony from death, famine, and utter confusion," testified Captain Smith.

At the time of her kidnaping she was seventeen years old and married to a warrior named Kocoum of whom nothing more is heard, for she married the next year one of the leading men of the colony, John Rolfe, a widower with one child. Rolfe married her, he wrote, "for the good of the plantation," denying the allegation of vulgar persons that it was merely to gorge base carnal desire, Pocahontas being "a well-featured but wanton young girl," as Secretary Strachey had described her, and evidently much in English reveries since the early days when, half grown, she would "get the boyes forth with her into the market place, and make them wheele, falling on their hands, turning their heels upwards, whom she would followe, and wheele so herself, naked as she was, all the fort over." The marriage was a smashing success for all concerned. The bride, "O princess whose brown lap was virgin May" (as says the best of her hundred poets), was crowned with English immortality; and even the father of the bride was eminently pleased, and real peace resulted.

More significantly, John Rolfe forthwith learned, presumably with Indian help, the cultivation of tobacco. He became the colony's first tobacco planter, and the colony had what it needed, a fortune-founding cash crop.

John Rolfe took his bride to London, where she was a sensation and where tradition still remembers her as the first lady of quality to enter a pub; the many pubs still named The Indian Queen supposedly honor this wanton breakthrough. She met everyone from the English queen to drunk Ben Jonson (who had a character remark in a play several years later that the "great King's daughter of Virginia, hath/ been in womb of tavern. . . ."), and she died of smallpox in the spring of 1617, at the age of twenty-one or twenty-two, on shipboard just at the start of her return trip to America, leaving an infant son from whom a whole hallful of illustrious Virginians have claimed extraction.

But it was tobacco that fathered all Virginia, and had its effect in turn on the broader future of the English elsewhere in America. It had an even profounder effect on the future of Powhatan's people.

It was not a king, nor Christianity, nor knighthood gone adventuring that muscled the conquest of the Atlantic seaboard north of Florida. It was the joint-stock company. The joint-stock company was organized and operated simply for profit and nothing but profit, and recognized no other purpose, higher, lower, or in between. This attitude was the foundation of colonial Indian policy in non-Spanish North America.

Bows were made in the direction of patriotism and piety, but for the most part they were frankly cynical. Said an early promoter (Sir George Peckham, High Sheriff of Buckinghamshire, whose promotions left him broke in 1595): "First and chiefly [are those benefits to the Indians] in respect to the most gladsome and happy tidings of the most glorious gospel of our Saviour Jesus Christ, whereby they may be brought from falsehood to trueth . . . And if in respect of all the commodities they can yeelde us (were they many more) that they should receive this onely benefit of Christianity, they were more than fully recompenced." Said Sir Ferdinando Gorges, arch-genius of early English colonization efforts: ". . . what can be more pleasing to a generous nature than to be exercised in doing publique good . . . and what more pious than advancing of Christian Religion amongst People, who have not known the excellency thereof, but seeing works of Piety and publique good, are in this age rather commended by all, then acted by any; let us come a little near to that which all harken unto and that forsooth is profit."

The earliest ventures into Virginia, from Raleigh onward, envisioned profits from gold mines, peltries, a passage to India, or such commodities as sassafras, believed at the time to be a specific for syphilis. William Strachey, Gent., proposed that the Virginia Company get a monopoly on sassafras, hold it until the price skyrocketed, and then sell to all Europe "thereof at good rates."

Tobacco offered the first genuine indications of a profit, a real profit, indeed a stunning potential for instant riches, to the new Virginians and their stockholders. Tobacco, introduced to Europe via Spain and Portugal (and the French ambassador to Portugal, Jean Nicot, whence nicotine) in the 1500s, had become the rage of fashion to Englishmen of 1600. No devout Indian offering tobacco to the gods of the four directions could have equaled English eulogies bestowed on "This pretious herbe, TABACCO most divine . . ." "The sweete and sole delight of mortall men . . ."—to quote some laudatory verses of 1602. It was believed at first to possess more or less miraculous powers for healing and well-being (an early name in Europe was *herba panacea*) and was also believed to bring "the pleasure of drunkenness" because with it the Indians "unsettle all the fibres of their brain, and intoxicate themselves as if they had been drinking wine to excess." With this kind of promotion it became a best-seller everywhere, in spite of the usual opposition of the authorities which included stringent penalties sometimes even unto capital punishment or even excommunication. Tobacco quickly became the Virginia colony's only export, and Sir Thomas Dale had to force the colonists to give some of their time and land to the planting of grain, since they couldn't eat money.

Not only did the potential profit call for constantly expanding acreage, but tobacco used up the soil, and new fields had to be found every two or three years. It was usually easier to take fields from the Indians than to clear new land: early in the life of the colony Captain John Smith succeeded, by herculean efforts, in having forty acres of land cleared, but not long afterward, the village of Kecoughtan at the mouth of the James River was seized and its inhabitants driven away, its cornfields (according to Secretary Strachey) encompassing two to three thousand acres. Even allowing for a tenfold exaggeration on the part of the Honorable Secretary, it wouldn't take a canny eye long to see in this the birth of a pattern. The Americans loved their homes but they loved their peace and quiet (to say nothing of their lives) more. They wept but they moved.

It was easy to believe, each time, that the Coat-wearing People (the commonest Algonquian term for Englishmen) would now have all the land they could possibly want, but if the Indian mind grasped only dimly the European notion of land title it grasped not at all the European notion of great personal estates. A strong feudal flavor lingered in those early joint-stock companies. Some were given the right to grant titles of nobility; all had the right to grant landed estates. The principal officers of the Virginia Company were to be put in possession of personal estates of no less than 1,500 acres each—more if they owned extra "great shares," which brought the estates of some officers to 5,000 acres. Junior executives were granted 500-acre estates. The company created a 12,000-acre estate for itself. Other promoters who guaranteed to send out certain numbers of settlers were given large tracts of land.

Land encroachment was not the only cause for conflict on this first Virginia frontier. Livestock introduced by the settlers damaged the unfenced Indian gardens, hogs being the worst offenders. But if you damaged the hog, the hog's owner would damage you, and if your friends damaged the hog's owner, the English would then burn an Indian town and put a dozen people to the sword (the second most common Algonquian name for Englishmen was "cutthroats"), and another little war was afire that took all old Powhatan's influence to smother.

Trading, theft, rowdyism, liquor, women, and attempts at taxation brought contentions, and as the English grew more numerous and bolder, and the inevitable felons, toughs, and whores were swept over from London streets to fill colonist quotas, contentions grew more common, regrettable outrages more outrageous, and exactions of the English always more exacting.

Nothing personal was involved, and it is a mistake to think of Indians and settlers as making two hard and fast opposing camps; the "old settlers" of the colony often had closer ties among the neighboring Pamunkeys or Appomatocs or others of the Powhatan league (or even more so among such as the anti-Powhatan pro-English Chickahominy) than among the john-

ny-come-lately new settlers. What was involved was the inexorable trending of the colony's basic official policy. Founded
purely on economic considerations, this policy conciliated the
Powhatan people while they were of use, and pressed them
remorselessly, facelessly, mechanically, as innocent of conscious ill will as a turning wheel, when they became of less value
than their land.

Old Powhatan died in 1618 (the year after Pocahontas' death
in England). Some time passed, during which the councilors of
the Powhatan Confederacy may have fought out a behind the
scenes battle between pro- and anti-English factions. The aged
Opechancanough, a brother of Powhatan's and an implacable
English-hater ever since the days of 1607-1608 when he and
Captain John Smith had taken turns capturing each other, came
out the winner. (An entertaining Virginia legend makes
Opechancanough the youthful Don Luis of the Spanish Jesuit
mission in 1570.)

In the spring of 1622 Opechancanough's Powhatans exploded
under the unrelenting English pressure in a savage flash that left
nearly 350 colonists dead and a number of settlements destroyed
in the space of a few hours.

The English population just before Powhatan's death had
been at this same figure, 350, scattered in a half-dozen villages.
But in the five years since, the number of colonists had
quadrupled, while the Indians had suffered disastrously from
pestilence. Opechancanough was four short winters late.

The surviving English swore to scourge the Powhatans from
the face of the earth, and did succeed in practically exterminating those along the lower James and York rivers. Three punitive
expeditions a year were carried out, year after year, giving the
Powhatans no chance to plant or harvest corn or rebuild
destroyed towns. Men, women, and children were slain without
quarter; the English captains were under oath to make no peace
on any terms whatsoever. The heaviest Indian losses were
achieved when numbers of them were slyly persuaded to return
to their villages, under promises of peace, and were then trapped
and massacred. The greatest single victory came in 1625, with
the defeat of 1,000 Pamunkeys and the burning of their town.

The campaign continued for fourteen years, and ended with a
peace of mutual exhaustion. During this time, King James had
secured an annulment of the Virginia Company's charter in the
courts (for reasons having to do with European politics), and

Virginia had become a Crown colony, but the Indian policy established by the original joint-stock company remained substantially unchanged.

After a few years of peace, land-grab pressures again rose past the danger point; the outbreak of the English civil war in the year 1642 was also apparently a factor in Opechancanough's plans, as were wars and rumors of wars in other new colonies up the coast, and freer availability of firearms from various European traders. On April 18, 1644, the aged chieftain, now in his nineties and so feeble he had to be carried in a litter, struck once again. Again, hundreds of English lives were lost in a single flaming day, in a carefully coordinated sneak attack that took the colonists completely by surprise, There is a tradition that after this first attack the Powhatan war parties slacked away without pursuing their advantage, possibly frightened by an omen.

Opechancanough was eventually captured, shot (against orders) by a guard, and the war came to an end; this time the Powhatan Confederacy came to an end with it. The English broke up the league, made peace separately with the various tribes and assigned them to reservations which were subsequently whittled down at the colony's pleasure, and—within less than forty years after Jamestown's founding—the once mighty Powhatans turned their faces toward the oblivion of beggary.

At the time of the American Revolution there may have been perhaps a thousand persons left of all the "three or fower and thirty" provinces, most of them moved by then to the more thinly settled Eastern Shore of Chesapeake Bay, with only a very few tribal societies, notably the Pamunkey, Chickahominy, and Mattapony, still functioning.

A traveler wrote of late colonial Virginia (1759): ". . . Indians and Negroes . . . they scarcely consider as of the human species; so that it is almost impossible, in cases of violence, or even murder, committed on those unhappy people by any of the planters, to have the delinquents brought to justice. . . ."

With local variations, this is the story of most of the nations of the Atlantic seaboard from the Carolinas to New England during the period of early European colonization.

Unlike the Spanish attitude, there was little official English interest in the Indians as a labor force or as souls to be saved. Here, where plantation exports rather than mines or Indian trade became the infant colony's main road to profits, and where other European rivalry was not imminent enough to be a commanding factor, dealings with the Americans followed a fairly simple and generally uniform course: initial friendship and cooperation, followed by dismissal of the Indians, so to speak, when their help was no longer needed. This dismissal usually took the dramatic form of growing hostility, massacre, war, and eviction, but in essence it was, as previously described, merely a matter of business. It was not complicated by any of the soul-searching agonies that beset the Spanish conscience; there was exceedingly little self-criticism of the Las Casas genre.

There was no body of law designed to protect the Indians from exploitation or deliberate extermination. The governor and council (corresponding to president and board of directors) of the parent joint-stock company were answerable to no one for any action against Indians, up to and including enslavement or annihilation. There was, in the beginning, little control by central authority, and an almost total lack of home-government concern with Indian welfare.

Some of this was to undergo considerable modification after the colonies were taken over by the crown—which customarily happened as soon as the parent colonization company had gotten the colony reasonably well established and more or less able to stand on its feet. Indian policy was to remain for generations a major problem in colonial politics. But at heart it was to remain what the hard-headed company-directors in their paneled council-rooms in Europe's capitals had first made it, a matter of business, basically a problem in economic expediency.

A local variation in the Powhatan story was the meager use of Indian allies by the Virginia colonists when war came. More commonly, Indian auxiliaries made up the bulk of the little European armies, as was the case in Spanish America.

Next door southward, in North Carolina, the Iroquoian people who composed a confederacy known as the Tuscarora were effectively dismissed, when the time came, by two English -led invasion forces, the first made up of thirty-three Europeans and 498 Indians from eighteen nations, the second numbering again some thirty white men, and more than 900 Indian auxiliaries. These figures are as of the formal organization of the two expeditions, and were subject to fluctuation as the campaigns progressed. In the informal warfare of the time, many campaigners—white or red—headed jubilantly for home as soon as they had taken slaves or loot, while new recruits joined up along the way.

North of the Powhatans, along the Maryland shore, were a

people known as the Nanticoke (their own name, meaning "tidewater people"), nucleus of a confederacy that had existed, so they said, for thirteen generations before the English colonization of Maryland. They were reputed to be of unusual skill in hunting, fishing, and witchcraft, and of unusually dark skin, although they were near relatives of the Powhatans, Delawares, and Shawnees. A local variation in their story is the brevity of the initial interlude of peace after the arrival of European colonists. The first English settlement in Maryland was founded in 1634 (on cleared Indian fields), and only five years later the colonists were sending an annual war party against the Indians. By the end of the seventeenth century the remnants of the Nanticoke were placed on reservations, where a few hung on, but most of them, during the next generation or two, forsook their homeland and entered other countries as suppliants.

The leading people of all the eastern Algonquians, known to their relatives, friends, and even some of their enemies as the Grandfathers, were the Lenape, as they called themselves, a word meaning "real people." They were usually called Delawares by the Europeans, after the English name for the river along which their principal towns were located. Their confederacy (made up of three large divisions and numerous subdivisions) spread over a vast territory centering in New Jersey, eastern Pennsylvania, lower New York, and Delaware. The capital of their country, the meeting place of the confederacy council, was (during early colonial times) on or about the site of the present Philadelphia suburb of Germantown.

The Delawares possessed, incised in wood, a pictographic version of their migration legend, known as the Walam Olum, or Painted Record. It is not until the last of its five "books" that such incidents as the splitting-off of the Shawnee and Nanticoke to go "to the south lands" are mentioned, bearing out the traditions of both these tribes that they, and a number of other eastern Algonquian peoples, were formerly one with the Delawares. Incidentally, throughout this long historical record there are only twelve symbols for war, and most of those are concerned with a single, specific conflict—for what this may be worth as an insight into pre-European ways of war and peace.

Hollanders of the Dutch West India Company and Swedish colonists sent out by the New Sweden Company were the first Europeans to establish themselves in the country of the Delawares (in 1614 and 1638). The Dutch came primarily as fur traders and the Swedes were never numerous; consequently their relations with the Delawares were generally peaceful. Both Dutch and Swedes bought Indian land, perhaps to legalize their occupancy in the eyes of other Europeans. The prevailing English usage (with some exceptions) at the time of earliest colonization was simply to seize, when they could, what was wanted, claiming English ownership of all North America by right of prior "discovery"—even the Indians, in this view, could only clear title to their lands by grant of the English king.

In 1749 Old Nils Gustafson, then ninety-one years of age and the son of one of the original Swedish settlers, related that "At the time when the Swedes arrived, they bought land at a very inconsiderable price. For a piece of baize, or a pot full of brandy, or the like, they could get a piece of ground, which at present would be worth more than four hundred pounds, Pennsylvania currency."

Old Nils also recalled walking with an Indian and meeting a red-spotted snake on the road; Nils got a stick to kill it, but the Indian begged him to let it live "because he adored it. . . ." On hearing that it was the Indian's deity, Old Nils killed it "in the presence of the Indian, saying: because thou believest in it, I think myself obliged to kill it."

The Delaware tradition of peace with the foreigners was maintained after the appearance of the English Quaker colonists and the famous treaty meetings with William Penn in 1683. The best known Delaware leader at these meetings was the councilor Tamanend; of this man a missionary wrote more than a century later, repeating Delaware yarns: ". . . he was an ancient Delaware chief, who never had his equal. He was in the highest degree endowed with wisdom, virtue, prudence, charity, affability, meekness, hospitality, in short with every good and noble qualification. . . ." The English spelled his name Tammany.

A local variation in the Delaware story is that the initial interlude of peace lasted for more than a century of expanding European settlement—peace with the whites, that is. The Delawares endured much, in the middle 1600s, from a war of conquest by their western neighbors, the Susquehanna, an Iroquoian people in the interior of Pennsylvania; of which more later.

People of the Delaware confederacy inhabited Staten Island and the western end of Long Island, where a Delaware subtribe called the Canarsee sold Brooklyn to the Dutch. But the region generally east of the Hudson River, which would have included the present Manhattan (apparently only used as the site of a few hunting and fishing villages), the Bronx, and Westchester, was the territory of another Algonquian-speaking union, the Wappinger confederacy. These were relatives of the Delawares and also of the people of the Mahican confederacy (Mohicans, they were called, in J. Fenimore Cooper's time) who lived north of them up the Hudson. It seems to have been one of the Wappinger groups, with its central town at the site of modern Yonkers, that participated in the famous sale to the Dutch of the woodland island that is now the center of New York City—this was the Manhattan group (the name probably had something to do with *munnoh* or *manah*: "island"). The often quoted price of $24.00 may be based on a questionable exchange rate; a modern economist has estimated the sixty gulden worth of trinkets would have been closer in contemporary buying power to several thousand dollars.

The Dutch traded for furs with people of inland regions, notably the Iroquois; the coastal people had supported the first *swannekins* (Algonquian for Dutchmen) with gifts of food, but now, hanging around the farms of the colony at New Amsterdam, they were of no use and became a nuisance. Their odd ideas of land tenure evidently led them to believe they were only selling the use of land for a season or so, and eventually even led to some re-purchase of lands by the Dutch. The usual sort of unpleasant incidents occurred, and multiplied. The half-naked natives were indolent, insolent, and as thievish as monkeys, but when a farmer caught and killed one of their females who was stealing peaches, her relatives or friends wantonly slew the farmer, and the tribes refused to turn these murderers over to the Dutch authorities.

In 1643 (seventeen years after the purchase of Manhattan Island) the Dutch governor, according to some accounts not only exasperated but inebriated, ordered the massacre of a number of Wappinger people who had run to the Dutch for protection from raiding Mohawks. The Indian refugees were lulled by friendly Dutch treatment for several days and then were attacked by Dutch soldiers while they slept (in a village on the Jersey side of the Hudson), and eighty heads of men, women, and children were brought back to Manhattan, to Fort Amsterdam, where a New Amsterdam dowager played kickball with them in the street. A captive Hackensack Indian was publicly tortured, charged a contemporary pamphleteer, by being skinned in strips and fed with his own flesh while the "poor, naked, simple creature" stubbornly tried to keep up his death song, until at last, flayed from his fingers to his knees, castrated, dragged through the streets, but still alive, he was placed on a millstone and his head beaten off by the soldiers.

In the war that followed, the Wappinger villagers were stamped out by hundreds, but even so only some 1,500 of their total population of (maybe) 5,000 had been liquidated at the end of a year. But Dutch losses had been heavy, especially in outlying settlements; and the war was expensive. The Dutch governor requested permission from the Dutch West India Company to keep on until "the Indians who waged war on us should . . . be utterly destroyed and exterminated . . ." but the company directors were far from pleased by the "bloody exploit" of the massacre that opened the war and had no intention of authorizing complete extermination, "since it would necessitate so heavy an expenditure on so uncertain an event and so little appearance of profit."

A wall built across lower Manhattan in the course of this war gave its name to Wall Street.

The New England coastal area, roughly from New York to Boston, is regarded as having been the most densely populated section of eastern North America in aboriginal times. East of the Wappinger country, in Connecticut, were the Mohegan, a separate, eastern branch of the Hudson River Mahican (the same name, of course, through different ears; it meant "wolves"); above the Mohegan, in the region of Rhode Island, the Narraganset made up the principal nation; above the Narraganset the Wampanoag (a word cognate with Wappinger, both meaning "Easterners"); and above the Wampanoag the Massachuset. All these were Algonquian-speakers, and generally similar peoples.

Dutch traders had been active in the Hudson River area since 1610, and European deep-sea fishermen had been visiting the New England coast since the early 1500s. English traders had been appearing there at least since 1602. English shipmasters had been pausing here to pick up an occasional slave or guide, either by kidnaping or smooth speeches, at least since 1605, when five New England Indians were brought into Plymouth in England; one of them, named Tasquantum, was "seized upon" by Sir Ferdinando Gorges, then governor of Plymouth.

The Plymouth (joint-stock) Company was actively interested in the New England coast a few years later when they employed the redoubtable Captain John Smith to explore it for them; Captain Smith, exploring his way along in 1614, renamed a Wampanoag village in honor of his employers—the Indian name of the town was Patuxet, the new name bestowed by Captain Smith was Plymouth.

In the next year (1615) an English slaver, one Captain Thomas Hunt, kidnaped a Patuxet citizen reportedly named Tisquantum and sold him into slavery in Malaga, whence he escaped to England. In 1616, the year after Captain Hunt's visit, an epidemic, probably smallpox, broke out among the people of the New England coast "with such a mortall stroake," wrote an English trader, "that they died on heapes . . . and the living . . . would runne away, & let them dy, and let there Carkases ly above the ground without buriall." It raged for three years. The Wampanoag and their nearest neighbors, the Massachuset, who lived just north of them in the region of modern Boston, seemed to be in the center of this long storm of sudden death. The Massachuset were so nearly destroyed that, according to some estimates, their population fell from ten thousand to one thousand persons.

In 1620 a band of English colonists, organized into an unchartered joint-stock company financed by a group of business men, left England for the northern reaches of the territory assigned to the Virginia Company. The Virginia Colony's new tobacco prosperity had influenced the choice of a destination; Guiana in South America (subject of Sir Walter Raleigh's final golden tales) had also been considered. But the Virginia Company's northern territory was within the sphere of Dutch trade, and the master of the colonists' ship landed them still farther up the coast, "having been bribed by the Hollanders to carry them and land farther to the northward," according to gossip later current in England.

These colonists were the Pilgrim Fathers of the schoolbooks, a sect of religious revolutionaries, a grim and bitter people, enormously industrious, and as mercenary as purses.

They found the forest clearings of their new country bespangled by the scattered bones of plague victims, and the village of Captain John Smith's Plymouth, née Patuxet, was a ghost town, the population dead in the houses or fled from the plague in horror and despair. The colonists made the village and its fields their own, fields so handsomely cleared, said a delighted colonist later, there was "scarce a bush or bramble, or any cumbersome underwood to be seene in the more champion ground. . . ."

And behold, a solitary survivor of Patuxet's people appeared and spoke to them marvelously in English. This was, says orthodox history, the ex-slave Tisquantum kidnaped by Captain Hunt in 1615. But Sir Ferdinando Gorges said that his Tasquantum, brought to Plymouth in 1605, "must be acknowledged the meanes under God of putting on foote, and giving life to all our Plantations . . ."

Whoever he was, to the Pilgrims he became ". . . a spetiall instrument sent of God for their good beyond their expectation," as wrote the historian of the colony. "He directed them how to set their corne, wher to take fish, and to procure other comodities, and also their pilott to bring them to unknowne places for their profitt. . . ." The English shortened his name to Squanto, and until he died of an "Indian feavor" in 1622 he was of inestimable use to the struggling colony.

A local sachem, or chief, named Samoset, who had picked up a few words of English from (presumably) previous traders, was perhaps even more the colonists' salvation by introducing them to the noble Massassoit, grand sachem of the Wampanoag people. (Massasoit, again, was only a title of address, as we would say Senator; the grand sachem's real name was Wasamegin, meaning "Yellow Feather.") The noble Massassoit and his equally noble councilors remained fast friends of the English, notwithstanding repeated English "usurpations," as a nineteenth century authority put it, upon Wampanoag lands and liberties.

Seven years after the founding of Plymouth, a combine of the colony's leading men bought out the stock of their financial backers and formed a joint-stock company of their own. The considerable debt from this purchase was paid off in six years from the profits of trade, primarily Indian trade.

There was serious trouble from the first in regard to management, jurisdiction, competition. The Pilgrims having been landed north of their proper jurisdiction necessitated not only the Mayflower Compact but a good deal of adjustment among the stock-managers of the Virginia Company and the Plymouth Company back in England. In 1623 there came the beginning of the Puritan colony at Massachusetts Bay which eventually settled at Naumkeag, later Salem, and which from the first quarreled piously with Plymouth. Thomas Morton, agent for Sir Ferdinando Gorges, founded in 1622 with thirty followers his colony of Merry Mount, meant to be Episcopal and regarded as utterly godless by both Plymouth and Massachusetts Bay, who at last seized his goods, burnt his buildings, and sent him a prisoner to England. Morton blamed their hostility less on piety than on profit, saying he had harmed "the benefit of their beaver trade," which "action bred a kinde of hart burning in the Plimouth Planters . . ."

Between 1629 and 1642 the joint-stock company of Massachusetts Bay brought over more than 17,000 settlers. They were lured by such promotional literature as the Rev. William Morrell's verse description of New England, published in 1625: "The fruitfull and well watered earth doth glad all hearts . . . And yeelds an hundred fold for one . . ."

O happie Planter if you knew the height
Of Planters honours where ther's such delight. . . .

The churchly colonists exulted, with reverence, over the frightful epidemic of 1616-1619 that had cleared so many heathen from the path of the Chosen People. "The Wonderful Preparation the Lord Christ by His Providence Wrought for His People's Abode in this Western World," wrote a Puritan chronicler, pointing out with particular satisfaction that the plague had swept away "chiefly young men and children, the very seeds of increase." Even Thomas Morton of Merry Mount, who had more affection for the Indians than for the Puritans, observed that in "this, the wondrous wisedome and love of God, is shewne, by sending to the place his Minister, to sweepe away . . . the Salvages. . . ."

But there were still enough seeds of increase left to be troublesome, as happie planters multiplied, trade moved inland, and the nations near the coast became of no benefit whatever. In 1636, sixteen years after the first beginnings of colonization, the Massachusetts Bay Puritans sent a force to smite the Indian nation that had become the strongest in New England, a division of the Mohegan known as the Pequot ("destroyers"). The Massachusetts Bay people massacred a village, and having thus declared war went back home. (The Seal of the Massachusetts Bay colony was the figure of an Indian with a label at his mouth saying, "Come over and help us.")

The Pequots had attacked no English settlements. Will Wood

said of them, two years before the opening of these hostilities, "The *Pequants* be a stately warlike people, of whom I never heard any misdemeanour; but that they were just and equall in their dealings; not treacherous either to their Country-men, or *English*. . . ." The war against them was begun on the flimsiest of pretexts and was rather clearly a matter of political and economic expediency.

During the time of first English settlement the Pequot people were busy conquering their weaker Indian neighbors, and by the middle 1630s their great sachem, Sassacus, ruled over more than two dozen subchiefs and claimed dominion over most of Connecticut and Long Island. Being on the border between the Dutch and the English, Sassacus played shifty politics with both, growing more and more arrogant and independent with everyone in sight as Pequot power increased. The Dutch and the various English colonies in return played shifty politics with the Pequot and the other Indian groups, notably the powerful Narraganset with whom the Pequot people were frequently at odds; for example, Plymouth Colony disputed Pequot rights to lands on which the city of Hartford now stands in order to strike by this means at the Dutch, who had just bought land in this region from the Pequots—Plymouth claimed the land still belonged to Indian groups who had held it previous to Pequot contest. The Pequot war came into being behind such devious jurisdictional screens, and with sudden demands on the part of the Massachusetts Bay colony for the supposed Pequot murderers of two lawless Virginia traders whose disappearance more than two years earlier had heretofore been ignored. But all these were cold political moves, and it takes hot blood to go forth and kill: in this case blood was heated by religious lust, a moving emotional force in the New England colonies.

The English settlements in Connecticut and at Plymouth were dragged into the war by the precipitate action of the Massachusetts Puritans. A splinter party of Sassacus' own people had broken away, under a malevolent leader named Uncas, and become the Pequots' bitter enemies; this small group retained the name of Mohegan. They entered the fray on the English side with pleasure.

The strongest English allies, and perhaps decisive in the conflict, were the Narraganset, obtained through the intercession of Roger Williams, who the year before had been banished from Massachusetts for advocating the eccentric heresies of religious tolerance and Indian land rights. He had been given shelter in what is now Rhode Island by the noble Canonicus, the leader (with his nephew Miantonomo) of the Narraganset tribe.

In June 1637 the English army (240 colonists; 1,000 Narragansets; 70 Mohegans) made a stealthy night attack on a stockaded Pequot town near the Mystic River in Connecticut, burned the town, and slaughtered its 600 inhabitants. Wrote the Plymouth governor: "It was a fearful sight to see them frying in the fire . . . and horrible was the stink and stench thereof. But the victory seemed a sweet sacrifice and they gave praise thereof to God . . ." The only other engagement of the war was the surrender of a crowd of Pequots trapped in a swamp; the adult male captives were killed, the boys sold to the West Indies, and the women and the girls parceled out among the colonists as slaves.

The Pequot nation was broken. Refugees fled in all directions. Survivors were placed under the sovereignty of their old enemy, Uncas, and so sweet was the savor of his revenge thereof that the colonies mercifully took them away from him a few years later. Sassacus escaped to the Mohawks and begged sanctuary; they deliberated, and put him to death.

The year following this war the New England colonies, pursuing the idea of united action that had worked so well against the Pequot, began negotiations that led to the federation in 1643 of the United Colonies of New England, the first union of English settlements in America.

The Pequot defeat left the Narraganset the strongest nation in New England. Uncas, commanding only a handful of warriors in comparison with the Narraganset military potential, was nevertheless able to maintain an Indian balance of power by the threat of his influence with the English. He boiled with ambitious plots, and ceaselessly stirred up English suspicion against the Narraganset and Wampanoag. The usual hostile incidents accumulated. But an uneasy peace, of a sort, was sustained for a generation.

It must be pointed out again that many individual settlers and Indians were not only peaceful neighbors but close friends. It was from these various Algonquian people of New England that most of the common Indian words in the English language were borrowed: squaw, papoose, moccasin, wigwam, succotash, and a great many more. The settlers adopted New England Indian cookery from clambakes—a clambake on the beach was a "squantum," perhaps from the name of a favorite picnic spot—to baked beans. The Indians adopted European designs in beadwork. A colonial dancing-match, or play party, was called a "cantico," from a word of Algonquian root, and many a time Indians and settlers cut a cantico together, as the phrase had it.

The period's friendliest view of Indians comes from trader Thomas Morton, whose Maypole at Merry Mount so scandalized the Puritans, and who said, ". . . it was my chance to be landed in the parts of New England, where I found two sorts of people, the one Christians, the other Infidels, these I found most full of humanity, and more friendly than the other. . . ." He sums up, with typical Merry Mount philosophy: ". . . their life is so voyd of care, and they are so loving also that they make use of those things they enjoy (the wife onely excepted) as common goods, and are therein, so compassionate that rather than one should starve through want, they would starve all, thus doe they passe away their time merrily, not regarding our pompe (which they see dayly before their faces) but are better content with their owne, which some men esteeme so meanely of . . . They may be rather accompted to live richly, wanting nothing that is needefull; and to be commended for leading the contented life. . . ."

John Eliot studied the Algonquian languages with a captive from the Pequot war, and after thirty years of labor published the Bible "translated into the Indian language." He founded at Natick on the Charles River the first of his villages of "praying Indians," and by 1674 had four congregations totaling two thousand persons, mostly, alas, from the weaker Indian towns located between the proud and pagan Narraganset, Wampanoag, and Mohegan. The missionizing Mayhew family worked among subjects of the Wampanoag confederacy on Martha's Vineyard: four generations of this family remained in business as missionaries there for a consecutive 116 years. At Providence (where church and state were impiously kept separate) Roger Williams continued to agitate for Indian land rights so successfully that purchase of Indian lands, on the Dutch model, gradually became the accepted practice up and down the coast in the English colonies.

But the New England settlements grew in strength and property. The weighty, propertied men at the direction of affairs waxed inexorably weightier. The wheel of basic policy inexorably turned, to complete its inevitable full circle.

The noble Narraganset Canonicus, whose help had saved impetuous Massachusetts from disaster in the Pequot war, died in 1647, full of years. The noble Wampanoag Massassoit, who had succoured Plymouth Colony in its first years, died in 1662. The proprietors of Plymouth Colony then began a campaign to place the Wampanoags under outright subjugation. The Wampanoag people were willing to profess themselves subjects of the English king, but Plymouth demanded that they also admit themselves subjects of Plymouth. Massachusetts on the other hand supported the Wampanoag view of equality with Plymouth. The Wampanoag leader known as Alexander, eldest son of Massassoit, died suddenly on his way home from a more or less forced conference at Plymouth—his young wife Wetamoo believed he had been poisoned. Plymouth now threatened Alexander's younger brother (twenty-three years old) Metacom, known to the English as King Philip, with war if he refused to acknowledge Plymouth sovereignty. Philip at last bowed to the yoke, committing his nation to pay one hundred pounds a year tribute to Plymouth. This was in 1672.

Probably war was a certainty from this moment on, Philip very likely having only submitted to gain time. But English pressure increased, regardless. The drum-blows of hostile incidents came at a faster tempo. If covert competition between Plymouth and Massachusetts Bay had been a factor to begin with it was superseded as the real possibility of general war developed; the colonies joined together and both Philip and the United Colonies maneuvered for allies. Philip showed an unexpected gift for statecraft in these preliminary machinations. The neutrality of the dreaded Mohawks (far to the west in New York, beyond the Hudson, but nevertheless a significant power element even unto the Plymouth coast) was secured by both sides.

When war burst out, in 1675, the mighty Narraganset threw in with Philip, as did nearly all the lesser tribes nearby. Uncas, delighted at the prospective ruin of his last American rivals, brought 500 Mohegan gun-men and bow-men in on the English side. The Praying Indians remained loyal to their missionaries—although they had to be moved to Boston for protection from the enflamed populace, after the war got rolling.

For it was the most devastating war New England has ever

experienced, before or since, ancient or modern. Philip had been underrated. The Indians had not yet learned proper battle tactics but they were better armed with muskets than had been expected, and they had made some progress in learning how to do their own gunsmithing—not enough, for inability to repair their arms remained a handicap, but enough so that Indian forges in the forests became prime military objectives for the English. (And some Indian war chiefs were resplendent in English armor.) In matters of larger strategy Philip revealed another unexpected talent. Clearly the Wampanoags and Narragansets believed they could win. Their remarkable courage—apparently born of optimism as much as desperation—is mentioned prominently in contemporary accounts.

The value of Mohegans and Praying Indians as English scouts and spies is instanced by some later historians as a valuable if not decisive factor in the ultimate English victory. Perhaps they romanticize. There were now more than 50,000 European colonists in New England. The total population of the Indian states allied against them could not have exceeded 20,000, and was probably much less. English superiority in basic military ability was unquestioned. The European organization for war—as in stable sources of supply—was infinitely superior; there were probably more Indian casualties in the long run from exposure and malnutrition and the illnesses incident thereto than from military action. King Philip's "genius" notwithstanding, the final issue could not be in doubt. That is easy to say now, of course, totting up statistics out of books, but those on the scene at the time, both red and white, were a little too busy wiping the sweat (and fear) out of their eyes to see how simple and clear it was all going to look in books, later on. In the first few months of the war the outcome appears to have been felt in real doubt.

As before, the Puritans distinguished themselves by wholesale massacres of non-combatants that could scarcely be credited if not for the fact that it is the Puritans themselves who record them, often with relish—although not always: the shrieks of several hundred victims, mostly women and children, dying in the burning of a large Narraganset village in the winter of 1675, "greatly moved some of our soldiers. *They were much in doubt* and afterwards inquired whether burning their enemies alive could be consistent with humanity and the benevolent principles of the gospel." Some modern scholars, suckled on Freud, have made much of the dark side of Puritan psychology, which exhibited a holy ferocity toward dissenters as well as Indians— four Quakers, including the renowned Mary Dyer, having been hanged on Boston Common in 1660. But in their day Puritan psychologists were stricken with horror at the triple Tyrant's bloody Piemontese, that rolled/ Mother with infant down the rocks;* as possibly future psychologists will puzzle over nice Americans burning Vietnamese mothers with infants monotonously year after year.

The colonists needed no blood-warming this time, with fifty-two of New England's ninety towns attacked, a dozen utterly destroyed and others heavily damaged, and 600 men— "the flower and strength of the country"—killed, and unknown numbers of unrecorded noncombatant losses. But it was warmed again anyway by the divines of the New England theocracies, who repeatedly proved by Biblical interpretations that it was the sacred duty of the Christian English to root out the godless Canaanites.

Canonchet, a Narraganset sachem, great-nephew of the noble Canonicus and Philip's most famous field general, was trapped by the English and taken into Stonington and there executed, technically by the Indian allies of the English although the obsequies performed upon his body, drawing and quartering, hath an English smack. The month following this loss Philip's forces suffered a critical defeat in a battle near the falls of the Connecticut River (Indian dead 100 to 200, but including many women and children). This was, by now, the summer of 1676, and the war had been going on for more than a year. Anawon, an old man, one of the noble councilors from the time of the noble Massasoit, surrendered to the English on promises of quarter and was executed, over the bitter protests of Captain Benjamin Church, who had taken him prisoner. The same Captain Church captured, early in August, Philip's wife and nine-year-old son, at which Philip is reported to have cried out, "My heart breaks; now I am ready to die . . ." while the Reverend Increase Mather said with gusto, "It must be bitter as death for him to lose his wife and only son, for the Indians are marvellously fond and affectionate towards their children."

Later in August, in what proved to be the last battle of the war, Philip himself was killed. The confederacy was shattered.

*John Milton, "On the Late Massacre in Piedmont" (1655).

Survivors, as usual, fled or were hunted down; refugees turned up a half dozen years later far to the west, in the Mississippi valley, working as hunters for La Salle. Hundreds were sold as slaves, 500 being shipped from Plymouth alone. Proceeds from these sales were divided among the colonies (Uncas was dismayed at not being cut in, but there was no more need of him now) to help defray in some small part the expenses of the war, usually called the most costly Indian war in U.S. history. The part would have been a tiny fraction of the total; outright military expenses alone have been estimated at 100,000 pounds (Philip's tribute for a thousand years?), plus the immense damage—said the orator Edward Everett a century and a half later, "No period of the revolutionary war was to the interior of any part of the United States so disastrous." And for nearly a hundred years thereafter no village or farm in the Connecticut valley was safe from, in Mr. Everett's rolling tones, the incursions of the savage foe.

Philip's wife and son, held prisoners in Plymouth, where Philip's head was exposed on a pole (along with others of the slain enemy, men and women, in a New England version of the skull-rack that remained in place for at least more than twenty years), became the subject of high deliberations as the clergy decided their fate.

The Reverend John Cotton of Plymouth and the Reverend Samuel Arnold of Marshfield quoted Deuteronomy 24:16 as authority for sparing the boy's life but the "scripture instances of *Saul, Achan, Haman*, the children of whom were cut off, by the sword of Justice for the transgressions of their parents," as deciding their vote for death to the child of him who had dared to attack the "whole nation, yea the whole Israel of God." The Reverend Increase Mather of Boston also voted for death, quoting the instance of "Hadad, who was a little child when his father (the chief sachem of the Edomites) was killed by Joab; and, had not others fled away with him, I am apt to think that David would have taken a course, that Hadad should never have proved a scourge to the next generation . . ." The Reverend James Keith of Bridgewater urged milder treatment, writing, "I know there is some difficulty in that Psalm, 137:8, 9 . . ." but, "That law, Deut. 24:16, compared with the commended example of Amasias, 2 Chron. 25:4, doth sway with me . . ." Mildness prevailed, and Philip's wife and the grandson of the noble Massassoit were sold as slaves to the West Indies.

Northward from New England, northward through the un-broken Maine woods, there lived other Algonquian peoples, and still others dwelt farther north, north as far as corn could grow and farther still, all the way to the freezing black spruce forests and the treeless sub-Arctic plains encircling Hudson Bay.

From the Abnaki of Maine through the Micmac of Nova Scotia and the Montagnais and Naskapi of Quebec and Labrador, hunger was increasingly a part of life and legend, in direct proportion as farming dwindled and hunting became the only gainful occupation. Even in a country teeming, as the saying goes, with game, the chase is bound to be a shaky provider, there being nothing stable about a supply of wild meat.

But through fat times and lean, snows and spring, meat had to be brought in. Inevitably there were strings of empty-handed days. Then starving times, always waiting, the veritable wendigo, the mythical monster of the north woods, moved in to creep among the lodges. Especially at the end of the long winters there were weeks when the woods seemed to grow magically still and all game vanished, and the world sank into the semblance of death that preceded the first stirrings of spring. Famished people ate broth made of smoke, snow, and buckskin, and the rash of pellagra appeared like tattooed flowers on their emaciated bodies—the roses of starvation, in a French physician's description; and those who starved died covered with roses.

Naskapi and Montagnais are umbrella-names for a considerable number of related groups that roamed over their immense northern territory. The Micmac, remote in the Nova Scotia land's end country that sticks out like a sore thumb into the Atlantic, spoke an Algonquian dialect only remotely related to the Algonquian languages of their neighbors, but provided excellent exemplars of the old Algonquian institution of the family hunting territory; some geographers have speculated they may have been descendants of very early arrivals in the Americas, gradually pushed to the outermost fringes of the continent. Although not quite the last outermost fringe—the little-known Beothuk, a timid, retiring people who painted their unusually white skins red with ochre, were still beyond, on the island of Newfoundland.

The Abnaki of Maine (another variation of the word for "Easterner") were rather close kin, in language, with the Algonquian peoples hundreds of miles to the west, around the Great Lakes.

But between the Algonquian-speaking nations of the Atlantic coast and those of the Great Lakes there stretched another world, the world of the Iroquois.

Archaeological evidence seems to show that Iroquoian people had lived in the region of the lower Great Lakes and present New York for perhaps a thousand years before the time of Columbus. Their original ancestors may have been in the area much longer, but earlier (and later) discernible strains appear from the Ohio Hopewell and from the Southeast, possibly only an influx of ideas, possibly of peoples.

At some unknown time, an unknown number of centuries ago, five Iroquois nations inhabiting all of central New York, from the Genesee River to Lake Champlain, organized a confederacy. They were, reading from west to east, the Seneca, Cayuga, Onondaga, Oneida, and Mohawk. In the customary frame of reference, these five nations are regarded as the Iroquois proper. Other Iroquois nations and confederacies north, west, and south of them are usually fobbed off with the qualificative Iroquoian. The confederacy formed by these five New York nations was the far-famed League of the Iroquois.

North of the Five Nations were the Hurons, a populous confederacy made up of four aristocratic tribes, richest in tradition and ceremony of all the Iroquoian people, and a number of dependent tribal groups, one of these an Algonquian community.

West of the Five Nations was the Iroquoian state that came to be known as the Tobacco nation, and the Iroquoian confederacy that came to be known as the Neutrals.

Southwest of the Five Nations were the Erie, also known as the Cat nation, from the meaning of their full name in Iroquois: "People of the Panther."

South of the Five Nations, in central Pennsylvania and adjacent regions, were the Susquehanna, also known as the Conestoga.

The Five Nations Iroquois were traditionally hostile toward most of these surrounding Iroquoian peoples, according to early reports. According to most reports, they were also traditionally hostile to surrounding Algonquian peoples. According to legend, the Five Nations were traditionally hostile even to each other before the founding of their League.

Legend says the League was organized by the saintly statesman Dekanawida (son of a virgin mother), assisted by the great and noble councilor Hiawatha, a Mohawk, for the purpose of putting an end to the constant broils and battles among the Five Nations and establishing a universal peace based on harmony, justice, and a government of law.

From the earliest days of contact with Europeans, the various Iroquoian peoples were subjects of superlatives. Said Captain John Smith in speaking of the Susquehanna: "Such great and well-proportioned men are seldom seen . . ." Will Wood wrote that the Mohawks "be people of a tall stature, of long grimme visages, slender wasted, and exceeding great armes and thighes . . ." Jacques Cartier's men in 1535 were as much impressed by the fearlessness as by the strength of the five Iroquoian hunters (probably Hurons) they met on an island in the St. Lawrence, one of whom carried Cartier ashore as "lightly and as easily as if he had been a child of five years old; so strong and sturdy was this fellow . . ."

Numerous French writers remarked on the exceptionally fine minds of the Hurons, an early French missionary describing them as of such nobility and superior potential that French peasants should be imported to work for them. Other reports speak of the impressive farms of Iroquoian people, the miles of fields of corn and beans and squash, and of their well-built multifamily longhouses and their log forts (their "castles" as the English called them)—and still other reports emphasize the dirt, the dogs, and the eternal racket of laughter, horseplay, and constant multifamily chatter.

But for the Five Nations the choicest superlatives, in early accounts, are reserved for their ferocity, and of the Five Nations the Mohawks in this repute led all the rest (the name "Mohawk" came from an Algonquian term meaning "maneaters"). One reason the Mohawks in this repute led all the rest was their geographical location; the most easterly of the Five Nations, they were the nearest to the frontiers of the first European colonies, and so better known to the first European reporters. Some early records refer to all the Five Nations Iroquois indiscriminately as Mohawk, thus giving the Mohawks credit for all the rip-roaring deeds of the whole confederacy.

The Iroquois were an "evil people, who go all armed even to their fingers ends," Cartier was told by some of their neighbors in 1535; a century later Will Wood, quoting other neighbors, referred to the Mohawks as being "more desperate in warres than the other Indians . . . a cruell bloody people . . ." This reputation grew for a hundred and fifty years and reached perhaps its highest point during the American Revolution.

Iroquois cruelty in torturing captives was notorious. There is a description of a woman burned as sacrifice to Arekwaskwa, god of war, but, in general, tales of Iroquois cruelty were told simply to raise the listener's hair, and any underlying religious significance, if present, was not mentioned.

As among the people of the Southeast, a captive was supposed to perform a ritual dance after entering the town— while gold-star mothers showered him with blows, paying the accompanying soldiers a little tobacco for the privilege. Then, lashed to an elevated platform, he was supposed to continue singing his defiant death song while the jubilant, screaming women and children burned him with torches, gouged out bits of his flesh with jagged pieces of seashell, or while a warrior tore off his scalp and poured red-hot coals over his bleeding skull, all this cunningly managed so as to delay as long as possible the moment when the last glint of life, like a melting snowflake, died from the body.

This high estate of torture may have sometimes made a reputation for public sadism a political advantage, as with one Aharihon who (ostensibly collecting vengeance for a brother killed in the Erie wars) developed down through the years refinements of psychological torture that would have done credit to a modern police state, and by 1663 boasted that he had tortured a total of eighty persons to death with his own hand—and attained a responsible and eminent position as an Iroquois leader.

The best early ethnography (published 1724) on the Iroquois, though, presents some reservations: ". . . When one burns a Slave [captive] among the Iroquois, there are few who do not show pity, and who do not say that it is worthy of compassion. Many, especially the women (if one excepts some furies, as are everywhere more savage than the men), have not the courage to be present at such an execution. Among those men and women who are present, some do nothing; those who torment the victim, often do so . . . because they feel obliged to; some, passing above this respect of custom, solace the victim when he asks for something . . . At last, after a certain time, someone authorised by age and position gives the victim the coup de grace, and saves him from tortures he might still suffer . . ."

Maybe Iroquois torture was a trifle too notorious, considering that most of their neighbors indulged in similar delights. Also considering that the Iroquois were particularly noted for adopting captives into their nations, to the point that at various periods naturalized Iroquois may have outnumbered the native-born: it seems reasonable that such wholesale adoptions must have cut into the torture supply. And also considering that Iroquois cruelty, like the "black legend" of Spanish cruelty used by the English and Dutch to excuse their own more conscience-less behavior, served various propaganda purposes for some of those who passed along the tale and let it lose nothing in the telling.

In later accounts and subsequent history superlatives have been lavished on another aspect of the Five Nations Iroquois—their political sophistication. The League of the Iroquois is sometimes said to have been the best organized, in certain political respects, of any of the many confederacies north of Mexico.

It was operated by a council of fifty, made up of the ruling councilors of each of the Five Nations. These sachems were chosen from specific families by the mothers of their clans (groups of related women and their families), and were appointed for life—although the matriarchs of his clan could have a sachem deposed if he turned out to be a bad choice.

Dekanawida, the organizer of the great League, had been only a naturalized citizen (born a Huron, according to tradition), and so ineligible for a place among the council of fifty, but had become a chief on his merit, and had forbidden the appointment of a successor to his office. This may have given rise to the second class of sachems to which anyone (man or woman) could aspire by merit, rather than birth: the "solitary pine trees," they came to be called. These Pine Tree chiefs had the right to speak in council and made up a house of representatives, so to speak, as against the senate of the hereditary chiefs. The usual road to Pine Tree honor was, as might be expected, via fame in war.

Each of the Five Nations was left alone in its own domestic affairs, but theoretically they were to act together in matters international. They seldom did. Individual nations, or even factions within the individual nations, went their own jolly way again and again in making peace or war—except when it came to fighting each other. The League, or the Great Peace as its founders called it, did keep the peace among its members.

No doubt it was also of value as a shadowy bugaboo for use in power diplomacy—My tongue speaks for all the Iroquois, said the Mohawk ambassadors, when they didn't even have authorization to speak with finality for their own nation.

One other value that perhaps should not be minimized was the spiritual sense of union. However often the League may have proved a fiction in actual political practice, it was a reality in the minds of the honored old men who composed the council, and doubtless in the mind of the general nonpolitical public.

The great council of the League held each summer at the principal Onondaga town (the Onondaga also furnished fourteen of the fifty councilors, and the council's presiding officer) was an impressive show that could not have helped but instill this sort of feeling, as it continued year after year, generation after generation.

A pooling of the religious power of the Five Nations— cooperation in prayer as well as in war—had been one of the main objectives of the League's founders. This objective was never achieved either. But to some degree the magic of friendship was established, the emotional (even if unsound) conviction that come what may one's country did not stand alone, that all the way from the Seneca to the Mohawk the west wind streamed over a forest of brothers.

VIII

The Anvil
of America

The performance record of the Great League notwithstand-ing, the Five Nations Iroquois wrote a crucial chapter in the story of colonial North America. This came about in the following way.

North of Maine the first European colonies were French, and their reason for being was fur, primarily beaver. By 1608 when the first permanent colony, Quebec, was founded, French fur traders had already been active around the Gulf and the lower St. Lawrence for seventy years or so, and Grand Banks fishing crews from the French port of St. Malo had been pulling ashore for casual trading for a generation before that. Fur, primarily beaver, remained the grand preoccupation of the French in Canada.

Furs were obtained by trade with the Indians. French fur traders courted the Indians with whom they did business. They were partners. The Indian nations were essential to the enter-prise. The Indians wanted the wonderful kettles and hatchets of the foreigners, but the French wanted even more the help and good will of the Indians, their woodland skills, their knowledge of winter snowshoe traveling, their birchbark canoes (up to forty

216

feet in length) and the paddlers to man them, their familiarity with the river-and-lake waterways to still more treasures of fur, and above all the French wanted to maintain in working condition the tribal channels of trade.

Whereas the English colonies usually destroyed, as soon as convenient, the Indian cocoon around them, the French more often supported and sustained the Indian world in which they found themselves, for out of that world came fur. Thus Indian communities here were in many cases strengthened and enriched by white contact.

The first fur-trading partners of the French were the Hurons and the Algonquian people of the lower St. Lawrence, principally the Montagnais and the numerous bands next above them on the river who were known collectively as the Algonquian proper—one of these bands, the Algonkin, being the original bearers of the name later applied by anthropologists to an enormous network of related languages.

Hurons and Algonquians had been friends of the French for some time when in 1609 Samuel de Champlain, founder of Quebec and lieutenant of the owner of the French fur trade monopoly, went with a Huron and Algonquian war party on a long journey to the lake now known as Lake Champlain. There he won a battle for them, single-handed, against a little army of their hated enemies, who had never before met firearms. The foe were bold in arrow-proof body-armor made of plaited sticks, but Champlain killed two of their three war-captains and wounded the third, and the bold foe broke and ran. And the thunder and lightning of his arquebus echoed for a hundred and fifty years. The bold foe had been Mohawk. The Five Nations Iroquois nursed a dogged animosity toward the French, with only a few interludes of genuine peace, from that time onward.

In 1614, five years after this little battle with big consequences, Dutch fur traders built a trading post up the Hudson, near the present location of Albany, on the doorstep of the Mohawk country. The Dutch were also primarily in the beaver business, eager to uphold and sustain the forest nations who might act as district jobbers for them. Within twenty years or so, Iroquois fur salesmen were procuring guns from Dutch, English, and French traders.

During this period trade in firearms to Indians was usually illegal, but the Five Nations Iroquois were favored in it by their location, remote enough from principal Dutch and English settlements to seem harmless, and remote enough from any European settlements to make trade-supervision impossible.

It was standard colonial practice, naturally, to be more watchful about keeping guns from nearby Indian neighbors than from distant nations, safely distant in their far-off woods, who had a legitimate use for guns anyway in coaxing more furs out of the gunless people still beyond them, and for use in attacking (one might hope) rival European trading posts. The Swedes of the Delaware country were chary of handing guns to the Delawares but freely armed the Susquehanna of the interior, even supplying their forts with cannon and professional military instructors.

As spheres of trade expanded, a clear area of conflict came into being between French, Dutch, English, and Swedes. Likewise a clear area of conflict came into being between Indian nations stimulated and aggrandized by trade with Europeans, yet far enough from centers of white settlement to remain reasonably independent.

The earliest frontier did not move with westering European settlement but with the aggressive expansion of Indian nations who were in business with Europeans.

There were, in effect, two frontiers: one strictly Indian, the other, following years behind, European. Out of the hurricane belt of that Indian-versus-Indian frontier came winds that affected and sometimes determined the course of American history.

The Five Nations Iroquois became the determining force of this Indian-versus-Indian frontier in the Northeast. Perhaps favored by their strategic location, they were no colony's creature. They were from the beginning their own master. They traded, when all the magnificent oratory of the councils was done, with whoever offered the best deal, all things considered. All the things considered made for a bewildering tangle of loyalties, emotions, and motives, as does any political action. But no European business partner could be confident of calling the tune, either for any of the separate Five Nations who so often went their separate ways, or for the broad policy of the confederacy as a whole.

During the first half of the seventeenth century the Five Nations, singly or otherwise, were sometimes at war, sometimes at peace with the French and the "French Indians" to the north: Montagnais, Algonkins, Hurons, and the long-established river traders westward of the Hurons known as the Ottawa (from an Algonquian word meaning "he buys"—evidently the Ottawa were professional traders even in pre-European times).

There were several Iroquois attempts in this period to form a coalition with the powerful and populous Hurons. Failure of these efforts may not have been due to Mohawk and Seneca resistance among the Iroquois, and French machinations among the Hurons to keep them at odds with the Five Nations, but these things at least played a part.

The Hurons funneled through to New France whole canoe-flotilla-loads of pelts taken in trade from the country north and west of the Lakes, a limitless country sparkling with streams and beautiful with beaver. The French felt they had the Hurons, and this trade, in their pocket. They feared to lose them to the more independent Five Nations.

The Hurons had accepted missionaries, who from the times of Champlain had acted as the governor's agents in stirring up anti-Iroquois sentiment when needed. The Hurons themselves being an Iroquoian people, the priests distinguished between them and the Five Nations by calling the Hurons the "good Iroquois." Letters of missionaries published in France were loaded with extravagant praise of the Hurons (for all that the name Hurons, bestowed by the French, was an old French word with a meaning similar to "slobs"), and a continuous propaganda barrage against the Five Nations Iroquois.

In the summer of 1639 the Hurons captured and burned a total of 113 Iroquois, some from roaming war parties, some casual Iroquois travelers. Nevertheless, the Hurons remained to the French the good Iroquois, while the Five Nations were those demons, those tigers, those wolves. "Did I not hope that you Frenchmen will wreak vengeance for such cruelties, I would be unable to speak," a French Jesuit quoted a weeping Algonquian woman, ex-prisoner of the bad Iroquois, as saying, while she related atrocities. When in the 1630s repeated epidemics swept through the Hurons, reducing their population from an estimated 30,000 to an estimated 15,000, French administrators, writing home for more money, sometimes forgetfully attributed these plague losses to battle deaths at the hands of the bad Iroquois. Some twenty years after this, a French governor mentioned, "It was politic to exaggerate more than ever the cruelties of the Iroquois," revealing more by the qualifying phrase than by the statement.

Spheres of power swelled. Guns became more common. Cardinal Richelieu's joint-stock company, which had taken over (and kept until 1645) the French fur-trade monopoly, permitted trade in guns to Christian Indians and there were thousands of baptized Hurons who could have qualified, but the French monopoly policy, with its attendant high prices, may have made them too dear a luxury. The usual view has it that the Hurons were not as well armed as the Iroquois, who are made the possessors of some 400 muskets by information as of 1643. But the tensions rising on the Iroquois-Huron frontier seem to have come from equally aggressive pressure on each side.

In 1648 Mohawk and Seneca war parties deliberately broke a truce with the Hurons that had been made in the name of the League—their reasons for doing so are unfathomable, but intra-League politics may have played a part. Economic factors involving the fur trade are sometimes emphasized by historians, sometimes to the exclusion of any other factors at all, but while it seems likely hostilities were heightened, or perhaps even genuine war first introduced, by the glittering presence of European trade, it also seems likely that other factors— religious, emotional, fraternal, national—continued to exist. At the Mohawk-Seneca action a statesmanlike Onondaga councilor, Scandawati, who had pledged his word to the truce, invoked the ultimate diplomatic protest of killing himself. To no purpose. In the dead of the following winter, in March, 1649, an overwhelming army of no less than 1,000 Mohawk and Seneca warriors suddenly invaded the heart of the Huron country in the area of Lake Simcoe and Georgian Bay, north of modern Toronto. Most of these troops are said to have wintered in Huron country, living off the snow-drifted land, without the Hurons suspecting their presence, while the massive strike was being prepared.

In two days of fighting they took and burned two Huron towns, were repulsed from a third, and vanished with many captives and much loot. The Huron losses could not have been ruinous; their casualties were perhaps 300 warriors killed as against 200 of the enemy. But panic followed. With no thought of provisions or shelter, the Huron people fled from their towns. Before the long northern winter ended many had died from starvation and exposure. Survivors kept on fleeing, literally, for years. In those two days of invasion the mighty Huron confederacy had been smashed. The ancient desultory war that had gone on so long between the Hurons and the Five Nations, those evil people all armed even to their fingers' ends, was over.

Some Huron refugees went to join their conquerors, occupying a town to themselves among the Senecas, and identifiable Huron groups turned up among the Mohawks and Onondagas. Others emigrated to the Iroquoian nations of the Tobacco-growing people, the Neutral people, or the Erie. Others scattered to the four winds, sometimes calling themselves by what had been their own name for their confederacy—Wendat: the name became Wyandot in white literature.

The sense of utter defeat when there had been no defeat, the nightmare demoralization that so suddenly destroyed the Huron state, is inexplicable. Maybe it was the roll of thunder in the air, for from now on the Iroquois frontier was alive with lightning.

Neighbors of the Hurons were thrown into panic, and the Iroquois interpreted their panic as hostility and anti-Iroquois agitation, as no doubt it sometimes was. The Tobacco people living at the western door of the Huron country were blasted by the Iroquois thunderbolt in December of 1649. These people appear to have been Hurons in everything but the name, and were famous for cultivating, besides tobacco, immense fields of corn and large quantities of hemp, used for making fish-nets. They seem to have been a larger nation, in population, than all the Five Nations put together. Each of the opponents the Iroquois demolished, one after the other, seems to have outnumbered the Five Nations, whose combined population at this time probably didn't exceed 12,000.

The next great Iroquoian confederacy to the southwest of the Hurons, called the Neutral confederacy by the French because of its neutrality in Iroquois-Huron troubles, was shattered by the Iroquois in 1651, with mopping up continuing for several years more.

The next people to the south, the People of the Panther, the Erie, another powerful Iroquoian nation, apparently a Goliath in size compared to the Five Nations, struck first at the Great League in 1653. An Iroquois counter-offensive the following summer, led by Onondaga soldiers, won a desperate battle in taking by storm an important Erie town located near the present Erie, Pennsylvania.

Here 3,000 to 4,000 Erie warriors were defeated by an army of 1,800 Iroquois (whose guns probably made the difference) in a victory that should have won the war on the spot, but this time the enemy reformed and fought back again and again, and two more years of fighting were required before the Eries, too, were finally vanquished.

One of the temporary Iroquois-French friendship pacts was in effect during the Erie war; a couple of the Iroquois war chiefs even wore French uniforms, and a French Jesuit mission was attempted, very briefly, among the Five Nations. This peace ended in war, and in 1666 the French made a full-scale, organized military invasion of the Iroquois country, burning towns and cutting a swath of devastation that should have been enough to destroy any nation. The Iroquois, furthermore, were in a disastrously weakened condition. There had been too much war. The Iroquois were bled white by war. In the expert opinion of the Jesuits the native-born Iroquois were by now reduced to a minority in their own towns, outnumbered by the immigrants they had adopted. They were still further reduced by a death-dealing epidemic in the 1660s. But they made their enforced peace with the French, and somehow the Great League still stayed on its feet.

It faced continual wolf-pack attacks from remnants of the shattered nations to the north and west, and now a new major threat appeared from a new direction: from the south. The Susquehanna, armed with the best of guns and tall from easy conquests among their unarmed eastern neighbors, the Dela-wares, gave a humiliating beating to the Senecas and Cayugas and very obviously prepared to sweep the Five Nations from the face of the earth.

It has been observed that Europeans had furnished guns to the Susquehanna who in return had formed a firm alliance with the colony of Maryland, an alliance of mutual defense against the Iroquois. Maryland occasionally sent detachments of militia to aid the Susquehanna, the Swedes gave them cannon and military engineers, and on one occasion Maryland even con-scripted every tenth man in the colony to raise a company of 410 men for Susquehanna assistance. This had been going on since the 1650s. Now, lording it over the grandfatherly Delawares become their humble vassals, and with such powerful allies at their back—and with the Dutch friends of the Iroquois out of business in New York (since 1664), the Susquehanna might reasonably have expected a final victory over the Seneca, their special foe, and the rest of the enfeebled League.

Something intervened—perhaps fate, perhaps Tahiawagi,

Holder of the Heavens, the Iroquois national deity. The Susquehanna lost staggering percentages of their people in waves of epidemics. By 1674 they were reduced to only one village of a few hundred people in Maryland and not many hundred more in Pennsylvania. White opportunists along the borders of the Maryland and Virginia settlements attacked (in 1676) these helpless remnants—in direct contravention of the official policy of their colonial governors, who had so long valued the Susquehanna as a frontier buffer. But Maryland had already (1674) discreetly forgotten its mutual-defense treaty with the Susquehanna and come to terms with the Iroquois, acknowledging them masters of Susquehanna territory by right of conquest, a victory assumed without even the necessity of a major battle.

And with this their Indian-versus-Indian wars, the big ones at any rate, ended, and the Iroquois were king of the hill. From their worndown low point of the 1660s they bounced back with astonishing rapidity, strong with adopted immigrants, lords of a vast woodland "land of Souls, where all was laid waste by war and terror, where on the fields was only blood, in the cabins only corpses," in the words of an orator from one of the nations they had destroyed.

Ghost-filled it may have been, but in this paramount area of conflict between rival European invaders the Great League now stood alone, the ruling power, holding the key to the entire interior of the continent.

During the 1680s and 1690s the French, with Indian allies, smashed again and again at this Iroquois barrier, sending invasions that again and again should have broken forever the confederacy of the Five Nations, but did not. Iroquois crops and towns were destroyed and Iroquois souls went to join the wandering dead of their recent victims but the Iroquois state remained, frequently still capable of delivering heavy reprisals. ("Men make a state," wrote Alcaeus, "not walls nor empty ships.")

The Tree of Peace (as the Iroquois orators also liked to call their Great League) still stood.

It was from this point on that the League really began to function as a more or less unified force. At no time in the thirty years of great wars had the Five Nations all worked together—the Seneca at the western "door" and the Mohawk at the eastern had followed the devious paths of their own intricate interests, sometimes bitterly opposed to each other, sometimes making

common cause against the Onondaga in the center, who had
sometimes conspired against other League members with the
Hurons or Susquehanna or even with the French. But now, it
seems, all the Five Nations began to realize the strength of their
position and made the most of it.

Swedes and Dutch were gone, as official entrants among the
European invaders: English and French remained. The Iroquois
learned to play them off one against the other with a certain
amount of artistry.

They could never be true friends of the French:
". . . between us and them there is no more good faith than
between the most ferocious animals," said an astute French
administrator. At bottom, Iroquois sympathies were with the
English, as they had been previously with the Dutch; this was
especially true of the Mohawks, with what influence (frequently
plenty) they could bring to bear on the rest of the League, for
English trade, as had the Dutch, came first to their eastern door.

But the Mohawks as well as the League in toto fashioned a
broad policy of independent neutrality that kept the balance of
power in their hands for nearly a century.

"We are born free," a French governor was told in 1684 by
Haaskouan, known to the French as La Grande Gueule (both
names meaning "Big Mouth"), renowned Onondaga spokesman.
And he spelled out exactly what he meant: the Iroquois would go
where they wished, allow passage through their country only to
"those who seem to us good," buy and sell with whom they
pleased, English as well as French, or anyone else. They wore no
muzzle, neither French nor English. "Listen, French Governor,
my voice is that of the five Iroquois houses." And in this case it
really was. The French governor retired to his tent to rage and
curse (so a witness reported), and a long line of French and
English empire-builders raged and cursed, threatened, whee-
dled, devised, conspired. The Iroquois, those "subtle, adroit, and
arrant knaves," (in the accolade of a French Jesuit), remained
blandly independent and in command.

Their country lay athwart the one good water-level route to
the interior and dominated the St. Lawrence and Ottawa River
trade routes, the lower Great Lakes, the Ohio country, and the
wilderness threshholds of New York, Pennsylvania, Maryland,
and Virginia. In every plot and plan of French or English
expansion, in every scheme to penetrate the interior or secure
the alliance of the interior tribes, in every move of complicated

fur-trade politics, the position the Iroquois would take had to be considered, often as the problem of foremost importance.

There was no help for it. Neither side could afford to let the other take possession of the Iroquois and their country, highroad to the center of the continent. Neither side could afford to let the other become the Iroquois' one and only friend.

And so the latest decisions from the council of the Great League of the Iroquois became matters of moment to the busy strategists of St. James and Versailles. A French frontiersman was elevated to the peerage for his valuable work as interpreter to the Iroquois. Thirty-six Iroquois councilors, seized during a parley and sent in chains to the galleys of Marseilles as a means of cutting their arrogance down to size, were apologetically freed, dusted off, dressed in "gorgeous French" robes, and returned in state to the dignity of their senatorial mats. ("A dirty troupe squatting on their behinds like monkeys, knees at ears, or sprawling back belly in air, everyone his pipe in his mouth, treating the affairs of State with as much coolness and gravity as the Junta of Spain or the Council of Doges at Venice.") In even more state, four Iroquois councilors were escorted to London to visit the Queen—Queen Anne, this was, in 1710, and they were showered with gracious attentions and official favors, for, it was said, they were about to sign an important treaty with their friends, the English. The governor of New York, at about this same time, spoke glowingly of the Iroquois as the "bulwark between us and the French." The New York Indian commissioners at Albany reported that the Iroquois held "the balance of the continent of North America," and a French missionary in Canada recorded the same thing in almost the same words. The secretary of the Pennsylvania colony wrote to William Penn, "If we lose the Iroquois we are gone." The Iroquois were even a factor in the temporary reversal of French colonial policy in 1696 when all traders (except Henri de Tonty and his partner) were recalled from the forests and all expansionist activity ceased, although the mainspring of this extraordinary interlude was the brief rise to power of the Abbé Fénelon and his League of the Public Good with its revolutionary ideas ("I love my family better than myself, my country better than my family, the human race better than my country").

Colonial delegates from New York, Massachusetts, Virginia, Maryland, Pennsylvania, and the Carolinas traveled to the Iroquois eastern door at Albany to meet with the representatives of the Great League. The Iroquois themselves are said to have urged the colonies' concerted participation in these assemblies, expressing wonder that the colonies did not meet together over common interests, as did the Five Nations. Such irregular meetings had gone on for seventy years when, in 1754, the first great intercolonial conference (outside New England) was held to work out a design of colonial union; it took place, as a matter of course, at Albany.

The Tuscarora, driven from North Carolina in the years following 1712, were an Iroquoian people ". . . they were of us and went from us long ago, and now are returned . . ." said the Five Nations, who gave them land for a new home, and made a place for them in the council of the Great League. Thereafter, the Five Nations were the Six Nations. The event caused concern among the colonies, for fear that it would embroil the Iroquois in southern Indian troubles. To prevent this, the governors of Virginia and Pennsylvania together with Indian ambassadors from the South went to Albany in 1722 and persuaded the Six Nations to agree to a dividing line between North and South. The line was laid down from the high ridge of the Alleghenies to the Potomac—forty-five years before the portentous Mason and Dixon survey to establish a Pennsylvania-Maryland boundary in the same area.

Iroquois power and glory during the eighteenth century reached the highest point attained (so far as history knows) by any Indian nation north of Mexico. An English chronicler writing in 1727 draws a picture of an Iroquois tribute-collector at an Algonquian village on the New England coast ("An old Mohawk sachem, in a poor blanket and dirty shirt . . . issuing his orders with as arbitrary an authority as a Roman dictator") that calls up Aztec memories. Although the impressive old Iroquois councilors, sincerely respected by the generations of Europeans who dealt with them, had no magnificence to display other than their simple presence: "The chiefs are generally the poorest among them," wrote a Dutch pastor at Albany in the 1640s, "for instead of their receiving from the common people . . . they are obliged to give."

For the people in general, there was prosperity: calico dresses and hickory shirts, log houses, barns fat with farm produce. Missionaries and rum came among them and the French never tired of fomenting trouble at home and wars with the "far nations," but all these classic destroyers, while wreak-ing much havoc, could not succeed in destroying the Great League. Said Lafitau, writing in the 1720s, "... under the uncultured and gross appearances, you will see everywhere among these Peoples a love for their Country engraved in their hearts, and a greatness of soul not only in the face of peril but even proof against unhappiness ..." And of the Iroquois women: "... It is in them that resides all real authority ... they are the soul of the councils, the arbiters of peace and war ..."

Vainglorious young men could and did go forth on war parties, sometimes to very distant lands, and the gaudy round of ceremonies and councils continued as before, but the old days of incessant war, of furiously painted soldiers with high-roached scalplocks, receded into the past. The old, old men recited their deeds against the Susquehanna or against the French, and taught the young men how to dream a proper death song; but why should the young men take them seriously? In the old days, you took your death song very seriously indeed because you fully expected to sing it some day roped up before glistening enemy eyes, and many, many friends the old men loved so long ago had done so; it was strange (the old men must have thought) that theirs were still unuttered. Sometimes the old men wept when they heard recited the rite of the Great League's founding: "... You see the footprints of our forefathers/ ... all but perceptible is the smoke where they used to smoke the pipe together ..."

The union lived, triumphant. The hurricane belt had subsided to soft showers and golden days. But the violent disturbances of its years of storm had sent repercussions bounding across the lakes and forests of the wilderness as far as there were missionaries or traders to record them. There's no reason to suppose they didn't roll on farther still, toppling ancient societies, uprooting peoples, tumbling together fugitives and invaders, littering the whole middle of the continent with wreckage left by the tumultuous winds of change.

Bands of Hurons and Ottawas straggled westward to the upper Mississippi, quarreled with the forest Sioux and were driven back eastward. They joined with other Huron and Tobacco people calling themselves Wyandot, and with Algonquian groups from the eastern St. Lawrence who had adopted themselves into the loose nationality of the Ottawa; they joined and divided again and again. Some planted villages near the French trading posts of the far Lakes: Michilimackinac, Sault

Ste. Marie, Detroit. More and more these dislocated peoples tended to coagulate around French forests forts or end-of-the-world French trading towns, little settlements that were Indian in everything but the language.

The aloof people known as the Foxes were an exception and fought off the French, but the Ojibwa then pushed the Foxes southward to settle with their brothers, the Sauk, in the rich, gorgeous country of lower Wisconsin. The Ojibwa, armed with trade guns, then began a hundred years' war against the Sioux, eventually forcing them westward clear across the Mississippi and out into the plains of Minnesota and the Dakotas. The Cree of the northern forests, armed with trade guns and hunger for all the beaver country in the world, assaulted and dispersed the wandering people of the woods to the north and west of Hudson Bay, raiding northward down the Mackenzie River almost to the Arctic Ocean.

The fierce Winnebago west of Lake Michigan were crushed by pestilence and by a war they provoked with the Illinois. The Illinois, Potawatomi, and Miami, jostled here and there below the Lakes, were subject to Iroquois onslaughts in the 1680s. For many years afterward displaced Erie, Susquehanna, Delaware families at last dispossessed of their Pennsylvania lands by European real-estate developers operating with Iroquois connivance, and Shawnee bands with their brothers the mystic Kickapoo drifted into the Miami and Illinois country, sometimes settling, sometimes gathering around the French posts that were coming into being along the Mississippi, sometimes traveling away southward down the Warrior Trail, while displaced persons from the South passed them traveling hopefully to the North.

The land was filled with Ishmaels. They transmitted their restlessness wherever they went; they brought strange ways with them and learned strange ways as they wandered. But they found new homes and settled, at last, among nations with whom they could live in brotherhood, and, in the words of a French observer, tried "to forget what was past for their own preservation."

East, south, and north of the Iroquois the turbulence of the Indian-versus-Indian frontier coincided with the frontiers of European settlement. French frontiers were directly affected by the Indian organization of the fur trade. But events and attitudes within the Indian world also had much to do with the subsequent movements of the English colonial frontiers.

The usual picture of land-hungry white settlers irresistibly pushing the Indians back, "clearing the Indians out," is naively oversimplified for any period, and basically wrong for the decisive years before 1800.

In its early phases the progress of the North American frontier was at least as much a creation of Indian politics and attitudes as white pressures. Many forces within the Indian world operated on this far from inexorable advance, sometimes in such obvious ways as an Indian nation encouraging white settlement in order to gain European support and auxiliaries, or storms among Indian states leaving a shattered borderland that invited occupation. It was no accident that the first frontiers of English settlement to move westward across the Alleghenies, in the mid-1700s, happened to move into the country south of the Ohio, centering in Kentucky, that was, as previously noted, uninhabited by any Indian nation.

The first tendrils of the white frontiers, Dutch *boschlopers*, English traders and "long hunters," French *coureurs de bois*, were directed from here to there not only via devious Indian trails but for devious Indian purposes. No white frontier before 1800 was initiated in the face of opposition from an intact Indian nation being pushed back from it. The first frontiers in Virginia and New England and New York, for example, were the original colonies, and their founding was not only tolerated by the Indian nations at hand but, as has been seen, given some Indian assistance. By the time Indian opposition developed, these frontiers were too strongly established to be dislodged.

For after the initial invited penetration, the story, as a rule, quickly changed. But in the subsequent destruction of such penetrated Indian nations, Indian politics continued to play a large part, both for the whites and for the Indians allied (for reasons of their own) with the whites.

The white frontiers moved where these factors wist. White population pressure was only a minor force in determining their direction or setting them in motion.

But once begun in any area, the seepage of settlement over the border into Indian country became a clamorous factor all its own, unimportant at first but ultimately to become the most explosive ingredient of all, both for the Indian and white worlds.

Most of these frontier outposts were settled by recent immigrants from Europe too poor to afford a place within the recognized boundaries of the colony (or were established by the leaders—real-estate developers—of such immigrants). The frontier was the low-rent district, the slums of colonial days. From the beginning the frontier also attracted outlaws, runaways, malcontents, freethinkers, and other such undesirables.

The border-jumpers brought trouble with them, and the region into which they intruded was often a troubled, unstable sector of the Indian world to begin with. When they and their troubles had sufficiently multiplied, a policy of clearing the Indians out came into being automatically. This was primarily a vocal policy, a matter of political agitation: they wanted, of course, the government militia to come and do the clearing out for them.

But their desires were quite often at variance with the policy of the colony's government or of His Majesty's government across the sea, who with their sights set on grander strategy had more often than not done everything possible to keep the settlers from settling in the frontier country in the first place.

If the borderers resented the Indians' presence on what they regarded as their land, they resented fully as much the rich, bloated, unfeeling, profiteering, tyrannical colonial governors back yonder in their brick colonial mansions, and the bloodsucking Lords of Trade in their lordly London halls. These fine gentry, lolling safe in their lace and powdered wigs, refused to give white men sufficient protection against the bloody savages because they didn't want to hurt their trade with the savage nations or endanger their dangling war schemes against the distant French, accusations which were usually true.

Not surprisingly, these pioneers were more inclined to be vicious than brave, and as far as they themselves were concerned their policy of clearing the Indians out was only exercised against tame Indians or the crumbled remains of previously broken Indian nations among which the frontiersmen so often settled. Making a dent in an unbroken Indian nation was a job for the troops (with Indian auxiliaries), then and later. The frontiersmen's direct effectiveness in advancing the frontier, in a sense of Indian conquest, was never important.

But their indirect effectiveness, in the truly inexorable expansion of their influence in official government policy, was something else again. And their spirit of hatred for the established order, the citified and pompous central government that spurned their needs and arrogantly repressed their demands, springing from however small a source grew to wield extraordinary power. It became the traditional spirit of the border, the spirit of the West, and the left wing of the angel of the American Revolution.

An early example of this feeling showed itself in Virginia in what has been known since as Bacon's Rebellion, its leader being one Nathaniel Bacon, a young American cousin of Francis Bacon. It was touched off by the murder of several white men on the northern border of Virginia, which brought out a detachment of Virginia militiamen under Colonel John Washington, great-grandfather of the president (this took place in the autumn of 1675). The few surviving Susquehannas, by then congregated in a village at the head of the Potomac, were accused of the murders but blamed an Iroquois war party recently in the neighborhood. The Virginia militiamen, together with a troop of cavalry from Maryland, discussed the matter with a half dozen elderly spokesmen who came out from the fortified village under promises of safe conduct, which turned out to be something less than safe when the militia concluded the affair by shooting down the half dozen elderly spokesmen. The rest of the Susquehannas later escaped from their besieged village, killed a reported sixty frontier settlers—ten for each murdered councilor—and sent a message demanding damages from Sir William Berkeley, governor of Virginia.

Berkeley neither answered the Susquehanna complaint nor, enraged at the murder of the sachems under a flag of truce ("If they had killed my grandfather, my father, my mother, and all my friends, yet, if they had come to treat in peace, they should have gone in peace") would he field troops against the rampaging Indians. Young Bacon, a member of the governor's council, formed an unofficial army that killed a reported seventy Susquehannas (". . . well nigh exterminated the Indian tribe of Susquehannocks," wrote historian Woodrow Wilson) and then slaughtered remnants of the peaceable Powhatans at what has been known since as Bloody Run, near the Falls of the James River—in fact, modern experts suspect Bacon was principally interested in killing friendly Indians to get their land. The frontier army then went on to take over the whole Virginia colony, chasing out the governor and burning Jamestown before the frontier dander simmered down. This happened in 1676.

It is not unlikely that resentment over the Navigation Acts of 1651 and 1660, which had brought about lower tobacco prices and higher commodity prices all for the benefit of English shippers, had as much as Susquehannas to do with the temper of rebelliousness. A principal figure from another Year of '76, Thomas Jefferson, putting his finger on not the Indian policy involved but the spirit of protest against unresponsive centralized rule ("insurrections proceed oftener from the misconduct of those in power, than from the factious and turbulent temper of the people"), suggested more than a century later that Nathaniel Bacon would "no longer be regarded as a rebel, but as a patriot . . ." A recent authoritative study, though, argues that the spirit of self-government in Virginia was born not during the rebellion but in response to the tyrannical acts of a subsequent royal commission sent out to investigate. Whatever righteous rebellion's other wellsprings, slaughter of Indians was for generations a popular frontier refuge for patriotism.

In sum, white frontiers were set in motion with the considerable assistance, voluntary and involuntary, of forces within the Indian world. Once in motion, any frontier developed a growing force of its own, exerted primarily to impose its policy upon its own reluctant government. One desired feature of that policy was to clear the Indians out. This process formed the pattern of the Indian story on the white frontier. Sufficiently repeated, this process helped eradicate European government, along with eradicating Indian nations.

Frontiersmen sometimes became genuinely industrious about cleaning out the debris of demolished Indian societies caught in the tide of this process—I've shot and chopped and drowned the critters, I've fried 'em by the houseful and roasted 'taters in their grease, ran the Davy Crockett school of stories— but their efforts only amounted to casual rape as against the total score.

Drink and the devil did for the rest, a devil crowned with the three heavy horns of degradation, prostitution, and disease. Religion helped by destroying the comfortable elastic world of the old gods and by providing the circumstances for point-blank epidemics among converts crowded in squalid imitation-white housing. (There were exceptions, such as the thriving Indian villages founded in Pennsylvania by Moravian missionaries; the villages were destroyed one after another by indignant white frontiersmen or equally indignant non-Christian Indians.)

Descendants of friend and foe alike shared the common Indian fate within the white world: by about the year 1800 neighboring Connecticut villages were occupied by the few forlorn survivors of the anti-English Pequots, less than a hundred strong, and the few forlorn survivors of their tribal brothers, the pro-English Mohegans, also less than a hundred strong.

Some, maybe many, escaped from the long nightmare to the intact tribes beyond the borders; Narragansets went to Maine and turned into Abnakis by the hundreds, maybe thousands, after King Philip's War, and the parade of Tuscarora plodding north to the Iroquois took a hundred years to pass.

But one after another of the intact tribes marched to destruction in their turn in the major colonial wars from 1689 to 1763, echoes for the most part of European wars between France and England, but in America fought on the American plan, with as much use as possible of Indian allies. The brunt of these wars was felt on the frontiers, with enough wanton hatcheting of settlers and burning of farms and villages, enough wives and children carried away into captivity, to madden a people with far less motive for madness than property-minded frontiersmen. The stories can still communicate the reality of agony behind the archaic phrases. Wrote a mother, of parting from her six-year-old son, both made captives by "French" Indians at Charlestown, New Hampshire, in 1754: "The inexorable savage . . . forced him away; the last words I heard, intermingled with his cries, were 'Ma'am, I shall never see you again.' The keenness of my pangs almost obliged me to wish that I had never been a mother. 'Farewell, Sylvanus,' said I; 'God will preserve you' . . ." It is good to note that God did, and Sylvanus, although by then as Indian as English, came back when grown to live near his mother in Charlestown.

Typically, though, much of the understandable fury of bedeviled frontier settlers was turned inward against their own governments, their grievances used as levers to secure various official concessions. One of these was the scalp bounty, sometimes extracted by the radical frontier bloc as a sop for damages claimed from Indian depredations. Scalp bounties had been used first by the Dutch, and were adopted at one time or another by most of the colonies. It was an expensive business—Massachusetts paid from twenty shillings in 1675 to twelve pounds per scalp in 1703, which was a lot of money, and a hundred pounds in 1722, which was a lot more—but effective. Of course, no one could be sure the scalps brought in were the scalps of whatever Indians happened to be enemies at the moment. Missionaries had to keep a frantic guard over their Indian flocks during bounty years—when you could collect hair worth $1500, as did some Pennsylvania frontier militants in 1763, simply by hatcheting a score of Indian men, women, and children who plied the basket-making trade in a nearby town. Murder of Indians here again was only a convenient expression of a broader conflict, in this instance a political struggle between poor frontier Scotch-Irish Presbyterians and the wealthy urban Quakers who controlled the Pennsylvania colonial Assembly. The Indian victims were the last shreds of the once mighty Susquehannas, a tiny band inhabiting a village named after one of their ancient tribal appellations, Conestoga.

The French used the scalp bounty to have the inoffensive Beothuk of Newfoundland Island cut off, as the phraseology of the time had it, by the Micmac of Nova Scotia. The Beothuk were a minor nuisance to the French, who offered the Micmac a bounty for Beothuk scalps. After a generation or so not a single Beothuk was left alive, at any rate none who would admit their tribal identity; some may have escaped across the Strait to join the Naskapi of Labrador.

Those Indian nations left in shambles by the stress of colonial wars were, if within reach, swallowed up and digested by the European frontiers—at an accelerated rate as the frontiers and the shambles spread. In each instance the cycle of disorder, decay, and fitful extermination was scrupulously repeated, only faster.

The fissures opened in intact Indian nations by the disruptive effects of Indian-versus-Indian wars and European colonial wars are seen in white history as the "opening to settlement" of the trans-Appalachian country, the Ohio country, and the country northwest of the Ohio known as the Old Northwest.

Previous Iroquois conquests in this back country made possible the first tentative entry of English traders and settlers. The principal avenue of the march of settlement was through Delaware territory, cracked open by Susquehanna wars of conquest in the middle 1600s. The Iroquois, after their tacit conquest of the Susquehanna in the 1670s, claimed to have inherited thereby sovereignty over the Delawares and by the 1730s were freely selling Delaware lands to the proprietors of Pennsylvania. The Delawares objected but Pennsylvania, not surprisingly, sided with the claims of the generous Iroquois land agents.

The Delawares particularly objected to a slick operation known since as the Walking Purchase which had cheated them out of an immense tract of land running some hundred miles into the interior north and west of Philadelphia. Early purchases made by William Penn from the Lenape (Delaware) Confederacy had been based on the stretch of land a man might walk over in a given period, a day or a day and a half; tradition says (mistakenly, alas) that Penn himself marked out the first of these purchases with a day's walk of twenty to thirty miles, a leisurely walk "after the Indian manner, sitting down sometimes to smoke, eat biscuit and cheese . . ." But after Penn's death one such purchase was executed, in 1737, by men specially hired as the fastest walkers available, who clocked eighty-six miles in the day and a half of the deal, to the indignation of the Indians—who also protested the legality of the transaction on several other counts, including the place and directions involved. And here, says a modern study, was the real point of fraud in the Walking Purchase: James Logan, chief justice of the Pennsylvania supreme court, had a personal interest in obtaining land to the northwest and showed the Indians a map which appeared to designate land farther south than the wording on the map— which the Indians could not read—said it was; and on this map the purchase was based.

When during the next few years surveyors and settlers appeared even among the northerly Delaware towns at the forks of the Lehigh River the Delawares threatened war, and Pennsylvania besought the connivance of the Iroquois, at a Philadelphia meeting in 1742. "The record says that handsome dinners were provided, and the health of King George, the proprietaries, the governor, etc., were drank in high good humor, and at a certain time, at one of these sociable canticoes, the subject of the walk was introduced, and the several deeds and writings shown and explained by way of appeal to the high authority of the Six Nations, against the conduct of their cousins the Delaware, etc." (This in the words of a chronicle written a half century or so later.)

The Iroquois were won over to Pennsylvania's point of view and at a council session on July 12th (official text printed by Benjamin Franklin) the Onondaga orator Canassatego delivered a blistering rebuke to the Delawares present, ". . . Your Cause is bad; your Heart far from being upright; and you are maliciously bent to break the Chain of Friendship with our Brother *Onas*

[Governor of Pennsylvania] and his People . . . But how came you to take upon you to sell Land at all: We conquered you; we made Women of you; you know you are Women, and can no more sell Land than Women . . . This Land you claim is gone through your Guts; you have been furnish'd with Cloaths, Meat and Drink, by the Goods paid you for it . . . You act a dishonest Part . . . And for all these Reasons we charge you to remove instantly; we don't give you the Liberty to think about it. You are Women . . . We therefore assign you two Places to go, either to *Wyomen* or *Shamokin*. You may go to either of these Places, and then we shall have you more under our Eye, and shall see how you behave. Don't deliberate; but remove away. . . ."

Canassatego then took the Delaware leader Sassoonan by the hair and threw him out of the council room; the other Delawares at the council followed "in great and silent grief," went to their homes and burned their cabins to signify they would never return, and moved across the Susquehanna to the Wyoming valley.

Although "no doubt there were some land speculators, and those who had conducted the business to such an issue, who enjoyed the triumph with unfeeling satisfactions" it was nevertheless "seriously apprehended that mischief would sometime" result from this "shameful imposition," and in due time grievous mischief indeed did.

But for the moment many outraged Delawares only drifted on westward all the way to the region of the upper Ohio, accompanied by their brothers the Shawnees and remnants of other dispossessed peoples, and there became the nucleus of bitter anti-English (and anti-Iroquois) feeling.

It was also in the 1740s that the Iroquois granted control of the country of the upper Ohio to the English, and several land-promotion companies were formed to subdivide tracts in this area and sell them off to settlers; English fur traders and explorers roamed as far west as the Mississippi, trading posts were established on the Ohio and the Allegheny and the Monongahela, and a settlement was planted in 1748 across the first range of the Blue Ridge mountains of Virginia. Christopher Gist, a fur trader exploring for a combine of wealthy Virginia land promoters known as the Ohio Company, was at the falls of the Ohio (present Louisville) in 1750. Some of this country, as previously noted, had been regarded by the various Indian nations for a long while as a sort of no man's land, owned by no one—not even the Iroquois. Refugees from the Iroquois and the English were plentiful in the surrounding regions. These "western" Indians encouraged French resistance to the English occupation of their country; the French informed Virginia in 1753 (via twenty-one-year old George Washington, guided to the French forest forts by Christopher Gist) that if the English wanted the Ohio country they would have to fight for it.

The immediate cause of the French and Indian War, the final struggle between France and England in the New World, was rivalry between Virginia and France for control of this upper Ohio country, specifically the key point at the forks of the Ohio where the French, at the opening of hostilities in 1754, built Fort Duquesne (now Pittsburgh). Two British forces sent against this point, Frye's in 1754 and Braddock's in 1755, were cut to pieces by the French and their Indian allies.

Perhaps the most influential of these allies were exiled Delawares from Pennsylvania (in the scalp bounties General Braddock offered his troops, the scalp of the Delaware leader Shinngass rated by far the highest price, 200 pounds, forty times the price for an ordinary French soldier's hair, and even twice as much as was offered for the scalp of the Jesuit missionary among the Ohio Indians). After Braddock's defeat the entire western border of Pennsylvania, Maryland, and Virginia was laid bare to these Delawares and their friends, who skinned it alive with pleasure. Outposts and settlements were abandoned and the English frontier recoiled, on the average, a hundred miles.

The exiled Delawares were eventually appeased by the desperate diplomacy of Conrad Weiser, Pennsylvania's wily interpreter and ambassador extraordinary to the Indians. It had been Weiser's support of shady Iroquois claims to Delaware lands that had helped to cause the trouble in the first place; it was widely believed on the frontier that land frauds such as the Long Walk were the only cause of the "great public distress" of the Indian War ("there could be no doubt but that it was occasioned by the imposition of the walk"). Now Weiser and the Pennsylvania authorities reversed their position and managed to win the cooperation of Tedyuskung, leader of the Delawares still living in Pennsylvania. (Weiser and his associate, George Croghan, Pennsylvania trader and England's deputy superintendent for Indian affairs in the northern colonies, first tried working on Tedyuskung with liquor, but although Tedyuskung got gloriously drunk with them each night he always had a clear head each morning, with his fantastic memory for each detail of dubious land deals quite unimpaired.)

In 1758, after numerous conferences, Tedyuskung and the governor of Pennsylvania sent Christian Post, a Moravian missionary, on an urgent journey to the western Indians in the vicinity of Fort Duquesne bearing Tedyuskung's plea for peace and Pennsylvania's guarantee that fraudulent land sales would be corrected. Post succeeded, not only in his long trip on foot through hostile forests, but also in winning of enough support from the western Indians to break the French alliance— the great Delaware warrior Shinngass (assured the English price on his head was withdrawn) traveled with him and did "all in his power to bring about a peace." Post returned to Easton in October, 1758, and in November of that same year Fort Duquesne fell to a new English expedition without a shot being fired.

The Walking Purchase was never re-negotiated (which would have meant the re-negotiation of a large portion of the settled parts of the province). Tedyuskung, much involved in politics (as front man for the Quaker faction in the Quakers versus Proprietors conflict, local production of the eternal Colonials versus Britishers alignment) did not insist—there is also evidence that he received a sizable "present" from Pennsylvania to drop this particular case. But Pennsylvania's efforts to rectify some of the land frauds, even to the point of sending troops to evict white settlers, helped in its small way to fire up frontier resentments that would find outlet in the American Revolution.

Various of the Indian nations who had not entirely used themselves up by 1763 were drawn into further debilitating hostilities by the grand Indian alliance on the western border under the Ottawa leader Pontiac, who fought a last-ditch campaign to retain the status of sovereign and equal associates they had held in the French beaver trade (by what right could Europeans "give away their country" ceded to England at the close of the French and Indian War?). A Delaware prophet known as Neolin ("the Enlightened") gave a message from the Master of Life to all Indians to suffer no longer "those who are come to trouble your possessions. Drive them away; wage war against them. I love them not." French traders stirred up Indian hostility toward the new English intruders and promised (vainly, of course) French support. Land speculators, with their "low,

cunning tricks" in gaining control of Indian lands, helped make
the English unpopular, and the postwar policy of the English
governor-general, the obtuse Sir Jeffery Amherst, who wrote his
field commander, "I wish to hear of no prisoners . . ." and
"Could it not be contrived to send the Small Pox among those
disaffected tribes . . .?" was even more effective in creating
anti-English feeling among the native Americans of the Lakes.
Essentially, though, Pontiac's war was in protest against British
encroachment in the country of the lower Lakes, with a string of
forts hundreds of miles west of the line of settlement.

The Seneca, traditionally the only one of the Six Nations
Iroquois with a noticeable pro-French faction, were charter
members of the Pontiac alliance, but the alliance in general was
composed not of intact nations but of bits and pieces of many
tribes; the country from Niagara to the Illinois seized by the
alliance had been open as a European frontier (French, mainly)
for more than sixty years, a process usually disastrous, as we
have seen, to Indian residents. Even so, the Pontiac war stood
off the British for nearly three years from the Illinois country,
captured nine forts, and caused far heavier losses among the
British than were suffered by the Indians, and maintained at Detroit one of the longer sieges in American history; the war was
finally settled only by bribes, conciliation (from Amherst's
successor, and unkeepable promises on the part of the English.

This was clearly a war between equals, for all that nineteenth-century historians settled on the terminology of a "Conspiracy" to describe Pontiac's war, with its implication of an
unlawful rebellion of subject peoples against their duly constituted ruling government.

The English government, in the Proclamation of 1763,
capitulated to Indian demands by closing the trans-Allegheny
country to settlement, and while few businessmen in the colonies believed the prohibition would last long there were anti-
expansionist elements in the British government that took it
seriously and meant to make it stick—the government did its
official best to make it appear to the Indians "as fixed and
immutable as the ground for which they were fighting." England
added further unkeepable promises guaranteeing to restrain
English settlement if Pontiac would demobilize his allies and
leave the restraining up to the English. Genuine efforts by some
elements in the British ministry to keep the unkeepable promises
infuriated the frontier West, which, as usual, had suffered the

most from the war, to the point that the Border became openly seditious toward the Crown and a noisy and obvious factor in the outbreak of revolution ten years later. Reported an experienced frontier official in 1765 of rebellious frontier residents who had destroyed Indian trade goods and attacked a party of his majesty's troops: ". . . from their conduct and threats since, there is reason to think they will not stop here . . ."

With a few exceptions such as the Seneca in Pontiac's war, the Iroquois, as steadily neutral as their subtle, adroit, and arrant knavery could manage, avoided serious involvement in most of the colonial wars. In 1754 at the start of the French and Indian Wars, the French made desperate efforts to win Iroquois alliance. Quebec and Louisiana were like two stones at either end of a 2,000-mile string, a string that had to make a wide, difficult detour by way of the Great Lakes around the Iroquois country. With Iroquois help, the French could have used the waterways of present New York State not only to shorten and straighten and reinforce that impossibly long front, but also to drive a wedge into the heart of the English colonies.

The Iroquois stuck to official neutrality, a neutrality that in itself was of consequence in deciding the outcome of the French and Indian War. Worse, they gave some unofficial help to the English.

An English fur trader named William Johnson had settled in the Mohawk Valley and become such a friend of the Iroquois that the English had commissioned him "Colonel of the Six Nations" in 1746. He was later placed in charge of all northern Indian affairs for the English crown, and was given so many bosomy grants of their beauteous land by the Six Nations that he became one of the largest landowners in all colonial America. The last two of his three wives were Mohawk girls, the last being Molly Brant, whose young brother, Joseph, became Johnson's special protégé. The most renowned Pine Tree of the Mohawk at the time of the French and Indian War, Hendrick (son of a Mohegan), was also related to Colonel Johnson by marriage.

In 1755, the year that Braddock's defeat threw most of the wavering Indian nations into the French and Indian War on the side of France, Colonel Johnson flung a painted war belt among the Six Nations council, in the manner of a war chief, and asked for some of their briskest men as unofficial allies. Hendrick himself volunteered, and several hundred warriors came with him. Their effect in the battle of Lake George which followed has perhaps sometimes been overestimated—there were 2,000 or 3,000 English militiamen in Colonel Johnson's command as well as the 200 or 300 brisk Iroquois—but the propaganda value of their presence was undoubtedly important.

At this battle Hendrick, then an old man of about seventy, is supposed to have made one of those battlefield remarks that have a way of reappearing down through the ages: "If they [his warriors] are to fight they are too few; if they are to die they are too many." They fought and they died. Hendrick himself was killed, and the Iroquois casualties were exceedingly heavy. But the battle was won. English America was saved, the war could go on to ultimate victory and the finish of France in the New World. Two months after the crucial Lake George action, Colonel Johnson was elevated to a baronetcy.

The finish of France in the New World was also the finish of the Iroquois as a determining weight in the balance of power, there being only one great power left—England. But the friendship of Sir William Johnson and that of his son-in-law and successor, Colonel Guy Johnson, could cut both ways, and the Iroquois (most of them) enjoyed an amiable hour of prosperity and peace after the close of the French and Indian War in 1763, in spite of continuing cessions of land to Sir William for white settlement.

Sir William placed his youthful brother-in-law Joseph Brant (who had been at Lake George as a thirteen-year-old warrior) in Moor's Indian Charity School, recently opened in Connecticut by the Reverend Eleazar Wheelock. The young man came forth with an education and a religious bent, and assisted various missionaries in revising the Mohawk prayer book and in translating the Acts of the Apostles into the Mohawk tongue.

During the French and Indian War the British Crown took exclusively unto itself the management of Indian affairs. It also reserved to itself the right to purchase or treat for Indian lands, forbidding these dealings in the future to colonies, land companies, or individuals—the United States was later to continue this same policy. In the late 1760s, after the French and Indian War, the British government secured permission from such intact Indian nations as the Iroquois, Cherokee, and Creeks, and expanded settlement once again into the Ohio country of broken tribes.

New land-promotion companies were formed, some getting

charters and grants from the British Crown, some evading the law by privately "leasing" Indian lands. One such group of speculators, the Transylvania Company (as it was later called) of North Carolina, employed a land prospector named Daniel Boone, who spent six years "in quest of the country of Kentucky" before his employer, Judge Richard Henderson, bought it for the company in 1775, paying 10,000 pounds to the Overhill Cherokees for what was at best a doubtful title.

The various Indian bands in the Ohio country, under such leaders as the Shawnee Cornstalk and the expatriate Iroquois Logan, son of a famous Iroquois sachem, made occasional resistance to the fairly frequent discourtesies of the incoming settlers, the most notorious of these being the unprovoked murder of a little group of Indian hunters and their families by a band of land jobbers led by one "Colonel" Michael Cresap. Several of the victims were relatives of Logan or of his Shawnee wife, and Logan, the "Great Mingo" (Mingo being derived from a Delaware and Shawnee term for Iroquois), led retaliatory raids against white settlers on Indian lands. Real-estate patriots howled for rescue and Lord Dunmore, governor of Virginia, defeated the "hostile" Indians in a formal war in 1774, thereby incidentally strengthening Virginia's claim to the newly opened country (as opposed to the claims of other colonies or speculators)—which may have been the real reason for Lord Dunmore's formal little war in the first place.

High prices asked by land speculators prompted poorer settlers to cross the legal line and take their chances as squatters on Indian lands. In the case of the Transylvania Company most of the incoming settlers simply ignored the company altogether and settled where they pleased, but numbers of emigrants did cross the Ohio into the territories of the broken nations northwest of the river, and the pattern for further Indian "wars" was once more established.

There is a poetic symmetry of a sort in the fact that the American Revolution, with the genesis of which the Iroquois had for so long been indirectly and directly involved, should have brought about the death of the Great League. Joseph Brant, who had become a leading young chief of the Mohawk (his proper Mohawk name was Thayendanegea), insisted on alliance with the English. Sir William had died, but the Johnson influence was still strong: Colonel Guy Johnson and the Brants, Joseph and Sir William's widow, Molly, succeeded in bringing most of the Mohawk, Cayuga, and Seneca, and some of the Onondaga, into the war on the English side.

The Tuscarora and the Oneida sided with the Colonies. Thus, finally, the Iroquois were openly divided against themselves in war. Although its shadow-play persisted, it was the end of the Great League as an operating reality.

Joseph Brant led his Mohawks in border raids that were seized upon and magnified, according to his biographer, by the "public writers," until his "name was terrible in every ear . . . associated with every thing bloody, ferocious, and hateful . . ." the idea being that "accounts of such deeds of ferocity and blood" would keep "alive the strongest feelings of indignation against the parent country, and likewise induce the people to take the field for revenge, if not driven thither by the nobler impulse of patriotism." ". . . the Monster Brandt," wrote the world-famous English poet Thomas Campbell, "with all his howling desolating band. . . ." ". . . a banditti of robbers, murderers, and traitors," stated a military proclamation of 1777 signed by Major General Benedict Arnold, in command of American forces at the time on the Mohawk River.

The most resounding of the Revolutionary War deeds attributed to the Monster Brant were the full-fledged battle of Oriskany, New York; the Wyoming, Pennsylvania, battle and "massacre"; and the Cherry Valley, New York, raid and "massacre." At Oriskany Brant and his Iroquois participated in an ambush of a vastly superior American force, both sides suffering heavily—it was the bloodiest battle of the Revolution—perhaps a hundred Iroquois warriors were killed. At Cherry Valley thirty-some civilians, including women and children, were killed (despite the efforts of Brant and the allied English commander to avoid deaths of noncombatants), and thirty or forty prisoners, mostly women and children, were taken, later to be exchanged for the families of New York loyalists being held by the Americans as hostages.

Brant was not even present at Wyoming, the Indians accompanying the British on this attack being principally Seneca, not Mohawk. A body of militia was defeated at Wyoming with immense losses, settlements in the Wyoming Valley were then looted and burned, and the settlers fled to the hills, but there was no massacre of civilians and no torture of prisoners. The Wyoming attack was not, as far as the Indian participants were concerned, prompted only by Revolutionary War considerations: the causes were deep in long-standing conflicts of the Indian-versus-Indian frontier. The Iroquois—or some Iroquois—had sold land in the valley (in 1754) to a Connecticut combine of land speculators; Delawares, and other inhabitants (including neighborhoods of Shawnees, Nanticokes, Mahicans, and Mingos), objected strenuously, among the most strenuous objectors having been Tedyuskung, who made his home in the valley. Pennsylvania complicated matters in the early 1770s by trying to drive out, with troops, settlers from Connecticut who had arrived in he wake of questionable land sales.

But in the summer of 1778 white squatters and Indian residents alike sallied forth from their principal settlements (site of the present Wilkes-Barre) to give fight to the invading British and Iroquois. They were routed, and the purely imaginary massacre that followed was given top atrocity billing in border song and story for a long time to come.

American troops in reprisal laid waste the Iroquois country (starting with Onondaga towns that had been struggling to stay neutral), as the French had done so often a hundred years before; although now there was more in the way of homes, corn (there is a tradition that sweet corn was first discovered for whites by a farmer-soldier along on this campaign), barns, farms, livestock, and orchards to lay waste. Of the thirty or so "thriving villages" of the Six Nations, only two survived by the spring of 1780.

After the war, Joseph Brant and the Tory Iroquois were given lands on the Grand River, Ontario, and the fearsome Brant returned to his occasional hobby of translating the Scriptures into Mohawk. He also made a return visit to England, where he had been at the start of the Revolution, and where he was a lion of society; he was taken up this time as an intimate friend of the Prince of Wales.

The fragments of the Six Nations who had given their loyalty to the "Yankeys" remained in New York. The Seneca, last of the Iroquois to retain their ancestral lands, sold most of these in 1797 at the bribe-riddled Treaty of Big Tree to Robert Morris of Philadelphia, who was repaid for financing the American Revolution by being handed this choice land-speculation plum. The split between the Canadian and New York Iroquois widened during the Indian wars of the Old Northwest that followed the end of the Revolutionary War, and from the early 1800s on there were two Iroquois "great council" fires, one on the Grand River in Canada and one at Onondaga in New York.

The rites commemmorating the founding of the League of the Iroquois repeat in their closing lines: "Now listen/ you who established the Great League/ Now it has become old/ Now there is nothing but wilderness/ Now you are in your graves/ you who established it/ . . . There you have taken your minds and your souls/ . . . What you established you have taken with you/ You have placed under your heads what you established, Great League."

IX

The Dispossessed

Part One: The Arrival

In 1790 the government of the brand-new United States of America succeeded in negotiating a treaty with the Creek Indians of the Southeast. This treaty was much desired to assure the peace and safety of the southern border against the machinations of the Spanish then in Louisiana and Florida. The "Case of the Creek Nation is of the highest importance," said President Washington to the Senate, and "the proposed Treaty is of great importance to the future tranquility of the State of Georgia as well as of the United States." President Washington even went so far as to say that "the fate of the Southern States . . . may principally depend on the present measures of the Union towards the Southern Indians. . . ." In the treaty the Creeks ceded certain lands north of the Thirty-first Parallel, and the United States government took its solemn oath to guarantee the remaining boundaries of the Creek nation.

In 1791 an Indian agent newly appointed by the American secretary of war traveled through the territory of the Creeks (highland Georgia and environs) and reported that it "must, in process of time, become a most delectable part of the United States."

The territory was large, some 84,000 square miles, and "remarkably healthy . . . The constant breezes, which are probably occasioned by the high hills and numerous rapid watercourses, render the heat of summer very temperate; and towards autumn they are delightfully perfumed by the ripening aromatic shrubbery, which abounds throughout the country . . . The winters are soft and mild, and the summers sweet and wholesome . . . The country possesses every species of wood and clay proper for building, and the soil and climate seem well suited to the culture of corn, wine, oil, silk, hemp, rice, wheat, tobacco, indigo, every species of fruit trees, and English grass . . ."

But this warm and charming land might give pain to a traveler at present, he reported, since its many resources and natural beauties were "only rendered unpleasant by being in possession of the jealous natives." In the 1790s that possession was still strong and secure, after generations of high living in the fast company of Europeans.

The position of the Creek confederacy in the Southeast was somewhat similar to that of the League of the Iroquois in the Northeast: a ranking Indian power strategically located in an area of conflict between European rivals.

The heart of the Creek country was near enough to early European settlements for trade but not near enough for serious trouble; the center of the Creek world was 300 miles inland from the nearest early settlements along the coast. The loose confederacy seldom acted with unity, and there was sometimes serious hostility between the two main divisions of the Upper and Lower Towns, but in general the various Creek towns threw themselves into active, on occasion enthusiastic, alliances with Europeans, more often pro-English than otherwise.

Studies of the relations with Europeans of such tribal nations as the Iroquois and Creeks and the Creeks' northern neighbors, the Cherokee, native American states that were of importance in colonial history, have at times made much of the trade motive, the obvious enrichment to be gained by any native state in cornering as much of the European trade as possible.

Motives of all kinds were no doubt present in the making of Indian alliances with Europeans and in Indian efforts to open European trade, even in Indian requests for European missionaries. But the motive most commonly advanced by Indian orators for wanting to establish relations with Europeans was that of learning the Europeans' higher wisdom. The tall and turbaned Creeks as well as the tall and strong-armed Iroquois were, by most accounts, superior people, and it seems reasonable that some of them may have been sincerely motivated by nothing more than a wish to sit at the feet of the people from heaven and learn better things.

Said Yahou-Lakee, Micco ("king" in the English interpretation) of Coweta, principal town of the Lower Creeks, when the Creeks visited James Oglethorpe on the site of Savannah in 1732: "We are come 25 days' journey, to see you . . . when I heard you were come, and that you were good men, I knew you were sent by HIM who lives in heaven, to teach us *Indians* wisdom. I therefore came down, that I might hear good things: —for I knew, that if I died in the way, I should die in doing good; and what was said, would be carried back to the nation, and our Children would reap the benefit of it. . . ."

And said, on the same occasion, the very tall old Honored Man the English called Long King: ". . . that though they [the Creeks] were poor and ignorant, HE, who had given the English breath, had given them breath also. That HE, who had made both, had given more wisdom to the white men. That they were firmly persuaded, that the GREAT POWER which dwelt in heaven, and all around, (and then he spread out his hands, and lengthened the sound of his words) and which hath given breath to all men, had sent the English thither for the instruction of them, their wives, and children. . . ."

This was the reason stated by the Creeks for giving land along the coast and the Savannah River ("where the Savannah bends like a sickle before rolling to the sea") for the founding of the colony of Georgia.

The Creeks had first come in tenuous contact with Europeans in the 1500s, with the Spanish explorations and the early Spanish and French attempts to establish beachheads along the coast of the Carolinas and Florida. In the first half of the 1600s Spanish missions prospered sporadically, between outbreaks of pestilence and uprisings of the catechumens, among the Timucua and Apalachee of northern Florida, and among the Guale of the Georgia coast: perhaps 30,000 Christian Indians were by 1635 gathered around more than forty mission stations, missions that were by report fully as rich, gracious, and idyllic as the later and better known Spanish missions of California.

It seems likely the Creeks would have known Spanish traders by this time—the Cherokee in the mountains north of them, when visited by Virginia traders in 1673, already possessed several dozen "Spanish flintlocks" as well as some Spanish wives. But English traders from Virginia must also have appeared early among the Creeks: a Creek word for white Americans was and still is *Watcina*, meaning Virginians.

After 1670, with the founding of the English colony of Carolina, more English traders and explorers probed into the Creek country toward the Spanish frontier of the Florida missions, and in 1680 Spanish missionaries responded by probing northward into the Creek country toward the English frontiers. In the military expeditions that naturally followed, a Spanish commander burned four Creek towns, including the important Lower Creek towns of Tuskegee and Coweta, and the Creeks drew back from the Spanish and resettled nearer English sources of trade.

During the next generation many Creeks, together with some neighbors known as the Yuchi, who spoke a language unrelated to any other and seemed to be absolutely devoted to fighting, happily joined English slavers in raid after raid on the Spanish missions.

The Spanish abandoned their missions on the Georgia coast before 1690 and moved what was left of the converts there to the region of St. Augustine in Florida. In 1704 the sadly tamed descendants of the athletic Apalachee were the principal victims of a crushing English-Creek (fifty English, one thousand Creeks) attack on the northern Florida missions: 6,000 head of livestock were butchered; 5,000 or more mission Indians were captured; fourteen mission Indians and three Franciscan missionaries were burned at the stake. Captives taken by the Creeks were bought by the English as slaves, and everyone was satisfied. The English wanted the slaves for the Carolina plantations, and they wanted to punish the Spanish not only for being Spanish but for providing in Florida a refuge for runaway slaves—by Spanish law, any foreign slave became free on reaching Florida.

In Florida the Spanish were attempting an experiment: a Christian Indian state. No colonies of Europeans were permitted. The tiny garrisons (thirty soldiers for the entire province) were only for protection of the missionaries and could not be used for conquest. Firearms were not allowed among the mission Indians. This last oversight made the Florida mission Indians sitting ducks for the English slavers and their Creek,

Yuchi, and occasionally Cherokee auxiliaries, whom the English not only armed but trained.

By 1745 the flourishing missions of northern Florida were in ruins, their thousands of converts wildly scattered, and immigrant bands of Yuchi and various peoples from the Lower Creek towns were moving into the country thus left vacant. They mixed with the few feral survivors of the mission Indians, with runaway slaves of all kinds that kept appearing from the colonies to the north, and with later immigrants from the Lower Creek towns. As the years passed an amalgamated society was formed by all these elements, a loose confederacy of many groups speaking many languages but with dialects of Muskogian, the great language family of the Southeast, gradually becoming the basis of the common tongue. This new-made tribe spread on southward down the peninsula of Florida and came to be known as the Seminoles (originally pronounced Seminolees), from a Creek word meaning something like "outlanders."

The English, French Protestants, and Scots who settled in the Carolinas had an unquenchable thirst for slaves. Blacks were expensive, although plentiful, but anyone could snare for free an Indian or two. Many Indian parents were anxious to have their children given an education by Europeans, and it was easy to take a child or two away and have the parents' grateful blessing into the bargain. The child or two duly sold, one later told the parents an affecting tale of a sudden illness, fatal in spite of all one could do, and with a few honest tears another child or two might be picked up on the same visit, to repeat the process.

Outright kidnaping of children was simpler and quicker, and thus deservedly more popular. The large Tuscarora confederation of North Carolina suffered from this industry for years and finally, in 1710, sent ambassadors to Pennsylvania asking for permission to emigrate there, for the safety of their children and the children yet to be born. The Pennsylvania commissioners regretted that it could not take them without a certificate of "good behavior" from the authorities who had for so long winked at the kidnaping, i.e., the Carolina government.

In September of the next year, 1711, the Tuscarora solved their dilemma with a savage attack on the North Carolina colonists, opening the war, ironically enough, with the capture and execution of John Lawson, Surveyor-General of North Carolina, the one Englishman of the region who knew the Indians best and felt the warmest affection for them. "We look upon them with disdain and scorn," he wrote, two years before his death, "and think them little better than beasts in human form; while with all our religion and education, we possess more moral deformities and vices than these people do." But ironically enough the Surveyor-General, at the very time he was writing, was selling an extensive tract of Tuscarora territory to a European promotor without mentioning the transaction to the Tuscarora—the crime for which the Tuscarora condemned him to death. Swiss and Palatine colonists were settled on the land just before the Tuscarora uprising, and suffered grievously in death and destruction therefrom.

A military expedition of colonists and Indian allies brought the Tuscarora to terms, but as the expedition felt insufficiently rewarded by North Carolina for its efforts the English commander violated the truce just made with the Tuscarora and trapped a large number who ingenuously responded to his invitation to a general friendship parley. These captives went to the slave ships and the Tuscarora went back to war, to be defeated by a second expedition the next year, 1713. By this time the Iroquois had offered the Tuscarora a new home in the Five Nations country, and the Tuscarora began migrating northward.

The numerous little coastal tribes who had joined with the Catawba, a South Carolina confederation of two fairly sizable eastern Siouan peoples, in helping the English against the Tuscarora had been promised certain trade preferences as a reward. That these trade matters were deadly serious to the Indians as indicated by the previous national disaster of the Sewee, a little coastal tribe that undertook to open direct trade relations with England and lost a large portion of its population at sea in the attempt.

However, the promise of trade preferences wasn't kept. This led to the mass murder of several hundred settlers by the little coastal tribes, culminating in the lengthy hostilities known as the Yamasee War (also known as the "Grand Conspiracy"), which was the finish of the little coastal tribes.

The defeated Yamasee, a people living just inland from the Georgia coast, emigrated to Spanish Florida and became Spanish allies (as they had been once before, until 1685, when they had migrated up from Florida to become English allies). The Catawba went back to being steadfast friends of the colonists, and being the largest nation left in the coastal region now that the Tuscarora had been dispersed, received many refugee bands from the shattered little coastal tribes. The far eastern division of the Shawnee who had lived on the Savannah River (the river's name was a variant rendition of "Shawnee"), having chased the Yuchi therefrom sometime about 1680 and performed thereby a "great service" to the new colony of South Carolina, moved out in their turn, drifting northwestward.

All these turmoils operated rather to the benefit of the Creeks, safe in their secluded hills. Their population was enhanced by refugees, and their prosperity enhanced by the unhindered spread of European trade. The Catawba declined with astounding rapidity under the onslaught of drink, disease, and attacks by any gangs of Shawnee or Iroquois or other wild Indian juvenile delinquents who happened along, and for the frightened Catawba as well as the displaced persons who had taken shelter with them there was no further escape except to the Creeks or Cherokees.

The Creeks waxed stronger, and the Carolina colonies grew in wealth and colonists. By the 1730s, upward of 200 ships a year were sailing from Charleston, "laden with the merchandize of the growth of the country . . ." rice, pitch, tar, turpentine, corn, peas, beans, beams, planks, timber, and deerskins (more than 200,000 a year). "They carry on a great trade with the Indians, from whence they get their great quantities of deer-skins, and of other wild beasts, in exchange for which they give them only lead, powder, coarse cloth, vermillion, iron, strong waters, and some other goods, by which they have a very considerable profit. The great number of slaves makes another part of the riches of this province, there being above 40,000 negroes, which are worth, one with another, 25 pounds each. . . ."

It was natural that speculators in England would look with interest on the uncolonized territory just below the Carolinas, "the Most Delightful Country of the Universe," as it was called in a prospectus of 1717. In 1732 its colonization was successfully undertaken by General James Oglethorpe, a wealthy philanthropist, who declared that "In *America* there are fertile lands sufficient to subsist all the useless poor in *England*, and distressed Protestants in Europe . . ." and established the colony of Georgia as a land of opportunity for imprisoned debtors. It would also serve as a buffer state for the rich Carolinas, and as an obstruction across that beaten path to freedom that was still being taken by so many Carolina slaves running away to Florida. Slavery was prohibited in the new colony (at first), which fit in splendidly both with Oglethorpe's humanitarian sentiments and the idea of an all-white cordon to fence in Carolina's slaves.

The proprietors of Georgia and the statesmen of England had use for the Creek Confederacy, as an instrument of trade and as a line of defense against the Spanish to the south and even more usefully against the French by now ensconced in Louisiana. The French, following their customary policy of vigorous Indian diplomacy, had kept Carolina, Virginia, and Maryland in an endemic state of alarm for thirty years, with recurring rumors of a general attack by "thousands" of French-allied warriors from the Mississippi River tribes.

Since 1703 the English had been endeavoring to form various anti-French combinations with the four great nations, Cherokee, Chickasaw, Creek, and Choctaw, located in the touchy Southeastern area between the Atlantic and the Mississippi. Their most enduring success was with the bellicose Chickasaw, who remained pro-English from first to last and were almost as valuable for the English cause in the Southeast as the Iroquois were in the Northeast.

Chickasaw country bordering on the Mississippi, the Chickasaw were a never-ending menace to French voyageurs going up and down the river; the French waged a total of five full-dress wars against them from 1736 to 1753 and were soundly whipped each time. One of these, a solid defeat administered at the Battle of Ackia (near present Tupelo, Mississippi) against the great Bienville, was called by a perceptive early chronicler one of the most decisive battles in American history, in holding the country of the Cumberland and Tennessee rivers for the English, an important factor in the outcome of the French and Indian War.

For good measure the Chickasaws also handed thundering defeats to the Creeks and Cherokees at various times in major wars, although both these nations had the Chickasaw people ridiculously outnumbered. As far as known history is concerned the Chickasaw nation, by far the smallest of the four "Civilized Tribes" of Cherokee, Chickasaw, Creek, and Choctaw, never lost a first-class battle, starting with a whirlwind attack that hastened the march of Hernando de Soto's expedition in 1541 and including the destruction of an Iroquois war party in 1732.

But the Chickasaw, although a most useful salient in French territory, were far away from the English colonies; the Choctaw (hereditary Chickasaw enemies) were generally more friendly to the French than to the English; the mighty Cherokee, in their mountain fastnesses of northern Georgia and the Carolinas, were off on the northern periphery of the theater of conflict and were inscrutable to boot—"humorsome" was young George Washington's word—in the way of mountaineers. If the Southern English colonies were to stay healthy and grow, and above all if the new colony of Georgia was to survive at all, the continued friendship of the powerful next-door neighbors, the Creeks, was essential.

The Creeks, as previously noted, were delighted to give it, and to give land as well for the establishment of the new colony. More, a dozen important men from the Creek confederacy, and a Yuchi chief, went to England in 1734 with General Oglethorpe to publicize the new colony, at which they were a huge success. Costumed in scarlet and gold and furs, wearing moccasins, and with feathers hanging in their hair, they went to court in royal six-horse coaches for a state visit with George II and his Queen Caroline. Seven Cherokees of doubtful rank had been brought to England in 1730 by a private individual, and had supposedly agreed to a "treaty" that no other Cherokees ever bothered to take seriously. Moreover, their trip had been clouded by a dubious carnival air. The Creeks, now that they too had a European colony of their own, showed their ancient Cherokee rivals how such matters should be handled, solemn protocol preceding every step. The only interruption for a commercial was a dignified address by the doyen of the Creek delegation, Tomochichi, said to be more than ninety years old, who asked "a fair and substantial basis for trade; standard weights and measures; standardized prices; favored-nation treatment; free repair of firearms; and the prohibition of rum." He also asked for missionaries. With the Indian's comical blindness to property he also observed that the English houses were built to last too long for the short lives of the people who lived in them. On their return to America the Creeks sent a bread-and-butter letter of thanks painted on the dressed robe of a young buffalo; it hung for years in the Georgia offices of the colony's Trustees.

Tomochichi's modest and sensible requests for fair trade practices could not be met, of course, even by colonial administrations genuinely willing to try (most did try to effect some kind of controlled system, but efforts and results alike were so spotty as to be all but imperceptible). The only really workable trade regulation was that enforced by the Indian towns themselves; since the Indians were ignorant of the finer trimmings of civilized misconduct, this regulation was usually confined to the immediately apparent evil of rum-running. ("Brandy goes off incomparably well," concluded a typical eighteenth-century list of "goods that are proper for the savages.")

English traders swarmed into the Creek country. They were not ideal preceptors of that higher wisdom the simple Indians sought. From the beginning the English trader—more commonly Irish or Scottish—was notorious for trickery, vices, brutality, and trouble. As it was put by Benjamin Franklin, "many quarrels and wars have arisen between the colonies and the Indian nations through the bad conduct of traders. . . ." The French, their monopoly system permitting a big-business setup with attendant close control of all trade employees, had a better record for fair dealings; but English goods were cheaper and better, to balance the score.

But good and bad, French and English, the traders brought new ideas, and, in the main, the intact nations of the Southeast prospered during the eighteenth century. They acquired live-stock, improved farming methods. Many took to European clothes and houses. The Chickasaw developed the locally fa-mous Chickasaw horse, a breedy and nervy strain apparently based on a superior stock imported from New Mexico in the Santa Fe trade—an Indian-operated trade in the 1700s. The Choctaw (in keeping with the sturdy, down to earth Choctaw character) developed the Choctaw pony, claimed by its admirers to have more bottom to the hand of height than any other horse on earth, although the better known Chickasaw horse was said by *its* admirers to have greater "powers of continuance" than any of the thirty-six "breeds" imported into Virginia before the Revolutionary War.

In the Indian towns the old ceremonies, the black drink, the busk or green corn festival, the eternal games of chunkey and ball-play, went on as ever. The red-painted war post still called men to battle, and if the battles were fought more and more in the interests of European politics—why not? Obviously the Europeans were on hand to stay, an important part of the future. All in all, that future looked good.

Not that the century was a placid one. The world crackled with change and opened many rifts of unrest. A typical report of 1753 to the governor of South Carolina gives a glimpse into the daily reality of many such problems, beginning with talk of the end of current trouble between the Creeks and Cherokees:

"... there came a Coweta Fellow [a Creek warchief] to the Warriour's Camp [Cherokee warchief] and told him that ... now it was Peace, and his People were ordered to go no more to war against the Cherokees. At which the Estertoe [a principal Lower Cherokee town, on the Tugaloo River] Warriour thanked him, and promised to send through the Nation and forbid his People to go any more to War, and withall gave the Creek Warriour Presents ... Pipes, Beads, and Tabacco in Token of Peace, and desired he should give them to his Warriours and beloved Men [chiefs and councilors] ... Again there is considerable Quantities of Rum imported by the Georgia Traders into this Nation [Cherokee], which if not hindred will certainly be of dangerous Consequence. Several of the Indians ... complain much of it, and say ... that if the Traders brings any more and offer it to Saile, they will certainly seize it themselves for they believe the Georgia Traders to be Rogues ... I hear likewise that the Emperour [principal chief of the Cherokees] has sold to the Government of Virginia a large Quantity of Land which they say was their Northward hunting Grounds, and that the Emperour had not Power of himself to dispose of any Land ... The Indians of this Nation grumble very much as I hear. The Emperour, they say, besides the Price of the Land received rich Presents of the [Virginia] Government ... The Little Carpenter [regarded as second chief, at that time, of the Cherokees] is come in, and brought in 3 or four Cagges of Spirits ... There are two French Men at Chote [Echota, an important Overhills Cherokee town just west of what is now Great Smoky Mountains National Park] and Toquo [a neighboring Overhills community; both these towns were on what is now called the Little Tennessee River]. The one is dangerous to be in this Nation. He talks the Tongue, goes to War with them, and in Time may conduct them to his own Nation. ..."

The Cherokees—or some Cherokees—ceded a large amount of territory to the English two years later, in 1755, but only a few years after that full-scale war flared up between them and the English, its climax the capture of Fort Loudon by the Indians in 1760 (on which occasion the bantamweight chief Attakullaculla, called by the English the Little Carpenter, ransomed a captured English friend by giving his own gun and the clothes off his back to the warrior who had made the capture). The Creeks in 1752 had been within a hair's breadth of a major war with the Savannah colony, brought on by the intrigues of a South

Carolinian, the Reverend Thomas Bosomworth, who had married a highborn Creek woman and attempted to use her political position as a lever to extort money from the Georgia English.

A great many Europeans married into the Indian nations of the Southeast, principally Englishmen everywhere except in the western Choctaw towns, which were strongly pro-French. Traders who were reasonably honorable or able, or both, won the absolute trust of the Indians, married into leading families, amassed political power as well as wealth; and the rise of an oligarchy composed in large part of such families created an invisible revolution in both Creek and Cherokee societies, and to a lesser extent among the Choctaw. But it was an aristocracy based not on descent but on power—the distinction is important. As said the great Choctaw leader, Pushmataha, "I had no father, I had no mother. The lightning rent the living oak, and Pushmataha sprang forth."

The half-European princes who evolved lived by Indian customs but their ambitions were frequently European; many became personally wealthy in livestock, slaves, and goods; some became petty tyrants, manipulating Indian law for their own purposes; some became tribal statesmen of the first rank, of the greatest value to their nations, and of note in American history.

The ascendancy of the chief was a phenomenon that accompanied European invasion everywhere. The Europeans needed some one responsible official to deal with in Indian negotiations, and if no real chief existed, as was usually the case, they invented one. Sometimes the fictitious power thus invested in these "treaty chiefs" was accepted by the other Indians and became actual. More often it led to discord.

Among the Creeks, favored by their key location (". . . they have the French and Spaniards to apply to in Case you won't supply them," as a Cherokee reminded the English in the 1750s), personal diplomacy became a constant necessity, with a consequent accretion of real authority around those Beloved Men who were of influence with Europeans. This emergence of strong political leaders brought on a struggle for ultimate power between various "chiefs" of the two divisions of the Upper and Lower Creek towns, which at times had an effect on the twists and turns of Indian politics throughout the whole region. To a lesser degree, a conflict came into being between full-blood conservative tribal members and mixed-blood progressives, particularly over the incessant question of land cessions to the whites. Similar problems, but with variations, beset the Cherokee and Choctaw towns. The Chickasaw, with their smaller population unified by unswerving loyalty to the English and persistent wars with the French, were perhaps a little less disturbed by such dissensions.

The French, English, and Spanish were constantly busy with agitation for this or that course of Indian policy, and with wrangle-making bribes and payoffs to the chiefs. However, the overriding exigencies of trade and empire demanded that the European colonies do their utmost to sustain "their" Indians, and so through it all the four nations not only survived but flourished. In the interaction of these many forces the New World took shape in the delectable land of the Creeks and their neighbors.

The horse-trading of the Peace of Paris at the close of the French and Indian War in 1763 brought vast changes to the Southeast. French Louisiana was divided between England and Spain: New Orleans and the Louisiana territory west of the Mississippi to Spain, and the Louisiana country east of the Mississippi to England. Florida went (temporarily) from Spanish to English control. French settlers here and there up and down the Mississippi crossed to the west side of the river to avoid English jurisdiction, and crowds of Indians went with them: Kaskaskias and Peorias from the Illinois country, Alibamus, Biloxis, ancient refugee Apalachees, and many others from the smaller nations along the lower Mississippi. Natchez remained all but deserted, as it had been since 1729, soaked with blood and bitterness, overgrown by the fragrant southern forest, until the first English plantations appeared—one of the first English houses was built on the sacred mound of the old Natchez White Apple village.

Spain was rejuvenated as a colonizing power under the aroused administration of the Bourbon Charles II, and brought more prosperity to Louisiana than the region had known under France. The Indian nations were skillfully wooed, maneuvered, and deployed, and became more valuable than ever to the colonial contenders.

Majority parties in the Creeks and Cherokees stood loyal to England in the Revolutionary War, although the Little Carpenter raised 500 gun-men for service on the American side. Spain regained Florida at the end of the American Revolution, and carried forward an accelerated and increasingly successful campaign to win Indian friends, helped by Indian reaction to the upsurge in American frontiering that came with the defeat of the Lords across the Sea. Important pro-Spanish factions appeared among the Creeks and Shawnees and even among the Cherokees and Chickasaws; and for that matter even among some of the American frontier settlers in the south and west.

But a new and weaker king came to the throne of Spain, and the brief, brilliant Spanish renaissance was over. Napoleon set foot on his star-wagon; France took Louisiana back and sold it to the new United States. Spain faded into empty Florida. The few Spaniards left there, mechanically pursuing small-time intrigues with the Seminoles and the Lower Creeks, were no longer El Greco knights or even Velasquez dwarfs but desolate, sun-dazzled, spiritually enchained little figures out of Goya.

In the 1790s, in South America, the last of the Conquistadors rode away fittingly enough on the last gallop of the champion chimera, with the failure of two final Spanish expeditions sent to hunt again through Patagonia for the City of Caesars. The pursuit of this glittering mirage had been carried on by some twenty formal expeditions and many more private explorations for some 250 years.

With the influx of new settlement into the southern states (colonies no longer) the world of change spun still faster for the Civilized Tribes, who adopted more and more of the ways, fashions, and ideas of their white neighbors. A traveler of 1818 reported that 2,000 spinning wheels and several hundred looms had been made and distributed in the Choctaw nation, and that the Cherokee council had promised a set of tools to every young man who would become acquainted with some "mechanical art . . . Rapidly are they coming into habits of industry."

Among those who did not change to European clothes, quite a few took to wearing a long shirt in the manner of a flowing tunic (a "sweep," the Creeks called it in English) which, with the customary headband or turban, was curiously like a costume prevalent in ancient Mexico. Cherokee women, however, were said to dress "almost universally" in European style, "in gowns manufactured by themselves, from cotton which they have raised on their own plantations."

Several years before that time the Cherokee reportedly possessed more than a dozen grist mills, several saw mills, a powder mill, plows, wagons, spinning wheels and looms, thousands of cattle and horses and hogs and sheep, and, wry finishing touch of white acculturation, 538 black slaves. The Cherokee built roads, schools, churches, and adopted a system of government modeled on that of the United States; and a middle-aged Cherokee silversmith perfected a method of writing the Cherokee language. His name was Sikwayi, in English usually spelled Sequoya. He developed a set of eighty-six letters, each standing for a syllabic sound, making Cherokee the first of the hundreds of American Indian languages to be put in writing via a really workable alphabet (more properly, syllabary) of its own. The system was made public in the early 1820s, and, said a missionary, "In a little over a year, thousands of hitherto illiterate Cherokees were able to read and write their own language, teaching each other in cabins or by the roadside. The whole nation became an academy. . . ." Everyone learned, and learned with fantastic speed, the syllabary providing a system of phonetic spelling reduced to utmost simplicity. Contemporary records attest to the fact that a week or so, or even three or four days, was enough time for the average Cherokee to learn to read and write with Sequoya's letters. This mass rush of instant learning appears to be unique in history.

The result of all this enthusiastic adoption of new things and new ways was a movement toward an actual new "third world" created of the Indian world and the European world combined, since these various modernized Indian peoples retained basic Indian ideas and beliefs as well as language. In return for the world of saws and mills they offered a world of the Indian spirit, a world in which religion was practiced with each planted grain of corn, poetry sung with every sunrise.

The Cherokee nation established a Cherokee government printing office, and in the course of years millions of pages were printed in Sequoya's characters, ranging from religious tracts and Bible translations and Cherokee history to newspapers, legal documents, a very popular annual almanac, and even fiction written by Cherokee novelists. Medicine men readily adopted the written language for recording rituals and sacred lore, to the dismay of missionaries and the delight of later ethnologists. Sequoya became famous among both Indians and whites, and the Cherokee nation presented him with an annual pension, the first literary pension in the United States. But he pursued success in Indian terms, not the terms of the white world, devoting himself to labors toward universal communication and universal peace among Indian peoples. "His air," wrote John Howard Payne in an interview, "was altogether what we picture to ourselves of an old Greek philosopher." It is noteworthy that even before he had perfected his syllabary he associated himself with the Cherokee conservatives, distrustful of all the radical changes and newfangled innovations, who migrated west of the Mississippi—by the 1820s perhaps a fourth of all the Cherokee people, some 6,000 persons, had moved to the west, mainly Arkansas.

Among the Creeks, Alexander McGillivray, son of a trader-father and a half-French Creek mother (a famous beauty named Sehoy, of aristocratic lineage from both parents), had become undisputed leader of Creeks and Seminoles as well, with 10,000 warriors, so they said, under his command; at the time of his death in 1793 he was one of the wealthiest men in the entire South. In the early 1790s he was superintendent-general of the Creeks for Spain, agent to the Creeks for the United States, and a partner in a trading business importing $200,000 worth of goods a year. The United States paid him $1200 a year for acting as agent, and Spain $3500 a year for being superintendent-general. When occasion warranted he wore either his Spanish military uniform, or his British colonel's uniform, or the uniform of an American brigadier-general presented him by Washington. He negotiated in 1790, amid much fanfare, the aforementioned treaty with the new American government in which the United States, in return for concessions, gave its solemn guarantee to the adjusted boundaries of the Creek nation. McGillivray's principal interest in this treaty seems to have been provisions giving him duty-free trade goods, and thus a monopoly of the Creek trade; he encountered, however, a great deal of trouble over the treaty from the Spanish and the pro-Spanish Creeks, and the provisions ceding lands to the United States were not carried out until a half dozen years later, after his death.

Part Two: The Removal

Pro- and anti-American parties in the Creek towns, aided and abetted by American and English politicians, squatters, vagabonds, and traders, split the nation into open civil strife at the time of the War of 1812. An anti-American war party under the half-Scot chief Weatherford descended on Fort Mims, about forty miles north of present Mobile, and massacred most of the 350 or so people there—troops of the Mississippi militia and families of settlers with their slaves. The principal pro-American leader William MacIntosh, son of a Scots trader and a Creek mother, who had climbed ruthlessly to the position of head chief of the Lower Creek towns, replied by leading his followers in a massacre of some 200 people of the anti-American party.

Another mixed-blood war captain, Menewa, celebrated for the exploits of his wild and reckless youth when his name had been Hothlepoya (Crazy War Hunter), was one of the ranking commanders of the "Red Sticks," or anti-American faction. The so-called Creek War, in the closing days of the War of 1812, was in at least some part a personal struggle between Menewa and William MacIntosh.

Surrounding states organized militia to march against the

anti-American Creeks, and five separate volunteer generals took the field, one of these being an obscure backwoods politician from west Tennessee named Andrew Jackson. Tennessee's Governor Blount "bawled for permission to exterminate the Creeks," in General Jackson's words, and General Jackson's command won the race to exterminate a pretty fair passel of them in the battle of Horseshoe Bend, Alabama, which polished off the Creek War.

Menewa had dug in some 900 Red Stick warriors on a tongue of land surrounded by the Tallapoosa River, except for a narrow neck fortified by a breastwork of logs. A number of women and children were in a village at the river's edge. Indian auxiliaries with General Jackson's Tennessee militiamen were several hundred Creeks under William McIntosh and Timpoochee Barnard, chief of the Yuchi then united with the Creeks, and perhaps 600 Cherokees—and with them a long young white man who had been living with the Cherokee up in Tennessee, Sam Houston. Before the battle started, General Jackson's Indian guides and "spies" were both able to place his 2,000 men so as to surround the Red Stick position on both sides of the river. The artillery—two cannon—were placed to enfilade the breastwork at a range of eighty yards, and opened the engagement with a two-hour barrage. The Cherokee and American Creeks then attacked repeatedly from across the river, burning the Red Stick village in one of the first attacks.

When it was clear the Indian auxiliaries would not be able to overcome the Red Sticks alone, the main body of militia stormed the breastwork. The remaining Red Sticks were driven to a thicket in the center of the peninsula and the cannon brought up to finish them off in another barrage of several hours. At length the battered thicket was fired and the few survivors shot down as the flames drove them out.

More than 300 women and children were taken prisoner, all captured by the Indian auxiliaries. Of the 900 Red Stick soldiers, only seventy were left alive, and of the seventy only one escaped unwounded—he jumped into the river and escaped at the first cannon-shot. General Jackson lost forty-nine killed (twenty-three of these Indian auxiliaries) and 154 wounded (forty-seven Indians). One of the American casualties was Sam Houston, whose wounds from this battle plagued him the rest of his life.

The Red Stick chief Menewa fell, hit seven times by rifle fire.

He recovered consciousness sometime after the battle was over, shot a soldier passing nearby and was in return shot through the head, the bullet going in one side of his face and out the other and tearing away several teeth. He came to again in the night, crawled to the river, found a canoe, and floated downstream to a swamp where other Red Stick wives and children had remained hidden. By the time his wounds were healed the Creek War was long ended, and the Red Sticks' land had been opened to white settlement. Menewa's store, 1,000 head of cattle, and hundreds of horses and hogs, at his town of Okfuskee, had vanished: William MacIntosh had won the contest between them, for the time being. But Menewa was still alive, and still very rugged, and as far as he was concerned the polls were not yet closed.

The brilliant victory brought General Jackson wide recognition and an appointment as major-general in the regular army, which opened the way for his triumph in the battle of New Orleans the following winter that made him a national hero.

Anti-American Creeks escaped to Florida in such numbers that the Seminole population was doubled or tripled, and mounting disturbances there brought an invasion of Spanish Florida in 1817 by General Jackson that in turn caused enfeebled Spain to cede Florida to the United States.

This was the end of Spain in the Southeast, the end of all foreign menace in the Southeast. And finally the Indian nations of the Southeast were not needed any more.

They were no longer of use as buffer states; there were no rival European nations left to buff against. White settlers were all over the back country; Indian trade and Indian middlemen east of the Mississippi were of no further importance—and the easy win in the Creek War revealed that even the strongest Indian nations were too uncertain about fighting to resist anything the whites might decide to demand. The spirit of the frontier—clear the Indians out—had already outgrown opposition to become the principal vector of force behind American policy when in 1828 it took over the government completely with the election of Andrew Jackson, the embodiment of the frontier spirit, as President.

The idea of uprooting all eastern Indian tribes and resettling them in the "wilderness" west of the Mississippi seems to have entered official government councils with Thomas Jefferson at the time of the Louisiana Purchase, as an idea that would offer some use for the newly acquired great West along with conveniently freeing eastern Indian lands for white immigrants. A widespread idea of the "nomadic" character of Indians—utterly erroneous in the case of the settled woodland peoples of the East—led to a widespread notion that Indians would troop away westward with "cheerful acquiescence" if tempted with the western lure of new and better "hunting grounds." Perhaps this arose from the fact, most striking to property-conscious whites, that Indian villages were sometimes moved now and then rather casually—although always within a homeland district, which may have escaped notice. Or perhaps the error was founded less on superficial ethnography than on self-interest. Jefferson wrote quite frankly in 1803 that the primary purpose in keeping agents among the Indians was to obtain their land, and indicated that he was not particular about the methods used in accomplishing same: one method he encouraged was for government traders to entice influential Indians into running up debts that could only be paid by land cessions, a method followed ever since (and from long before Jefferson's time, for that matter) with splendid success.

The defensive colonial device of using Indian nations as buffer states extended into Jefferson's proposal of "colonies" of eastern Indians in the new West of the Louisiana Purchase, and the formal suggestion of Great Britain, in the peace negotiations after the War of 1812, for a neutral belt of Indian nations along the Canadian border in the interest of Canadian national security. However, Thomas Jefferson and Andrew Jackson and some other would-be removers in between also alleged national security (this time, though, requiring white populations along the frontiers) as one pretext for Indian removal, Jefferson instancing the menace of Napoleon in 1803 and Jackson the menace of England in 1815. But the removal policies did not decline with the decline of these stated emergencies. Nor, after obtaining Indian lands along frontiers and along routes of communication to frontiers—such as the famous Natchez Trace—did these removers become any less insistent on seizing Indian lands in the interior, where purported national security could scarcely offer any validity at all as an issue.

Perhaps the cruelest jest in the long farce of removal pretexts was the frequent official assertion that dispossessed Indians were in fact only being "rescued" from the destructive vices of civilization by being separated from the propinquity of said vices as well as, incidentally, from their lands. This claim was often stated in public by Andrew Jackson and such of his cohorts as his latter-day secretary of war Lewis Cass, who having enriched himself on Indian land in Michigan Territory may be presumed to know whereof he spoke when he referred to Indian removal as "this gigantic plan of public charity."

It is impossible, however, to reconcile this ostensible official concern for Indian welfare with the official actions—from the same officials—bringing immediate and wholesale demoralization, destruction and disaster to the Indian nations. Since actions are presumed to speak louder than words, these words, no matter how piously declaimed, must be adjudged deliberately false, and the reigning motive of removal was that ". . . we may secure a part or maybe getting the whole territory . . ." as Jackson wrote privately to a secretary of war in the midst of such pious public statements.

Nevertheless, some commentators sufficiently unsympathetic to the Indian way of life have defended this *pro forma* excuse, arguing that the Indian nations either had to surrender to advancing "civilization," disband their tribal societies and turn fully into imitation white men, or inevitably perish—from which dilemma they could only be saved by surrendering their lands and getting far out of civilization's way, as in removal.

Indian leaders in the southeast argued that peaceful coexistence with the whites was perfectly possible and that they should be allowed to remain on a portion of their native lands, where the new third world they were building was predominantly friendly to whites and white ways. White emigrants into the Indian nations could be accepted and adopted, as could black emigrants, even runaway slaves—or even runaway white slaves (indentured servants). The hospitable Indians would even accept escapees from debtors' prison, and in some instances go so far as to pay their debts and give them land. One argument used for driving the Choctaw nation out of its Mississippi homeland was, as stated by Mississippi Senator Thomas B. Reed, that the Choctaws must not be permitted to "convert their country into an asylum for vagabond debtors." White Indians found one ironclad prohibition, though, in the midst of their vagabond freedom: they could not sell the land that might be assigned for their use. Herein lay the crucial Indian/white difference.

Agitators for removal made much of the "hunter state" of the Indian world as against the settled agriculture, the thrifty farms, of the whites. This was an enormous fallacy—but Indian men did seem to make an art of loafing, leaving much of the crop-work (and crop ownership) to the women, and above all there was that free and easy feeling about land use, that apparent lack of interest in private property: how could people so indifferent to property be anything other than savages? But as we have seen, agriculture was an ancient institution among the woodland Indians in general, and particularly successful in the southeast, where a numerous population had sustained itself for century upon century while the bounteous land, like an eternal bride, remained not only bounteous but beautiful. The tobacco and cotton plantations of the whites, on the other hand, had in a brief time laid the land along the coastal plains of the South in ruin, dead-red, eroded, "galled and butchered," and were now reaching for the fertile, virgin soils of inland Indian country.

Pressure from a crowded population of "land-hungry frontiersmen" was even more of a fiction in the South than in the North—even unto the 1840s open lands of the South were twice those of the North, and the white population only half as great. Precisely the opposite argument, in fact, was raised at the time: that Indian lands were needed to "encourage immigration." The white pressure that did exist, even unto the farther southern frontier—Mississippi—was from the start pressure from planters, some small "yeoman" planters, many large prosperous operators eager to move bag and baggage, slaves, "mansion house" and all, from the worn-out littoral to the rich Indian-preserved interior.

"Civilization" in white terms meant many other things as well: worshiping the white god, wearing "civilized" clothes, following "civilized" marriage and family customs, but one point never omitted was that of learning to hold private property, abandoning the "savage" concept of communal ownership of land.

In general the people of the Indian nations were bitterly reluctant to accept this change—to destroy tribal ownership of land was to destroy the basic tribal fabric—and many finally preferred to give up their native land and move to a raw new country where they might still be permitted to preserve such sacred institutions.

The stubborn refusal to allow an occupant of Indian lands to transfer his holdings without the consent of the full nation, the total interdiction against private buying and selling of land, excited an understandable fury among the dominant faction of white Americans, where profit and speculation were their sacred institutions.

Speculation in Indian lands was for generations the prime business of the American frontier. It was intolerable that it should be even hindered, let alone halted, just when King Cotton was hitting his stride with some of the highest, widest, and hansomest profits in agricultural history—totally intolerable that "a few naked wandering barbarians should stay the march of cultivation and improvement" as it had been put so neatly by Lewis Cass, a virtuoso of the cliché in an age jampacked with competition.

Speculation in Indian lands was not only the principal frontier vocation, it was the principal motive behind white frontier politics both North and South from the very inception of the United States, as a Congressional grant of Indian lands in 1787 to the Scioto Land Company bears witness. The grant was made without consulting the Indians concerned and led to years of war and political wrangling exercising a profound effect on an entire generation of frontier history. On the southern frontier land developers and plantation owners along with land specu- lators were the men of power, and it was their influence the public officials responded to with Indian removal. Being human (all too), the politicians did now and then look to their own pockets in the midst of so many massive Indian land grabs— General Jackson himself took flyers in real estate promotion, and gave tips to pals ("I have no doubt . . . that in ten years it will gain 1000 per cent")—but the evidence does not support any supposition that personal gain constituted an important motive for the principal federal officials involved. Political gain, yes; and Jackson particularly, who could seldom see any other side to an issue than his own, regarded Indian removal as an absolute political necessity. His influential constituents said so, and, besides, he heartily agreed with them.

Vast Indian land cessions, in fact the vastest, were made in the southeast before 1820. Although Andrew Jackson served as commissioner in making some of these immense deals and gained a reputation thereby as an "unscrupulous Indian baiter" willing to use intimidation, deceit, and secret bribes, the basic policy of Indian land acquisition preceded his administration and most of the Indian land of the southeast was obtained well before he became president.

The Choctaw confederacy, for example, ceded some two and

a half million acres to the United States in 1801, five million more during the next four years, and under Pushmataha, principal leader of the pro-American faction, sent several hundred Choctaw volunteers to assist the Americans against the Red Stick Creeks in 1812, and a thousand to join Andrew Jackson at the battle of New Orleans. At this famous battle Pushmataha was a brigadier general (commissioned by the United States government) and had personally raised the majority of the Choctaw contingent from the district known as the Six Towns, where his influence was strongest; during the battle the Choctaws carried out a successful flanking movement against seasoned British troops that won high praise from General Jackson. The Mississippi territorial legislature not only voted thanks to Pushmataha and his people for these various favors but also voted gifts of a "Rifle gun" and a blanket to Pushmataha and certain of his warriors as concrete evidence of the territory's gratitude.

In the warm air of camaraderie created by all this the leaders of the Choctaw nation appeared to hope that they could now live on the remainder of their lands side by side with friendly Americans—indeed they were given an official promise to this effect by the United States government in 1816. But in 1817 Mississippi was made a state, political ambitions were engendered thereby that cooled marvelously the air, and in 1820 General Jackson (wearing his treaty commissioner's hat) extracted from his recent comrades in arms, by the uncomradely but customary means of bullying, bribes, lies, and guile, an additional five million acres or so, creating such jubilation among Mississippi politicians that their new state capital was baptized Jackson in the general's honor. The Choctaw people were granted a much larger tract of land in exchange, but west of the Mississippi, with the explicit agreement that while those who wished to emigrate to this new land were most warmly invited to do so, still those who wished to remain in their reduced homeland would be equally free to do so.

Under preceding administrations, from Jefferson's onward, the notion of Indian removal had been predicated on voluntary Indian agreement, but voluntary removal simply did not work. The total number of Choctaws who removed under the foregoing agreement was, over a period of ten years, either eight or fifteen or fifty persons, depending on which report you believe (out of a total population of nearly 18,000).

The great change brought by the Jackson administration was a policy of remove or else. One of its first pieces of business was passage of what was known as the Indian Removal bill, which became law in the spring of 1830 after Congressional debate of exceptionally hot-tempered style, even for those hot-tempered Congressional times; it also became law by the narrowest of margins (102 to 97 in the House), reflecting the considerable size of the opposition. Two opposition measures, likewise defeated by close votes, called for a guarantee of Indian sovereignty over all lands then in Indian possession, and that Indian lands could be acquired only by a treaty negotiated and accepted by both sides, a revealing comment on the custom of forced "treaties" even under the "moderate" policy of the past.

The Indian Removal bill did not authorize enforced removal of any Indians, but merely gave the President power to initiate land exchanges with Indian nations residing within the states or territories. However, force was ultimately necessary—indirect and unacknowledged at first; at length, under any pretext no matter how thin, all too open and direct—since otherwise the nations would not remove, regardless of persuasion, harrassment, or short-of-gunpoint coercion.

The states principally involved, Georgia, Mississippi (created mainly from Choctaw and Chickasaw country), and Alabama (created in 1819 mainly from Creek and Cherokee country), passed legislation outlawing tribal governments and placing the Indian nations under the jurisdiction of state laws. This was in violation of securities granted the Indian nations by treaties with the United States, which had promised protection under federal jurisdiction, rather as army posts or other areas of federal rule are immune from state or local interference, and the Indians appealed to the federal government for the protection promised. General Jackson and his secretary of war told them the federal government was unable, alas, to comply with its treaty pledges. This was a threat Jackson had been making for years in "negotiating" with Indians—either see it our way or the government may find itself unable to "restrain" local politicians or squatters.

Now the threat was reality. State law prevailing within the Indian nations, the Indian lands were wide open for trespass by anyone, including liquor dealers. This too was in violation of federal law as well as tribal regulations, but again General Jackson and his secretary of war said they simply could not enforce the federal law. Bootleggers crowded into the nations, grog shops bloomed like the blossoms of spring, and large numbers of Indian citizens, dispirited, not surprisingly, with the course of events, went on a drunk that didn't quit until they found themselves either removed or dead.

Actions could now be brought against Indians in the state courts and their goods attached for debt by sheriffs and constables. State laws were enacted prohibiting a court from accepting the testimony of an Indian against a white man, so that a claim, no matter how fraudulent, brought by a white man against an Indian could not be legally contested.

In spite of all these persuasions the Indians remained immovable until inducements were added giving allotments of land, to be owned white style, to any and all individual Indians who still insisted on remaining behind when the nations should at last remove. One could, in other words, give up his tribal life in order to keep his home. This offer had a special appeal for the well-to-do, frequently half-bloods, who occupied improved property of potential value, but it also appealed to a great many full-bloods who intended to take allotments by the whole district and maintain themselves as Indian communities regardless. Government officials, though, were sometimes able to circumvent the allotment provisions fairly easily (when the provisions were not abrogated outright by the government, once removal was under way), while allotments that actually did manage to get allotted turned into the finest bargain opportunities for wholesale fraud in all the variegated removal swindles, white squatters and land speculators moving in by the swarm to strip the Indians of their properties by trickery, liquor, or force (Choctaw "floats"—allotment rights—figured in deals within deals for years). Large numbers of Indians, many of whom had been comfortable or even prosperous, took to the woods or the swamps in flight, divested of their possessions and driven from their homes. Occasionally they were divested of the clothes they were wearing by frolicking white men armed with writs or rifles.

Drunkenness, panic, privation, and starvation brought a terrifying boom in Indian-versus-Indian violence. Crimes of violence by whites against Indians could not ordinarily be brought to court and so are not recorded, but under the circumstances there may have been more than a few. A renowned Chickasaw warrior and councilor, Emubby, who had served with General Jackson in several campaigns, was killed rather casually by a white man named Jones; the incident got into the papers because of Emubby's prominence: ". . . he had been murdered without any provocation . . . When Jones presented his rifle at him, he leaped from his horse, opened his breast, and said, 'Shoot! Emubby is not afraid to die.' The wretch did shoot and the Indian fell. . . ."

Appeal after appeal to General Jackson and his successive secretaries of war brought the fixed reply that the federal government was not able to restrain either the squatters or the state legislatures, even though it had admittedly bound itself to do so by definite guaranties in previous treaties. All appeals were referred to a statement of General Jackson's that the matter was not one of right but of remedy.

The remedy, in the opinion of General Jackson and his faction, was removal of the Indian nations to the West, where they would be given land grants that would endure, said government spokesmen, "while the trees grow, or the streams run."

It is important to note that this extremist attitude in favor of removal at all cost was by no means unanimous throughout the United States (as the close votes on the Removal bill had made clear)—or even throughout the South. There was dissent and plenty of it, some of obvious political origin but some evidently proceeding from a plain and simple feeling of honest morality. In the deepest South a newspaper editorialized that "the day of retribution may come" to "visit on some future generations the despotism which the present has exercised over the hapless and helpless Indian." And said a Mississippi planter, "it involves the faith of this whole nation . . . it involves the principle of *right and of justice. . . .*" The people concerned with honesty, though, scaled lighter in political weight and, when the chips were down, produced considerably less moxie than the people moved by profit, power, and the rabid ethnocentricity of the period: declaimed a Mississippian, arguing that all Indians were inferior to whites, ". . . we have had plenty of Indians in Natchez, and can you show me one who has been civilized by being brought among us?"

Choctaw leaders accepted a provisional treaty of removal in 1830, after a battle-royal of behind-the-scenes infighting among and between Indians and whites, missionaries, politicians, traders, half-bloods, full-bloods, chiefs and would-be chiefs of the three major Choctaw divisions, and "captains" and subcaptains of the various tribal districts. Greenwood LeFlore (Le Fleur as processed through frontier Anglo-Saxon ears), nephew of the great Pushmataha and previously an arch-enemy of removal, maneuvered himself into a winning position as chief of the whole nation (an office never before existing among the Choctaw) and principal architect of a removal agreement, earning thereby the "handsome" plantation in Mississippi promised him by the War Department for his cooperation. Other chiefs, captains, and subcaptains received extra land grants of considerable value, cash annuities, and government financed education for their children at private schools and universities in Georgia, Ohio, and Virginia.

The tangled Choctaw political scene had included organized persecution, occasionally even public whippings, of pro-removal people, and a marvelously intricate role for religion, mission variety. The spontaneous combustion of the Great Revival at the end of 1828 created an alignment of "hot-gospel" Choctaw preachers and anti-removal half-bloods, with a motto of "Join the church and keep your country." This movement helped convince Jackson and others that the "common Indians" could be brought to favor removal if not for the baleful influence of half-blood leaders and empire-building missionaries; in truth, however, the anti-removal majority and the pro-removal minority cut through every sort of category, and some of the missionaries were decidedly pro-removal, seeing a better chance for empire-building in the West than in the East, some even dreaming of an all-Indian state (under missionary supervision). But others of the older missionaries, particularly of denominations long established in the Choctaw nation and with an empire already there begun, were said to be a crucial power in the councils and inflexibly opposed to removal. Perhaps for this reason all missionaries were barred by the secretary of war from the meeting ground when the removal treaty was presented to the Choctaws, the secretary's excuse being that their presence was "improper"—the presumably more proper presence of liquor dealers, whores, and gamblers was permitted, however, "under the assumed protection of the United States government."

In spite of such good-time prospects, something less than 6,000 Choctaws gathered for the treaty "negotiations"; many of these walked out on the meeting before the treaty was concluded, and most of the Choctaw people over the nation as a whole, says the best evidence, opposed the removal agreement (for at this moment the nation was "literally in mourning") that was finally signed. But when new chiefs were elected to protest the treaty President Jackson refused to recognize them; they were forced to resign and return their offices to the pro-treaty chiefs they had just defeated. The United States Senate added to the confusion by refusing to ratify a "whereas" in the treaty wherein the President avowed the United States could not protect the Choctaws in previous treaty rights against the state of Mississippi. Difficulties were ironed out, more or less, and in November of 1831 the first official contingent of Choctaw exiles, some 4,000 people, started for the new lands they had selected in what were then the western regions of Arkansas Territory. Other parties followed the same winter.

It happened to be an unusually hard winter. The Mississippi at Memphis was so choked with ice as to be impassable for days at a time to flatboats and most steamboats. There was zero weather and heavy snow in the Great Arkansas Swamp through which the emigrants, some of whom had left their homes destitute, barefoot, and nearly naked, had to struggle. The hardships were incredible, the sufferings extreme, the all too frequent deaths most distressing, say the monotonous reports. Some residents along the migration routes sold food to the starving people at exorbitant prices, squeezing out bits of cash or property that had been smuggled past the deputies and constables of Mississippi; other residents along the route gave freely what they could spare of help and supplies and scoured the country to raise more, and wrote indignant letters to their government at Washington, pointing out particularly the animal miseries of old people and young children, and questioning in particular such details as the government policy of issuing one blanket per family to the emigrants instead of one blanket per person.

Matters were greatly complicated by lack of funds. Congress had appropriated money to pay the expenses of Indian removal (rather, Congress had advanced the money, eventually to be paid by the Indians themselves from the public sale of their lands); these funds were to be disbursed through white agents and contractors who signed to "conduct" so many emigrants to the new Indian Territory for so much a head and of course expected to make a profit; some of these contracts, at least, were given as political plums. Major Francis W. Armstrong, of General Jackson's home town of Nashville, Tennessee, was appointed Choctaw Agent in the autumn of 1831 and left Washington in

November with $50,000 in cash to meet the expenses of that first desperate winter of Choctaw removal. The Choctaws and their conductors were obliged to make their chaotic journey without funds, however, since Major Armstrong didn't arrive with the money in Arkansas until the end of February. He had spent the worst of the winter at home in Nashville because it had been too cold, he said, for him to travel. Major Armstrong was put in sole charge of the rest of the Choctaw removal in the following years and was the subject of angry albeit futile complaints from the young Army officers sent along with the exiles to see that treaty provisions were fulfilled. (Major Armstrong forced the Indians to leave pet dogs behind on steamboated segments of the trips, and for some odd reason refused to allow his crowded passengers to go ashore at woodyard stops to relieve themselves in the privacy of bushes but stationed men with clubs on the bank to keep the passengers aboard, a situation neatly creating the "disgusting sight of a vessel loaded with human beings . . . leaving their evacuations in every direction through the whole range of the Cabins and deck. . . .")

And so removal began. It went on for years, and it developed that the experiences of this first winter were the easiest of all—with the single exception of the Chickasaw migration; the Chickasaws couldn't be entirely defeated, even in this.

Cholera appeared in the summer of 1831, centering around Vicksburg, and came back each summer until 1836, setting up a belt of death that halted most traffic but through which the armies of Indian exiles had to be moved, the federal government and the states concerned being inflexibly opposed to any delays.

Pressures and harassments notwithstanding, the removed people left their homeland with the greatest reluctance. They bore, be it remembered, the weight of time on their eyes; they were the descendants of the temple mound people of this region of long before, and perhaps of the burial mound people of still longer before. They had lived for countless generations in this sweet and luxuriant land, and did not share the white frontiersman's restless passion to be always moving on. Likewise the whites could not comprehend the Indians' emotional attachment to a particular piece of the earth. "They cannot appreciate the feelings of a man that loves his country," so Washington Irving quoted the Creek chief Eneah Emathla. Some watching whites were moved and some amused when departing Indians went about touching leaves, trees, rocks, and streams in farewell.

The conspiratorial treaty politics left an added legacy of

distress by setting friend against friend and family against family, so that some groups went west carrying dissension with them and feuded angrily for years in their new country, sometimes in all but open civil war.

Hostilities had the best of growing seasons as the educated and the ignorant, the good and the bad, those used to high-style gracious living and those from huts in the wildest depths of the forest were herded together, reduced to the lowest common denominator by corn likker, degradation, and despair, and driven like cattle, like wild animals, so they said: "We were drove off like wolves . . . and our peoples' feet were bleeding with long marches . . . We are men . . . we have women and children, and why should we come like wild horses?"

Rotten boats were occasionally hired for river passages, being cheap, but being rotten as well as overcrowded they were unmanageable and occasionally sank, with most melancholy loss of life (to use the favorite term of the time). A number of emigrant parties lost many of their people, and aged and children first, always, from deaths on the march.

White heroes of removal were not plenty (in another favorite word of the time) but there were a few, principally young officers such as Lieutenant Joseph W. Harris of New Hampshire, an 1825 graduate of West Point, who wrote in 1834 in the midst of a cholera epidemic among his Cherokee emigrants (he had cholera himself at the time), "I am not much of a physician and feel that I am but a poor prop for these unfortunates to rest upon—but I have done and will do my best." Lieutenant Harris's best, in the whole story, was resplendent with humanity and valor, although not always according to the regulations. He kept on giving his best in the work of Indian removal until his death in 1837 at the age of thirty-two and may have received his Order of Merit from Higher Headquarters later.

The Chickasaw made removal treaties in 1832 and 1834, insisting on provisions by which the government would sell their lands and hold the money for their use, and by which a commission of Chickasaw councilors would pass on the competency of any tribal member making a private sale of property. Even with these safeguards the Chickasaws did not escape unscathed. But as a whole the nation appears to have gotten away with more wealth and in better order than any of the others.

When they moved west in 1837 they took along thousands of

their horses, and got a fair percentage of them through—gangs of white horse-thieves hanging on the flanks of Indian emigrant parties that had any horses at all were the chief livestock menace; the swamps were next. Their horse herds made for slow travel, and the superintendent in charge of Chickasaw removal wrote: "The Chickasaws have an immense quantity of baggage. A great many of them have fine wagons and teams. They have also some four or five thousand ponies. I have used all the influence that I had to get them to sell off their horses, but they would about as lieve part with their lives as part with a horse."

In 1821 and 1823, some years before the push for removal, William MacIntosh of the Creeks had made treaties with citizens of Georgia ceding 15,000,000 acres of Creek land. He had been supported in these treaties by twelve other Creek chiefs under his control, but opposed by thirty-six chiefs representing nine-tenths of the Creek nation. MacIntosh was in the pay of the Georgia commissioners, and in 1825, said emoluments being fattened, MacIntosh and his followers signed a treaty ceding the remaining Creek land—10,000,000 acres—to Georgia. These treaties were not only in violation of Creek custom—"Among the Creeks there is no such thing as selling or ceding of lands. 'It is for me, for thee, and for all'. . . ." but the MacIntosh treaties were also in violation of a specific Creek law that provided the death penalty for any Creek who sold land without the consent of the entire nation in council. Formal sentence was passed on MacIntosh after the signing of the 1825 treaty, and on the morning of May Day, 1825, a party of Creek soldiers went to his house and shot him to death, and his son-in-law as well for good measure. The appointed executioner who killed William McIntosh was Menewa, the ex-Red Stick commander.

The illegal treaty of 1825 was annulled, and the following year Menewa went to Washington and signed a new treaty, supposedly securing the Creeks in the possession of their remaining territory, and promising his loyalty henceforth to the United States.

Governor George M. Troup of Georgia, William MacIntosh's cousin, was enraged by his murder and became one of the leaders in the subsequent large-scale and extralegal campaign to drive the Creeks out of the country regardless of treaty rights.

By 1831 this campaign had progressed to the point that the Creeks were reeling from waves of white squatters, land speculators, and bootleggers who were invading their country under the protection of Georgia and Alabama state laws. There were 1,500 such intruders in December, 1831, according to a protest made by Eneah Micco, principal chief of the Lower Towns. They included "horsethieves and other criminals" and also included men of heretofore respectable position.

The President and his secretary of war openly stated that they had no intention of trying to keep the government's treaty promises and insisted on a treaty of removal to the West as the Creeks' only hope of relief. In 1832 (two months short of the one hundredth anniversary of their first cordial treaties with Ogle-thorpe) the Creeks, driven to desperation, finally accepted a removal treaty, with the provision that white intruders were to be removed from their lands for five years while the tribe prepared to depart.

But the treaty also contained a provision giving each tribal member the right to sell his individual selection (or remain on it, if he wished), each sale to be protected from fraud by being subject to approval by the President. Under the new state laws this could mean that the land and property of any individual Creek were now legally up for grabs to the first white man who might present a claim for it, no matter how plainly fraudulent—unless the federal government enforced these protective provisions it had just agreed to.

General Jackson and his secretary of war did not enforce these provisions—while enforcing with rigor the provisions of cession by the Creeks. If the Creeks had been troubled before by intruders, now they were being overwhelmed.

Six months after the signing of the 1832 treaty, the Creek council said in a memorial to the secretary of war: "Instead of our situation being relieved as was anticipated, we are distressed in a ten fold manner—we are surrounded by the whites with their fields and fences, our lives are in jeopardy, we are daily threatened . . . We have for the last six months lived in fear, yet we have borne it with patience, believing our father, the President, would comply on his part with what he had pledged himself to do."

The Creeks were driven into the forests and swamps, their crops and homes were seized; many were reduced to starvation. Said newspaper stories of the time: "To see a whole people destitute of food—the incessant cry of the emaciated creatures being *bread! bread!* is beyond description distressing. The existence of many of the Indians is prolonged by eating roots and the bark of trees . . . nothing that can afford nourishment is rejected however offensive it may be. . . ." "They beg their food from door to door . . . it is really painful to see the wretched creatures wandering about the streets, haggard and naked. . . ."

White speculators had their capital in Columbus, Georgia, across the Chattahoochee River from Coweta, the capital of the Lower Creeks. A leading business, of course, was fraudulent certification of land titles, but a thriving sideline was grabbing title to the property of Creeks who died, since according to state laws only a white man could administer the estate of a deceased Indian. These businesses sometimes assumed the rather jolly air of a mass sports event, and while a United States marshal said they attracted "some of the most lawless and uncouth men I have ever seen" they also involved "men of every degree," as another investigator reported. A special agent wrote to the President: "A greater mass of corruption perhaps, has never been congregated in any part of the world. . . ."

The capital town of the Lower Creeks eventually taken over by these whites became the present Phenix City, Alabama, famous in recent years as the "most lawless" town in the country.

Legal aspects of the situation received much national attention. Georgia claimed technical justification for its aggressive actions by pointing to the Compact of 1802 between Georgia and the federal government in which the United States agreed to extinguish at its own expense, "as early as the same can be peaceably obtained, on reasonable terms," Indian title to lands within the state of Georgia, although the phrase applying this agreement to "all" Indian lands within the state was an ambiguous rider pinned peculiarly to an Article dealing with lands already at that time ceded by the Creek nation—and although the agreement as thus constituted was in direct contradiction to previous treaties between the United States and the Indian nations, such as the Creek treaty of 1790 in which the "United States solemnly guarantee to the Creek Nation, all their lands within the limits of the United States. . . ."

General Jackson's pronouncements repeatedly invoked the principle of states' rights, insisting, in contravention of nearly all previous Indian treaties, that the states must have jurisdiction over the Indian people within their borders ("*Sir, the sovereignty of the States must be preserved*"), although on other occasions —occasions dealing with other than Indian matters—he announced himself stoutly opposed to that principle ("Our Union, it must be preserved"). He repeatedly asserted that the federal government was simply too feeble to enforce federal law in the states of Georgia, Alabama, and Mississippi, but in the contemporary action of South Carolina in nullifying the federal tariff ("This abominable doctrine that strikes at the root of our Government and the social compact, and reduces every thing to anarchy, must be met and put down or our union is gone, and our liberties with it forever"), General Jackson reacted with his customary flaming vigor (". . . treasonable conduct . . . positive treason . . . I will meet it at the threshold, and have the leaders arrested and arraigned for treason"), sent General Winfield Scott and heavy troop reinforcements into South Carolina and a naval force to anchor off Charleston, and avowed that if need be he would arrest and execute not only John C. Calhoun, leader of the South Carolina nullifiers, but every member of Congress from South Carolina who had taken part in the nullification proceedings. Years before becoming President, General Jackson wrote hotly to President Monroe that if he had been in command of the eastern division of the army when the Hartford convention met (in 1814, to present a doctrine of states' rights) he would have brought its members to court-martial, even though the rebellious New England states were at that moment so strong and the federal government so weak that, as said a Boston newspaper, "it would have been the last act of his life. . . ."

Obviously General Jackson's administration only countenanced the open defiance of Georgia, Alabama, and Mississippi because in this case it was in sympathy with their objective—clear the Indians out. That objective was as much the baby of General Jackson's administration as of the various states involved, but the independent extralegal actions of the states were necessary both in pressuring the Indians and in furnishing an excuse of sorts to the administration, which after all needed some kind of pretext in asking the nation to wink at violations of the national word of honor and the President's oath of office.

Some aspects of the situation are of more than ordinary historical interest. For one example among many: an Alabama citizen named Hardeman Owen, a tough boy noted for his exceptional thoroughness in beating up Indians when chasing them off their lands, made an unsuccessful attempt to murder a Unites States marshal. Troops from Fort Mitchell, Alabama, ran Owen down and killed him when he fired upon them. An

Alabama grand jury then returned indictments against the soldier who shot Owen, the other soldiers and officers present, and the United States marshal who had called out the troops; and a court order was issued attaching the person of the army major commanding Fort Mitchell. Alabama's basic objection was to the molestation of white intruders in the Creek country by federal officers, some of the officers having made a nuisance of themselves by individual efforts to enforce the protective provisions of the recent treaty.

General Jackson sent Francis Scott Key to Alabama to calm the situation, and Alabama at length dropped the indictments in return for certain federal concessions: the terms are less important than the fact of the capitulation by which the star-spangled banner refrained for the nonce from waving over the state of Alabama. Such incidents, and encouragement from the highest government sources for the idea that in Indian matters state jurisdiction took precedence over the national jurisdiction guaranteed by treaty, very possibly added a few states' rights vineyards to the grapes of wrath that would be harvested a generation later in the Civil War.

In spite of pressures and harrassments the Creeks delayed their departure for four of the five years allowed them by the removal treaty, being unable to decide on the specific lands of destination. But in 1836, when a resistance movement against their sufferings spread among some of the Creek people under the general leadership of Eneah Emathla, the secretary of war immediately gave orders to the military to remove the whole tribe at once as a military measure. An army was ordered into Alabama, to "inaugurate an operation of war" against the Creeks, "subdue them and remove them to the West."

Menewa, true to his promise of loyalty, joined this army in rounding up the insubmissive Creeks, as did nearly 2,000 other Creek warriors.

The captured "hostiles" were started west in a double-file procession, manacled and chained together, eighty-four-year-old Eneah Emathla among them: ". . . I was informed . . . that he never uttered a complaint," said a reporter in describing the first leg of the march.

And so the nations departed. The Cherokee resisted with incredible tenacity in the face of concerted oppression that mounted year by year. (It had its entertaining incidents—the extraordinary Cherokee leader John Ross, evicted from his beautiful Georgia mansion and living in a dirt-floored log cabin across the line in Tennessee, received as a guest there John Howard Payne, the author of "Home, Sweet Home." The Georgia State Guard happened to cross the border at that time to abduct Ross and kidnaped Payne too as a suspicious character; he was held in a Georgia jail for twelve days.) The Cherokee nation pushed a legal fight until it won its case in the United States Supreme Court, Chief Justice John Marshall delivering with the opinion a blazing denunciation of the wrongs perpetrated by the state of Georgia upon the Indians, and finding the acts of the state of Georgia unconstitutional and in violation of solemn treaty rights. The decision was wildly celebrated by the Cherokees.

However, President Jackson refused to execute the decision of the court.

The state of Georgia also flatly refused to carry out the court's order.

From the beginning the Cherokees (and the uneasy moderate segment of the American public) had been assured by the Jackson administration that removal by force was the furthest thing from the administration's thoughts ("NOTHING OF A COMPULSORY COURSE, TO EFFECT THE REMOVAL OF THE UNFORTUNATE RACE OF PEOPLE, EVER HAS BEEN THOUGHT OF BY THE PRESIDENT"); in repeated treaties the Cherokee had been assured by the most solemn guarantees that lands not ceded would be secured to them "forever" and "the authority and power of the United States were solemnly pledged to protect the Cherokees from intrusions and trespasses" and "from all encroachments upon the lands not ceded." From George Washington onward ("Rest, therefore, on the United States, as your great security against all injury") principal officials of the United States had personally reiterated these pledges and the government had regarded these treaties as the law of the land that could not be annulled, so stated President Washington, by a later President.

All these assurances were systematically and openly broken, although never openly repealed, and still the Cherokees hung on ("It is impossible to conceive of a community more miserable, more wretched," said Henry Clay, adding that even "the lot of the African slave is . . . far preferable" since the "interest of the master prompts him to protect his slave"), and still John Ross sought patiently for legal means to save his people, suggesting in

1835 that the Georgia Compact dilemma (illegal or not) could be solved by the United States buying the land of the Cherokees in Georgia and granting them "a sufficient portion of it in fee simple" and also giving Cherokee people full citizenship to protect them against discriminatory state laws. But the Jackson administration insisted on nothing less than total removal, and in that same year (1835) obtained an openly fraudulent removal treaty (backed by ninety-seven Cherokee delegates against 1,269 opposed, supported by "300 to 500 men, women and children out of a total population of about 17,000"), railroaded it through Senate ratification (by one vote), and the following year for fear that this Treaty of New Echota "would not be carried out by the mass of the Cherokee nation" assigned a military force to the Cherokee country with orders "to reduce the Cherokees to submission if they should begin any hostilities." Two years later, at expiration of the time allowed by this false treaty for the Cherokees to get out, the Eastern Division of the U.S. Army was ordered to the Cherokee country "with a view to the fulfillment of the treaty" and the Cherokees were gathered in concentration camps from which at last they departed westward on their own—with the exception of a few hundred who hid in the mountains of North Carolina, where their descendants still live.

The Cherokee people, having resisted longest, suffered the most, nearly one-fourth of their entire population dying along the western route of "The Trail of Tears." Furious division went west with them, resulting eventually in the murder of the leaders of the splinter party that had agreed to the removal treaty (at the report of the first of these murders General Jackson, enraged, announced that "The Government of the U.S. has promised them protection, *it will perform its obligations* to a tittle"). But even in this most earnestly intended instance the government did not perform its obligations, and occasionally violent feuding went on for years. The banished nations were greeted in their new homes by another government benefit prepared (so said its preparers) for them—the Indian Trade and Intercourse Act of 1834, designed to protect the Indians by a strict supervision of traders permitted among them. But the act (said its Indian critics) made of the isolated Indian peoples a captive market to be delivered as a political plum to politically deserving whites or politically influential trading companies (no Indians as traders need apply).

In the face of all these difficulties the difficult work of

Cherokee national reconstruction was patiently, if painfully, carried on—it was begun under two elected leaders, a president of the eastern and a president of the western Cherokees, the latter office being filled by the universally respected peacemaker, Sequoya.

General Jackson's superintendent of Indian affairs stated bluntly ten years later that this gunpoint-removal of the Cherokees "proceeded from a fraudulent act, connived at by the Executive of the United States," and since the superintendent had been involved in a good deal of the preliminary conniving himself (he was fired early in the game), and was a religious man, he spoke of divine justice, of atonement, of apprehension of a day of retribution . . . "What an accumulation of wrath!"

An effort was made to include the Seminoles of Florida in the general removal from the Southeast—this brought on war, which lasted until 1842 (officially, but simmered along unofficially for quite a while longer) and cost the lives of 1,500 American troops and the stupendous (for the times) total of $20,000,000 in military expenses. Its most publicized feature was the capture of the young Seminole chief Osceola by the American General T. S. Jesup, who had been temporarily relieved of his regular duties as Quartermaster General to try his hand in this nasty little southern war. When the much-wanted Osceola at last set up a conference under a flag of truce, General Jesup sent an officer to the appointed place, seven or eight miles from St. Augustine, and while the conference was going on had the conference ground quietly surrounded by a body of troops, who at a signal made Osceola and his followers (thirteen other chiefs, ninety-five persons altogether) prisoners.

This means of capturing prisoners was used repeatedly by General Jesup against the Seminoles—once with the inadvertent help of a well-intentioned Cherokee peace delegation. The shocked Cherokee chief John Ross wrote to the secretary of war, "I do hereby most solemnly protest against this unprecedented violation of that sacred rule . . . of treating with all due respect those who had ever presented themselves under a flag of truce." But, unfortunately, it was the only means that worked. Wrote General Jesup, "No Seminole proves false to his country, nor has a single instance ever occurred of a first rate warrior having surrendered." Osceola died in a military prison three months after his capture. But the war went on.

Seminole women (as some of the women of the Creek

resistance had done) killed their small children to free themselves to fight beside their men, and the war developed into a game of hide-and-seek in the swamps of the Florida Everglades; obviously it could never be won by either side.

Peace was finally offered on quite honorable terms worked out by Army Colonel Ethan Allen Hitchcock, who during the war wrote, "Five years ago I came [to Florida] as a volunteer, willingly making every effort in my power to be of service in punishing as I thought, the Indians. I now come, with the persuasion that the Indians have been wronged. . . ." However, resistance to peace on the part of influential whites (there was some feeling that determination of owners to recapture fugitive slaves living among the Indians was one of the subsurface causes of the Seminole War) caused the war to drag on and on, successive generals announcing light at the end of the tunnel (in effect) that was never quite reached, Army losses continually higher than Indian losses, "humanitarians in the North" setting up a "howl of protest" over such military expedients as the use of fighting bloodhounds, until at last in 1842 ("after some hesitation lest the honor of the country and the gallantry of the army be compromised") President Tyler simply declared the war at an end; in 1858, after further scattered and rather futile military operations, an army colonel declared it at an end for the second time. Most of the Seminole people moved west to Indian Territory, but several bands remained in the region of the Everglades and are still there, having resisted, down through the decades, inducements to emigrate such as had seldom been offered to any other tribe.

The old ever-faithful American allies among the Creeks and Cherokees, who had made possible the Horseshoe Bend victory that had launched General Jackson's national career, came off no better in the removal than the ancient hostiles. Ex-hostiles such as Menewa, who had become steadfast American allies (Menewa adopted the army uniform of an American general), fared no better than the implacable anti-Americans who remained implacable. Several hundred Creeks, including Major David Moniac, a Creek graduate of West Point, volunteered for service with General Jesup against the Seminoles, with the understanding that their families would be protected until their service ended and they could emigrate to the West—but while they were fighting in Florida, citizen companies from Alabama and Georgia overpowered the defenseless federal agents assigned to protect the waiting families, seized whatever property was available, made a number of the families prisoners on various pretexts, and clubbed to death with their muskets a ninety-year-old Creek who foolishly tried to prevent the rape of a fifteen-year-old girl. The Creek volunteers returned from Florida to find the last of their possessions gone, and their families already started West.

The terms of the Creek treaty permitted individual Creeks to elect to stay in their native land (if they were willing to brave continued persecution by the States) and quite a few meant to do so. However, these provisions were abrogated by the government, and all the Creeks were forced to leave, including Menewa, who had received a personal promise from high authority to the contrary. On the night before he left he went back to his town of Okfuskee and spent the night alone. He said to an old white friend the next morning, "Last evening I saw the sun set for the last time, and its light shine upon the tree tops, and the land, and the water, that I am never to look upon again." Then he walked away. He was an old man, and had been many times wounded. But those who believe that Indians don't cry haven't looked over the official reports of the Great Removal.

And so the nations were gone from their warm and charming land. But something more had happened than the mere uprooting of 50,000 or so people from their homes. The frontier spirit had clearly paraded the black horse of its evils coupled to the white horse of its virtues. Natural resources—in this case, people—had been merrily exploited in an open conspiracy involving the President of the United States and large portions of the population. Young America, in short, had been told a most effective bedtime story of crime without punishment. The nation, in short, had been exposed to quite a spectacle of dirty business, and it is reasonable to suppose the sinuous folds of the young American mind had picked up a new wrinkle or two.

X

The Image Makers

The statement has been made in foregoing chapters that the Indian story is of considerable historical importance, important to the history of both the Old World and the New. It might be well to pause and examine this point.

Christopher Columbus' first reports of the New World and its people were contained in two letters written in February and early March, 1493, in the course of the return trip from his voyage of discovery. On his way to Spain he touched at Lisbon, where he was given a state welcome and a royal cross-questioning by King John of Portugal, and the two letters were transferred to a courier to be rushed overland to the Spanish court, then at Barcelona.

A foreign agent in Spain had the gist of the first letter on the way to his employer, the Duke of Ferrara, by March 8, and by April the letter was in print in the Italian states.

The second letter was put into Latin and sent in April to Rome, where it also was rushed into print, in at least eight different editions, and by June was being published in a verse paraphrase of sixty-eight metrical stanzas for the common reader. This also went through a number of popular editions. It was sung in the streets—the news magazine for the illiterate—while learned scholars met to discuss the official Latin text.

Ego statim atque ad mare illud perueni prima insula quosdam Indos violenter arripui: "As soon as I had landed on the first island that I encountered in that sea I had several Indians taken prisoner. . . ." and the people of the New World were thenceforward Indians. Columbus had brought back six of those *quosdam Indos* with him; they were a "well-formed people and of fair stature . . . very comely" and created a sensation, especially among the Spanish ladies.

In Spain, holiday was declared wherever Columbus appeared. Business was suspended, bells were rung, the streets were illuminated with torches; and the Admiral of the Ocean Fleet, as he styled himself in the signature of the famous second letter, was granted the extravagant honor of being seated in the presence of the sovereigns; and his Indians ranked about his throne like wonder-bringing cherubim.

For wonders had arrived in the Old World from the New. From that time on, in a fairly real sense, they never ceased. Much has been said about the prodigious changes brought to the New World by the Old. Something needs to be said about the changes, perhaps less immediately obvious but no less prodigiously effective, brought to the Old World by the New.

Within a matter of weeks after Columbus' return Portugal was locked in a diplomatic struggle with Spain over rights to the new discovery. Portugal was the great seafaring nation, and the efforts of four kings, Prince Henry the Navigator, and many brave fleets had brought her various guarantees in the realms of the farther oceans that were supported by three papal bulls and the formal Treaty of Alcaçovas. (Columbus dodged trouble over this treaty and gained time for Spain by discreetly falsifying, at first, the latitudes of his discoveries.)

But the Discovery was Spain's. And the newly elected Pope, the licentious Alexander VI, was also Spain's—he was the Borgia Pope (father of Cesare and Lucrezia Borgia), and the Borgias were an Aragonese family.

By the end of summer, 1493, new papal bulls were cutting the ground from under Portugal's position, and Columbus was on his way back to the Indies with a hastily assembled expedition to seal the Spanish claim with commerce and colonies.

The Pope established a line 100 leagues west and south of the Azores, perserving everything beyond for Spain and confining

Portugal, in effect, to Africa. This line (enforceable, of course, by the fact that any Christian who disregarded it might be excommunicated) was too drastic to be realistic, and was revised more to Portugal's liking the following year by the Treaty of Tordesillas, agreements between Spain and Portugal "for the Partition of the Ocean Sea" that moved the Pope's line considerably farther west, to 370 leagues west of the Cape Verdes; thus, as it turned out, giving Portugal the hump of Brazil.

This, the first of many American matters to occupy the chief statesmen of Europe, was America's entrance on the stage of world history. The script thereafter was ceaselessly and sometimes hectically rewritten to give the newcomer an ever-growing role. The New World and its innocent people so easy to plunder went straight to the Old World's heart and became a star overnight.

Rich America played a part of many sides in the Reformation: in the expansion of the fur trade so important in the lives of England, France, and Russia; in the rise of English and Dutch mercantilism; and even in the foundation of modern international law, as laid down in the lectures of the learned Francisco de Vitoria at Salamanca in 1539 and the great debate between Las Casas and Sepúlveda at Valladolid in 1550, establishing the legal principle that any foreign people should be dealt with honorably even though they might differ in religion and culture from one's own people. All of Europe's plots and counterplots and the process of Europe's ideas after 1492 were in some wise altered and shifted by the New World and the peculiar character of the New World people.

The point to be emphasized here is that the role of the New World's people was not entirely passive. It was active in the sense that they so often welcomed their conquerors, nursed fledgling European colonies, and to such a degree helped the European conquerors in their business of conquering that, as has been previously noticed, the conquest of the New World was principally one of European-directed Indians conquering other Indians. In this respect the peculiar character of the American Indians was of some import in world affairs almost from the moment of Discovery.

In other obvious direct respects the impact of the world of the American Indians worked fairly rapid changes in the Old World: with the spread to Europe of such Indian crops and products as corn, tomatoes, rubber, white potatoes, tobacco (in all its Indian usages—pipe, cigar, cigarette, snuff, and chaw), a long list of medicinal drugs including quinine, and such essentials to modern living as peanuts, popcorn, and chewing gum. Chocolate, brought from Mexico, became so popular in Spain that church services were disturbed by worshipers sipping the chocolate they had brought along to Mass.

Some authorities believe that an influential item of another kind, syphilis, first came to Europe from the New World. Other authorities believe the opposite, that it was one more in the catalogue of disastrous diseases brought by the people from heaven from the Old World to the New. A recent theory suggests neither view (or both) may be right, and that with the rise anywhere of urban environment venereal syphilis may have developed from various other manifestations of treponemal infection (there are many) that were worldwide from the earliest times, a "dialogue" between such a "biological gradient" and its changing environment "that has run continuously since the Old Stone Age."

Indirectly, the peculiar character of the American Indians became profoundly operative upon the European soul, an operation which, in all its ramifications, still goes on.

The smell of gold and spice and azure jewels filled the nostrils of the first Spaniards in the New World, but, curiously, it is the childlikeness of the lovely people that most fills the first Spanish reports. They could almost imagine that the beautiful (and nude) island girls who came forth dancing and singing to welcome them at Caribbean towns were the fabled dryads, the wood nymphs sung by ancient poets, so said (in 1530) Peter Martyr of Anghiera, first historian of the New World. Simple childlikeness was transfigured into unearthly poetry when the Spaniards broke their way into the marvel-filled civilizations of the mainland, and the Maya sang of their coming (in the Book of the Jaguar Priest of Tizimin): "They are agitated by the drums. The Bat is awakened by the drums. The four Bacabs ride to earth on the back of a green rainbow. One by one the stars fall. . . ." The bearded invaders thrust with their swords and were pierced in return by words: "The warrior will employ his prowess on nobody. When they are taught about the abundant life, they will have compassion on the fields. They will have compassion on the mountains. . . ."

The childlikeness and the poetry seized on the imagination of Europe and remained a living force long after the plunging swords had crumbled into rust.

"I wolde think their life moste happye of all men, if they might therwith enjoye their aunciente libertie," to quote the language of Peter Martyr's first English translantion (1555), speaking of the Indians. "Emonge these simple sowles, a fewe clothes serue the naked: weightes and measures are not needefull to such as can not skyll of crafte and deceyte and haue not the vse of pestiferous monye . . . So that if we shall not be ashamed to confesse the truthe, they seeme to lyue in that goulden worlde of the whiche owlde wryters speake so much: wherein men lyued simply and innocentlye without inforcement of lawes, without quarrelingue Iudges and libelles, contente onely to satisfie nature. . . ."

The famous *Essays* of Michel Eyquem de Montaigne, published in France in the 1580s, contain in Chapter 30, Book I, a widely quoted dissertation on "the new world we have lately discovered. . . ." This essay was first translated into English in 1603, entitled "Of the Canniballes," and made to read in part as follows:

"I find (as farre as I have beene informed) there is nothing in that nation (the New World), that is either barbarous or savage, unlesse men call that barbarisme which is not common to them. . . ." Wishing that the Greek philosophers could have known of this people so "neere their originall naturalitie" and of a genuineness "so pure and simple" as an example of the ideal state sought by Plato, "It is a nation, would I answer Plato, that hath no kinde of traffike, no knowledge of Letters, no intelligence of numbers, no name of magistrate [which, incidentally, Montaigne was], nor of politike superioritie; no use of service, of riches or of povertie; no contracts, no successions, no partitions, no occupation but idle; no respect of kindred, but common, no apparell but naturall, no manuring of lands, no use of wine, corne, or mettle. The very words that import lying, falsehood, treason, dissimulations, covetousness, envie, detraction, and pardon, were never heard of amongst them."

Montaigne learned of Indians ("They spend the whole day in dancing") through reading the travel books of his time, talking with returned explorers, and questioning (through a highly unsatisfactory interpreter) three Indians who visited France in the time of Charles IX (1560-1574). These last were able to explain to him something of the common Indian custom of dividing the people of a town into moieties, two groups or societies with special and separate duties, such as the Summer and Winter people of various North American tribes. The

Indians were struck by the two opposing moieties they seemed to see in the towns of Europe: "They had perceived, there were men amongst us full gorged with all sorts of commodities, and others which hunger-starved, and bare with need and povertie, begged at their gates: and found it strange, these moyties so needy could endure such an injustice, and they tooke not the others by the throte, or set fire on their house. . . ."

Shakespeare, in writing *The Tempest*, took for the play's framework the Bermuda shipwreck of some Virginia-bound colonists in 1609; twisted the monster Caliban's name from an anagram of *canibal*; and in Act II, scene 1, gave the honest old Counselor Gonzalo this celebrated speech on the ideal commonwealth:

> I' the commonwealth I would by contraries
> Execute all things; for no kind of traffic
> Would I admit; no name of magistrate;
> Letters should not be known; riches, poverty,
> And use of service, none; contract, succession,
> Bourn, bound of land, tilth, vineyard, none;
> No use of metal, corn, or wine, or oil;
> No occupation; all men idle, all;
> And women too, but innocent and pure;
> No sovereignty . . .
> All things in common nature should produce
> Without sweat or endeavour: treason, felony,
> Sword, pike, knife, gun, or need of any engine,
> Would I not have; but nature should bring forth
> Of its own kind, all foison, all abundance,
> To feed my innocent people . . .
> I would with such perfection govern, sir,
> To excel the golden age.

Maybe Alcaeus could be paraphrased to say words change the world, not kings nor empty wars. Anyway, these same thoughts, multiplied in countless other minds (Sir Thomas More found details for his *Utopia* from listening in Antwerp to sailors talk of the South American Indian world) and filtered through the centuries, were in 1750 distilled by Jean Jacques Rousseau into his vision of the blessed state of the natural man, the noble savage, pure, simple, and above all free. "Man is born free, and everywhere he is in chains"—and the words almost literally undermined the thrones of Europe and sent them crashing into chaos with the French Revolution and the powder train of subsequent convulsions.

Rousseau's spiritual heirs pursued the glorious vision of natural freedom, idealistic liberty pure and simple, in the face of such worthy defenders of the traditional European faith as Goethe, who said in 1827: "Freedom is an odd thing, and every man has enough of it, if he can only satisfy himself . . . The citizen is as free as the nobleman, when he restrains himself within the limits which God appointed by placing him in that rank . . . Freedom consists not in refusing to recognize anything above us, but in respecting something which is above us. . . ." Hegel took his stand on the same dictum; but the dictum went the way of the thrones and it too was overthrown in the leveling sweep of the idea of liberty pure and simple, a sweep in which, as has been seen, the image of the American Indian was not entirely absent.

A divergent line of European thought gradually turned to the problem of property and, clearly not altogether unaware of the ghosts of Montaigne's philosophical Indian tourists, proceeded to take some of the propertied moiety by the throte and set fire on their house.

A pioneer American anthropologist, Lewis Henry Morgan, was an authoritative student of the Iroquois and unbefuddled with naive notions of an Indian golden world, but the peculiar character of Indian society, the propertyless society of the "ancient gentes," nevertheless gave him a message he felt was important. He wrote in his most ambitious book, *Ancient Society*: "Since the advent of civilization, the outgrowth of property has been so immense . . . that it has become, on the part of the people, an unmanageable power. The human mind stands bewildered in the presence of its own creation . . . A mere property career is not the final destiny of mankind, if progress is to be the law of the future as it has been of the past . . . The dissolution of society bids fair to become the termination of a career of which property is the end and aim; because such a career contains the elements of self-destruction. Democracy in government, brotherhood in society, equality in rights and privileges, and universal education, foreshadow the next higher plane of society to which experience, intelligence, and knowledge are steadily tending. It will be a revival, in a higher form, of the liberty, equality and fraternity of the ancient gentes. . . ."

This was published in 1877, in time to be of use to Karl Marx and Friedrich Engels as a corroboration of Marx's materialistic theory of history. Marx was particularly impressed by Morgan's basic point, that primitive society is organized on a structure of family relationships while modern society is based on property relationships, and made notes for a book on Morgan's researches but did not live to write it. Engels did so, in his *The Origin of the Family, Private Property, and the State in the Light of the Researches of Lewis Henry Morgan,* published in 1884, in which he described the notion he had gathered of the Indian way of life with a restatement of the old familiar pattern: "And a wonderful constitution it is . . . in all its childlike simplicity! No soldiers, no gendarmes or police, no nobles, kings, regents, prefects, no judges, no prisons, no lawsuits . . . There cannot be any poor or needy—the communal household and the gens [related family groups] know their responsibilities towards the old, the sick, and those disabled in war. All are equal and free—the women included . . . And what men and women such a society breeds is proved by the admiration inspired in all white people who have come into contact with unspoiled Indians, by the personal dignity, uprightness, strength of character, and courage of these barbarians. . . ."

The Indian image operative on the European soul was often a far cry from Indian reality. The European soul thus altered often achieved an even farther cry from its expressed aim. But the fact remains that an undeniable reality, the peculiar character of the American Indians, was the kernel of this process, and, for good or ill, did have its effect on the changing world of Europe.

The Indian image that touched Europe with its shadow was of course more directly influential still in helping to shape the new countries and peoples that came into being in the Americas. Mention has already been made of the important and sometimes decisive Indian participation in colonial history, and in the action and reaction that set white frontiers in motion.

Not surprisingly, the leveling sweep of the idea of liberty pure and simple ran first through America before making its tour of Europe and then the world. In America this idea sometimes manifested itself in outright Indian costume, such as in the various pseudo-Indian political, military, and fraternal societies organized from the time of the French and Indian War onward. The most famous of these was the Tammany Society, taking its name from the great Delaware councilor Tamanend and calling its different lodges "tribes," its officers "sachems," and its meeting place the "wigwam." It came into prominence shortly after the Revolution, dedicated to promoting "the independence, the popular liberty, and the federal union of the country," in particular opposition to the powerful elements working to make the new country a kingdom or an oligarchy. The Tammany Society earned a fair share of credit for the eventual triumph of libertarian ideals in the United States; it also eventually managed to force through universal manhood suffrage in New York State in 1826, and abolish imprisonment for debt in New York City in 1831. It was also principally responsible for securing the 1790 treaty with the Creek Indians that was so useful at the time in ensuring the peace and safety of the southern borders of the new United States. In later years, after the Civil War, the Tammany Society degenerated into the New York City political machine familiar to our own day.

Mention has also been made of the possible influence of Indian confederations on the conversion of European colonies into new American states. But there may be still other less apparent traits in the makeup of modern American nations that perhaps owe something to the peculiar character of Indian society. The policy of free immigration, for example, among the countries of the Americas, is scarcely in the European tradition. No doubt the free land of the frontier contributed to this policy, but what then of Australia, with vast free frontier lands but never a policy of free immigration? Could the common Indian tradition of free access into the tribe be at work here? The speculation seems permissible. There may be a number of other such permissible speculations. Again and again Indian tribes sent food to starving European colonists; again and again early European writers remarked on the fact that among the Indians if one starved they all starved. Could this have anything to do with American traditions of charity on mass, even international scale? Are there clearer European sources for such traditions?

At any rate, it seems clear that the peculiar character of the American Indian constituted a force in history deserving of serious consideration.

The question of what that peculiar character was, what made the Indians behave as they did, is involved with the total picture of Indian life and thought, and lends historical importance to that study. The question *in toto* is exceedingly complex. But a speculation may be permitted here as to the essence of it, the essential peculiarity of the Indian character, the basic difference between the Indian and the Old worlds.

The European culture that invaded the New World was infinitely superior to the culture of the Indians in the broad field of mechanics. In concepts of virtue, ethics, justice, and wisdom the two cultures frequently differed, but seldom widely.

The one great Indian difference appears to have been rooted in the matter of property: the general Indian view (with exceptions) of cooperation in the use of property in common as against the general European view (with exceptions too) of competition for the acquisition of private property.

This encouraged an appearance of classless freedom in Indian society, encouraged a strong group identity, and encouraged a prevailing interest in matters other than work. The bohemian, impractical attitudes that resulted acted against material progress, but Indian life, in its preoccupation with rituals, games, the beauty of soft spring rain, the making of pretty gewgaws to wear in the hair, or other such folderol, may have been quite a bit of fun.

Railed Cotton Mather of Indians, writing in the 1690s: "They are *Sluggards* to a Proverb; they are for any way of Living rather than Work . . . They are abominably indulgent unto their *Children*; there is no *Family Government* among them." And he demanded of his Puritan audience to *"Enquire*, Sirs, how far we have *Indianized* in every one, but especially the last of these *Evil Manners. . . .*" During the colonial wars European captives frequently Indianized to the point of refusing to part from their captors and return to "civilization" when they had the chance. This was a subject of indignant remark by generations of uncaptured Europeans. Said the historian of an Ohio Valley campaign in 1764, when a number of white captives had to be forcibly repatriated: "For the honour of humanity, we would suppose those persons to have been of the lowest rank, either bred up in ignorance and distressing penury, or who had lived so long with the Indians as to forget all their former connections. For easy and unconstrained as the savage life is, certainly it could never be put in competition with the blessings of improved life and the light of religion, by any persons who have had the happiness of enjoying, and the capacity of discerning, them." But a surprising lot of white captives opted for it, nevertheless. What did it profit a man to work the fat off his back for the blessings of improved life, when the twinkling stars were equally bright for everyone lost in the dark? Indian life may have had an edge in the pursuit of happiness precisely because it would not race.

In a word, the Indian world was devoted to living, the European world to getting.

This, the essence of the peculiar character of the American Indian, was the essence of the force that, hidden in the image of the noble savage, helped change the course of history. It was also the essence of the weakness that destroyed the Indian nations. It was also, as has been mentioned before, the unbridgeable gulf separating whites and Indians from direct communication and understanding.

Thomas Jefferson, among many others, proposed a bridge for this abyss and described it quite accurately in a Washington speech to certain Indian leaders: ". . . temperance, peace, and agriculture . . . will prepare you to possess property. . . ." It seemed so simple, this bridge, but it invariably collapsed in an inextricable tangle.

Bishop Landa admired the idyllic sheen of the Maya world, their women nursing fawns, their "good habit of helping each other in all their labors," but like other missionaries and civilizers for the next 400 years he was frustrated by their indolence. "Indolence" is probably the most used single word in all the reports written by non-Indians about Indians from discovery to the present day. It is the key word for the white point of view. Why wouldn't they work? Why didn't they want to labor to acquire things? The European simply could not comprehend a view of life (at least for respectable people) in which this objective was not paramount.

The gulf between the Indian and white view of life was at its most unbridgeable in the region that became the United States, colonized mostly by a people to whom diligent labor, thrift, Benjamin Franklin's advice to "Remember, that time is money," became the highest virtues, and work was literally man's sacred calling. The colonies of Catholic Spain to the south and Catholic France to the north, while by no means less interested in reaping golden pesos or gross sous, were less devoted to the principle of absolute utilitarianism—measuring fields, woods, streams, people, and above all time, only by the yardstick of potential profit. In Protestant America this principle emerged as a ruling ethic. The *summum bonum* of this ethic, in the words of the economist Max Weber, was "the earning of more and more money, combined with the strict avoidance of all spontaneous enjoyment of life," leading to gain, profit, acquisition that was thought of "purely as an end in itself." In the light of this ethic the Indian attitude was more than troublesome, it was downright sacrilegious.

This basic conflict in points of view helps explain some otherwise puzzling matters: why, for example, Indians were so seldom used as settlers or even as laborers in the Atlantic seaboard colonies. Colonizers ransacked central Europe and the savage backwoods of Scotland and Ireland to find and transport colonists, sometimes at considerable expense, instead of making any serious attempt to transform the Indians, who were already on the scene and who are often described as being superior physical and mental types, into supplemental colonists.

Sometimes the heterogeneous colonists quarreled bitterly among themselves, Catholics versus Puritans in Maryland, Scots-Irish versus German Pietists in Pennsylvania, but in the last analysis they could understand each other and make common cause since in the last analysis they were all after the same thing.

Frontiersmen became more Indian than white in many respects, and in many deeper respects than simply borrowing such gadgets as snowshoes or canoes, but they never forgot the basic objective of their life—property—so different from the basic Indian objective that the two could never hope to be members of the same club.

Spain, in general, was far more tolerant in making use of the Indian peoples, who were absorbed in large numbers into the population of Spanish colonies, to such a degree that what is today called Spanish America could almost equally well, with a few regional exceptions, be called Indian America. In much of Protestant America the Indian nations were stamped out to the point that a nineteenth-century synonym for the Indian race became the Vanishing American, and it was generally believed that some inscrutable natural laws were at work by which the Indians automatically perished under the withering touch of white civilization (ignoring the millions of unwithered Indians in Spanish America).

The inscrutable natural laws at work may well have been the aforementioned ultimate conflict in points of view, at its sharpest in the United States, and the various Indian images created under the fire of this conflict in the white mind.

The noble savage gave way to the bloodthristy savage, reeking with gore. An 1837 volume entitled "Indian Anecdotes and Barbarities . . . Being a description of their customs and deeds of cruelty, with an account of the captivity, sufferings and heroic conduct of many who have fallen into their hands, or who have defended themselves from savage vengeance; all illustrating the general traits of Indian Character . . ." describes a massacre at Schenectady in 1690: "They ravished, rifled, murdered and mutilated the inhabitants, without distinction of age or sex, without any other provocation or excitement than brutal lust and wantonness of barbarity. Pregnant women were ripped open and their infants cast into the flames or dashed against the posts of the doors!!"

The insensate barbarian gave way to the Red Brother Asking for Guidance of the missionaries, the Return of the Son of Noble Savage of the sentimentalists, the whiskey-begging, beetle-eating derelict of the realists, the culture-index cipher of the scientists. There were infinite varieties of the Indian image. Some left a pronounced impression on the American character (the psychiatrist Jung has said he could detect an Indian streak in all his American patients). Most had an even more pronounced effect on the fate of the Indians.

Town-dwelling Indians, rich in culture and cornfields, were transfigured in the popular (as well as the political) mind into nomadic hunters, rather dirtier and less desirable than gypsies—which of course made it easier to drive them away, or shoot them if they became dangerous. Well-meaning citizens—good people—had to keep reminding themselves that the dispossessed Creeks or the dispossessed Sauk and Foxes of the particularly synthetic Black Hawk "War" were savages.

But at the same time sizable sections of public opinion magnified the Creeks and their neighbors into romantic heroes. The indignation of idealists in the North to the methods of Indian removal in the South may be supposed to have added fuel to the various heated reform movements of the time, among them the militant American Antislavery Society, the Abolitionist movement, formally launched in Boston in 1833. To be sure, the North also had its full share of practical men, but while Illinois militiamen were shooting Sauk and Foxes to persuade them to stay west of the Mississippi in accordance with the terms of a dubious treaty ("It was a horrid sight to witness little children, wounded and suffering the most excruciating pain, although they were of the savage enemy"), the Sauk and Fox leader Black Hawk was becoming a national celebrity. After his catpure at the end of the "war" in 1832, he was taken on what can only be described as a triumphal tour of the cities of the East (and after his death in 1838, his bones were stolen for exhibition). In an epic poem written in his honor he was compared, "As soldier, patriot, soul magnanimous," with Napoleon and Wellington:

> And sure they had no better cause,
> Than fight for country, kindred, laws!"

The mid-nineteenth century found its Indian heroes in fact as well as in Fenimore Cooper fiction, in the past as well as the present, in biographies, novels, dramas dealing not only with such superstars as Tecumseh, Pontiac, King Philip, Moctezuma, but with relatively obscure Indian sages of long before such as Big Mouth the Onondaga. What is by many regarded as the best book by America's best historian (*The Oregon Trail*) was undertaken by Parkman in 1846 simply for the purpose of "studying the manners and character of Indians in their primitive state. . . ." The last work of the age's most enduring sage, Thoreau, a work left unfinished at his death, dealt with Indians.

A look at minor Indian luminaries of the age may be revealing. One such, a sensation in Washington during his visit there in 1821, was the young, dashing, and intrepid Petalesharo, son of a chief of the Skidi Pawnee. The Pawnee, a confederation of Caddoan peoples that in recent centuries had moved up the west bank of the Mississippi and the Missouri to Nebraska and beyond, retained a showy collection of (seemingly) temple-mound religious practices, splendid with symbolism and poetry and culminating, at least among the Skidi Pawnee, in a splendidly gruesome human sacrifice at the time of the summer solstice, an arrow-shooting sacrifice reminiscent of similar rites pictured in pre-Columbian codices from deep in Mexico. Petalesharo put a stop to the practice by rescuing an intended victim, a Comanche girl, in the best last-minute tradition, so it was reported ("Who was it that intrepidly released the captive maid? It was the young, the brave, the generous PETALESHARRO"), dramatically defying priests and thunderbolts and the assembled faithful. A figure of the Washington social season of 1826 and 1827 was an Ojibwa confidence woman, Tshusick, who ran a sanctimonious racket on high government officials and their ladies, including the lady of President John Quincy Adams. A contemporary, Eleazar Williams, a Christianized Oneida called by a biographer "the most perfect adept at fraud, deceit, and intrigue that the world ever produced," was alleged to have looted the Oneida and several missionary societies of thousands of dollars during the 1820s (while moving most of the Oneida against their will from New York to Green Bay, Wisconsin, into the bargain), and turned up in the 1850s as the pretended Lost Dauphin of France, son of Louis XVI, immediately gaining a large claque of white followers.

Obviously, in areas mystical and romantical a certain cachet attached to being an Indian, and it is not surprising that Indian-model mumbo jumbo played a part in the founding of various religious sects during the period. The Book of Mormon, adopting the then current theory that the Indians were remnants of the Lost Tribes of Israel, dubbed them Lamanites, and offered a history for their movements from 600 B.C. until after the Resurrection, when Christ appeared to them here and there under the guise of Viracocha, Kukulcan, or Quetzalcoatl. The sects of the Shakers and the Spiritualists gave quite a bit of attention to Indians, generally regarding them as virtuous and mystically powerful simply because they were Indians, in contrast to the wicked (fallen) Lamanites of the Mormons. A natural counterpart to the virtuous Indian mystic was the Indian herb doctor (sometimes a very good doctor indeed), forerunner of the Kickapoo Medicine Show of a generation or two later.

In the various images the Indian was sometimes wondrous wise, and a virtue attached itself to Indian wit as well as to Indian yarbs and roots: when a Jesuit priest reproached an Algonkin priest with the immorality of his people saying, "You don't even know which of the children around you are your own," the old Indian replied, "I will never understand you Frenchmen—you love only your own children, but we love all children." When a Dutch pastor told some Iroquois that in his sermons he reminded the Christians each week "that they must not steal, nor commit lewdness, nor get drunk, nor commit murder," the Iroquois (puffing on their long tobacco pipes) said he did well but asked in pretended amazement, "Why do so many Christians do these things?" A Seneca sachem, objecting to Christian missionaries among his people, said he had been to Buffalo and seen how the white people lived, and they needed missionaries more than the Seneca did. These and other bright sayings from the past were given wider than usual circulation in the mid-nineteenth century, almost for a time threatening to replace the dominant but spurious wooden image of the dour and humorless Indian with one a little nearer to reality; although in reality the favorite ironic wit of the Indian was not always either so virtuous or so printable.

In the various images a romantic virtue sometimes attached

even to Indian savagery, so that London street brawlers of the eighteenth century proudly called themselves "Mohocks," as Parisian toughs of a later period were given the name Apaches. And a real honorary Mohawk, the English Duke of Northumberland who had been adopted into the Mohawks as a warrior during the Revolutionary War, wrote in 1806 from England to the Mohawk leader Joseph Brant: "There are a number of well meaning persons here, who are very desirous of forming a society to better (as they call it) the condition of our nation, by converting us from warriors and hunters into husbandmen. Let me strongly recommend it to you, and the rest of our chiefs, not to listen to such a proposition."

In the various images a certain scientific virtue even attached to strong-stomached primitivism (the long fingernails of an old Montagnais woman scraping a greasy pot, and the professionally long fingernails of the official Choctaw bone-pickers who cleaned the bones of the dead for burial; and the Creek Honored Men vomiting with punctilio the black drink), for the age was intellectually elevated as well as refined.

Intellectual curiosity probed Indian mythology, legend, and folk history, and a scholarly treatise accidentally transferred the name of the great Iroquois political reformer Hiawatha to the story of the Ojibwa demigod Manabozho, and the accident was sealed in marbled meter for posterity in Longfellow's poem (would it have been as deathless under its right name of Manabozho?).

As the Vanishing American vanished from the eastern states he became a figure bathed in nostalgic fable and the rush of poignant affection that one feels for the dying. Sang Lydia Sigourney ("The Sweet Singer of Hartford"), America's most popular poetess of the first half of the nineteenth century:

> Ye say that all have passed away,
> The noble race and brave
> That their light canoes have vanished
> From off the crested wave;
> That 'mid the forests where they roamed,
> There rings no hunter's shout;
> But their name is on your waters,
> Ye may not wash it out.
> . . . Ye say their cone-like cabins
> That clustered o'er the vale,

Have disappeared as withered leaves
Before the autumn gale:
But their memory liveth on your hills . . .

Mid-nineteenth-century images of the Indian in history emphasized tribes melting away at a touch, or skulking savages being eradicated like other agricultural pests. The war was over, the conquest won, and a curious blindness blacked out the long and important Indian role in the American story, relegating it to a minor, if colorful, bit of business. The central mystery of the Iroquois, for example, their tremendous staying power that had been so influential in the course of American events, was obscured by the noisy sideshow of Joseph Brant's howling desolating band. The similar staying power and historical importance of the Chickasaws and Creeks was lost in the emotional sideshow of their removal.

The tumbling phantoms of the jumbled Indian images occupied the popular fancy to an amazing degree in literature, laws, and the practice of the comfortable nineteenth-century morality. In the official image the Indian problem was a purely economic matter to be handled as economically as possible; the starched missionary image saved the Indian child and killed the Indian poet and created pious, if rather childish and indolent, Christians of the second class; academicians, always correct and seldom right, created a rattle-shaking taboo-conditioned automaton that had nothing whatever to do with the stagey ghosts of Those Who Have Gone to whom the sentimentalists strewed grateful garlands, using thank as the past tense of think.

But all the tumbled phantoms of all the jumbled images could not bridge the gulf to a comprehension of the Indians as people to be taken seriously, as people who were part of the national history and their own incomprehensible world part of the national life. Admirable as the images were, the public could comprehend the practical necessity of the removal of the eastern tribes, tragic and not quite legal though it might be. Practical men, at least, could comprehend the need and condone the conspiracy, as practical men before and since could condone other instances of rapacious exploitation of America's natural resources; the curious schism in the American character between private right and public wrong was not born with the dirty business of the Great Removal, although it received a resoundingly helpful whack therefrom. The tragedy of the exiled Civilized Tribes brought sympathy, and the long and heroic resistance by the Creeks and Cherokees to a persecution that should have crushed an ordinary people in six months brought admiration; but even the most indignant idealists could not perceive the other side of the tragedy—the costly loss to the states of Georgia, Alabama, and Mississippi of such potentially superior citizens.

"Why should you take by force from us that which you can obtain by love?" Old Powhatan had asked. "Because thou believest in it, I think myself obliged to kill it," Old Nils had said to his Indian companion.

But the old men were long gone, while wild roved an Indian girl, bright Alfarata, where sweep the waters of the blue Juniata, and she was swift as an antelope through the forests going and loose were her jetty locks in wavy tresses flowing, and it would be a safe bet she'd never pounded hominy. But what difference? Phantoms live on memories, not food. Phantoms looked from the Alabama hill that broke Menewa's heart, and danced a solemn step or two in the busy streets of Plymouth, among the phantom lodges of Patuxet, and phantoms grinned at phantom jokes in a thousand phantom councils. Phantoms settled down to live in the names of the land, as the Sweet Singer said; but also, perhaps more than most American suspected, in the heritage of their past and the dream of their future.

XI

The Speculators

In the meantime the real Indians, most of them, were jumbled west of the Mississippi. The Great Removal from the Old Southwest was matched by a Lesser Removal from the Old Northwest, but lesser only in the sense of driving out fewer numbers of people. In certain respects, in gigantic swindles by traders and "treaty" makers, in the part played by land speculators, even in incidents of ferocity and atrocity, the North easily equaled the South.

William Henry Harrison, governor of Indiana Territory in the early 1800s, "held treaties with factions, with isolated bands; in short [says the principal authority for this area] with **any** Indians over whom he could exert a temporary influence, quite in defiance of Indian usage, which required the consent of a general council." The conduct of Governor Hull, of Michigan Territory, was "scarcely less reprehensible than that of Harrison."

Throughout the 1830s in the Old Northwest Indian traders received, as a provision of such land-sale "treaties," sums in cash for debts claimed against Indian leaders or communities, a practice that diverted to the traders a total of more than $2,000,000 of Indian money between 1825 and 1842, when the

U. S. Senate, questioning the legitimacy of many of these claims, refused to ratify their inclusion in subsequent treaties. A considerable share of this enormous sum went to the American Fur Company, recipient of so many signal favors from Lewis Cass (territorial governor, secretary of war) that their warm friendship has been a subject of remark by historians ever since.

Land as well as cash was transferred to trading companies or other interested parties by these treaties, which usually reserved special allotments of choice land for tribal leaders, which allotments were then passed on, by prior agreement, to the white creditor or land speculator. Government Indian agents sometimes thus enriched themselves from treaties they themselves helped negotiate, one such being U. S. Senator John Tipton of Indiana, ex-government agent for the Potawatomi and Miami people whose rich lands north of the Wabash were the last big plum of the region. Peshewah, better known to the whites as Jean Baptiste Richardville, a principal chief of the Miami, was "showered" with individual reserves of land that, by 1838, totaled nearly forty-five sections, and in the crowning final treaties extorted from the Miami during the next two years was bribed with more than $30,000 in cash and additional individual lands. Other favored Indian leaders received similar benefits. The cash went to the trader's barrelhead and the individually reserved lands to the powerful trading houses and speculators such as Tipton, who with his trader accomplice was so fearful that other traders would outbid them for control of Richardville's reserves that "all rules of fair play were abrogated." In this way "valuable lands in the regions east of the Mississippi passed by hundreds of thousands of acres to speculators, without ever having been part of the federal domain."

Speculation in Indian lands, as has been noted previously, was the principal frontier occupation; it should be emphasized that such speculators ("Tipton, like most contemporary Hoosiers, speculated in land to the extent of his means") were not exceptional but typical, although Tipton to be sure was a much bigger winner than most. A recent study of Midwestern pioneering concludes, "On the mid-continent frontier, then, almost all the early comers to any area were speculators first and home-seekers second or not at all."

The Indian wars of the Old Northwest that broke out after the American Revolution sprang more from such "treaties" and questionable grants—beginning with the completely illegal congressional grant to the Scioto Land Company in 1787—than from the British agitation usually blamed by American politicians at the time. Little Turtle, a Miami, in command of combined Indian forces, opened these wars with victories over two American armies in the years 1790 and 1791 but met the inevitable defeat in 1794 against a third American army, under Mad Anthony Wayne, who then forced from the Indians the Treaty of Greenville, which was "so framed as to be productive of the very evils it sought to avoid"—that is, collisions between Indians and whites. Indian despair and further extortionist treaties multiplied side by side in the Old Northwest between 1794 and the final Indian convulsion in the region, the unsuccessful resistance raised by the Shawnee chief Tecumseh in 1811.

Tecumseh made an effort to engage every border nation or remnant thereof from the deep south of Florida to the far north of the upper Missouri River, his object being to hold the Ohio River as a permanent Indian boundary line. Above all he argued that the land, especially the Ohio valley, belonged to all tribes in common and that no portion could be sold or ceded by any single nation without the consent of all.

He made amazing progress in four short years in organizing the basis of a genuine pan-Indian union, assisted by such continuing outrages on the part of white Americans as the second treaty of Fort Wayne in 1809, the last and perhaps the most unjust of the series engineered by William Henry Harrison—this one ceded a large tract of Shawnee land on the Wabash but overlooked the formality of obtaining even a single Shawnee signatory.

Tecumseh and his allies tended, not surprisingly in the light of these American-made "treaties," to be pro-British as the War of 1812 rose on the horizon, and in the summer of 1811 Harrison called a council at Vincennes with the hope of persuading the Indians to remain neutral. (When the warmly disliked Harrison offered Tecumseh a chair saying, "Your father offers you a seat," Tecumseh is said to have exclaimed in indignation, "*My father! My father!* The Sun is my father, and the Earth my mother; she gives me sustenance, and I will rest on her bosom!" whereupon he seated himself on the ground "with as lofty and commanding an air, as if the green sward beneath him had been the throne of the Caesars.") Tecumseh later, after a speech of "impassioned eloquence, which has rarely been equalled, and never, perhaps, surpassed, by any native orator," broke up the meeting, accusing Harrison of falsehoods.

Harrison subsequently chose a time of Tecumseh's absence to lead troops against his headquarters, the large Indian village of Tippecanoe on the banks of the Wabash. Tecumseh's brother, Tenskwatawa; called the Prophet (one of the many messiahs springing up among a people beginning to sense the numbing odor of genocide), ordered an overhasty attack, instead of playing for time until Tecumseh's return. Losses were about even (and heavy) on both sides, but the Indians were forced to retreat and the Prophet was discredited, with some resultant damage to Tecumseh's plans.

His vision of a total Indian confederation was ultimately smashed by the War of 1812, in which Tecumseh, leading some 2,000 warriors and commissioned a British brigadier general, fought as subordinate to an inept English commander and was killed at the Battle of the Thames, October 5, 1813. There is a story, perhaps legendary, that he had a presentiment of death before the battle and discarded his general's uniform for Shawnee buckskins.

Land cessions and removal treaties continued for years, but they became more and more hollow formalities, signed by treaty chiefs without authority in the name of nations that had become little more than memories. The paper storm of these purported agreements rolled all the way west to the Mississippi, driving the scattered survivors of the nations before it or leaving them here and there as islands of paupers, and rarely meeting resistance.

A string of treaties negotiated by Keokuk as chief of the Sauk people (which he was not) giving up the Rock River country of the Sauk and Foxes did bring a show of something the authorities construed as resistance from Black Hawk, the legitimate leader of an important Sauk band. (When Keokuk announced in council that the United States government had made him supreme chief of the Sauk, Black Hawk, so they say, struck him across the face with his breechclout.) In any case, Black Hawk's reluctance to keep his village west of the Mississippi in obedience to the terms of Keokuk's agreement brought on some excitement and the shooting up of Black Hawk's fleeing people by the military. This holiday excursion of the frontier militia took place in 1832. It is embalmed in the history books as the Black Hawk War, a rather unfortunate example to serve as the last of the Indian wars of the Old Northwest.

No resistance was even alleged in the case of the Potawatomi a few years later, rather it was the impatience of white squatters on their land demanding the final removal of the Indians. The few bands left in Indiana of the once powerful Fire Nation (Potawatomi: "People of the place of the fire") promised in treaties "extorted from them under duress or when they were too intoxicated to realize what they were doing" to get out of Indiana by 1839, but in the summer of 1838 Senator Tipton, alarmed, so he said, by threats from the impatient squatters, received authority from the governor to raise an armed force to "police the frontier and, if possible, to secure the consent of the Indians to their own removal." He gave this authority a splendidly cavalier interpretation in assembling the Potawatomi people under pretext of having an important pow-wow, and then without any adequate preparation marching them all off westward. Seven or eight hundred persons were thus kidnaped; forty-nine, mostly children, died within the first two weeks, and at one time on the nightmare march some three hundred were incapacitated with illness. They were turned loose in their new lands west of the Missouri where "they found no welcoming homes or cultivated fields such as they had left in the Wabash country."

Some of these exiled nations, including the Potawatomi bands driven out of Indiana, were barely given time to pause in the new lands that were to be theirs "forever" before the paper storms of the speculators were upon them again—the Indiana Potawatomi were forced to "re-cede" their new reserve in eastern Kansas and go on farther west only a few years later. Two series of new treaties were wrung from most of the "intruded" Indians for their reservations in what turned out to be the valuable country of eastern Kansas, the first series in the middle 1850s, the second from 1859 to 1868. Lands ceded under the first series were seized in the good old way for Indian debts or under the newer pretext (wholly illegal) of tax delinquency; the second series provided as a rule for the specific purchase of specific reservations, often naming the prospective purchaser and the price of purchase—the purchasers in the 1860s being railroad groups.

Railroad promoters spared no punches in competing for influence with the Indian Office and for influence in the Senate for ratification; the Indian lands, thus bought for a token price, were preferred to the wholly free grants of land made so

generously by Congress to the railroads, since the Indian
reserves were not affected by the alternate-section provision of
the congressional grants. Wide-open corruption eventually
reached a point even the Grant administration could not stomach, and Congress in 1871 passed a law ending the Indian
Office's control of the Indian-treaty racket and taking unto itself
all future acquisitions of Indian lands. By this time railroads
already possessed one-fifth of the state of Kansas, and roughly
half of Kansas' total 50 million acres had gone, via various
dodges outside restrictions of the general land laws, to speculators large and small—the best half; legitimate homesteaders
got the dusty slim pickings left over. (Wrote Horace Greeley on
a visit to Kansas in 1859: "As to the infernal spirit of Land
Speculation and Monopoly, I think no State ever suffered from it
more severely than this.")

The nations beyond the Mississippi intruded upon by the
exiled nations of the East were, most of them, made up of
peoples who lived a life similar in some respects to that of the
eastern woodlands, similar in other respects to that of the great
plains farther west. The Caddoan tribes of east Texas and
adjacent country were farmers, villagers, mound-builders, and
guarded sacred fire in their temples, but their dome-shaped
houses were usually of grass. These, and other, westward
representatives of the group as the Wichita confederacy were
almost transformed into buffalo-chasing people of the plains—
these were the people of Quivira (Kansas) found by Coronado in
1541.

The Siouan Quapaw (also known as the Arkansa) were
prairie Sioux who nevertheless built forest-style stockades
around their towns. The Siouan Osage of present Missouri, one
of the most powerful of the trans-Mississippi nations, lived in a
country of prairie and cross-timber woodland and were prairie
Sioux in their clan divisions but southeastern woodland in their
arrangement of peace and war moieties. Both the Osage and the
Quapaw were famous for the bow wood of Osage Orange that
came from their country: the name Ozark is an Americanization
of the French *Aux Arcs*, meaning "at the (place of the) bows."

The Kansa, relatives of the Osage and Quapaw, as well as of
the Omaha and Ponca to their north, were prairie villagers,
familiar during the mid-nineteenth century to travelers along the
eastern stretches of the Santa Fe Trail, the men always recognizable by their distinctive haircut: the head shaved or plucked

except for a lock at the back. The Pawnee, Caddoan village people living at the border line of prairie (tall grass and islets of woods) and plains (short grass and treeless), have been previously mentioned. Three related Siouan groups ranged northward of the Kansa: the Missouri, Oto, and Iowa (this last name supposed to be from the Dakota term *Ayuhwa* meaning "Sleepy People"), all three small tribes of, probably, no more than a thousand or so souls each in their best days. The Missouri were almost destroyed in a war with the Sauk and Foxes in 1798, and in the early 1800s suffered another disastrous defeat from the Osage which ended the tribe as an independent unit, survivors going to live with the Oto and Iowa.

North and west up the Missouri River began the country of the Sioux par excellence, the various divisions of the Dakota. But far up the Missouri, deep in the short-grass plains of modern North Dakota and environs, were three tribes of village people stubbornly clinging to many of their village ways, farming and living in earth houses. These were the Caddoan Arikara, an emigrant group from the Skidi Pawnee, and the Siouan Hidatsa and Mandan. Very well known to early fur trappers, traders, and explorers along the upper Missouri, these three nations were almost wiped out by the terrible smallpox epidemic that came up the river in 1837. Some accounts say there were only 30 to 150 people left alive in the two Mandan towns out of a pre-epidemic population of some 1,600.

To the west of all these nations there were still others, seemingly endless ranks of tribes, each with its own territory and its own way of life, stretching across the seemingly endless western plains and mountains; when Lewis and Clark made their flea-plagued three-year trip to the Sea of the West from 1804 to 1806 they met these differing peoples all the way. They were in fact guided by one of those distant people, a Shoshoni girl from the Rocky Mountains named Sacagawea who left an enduring image in a very literal sense: there are said to be more statues erected to her honor than to any other woman in American history.

XII

Kayakers and
Cannibal Dancers

Westering exploration and trade by sea outstripped that by land, and the strange faraway tribes of the Pacific coast were generally known to eastern America while the nations of the plains and mountains in between were still no more than shadowy half-realities. New England deepwater sailors of 1800 knew the outlandish whale-hunting Indians of Nootka Sound better, no doubt, than they knew the Indians of New England. Whalers, fur traders, and missionaries had known the furclad peoples of the far North for more than 200 years when in 1848 the vanishment of Sir John Franklin's great Arctic expedition turned the eyes of the world on the land of the Eskimos. Thirty-eight relief expeditions were sent out in the next ten years (it was later discovered that Franklin's large party had perished, to a man, of starvation); 7,000 miles of new Arctic coastline were incidentally explored; and the Eskimos were solidly implanted in the consciousness of America and Europe.

Due to their distinctiveness the Eskimos probably remain the most widely known of all America's native peoples. European provincials who may never have heard of the Iroquois or the Aztecs are likely to know about Eskimo igloos and dog-sleds.

Nevertheless, in spite of the exhaustive ethnologizing and publicizing they have received, the Eskimos remain, in a sense, semiconcealed, hidden by the fearsome unfamiliarity of their country. One can picture the people but not the life, the life of long dark winters and incredible cold, hardships, and dangers. It is especially difficult to conceive of this bitter, anxious life bringing forth a people usually described as placid and rather jolly and who created, within the limits imposed by their harsh if vivid world, a culture of spectacular richness.

One further uniqueness, as far as European views of the Eskimo are concerned: long before the early Greenland whale fisheries, long before the first voyage of Columbus, Eskimos and Europeans commingled in an association that lasted for centuries. The Norse, Irish, and Vikings who settled in Iceland from circa A.D. 850 to 1100 planted colonies in Greenland, the far eastern frontier of the New World and the Eskimo world. In contrast to their brief and dreamlike excursions to the coast of North America, Norsemen established settlements in Greenland and lived in some contact with the Eskimos there for several centuries. These settlements were eventually either wiped out by the Eskimos or abandoned, but until the mid-1300s, if not somewhat later, they remained in fairly frequent contact with Europe.

But the two peoples met, so to speak, incognito, neither realizing that the other was from a different world. Europe was unaware, and the Eskimos were unimpressed. A few words of Old Norse or Old Icelandic origin found their way into Greenland Eskimo dialects, a few hammers were made of church-bell metal, a few tubs were coopered (with hoops made of the corset whalebone known as baleen), and a few Greenland Eskimos of the time learned to write a few lines in medieval runic rhyme.

Otherwise the kayaking life of summer and the snow-goggled life of winter went on as always, and to the New World people of Greenland the generations of intruding Europeans were as if they had never been. This long and bootless contact reveals something of the difficulty of transferring elements from one culture to another, and something of the difficulty of discovering a New World before the discoverer is ripe for the event.

The Eskimo are generally reckoned to be relatively recent arrivals among the American peoples. There were previous inhabitants of the Far North, but whether these were distinct and separate predecessors or remote Eskimo ancestors is not known; the most ancient relics of these earliest people constitute the British Mountain complex, centering apparently in north-western Alaska and on the Arctic coast of the Yukon, and featuring rather crudely made stone tools that may be of enormous age, in any case probably dating from more than 10,000 years ago, possibly much more. Archaeologists have identified several other distinct technological traditions down the immense avenues of time in the subsequent thousands of years, some with similarities to the tools and spearpoints of the big-game hunters on the western plains of 6,000 years and more ago, some with obvious similarities to work produced in equally ancient Siberia. One of the latest such traditions before the appearance of undoubted Eskimo objects is now called the Arctic Small-Tool tradition, its most representative culture, known as Denbigh, centering along the coast of the Bering Sea, particularly noted for minute, exquisitely tooled microblades that are also found in some of the first Eskimo cultures. The established antiquity of the Eskimos themselves is fairly re-spectable, since they were definitely occupying some of their Arctic homesites at least 3,000 years ago if not earlier; in other words, pointing up once more the vast scale of time in the Indian story, somewhat longer than the Romans have been in Rome, and considerably longer than the French have been in France.

They have an Asiatic look but are a physical type unto themselves (average in height, plump, massive-faced, narrow-nosed, longheaded) and are not usually classified by anthropolo-gists as Indians, nor do they regard themselves as Indians. Anthropologists classify them as Eskimo, and the Eskimos regard themselves as the race of Inuit, which is to say The People. (The name Eskimo may have come from an Algonquian word meaning "raw-meat-eaters" or then again from a term applied by early French missionaries meaning "the excommuni-cated"; the Norsemen called them *skraelingar*, meaning "little people"; most of their Indian neighbors to the south speak of them by the usual Indian appellation for foreigners, some term or another meaning "snakes" or "enemies"; the central Eskimo retaliate by calling the Cree and Chipewyans south of them *itqilit*, meaning "lousy.")

Their language is believed to be unrelated to any other language on earth. Occasional loan-word parallels hint at con-tacts in bygone ages with such languages as Finnish, Lapp, Pequot, and even the Aztecs' Nahuatl, among others, but no real kinship has been demonstrated. One eminent authority has discerned possible deeper connections with Indo-European and suggests a very tentative but tantalizing possibility that the Eskimos might be descendants of a people originally from inner Asia still speaking a form of proto-Indo-European, parent language of Sanskrit, Greek, Latin, German, English, and a galaxy of other more or less cultured tongues. Thus the English word "ignite," for example, from the Latin *ignis* meaning "fire," may stem ultimately from the Eskimo *ingneq* meaning "to make fire by twirling a stick in a block of wood." But the hypothesis is only suggested, and Eskimo is still officially listed as unrelated to any other language. This is a reasonably good place to mention, by the way, that "primitive" languages are usually far from primitive in structure or capability, being often more complex and a fitter instrument for abstract thought and poetry than the streamlined and busier languages of technologically advanced peoples.

For a swing of 5,000 miles across the Arctic and sub-Arctic seacoast, islands, tundra, and forest, from Siberia across Alaska and the immense reaches of the north of Canada to Greenland, the isolated villages of the Eskimo were the only sign of man. Their total population in this enormous area perhaps never exceeded 100,000, perhaps seldom exceeded 50,000. There were no tribal governments, no real village governments, and consequently no war and no law, other than observance of custom and taboo. (Murder was punished by the victim's relatives, if they felt up to it.) The real unit of government was the family.

And yet there was a remarkable uniformity among the people—with a few exceptions, notably the Aleuts (pronounced Alley-oots) of the Aleutian Islands. There was a remarkable basic similarity among the various dialects of the language, Aleut again excepted. And there was a remarkable similarity in the way of life, allowing for differences necessitated by variations in the food supply.

More, there is a remarkable similarity down through the centuries—the rise and fall of Eskimo culture follows a curve so slow as to be almost imperceptible unless it is measured from stations a thousand years apart. In some regions it has been difficult for archaeologists to detect much change at all: Aleut culture of 2000 B.C. was very similar to that of A.D. 1700. In other regions periods of gradual cultural development have been distinguished, reaching a high point (and a brilliant one) not long after the time of Christ.

Investigators divide the Eskimo into geographic groups for

purposes of identification, but the basic Eskimo division is between the whale and walrus and seal hunters of the coasts and the caribou hunters of the interior (some groups hunt both at different seasons, still today as 2,000 years ago). And the basic question in Eskimo ancient history is which came first—the coastal or the inland way of life. The answer is not yet known. Further unanswered questions concern how much of the Eskimo way of life came from Asia and spread eastward over the Eskimo empire, and how much was originated in America and spread back to Asia. The famous vaulted snow house, for example, never observed in Asia, would seem to be one of the definite Eskimo inventions. Some experts trace lines of cultural influence to and from the south, involving such ancients as the Great Lakes Old Copper people of more than 5,000 years ago.

In a very general sense the earliest Eskimo cultures so far identified appear to be somewhat more elaborate toward the west, more simplified toward the east, until, after a thousand years or so, new high-culture developments in the central Arctic fed back westward, leading to the coast-to-coast manifestation of the aforementioned uniformity. But even in the somewhat varying earliest cultures most of the familiar Eskimo elements are already present: boats made of skins sewed over wooden frames, the decked one-man kayak and the larger open umiak; sleds with runners of bone or ivory, probably for use with dogs (according to observed custom of later times, the dogs were hitched tandem in the west, fanwise in the east); ivory snow goggles, at first with round holes, later with slits; hobnails of bone or ivory for lashing to your boot soles in working your way over ice, very similar to the crampons of the modern mountaineer; ice scoops and ice picks; plugs to stop up the wounds of animals and save the precious blood; specialized fishing gear, specialized harpooning gear for use with floats of inflated bladders, specialized bird-catching gear; bows and arrows for hunting musk ox, caribou, and other big game; and usually the seal-oil lamp, the center of the Eskimo household from time immemorial. This, the only lamp known in the Americas, a saucer of oil floating a wick of moss, was at first used only for light, later for heat and cooking. Traditionally its small, smokeless (if trimmed properly) flame was the only heat in Eskimo homes of woodless areas—where the temperature could settle down and stay for a while at 50 ° or 60 ° below.

Present day archaeologists have suggested various broad

divisions for the basic ancient Eskimo cultural tradition, usually turning on certain differences between the cultures of the Pacific coast Eskimo communities (including the Aleutian Islands) and ancient communities fronting on the Arctic Ocean, although with numerous correspondences and connections in between, which sometimes cause a great deal of overlapping in proposed divisions. Best known specific cultures in these various sub-traditions (all pretty much climaxing in the centuries between A.D. 1 and 1000) are known as Old Bering Sea centering on the Bering Strait, both the Alaskan and Siberian side and the islands in between, especially St. Lawrence Island; Ipiutak in northern Alaska; the latest phases of Kachemak Bay culture on Kodiak Island, the Aleutians, and the neighboring mainland; and late Dorset and early Thule in the eastern Arctic and Greenland. All produced decorative work in bone and ivory, sometimes of a high order; possibly the finest of all Eskimo carving and engraving is found in the exquisite ivories of Ipiutak, where the dead in their log tombs were furnished with artificial eyes of inlaid ivory, mouth-covers and nose plugs of carved ivory, and accompanied by elaborate ivory masks, fantastic carved animal figurines, carved ivory spirals and chains. These last are believed to represent imitations of the metal chains and swivels hung as magic gadgets to the gowns of shamans far to the west in Siberia. The artificial eyes are thought to resemble jade eye-amulets of Han dynasty times in ancient China. The mysterious ivory winged figure (looking a little like a butterfly) prominent in the art of the Old Bering Sea people is reminiscent of nothing known before. They may have been used as stabilizers, bomb-wings in effect, on the tail end of dart or harpoon shafts.

During this time pottery appears to have been introduced, and—probably the one great revolutionary event in coastal Arctic history—the virtuoso profession of whaling from an open boat was developed.

During this time, so the central Eskimo say, another race lived among them, a mighty race with mighty ancestors, men so powerful one of them alone could haul a walrus across the ice as easily as an Inuk (Eskimo man) could drag a seal, people known as the Tunit, or Tornit. For some reason they went away, but ". . . so greatly did they love their country, that when they were leaving . . . there was a man who, out of desperate love for his village, harpooned the rocks with his harpoon and made the stones fly about like bits of ice." There are indications that the

Tunit may not be mythical but historical (perhaps the bearers of the Thule culture), but if so who they were or where they went is not known.

Possibly there were other non-Eskimo groups in the Arctic past of this period: some features of the Dorset culture are thought to hint at the now extinct pale-skinned Beothuk Indians of Newfoundland. Possibly among the Inuit (Eskimo people) themselves there were varying peoples; possibly the inland and coastal tribes were then distinct in physical type; the Aleuts are so different from other Eskimos, possibly due to Asiatic immigrations from the Kamchatka peninsula, that they almost (but not quite) seem to represent a separate people.

In many respects the ancient way of life changed in the centuries after A.D. 1000. The quality of art, while still impressive, nevertheless exhibits a definite decline. Tools and weapons became more specialized. There were a few further innovations—such as pipes and tobacco, that traveled around the world after the discovery of America to reach at last the Eskimos via Siberia in the 1700s and 1800s. But essentially the pattern of living remained the same. Depending on what was available, winter houses were built (usually over a dug-out floor) of driftwood, whalebones, sod, stone, or snow. The domed snow house (rare in Alaska) is most typical of Canada, where modern explorers have visited vaulted halls of snow roomy enough for dancing parties of sixty people, and noted that the roaring sheet-iron heating stoves in use today—their rusty chimneys elbowing out through the domed snow ceilings—did not melt the well-built walls or roofs. Skylights were paned with stretched walrus gut. The prinicpal piece of furniture was the drying frame, for drying the constantly wet clothes. The great winter amusement (next to sex, in which the Inuit by report have always taken a frank and enthusiastic interest) was gymnastics performed on stretched ropes of sealskin.

Summer dwellings were sometimes skin tents, conical in the western regions, ridged in the east. Winter clothes were commonly tailored from caribou skins, boots from sealskin. Sea-mammal gut was also used for waterproof coats—a man hooded with it and lashed watertight in his kayak might drown but he would not get very wet.

In the winter, seals were hunted at the ice edge or breathing holes (a freezing job, waiting motionless for hours with harpoon ready); in the summer they were harpooned from kayaks in the open sea. Kayakers became desperately expert at handling their

fast and maneuverable craft, but even so Arctic waters are wild
and dangerous, and it is not surprising that one of the Eskimo
words to travel farthest among neighboring people is *pivoq*,
meaning "he lost his life by upsetting in his kayak." In the
summer the whalers put out in their umiaks (which were
occasionally rigged with grass-mat sails), sometimes operating
almost out of sight of land, and where there were no whales
whole villages moved inland to hunt the caribou:

> Glorious it is
> To see long-haired winter caribou
> Returning to the forests . . .
> . . . While the herd follows the ebb-mark of the sea
> With a storm of clattering hooves.
> Glorious it is
> When wandering time is come.

The song may be old, but no one is sure. It was sung for (and
translated by) the late Knud Rasmussen, one of the greatest
of interpreters of the Eskimo mind and poetry, a poetry which
in his hands at least shimmers and flames like the northern
lights.

All activities were ringed with taboos. Illness, misfortune,
lack of game were certainly caused by some broken law that had
thrown the world out of balance. A shaman would find out what
had gone wrong and correct it. Had the sick woman's husband
perhaps speared a salmon at a time when he was restricted?
Then of course the salmon were indignant and would not let
themselves be caught. Or perhaps a sin had floated down to the
bottom of the sea, to fall like dirt in the hair of the great goddess
known as "She Down There." Then of course she was indignant
and was keeping the fat creatures of the sea out of reach of those
on land, and the shaman would have to make a spirit journey
down to her and square things. The shaman, common among
many Indians as well as among Siberians, was particularly
popular among the Eskimos. Shamans could be women as well
as men, maybe better. They performed magic, secured revenge,
cured illness, sometimes by a method very widely known among
the peoples of both North and South America—sucking out
the illness and spitting forth a pebble or some such object to
prove it.

The ages passed, and the Inuit moved with the same age-old
acts and gestures through the summers as swift and brilliant as
flights of ravens and wild geese, through the winters of intermin-

able night, when they harnessed their sled dogs by the green light of the aurora. Perhaps the ancient life of men in caves still lived in their names for constellations: the Caribou and the Wolf (in the Big Dipper region of the sky); the Pleiades were "Branches on Antlers." And a magic song ran:

> I will take care not to go towards the dark.
> I will go towards the day. . . .

Among the Eskimos of the seacoast, as among nearly all people who live from the bounty of the sea, there was little tradition of famine. Among the comparatively few Eskimos who lived permanently inland, particularly among the caribou hunters of the Barren Grounds, winter was only another name for hunger.

The inland Indians of the great black forests bordering the treeless tundra on the south also knew seasonal starving times, although the season varied with the pattern of game migration—it will bear repeating that Eskimos are regarded as distinct from Indians, and that Indians also inhabited some regions of the Far North. These tribes were the Naskapi in Labrador, the (Algonquian-speaking) Cree and (Athapascan-speaking) Chipewyan around the south and west shores of Hudson Bay (with a long history of border wars with each other), and various wandering Athapascan groups stretching across the broad interior of northwest Canada from Hudson Bay almost to the Pacific.

The Athapascan language family derives its name from a Chipewyan band, the Athabaska, who lived in the area of the lake of the same name; the Athapascans of northwestern Canada, still today the least-known Indians of North America, are divided by ethnologists into twenty-one main tribes, some of them bearing such traders' names as Yellowknives, Dog-ribs, Slaves (so called by the Cree), Beavers, and Carriers—this last from a tribal custom demanding that a widow carry the ashes of her dead husband for three years in a basket.

The northern Athapascan hunters may have been the last important body of people to drift into America by way of Bering Strait and become American Indians. Since the Athapascan language family is the most widely distributed of all Indian language families in North America, this entrance could hardly have been really recent. But some students believe Athapascan-speaking people may have been entering America as late as the middle of the first millennium A.D., or about the time the Angles and Saxons were entering England.

Among these people men sometimes wrestled for wives (winners got harems and losers slept forlorn), and the soul of a slain bear was propitiated with solemn ceremony, as among some Eskimos and some other Indians and the Ainu of Japan, and as among Old World paleolithic men of more than 50,000 years ago.

The foggy, raw, and windy climate of the Aleutians and the southwestern coast of Alaska, while often defined by its denizens as miserable, is much less rugged than that of the rest of Eskimo country. ("It doesn't rain in the Aleutians, it rains in Asia and blows over," said the GIs of World War II.) The Eskimos here have certain marked differences in dialects and styles of life (with the Aleuts the most extreme variants, as already noted), so much so that two broad Eskimo divisions, rather as in the case of Arctic archaeology, have been suggested: Arctic Ocean Eskimo and Pacific Coast Eskimo, with the breaking point in the vicinity of Norton Sound in Alaska.

Coastal Inuit below this point are still kayakers, of course, and some are whalers, using poisoned harpoons, but the principal food for some villages becomes salmon and birds; an un-Eskimo interest in social status appears; hats and ceremonial masks are elaborately carved in wood.

All these things reflect the ways of the people living next door south, the Indians who developed the remarkable culture of the Northwest Coast.

The Northwest Coast people are marvelous on several counts. They produced a genuinely high culture (ranking with that of the Pueblos of the Southwest or the temple-mound people of the Southeast) without benefit of either agriculture or pottery, usually the chiefest handmaidens of cultural progress. Alone among such high cultures in the New World, it was uninfluenced by the ancient civilizations of Mexico and points south; its ultimate affinities were more with northeastern Asia, although the Northwest Coast people vigorously disguised borrowed elements into their own highly individual patterns.

Amost alone among such high cultures in the New World, it seemingly reached its zenith after contact with Europeans, rather than some centuries before (possibly with an assist from the steel wood-carving tools the Europeans brought).

And almost alone among American Indians, various peoples of the Northwest Coast area placed an inordinate value on the acquisition of private property, the purpose being a bizarre and inordinately pompous display of personal munificence.

In its purest form the Northwest Coast way of life was seagoing and fishing (salmon, cod, halibut). Roots and berries in the tall, lush, coastal forests furnished variety, camas root first of all, and cranberries and blueberries, and the Saskatoon berry that contains three times as much iron and copper as prunes and raisins. Food was plenty, and easy to come by. Work in the spring and summer laid up enough for a year. The mild, idle winters were for luxury, a luxury that created fantastically intricate systems of ceremonials; of clans and the groups of clans known to the anthropological trade as phratries; of secret societies; a wealth of decorated blankets, baskets, and boxes; an outpouring of fantastic wood carving; and a fantastic elaboration of social climbing.

Related families lived together in gabled plank houses, with the house posts and door poles carved and painted with the family crest—from which developed the wooden memorial monuments we call totem poles (the word is from central Algonquian and means literally "family" or "clan" or the armorial bearings thereof). Trees were hollowed out by fire and adze into great sixty-foot canoes of admirable workmanship, bounteously adorned with carving, "carved in grotesque figures and remarkably well handled," in the expert testimony of a British sea dog, Captain Sir Edward Belcher, R.N., C.B., referring to some Tlingit crews he saw in action in 1837.

A few of these people, notably the Nootka of Vancouver Island, used their barbaric longboats for harpoon whaling, the real McCoy, in which the whale was harpooned again and again and finally killed with a thrusted lance and then towed to shore. Slat armor was worn in warfare, and wooden helmets, and (maybe) terrorizing carved masks. Mustaches and occasional beards were in fashion among some tribes, as among some Eskimos. Slave raids and the resultant slaves were common; in ultra-rich villages slaves were said to make up nearly a third of the population; a Nootka chief of the early 1800s had "nearly fifty male and female slaves," reported an American captive. Social classes (above the slaves) were divided into commoners and nobles, with here and there, as among the exceptionally powerful chiefs of the Haida of the Queen Charlotte Islands, a sort of embryonic royalty.

These were an emotional people (like many Indians), much given to weeping, melodrama, and soaring imagination. Mighty spirits, beings of boundless power, walked the earth—at least in the stories told in the winter, when the North Wind smoothed the sea: "Something wonderful came in and stood there. His large eyelids were too powerful to look at. Where he placed his foot he stood for a while. When he took another step the earth and the house shook. . . ."

The nations of the Northwest Coast culture area extended from the Tlingit in the north, along the southernmost islands and coastal reaches of Alaska (its center about at the present Sitka, which is the name of a Tlingit subgroup), down through the Haida, Tsimshian, Kwakiutl, Bella Coola, Nootka, and Coast Salish of the coast and islands of British Columbia, the Salish and Chinook of Puget Sound and the lower Columbia River, to the Yurok, Karok, and Hupa of northern California.

Ways of doing things of course varied considerably throughout this long strip. The heart and high point of the Northwest Coast spirit was toward the north, with the Tlingit and Haida its best representatives for certain aspects, the Kwakiutl or Tsimshian or Nootka for others. Among other front-ranking activities, Tlingit and Tsimshian people made the famous Chilkat blanket, woven from cedar bark and the hair of the wild mountain goat into a mystic design that was inbued, so they say, with the power of speech. The Haida and Kwakiutl were the premier wood carvers. The Tsimshian were the great traders, dealing in copper from the north and captured Salishan slaves from the south, otter skins from the Haida, dentalium shells (a kind of West Coast wampum) and candlefish oil from anywhere. The Kwakiutl apparently originated the secret societies, each paying dramatic ceremonial homage to its protective supernatural being, that spread throughout the Northwest Coast.

Most of these national names meant, as usual, "people," and the Northwest Coast styles spread over many varying peoples speaking varying languages. These language groups, large and small, became more complex and tangled toward the south, approaching the Babel of tongues that was California.

The Columbia River region was another great aboriginal crossroads, similar to the lower Mississippi, and the language of the Chinook people there was used as the basis of a trading jargon spoken far and wide over the Northwest. It was eventually spoken from California to Alaska—but oddly enough the Chinook themselves merged with another tribe (the Chehalis) in the mid-nineteenth century and dropped their own language entirely. But the Chinook jargon continued in use. One of its later words, *hootchenoo,* meaning homemade liquor, was the origin of the slang term "hootch."

It was the Chinook jargon that changed the Nootka word *patshatl,* meaning "giving," into "potlatch," the best known feature of the world of the Northwest Coast. The potlatch was a feast given to celebrate any sort of an occasion (often a coming-out party for a debutante daughter) extravagant gifts were distributed—blankets, cedar chests, sea-otter furs; wealth was wasted with the greatest ostentation possible, all of which redounded to the prestige of the potlatch giver. Potlatches became contests of squandering between rival clan chiefs. Precious oil would be thrown on the fire at a "grease feast" until guests were singed by the flames, and perhaps an opulent chief would kill a valuable slave with the special club known as a "slave killer' and contemptuously fling the slave's scalp to his opponent, or break and destroy an even more valuable "copper" (plates of wrought copper, used as very high-priced currency), an act roughly equivalent to lighting a cigar with a thousand-dollar bill. All the gift giving and destruction were carried out with immense formality, and the rival clan leaders sang songs of insult to each other:

"What will my rival say again, that 'spider woman', what will he pretend to do next? . . . Will he not brag that he is going to give away canoes, that he is going to break coppers? . . . Do you know what you will be like? You will be like an old dog, and you will spread your legs before me when I get excited. You did so when I broke the great coppers 'Cloud' and 'Making Ashamed', my great property . . . This I throw into your face. . . ."

The humiliated loser sometimes sailed off to war and deliberately threw away his life, out of sheer chagrin. More important-ly, the entire clan of the chief won or lost face as a result of these contests, and the whole clan more or less participated to make the really grand potlatches possible, a spur to industry that may have played its part in the growth of the Northwest Coast culture.

The Kwakiutl complicated the potlatch system with an interest rate of 100 per cent—gifts had to be repaid double at the return potlatch. This interest rate (the practice—not necessarily the 100 per cent rate—may have been picked up from Hudson's Bay Company practices) saturated all Kwakiutl business customs, producing involved deals that would try the acumen of a Hollywood agent.

Obviously among the Northwest Coast people wealth was, as said an early authority, "considered honorable, and it is the endeavor of each Indian to acquire a fortune." The purpose, though, being "not as much the possession of wealth as the ability to give great festivals. . . ."

The idea of gaining prestige by giving away things of value is a thread noticed before (as among the Iroquois chiefs who kept themselves poorest of all by constant giving) in the basic Indian fabric of life, and the specific idea of a grand ostentatious giveaway in celebration of some specific event, a naming, a coming of age, a grief at death, existed far beyond the Northwest Coast area, reaching, for one example, more than a thousand miles to the east, to the buffalo-hunting people of the high plains.

But on the Northwest Coast the notion of property also extended to a variety of intangibles, possessions that could not be so freely given away and remained individual possessions until (usually) bequeathed as individual inheritances, so that titles, society memberships, professions such as carving or boatbuilding, ownership of certain songs or dances, could be handed down from the mother or the father, depending on the custom of reckoning descent—or, among the northern Kwakiutl villages, in a hybrid arrangement that passed inheritance from the father to his son-in-law, then to the son-in-law's son, and so on, descent progressing like a flight of stairs.

Young men and women of many Indian nations went alone into the forest to fast and pray and seek a guiding vision, but on the Northwest Coast the right to do so and sometimes the blessing of the vision as well (transformed into the ritual of a secret society) became an item of property to be inherited. Membership in a secret society brought as much high prestige as high drama, and the drama was the keen clear note of life itself, life unchanged from ancient ages: for here again the cult of the Bear appeared, and the cult of the Cannibal, echoes from the dawn of man.

Sang the people, while the Bear dancer danced and juggled glowing coals and threw them among the onlookers, sometimes setting fire to their cedar-bark clothes, and while the Bears of the Bear Society, wrapped in their great black bearskins, angrily clawed the earth:

How shall we hide from the bear that is moving
all around the world?

> ... Let us cover our backs
> with dirt that the terrible great bear from
> the north of the world may not find us. ...

The initiate of the Kwakiutl Cannibal Society fasted in the woods until, emaciated and hysterical, he appeared for the frenzied dance of initiation. He was lured into the house of the Society by a naked woman, dancing backward, enticingly, holding in her outstretched arms a corpse. The Cannibal dancer followed her step for step, trembling, drawn on as if against his will, and in the house was seized with wildness and bit flesh from the arms of the communicants around him, and in ecstasy he danced, while the people sang for him:

> Now I am about to eat,
> My face is ghastly pale.
> I am about to eat what was given me by Cannibal
> at the North End of the World.

The ceremony ended with a ritual feast of dog, stand-in for man in mock-cannibal performances among a number of Indian peoples.

But anyone could see spirits in secret dreams, and the spirits could be prayed to. Toward the southern periphery of the Northwest Coast world, below the present Canada-United States boundary, this spirit dreaming was of much moment; and reverent young dreamers deep in the cathedral forests of Douglas fir or towering redwood prayed, with all the devotion of their being, "I want to be rich."

The fur trade was the great bringer of technological civilization to the people of the North, Indians and Eskimos alike. Its chief apostles were the agents of the "Governor and Company of Adventurers of England Trading into Hudson's baye," organized in 1670 to compete with French *coureurs de bois* for the prime "oiled beaver" (skins worn next to the body, for a season, hair side in) of the Cree and their northern neighbors. The other great English-backed fur combine, the North-West Company, began to get under way in the 1770s; in 1796 it split temporarily into rival factions that spent no less than 195,000 gallons of liquor on the Indians during a two-year trade war. The inevitable conflict between the North-West Company and the Hudson's Bay Company reached a bloody climax in 1816, with a veritable war on the Red River of Canada; the two companies merged five years later.

The usual new diseases took their toll, consuming the people of the northern forests "as the fire consumes the dry grass of the fields," in the words of the first known European to cross the continent from coast to coast, the North-West Company's Alexander Mackenzie in 1793. Among the Eskimos, tuberculosis became the high-scoring killer. The usual inter-Indian disruptions ran their course. But the deepest changes were wrought on the people of northern Canada by H.B.C. (Canada's name for the Hudson's Bay Company), which transformed the Indians and Eskimos it touched from a hunting economy to a commercial fur-trapping economy, and their supply of winter food from caribou or seal meat to flapjacks from the trading post's supplies (or today to potato chips and pop)—caribou, butchered by the herd for their hides in the nineteenth century, virtually disappeared from some parts of their range.

Missionaries and whalers contributed to the European infiltration of the north country. The Moravian United Brethren, after much difficulty and some loss of life, established in 1764 their influential mission among the Labrador Eskimos. Danish missionizing in Greenland, begun in 1721, developed a series of trading posts and Danish colonization and the world's first relief fund, set up in Greenland in 1783 for the support of the aged and poor. Nineteenth-century whalers summered so regularly with the Polar Eskimos that their local nickname was *upernagdlit,* "harbingers of spring." New Bedford whalers plowing the waters of Hudson Bay were frequently crewed by Aivilik Eskimos of the bay's far northwestern shores.

In the west, in the Aleutians and Alaska, the fur trade came from Russia, led by the freebooting Siberian frontiersmen called the *promyshleniki,* who killed with true frontier abandon whatever they found on the beaches—seals, the six-foot Bering Sea king crabs, or the artistic, "mild, polite, and hospitable" Aleuts.

Freebooting was brought under organized restraint when the Russian American Company was given a fur monopoly by Russian imperial decree in 1799. By that time the Aleuts were said to have been reduced to one-tenth of their pre-promyshleniki population.

The survivors were put to work as sea-otter hunters and voyaged under Russian command as far south as Santa Barbara in southern California, and eighty Aleut sea-otter hunters helped colonize the Russian post of Fort Ross in northern California in the 1820s. The Eskimos of Alaska's Pacific coast got off easier, only having to pay a tax in furs.

The Tlingit fought the Russian fur company for many years, although a Russian fort was established at Sitka, at great expense in powder and ball.

The Russian company made some real effort to look after the welfare of the remaining Aleuts, and in the years following 1824 Russian missionaries converted them to the Greek Orthodox Church: tradition records that the Aleuts said to each other, "Any religion which can save the Russians must be very strong," and they joined the church to a man.

The Russian advance into the New World brought a hurried response from the Spanish in a voyage up the Northwest Coast to Alaska in 1773 and 1774. Thereafter Spanish, English, and, later, American ships called with increasing frequency at Nootka Sound on Vancouver Island; fast and loose trade with the Nootka people resulted in several savage massacres—a Yankee vessel, the *Boston*, was attacked and destroyed in 1803, and another, the *Tonquin*, in 1811—and earned for the whale-hunting Nootkas a reputation for toughness which they richly deserved. But it was this trade that brought the previously mentioned steel tools, sending the art of the Northwest Coast into a most glorious sunburst.

But it came at sunset. The Russian advance also brought a response in Alexander Mackenzie's transcontinental journey, and in the arrival of Lewis and Clark at the Pacific twelve years later, in 1805, and the subsequent establishment of English and American trading posts roundabout the lower Columbia River. In the 1830s American and Canadian missionaries appeared in Oregon, and in the 1840s settlers; the world of the Northwest Coast, its potlatches and its arrogant nobles, entered upon the days of its decline.

The Crimean War (raising justifiable fears that Great Britain would lay hands on Russian possessions in America) set Russia to dickering with the United States for the sale of Alaska. The sale was finally made at a price of $7,200,000, one ninety-fourth of the amount since taken out of Alaska in gold alone.

Transfer officially took place on Friday, October 18, 1867, at Sitka, when American officials and troops arrived by a steamer which also brought one Hayward Hutchinson, a Baltimore business man who did a little business that day with representatives of the Russian sealing monopoly. Back in San Francisco he helped organize the Alaska Commercial Company, which obtained from the Grant administration in 1870 a monopoly lease of the Pribilof Islands with their priceless seal fisheries.

During the twenty years of its lease the Alaska Commercial Company netted many millions of dollars for its few (sixteen in 1872) stockholders and left the seal herds generously depleted. It claimed, however, to have improved the lot of the Aleuts who lived on the Pribilof Islands. Missionaries claimed otherwise. The company was the subject in 1876 of a Congressional investigation which got nowhere; a United States Treasury agent stationed in Alaska to guard the public weal against overexploitation happened also to be the company's Superintendent of Seal Fisheries. Would-be competitors kept the company under a fairly constant fire for years, charging in effect that Alaska was maintained as its private pork barrel and subjected to merciless plundering. Since the company controlled Alaskan trading posts and shipping, and thus exerted almost total control over travel in those parts, the charges were difficult to investigate.

But it was at this same epoch (1884) that an American Presbyterian missionary, Dr. Sheldon Jackson, set up shop in Alaska as Superintendent of Education. He found that whiskey, prostitution, and disease, liberated from the more rigid controls of Russian times, had drastically reduced the Inuit population. The thousands of Eskimos that in the 1820s had inhabited the Alaskan north and northwest coasts were only hundreds in the 1880s.

Disease had probably done the greatest damage, but the most dramatic destroyer was the new institution of the summer drunk. Summer was the time of preparation for winter, and really not a time to gambol. But Eskimos, swapping their furs and ivory for whiskey with the summer traders, would go on a mighty drunk during the short, vital hunting season, and wake up to find winter at hand and nothing in the meat pit. They would then starve. In 1888 a revenue ship visiting St. Lawrence Island, at the southern entrance of Bering Strait, found the entire population of three neighboring villages—400 men, women, and children—dead from these causes.

Even for a sober man, meat was hard to come by. In many areas the rifle had all but done for the walrus and the whale, the seal and caribou. Dr. Jackson set about to replace the vanished caribou with tame reindeer, change the Eskimos from hunters to herdsmen, and bring to them some education in the white man's money-oriented ways, some medical assistance, and some legal protection.

Hercules never faced a task more beset with discouragements and opposition—passive from the Eskimos, violent from frontier whites who could not see any earthly reason for helping the dirty and wretched natives to survive. But in 1892 the United States government brought in the first sizable herd of reindeer, and hired Lapps from Norway to teach their care and breeding; and to everyone's amazement except Dr. Jackson's the experiment began to work.

No doubt it is an oversimplification to say, as some do, that Sheldon Jackson (an eyeglassed, diminutive, Teddy Roosevelt sort of man but "by inside measure a giant," as a contemporary wrote) saved the Eskimos in Alaska. But since his time, anyway, the United States has hung up a better record in its dealings with the Alaskan Eskimos than before—at least the Danes and Canadians in the Arctic think so, with praise that is rarer than rubies, examples for it being so exceedingly scarce.

XIII
Beulah Land

The land ran down in golden hills from the mountains to the sea, with green groves of oaks in the folds between and poppies red on the slopes in their season. A little river, dry for half the year, curled along the bottom of the valley. This was the site of the present Los Angeles, and in the year 1602 there were probably a couple of dozen villages scattered here and there over its area, impermanent-looking clusters of mat-made huts and trash and tumbled baskets. People speaking the same language (a Shoshonean tongue) also lived on a couple of islands off the coast, the nearer now known as Santa Catalina or, in song and tourist promotion, as Avalon.

Three Spanish ships, commanded by a Basque navigator named Sebastian Vizcaino, put in at the nearer island on Santa Catalina's day (November 25th) of the year 1602, and the recorder of the expedition wrote of the people who lived there: "*The women are very beautiful* and virtuous, the children are fair and blonde and very merry."

Some days later the same three ships anchored in an "excellent harbor" 325 miles up the coast; Vizcaino named this bay after the Count of Monte Rey, the viceroy of New Spain who

331

had sent out the expedition. The crews of these three ships were riddled with scurvy, and sixteen men had already died since their departure from Acapulco, Mexico, seven months before; the explorers were scarcely in a condition to look at this particular new world (perfumed by a dead whale washed ashore, upon which bears fed by night) through rose-colored glasses. Nevertheless, the Carmelite friar who was keeping the journal of the expedition wrote that the people of Monterey Bay were ". . . affable, generous Indians, friendly to the point of giving whatever they had; they much regretted the Spaniards' departure, because they had so much affection."

The people of the California coast had been encountered now and then by other Europeans—English pirates, Manila galleoneers, previous Spanish explorers—for at least sixty years before the time of Vizcaino, and in general had been described as friendly, frank, handsome, lightskinned, of good stature and extraordinary strength. They could stride along for a mile carrying a weight an Englishman could scarcely lift, wrote a companion of Francis Drake's in speaking of the people north of San Francisco Bay; and he added that they were marvelous runners. Vizcaino in a letter to the Spanish king spoke of the plank canoes used by some of the southern California coastal and island people "in which they go to sea with fourteen paddle-men of a side, with great dexterity—even in very stormy weather," darting over the water with such speed "that they seemed to fly."

The life described by these first foreign observers—the nearly naked men occasionally dressed in skins and the women in "aprons" of rushes, the fishing and acorn gathering, the multitudes of baskets (and the little round basketry hats of the women), the dancer with a belt of deer-hoof rattles, the sweathouses in which the men sweltered of an evening before plunging into a cold stream for a bath—had been going on basically unchanged for a very long time.

In many material aspects this life of most of the California people was exceedingly spare and austere, "primitive," as the terminology used to have it, more primitive than that of any other region in the area of the United States with the exception of the Great Basin—the Nevada-Utah deserts—next door east. Over most of California there was no real agriculture, only scarce and as a rule rather crude pottery; no general wealth of art, except in basketry; few elaborate dance costumes, no carved and painted masks; no leagues and confederacies and formally organized governing councils.

And yet California was, as a whole, more densely populated than any other region north of Mexico, with a bewildering variety of peoples, and with a notable stability as to their location—each little group usually inhabiting a tiny country marked out with some precision and regarded as having been forever theirs. There were comparatively few migration legends among the Californians—most asserted they had sprung from the earth where they had always lived.

Food was abundant, in profuse variety, and provided by nature free for the taking. Wild seeds and grain and nuts of all kinds were gathered, wild plants and roots, fish and shellfish and game; grasses of some two dozen genera and some three dozen species and even more varieties of the aster family, such as dandelion, goldenrod, sunflower, were threshed for grain. Acorns, where they grew, made the leading crop, acorn flour the staff of life, made by a fairly intricate process of pounding the acorns and then leaching out the tannic acid. Other staples took the place of acorns in lands where oaks were scarce: mesquite beans in the desert, pine nuts on the slopes of the Sierra. The California buckeye, containing knockout-drops (of hydrocyanic acid) so powerful that it was sometimes sprinkled in streams to stun fish, rivaled the acorn as favorite flour in some regions, after the poison was extracted by leaching.

The living was easy, and this made for leisure. Leisure and dense population are supposed to make for material progress. But here there was an almost inconceivable sameness century after century, penetrating enormous deeps of time. As in the case of Eskimo history, it is necessary to set up stakes a thousand years apart to catch the slow motion of change.

There is a feeling among some experts that the California life remained relatively primitive and changeless because it had reached a comfortable state of balance with what the pleasant environment had to offer. The lotus-eaters may have spent part of their free time in contemplation of spiritual matters—then as now California seems to have been a spawning ground of religions. But mostly they appear to have been content with drifting and dreaming on their sunny oceans of time. Maybe the principal occupation was being very merry.

The oldest inhabitants of California had probably been there a long time indeed, very possibly being descendants of some of the earliest people to inhabit the hemisphere so many thousands of years ago. Likely candidates as the most ancient ancients were peoples speaking the dozens of various languages now gathered into the language family called Hokan. Among these widely scattered groups were the Chumash of the coast and islands around Santa Barbara (Vizcaino passed by there on Santa Barbara's day); the Pomo, along the coast north of San Francisco Bay, and the Shasta, north of the mountain of the same name; and the Salinans, who ranged the highest coast line in the world, the coastal mountains south of Monterey now known as the Santa Lucia mountains (Vizcaino passed by there on Santa Lucia's day).

Perhaps equally ancient were other groups speaking the dozens of various languages now classified in the language family called Penutian, such as the many tribelets (each with a distinct dialect) of the related Wintu, Wintun, and Patwin in the Sacramento Valley; the forty or fifty distinct tribes of the Yokuts of the San Joaquin Valley; the Maidu and Miwok just eastward of these central valleys in the lower slopes of the Sierra; or the many villages of the Costanoans along the coast from San Francisco Bay to below Monterey

It is thought that newcomers spread into California from the north and from the southeast in the thousand years between 500 B.C. and A.D. 500. In the north some of these may have been such Athapascan-speaking peoples as the Hupa, of the picture-post-card Hoopa Valley on the Trinity River, and in the south numerous groups such as the Cahuilla of the mountains and deserts east of modern Riverside, and the aforementioned people of the region of present Los Angeles, these speaking various Shoshonean tongues.

There was occasional gardening of sorts in some of the communities, and in what is now called Owens Valley, east of the Sierra Nevada, the Paiute people along Bishop Creek near the present Bishop, California, practiced their remarkable (remarkable because unique in all the world) irrigation of large tracts of wild grasses and grass nuts ("Their ditches for irrigation are in some cases carried for miles, displaying as much accuracy and judgment as if laid out by an engineer, and distributing the water with great regularity," says an account of 1859—some of the ditching is still in use today, one still known locally as Paiute Ditch), but full-scale agriculture was practiced only by the Yuman peoples living along the Colorado River bottoms in what is now the far southeastern corner of the state.

"My country is abundant in wheat, maize, beans, cotton, tobacco, watermelons . . ." wrote Quechan "captain" Salvador Palma to the Spanish viceroy in 1776, and indeed, said the earliest European explorers, Yuma crops were the finest ever seen in the New World. But even so the Yuman peoples were solidly Californian in their neglect of material goods (". . . the tallest and most robust people that I have seen in all the provinces, and their nakedness the most complete," said a Spanish explorer) and in their preoccupation with religious ideas. Songs, the "dream-songs," of Yuman-speaking people are still today among the marvels of American Indian literature, some of the Mohave song-cycles requiring several days and nights to perform, consisting of intricate surrealistic patterns improvised on a theme that frequently has no meaning except as a foundation for this rich decoration. Related people speaking Yuman dialects—but not farmers—lived in the Mojave Desert of California, in the region of present San Diego, and down most of the peninsula of Lower California.

All these different people and many, many more had become solidly settled by about A.D. 1200 in their diverse little homelands. During the same long epoch, from about A.D. 500 onward, other broad, gradual changes took place. The Northwest Coast culture reached down from the north to embrace a few river and coastal groups below the present Oregon boundary and perhaps to communicate the worship of the raven to the Santa Barbara country, where it became the worship of the giant California condor, and from someplace the Chumash seamen there learned to make their extraordinary plank boats—the pine planks joined with lashing of sinew and caulked with asphaltum. These plank canoes were unique in North America, and only known elsewhere in the hemisphere at a spot on the coast of Chile.

Among such people as the Pomo the art of basket making reached a phenomenally high point, producing extravagant work dripping with feathers and beads. At Drake's Bay in 1578 these people showed Drake one of their famous feathered baskets "so well wrought as to hold water"; virtuoso examples exist of tiny baskets the size of a pinhead, made with stitches too minute to be counted with the naked eye.

Everywhere, the ancient fears and placations—fear of speaking the name of the dead, fear of the shaman's magic power, fear of the mysterious force that touched adolescent girls—were overlaid with refinements and new religious ideas.

Most of these new cults were highly localized. Feather-veiled

Kuksu dancers, so important to the Patwin, Pomo, and Maidu, were practically unknown to their next-door neighbors, both north and south. Stylized deer dancers were limited to the Yurok, Karok, and Hupa, who had most fully absorbed the Northwest Coast ways of splendor and display. Annual rites to renew the world (with sometimes a New Fire ceremony) were limited to the northwest, and periodic rites of public mourning for the dead were limited to the central and southern regions. Singing protectively over the adolescent girl and forcing her to hide her dangerous eyes so she would not wither trees or drive away the game were alone universal, as those customs were practically universal over all of western North America. Otherwise, the threads of the different California religions are difficult to untangle.

Shamans held contests in which they tried to out-wizard each other, and perhaps from these came group· ceremonies that became sacred dances, repeated each year in dance cycles that went on all winter. Some of the dance cycles were based on voluminous, dreamlike creation and animal myths possibly composed by unknown Homers among the mystical, myth-making peoples of southern California. The *toloache* initiation ritual, a religious system involving holy visions induced by the narcotic Jimson weed, is believed to have originated on Santa Catalina Island—although ground-painting ceremonies connected with it doubtless came from the Southwest of the Pueblos. The bear-dancing shamans (who really turned into bears), and the dying god here and there in the theologies, and the spirit-impersonators of the Kuksu societies reminiscent of, among others, the Kachina dancers of the Pueblos, may also have been importations from other places. But on the whole, imported ideas were not very prominent. In a very general sense the California religious ideas, dark, obscurantist almost as if consciously artistic, were growths from the California soil.

Spain left the upper California coast more or less unattended for 166 years after the voyage of Vizcaino in 1602 and 1603. During that time the Spanish frontier of missions and mines, Indian vaqueros and leather-jacketed border soldiers, crept laboriously up through northern Mexico to New Mexico, eastward into the "kingdom of the Texas," westward into southern Arizona and the desolate penninsula of Lower California. As swollen Spain grew older and more tired the movements of such expansion became more and more reflex responses to alarms real or imaginary: to the menace of the French in Louisiana, or of the Illinois French working their way westward to the Rocky Mountains, or of the Canada English working their way westward to the Pacific. In the middle of the eighteenth century a new threat appeared—the Russians in the Aleutians and Alaska, seemingly ready to swallow up the whole Pacific coast. This coincided with the Spanish colonial renaissance under Charles III, when for a brief generation new vigor surged through the veins of the Spanish empire. The Spanish occupation of Upper California resulted.

In the spring of 1769 Spanish frontiersmen, priests, soldiers, and Indian allies were at San Diego, and in the spring of 1770, after many difficulties, a Spanish expedition was at Monterey "to occupy and defend the port [said the expedition's commander ironically] from the atrocities of the Russians. . . ." During the next fifty years or so, twenty-one mission stations were planted from San Diego to San Francisco Bay, accompanied by six tiny garrisoned presidios and settlements of colonists.

The missions gained their sustenance from Indian lands and Indian labor, and in return undertook to educate the Indians in the ways of Christianity and Spanish civilization and thus prepare them to become responsible colonial subjects. The "Mission Indians," the people of about 700 miles of coastal country, were only a fraction of California's total Indian population, and of these only a part became Christian. Converts numbered 21,100 in the missions' best year, 1820. They lived in large pueblos at the missions, laboring at every trade from adobe making to soap making, sheepherding to pigeon tending. They were restrained from going back to the "monte"—back to their old free life, although groups would now and then be given a few weeks off to gather wild fruit in the woods and the hills, both literally and figuratively: figuratively in proselyting for new converts or coaxing runaway neophytes to return.

Discipline was maintained by such corporal punishments as shackles, hobbles, stocks, imprisonment, or flogging—although no more than twenty-five lashes a day; and women, says a report of 1800, were only rarely flogged. Runaways were a constant problem, and the terrible death rate ("sickness and death dealt unsparingly among them," in the words of one observer) a greater problem still: on the basis of mission records the total loss of the Mission Indian population between 1779 and 1833 has been estimated at seventy-two percent.

In the main the myth-shrouded world of the California coast

people, idle and merry, appeared to collapse almost at the first toll of a mission bell; there were a few armed revolts, but none of any consequence—these people were hopelessly simple when it came to making war: indeed the superior Chumash, the matchless artists of the coastal country, were rated by some early writers as "dull of intellect" because of their low grade "progress in warfare" and defended by another local authority on the basis that the Chumash "scarcely understood the use of arrows" not because of stupidity but merely because "his life was gentle." Resistance, where it occurred, tended to emphasize such passive measures as the persistent abortions practiced by the sullen women (also Chumash) of a mission district near Santa Barbara, as noted in a report of 1810; abortion and infanticide presumably played some part in the spectacularly low birth rate at the missions (29,000 in a cumulative total from 1769 to 1833, as against 62,000 deaths in the same period, and of those relatively few births some three-fourths died in infancy).

It would seem that the collapse of their world changed the very look of the people. Travelers during mission times describe Indians markedly different in appearance from the tall, candid, handsome natives seen by the early voyagers two hundred years before; the Mission Indians are invariably pictured as short rather than tall, dark rather than fair, and above all dirty and spiritless. The motivation of the describer may have played some part in this—early explorers, anxious to encourage further expansion, exploration, missionizing, often larded their reports with pointed praise of the new country and all its works, while later observers, frequently foreigners having an irritable time of it with everyone, just as often found all they encountered, including the people, detestable (as irritable foreigners, including Americans abroad, are still inclined to do.) In reality the Costanoan people of part of the coast undoubtedly were short and dark, but the Chumash and Yuman and Pomo people of other coastal regions were undoubtedly not. Possibly crowded living, heavy new clothes, drudging labor, altered diet, and the suppression of the cleansing sweathouse helped make the people dirtier and less cheerful, and possibly suppression of such pagan (but incidentally bleaching) cosmetic aids as washing the hair with urine, or plastering the hair and face with clay or mud for several hours—to give gloss to the hair and kill vermin—made the people darker. Possibly shrinkage of the spirit made them shorter.

A European artist writing of San Francisco Mission Indians in 1816 said the mission Fathers characterized their native charges as "lazy, stupid, jealous, gluttonous, timorous," and he added, "I have never seen any of them laugh, I have never seen a single one look anyone in the face. They have the air of taking no interest in anything."

The missions flourished mightily, however, in a material sense, with an easy commodity prosperity that combined with the stringent discipline to produce a society of closed minds and open hands, a plump insular society almost hermetically sealed off from the rest of the world, especially after 1781 when the Yuman people along the lower Colorado River closed the overland route between Mexico and California. Thousands of horses and hundreds of thousands of cattle and sheep grazed on the millions of acres of mission lands, and crops of wheat, corn, and beans ran to 120,000 annual bushels; mission storerooms were treasure houses of wine, leather, wool, oil, and other such riches. Given time enough such going concerns might still have transformed the Mission Indians, shrunken spirits notwithstanding (and even shrunken population—the general mission population appeared to be making a slight actual upturn along toward the end) into the solid basis of an Hispanicized native people in the typical Spanish colonial pattern. But time ran out for Spain while the colony of California was still a raw, unassimilated frontier. The missions were in business, on the average, only a bare half century.

In the early years of the nineteenth century a wind of revolt, born of the American and French Revolutions, ran around the world. Rather suddenly, the 300-year-old Spanish empire was blown apart. Between 1811 and 1825 most of Spain's New World colonies fought for and won their independence; Mexico became an independent kingdom in 1821, and a republic only three years later.

In California, for the moment remaining a possession of Mexico, revolution first made itself felt in the destruction of the wealthy missions, which were secularized in the middle 1830s. Theoretically this secularization was supposed to give the mission lands back to the Indians, thus making the Mission Indians a self-sustaining people. In practice, the missions were carved up to form the great California ranchos ("a wild carnival of looting"), and the Mission Indians were scattered like quail. A great many, especially among the people who had been brought from the inland valleys, returned to their homes and tried, for the time, to resume their ancient life; other survivors turned into peons on the ranchos or free-lance vagrants about the coastal settlements.

This was California's pastoral interlude, this Mexican epoch of the great ranchos, when the rancheros and their enormous families and a few handfuls of urban families, some 4,000 persons all told, lived a gracious, leisurely life, a life of music, horses, abundant love-making and ever-ready prayers, an idle, merry life, in fact, preoccupied with games and religion, over the bones of the thousands of coastal Indians who had lived their idle, merry life, preoccupied with their games and religion, on the same hillsides, on the same rivers and coasts and town sites, so short a time before. A few old people, both Indian and white, could easily have still remembered in the 1830s the first meetings forty or fifty or sixty years before; it must have seemed to them that only a moment had passed since the Indian had looked up, all nature teeming in the prism of his eye, to welcome the strangers and their gods.

Recruited from both ex-Mission Indians and gentiles (wild Indians) the Indian peons worked as tanners, saddlers, farmhands, blacksmiths, and above all as vaqueros. To this day on California ranches a Spanish-speaking cowboy who wants to lay claim to being a top hand states the proverbial boast, "*Me crié entre los Indios* (I was raised among the Indians)". A British travel writer described a California Indian he met on the Santa Fe Trail in the 1840s as ". . . a young centaur, who handled his lasso with a dexterity which threw all the Mexican exploits I had previously seen into the shade."

In general, though, the Indian peons, relegated to a servile status seldom better and sometimes worse (they had no cash value to their master) than that of black slaves in the American South, did not share too well in the gracious living of the period.

The distribution of the immense mission spoils was only being completed at the time of the American conquest of California in 1846, during the Mexican War. The discovery of gold came two years later, the stampede of the California gold rush followed, and by the autumn of 1850 California had become a full-fledged American state. The non-Indian population jumped from less than 10,000 in 1845 to nearly 93,000 in 1850, according to the federal census of that year—or to some 260,000 according to a claim by the state government after a census of its own in 1852.

The population of Indian California before the arrival of any Europeans is estimated to have been something more than 300,000 persons. The epidemics and the attrition of Spanish and Mexican times may have reduced this figure by 1848 to 175,000, most of whom were in the mountains and interior valleys where they had not yet fully enjoyed the experience of white "contact." The newly arrived gold-rushers and companion pioneers killed these people off in what seems to have been the biggest single spree of massacring in United States history. Some guesses say there were perhaps as many as 100,000 still left by 1851, perhaps 30,000 by 1859. A fairly dependable count in 1880 gives no more than 20,000 left at that time; these may have dwindled away to still somewhat less by the end of the century.

The thousands of newcomers to California brought with them the Indian policy of the American frontier—clear the Redskins out. The California Indians obligingly furnished depredations, occasionally killing or robbing the bearded miners or isolated settlers driving off livestock. The California Indians were, as a whole, even more obliging by being so far from formidable in a fight. Whooping bands of the new California citizens formed companies of Indian fighters and butchered Indians with abandon in a long series of Indian "wars" that are all regarded as illegitimate by modern California historians. However, the Indian fighters asked and received pay and expenses from the government, a point that became increasingly important as the diggings played out and times grew hard. The United States government reimbursed the state of California $924,259 for this sort of semi-pro Indian killing between 1850 and 1859, exclusive of the expenses of the United States Army in policing California Indian country and suppressing "uprisings."

Prostitution and venereal diseases ran rampant among gold-country Indians, and gang rapes of Indian women became so flagrant that even the white press took cognizance. Indians of course had no police protection, were not permitted to testify in court, could not bring a damage suit or accuse a non-Indian of any legal infraction, could be picked up and jailed indefinitely without warrant, bail, or any charge, held no property rights, and could be driven away wherever a non-Indian wished to prospect or settle. Above all, an Indian's life was of no moment whatever to the new society—no non-Indian, "of whatever ethnic origin, could be held responsible for the death of a native, nor could any legal action be taken against him." Thus the 1858 obituary of a Sacramento valley citizen could read: "Bill was a terror to the Indians, having killed a great many in his time; some of whom, as he said himself, he shot to see them fall."

Kidnaping of Indian children to be sold as servants or laborers was common—one recent authority, in a careful calculation from such records as exist, has estimated that between 3,000 and 4,000 Indian children were stolen in the years from 1852 to 1867, "not counting women taken for concubinage or adults for field labor." A Sacramento newspaper stated in 1862 that some "pestilent" characters were killing the Indian parents in order to seize the children for sale, the price running from $30 to $200 per child.

It was not good to be a California Indian in the 1850s and '60s. And yet, in the discussions of the time as to the propriety or necessity of extermination there were many who spoke for the Indians, not only on the grounds of humanity but on the perhaps more telling grounds of economy. An official report to Congress in 1850 summarized that it was "*cheaper* to feed the whole flock for a *year* than to *fight* them for one week." Said Benjamin D. (Don Benito) Wilson, ex-Rocky Mountain trapper who had become a prosperous rancher in southern California, "None here but see and lament their sad condition . . . Humanity, not war is the true policy for them."

Southern California, relatively untouched by the swarms of immigrants hot-footing it for the northern gold fields, was inclined to be less bloodthirsty about extinguishing all the Indians in sight; there were troublesome, half-wild Indians in the deserts not far distant from Los Angeles, but a reasonable peace was enforced by such peacemakers as Don Benito Wilson and Juan Antonio, noted chief of the still consequential Cahuillas. The debauched ex-Mission Indians of Los Angeles furnished a revolving slave-labor force for years, regularly arrested for drunkenness on Saturday night in Nigger Alley and bailed out on Monday morning for $2 or $3 a head (paid to the court, not the Indian) by anyone who could use an Indian for a week's work. "I wish you would deputize someone to attend the auction that usually takes place on Mondays and buy me five or six Indians," wrote a ranch foreman to a Los Angeles associate in 1852.

The *aguardiente* sold to the Indians was real firewater, being sometimes mixed with corrosive acids, and gave rise to wild weekly jamborees in which Indian men, women, and children brawled tooth and nail. "Those thousands of honest, useful people," wrote a Los Angeles resident of the 1850s, speaking of the local Mission Indians, "were absolutely destroyed in this way."

Eventually, most of the surviving California Indians were placed on tatterdemalion little reservations that grew steadily littler, there to finish dwindling away in comparative peace. They didn't, quite, although many once-populous stocks became extinct. They were sacrifices, said a government inspector in 1858, for the "great cause of civilization, which, in the natural course of things, must exterminate Indians." But mass extermination by the gun still went on, here and there, into the 1870s—an old-timer with a Mark Twain touch recalled years later an incident of 1871, when some ranchers in the Sacramento Valley found a steer wounded by Indians, trailed the Indians with dogs, cornered them in a cave, and killed "about thirty. . . . In the cave . . . were some Indian children. Kingsley could not bear to kill these children with his 56-calibre Spencer rifle. 'It tore them up so bad.' So he did it with his 38-calibre Smith and Wesson revolver."

The entire frontier process was so accelerated in California that the California people seem scarcely to emerge from the tentative contact of the Mission period before they vanish in an instant. It was in fact quite possible for an aged Indian to have encompassed the entire story, from the first coming of the Spanish colonizers to the destruction of the Fifties, in a single lifetime.

One island woman from San Nicolas, farthest offshore of the Santa Barbara Channel Islands, did even better in living the full circle of the drama. In her time she had seen the Russian and Aleut sea-otter hunters bring death and carnage to the island, and press gangs from the missions had rounded up and taken away all those who could be caught. In 1835 Mexican authorities removed the last of the natives still living on the island, and the woman was left behind when she ran back from the boat to find her child, who had been overlooked. The boat departed, and, although there was some talk of returning for her, no one really wanted to bother. The child soon died, and the woman was alone and forgotten on the island for eighteen years.

She had the houses of her people to live in, houses made of the ribs or jawbones of whales, walled with skins. There were seals, birds, fish, shellfish, and roots, and the island's ancient gods belonged to her alone. The island is wrapped in incessant winds and fogs, at their worst in summers when the young hair seals cry like babies; and the woman dressed herself in warm but delicate gowns of bird skins.

She was found by hunters and taken into a Santa Barbara that had become an American town, and efforts were made to locate some of the remnants of the thousands of Chumash and Santa Catalina Pepimaros who had inhabited the other offshore islands not so many years before. A number were turned up and brought to see her, but no one could understand her language. She was good humored and frequently sang and danced but something in the strange new world, perhaps its food, perhaps her multiform isolation within it, was too much for her and she died within a few months.

East of the great wall of the Sierra Nevada that separates California from the ordinary world there roamed numberless bands of primitive people, picking an arduous living from the pastel-colored deserts and the brilliant, flowery, barren desert mountains. Their manner of life—gathering wild seeds and grasshoppers, digging roots, hooking lizards out of their holes, making baskets and brush huts, circulating forever over a given territory around a recognized village site—apparently preserved the beginning ways of long, long ago on which had been built the somewhat more developed cultures of California.

It is usually assumed these people of the Great Basin were too busy finding food to build much of anything cultural or otherwise. Their ceremonies were slight family afairs—there was not enough to eat in any one place for large gatherings. They sang their dreams, and sometimes performed a public mourning for the dead. In common with many other people of the Americas and elsewhere they believed that illness came from theft or loss of the soul—a belief curiously missing, by the way, from much of California.

As in the case of California, the various unorganized bands are customarily grouped on the artificial basis of language. All those within the Basin country proper spoke some Shoshonean tongue, and most had a Shoshonean look—short-legged and dark-skinned. The people known specifically as the Shoshoni occupied a great arc of country all the way from the Panamint Mountains and Death Valley in California through a wide swath in Nevada and contiguous belts in Utah and Idaho into the heart of the Rocky Mountains in Wyoming. Some of the desert Shoshoni, such as the Gosiute of the shores of the Great Salt

Lake, were abysmally poor; some of the Rocky Mountain Shoshoni were gorgeously rich and showy, as befitted people living in some of the most gorgeous and showy mountain country on earth, that of the Grand Tetons.

The Utes ranged up and down Utah and eastward into the Colorado Rockies. The people known as the Paiute (sometimes said to mean "true Utes") inhabited most of those parts of Nevada and its borderlands not occupied by the Shoshoni; a mountain branch of the Paiute, in Idaho and Wyoming, were known as the Bannocks.

Around the edges of the Great Basin there were some peoples of non-Shoshonean language who nevertheless seemed to be Basin types in their manner of life. Such were the Washo, of the region between Reno and Lake Tahoe, and the conspicuously fierce Klamaths and Modocs of the California-Oregon border. The Klamaths made the most beautiful and warlike arrows that he had ever seen, said Kit Carson, and their bows could send those arrows, said a veracious missionary, clear through a horse.

Most of the dwellers in the limitless mid-Basin deserts were desperately poor and correspondingly weak. They made a little trouble, but not much, when miners and ranchers moved into their country. In the end they usually attached themselves to ranches or towns as casual laborers or beggars, and thus remained on the sunburned native soil where they had lived for unnumbered thousands of years. Whites called them Digger Indians and generally regarded them as scarcely worth kicking out of the way.

To many of the perennially hungry mid-Basin people a horse was only something to eat. But in the far western reaches, in the 1850s and 1860s, Paiutes and friends raided California ranchos in great horse-rustling expeditions, fought a pair of formal little battles with the whites at Pyramid Lake in 1860, and gained signal remark by making elegant horse-race pursuits of such desert interlopers as Pony Express riders and stagecoaches. On the eastern and northern periphery a number of tribes acquired the use of horses and became rather splendid horse Indians, most notably some of the Northern Shoshoni of the slopes of the Rockies—one migrating branch of these people, known as the Comanche, were ranked as the finest horsemen and the most redoubtable warriors in America by quite a few experts who had had the hair-raising pleasure of their acquaintance.

Lewis and Clark's providential and beloved girl guide Sacagawea came from the Shoshoni of the Rocky Mountains, having been captured in 1800 by Minnetarees (a name applied to both Atsinas and Hidatsas) in Atsina country on the plains and having wound up, by a set of curious chances, at the Hidatsa towns on the Missouri far to the east three years later, at the moment Lewis and Clark were in the neighborhood preparing to head west. The historical importance of this happy accident can be overestimated: maybe the Lewis and Clark expedition could have made it to the coast anyway, without her services as interpreter, and without the horses she was able to get from her people when they reached the Shoshoni, and maybe Clark's parrty could have extricated itself anyway from the Montana mountain passes on the way back without her help, and maybe subsequent constant friendship of the mountain Shoshoni for Americans, with its effect on far-western colonization and American possession of the Oregon country, would all have come to pass anyway. On the other hand, maybe not.

It is certain that Sacagawea had no sense of directing destiny. Meriwether Lewis said of her, ". . . if she has enough to eat and a few trinkets to wear I believe she would be perfectly content anywhere."

The destiny of western America received a few other nudges from people around the Great Basin who were quite innocent of any such intention, as so often seems to be the case in the making of history.

The tall and naked Yuman-speaking people of the lower Colorado River became great friends of the Spaniards and contributed to the success of overland colonizing expeditions that marched from Sonora, Mexico, to California in the 1700s—the largest of these expeditions, made up of 240 people (more than half of them children) and a long train of animals, colonized the San Francisco area in 1776. The good will of these river people was vital to California's land connections with Mexico, and missions and a few settlers were planted among them to cement that good will. But trouble came between the Indians and the settlers; the foreigners along the river were slain in 1781 and the trail was closed, and never reopened during Spanish times, and as has been previously suggested this may have left cut-off California at least to some degree weaker and more remote, perhaps to fall the more easily into American hands in 1846.

In 1805 the Spanish governor of New Mexico sent his top scout, a Frenchman named Pierre Vial who had a twenty-year string of superb feats of frontier exploration to his credit, to raise the northern Indians against Lewis and Clark and thus parry the thrust of the United States toward the Far West. But Vial was attacked on the Arkansas River (probably by Pawnees) and turned back. He tried again in the spring of 1806, and again the experienced Vial failed—while the greenhorns Lewis and Clark had already, by that time, won through to the Pacific.

Westward of the mountain Shoshoni, ranging over much of central Idaho and the eastern sections of Washington and Oregon, there lived a number of neighboring tribes speaking various related languages now known collectively as Shahaptian. These included among others the Nez Perce, most easterly of the group, centering in Idaho and the Snake River country where Idaho, Oregon, and Washington come together; and the Palouse, the Walla Walla, and the Yakima, the latter among the most westerly of these people, living along the Yakima River westward of the great bend of the Columbia. All these had been river people, living pretty much on salmon, camas bulbs, and roots, but they took enthusiastically to horses when horses became available. This was probably in the very early 1700s; the horses probably came from the Spanish settlements of New Mexico and were probably passed along to this upper country by the Northern Shoshoni. By the early 1800s the Nez Perces were more skillful than Virginia hostlers at handling horses (so said Americans who had seen both), and had alredy become identified with a famous breed earlier developed in the region, the Appaloosa horse—the name coming no doubt from the neighboring Palouse. A small, distantly related tribe living south of the Yakimas, known as the Cayuse, built up such a trade reputation as horse-dealers that "cayuse" became another name for horse among early Oregon settlers.

These were proud, warlike people, and of them all the Nez Perce were the most numerous (Lewis and Clark guessed their population at 6,000) and most powerful. But like the Shoshoni, not only were they friendly and hospitable and helpful to Lewis and Clark in 1805 and 1806, but also to the other Americans who passed through their country during the next fifty years, and whose name in that time became legion. The stubborn, although sometimes sorely tried, Nez Perce friendship for Americans—through all that fifty years, and more, not one American lost his life at Nez Perce hands—was of considerable influence, due to their position of leadership in the region.

The Nez Perce were minor instruments of history in still

another manner, which came about in the following way. In 1825 Canadian fur traders arranged to have two deserving Spokan and Kutenai youths sent to the Red River of Canada for schooling. The Kutenai and Spokan were neighbors living to the north of the Nez Perce. Later three Nez Perce youths also attended the Red River Mission School. Apparently the Nez Perces became increasingly interested in obtaining the advantages of formal education for their young men, and some Nez Perces visiting St. Louis in 1831 asked this boon of General William Clark (of Lewis and), then governor there.

Somehow the story of their request got a little twisted in the telling, and the deputation of distant Indians was represented as coming all this way to seek the white man's religion. As a matter of fact there had been Christianized individuals here and there among the Nez Perce and their neighbors since before 1820, due to the amateur missionary work of Christianized Canadian Indians (particularly Iroquois from Caughnawaga, a settlement of Catholic Iroquois in Quebec) brought to the Far West in fur-trapping brigades. On the other hand, a request for teachers and a request for missionaries were one and the same thing, there being no other kind of white teacher known to trans-frontier Indians anyplace in the hemisphere.

In any case, the tale of the "Four Wise Men of the West" journeying so far to deliver their appeal for "The Book" of the white man was widely reprinted, and the eastern religious press became much exercised.

The missions to Oregon of the Reverend Jason W. Lee (1834), Dr. Marcus Whitman, and the Reverend H. H. Spalding (1836-1837), and others, followed, with some effect on the opening of heavy American emigration to Oregon during the next ten years. This in turn, by installing the nucleus of a settled American population in Oregon, had its effect on the boundary question then in dispute between England and the United States as to which was to have possession of the Oregon country. The boundary issue was settled in 1846, and the Oregon country— embracing the entire region that had been the real bone of contention, that between the Columbia River and the 49th Parallel—was turned over to the United States.

Among most of the people of the far Northwest fishing was usually the mainstay of life—Lewis and Clark in October of 1805 found the broad Columbia almost continuously lined with fish racks and bands of salmon fishers. But toward the east, toward the sweeping Rockies and the sweeping winds of the Great Plains, the coming of the horse brought changes: hunting became more important, especially the annual buffalo hunt, and clothes and customs took on some of the dash and flamboyance of the wild horsemen beyond the mountains. A house became a tipi, full-dress fringed skins and feathered warbonnets came into fashion, and flowered bead designs blossomed on anything that would hold still to be stitched.

Such were the Nez Perce and their neighbors, such as the Bannocks to their south, and the Flatheads to their northeast, centering around Flathead Lake in present Montana. The Flatheads were, in their own name, the Salish; the name was later applied to one of the largest language families of the Northwest, Salishan. The Flatheads did not flatten their heads but left them as nature made them. However, an undeformed head appeared flat on top compared to the tapered skulls of various Salishan and Chinookan people farther west who did practice ornamental skull deformation. Hence the misnomer, applied to the Flatheads by these richly cultured neighbors who thought of a pointedly deformed skull as a mark of proper upbringing, of having been "well-cradled."

Most of these tribes of the Northwest plateau country—Lewis and Clark counted twenty-five along their route through the area—were unfailingly friendly to the first American settlers. The first nucleus of permanent American establishment in Oregon, the trading post of Astoria, was set up by an expedition that labored its way westward in 1810-1812 and would have perished three times over if not for Indian provisions and Indian guides—some of whom showed the whites for the first time what was later to become the vital Farewell Bend link of the Oregon Trail. But it was when waves of settlers began arriving, a generation after the Astorians, that Indian friendship was most decisive. The Nez Perce and the Northern Shoshoni, as mentioned, were particularly distinguished in this regard—Washakie, the illustrious war chief of the Eastern Band of the Wyoming Shoshoni, was given a memorial of gratitude signed by some 9,000 emigrants, having helped them cross difficult fords or recover strayed stock, and having kept his people out of quarrels even when an occasional unruly emigrant seemed bent on same.

But in general the first settlers to the Oregon country were not looking for trouble with anyone (unless it might be with the British); they were looking for a Promised Land of corn and wine, green grass and fertile loam—Beulah Land they called it in their hymns, after the land of heavenly joy described by Pilgrim in his Progress. They were for the most part earnest, honest, pious people, and they met the Indians' friendship with a friendship no less genuine in return.

Perhaps as many as 10,000 came to settle in the Oregon country in the early 1840s, mostly in the Willamette Valley, with a few in the valleys of the Columbia and the Cowlitz and on Puget Sound. If the river tribes restrained themselves from any grave objections to this invasion of "Bostons" as they called the settlers, the Americans likewise invoked patience when a Klickitat passerby stopped at a farmhouse to demand a prepared meal, or a few roistering Smackshop Chilluckittequaws requisitioned an ox or a horse, or a drunken Chinook stopped respectable people to shout in the jargon, "Nah, six, potlatch blue lu!" ("Hey, friend, give me whiskey!")

The real first trouble came in 1847, with the destruction of the Whitman mission among the Cayuse (near modern Walla Walla, Washington), and the murder of twelve Americans there, including Dr. Whitman and his wife. The subsequent deaths from measles of two little girls among the surviving women and children—Mrs. Whitman was the only woman killed—are usually added to the total. The immediate causes of the Whitman massacre are not clear. The Cayuse are said to have been increasingly resentful of the missionaries as more and more Bostons swarmed into the country, believing that the missionaries were in league with the Bostons to dispossess the Indians entirely. Bitter competition between Protestant and Catholic missions caused angry controversies among the Indians themselves, making for quarrels, grudges, and high feelings. A measles epidemic just before the murders—killing perhaps two hundred Cayuse people in only a few anguished weeks—helped to overheat the atmosphere.

Settlers formed a volunteer army and exacted preliminary revenge, and Congress was importuned for military protection. To make peace the Cayuse eventually (in 1850) turned over to the Oregon authorities five of the Whitman murderers, or five Cayuse men who at any rate played the part for the sake of saving the rest of their people. They were duly tried and hanged in Oregon City.

The early 1850s brought a surge of new population to Oregon, much of it consisting of ex-gold-rushers from the California diggings looking for a fresh bonanza. The political machinery of organized territorial government got into high gear—Washington was split off and established as a territory unto itself in 1853, under the governorship of Isaac I. Stevens, regarded as a strong anti-Indian man. United States Army troops were on hand by 1850, as a result of the alarms of the Cayuse War, and were regularly augmented thereafter.

These circumstances set the frontier process of Indian disposal in operation more or less automatically. For the next ten years it clattered with remarkable celerity through its familiar routine.

There were the usual councils large and small, the usual treaty chiefs of doubtful authority, the usual stubborn bands who did not want to obey the treaty chiefs' treaties, the usual hostilities to force them to do so. There was the usual reluctance on the part of some tribes to make any land-ceding treaties at all, and the consequent overrunning of their country by unauthorized immigrants and the consequent hostile incidents and the consequent wars.

There were numerous sizable operations involving the military, as well as countless volunteer "wars" on the California model, with attendant expense accounts billed to the government. One of the least illegitimate of these volunteer activities was the brief foray against the Rogue River Indians of southern Oregon in 1853, resulting in the "purchase" of the entire Rogue River Valley, more than 2,000,000 acres, for a price of $60,000; $15,000 of this was to go to settlers for claims of war damages, $45,000 to the Indians, to be paid in annuities of approximately $2.75 per Indian for sixteen years. There was also an added bill to the government of $258,000 for the five weeks' service of the 200 to 500 volunteers involved. The Rogue River country was left far from pacified by this expense; an outbreak of 1856 cost the lives of many innocent settlers and officials, extensive military operations, and the near extermination of a number of the various groups known collectively as the Rogue River Indians.

As the Indians were increasingly cowed there was the usual increase of lawlessness on the part of opportunistic whites, which goaded new wars into being. Military commanders, sent to Oregon to protect American settlers, found that they had to spend much of their effort vainly trying to protect the Indians, and wrote repeatedly to higher headquarters that outrages by white men were responsible for the disturbances.

These outrages were sometimes deliberately intended to

keep the hostilities burning, due to a quite sincere belief in many quarters (and an eye on profit in others) that the Indians should be wholly exterminated. "Let our motto be extermination, and death to all opposers," said a newspaper in Yreka, a trading town in the California-Oregon border country—whose merchants, incidentally, sold goods to a volunteer Indian-chasing expedition in 1854 at such exorbitant prices that the commanding general on the Pacific Coast sent a protest to Washington against paying the expedition's expenses, alleging that the entire project was unnecessary and had only been drummed up as a speculation to benefit the suppliers.

The exterminators were noisy and given to ever more violent visions—saloon orators as well as the official newspaper of the Know-Nothing Party in Oregon called for the extermination of all Catholics as soon as the savages were finished off. They also committed quite a bit of personal exterminating in their own small way—three unauthorized squads in one sector of Oregon killed between twelve and eighteen savages per squad in less than a week in 1853, in each case by inducing the savages to lay down their arms under pledges of peace and then shooting them.

But it should be pointed out that a reasonable proportion of the Oregon and Washington settlers seems to have felt sympathy toward the Indians, sometimes when such an attitude was so unpopular as to be dangerous. There were members of volunteer companies who denounced with considerable fervor the killing of Indian women and children. There were farmers who hid Indian friends in their houses when the troops or the volunteers were on the warpath—and Indians who did vice versa when the Indians were uprising. However, the anti-Indian people were more actively interested in removing the Indians than the just and peaceful people were interested in peace in justice. As a result, the peaceable part of the public was not as a rule very effective.

A great treaty-making council was held in the rainy spring of 1855 with the tribes east of the Cascades. It took place on an ancient council ground of the Yakimas in the Walla Walla Valley, and was attended by 4,000 or 5,000 people of the Yakimas, Nez Perces, Walla Wallas, Cayuses, Umatillas, Palouses, and eight other tribes of the region. There was much talk about land-cession and confinement to reservations; most of the Indian spokesmen present were opposed to both ideas. (A Cayuse orator said, "I wonder if the ground has anything to say? I wonder if the ground is listening to what is said. . . .") Support for the treaties desired by Governor Stevens, who had been appointed a United States treaty commissioner, came principally from an influential bloc of the traditionally pro-American Nez Perce, under a leader known as Lawyer. Lawyer stated that he was in favor of a treaty because his father had agreed with Lewis and Clark to live in peace with the whites. Lawyer's political foes murmured that he was after the appointment as head chief of the Nez Perces, an artificial office created some years previously by the missionaries.

Kamaiakan, a leader of the Yakimas, headed the opposition, even though the United States commissioners offered to make him supreme chief of all the nations gathered there. But at last each band of the fourteen present was permitted to select its own favorite home valley as a reservation, and on these terms the treaties were signed.

Charges and countercharges of duress, deceit, and plotted treachery in connection with the treaties came in later years, but they were academic—for within three months after the council war broke out, the major and decisive conflict in the Northwest. Miners and settlers did not wait for the ratification of the treaties by Congress before streaming into the treaty lands (gold strikes in the Colville and Coeur d' Alène countries spurred them on), and the Yakima and a half-dozen neighboring tribes decided almost unanimously that they did not want to ratify the treaties at all. White squatters were attacked, an Indian agent was killed, and Governor Stevens called out the troops.

The war lasted for three years, spreading to engulf peoples as far away as the Haida of British Columbia and some member peoples of the Duwamish League of Puget Sound—although Chief Seattle of the Duwamish League remained a strong American ally. It featured innumerable actions by irregulars of both sides, two Indian victories over regular Army troops, two naval engagements—an attack of Yakimas and their allies on river steamers, and a hot assault on the town of Seattle fought off by a naval force then in the harbor—and ended with the defeat of the Indian allies by an Army force of more than 700 artillery, cavalry, and infantry troops. Two or three dozen of the Indian leaders were hanged. Kamaiakan, wounded, escaped to Canada.

Wars continued, official and otherwise, and raids and retaliations, but for most of the tribes of the Northwest there remained only the final phase of decay and dissolution.

Sometimes, though, they decayed hard, as in the case of

Captain Jack and his band of Modocs. By 1870 this was, according to some accounts, a degraded band that hung around Yreka getting drunk and selling children when it wasn't out in the country terrorizing honest farmers; according to other accounts, Jack carried letters from prominent Yreka citizens testifying to his good conduct and good faith with the whites. Captain Jack, as he was known to the whites—his Modoc name was Kintpuash—preferred the Lost River country south of Upper Klamath Lake to the Klamath reservation on the lake where all the Modocs were supposed to go, and where about half of the tribe was already installed. The Lost River country was his home, Kintpuash said, and besides that he didn't like the Klamaths and couldn't live with them. But settlers wanted the Lost River country too, and they didn't want Kintpuash and his people as neighbors.

When troops came in 1872 to remove him by force to the reservation, Kintpuash and his band killed as many soldiers and settlers as they could manage and then took up a position in the lava beds (now a national monument) south of what is today called Tule Lake, just below the California line. More troops were summoned, and still more, and were joined by Indian scouts and allies—some of them Modocs from the Klamath agency—until after seven months more than a thousand men were in action against Kintpuash and his handful of followers. The Modoc band consisted of perhaps 250 men, women, and children, with perhaps seventy or eighty men of warrior age— most of the men were well known to the whites, under such monikers as Humpy Jerry, Shacknasty Jim, or Curly-headed Doctor.

Attack after attack was trapped and shot to pieces in the nightmare lava beds, total Army casualties running to over a hundred killed and wounded. A peace conference was arranged, and Kintpuash broke up the proceedings by killing out of hand the president of the peace commissioners, and Army commander of the Department of the Columbia, the noted General E. R. S. Canby—Kintpuash wore General Canby's uniform in later engagements. A Methodist minister was also murdered, and the other peace commissioners barely escaped with their lives. The nation was shocked by this cold-blooded treachery; President Grant demanded commensurate action from his commander of the Army, and his commander of the Army, General William Tecumseh Sherman, replied, "You will be fully justified in their utter extermination." Field guns were finally brought up and the Modocs were shelled out of their lava beds and at last, in scattered groups, hunted down and forced to surrender. Kint-puash and three of his lieutenants were hanged, and that was the end of Captain Jack (except that his severed head, and the heads of his three executed companions, were sent by the U. S. Army to Washington for the "anatomical" collection of the Surgeon General whence they were later transferred to the collections of the Smithsonian Institution, where they still remain). The rest of Captain Jack's band drew a harder fate, being sent to the Quapaw agency in the malarial southeastern corner of Indian Territory, where in the next 30 years they quietly decayed in numbers to less than a third of the 170 men, women, and children who surrendered.

Among the Nez Perce (distant relatives by language family to the Modocs and Klamaths), so constant in their American friendship, there lived a man of importance named Joseph, the name having been given him by the Reverend Spalding, whose school Joseph had attended. Joseph was the son of a Cayuse father but his wife was a Nez Perce, and he had been at the great Walla Walla council of 1855 as one of the Nez Perce spokesmen. The treaty he signed there reserved for his Nez Perce band what it claimed as its ancient home, the Wallowa Valley along the Snake River at the mouth of the Grande Ronde, crossroads of the present boundaries of the states of Oregon, Washington, and Idaho.

After 1855 the Nez Perces stuck to peace and American alliance while all Oregon was on fire with war, rescued a body of American troops in 1858, and refused entanglement in trouble-making plots at the start of the Civil War.

In 1863 a new treaty was negotiated, in which Joseph's band did not participate, which ceded the Wallowa Valley to the government for settlement. Joseph protested that the other Nez Perces who had made this cession had acted without authority, and in violation of the previous treaty of 1855. He and his band stayed in the valley, although white settlers started moving in and the usual unavoidable hostile incidents occurred.

In 1871 Joseph died and the leadership of his band went to a son named Hin-mah-too-yah-laht-ket (Thunder Rolling in the Mountains), who was known to the Americans as Young Joseph, and later as Chief Joseph.

The Nez Perces are so often described as noble, handsome,

brave, truehearted, and in general excellent in all respects, that it seems likely they may have been, J. Fenimore Cooperesque though the assumption may be. When it comes to Young Joseph, the paean reaches crescendo. He was, so they say, of wisdom, eloquence, goodness, and mercy unmeasurable, and in his pictures as a young man he is obviously no mountain Indian, but a figment of Sir Walter Scott's imagination, or more likely George Sand's.

In the spring of 1876 a man of Young Joseph's own band was killed by a settler in the course of one of the unavoidable hostile incidents—all of which the Nez Perces had so far endured without retaliation. Young Joseph said of this murder: "As to the murderer I have made up my mind. I have come to the conclusion to let him escape and enjoy health and not take his life for the one he took. I am speaking as though I spoke to the man himself . . . I pronounce the sentence that he shall live."

The government offered allotments of land to be owned white style by individual Indians who might want to try staying on in their home valley as small farmers among white neighbors. But Young Joseph and his people were horsemen, with wealth that they very much cherished in their herds of horses, many of them the blue Appaloosas with five-finger-spotted rumps that had become traditional Nez Perce war and hunting horses, and the twenty acres offered under the allotment plan to each Indian man was far from enough for a stockman. The Indians wanted to stay in the valley as a community because they were a community and because the valley was their home. Political influence in Washington, however, was more responsive to those who wanted the Wallowa Valley turned over to white occupation, and this decision, after some backing and filling on the part of the Washington authorities, was adopted. To avoid a hopeless clash Young Joseph at last agreed to take his people out of the valley and settle on the Lapwai Reservation, where the government wanted them to go. This was in the spring of 1877.

Unfortunately some white neighbors took the opportunity to make away with several hundred of the Indians' horses while the Nez Perces were preparing to move. The departing people, already heartsick, homesick, and enraged, counted their multiplied grievances until at last a moment came when they could be restrained no longer. In a night and day of vengeance a mutinous party of a few young men murdered eighteen settlers, and out came the troops. After seventy-two years of peace the

Nez Perces were at war. Joseph, who had said, ". . . rather than have war I would give up my country . . . I would give up everything . . ." no longer had any other choice.

It happened that among the troops there was a twenty-five-year-old West Pointer, one Lieutenant Wood, who later, under the name of Charles Erskine Scott Wood, became one of the finest writers in America. The picture of Indian fighting scribbled in his journal might be dull but is probably real.

". . . hot stifling march across a dry prairie. No breakfast no water, men fainting and falling by the wayside." But, the next day: ". . . the afternoon march and camp on the prairie, grass to our knees, rolling hills. . . ."

And his first Indian battle: "The advance, more rains. Indians speckling the hills like ants. Firing. Sudden feeling of intoxication on hearing the shots nervous eagerness for the fight. . . ." But the fight was over. The ants speckling the hills and the distant slam of the shots was an Indian battle.

In a series of such fights the American commander, General O. O. Howard, found himself consistently outmaneuvered, suffering heavy losses, and unable to gain an advantage although superior in numbers, firepower, and mobility—Joseph being burdened with all of his refugee people and their belongings. It began to appear that young Chief Joseph might be a military prodigy—he was, according to the Army officers who fought against him. He decided to lead his band—400 to 500 people, with at the most something between 100 and 200 effective warriors—to safety in Canada, and for four months he fought his way through and around Army units (with their Indian scouts) that were rushed in from all sides to head him off, fought a running campaign of over a thousand mountain miles that has been compared to the Anabasis of Xenophon's Ten Thousand Greeks, conducted with a magnificent generalship that has been compared to Napoleon's best.

The question has been raised in recent studies as to how much of the credit for this campaign should go to Joseph and how much to the leaders of smaller bands or other chief men present during the march—the lean Looking Glass, famous warrior, who joined along with his band after Joseph's first startling victory had been achieved; or Too-hul-hul-sute, the aged and influential Dreamer priest; or White Bird, who at the last moment did succeed in reaching Canada with about 100 followers; or Joseph's brother, Ollokot, leader of the warriors in

Joseph's band, "he who led the young men," as Joseph spoke of him; or others among the ranking men.

Without written records from the Nez Perce headquarters it will never be possible to assign reasonably exact credit for the various battle plans—even in the presence of written records the same sort of question is raised among Napoleon buffs, wondering about the real contribution of such gentry as Marshal Ney.

Nor is it possible to assign exact commands to the various principal men. Indian rank and authority are slippery matters at best, when it comes to defining them in traditional European military terms. The custom of separate peace and war chiefs, common among some Indian peoples, was not followed by the Nez Perces and the neighboring people of the Columbia River plateau region, or by the people of the neighboring Great Basin area and the California region. Authority was instead likely to be rather informal.

Contemporary comment, at the time of the epic adventure of his fighting Nez Perces, associates the aura of principal authority with Joseph. He may thus be regarded as the inspired tactician of the march of his people, or, if one wishes, simply as the symbol of their inspired spirit.

He fought over a dozen engagements with four different Army columns, cut off pursuit by a daring night raid that left the pursuers without transport animals, or by an adroit feint that turned the pursuing columns around to run into each other, or simply fought and outfought the enemy with his handful of dazzling Nez Perce cavalrymen—". . . they rode at full gallop along the mountain side in á steady formation by fours; formed twos, at a given signal, with perfect precision, to cross a narrow bridge; then galloped into line, reined in to a sudden halt, and dismounted with as much system as regulars," said an Army general. The Nez Perces were hurt several times by heavy casualties—eighty-nine killed in one engagement, fifty of those being women and children. But they continued to march, and they continued to fight. They practiced one further novelty, novel for either red or white warriors, in the warfare of the time and region: Joseph had reportedly ordered no scalping in the battles that he was to command, and—from the Indians—there was none.

The war they fought, said General William Tecumseh Sherman, was ". . . one of the most extraordinary Indian wars of which there is any record. The Indians throughout displayed a courage and skill that elicited universal praise; they abstained from scalping, let captive women go free, did not commit indiscriminate murder of peaceful families, which is usual. . . ." General Nelson A. Miles, whose column finally cut off Joseph's retreat, was quoted as saying, "In this skillful campaign they have spared hundreds of lives and thousands of dollars worth of property that they might have destroyed . . ." and was moved to add gratuitously that Joseph's Nez Perces ". . . have, in my opinion, been grossly wronged in the years past." One gross wrong may be attributed to General Nelson A. Miles himself, who endeavored to make Joseph a prisoner during discussions under a flag of truce, an outrage that apparently delayed the Indian surrender for an extra added three days of needless suffering and casualties.

Joseph "led his tribe—men, women, and children, sick, wounded, maimed, and blind—through the Bitter Root Mountains, twice across the Rocky Mountains, through the Yellowstone National Park, across the Missouri River, to the Bear Paw Mountains, where, on Eagle Creek, within thirty miles of the Canadian line, he finally surrendered, October 5, 1877," wrote young Lieutenant Wood some years later, in a letter recounting the saga and its conclusion. Lieutenant Wood had been made General Howard's aide-de-camp and so was in at the finish, which came with the arrival of Howard and his additional forces at the end of the above-mentioned three days' standoff. Lieutenant Wood's letter continues: ". . . on the evening of a wintry day, the prairie powdered with snow, and a red and stormy sun almost at the horizon, Joseph surrendered, his people coming out of the burrows they had made in the hills, and where they had been living without fires, subsisting on the flesh of the dead horses. . . ."

"In the final attack, a surprise by General Miles, Joseph's little girl, about eight or nine years old, and of whom he was very fond, fled in terror out on the prairie, and at the time of his surrender she was supposed to have perished from cold and starvation. As a matter of fact, she was afterwards found among the Sioux as a prisoner or slave, and was restored to Joseph; but with little effect, as his express condition of surrender—that he should be allowed to go back to the reservation which had been provided for him—was broken by the government, and he and his people were sent to the malarial bottoms of the Indian

Territory, where all of his own children (six) and most of his band died." (An error, for the lost little girl did survive and grow up, although separated from her father—see Notes.)

"At the time of the surrender, the able bodied warriors were surprisingly few, in contrast to the number of sick, aged, and decrepit men and women: blind people, children, babies and wounded that poured out of their burrows in the earth as soon as it was known that they could do so with safety.

"Joseph came up to the crest of the hill, upon which stood General Howard, General Miles, an interpreter, and myself. Joseph was the only one mounted, but five of his principal men clung about his knees and pressed close to the horse, looking at him, and talking earnestly in low tones. Joseph rode with bowed head, listening attentively, apparently, but with perfectly immobile face. As he approached the spot where we were standing, he said something, and the five men who were with him halted. Joseph rode forward alone, leaped from his horse, and, leaving it standing, strode toward us. He opened his blanket which was wrapped around him, and handed his rifle to General Howard, who motioned him to deliver it to General Miles, which Joseph did. Standing back, he folded his blanket again across his chest, leaving one arm free, somewhat in the manner of a Roman senator with his toga, and, half turning toward the interpreter, said:

"Tell General Howard I know his heart. What he told me before, in Idaho, I have it in my heart. I am tired of fighting . . . My people ask me for food, and I have none to give. It is cold, and we have no blankets, no wood. My people are starving to death. Where is my little daughter? I do not know. Perhaps, even now, she is freezing to death. Hear me, my chiefs. I have fought; but from where the sun now stands, Joseph will fight no more forever.'

"And he drew his blanket across his face, after the fashion of Indians when mourning or humiliated, and, instead of walking towards his own camp, walked directly into ours, as a prisoner.

"After long delay, and when his band was reduced to a comparatively small number of people, he was (in 1885), with the remnant of his tribe, allowed to come north from the Indian Territory—not to his old ground in Idaho, but to Northern Washington. No supplies were provided for them. They marched from the Indian Territory to their new home, and arrived on the edge of winter in a destitute condition, experiencing great suffering. . . .

"I think that, in his long career, Joseph cannot accuse the Government of the United States of one single act of justice. . . ."

The above version of Joseph's surrender speech was written from memory, although it was Lieutenant Wood who took down the original at the time, in his capacity as General Howard's aide. The speech has become one of the most famous in Indian literature and has been many times quoted, in almost as many different versions.

XIV
The People of Dreams

Beyond the Spanish frontier in northern Mexico, in the year 1594, the chief of a village of Laguneros Indians rode out on horseback to welcome a venturesome Jesuit, the first missionary to appear in those parts. The exploring padre duly reported his cordial reception, in no wise making anything remarkable of the mounted chief. Obviously there was nothing extraordinary about wild Indians owning and riding horses. And yet this was only seventy-five years after Cortes had landed the ten stallions, five mares, and a foal who were the first Spanish horses to appear in horseless North America.

The prehistoric horse was born in the Americas, many millions of years ago, but for some reason became extinct in the New World at the close of the Ice Age. However, horses had long before spread to the Old World, no doubt across the occasional Siberian land bridge. Thus the horses brought by the Spaniards to the New World were, fairly literally, coming back home. Perhaps they knew it. In any case, they went forth and multiplied at an astonishing rate.

For horseless South America the principal early center of distribution was Peru, where horses first arrived in 1532. By 1535 they had entered the horse heaven that was to become Argentina. By 1600 they streamed over the Argentine pampas in herds too vast to count. The varying peoples there, and the people of the rolling, scrub-covered country adjoining on the north, known as the Chaco, became intense horsemen and utterly revolutionized the ways of their world in the process.

In North America the horse frontier jumped to northern New Mexico, to the heel of the Rockies, when Oñate's colonists drove up thousands of head of assorted livestock in 1598. The Santa Fe country remained for generations the chief dispersal point for the new American horse. Spanish officials now and then made efforts to enforce security regulations against letting Indians learn the use of horses, but the *mayor-domos* at ranches and missions had to reply that there were only Indians available to work as vaqueros. The Indians learned. The secret plans of the manipulation of that ultimate weapon, the horse, must have been stolen many times over by amateur Indian secret agents. And having learned, Indians liberated horses by the bunch, by the herd, by the multitude, from the huge ranches of Chihuahua and New Mexico.

The Pueblo revolt of 1680 threw all the horses in New Mexico on the open Indian market for a dozen years, and from this point on the horse frontier left the white frontier years behind. Bartered or stolen from band to band, ridden on terrorizing raids that covered 500 miles or more, galloped into hitherto unknown lands on wonderfully lucrative hunting trips, driven in herds to distant nations by Indian merchants, horses fanned out over the West, their hoofbeats a flourish of drums announcing a marvelous new life. The sun-cracked wastes of Utah and Nevada were too poor in graze and water for a man to keep a horse but the Utes of the Rockies' western slopes took to horses and passed them along (unintentionally, no doubt), and by the 1690s horses were being introduced among the Northern Shoshoni of Wyoming by someone, spies or tradesmen or exiles from horse-owning tribes, who could teach the mysteries of their management. And now, with Shoshoni war feathers tied in their flying tails and with Shoshoni bowmen on their backs, horses trotted eastward out of the mountains to sweep across the high plains, the seemingly endless plains that stretch from the Rockies to the Mississippi Valley prairies, in pursuit of the antelope, the buffalo, and the constant Shoshoni foes, the bold-hearted people of the northern plains known as the Blackfeet.

Intrepid or not, the trudging foot people of the plains were thrown into panic by enemies transformed into centaurs nine feet tall who could dash upon their victims with the speed of the screaming wind. Mounted Shoshonis were attacking the Blackfeet by 1730, according to the best recollection of a Blackfoot senior citizen more than half a century later; the Blackfeet asked for help from Crees and Assiniboins to their east, who came and defeated a Shoshoni war party with the aid of another fantastic new weapon—the gun.

The horse frontier, moving in from the south and west, and the gun frontier, advancing from the east, met on the Great Plains in a spectacular clash and created the figure that has obsessed the world ever since as the archetype of the American Indian: the feather-streaming, buffalo-chasing, wild-riding, recklessly fighting Indian of the plains.

This figure, shaped by the European's horse and gun, decorated from warbonnet band to moccasins with the European's beads, only reached full glory when the real Indian world was all but a memory. The Plains Indian was a late, last flowering of the ancient cultures already vanished or in ruins over most of the hemisphere. He was less sheer Indian than almost any of his predecessors down through the ages of Indian history, from the Ancient Olmecs and the Mayas to the Creeks and Iroquois.

But in some other respects the Plains Indian is an excellent happenchance choice as an Indian symbol. In his exaggerated world he intensified a whole palette of more specialized Indian colors common to some previous Indian societies although by no means to all: Warrior societies and elaborate codes of combat, fear of sex and grief for the dead and emotional excesses deriving from both, sacred objects and sacred rites deriving from dreams and inspired visions, and the omnipresent sacred power to be sought in dreams and inspired visions. In all these respects and many more the Plains Indian was the Indian carried to extremes. Finally, the boundless land in which he lived, confined only by the wide and starry sky, gave obvious emphasis to the pervasive notion of Indian freedom.

These modern Plains Indians sprang from several different roots, from farmers and hunters who had lived on the plains and their margins for untold centuries as well as from the diverse tribes and nations who poured into the plains with the storm fronts of the horse and the gun.

There had been buffalo hunters on the plains at least since

Folsom times, possibly 10,000 years ago. Mountains of bones from the herds they stampeded over cliffs or into ravines have been found from Texas to Alberta, Canada, sometimes in such quantities that present day Indians have made a business of selling the bones to be turned into commercial fertilizer. Eventually villages of farmers appeared along the river courses; some of the typical plainsmen for many hundreds of years seem to have been not hunters but pottery-making farmers who hunted as a sideline. Some ancient peoples along the eastern marches of the plains were clearly connected with the great Hopewell culture centering in the Ohio Valley far to the east, and there centering some 2,000 years ago in time. The plains were long a frontier between the two different farming worlds, the worlds to the east and west, worlds actually quite different from each other although their farming economies were founded on the same basic crops, corn and beans and squash; in the corn-pounding, hominy-boiling towns to the eastward the farm was principally woman's work and the holy places were summits of mounds or pyramids raised to the heavens, while in the corn-grinding tortilla-slapping towns to the westward men worked the farm fields as a rule and the holy places were more likely to be underground, in the kivas.

Later earthlodge villages in the easterly regions of the plains, dating back to at least more than 400 years ago, are identifiable as Pawnee, carrying associations from the Temple Mound people of the Southeast. In more recent times farming gave way to a return to nomadic hunting over most of the plains country, and some people who had once grown corn and made pottery forgot how to do both, and devoted their lives to hunting the inexhaustible buffalo.

Among the historic peoples of known location the Blackfeet (a literal translation of their own name, Siksika, possibly referring to black-dyed moccasins) are regarded as the ancients of the northern plains. Their language, a much-altered Algonquian variant, had obviously been separated for a long period from other Algonquian languages to the east. In the vague but seemingly not too distant past they appear to have expanded westward over the Alberta-Saskatchewan plains and later, perhaps at about the time they acquired horses, southward into what is now Montana, thrusting out a people then living in the plains in the region of the present Canadian boundary; these were the Kutenai, a tall, estimable race speaking a language unrelated to any other, who gradually moved westward across the Rockies and became northern neighbors of the Flatheads and Nez Perces. The Siksika, by the time whites became familiar with their country, dwelt along the eastern base of the Rockies throughout Montana and far up into Alberta, to the edge of the black northern forests that begin beyond the North Saskatchewan River.

Known collectively as the Blackfoot confederacy they were a numerous (estimated 15,000 in 1780) people divided into three tribes of common descent, common language, and (sometimes) a common front against a common enemy. These three tribes were, in the farthest north, the Siksika proper; next to the south the Kainah or Bloods (possibly from a former name for themselves, "Blood People," or possibly from their sacred face paint of red earth); and farthest south, generally below the present Canada line in Montana, the Piegans ("Poor Robes"). On the north a small Athapascan-speaking tribe, the Sarcee (Blackfoot for "No-goods") allied itself to the Siksika in later years for protection.

East of the Piegans another group speaking a highly aberrant Algonquian language roamed the plains of Montana and Canada between the Missouri and the Saskatchewan. These were the Atsina, brothers of the Arapaho of the Wyoming plains from whom they had separated perhaps as late as the seventeenth century; they may have been in the plains country— somewhere—well before that. Misreading the sign talk, early traders often called the Atsina by the various names of Minnetarees or Gros Ventres (French for "Big Bellies"). The same names were applied to a totally unrelated tribe speaking a Siouan tongue, the Hidatsa, who as village farmers along the Missouri River in what is now North Dakota may have been survivals of the plains farmers of an earlier time, and so also old residents of the plains at the time of the arrival of the horse. The Hidatsa were neighbored on the north and south by a few other villages of plains farmers, the Siouan-speaking Mandan upriver from them and the Arikara, an offshoot of the Pawnee, down the Missouri to the south.

A part of the Hidatsa who called themselves the Absaroke, meaning Crow-people or Bird-people, left the Hidatsa towns and traveled westward to settle in the country of the Yellowstone and its southern branches of the Powder and Big Horn rivers. This evidently happened several centuries ago. They stopped farming and building earth lodges and making pottery and became hunters living in skin tipis, and are known historically as the Crows. Their country ran so much to mountains that they are sometimes spoken of in the two divisions of Mountain Crows and River Crows.

These, then, were the principal known inhabitants of the high plains north of Kansas before the coming of the horse and the gun. The gun frontier drove in new peoples from the east, who seized on the horse and became thoroughgoing plainsmen almost, one gathers, overnight.

In the northeast a part of the Cree, snowshoe and canoe people when they were at home in their Canadian forests, pressed into the prairies and then the plains with Hudson's Bay Company guns, looking for beaver, and became the Plains Cree. They drew along friends from southern Ontario, the Assiniboin, a sizable tribe that had separated not long before from the great Siouan-speaking nation known as the Dakota.

The Ojibwa, triumphant with trade guns, drove the rest of the Dakota and the Algonquian-speaking Cheyenne out of the forests of the Upper Mississippi country in Wisconsin and eastern Minnesota. Both the Dakota and the Cheyenne were farming people as well as hunters, decorous and yet valorous, and were clearly of a high order in character, intellect, and ability. They became some of the most notable of the Plains Indians.

The Cheyenne crossed the wide Missouri into the short-grass plains, and in the space of perhaps fifty years or so roundabout the last quarter of the eighteenth century and the first quarter of the nineteenth transformed themselves into horsemen, constant hunters, magnificent warriors, in short into Plains Indians of the first class. They divided, after much wandering, into two groups, the Northern Cheyenne around the headwaters of the North Platte and the Yellowstone, and the Southern Cheyenne headquartering along the plains of the Arkansas within sight of the southern Colorado Rockies.

The Dakota, who formed a true confederacy (the word means "allies), were made up of seven tribes—their own name for themselves was *Ocheti shakowin,* "the seven council fires." Some of these tribes, such as several known collectively as the Santee, remained on the edge of the eastern forests and adjoining high-grass prairies and remained semi-agricultural. Others, such as the tribe known as the Teton, moved into the plains in the late 1700s and within a century or less were known the world over as the very embodiment of Plains Indianism—the famous Sioux. The French coined the name Sioux from an Algonquian term meaning "enemies"—in fact, referring as usual to "serpents" in its full original form. Out of all the different Siouan peoples the Dakota have usually been designated specifically as the Sioux, somewhat as the Five Nations Iroquois became the specific Iroquois.

The Sioux spread clear across the plains into the country of the Crows, who naturally resisted their invasion and became their inveterate enemies. At the height of Sioux power, the Northern Cheyenne were bordered on the north by the Oglala, the most westerly and one of the most renowned of the Teton subdivisions, which were also seven in number, and Dakota country included much of the territory of the present states of the same name, extending south into Nebraska and east into Iowa and Minnesota.

For all these people of the plains, newcomers and old residents alike, the horse brought a miraculously changed life.

Before the horse, families moved their possessions from place to place with the help of dogs, dogs bearing little packs or dogs dragging the A-shaped frame of trailing sticks across which baggage was lashed, the contraption named by French Canadians a travois. Possessions, therefore, could be neither many nor heavy.

After the horse, lodge poles could be as long as thirty feet, tipis (a Sioux word) could be made of as many as eighteen or even twenty dressed buffalo hides, enclosing a room some fifteen spacious feet across crammed with furnishings, riches, and relations.

After the horse, buffalo could be found miles away, surrounded at a gallop, chased down if they stampeded—although the formal hunt was still strictly regulated, as was the camp life, by a police society.

After the horse, dried meat and the everlasting pemmican (dried meat pounded up with suet, marrow, and some such added flavoring as wild cherries) could be kept and moved by the ton. One could own and carry along a wealth of buffalo robes, pots and skin bags and rawhide traveling trunks, tools, new clothes, spare time, and new delights.

The old custom Coronado had noticed in 1541 of Plains Indians trading buffalo robes for the corn and beans of farming villagers could be extended; traders could go a thousand miles after such luxury importations as jewelry or rare furs or the beautiful Nez Perce bows, made of the horn of the wild mountain sheep. The Mandan, Arikara, and Hidatsa towns became trading centers and entered upon a century of unexampled prosperity.

Better still, there was time for war, and horses gave it method as well as purpose. A man's fortune was counted in horses, a young man's future depended on horses, and so horses became the common goal of war, and the capture of horses the prime reality of war. War's other aspects, fighting and the danger of death, were gradually bound around with as much ceremony as a Japanese tea party. Elite soldier societies multiplied, each with special costumes, special grades, special manners, special sacred rites, and special taboos.

Wars called for fancy tricks, fancy riding, fancy fighting, as war songs called for fancy drumming. Two of the three finest feats of war were to capture by stealth an enemy's best horses, the valued stallion or fleet hunters he kept picketed close beside his lodge; or to touch an enemy's body in battle—this last, called via the French "counting coup," gave rise to rigid, complicated, and jealously administered systems of war honors. As in some other countries of the Indian world, a man introduced himself on the occasion of any public appearance by recounting his deeds of war, reciting his coups. Coup systems and soldier societies were brought to the plains from the Indian world of the forested East, but in the plains they reached their most elaborate development. The taking of scalps was not important—the Crees and the Teton Dakotas alone regarded a scalp as a first-class trophy. The Dakotas, if they had time, would take all the skin of the head and face, possibly similar to the "skins of five men's heads" shown to Jacques Cartier in Canada in 1535. Scalping was apparently very limited in extent before the coming of Europeans; scalp bounties undoubtedly helped spread it far and wide over the Indian world.

As in other parts of the Indian world (and as in the world of the ancient Greeks, for that matter), a war leader was usually guided by the auguries of dreams, and a sacred symbol— inspired by a dream—was carried with the war party like a banner. In this life where a man was expected to die young, and many did, the rare boon of old age could only come from divine protection, a supernatural power granted, along with instructions for its use, in a dream or vision.

For above all, the new world of the horse brought time and

temptation to dream. The plains are afloat in mysterious space, and the winds come straight from heaven. Anyone alone in the plains turns into a mystic. The plains had always been a place for dreams, but with horses they were more so. Something happens to a man when he gets on a horse in a country where he can ride at a run forever; it is quite easy to ascend to an impression of living in a myth. He either feels like a god or feels closer to God. There seems never to have been a race of plains horsemen that was not either fanatically proud or fanatically religious. The Plains Indians were both.

A man dreamed of the horse he would capture, and of what sort of feathers to wear in his hair, and the paint to put on his face, and the foe he would kill, and the girls he would marry, and the pattern to put on his shield, and the way he would die.

Sacred bundles and sacred objects, for the most part associated with dreams and visions, operated for the welfare of the group as a whole, and in particular guarded the welfare of the bundle's owner, as long as the rules were carefully followed, in other words as long as devoted attention did not lapse—as long, for instance, as the owner of a Blackfoot pipe bundle sang the correct ritualistic songs in sets of seven on the special occasions when the bundle was opened, and observed certain taboos such as never pointing at anything except with his thumb, and never picking up anything he found. A Cheyenne owner of a Thunder Bow, or Contrary Bow, had to do exactly the contrary of whatever he was asked to do, and in battle he could never retreat. Sacred objects were owned by persons of piety and consequence, and brought as much prestige as the ownership of a private chapel brought to a medieval baron. Sometimes the power of such objects was transferable, and their buying and selling constituted one of the uses of the new wealth that came with the horse; a man was respected not for the riches he possessed but for the riches he had spent on the holy objects that had passed through his hands.

With horse prosperity entire tribes could gather every year or two or three for observances of the greatest solemnity, when the tribe was reunited and renewed. Such observances took a variety of forms with different peoples, but the principal appeal to dreams and visions, the Sun Dance, was common to nearly all the people of the plains. For days and nights (usually four) the dedicated participants went without food or water and throughout all the dance stared fixedly at the top of a central pole, where

a red-painted buffalo skull or some other mystic object represented the sun. The Sun Dance was scarcely a dance; the
celebrants stood more or less in one place, rising up and down on
their toes or shuffling a little backward and forward. They held
eagle-bone whistles in their mouths, to sound with each breath.
For those who lasted long enough, a vision might be granted.
Some, in fulfillment of a vow or to wring pity from the gods,
tortured themselves by running skewers through the muscles in
their chests or backs and swinging from thongs until the skewers
were torn loose.

The Creator, the Old Person, God by whatever name, spoke
through dreams and visions over much of the Indian world; it
was merely typical of the plains people to go to extremes in this
conversation. These were people of emotional excesses. Blight-
ed love, or sometimes nothing more that a scolding from her
mother, might drive a girl to suicide. Humiliation could make a
man decide to embrace death by single-handedly charging an
enemy war camp. Death was always a matter of magnificent
emotion. Mourning brought wild excesses of grief. The third
great feat of war was bravery in rescuing a dead body from the
enemy, so it could not be mutilated.

In general there was a considerable sameness among the
people of the plains, in spite of the diversity of their origins; all,
too, lived in the same dream-haunted atmosphere. Many whites
found the Plains Indians remarkably alike, all as natural and
colorful as tigers. But within the general pattern there were also
considerable gulfs of difference, extending far deeper than the
differences in ceremonies, moccasins, arrow-feathering, or
styles of decoration—rich and varied as these last are. These
deeper differences might be represented at one end of the
spectrum by the relatively earnest and austere Cheyennes, very
much concerned with living up to an ideal of high-minded and
responsible behavior, and at the other end of the spectrum by
the relatively free and easy Blackfeet. A trader among the
Blackfeet in the era around 1800 wrote that they were the "most
independent and happy people of all the tribes E. of the Rocky
mountains. War, women, horses and buffalo are their delights,
and all these they have at command."

By 1800 French fur traders had been in the great plains for
more than two generations. In the early 1700s the Illinois
country was an important district of New France, producing
grain, tobacco, and Indian traders—a party of Illinois traders

made a try (although they didn't get far) at crossing the plains to New Mexico sometime before 1703. Lead mines were opened in the country of the lower Missouri in the 1720s—200 French miners and 500 Santo Domingo blacks were imported to work them—and traders were by that time already striving to ascend the apparently endless Missouri; a French expedition was at the Mandan towns in 1739 noting the riches of commerce there and talking with horse-owning plains people—possibly plains-newcomers Cheyennes and old resident Crows—who came to make long trading visits, hearing reports of the Rockies, the Pacific, and seeing with their own eyes trade goods, a bridle and bit, from the New Mexico Spanish. Some of the same explorers came within sight of the South Dakota Black Hills four years later, the French flag's farthest west in the New World. France's official fur-trading organization was dismantled by the defeat of France in the French and Indian War, but the French wilderness mechanics, the *voyageurs* and *coureurs de bois*, remained; they, and the Indians they had such a knack for getting along with, hired out their talents to English and Scottish masters and were the muscles of the two great English fur-hunting combines. Well before the end of the 1700s French traders had reached the Rocky Mountains by nearly every important river between the Saskatchewan and the Red, and before the end of the century had helped the two English companies string rival lines of trading "factories" from the Red River of the North to the Rockies. For much of the hundred years thereafter French or Indian-French assistance was an indispensable part of successful dealings with the nations of the northern Rockies and the upper plains.

Six veteran Frenchmen and two Indians accompanied Alexander Mackenzie on his trail-breaking journey to the Canadian Pacific in 1793, and five Frenchmen crossed the plains with the Lewis and Clark expedition in 1805—not counting the infant Jean-Baptiste Charbonneau, born to the Shoshoni girl guide, Sacagawea, two months before the start of the trip.

Lewis and Clark opened the way for a new specimen of foreigner in the plains and the "Shineing Mountains," as Captain Meriwether Lewis referred to the Rockies. This was the American trapper, the "free" trapper, the mountain man. The mountain men became a byword for knowledge of the wild Far West and how to survive therein; a few who survived gained fame in specialized circles as guides for later western explorers. One of the most remarkable, so much so that some students have thought of him as wholly legendary, was Sacagawea's son Baptiste, who was educated at the court of a European prince and returned to the Rockies to whack out a monumental mountain-man career, packed with the history of westward-rolling America, and at last went home to his mother's people, the Northern Shoshonis, to die in their Wyoming country of the Wind River Mountains.

The mountain men lived and worked with the Indians and constituted, in effect, a small, scattered tribe of their own, in some respects more Indian than the Indians themselves, so far from the civilization of the "States" they were scarcely recognizable as white Americans. With one implacable exception the Indians usually·dealt them more hospitality than hostility, the friendliest being the Northern Shoshonis, or Snakes, as the mountain men called them, using the name given them by the Sioux and the French. One of the few large-scale Indian battles the mountain men encountered took place in the valley of the Little Snake River, almost on the present Colorado-Wyoming line, in the summer of 1841, when a brigade of some thirty trappers, captained by a mountain veteran named Henry Fraeb, along with a number of Shoshonis, were attacked by a tremendous war party of several hundred Cheyennes, Sioux, and Arapahoes—for what reason is not known; perhaps horses, perhaps the Shoshonis, perhaps for coups, perhaps anything.

The mountain men forted up behind killed horses and logs and withstood charge after charge throughout the day, the Cheyenne and Sioux warriors galloping up furiously to within ten or fifteen yards while Fraeb yelled constant warning to his men to hold their fire and shoot carefully in turn, so there would always be some loaded rifles. The mountain men knew their business and were able to maintain a steady fire from their heavy Hawken rifles, slow to load but very deadly. Each charge broke with a vicious drive of arrows, as the army of attackers wheeled and dashed off, gathering up on the way their dead and wounded.

At the end of the day the Cheyennes and their allies stopped fighting and went away, but by then Old Fraeb had been killed, and, said one of his men years later, "he was the ugliest looking dead man I ever saw, and I have seen a good many. His face was all covered with blood, and he had rotten front teeth and a horrible grin. When he was killed he never fell, but sat braced up against a stump, a sight to behold." Three or four other trappers were killed in the same fight, commemorated by the trappers in strewing the names Battle Creek and Battle Lake and Battle Mountain over the vicinity, and calling the mountain just south, where they and the Shoshonis had sent their women to hide, Squaw Mountain.

The one implacable enemy of the American trappers in the early days was the Blackfoot confederacy. Principal source of the savage Blackfoot hostility was to be found, more than likely, among the Canadian companies on the Saskatchewan, where the Siksika people traded. It was considered a legitimate business tactic, in the fur trade, to urge one's Indian clients to kill off the competition. The Blackfeet did so with joyous abandon, and their very name was enough to make a mountain man swallow hard and think serious thoughts of his hair. Since they were the most powerful nation north of the Missouri, they effectively deflected American penetration to the north.

Finally, in the 1830s, American traders made some progress at winning Piegan trade from the Hudson's Bay Company, and some progress at making peace (with a great flow of rum), although trapper killing still went on. Most of the trade of the Piegans and their Atsina allies, controlling the country that is now northern Montana east of the Rockies, was in American hands by the late 1840s.

The mountain men, by this time, had vanished from the trapped-out beaver streams; their place, in the plains and the Rockies, was being taken by trains of West Coast-bound overland emigrants. The frontier stole in from the east like dusk, and by the 1840s the nations of the plains had already felt its touch, in the form of whiskey, plagues, syphilis, and a bewildering increase of war.

Throughout the 1830s the Southern Cheyennes and Arapahoes fought the Comanches and Kiowas along the Arkansas River; to the north, above the Platte, the Sioux and the Northern Cheyennes were at war with the Crows; most of the people of the farther plains were hostile to the Shoshonis, who ranged down from the mountains, and to the Pawnees, who ranged westward from the eastern reaches of the plains. The "intruded" eastern Indians, Delawares and Shawnees and Potawatomis and many others, driven west of the Mississippi, were fearful adversaries, expert with firearms at a time when the plains people had few guns, when they "would pay a good price for a barrel hoop to convert into knives and daggers," as a mountain man remarked of the early 1840s. The eastern intruders were sometimes attacked on sight, as numbers of fleeing survivors of Black Hawk's band were later "cut off" by the Sioux after they had reached the Mississippi's west bank.

Some of these numerous feuds were conducted with propriety and a regard for the laws of tradition, but some were not. Such Cheyenne warriors as Little Wolf, chief of the Bow String soldier society, and White Antelope, one of the chiefs of the Crooked Lance society, won great fame fighting the Comanches and Pawnees in the most honorable and decent manner, but in 1838 a group of Bow String men whipped with their quirts the aged and respected keeper of the Medicine Arrows, the Cheyennes' most sacred possession, in order to force him to perform the requisite ceremonies so they could go to war. This was an unheard-of thing. The chief of the Dog Soldiers, the principal Cheyenne soldier and police society, killed another Cheyenne in a drunken brawl. This was an unheard-of thing. He had to go into exile along with all of his relations. As a result of these things the Cheyennes suffered bitter defeats at the hands of the Kiowas and Comanches, until a peace was made between them in 1840. Thereafter the Arapahoes and Cheyennes made the Utes, westward across the Rockies, their grade-A enemies.

The incessant simmer of hostility was bad for trade and travel. In the early 1840s five Blackfoot chiefs took a three-year trip to see the world, traveling from the Alberta plains down the eastern curb of the Rockies all the way to Taos, along the Old North Trail—the very, very old North Trail, probable main route of the first people to enter North America so many thousands of years ago. Less than a century ago stretches of it were still rutted by travois and marked by countless generations of travelers, in particular by the circles of stones that sometimes represented lodge burial: the practice of honoring a great and brave man by leaving his body propped up in his lodge to receive death alone, and the tipi weighted with stones around the edges to resist as long as possible the whipping wind of the plains. The five Blackfeet may have been the last Indian tourists to travel the Old North Trail in peace.

Especially, wars bothered the trade and travel of Americans, filling the country with excitable war parties that menaced and frightened emigrants and sometimes stole their stock. American troops were marched up and down the plains several times in the 1830s and 1840s, to the delight of the Indians, who admired the show of color and guns and, most of all, the soldiers' swords. "Big Knives" was the polite name for white Americans among the plains people, as it was among many other Indians over the United States, and a saber was much valued by Plains Indians as a weapon. In 1849 two military posts were established along the Platte, and in 1851 ex-mountain man Tom Fitzpatrick, appointed United States Indian Agent, held a great council near the farthest west of these, Fort Laramie, a converted fur-trading post at the mouth of the Laramie River on the North Platte.

The council encampment was at Horse Creek, thirty-seven miles east of the fort, and was the scene of the greatest assembly of Indians in plains history, the number present estimated at from 8,000 to 12,000 persons, representing Assiniboins, Atsinas, Arikaras, Crows, Shoshonis, Sioux, Cheyennes, and Arapahoes, some of these nations never having met before within their memory except in battle.

All agreed on a general peace (Pawnees tacitly excepted, no Pawnees being present) and promised to be more considerate of emigrants, whose covered-wagon trains had by then been familiar along the Oregon Trail for ten years and during the previous two summers had filled all the westward trails to overflowing, rushing to the gold in California. The United States promised to keep troops in the plains, ostensibly to protect the Indians from white depredations, and the Indians authorized the building of roads and forts in their country—a point vividly protested later on by some of the membership, and a point fairly sure to result in Indian-white collisions, as had been clear at least since Mad Anthony Wayne's malignant Treaty of Greenville back in the Old Northwest nearly sixty years before.

Three years later, ten miles or so from the scene of this great peace council, the wars of the United States against the Plains Indians were opened.

The immediate cause was a dilapidated emigrant cow, allegedly abandoned, killed by a Minneconjou Sioux for the hide. The emigrant put in a claim at Fort Laramie for damages. Spokesmen from the Sioux camp offered ten dollars, the emigrant demanded twenty-five. The Sioux couldn't meet his price, and a lieutenant took thirty-two men and two howitzers and went to the Sioux camp, several miles down the river from the fort, to drag out the cow-killer. There were many lodges of Oglala and Brulé people, and among the Brulés a few lodges of Minneconjous, summer visitors from the Missouri; all these were subtribes of the Teton Dakota. Man Afraid of His Horses, the Oglala chief, was present and tried to pacify the lieutenant, as did the leader of the Brulés, Conquering Bear, who was considered a "good old man" by Americans who knew him, but an argument developed, and the lieutenant had Conquering Bear shot down on the spot. In the fight that followed, the lieutenant and all his men were killed.

This was not the first blood spilled between the plains people and the soldiers who had come to protect them. The summer before, a detachment of Fort Laramie troops had killed three or four Sioux in a regrettable misunderstanding, which the Sioux had recognized as such. But this was the first blood of American soldiers.

The American public (or at least its louder vocal segments) clamored for retaliation, which was provided the following summer, in 1855, when an army of 1,300 men marched into the plains from Fort Leavenworth and destroyed a Brulé village near the forks of the Platte, killing eighty-six persons. The number—unpublished—of women and children among the eighty-six brought a protest from higher army headquarters (General Winfield Scott) back east. But at a conference in the spring of 1856, the properly humbled Brulés promised to turn over the man who had killed the cow.

In the same spring of 1856 a controversy with a band of Cheyennes over one of several stray horses led to an attack by troops on a Cheyenne family that had had nothing to do with the controversy. Other Cheyennes then killed a stray trapper who had had nothing to do with the military attack. Troops from Fort Kearny then attacked a group of unsuspecting Cheyennes who had had nothing to do with any of the foregoing, killing a half dozen of them and seizing all their horses and property. Cheyennes then plundered two wagon trains, killing seven innocent persons, including a woman and two children.

This tragicomedy dragged along until the summer of 1857, when Colonel E. V. Sumner set out with a strong force to put a stop to it. On a July day in a handsome plains setting along the Solomon River, in present Kansas, he met the flower of the Southern Cheyennes in one of the few real picture-book battle scenes in all Indian history. Everything was as it should be; some 300 mounted warriors drawn up in battle line singing their war song, all in their full war costumes, colorful as fireworks; and they had all had time for all the necessary pre-battle ceremonies. Their great medicine man, Ice, had picked the battleground for them, and seemed to be certain that he had been granted the spiritual power to render the soldiers' bullets harmless. Accordingly, the Cheyennes were confident of victory. But Colonel Sumner charged with cavalry, and curiously enough decided to make the charge with the saber, possibly the only instance of a full-fledged saber charge in all the plains wars.

No medicine had been made against sabers. The Cheyennes fired a panicky flight of arrows, and fled. Losses on both sides were small, but there was no question as to who had won. A peace was made the following spring.

But war had settled down to stay. Peace, from now on, would only be intervals that could not last, like sunny days in winter. Everyone believed each time—at least they said they did—that peace this time was forever. The whites congratulated each other on having settled the Redskin problem at last and held foot-stomping jamborees to celebrate. The Indians rejoiced in their lodges and invited each other to company dinners; high-spirited social dances abounded, and young warriors became young dandies, dripping rich habiliments and waving turkey-feather fans and contriving elaborate strategies to get a word with their girls by the light of the moon. But then the whirlwind of hostilities would suddenly spring up again, spin to a climax and stop with a jolt at still another peace. As the frontier reached out to envelop the plains the intervals of peace grew briefer and more clouded, the rings of war more distended and more violent.

Some Cherokee gold-rushers had seen placer deposits in the Rockies on their way west in 1849; in 1858 they returned with other prospectors and discovered gold in Cherry Creek at the foot of the Rockies, near present Denver, Colorado. The Pike's Peak gold rush got under way the following summer, pouring an estimated 80,000 Pike's-Peak-or-Busters into the plains during the next three years. Other mining strikes followed; many of the Plains Indians seriously thought the crowds of would-be prospectors rushing hither and yon to new strikes real and fanciful were people who had gone insane by the bunch. Town founders and real-estate promoters appeared in the wake of the mining camps, with settlers following after, and within less than a decade railroads were being driven across the buffalo plains.

The frontier wrapped its coils around the Indians of the plains and in due time swallowed them up. Basically the story is no different from the penetration and destruction of Indian nations elsewhere. There were the treaties, the dissensions and factions within the Indian nations, the enforced new treaties, the quarrels, the wars, the clarion call for extermination and piecemeal attempts at same, and the long, agonizingly long, diminuendo ending.

The wars were founded on very much the same elements as in the Indian wars that had gone before. At bottom there was pressure for property—time after time agreements on reservations were upset by mining, railroad, or land-speculation interests that were able to bring sufficient influence to bear on the government. Orders went out to persuade the Indians to accept revised treaties and revised reservations. The Indians often had to be persuaded by force. Each of these occasions broke a solemn promise of the United States and led to a thorough Indian distrust of anything American. General George Crook, the most experienced of western Indian-fighters, summed up this process: "Greed and avarice on the part of the whites—in other words, the almighty dollar, is at the bottom of nine-tenths of all our Indian troubles."

There were the usual subsidiary causes, such as the refractory bands, sometimes making up the majority of a tribe, that denied the authority of treaty chiefs; wild warriors who would not be controlled; gangs of bootleg traders, buffalo hunters, prospectors, or amateur Indian killers who would not be controlled either and who overran Indian lands in defiance of government orders to stay out and keep the peace. Said the Superintendent of Indian Affairs for Montana in 1869: "Nothing can be done to insure peace and order till there is a military force here strong enough to clear out the roughs and whisky-sellers in the country." Five years later the Canadian North West Mounted Police were organized specifically to put down this whiskey trade north of the border; 150 "Mounties" ended it in less than three months, to the indignant howls of its Montana proprietors.

There were also some trouble spots that attained new prominence in the plains wars. The Bureau of Indian Affairs was transferred to the Interior Department from the War Department in 1849; conflict between its agents and the Army became frequent and sometimes serious, an occasional consequence being the dishonoring of Indian peace or surrender terms when one department triumphantly succeeded in overruling the other. "Indian Rings" of crooked officials and crooked suppliers made graft a big business, while Indian families imprisoned on reservations suffered concentration-camp privations, ate their gaunt horses or the bark of trees, and sometimes starved to death by hundreds. Large numbers of Indians were shifted from this agency to that, perhaps hundreds of miles from their homes into a foreign land, by whatever clique of whites happened to get momentary control of Indian matters—"I think you had better put the Indians on wheels," said one weary chief.

The disappearance of the buffalo is generally emphasized as a cause of war on the plains, perhaps too much so. As early as the close of the 1850s, when the buffalo could still darken the earth and their gigantic mirages fill the sky, numbers of Indian leaders foresaw the finish of buffalo hunting. The question was not if the buffalo would vanish, but when. Some thought soon; some thought not for a hundred years. It was the former who usually associated themselves with the treaty factions, anxious to make a deal for the sale of land and mineral rights that would subsist their people through the coming time of change.

But the buffalo motive is further diminished by the fact that the Blackfeet, Bloods, Crees, and Assiniboins of Canada, buffalo people from horns to hocks, made no war to save the buffalo. The only major Indian war in British Canada's history, in fact, was not primarily an Indian war at all, but was styled by Canada a rebellion, and had strong overtones of religious war: Protestant Ontario against the Catholic Métis of the Red River of the North. The Métis were mixed-blood French-Indian plainsmen, mostly French-Cree and French-Assiniboin; under the mystical Louis Riel they made a noble effort (in 1870, with an epilogue in 1885) to set up an independent semi-Indian state in Canada's great plains, and lost.

So much for the prosaic reality behind the Indian wars of the plains. In reality, like so many other Indian wars, they were dismal, dirty, and needless. But their reality has been largely forgotten, if it was ever noticed to begin with. The wars of the plains entered immediately into our folklore, and there they will remain, no doubt, until the end of time.

In our folklore they are all Indians and all Indian wars in one gaudy package. As the Plains Indians were amalgamations of other Indians of the eastern forests and the western mountains, and, with their horses and guns, were in part the white man's creation, so the folklore of their wars is an amalgamation of all such folklore from every point of the continent.

It is in the Plains Indian as the classic Indian warrior, as hyper-Indian, as the mythic Indian carried to extremes, that the folklore of the plains revels best. Never were such brave knights, such reckless horsemanship, never such tragic nobility, and when a general said, as a general did, that they were good shots, good riders, and the best fighters the sun ever shined on, one can see the mist of emotion in his eyes, and he'll shoot the man who doesn't bare his head. And above all, never was there such rainbow color brought to combat—the painted shields and war-horses, the painted eyes and bodies, the buffalo hats, the lynx-skin headdresses with an eagle feather for each slain foe, the rippling warbonnets, sometimes trailing down to the heels, the jewel-work of beads and porcupine quills, arrow quivers furred with the magic skin of the otter, hearts made strong by dreams that always came in the form of songs.

The wars of the plains are America's *Iliad*. It is sung in the jagged rhythm of a wild Sioux charge. It is all poetry, for poetry is really made of blood and not of daffodils. It will outlive sober history and never quite die, as poetry never quite does. Red Cloud and Roman Nose will, very likely, still touch a light to the spirit as long as America is remembered.

The Minnesota Sioux, the four Dakota subtribes known as the Santee, had signed a treaty in 1851. They felt cheated by the treaty and were cheated in their reservation life, and in the summer of 1862 they tried to kill all the whites in their country, under the leadership of one of their chiefs, sixty-year-old Little Crow. They murdered some 700 settlers and killed 100 soldiers before they were driven out of Minnesota to join the other Dakotas on the plains. Several dozen Santee chiefs and warriors were hanged. Fugitive Little Crow, foraging for berries, was shot by a farm youth.

The Sioux of the plains were asked to sign a treaty in 1865 to permit passage from Fort Laramie along the Powder River to the gold fields of Montana. Red Cloud (named for the red meteor of 1822), greatest of Oglala warriors, refused to sign and refused to cede. When the troops built forts along the trail, Red Cloud with his followers and Cheyenne allies closed the trail to supplies and held the troops under a virtual siege for two years at Fort Phil Kearny, at the foot of the Bighorn Mountains in what is now northern Wyoming.

There was a famous fight on a December day in 1866 when one Captain William J. Fetterman, who was reported to have said, "Give me 80 men and I'll ride through the whole Sioux nation," rode forth with eighty-one and was decoyed by a daring party of ten picked warriors—two Cheyennes, two Arapahoes, and two from each of the three Sioux tribes present—into ambush and annihilation. There was another famous fight the next summer when Red Cloud's finest cavalry stormed down to make meat of a wood-chopping detail from the fort—thirty-six men. Thirty-two managed to reach the shelter of a wagon-box corral and, armed with new breech-loading rifles, fought off repeated and suicidal charges throughout the day; twenty-nine were still alive and fighting when relief arrived from the fort.

But Red Cloud could not be pushed aside, the trail could not be used, and in 1868 the government at last surrendered. The forts were dismantled, the troops moved out, and the Powder River country, including the Black Hills, was reserved for the Dakotas forever. Red Cloud signed the treaty, and, true to his word, never again made war on the whites; he only tried to avoid them, and counseled his people to do the same. If you wished to possess the white man's things, he said, "You must begin anew and put away the wisdom of your fathers. You must lay up food and forget the hungry. When your house is built, your storeroom filled, then look around for a neighbor whom you can take advantage of and seize all he has." He was one of the foremost of Sioux patriots, and when he recited his war deeds it took a long time, because he had counted the incredible total of eighty coups; once he had returned from the wars with a Crow arrow driven entirely through his body, projecting front and back.

Peace had lasted very pleasantly through the early days of Denver for the Southern Cheyennes and Arapahoes even though troubled by emigrant traffic (the wandering Cherokee prospectors established a new main route westward through Colorado before they left the country, the Cherokee Trail, that after 1862 replaced the South Pass road as the most traveled highway). A large party of Arapahoes camped in the heart of Denver during the town's first couple of years around the turn of 1860, and left the women and children there while they went to make war against the Utes, for all the world like pioneers. And then a treaty was made in 1861—only a few chief men could be induced, with great difficulty, to sign, and some of those later claimed they had been misled as to what they were signing. The treaty ceded most of Southern Cheyenne and Arapaho territory, but worse than this it contained a clause that government officials later construed as permitting a railroad through what Indian lands were left. A railroad meant white settlements, and this meant an end to the last of their country, and the Cheyenne and Arapaho general public at length forced a number of treaty chiefs to repudiate the treaty, under pain of death. White politicians regarded this as hostility, and the refusal of some bands and soldier societies to sign the treaty at all was regarded as hostility. Buffalo hunters followed herds into the Indian country whenever the herds went that way, and this too brought hard feelings.

But peace dwindled along until the spring of 1864, when the Reverend J. M. Chivington, colonel of Colorado volunteers, reported that Cheyennes had stolen some cattle from a government contractor's herd. The report was suspect at the time and later—old mountain men said that whenever a greenhorn lost a stray he blamed the Indians—but Colonel Chivington took stern and instant measures, troops attacked families of the astounded Cheyennes, the Cheyennes attacked families of unsuspecting settlers, and another war was on.

Using the most eloquent persuasion, Colorado's governor managed by autumn to get some of the alarmed Cheyennes to come to Denver for peace talks. The peace party of the Cheyennes was headed by Black Kettle and the distinguished war chief White Antelope; they talked to the governor and, on the advice of the military commandant at Fort Lyon, established their village on Sand Creek, thirty miles from the fort. The village was then destroyed in a stealthy, sudden attack by Colonel Chivington and a force of something between 600 and 1,000 troops, mostly volunteers. Colonel Chivington had said, "Kill and scalp all big and little; nits make lice." The boys, as his reports refer to his soldiers, did so with enthusiasm.

Black Kettle ran up both an American flag and a white flag, but the boys were having too much fun. They butchered any Indian in sight (except for some Cheyenne men who managed to fort up on the creek bank, and who had rifles). Black Kettle's wife was shot down, and passing soldiers fired seven more bullets into her body; she had nine wounds, but lived. Another old woman was scalped but came back to life and was trying to walk but she couldn't see, for the skin of her forehead had fallen over her eyes. A child at the toddling stage brought merriment to some of the boys, testified an Army major later, as they took turns trying to bring it down at seventy-five yards; one finally did. A lieutenant, testified another officer, shot and scalped a captured group of three women and eight children, one after the other, while they begged for mercy. Black Kettle escaped. White Antelope refused to run. Some reports say that he tried to talk to the troops and some that he stood in front of his lodge and folded his arms and sang his death song. It was a good death song, and has been remembered. It went: "Nothing lives long, except the earth and the mountains." He sang until he was cut down by bullets and died. He was some years past seventy at the time.

Perhaps 200 Cheyenne women and children were killed at Sand Creek, and perhaps seventy men, and an estimated forty or more Arapaho people who were with the Cheyennes; but there was a great deal of dispute among the boys as to the number of dead, and the figures are not necessarily accurate. The boys went back to Denver and exhibited scalps and severed arms and legs in a theater (White Antelope's scrotum was later made into a souvenir tobacco pouch). The boys had reason to be proud. This was probably the greatest victory, measured by Indians killed, the whites were to record in the Indian wars of the plains.

Not all Americans were proud of the boys. One named Kit Carson spoke of them as cowards and dogs. A story was current that the volunteers had staged this Indian "war" to keep from being sent into Civil War action in the east. Nor were all the settlers jubilant. The Cheyenne plains went up in flames during the next three years; in two summer months alone 117 settlers were killed and their women and children dragged away as captives, in dozens of widely separated raids. And a government commission reported, four years after Colonel Chivington's victory: "It scarcely has its parallel in the records of Indian barbarity . . . No one will be astonished that a war ensued which cost the government $30,000,000 and carried conflagration and death to the border settlements . . ."

There were many men of valor among the valorous Cheyennes, including such leaders of exalted rank as Little Wolf and White Antelope. But none, surely, was more famous at the time to the ordinary public both Cheyenne and white than a hook-nosed 6-foot 3-inch warrior named The Bat. The Americans called him Roman Nose, translating thus his warrior name of Woqini (Hook Nose). Roman Nose was idolized by the young men and was especially famous because he was invulnerable in battle. He had a magic headdress, made for him by Ice, the medicine man, from a vision Roman Nose had seen during his vigil and fast, a headdress with forty red and black eagle feathers set in a tail so long it nearly touched the ground even when Roman Nose was mounted, and while he wore it bullets and arrows could not touch him. He proved this time after time, riding at a leisurely lope up and down in front of the enemy, while all the enemy shot at him and missed. This always inspired the other Cheyenne warriors. The war bonnet required elaborate ceremonies at each donning and was surrounded by various taboos, one being that Roman Nose must never eat anything taken from the pot with an iron instrument: fork or knife. If he broke this taboo he broke the war bonnet's medicine, and long rites of purification would be necessary to restore it.

It happened that in the summer of 1868 a company of 50 experienced plainsmen, enlisted in the army as scouts, was trapped by a large number of Cheyenne, Sioux, and Arapaho warriors, reportedly several hundred. Shortly before this battle started, Roman Nose was a guest in a Sioux lodge and the hostess, unaware of his taboo, took food from the skillet with a fork. Roman Nose did not learn of this until after he had already eaten (legend says the food was fried bread). When the fight began a day or so later he did not go to it. But the chiefs came to him and told him he was needed to inspire the warriors. A chief said, "All those people fighting out there feel that they belong to you." Roman Nose explained about his broken taboo. He said, "I know that I shall be killed today." Then he painted himself and performed the ceremonies attendant on unwrapping his war bonnet, offering it to the sun and the holy directions, and put on the war bonnet and mounted his horse and rode very fast at the enemy. He was shot from his horse, but lived to be carried back to the lodges, where he died at sunset.

The Indians made a few more desultory attacks, principally to recover the bodies of their dead, but they had lost heart and eventually went away. The company of scouts fought from an island in the dry bed of the Arickaree River, and the island has ever since been called (on the white men's maps) Beecher Island, after the name of the company's lieutenant, who was killed there.

Occupation forces fighting guerrilla terrorists are at a disadvantage, since they cannot often lay hands on the terrorists. If their government, or the spirit of the public back home, will stand for it they prefer the hostage system—executing all the people of a hostage town, in reprisal for acts of guerrilla resistance. When the War Department gained the ascendancy in its incessant conflict with the Indian Bureau it sometimes used this method. Unfortunately the village chosen for destruction, in the case of the wars of the plains, was more than likely to be a stronghold of pro-American peace party Indians endeavoring to be friendly, since such a village was likely to be the nearest one available.

Black Kettle had made unceasing and increasingly successful efforts for peace since the Sand Creek massacre, believing there was no other hope of survival for his people. In the winter of 1868 his village, which was camped on the Washita River in Oklahoma, was treated to its second stealthy and unexpected attack by troops, who were under orders to destroy a village and hang all the men and take all the women and children prisoner. Something between thirty-eight men, women, and children (Cheyenne figures) and 103 warriors (Army figures) were killed, and this time Black Kettle was killed too. But men from nearby Arapaho, Kiowa, and Comanche villages came to the rescue, and the American commander prudently withdrew, leaving behind a detachment of nineteen troopers who had gone prisoner-catching—all nineteen were slain. The American commander was Lieutenant Colonel George A. Custer, and this was his first major engagement with Indians. It might be called Custer's first stand.

The following winter the same Lidicesque technique of destroying a village as a lesson to the out-of-reach resistance was used by the military in northern Montana, on the Marias River, where a village of Piegan people, selected either at random or by mistake, was destroyed in a stealthy dawn attack. It developed that the village was that of the Piegan chief most noted as friendly to the whites, Heavy Runner, who was reportedly shot dead as he walked out to stop the troops, holding his hands above his head and waving his identification paper. It also developed that the casualties were overwhelmingly women and children, and that there had been no resistance—the four companies of cavalry involved lost one man killed, and another trooper broke his leg when he fell from a horse. It also developed that the village was in the midst of a smallpox epidemic at the time. These developments brought some rather angry criticism from the eastern press. General Phil Sheridan replied with the hostage philosophy in a nutshell: "If a village is attacked, and women and children killed, the responsibility is not with the soldier, but with the people whose crimes necessitate the attack." The frontier, with the usual frontier tendency toward a policy of extermination, generally approved.

The wars reached their climax in the 1870s, after the discovery of gold in the Black Hills in 1874. The Sioux had to be persuaded to sell out, the Black Hills having been guaranteed to them forever by the last treaty. The persuasion was a difficult job. It required many columns of troops and many scouts—Pawnees and Crows and Shoshonis who joined the white soldiers to fight their old interloping enemies of the plains.

In this war Red Cloud remained apart. The Sioux and their allies came gradually under the general command of two powerful and very different personalities. One was Crazy Horse, an Oglala warrior famed for his recklessness, who had led the decoy party that had beckoned Captain Fetterman and his eighty-one men into the hereafter. The other was Tatanka Yotanka, Sitting Buffalo, known to the Americans as Sitting Bull. There was a fashion for some years among western historians of belittling Sitting Bull's importance; recent scholarship seems to have restored him to the place of eminence he held in his own day. He was a dreamer of visions, a seer of the future, and war chief of the Hunkpapa division of the Teton Dakotas. He was also one of the most able, honest, and idealistic statesmen in Indian history.

In June of 1876 the main body of unpersuaded Sioux was found by General George Crook, leading 1,000 or so soldiers. A more or less equal number of warriors attacked him, everyone fought well, there were many individual acts of courage, it was a long and violent and well managed battle, the classic battle, perhaps, of the plains wars, but the ground kept growing Indians, and Crook at length had to withdraw and limp back to his base of supplies to await reinforcements. The battle was fought among wild-plum and crab-apple blossoms in the valley of Rosebud Creek, in southern Montana.

The Indians moved across the ridge to the next river west, the Little Big Horn, and established a large camp, made up of Crazy Horse's people and Sitting Bull's people and allies from the other Sioux divisions and the Cheyenne. Eight days after the battle with Crook, this camp was attacked on a Sunday afternoon by a regiment of cavalry. The attack was defeated. Crazy Horse himself, shouting, "Today is a good day to fight, today is a good day to die," led a rush that cut off half the attacking forces. Every man in this surrounded group of cavalrymen was killed in a desperate, blazing fight that lasted less than half an hour.

The attacking force had been the elite Seventh Cavalry, organized for the specific purpose of whipping the Plains Indians, destroyers of Black Kettle's camp on the Washita. It had been led by Lieutenant Colonel Custer, who died in the battle along with more than 260 of his men.

This battle was the sensational moment of truth in the wars of the plains, at least for the Americans. It was the kind of humiliating defeat that simply could not be handed to a modern nation of 40,000,000 people by a few scarecrow savages. Especially not in the very middle of the great centennial celebration—the first report appeared in eastern newspapers on the morning of July 5, 1876, and caught the country smack in the act of congratulating itself on its first 100 years. The Custer defeat was, in effect, the end of the wars of the plains, and Crazy Horse and Sitting Bull lost by winning. Troops harried their people without mercy, and the Indians had no means of keeping a standing army in the field indefinitely, Separated into small bands they were hunted down or driven into Canada.

The ending went on and on, like the dying wail of a death song. It went on for years, while the poetry and the romance evaporated, and these were seen to be not knights and paladins after all but only bedragged scurrying creatures rather like fugitive convicts. So they were turned over to jailers who knew how to handle tough prisoners, and the greatest of warriors is nothing more than any other weak-stomached man when he has nothing to do but crouch under guard and watch his people starve—as some 600 Montana Blackfeet died of "sheer starvation" in the winter of 1883.

But it was at this time, when the glitter and nobility were vanished, that the greatest feats of gallantry occurred, all the greater in that they were utterly hopeless. There were more of them than there were battles in all the wars put together. Some became famous, some did not.

In an obscure little police action a young Sioux, wearing a trailing warbonnet that is somehow comical, like his father's hat, paraded up and down and said to the soldiers, "I am a soldier walking on my own land. I will give up my gun to no man." A moment later he treacherously fired into a truce party of the soldiers. His uncle said sadly, "My friend is young." Then the uncle too fired treacherously into the soldiers. They were both dead in three minutes. Someone knelt and took careful aim and shot the young Sioux through the forehead, the bullet cutting the warbonnet's brow band. They were scalped and left to stay forever in their land. It was all so obscure the name of the young Sioux is not even certain. He might have been called Big Ankle.

Well, it all ended. Through the years it wavered away and ended. The New York *Herald* was still calling for extermination in 1879, saying editorialy, "The continent is getting too crowded." But no one really took that seriously anymore. Starvation, disease, and tough prison wardens were just as good anyway, and there were the noisy sentimentalists who kept insisting that sooner or later some of the Red Men could be saved by being civilized. And there was whiskey. That Indian trade whiskey, said Charles M. Russell, the old Montana cowboy turned world-famous painter, you could be shot and killed and you wouldn't die until you sobered up. So if you never sobered up you were bound to be all right.

At the very end the messiahs appeared, as they always do. One was a Nevada Paiute named Wovoka; his father (or it might have been his uncle) had been a messiah before him. His religion was called the Ghost Dance by the whites, because it preached that the ghosts of dead Indians were on hand to help living Indians in their hour of extremity. A great revival spread among the emotional people of the plains, and the authorities feared the excitement might lead to riot and violence. Sitting Bull was killed in the process of being placed under precautionary arrest (Crazy Horse had been killed a dozen years before, in 1877, bayoneted by a soldier while being held in captivity).

December 28, 1890, a unit of the Seventh Cavalry arrested 250 or 350 Minneconjou and Hunkpapa Sioux that an officer thought might be suspect, two-thirds of them women and children. The Indians were held overnight, camped in the center of a ring of 500 cavalrymen. Four Hotchkiss guns were set up and carefully sighted in on the Sioux camp. In the morning the troops formed a hollow square with the Indian camp in the middle and disarmed the Sioux men, who were called out from the others to form a line. Somehow, a disturbance began. It is said that someone fired a shot. In any case, the troops quite suddenly opened an intensive fire at point-blank range into the Sioux camp. The Sioux men seem to have been shot down first, and most of them finished off at once or in a few minutes, although enough people attacked the soldiers with their bare hands or what weapons they still had or could seize (or wild shots from the troops may have helped) that twenty-nine soldiers were killed. But the shooting went on as long as anyone, woman or child, remained to be shot at. The rapid-firing Hotchkiss guns may have terrified the people more than the simple fact of death. Some of the women were pursued as far as three miles over the plains before they were caught and killed. A few are said to have escaped.

There has been dispute about the total number of Sioux dead. The military commander of the department reported there were no fewer than 200. But it was at least the second greatest victory for American arms in the wars of the plains. The event took place on Wounded Knee Creek in South Dakota.

Stephen Vincent Benét wrote a poem in which he mentioned Wounded Knee, although there is no reason to suppose he was thinking of this incident. The last lines go:

> I shall not rest quiet in Montparnasse . . .
> I shall not be there, I shall rise and pass.
> Bury my heart at Wounded Knee.

They gathered up the frozen dead in wagons at Wounded Knee, and buried them all together in a communal pit.

XV
Apacheria

On the fourth of July, 1776, a Spanish friar sat beside his saddle in the plaza of ancient Oraibi, the principal Hopi pueblo. He had been sitting there for two days but no one had spoken to him except three traveling salesmen from Zuñi, and they had been fearful about it. The Walapai guides who had brought him had taken fright and disappeared. The Hopis were patient and peaceful people but they had not wanted Spaniards among them since they had killed their missionary priests nearly a century before. The friar was patient too, and he wanted very much to make peace with the Moquis, as he called them, using the name most other people in the Southwest gave to the Hopis.

During the day on the fourth of July the people in town stopped ignoring the priest and gathered in a crowd and watched him. Then four chief men came and told him to go away instantly. His mule was brought and he went away. He had expected to be killed when the crowd gathered. But the Hopis, who were connoisseurs of endurance, may have been impressed by his two long days of sitting there, in silence, beside his saddle.

The friar was Fray Francisco Garcés, a Franciscan, one of the foremost of North American explorers. Sometimes alone, but

391

most often with a single companion, a Lower California Indian named Tarabal, he had opened "roads" across the deserts and the mountains and the canyons to nearly everyplace a New Spain citizen of the 1770s might want to go in the Southwest. Said another priest of him, "Father Garcés . . . appears to be but an Indian himself . . . He sits with them in the circle, or at night around the fire, with his legs crossed . . . talking with them with much serenity and deliberation. And although the foods of the Indians are as nasty and dirty as those outlandish people themselves, the father eats them with great gusto and says that they are good for the stomach and very fine . . .

The road he had wanted to open this time was a road from Santa Fe to Upper California via some route north of the Gila River. Such a road would be more direct than the Gila, and it would be out from under the constant menace of the Apaches.

For the Apaches, by 1776, were already an old and familiar menace.

The Spanish mission frontier, laboriously pushing northward from Sonora toward what is now Arizona, had been stopped in the 1650s by a loose alliance of unconvertible wild tribes dominated by the Apaches. Garcés' illustrious Jesuit predecessor, Padre Eusebio Kino, had managed to move into the area in the 1680s, and for nearly twenty-five years had explored the Gila-Colorado River country, founding missions and ranches among the Pimas—the Apaches' most obdurate enemies. The Pimas themselves had later given this new frontier a considerable amount of rebellion trouble, apparently for good and sufficient cause, and the Apaches had remained predominantly hostile, a constant hindrance. A silver strike in the late 1730s in the region known as Arizonac had seemed for a time that it might ameliorate the Apache problem for the Spaniards by establishing a strong bulwark of mining towns. This was in the Altar valley below the present Mexican border, southwest of modern Nogales; giant nuggets of almost pure silver were found lying on the ground, some up to two tons in weight. But no important lodes were discovered, and the surface workings played out within five years. Apacheria—the Apache country—continued to be the perilous end of the world.

By the 1850s various Apache bands had dwelt on the frontier of European settlement for 200 years and throughout all that time had stayed completely independent. This seems to be a record unequaled by any other Indian people on the continent.

The impression should not be given that the Apaches were unremittingly hostile to whites during those long generations of living, so to speak, on the edge of town. There were intervals of peace and even alliance; eastern Apaches in what is now Texas were even missionized—briefly—in the eighteenth century, and on a number of occasions allied themselves with Spanish troops against the Louisiana French or against other enemies of the southern plains. The Apache record of hostility was perhaps no more constant than that of some of the Yaquis of southern Sonora. But the Yaquis, a farming people speaking a Piman language, had been beguiled into a general peace treaty in 1610 and thereafter had been pierced, disintegrated, and divided, and their outbreaks of serious hostility, continuing into the 1900s, had been the convulsions of isolated groups that simply refused to be subdued.

The Apaches remained generally unbeguiled; wild and untamed, in the usual sense of the words, which is to say, independent. Since they were regarded as a lost cause anyway, Spanish and Mexican administrators had no compunction about playing them false in negotiations or promises, if anything was to be gained thereby. The Apaches responded to such perfidy, naturally, with renewed hostility. Each side raided the other now and then for slaves and stock, in which industry the Apaches, being past masters of the art of the raid, unquestionably kept the score more than even.

The important point is that the Apaches, after these two centuries, were by no means strange mountain hawks wide-eyed at the wonders of a town, and savagely simple in their dealings with white men. They had had long experience in dealing with white men—while still contriving to keep themselves apart and free. They had had even longer experience at occupying a frontier of civilization, the frontier of the prehistoric Pueblo civilization. With the Pueblos too, there had sometimes been friendship and active alliance, traditionally more so with certain of the Pueblo towns than others; a long history of trade; and a frequent history of raids and enmity, traditionally more so with certain towns than with others.

The Apaches of the region of southern Arizona found their one irreconcilable foe in the Pima, this being Pima country which the Apaches had invaded. The Apaches centering in northeastern Arizona were on terms of basic hostility with such nearby people as those of Zuñi and the later pueblo of Laguna (founded 1699), for the same basic reason: invasion or trespass. The word Apache, from a Zuñi word meaning enemy, was first given as a name, it seems, to the specific invaders who took over the lands of an abandoned Tewa pueblo called Navahú. These invaders were called the Apaches de Navahú, or at least so it sounded to the ears of the early Spaniards. Eventually the name Apache was applied by extension to other related peoples all over the Southwest. The Apaches of Navahú, however, came to be known as the Navaho, or as the Spanish spelled it, Navajo, and in time were reckoned as an entirely distinct tribe, no longer included among the Apaches in general. The Navahos, indeed, did become a distinct tribe, gathering in new peoples and new customs until their ways, race, and language were considerably changed.

In the beginning all these, Apaches and Navahos, were Athapascan-speaking people who must have drifted down from the great Athapascan hive in the far northwest of Canada. It is assumed they made their way, over the course of generations if not centuries, down the eastern flank of the Rockies, some of them spreading gradually westward as they reached the latitudes of New Mexico. This may have taken place from 1,000 to 700 years ago. The epoch during which the Navahos and Apaches at last settled in their permanent homes in the Southwest is uncertain—it can only be placed sometime between A.D. 1000 and 1500 or thereabouts. Without doubt it was a very slow process, attended by much misery, prayer, and mayhem.

By the time Americans were beginning to get acquainted with the Southwest, in the early 1800s, most of these people had been long established in their desert and mountain fastnesses, and were as familiar with each rock and beast and useful plant as if they had been there forever—indeed they had long before named various local landmarks as the sacred places of their ancestors' original issuance from the center of the earth.

In a very broad view, the Apache tribes formed a rough ring around the country of the upper Rio Grande that was the center of the Pueblo world and of the early Spanish settlements. Nomadic in the sense of moving about quite a bit within vaguely localized ranges, the various groups of Apaches have been given at different times almost as many different names as there were Apaches. Recent classifications tend to reduce all this to some three dozen separate bands, exclusive, of course, of the Navaho.

Southward from the Navaho country, in and about the

mountain chains of central and eastern Arizona and the upper waters of the Gila and Salt rivers, was the domain of a number of bands or tribal groups, some of the best known, under their best-known names, being the Tonto groups between modern Flagstaff and Roosevelt Lake and the White Mountain bands roundabout the White Mountains and the midsection of the present Arizona-New Mexico line. Southward still, in southeastern Arizona and southwestern New Mexico, were a number of other groups, most notably the Chiricahuas of the mountains of the same name in southeastern Arizona, and the Mimbreños, of the Mimbres Mountains in southwestern New Mexico. In the mountains and plains of southern and eastern New Mexico were the Mescaleros, in several divisions; their name came from the custom common to most Apaches of roasting mescal (agave) to make a highly nutritious and much admired dessert—some Apaches carried on a trade in roasted mescal with under-privileged town-dwelling Pueblo people who didn't have mescal to roast.

The Apaches centering in Arizona, excluding the Navahos, are usually regarded as more or less alike. They got perhaps a fourth or a fifth of their food from farming, and the rest from hunting and an intensive use of wild foods: mescal and acorns first, and nearly innumerable others led by piñon, prickly pear, yucca, sunflower, mesquite, and saguaro. The Apaches east of the Rio Grande, such as the Mescaleros, placed more dependence on the chase of the buffalo. They are sometimes considered as forming a grand division separate from the Western Apaches.

To the north of the Mescaleros, in northeastern New Mexico and the mountains of southern Colorado, were a number of Apache bands considered a somewhat more separate group still, the Jicarillas (pronounced Heekareeyas, being a Spanish word, referring to little baskets which they made with great skill). The Jicarillas were in much contact with the pueblo of Taos, and through the centuries became as close as brothers with the Taos people, each making a point of attending the other's ceremonies—this in spite of the fact that the original Taos name for the Jicarillas was an uncomplimentary word meaning "filthy people."

The country of the Jicarillas extended on the west toward the country of the Navahos, and on the north, above the present Colorado line, bordered the ancient people of the southern Rockies, the mountain Utes.

The total population of all the Apache tribes—always excluding the Navahos—has been estimated at between 5,000 and 6,000, in prehistoric as in historic times.

For centuries during their slow migration southward, the Apaches and Navahos were among the most important occupants of the great plains—at various periods in the old pre-horse times, from the 1300s to the 1700s, they may have been the strongest force in the southern plains. They were sometimes enemies, sometimes allies, of the terrible Tonkawas of Texas, a ferocious plains people (cannibals, it was said) who were dreaded by all, and who were assiduously wooed by both the Spanish and the French. An Apache captured and adopted by the Tonkawa became their most noted chief, and in 1782 he brought about a great Apache-Tonkawa council for the purpose of unifying the two peoples to fight the Spanish. More than 4,000 Tonkawas and Apaches gathered for this meeting—and to trade stolen horses for French guns. The pact of unity failed to go through, and a couple of years later the Spanish succeeded in seizing the Tonkawa chief by treachery and assassinated him. They called him El Mocho (the cropped one), due to the fact that he had lost his right ear in a fight with the Osage.

This was one of the last high points of Apache presence on the southern plains. During the 1700s new people were invading from the north; these were the Comanches and Kiowas. The old name of Padoucas, prominent in the literature of the southern plains until the late 1700s, is associated by some authorities with the Comanches, by others with the Apaches, attesting the duration and confusion of their entanglement.

At last the Apaches of the plains, most of them, withdrew to the plains' western margins. This marginal country had probably been the center of gravity of the wide-ranging Apache people since their first appearance, with extensions eastward across the southern plains and westward into the Arizona country. A string of towns within this marginal area, the Tano pueblos, southernmost of the Rio Grande pueblos, had been devastated in 1525 by a war of hurricane pitch, believed to have been made by Apaches.

One Apache group stayed on the plains—the people known as Lipan, close relatives of the Jicarillas. They remained in west Texas, ranging westward to the Staked Plains of New Mexico, and went on fighting the Comanches the rest of their lives. They were also the only Apache unit of any importance to be really beguiled by the frontier of civilization. They accepted Spanish missions repeatedly (the missions were repeatedly destroyed by Comanches) and played politics with the whites rather eagerly, possibly because their anti-Comanche position left them so perilously exposed.

An Athapascan-speaking band that entered the southern plains with the Kiowa came to be known as Apache because of their language, and were called the Kiowa Apache. People of alien speech, they were nevertheless a fully accredited band of the Kiowa nation, and had a designated place in the camp circle.

The Comanches, as remarked earlier, were an offshoot of the mountain Shoshoni who came down into the plains with the acquisition of the horse. Short-legged, ungraceful people when on the ground, they turned themselves into some of the showiest horsemen the world has ever seen. Mystically certain of their superiority, in the way of born riders, the Comanches regarded other people, white and red, as inferior beings. This helped to make them tremendously successful in trade and war. With an estimated seventeenth century population of 7,000 the Comanches must have considerably outnumbered the Apache families on the plains, and were more than three times the strength of their constant allies, the Kiowas.

The Kiowas present something of a puzzle in their early history. Their traditions—and historical evidence—place their origin in the Montana mountains at the headwaters of the Missouri River. They were friends of the Crows in that area during the 1700s, and at the end of that century drifted southward to the Arkansas River, where they effected their alliance with the Comanches and thereafter occupied the plains eastward of northern New Mexico. Many students, however, feel sure that the Kiowas had originally come from the southern plains long before, so long ago that the memory has been erased from their traditions. This belief is based in part on the kinship of the Kiowa language with that of certain of the Pueblo people—a kinship deformed and wasted away by age, but nevertheless definite, according to recent studies. It is possible that at some unknown time in the past a people had emigrated to the plains from the Pueblo world, perhaps from the neighborhood of Taos; archaeologists have studied remains of some few farming settlements of centuries ago in and about what is now the Oklahoma and Texas Panhandles that echoed Pueblo ways, even unto houses built with stone slabs apparently in imitation of Pueblo

architecture. It is interesting to speculate that these archaeological unknowns may have been ancestors of the Kiowas, midway
in a long metamorphosis from corn-growers into plains hunters,
and, while thus speculating, to speculate further that these
émigré villagers may have begun moving north during long
drought periods of the middle 1400s, and, so callously abandoned by the gods of corn and rain, might have turned definitively away from farming during that same bitter time. Several
early names for themselves, remembered by the Kiowa people
from what are felt to be ancient times, refer to them as the
"going out" people, the "coming out" people.

The Kiowas were generally acknowledged as among the
most eloquent in the sign language, the international language of
the plains, by which Plains Indians from different tribes could
converse with remarkable precision. A similar sort of communication with signs made by the hands existed here and there
elsewhere in the Indian world, but it reached by far its most
elaborate form on the plains.

There may have been a connection between the perfection of
this sign language and the very ancient use of signals on the
plains: signals of smoke, fire, or signals made by waving blankets
or by moving in a circle or back and forth. On the level high
plains, where you can see forever, such signals would be a
natural development. Their use was noted by the first white men
to enter the Southwest, in the 1540s. In later years the Sioux
worked out a system of signaling with mirrors, and troops were
often only aware of the presence of Sioux around them by the
flickering of this mysterious heliograph on distant bluffs and
ridges. The Sioux are also said to have signaled at night with fire
arrows. Much of the paraphernalia of Plains Indian signaling, but
principally the heliograph, was adopted by the army of the
United States, and later the British Army, and used in early
operations of the Signal Corps.

The Comanches and Kiowas took over the southern plains in
parlous times. The dust raised in the Southeast by the French
and Indian War rolled across the Mississippi and far out on the
plains during the late 1700s. Spanish Louisiana, wanting buffers
against the mighty Osage, coaxed Indian colonists westward
from the lower Mississippi into the Caddo country on the
eastern edge of the great plains; such strong Caddoan people as
the Pawnee, Wichita, and the Kadohadacho confederacy welcomed the immigrants more or less peacefully, but the mighty
Osage took alarm and fought and formed war-making alliances.

A band of Cherokees moved west of the Mississippi in 1794, after killing a number of white men to announce the reason why. The band was headed by a leader named Bowl, a warlord of great repute; refugees from several other tribes later joined, and in the 1820s the augmented band went to Texas. There the Mexican government gave Bowl and his people a grant of land between present Dallas and Houston. After Texas was broken free of Mexico by its American colonists in 1835, Sam Houston made every effort to protect Bowl's Cherokee band. But most of the new rulers of Texas were opposed to leaving any part of the country in the possession of any Indians. Sam Houston's successor as president of Texas was the ex-private secretary of Governor Troup of Georgia, of Creek and Cherokee expulsion notoriety, and the policy makers of Texas thereafter were generally dedicated, in the highest degree, to the proposition of exterminating or clearing out all Indians.

Several regiments of Texas troops attacked and destroyed Bowl's town on the Angelina River in 1839; Bowl and many others were killed, and the survivors were driven across the border into Indian Territory (where, says tradition, they were dissuaded from bootless acts of retaliation by the aging Sequoyah). In the same year the Lipan Apaches delightedly sided with the Texans in fighting the Comanches; a few years later, however, Texas settlers drove the Lipan Apaches themselves into Mexico, where Mexican troops, aided by expatriate Kickapoos, almost annihilated the remnants of the tribe. Years afterward the Lipan survivors, fewer than two dozen persons, finally found a home among the Mescaleros in New Mexico. The miserably primitive people of the Texas coast, the Karankawan tribes among whom Alvar Nuñez Cabeza de Vaca and his companions were shipwrecked in 1528, were hunted into complete extinction, the last of them being killed off some time before the Civil War.

But it was in these parlous times, from the late 1700s to the middle 1800s, that the Kiowas and Comanches, like the other peoples of the great plains, reached their peak of power, wealth, and brilliance. Situated as they were, in contact with the Spanish settlements, some of them became practiced and prosperous middlemen. The trade relations of the Comanches were especially complex, however, due to the widely separated range of the various important bands. The southern division known as the Penatekas (Honey-eaters) and the Nokoni (Wanderer) band, did some trading with the Spanish settlements in Texas, but outlaw

American traders and filibusters trickling into the country before
1812 encouraged them in enmity and insolence toward the
settlements, an attitude of hostility that carried over into later
times. The Kwahadi (Antelope) Comanches of New Mexico's
Staked Plains kept pretty much out of touch with whites until the
very end of the free era, in the middle 1800s. A number of bands
toward the northern frontier of Comanche country, along the
Arkansas, became first great raiders and then great traders
among the settlements and pueblos of New Mexico. The Yam-
parikas (Root-eaters) was one of the principal groups in this
area; the western division of the Kotsotekas (Buffalo-eaters)
was another.

Ordinarily these bands did not constitute an Indian nation,
with a unified council or other machinery of overall government.
Some of the important bands were so far apart—700 miles or
even more—that they may hardly have been aware of each
other's existence. However, there were occasions when a man
of extraordinary ability and ambition became head chief of
several great bands temporarily confederated. One such seems
to have been the famed Cuerno Verde (Greenhorn) killed in a
battle with the Spanish in 1779 near the mountain in the southern
Colorado Rockies that bears his name. The leader of the 600
Spanish troops in this battle (259 of them were Indians) was the
New Mexico frontiersman Don Juan Bautista de Anza, who
encouraged the idea of a head-chiefship and gave Spanish
support to Ecueracapa (Iron Shirt), Cuerno Verde's successor.
Only with a genuinely authoritative chief, able to control his
people, could peace be lasting, in the usual European view.

Ecueracapa was said to represent 600 Comanche rancherias,
or villages, which means that either he padded the voting lists or
later estimates of Comanche population figures are much too
low, since this very large figure of 600 rancherias would only
have represented the western Comanches, exclusive of the
Texas Comanches in the east and south. Ecueracapa succeeded
in overcoming the leaders of the anti-Spanish party, killing one
of them with his own hands, and a Comanche-Spanish peace was
made in 1786 that was fairly real in the New Mexico region for
many years to come. Not that all the Comanches stopped
raiding, or even that the Spaniards wanted them to stop all
raiding. One of the Spanish objectives in this alliance was to
make use of the Comanches in fighting Apaches. The Comanches obliged with an excess of zeal, continuing their traditional

attacks on even the Jicarilla Apaches whom the Spaniards regarded as friendly; it appears that a shattering Comanche raid during this period on the once-populous pueblo of Pecos may have been made because Pecos was known to be harboring some fugitive Jicarillas.

Comanches had been admitted to the great Taos trading fair at least as early as 1749. Some Comanche go-getters occasionally enlivened business by early-summer raids on pueblos or settlements—not excepting Taos itself—to collect captives who were then brought in to the Taos fair to be ransomed, to the furious indignation of Spanish officials (but business was business). An equally indignant Spanish cleric wrote in 1761 of some unidentified "barbarians" that when they bring a certain number of Indian women to sell, among them many maidens and young girls, before delivering them to the Christians who buy them . . . they deflower and corrupt them in the sight of innumerable assemblies of barbarians and Catholics . . . without considering anything but their unbridled lust and brutal shamelessness, and saying to those who buy them, with heathen impudence: 'Now you can take her—now she is good.'"

A report of the late 1760s speaks of Comanches and Kiowas usually coming to the annual Taos fair ("There they trade buckskins, buffalo hides, and slaves from various Indian nations situated to the east for clothing and horses . . . Their arms are the bow and arrow and a few guns acquired from the French. . . ."). After the peace of 1786 these plains people were naturally much more in evidence still as traders, another Spanish objective in making the peace—in the late years of the century competition in better-made English trade goods was coming to the plains, and the Spanish needed all the trade-jobbers they could find; and the Taos trading fiesta, biggest doings in all the West, certainly helped to hold customers and keep them coming back. One of the most popular trade items, oddly enough, was a large size silver cross hopefully offered by the missionaries. The Comanches and Kiowas had no interest in Christianity, but the crosses were traded for high prices over the plains as emblems of military rank to be hung around the necks of soldier-society chiefs.

Horses were always the basic goods of trade. Some, probably the best blooded animals, were obtained by legitimate purchase from the Spanish settlements, and many more were stolen, particularly in raids on the Texas settlements. Comanches and Kiowas then went into winter camp on the upper Arkansas River with Cheyennes and Arapahoes and did a thriving business in horses and other trade articles, including captive slaves both red and white. A party of American traders camped with an enormous village—700 lodges—at a plains rendezvous of this kind in November of 1821. Crows were camped two days' journey away, on the Platte, and nearly every night brave young Crows would creep into the very center of this immense camp and steal some of the extra-fine horses that were kept there, under the most stringent security, in log pens.

A band of western Comanches known as the Jupes even tried settling down as farmers under Spanish guidance, early in the time of Anza's great peace. Spanish authorities financed the building of a model pueblo for them in what is now southern Colorado; the town was named San Carlos de los Jupes and was the envy of the mountain Utes, who began clamoring that they wanted pueblos too. But the project was a failure. Everyone had overlooked the fact that people of the plains moved their camp after the death of an important person. At the first such death the Comanches packed up and moved away, leaving the neat little adobe houses of San Carlos de los Jupes to melt into ruins.

Texas Comanches asked several times for a formal peace, after Texas had won independence from Mexico, but the Comanches insisted on a definite boundary line reserving their territory from settlement, and this the Texas politicians refused to consider. Texas land offices were open, settlers were pouring in by the thousand, and Texas' official position was that any Texas citizen could be settled on any land not already occupied by a white owner; Indians must withdraw and keep away from these settlements, wherever they might appear.

One early border settlement was established east of modern Waco by Elder John Parker and his numerous children and relatives, totaling nearly three dozen people. In the spring of 1836 Kiowas and Nokoni Comanches swept down from the north on the stockaded "Parker's Fort," killed several of its defenders, and took five captives. The tales of barbarities told by some of these captive women after their ransomed return were widely circulated and of considerable moment in making the name Comanche a byword for cruelty on the Texas frontier. One of the captives was not recovered for many years. This was Cynthia Ann Parker, variously reported between nine and thirteen years old at the time of her capture. She eventually became a wife of Nokoni, chief of the important Nokoni

Comanches, and bore him several children. Her brother visited her "in her Indian home" after some years but (rather out of keeping with the aforementioned atrocity stories) she could not be persuaded to return to civilization. Finally, in 1860, she was forcibly repatriated, together with an infant child, although both died soon afterward. A son named Quanah, about fifteen at that time, stayed with his father, who had extended his influence over other Comanche bands to become the most important of Comanche leaders. After Nokoni's death, Quanah, usually known as Quanah Parker, rose to become head chief of all the Comanches, apparently by virtue of his own outstanding ability rather than hereditary rights, there being no other recorded instance of inherited chieftainship among the Comanches.

In 1839, the Texas legislature having appropriated more than a million dollars for militia expenses, a number of citizen companies took the field against the Comanches, sometimes traveling several hundred miles to find and attack Comanche rancherias. In March, 1840, a small band of Comanches, invited to a peace conference in the San Antonio council house, was surreptitiously surrounded by troops of this militia and captured, several dozen of the Comanches and a few of the militiamen being killed in the process. This brought an outraged response from Isomania, one of the best known of the Penateka Comanche leaders of the time, who a week or so later rode into San Antonio with a single companion, like a medieval knight with his squire, lambasted the Texans for their treachery and roared challenges to the troops to come forth and fight the army of warriors he had left parked outside of town. No fight was forthcoming, the forted-up Texas citizen-soldiers explaining that a truce was in effect, and as usual the scattered frontier settlers, sitting ducks for any handful of angry young men, suffered the most in the long run.

Later in the summer Texas troops defeated a Comanche force in a pitched battle at Plum Creek, midway between Austin and San Antonio. But Comanche fighting remained a recognized profession on the west Texas plains for a generation longer. Officially, most of the Comanches kept peace with the United States, with only rare lapses, but it was a peace that did not include Texas, even after Texas' admission as a state in 1845; Comanches distinguished between Texans and other Americans. Murderous raids on settlers and travelers within the sphere of the Texas frontier became part of the standard way of life.

Essentially, such raiding parties were of two types: those

maddened by attacks of the whites and seeking revenge, and those looking for loot. As the attrition of years of white military operations took its toll, both types naturally increased. The ever increasing poverty of the Plains Indians has perhaps not been given its due in this connection; at each destruction of a village there went up in smoke not only the immediate food supply of jerked meat and pemmican but the product of years of hunting and work. Buffalo robes, beaded clothes, saddles and bridles and braided reatas, thousands of arrows, tipis and their hard-to-get poles, painted parfleches, possible sacks, painstakingly manufactured articles of all kinds, were burned by the museum-load. Horses, the real treasure, were stolen by the herd or killed on the spot, sometimes in vast numbers. A U. S. Army column reportedly killed 1,400 captured horses and mules after a raid on a Kiowa camp in the Texas Panhandle in 1874. Early reports from the plains speak of the wealth and prosperity of the people; later reports indicate, decade by decade, the advancing tide of poverty.

It was this long attrition that at last smothered the resistance of the Plains Indians, who had no other source of supply than what they carried with them. But it was also this long attrition that drove more and more men and boys to the business of looting, especially since the business of looting became constantly easier and more tempting as the plains filled up with green pilgrims and settlers.

There was, of course, no shortage of excuses for hostility. Some footloose parties, however, were quite honestly out for loot, an employment as old and honorable as humanity. One such, made up apparently of a few Comanche youths, was idling along the Cimarron cutoff of the Santa Fe Trail in the summer of 1831, and there met the Galahad of mountain men, Jedediah Strong Smith. They told someone later, it seems, that they joked with him while they casually used the mirrors hanging in their hair to blind Jed's horse, causing him to spook, and while Jed was busy trying to manage the horse they shot him in the back and then ran him through with lances; he killed two of them with his Hawken rifle, they said, before he died. Jed Smith was far and away the greatest explorer among the mountain men, with an unequaled map of the whole wide West etched in his brain; but he was always unlucky with Indians. His rifle and pistols turned up for sale in Taos.

In the middle 1850s the United States government set up several Indian reservations in Texas, for some of the Comanches and Kiowas as well as other peoples of the region, including the Tonkawas. The once terrible Tonkawas, much reduced by disease and evil times, had turned humble, and Tonkawa men had served the Texans faithfully as scouts in forays against Comanches and other Texas Indians. But Texas extremists reacted so violently against the reservations that the reservees, Tonkawas and all, had to be moved. The Tonkawas were established on the Washita River in Indian Territory, where in 1862 neighboring refugees from east Texas who had suffered at the hands of the Tonkawa-guided militia massacred more than 100 of them, leaving only 100 or so survivors.

The Comanches and Kiowas signed a treaty with the United States in 1865 reserving for them the Panhandle of Texas and sundry other lands. But Texas, which had pleaded from the outset of statehood the "perfectly irresistible" spread of settlement, insisted on the complete expulsion of all Indians, and the Kiowas and Comanches were persuaded to accept a revised treaty two years later and settled in Indian Territory. The irresistible wave of settlement for which the Indians had to give way was, in the Texas Panhandle, a team of Chicago investors, who shortly after the expulsion of the Comanches and Kiowas formed the largest single cattle ranch in the history of the West, the XIT Ranch, bigger than the state of Connecticut. Eight hundred miles of barbed-wire fencing were required to enclose this great domain. The irresistible pressure of settlement instanced all over the land as the inarguable reason for dispossessing Indian communities also did not seem to exist in the world inhabited by the railroads, which in the ten years before 1871 were given by Congress more than 131 million acres of choice land, to which various western states added grants of 49 million more, the whole adding up to more than all the land in the country then occupied by all the remaining Indian nations.

Not all of the Comanches and Kiowas went to live at the Indian Agency, and not all of those who went there stayed there. One who was still there in 1869 was an otherwise obscure Comanche chief named Tochoway (Turtle Dove), who stepped briefly into the limelight, according to a possibly apocryphal story, to play straight man for an immortal phrase. The time was six weeks after Custer's destruction of Black Kettle's Cheyenne village on the Washita, and the place was Fort Cobb, Indian Territory (where Black Kettle had gone in vain to ask for official camping instructions, just before the troops descended on his village). General Phil Sheridan, Custer's boss and patron since Civil War days, was at Fort Cobb and, so the story goes, Tochoway, introducing himself, explained that he was a "good Indian." Said General Sheridan, "The only good Indians I ever saw were dead." It was by no means the first expression of this staunch old frontier notion, but it was the one the general public took to its heart and made part of the language; it was the extermination philosophy epitomized, and given the sanction of high rank.

Quanah Parker, on the way to becoming the most influential of all the Comanche chiefs, refused to sign the reservation treaty of 1867 and remained on the buffalo plains, although within the area reserved for Indian use. His Nokoni band changed its name after the death of Chief Nokoni, since a man's name could not be spoken after his death; it was called the Detsanayuka, which referred to its hasty camps made in a life of constant movement. Apparently the Kwahadi Comanches also associated themselves with young Quanah Parker's leadership. When buffalo-hide hunters illegally invaded the Indian country by hundreds in the early 1870s, these two important Comanche bands seem to have spearheaded a desperate effort to drive them out. Hostilities began in 1874 and spread over five states, harmless settlers and travelers furnishing more victims than the guilty but tough hide-hunters. Troops immediately poured into the Indian country to put down the hostiles, and ended most of the fighting after a year. Quanah Parker surrendered with his band a couple of years later. His real career, and a long and distinguished one, began at this point, as the industrious, able, and devoted savior of the remnant of his people under the bitter new hardships of agency life.

The first two signers of the 1867 treaty were Setangya, known to the Americans as Satank, principal chief of the Kiowas, and Satanta, a noted orator and warrior some twenty years younger than Setangya, and regarded as the second chief of the Kiowas. However, both continued to lead raids into Texas—one story has it that Satanta went raiding for vengeance after a practical-joking army officer gave him a swig of an emetic in place of whiskey. Setangya's son was killed on one such raid, and the grief-stricken old man thereafter bore his son's bones along with him on a lead horse wherever he went. Both chiefs were arrested for their part in a raid of 1871; Setangya wrenched off his manacles, taking the flesh of his hands with them, and attacked his guards until he was shot to death—he meant the act for suicide, and sang his death song first. Satanta was given a conditional release from prison but was imprisoned again, for life, when the Kiowas joined the war against the invading buffalo hunters of 1874. He too killed himself, four years later, in the Texas state prison. Their deaths may have been meant to inspire the Kiowas with an iron will to survive during the iron subjugation facing them; this was what the Kiowas thought, at any rate.

The 1870s brought a number of despairing outbreaks from normally peaceful people, such as from some of the Utes of Colorado or the Bannocks of Idaho, as reservations were whittled away by "rings" of local developers and county officials, or Indian agents sprang a little too lustily at the task of "civilizing" their charges, or reservation inmates became discontented with enforced starvation—the Bannocks were being rationed at a cost of 2 1/2 cents per day per person.

In Arizona and New Mexico, however, the same period saw permanent peace envelop a people—the Navaho—who had been constantly warlike, by reputation at least, throughout all known history.

Navahos had long before created a unique society, in their country of magic mesas, vermilion cliffs, and painted deserts. Captives and immigrants made them a truly composite people and triggered a vigorous, thriving growth that had increased their numbers to perhaps 10,000 by 1860—more than the population of all the other Apache tribes put together. The only heritage they continued to share with their original Apache brothers was the Athapascan basis of their language, but even that was much changed by accessions from new tongues. One accession the language never picked up was the letter "v"—most Navahos, in consequence, found the word "Navaho" unpronounceable. Many Navahos, in fact, scarcely knew of the word until fairly recent times. Their name for themselves was and is Diné, meaning, as usual, the Folks, the People. All of the nearly four dozen Athapascan languages use some variation of this word as a tribal name.

At some time after the arrival of the Spaniards in the Southwest, the Navahos took to the raising of sheep and became herders and stockmen. Their women learned weaving and in time made the Navaho blanket world famous. They learned silversmithing and produced work of high excellence, for which Pueblo importers came to trade, bargaining in sign language.

They adopted the altars of the Pueblos—the much admired

"sand paintings" that the Navahos have made their own (intellectually superior, in the words of a recent international art
authority, "to any painting that has been done in Europe or
America within the last several centuries"). They never adopted
the formal, community-wide religious ceremonies of the Pueblos, although religious feeling sifted into every nook and cranny
of the Navaho way of life, and their religious songs became so
numerous, said an early investigator, that no one could ever
hope to collect them all. Religion was simply living the Right
Way, and entreating the world, by means of these inspired songs
led by priestly Singers, to behave in the Right Way. Sang the
Singer, in one of the Songs of Talking God:

> Now I walk with Talking God . . .
> With goodness and beauty in all things around me I go;
> With goodness and beauty I follow immortality.
> Thus being I, I go.

They farmed a little: peach trees and corn patches, Hopi
style, wherever a touch of moisture in the earth permitted. But
they never really formed villages. Their hogans—earth lodges—
were sometimes gathered in family clusters, houses of a mother
and her married daughters, but otherwise were anywhere; the
brush shelters of summer were as scattered as their flocks.

A house was customarily abandoned upon the death of an
occupant; usually the people would not touch a dead body, from
fear of the dead and of witchcraft. By custom they would not
touch even the body of a slain enemy; the Navahos, like most
other Indians, had not practiced scalping in original times, and
unlike many other tribes never did pick up the practice.

The keeping of family-owned flocks may have helped bring
about a sharper distinction between rich and poor than was usual
among most Indians; the Navahos, too, were much noted for an
industriousness uncommon to seminomadic peoples. These are
touches that blend well with the faintly Old World, almost Old
Testament, atmosphere that hangs about the early Navahos, as
the only pastoral non-village people in the Americas. But there
was certainly no Old Testament ring to their character—"Wit,
merriment and practical jokes enliven all their gatherings,"
wrote one nineteenth century observer, in an observation typical
of most. And in the testimony of generations of town-dwelling
neighbors, Pueblo Indians, Spanish colonials, and Mexicans
alike, the Navahos were raiders and warriors first and gentle

shepherds a distant second, finding far more joy in coming down like wolves on a fold than in patiently tending one.

It may be significant that the great majority of Navaho war names—war names being the only formal personal names in times past—made some use of the verb "to raid." This was true for girls' names as well as boys', although a very common girl's name was simply Warrior Girl.

But it is possible that the Navahos—and the Apaches also—were as much sinned against as sinning, in the matter of raids. The Spanish pronunciamentos picture New Mexico a martyr for centuries to the rapacious Navahos, the "Lords of the Soil," who reportedly boasted that they only tolerated the Spaniards' presence because the Spanish ranchos were so pleasant to plunder. Unquestionably Navaho raiders removed much movable property, including children and women, from the Spaniards and the Pueblos.

There must have been some plunderers from the other side, though, to capture the thousands of Navaho and Apache women and children who were commonly the slaves of the New Mexico settlements. Said a New Mexico resident in the 1860s, "I think the Navahos have been the most abused people on the continent, and that in all hostilities the Mexicans have always taken the initiative with but one exception that I know of." Kit Carson spoke of the way some Mexicans were accustomed to "prey on" the Navahos, but also mentioned the "continual thieving carried on between the Navahos and the Mexicans," which is probably the most accurate general summation.

Official American acquaintance with the Navahos came in the autumn of 1849, three years after the American conquest of New Mexico during the Mexican War. New Mexico was a land of uneasiness at this time. Early in 1847 an insurrection of Taos Indians, urged on by Mexicans who wished to overthrow the conquest, cost the lives of a number of Americans, including the acting governor, and was only put down with a hard-fought battle at Taos and the subsequent hanging of the *insurrecto* leaders. By the summer of 1849 new American arrivals, some of them emigrants on their way to California, were causing much anxiety by robbing and outraging the Indians, particularly the patient Pueblos. The Pueblos—"a more upright and useful people are no where to be found," said the Indian agent at Santa Fe—entreated the government for compensation and protection, but in vain, there being no way, said the American authorities, to control these lawless elements or make restitution for their misdeeds.

There were also endless complaints of Navaho raids and thefts, and to settle these the governor of New Mexico marched a body of troops westward from the Rio Grande to the Navaho country and made a treaty. Nothing like an authorized chief existed among the Navahos, each band operating with complete independence under an informally chosen head man. However, a local patriarch of considerable repute, known as Narbona, came with several hundred of his followers to meet with the Americans.

Narbona explained that lawless men were everywhere and that "their utmost vigilance had not rendered it possible for the Chiefs and good men to apprehend the guilty, or to restrain the wicked." This was rather the same situation as that just noted concerning depredations by lawless Americans, but unlike the American government Narbóna offered to make every possible restitution for Navaho thefts, and as an earnest of this intention turned over 130 sheep and four or five horses and mules.

A treaty of "perpetual peace and friendship" was signed, but then a Mexican with the American command demanded still another horse, the Navahos objected, the governor threatened, the Navahos wheeled their horses and "scampered off at the top of their speed," and the governor ordered his troops to fire on them. Six or seven Navahos didn't get out of range in time and were killed, including the patriarch, Narbona. Possibly his age, about eighty, slowed him up, or possibly the business of signing the treaty of perpetual peace and friendship had left him in an unhandy getaway position. The rest of the Navahos, "three to four hundred, all mounted and armed, and their arms in their hands," fled without offering any resistance. The artillery with the troops, noted a young army officer in his report, "also threw in among them, very handsomely—much to their terror, when they were afar off, and thought they could with safety relax their flight—a couple of round shot. . . ." He added, with a fine discernment, "These people evidently gave signs of being tricky and unreliable . . ."

This example of American statesmanship did not stop Navaho marauding, and a fort, Fort Defiance ("a wretched hole," wrote an experienced officer, "which deserves its name because its position is in defiance of nearly every principle of military science"), was established in the Navaho country in

1851. Thereafter reasonable quiet prevailed until 1858, when an altercation between a Navaho subchief and an army officer's black slave blew up a war. It featured a massed Navaho attack on Fort Defiance, and the country was strewn anew with garlands of wild-blooming violent deaths and disasters.

Exigencies of the Civil War intervened, and it was not until the winter of 1864-1865 that Colonel Kit Carson was sent to round up the Navahos and did so. In the impregnable Navaho stronghold of the Cañon de Chelly the troops cut down 2,000 to 3,000 peach trees and found, among other plantings, one field of corn that took 300 men the better part of a day to destroy. Flocks and herds were seized or butchered. Most of the Navahos were starved into submission and were removed to the Bosque Redondo, a reservation near Fort Sumner in eastern New Mexico, to be reformed from the incurable brigands everyone said they were. The idea was to turn them into peaceful farmers.

The idea was given up after four years of much Navaho misery, and the Navahos were allowed to return to their own country, or rather to a part of it which was made the basis of a permanent reservation. The government gave them 35,000 sheep and goats to put them back in the pastoral business. There were difficulties and hardships in getting started again, but in the main the tribe waxed greater year by year, sometimes prospered, and was at peace.

There was no peace for the Apaches. Spanish authorities had at various times drawn up rather grandiose battle plans for complete extermination of the Apaches, and the Mexican states of Chihuahua and Sonora occasionally paid very generous bounties for Apache scalps, as did some communities north of the border—in 1866 an Arizona county was still offering $250 for each Apache scalp. It was in a bounty boom year, 1837, that a party of American trappers invited a band of Mimbres Apaches to a fiesta at the Santa Rita copper mines, in southwestern New Mexico, and then massacred the guests, procuring many scalps. The Mimbreños had until then been friendly to Americans but were not exactly trustworthy thereafter, and killed a number of trappers who were working their country. The Mexican village at the Santa Rita mines was made untenable and the mines abandoned for several years.

South of the Gila River the peaceful Pimas had fought Apaches for generations, apparently always winning, by the traditions of both sides. The Maricopas, a tall Yuman people from the lower Colorado River, emigrated to the Pima country over a long period of time ending in the early 1800s, moving up the Gila to escape the attacks of their kinsmen the Quechan and other Yuman groups. It is said the Pimas made them promise to fight no wars except defensively, to which the Maricopas agreed; the two peoples thereupon lived together in perfect friendship, although neither spoke the other's language, and ran up frequent high scores in their defensive wars against the Apaches to the east and the Yuman bands to the west—of a sizable Yuman war party that invaded Pimeria in 1857, for one example, only three lived to get back home.

Other Yuman tribes lived above the Quechan on the Colorado—the numerous and valiant Mohaves, who "talk rapidly and with great haughtiness," meanwhile giving "smart slaps with the palms on the thighs," as Fray Francisco Garcés sketched them; and the smaller groups of Yuman peoples such as the Walapai, Havasupai, and Yavapai, living in western Arizona from the Grand Canyon to the Gila, were the only sizable bloc in the Southwest whose hands were not raised against the Apache. The Yavapais, in fact, mingled with the Tonto Apaches to such an extent that both were called Tontos indiscriminately; the Yavapais were also sometimes known as Apache Mohaves. It may well have been a gang of Yavapai hoodlums who in 1851 committed a famous massacre usually credited to the Tonto Apaches: the killing of the Oatman family of emigrants along the Gila, at what has been known since as Oatman Flat. Olive Oatman, twelve year-old daughter of the family, was sold into slavery to the Mohaves. She was rescued by a Quechan five years later and returned to white civilization, which made a sensation of her story and the Mohave marriage marks tattooed on her chin.

More than anything else, it was probably the incessant kidnaping and enslavement of their women and children that gave Apaches their mad-dog enmity toward the whites, from earliest Spanish times onward. It was officially estimated that 2,000 Indian slaves were held by the white people of New Mexico and Arizona in 1866, after twenty years of American rule—and some little while after the Great Emancipator had done his stuff elsewhere in the land. Unofficial estimates put the figure several times higher. More enslaved Apaches still were in Sonora and Chihuahua. "Get them back for us," Apaches begged of an army officer in 1871, referring to twenty-nine children just stolen by citizens of Arizona; "our little boys will grow up slaves, and our girls, as soon as they are large enough, will be diseased prostitutes, to get money for whoever owns them. Our women work hard and are good women, and they and our children have no diseases." Prostitution of captured Apache girls, of which much mention is made in the 1860s and 1870s, seemed to trouble the Apaches exceedingly. It was during this period—the 1860s—that Apaches are supposed to have taken generally to the custom of mutilating enemy dead.

Demure overtures of friendship characterized the usual Apache approach to the first Yankees who appeared in their country. The newcomers were very different from Mexicans—a common Apache name for Americans was White-eyes—and might prove to be allies against the constant Mexican foe. But the wonted hostile collisions were not long in occuring. Apaches, with their wild-flying hair (the usual custom was to shampoo it daily, which might make for cleanliness but not for neatness), their raggle-taggle bands sometimes consisting of only a few families, their dusty brush-hut rancherias in the dusty brush, looked miserably primitive. They had little of the finery of the Plains Indians. There was not much about them, at a glance, to command respect.

Furthermore, there was a great deal to create suspicion. They came and went with exceeding softness. They were often genial and talkative but without quite saying anything. The wandering American, everybody's buddy, could usually pick up a working knowledge of a strange tribe's customs in a week, but until the 1930s the Apaches remained the least known important Indian people in the United States—while "Apache" had been a worldwide household word for generations. In brief, Apaches were watchful. They were some of the most watchful people who ever lived, and that was the reason they had been able to go on living through centuries of playing dangerous big game for hunters with guns. To blunt White-eyes in heavy shoes their sly, grinning watchfulness had an air of menace and guilt.

Americans mining for gold in western New Mexico in the early 1850s were annoyed, or unnerved, by an Apache who persisted in hanging around their camp. He was an unusual Apache, a massive-headed giant of a man, comically bowlegged. The miners tied him up and lashed his bull back to ribbons, as a warning to keep away. He was an important man of the Mimbreños, a survivor of the Santa Rita scalp bounty massacre of 1837, related by marriage to chiefs of the White Mountain and Chiricahua bands who lived next door west. His name in Spanish was Mangas Coloradas (Red Sleeves). He was probably close to sixty years old at the time of his flogging, and he lived to be seventy or so; for these long last years of his life he warred against white men, Mexicans and White-eyes alike, without mercy.

In 1861 the Chiricahua people were not only friendly to Americans but were employed in cutting wood for a stage station in Apache Pass, on the stage line through the Chiricahua mountains. An impetuous young lieutenant leading a military detachment searching for depredators summoned the leading Chiricahua men to a conference in his tent, above which the lieutenant flew a white flag of truce, and during the conference attempted to make prisoners of the Apache conferees. The Chiricahua chief and several others escaped, and battle began; the troops withdrew from the pass after each side had executed its prisoners—the Apaches by torture, the Americans by hanging. The Chiricahua chief was named Cochise; he escaped from the conference tent, so they say, with three bullets in his body. For the next ten years he warred against the white men without mercy.

Together, Mangas Coloradas and Cochise laid waste the white settlements and promoted hatred of Americans throughout all Apacheria. At the opening of the Civil War, when garrisons were recalled from most of the forts in Arizona and New Mexico, Arizona was swept virtually clean of whites by triumphant Apaches. Only Old Tucson, in Pimeria, remained as a settled place of any importance, and its population shrank to no more than 200.

The White-eyes were occupied with menacing each other in the Southwest, as a brief and distant part of the early Civil War, until the close of 1862. General James H. Carleton, who had come with 3,000 California volunteers to take command in New Mexico, then set on foot a campaign of Apache extermination. This campaign got under way in 1863, reached all-out proportions in 1864, and continued, although gradually declining in energy, until 1871. In the first flush of enthusiasm, the cooperation of Sonora and Chihuahua was obtained; miners were encouraged to return to Arizona and were offered expenses, California style, for informal Apache-killing expeditions; Pimas, Papagos, and Maricopas were furnished with guns and American leadership; troops, at a wartime high, were employed to the full. Many of the troops were Californians, and California methods were adopted, which meant that any means whatever were acceptable as long as Apaches were killed. Thus there was no official objection if Apaches were coaxed to appear for "treaty" talks and were then shot—old Mangas Coloradas was one of the first to fall for this, dying in 1863.

Some officers, such as Colonel Kit Carson and Colonel John C. Cremony, who had known the Apaches for years, simply ignored the orders to kill all men and take the women and children prisoner, and accepted Apache surrenders. But in general the forces combined for the great extermination program went to their work with a will, and the peak year of 1864 recorded hundreds of armed encounters. However, the official score of a total of 216 Apaches killed in this big year was not terribly encouraging—and the rest of the score, 3,000 sheep captured by Indians as against 175 captured back, and 146 horses captured by Indians as against fifty-four recovered, was even less so. There was also a definite feeling in the Territories that the official white loss of sixteen was incomplete.

Mines were reopened in Arizona, settlements were reestablished, and the Apaches were driven deep into their mountains and made destitute by ceaseless destruction of their rancherias. But no Apache band was conquered, most of the Apache casualties were non-combatants, the life of a traveler was not safe in Apacheria, nor the lives of small groups of prospectors or settlers, and even settlements of some size lived in fear of bloodcurdling Apache raids. In effect, the old conditions of the Spanish frontier were restored, with the difference that there were more whites to be raided, and the methods of the war brought bitterness and cruelty to new highs. Some of the milder frontier tales of Apache atrocities spoke of captured women whose bodies had been literally torn apart, and of prisoners hung head downward over small fires, their uncontrollable jackknifing affording amusement for hours while their brains slowly roasted until they died.

We do not have, of course, the tales of white atrocities that Apaches may have told each other. Arizona in the 1860s and 1870s had the reputation of being the toughest territory in the West, filled with gentry who had departed other climes a quick jump ahead of the Vigilantes. There is no reason to suppose they dealt gently with an Apache, when they could get hold of one.

The 1871 massacre by a Tucson mob of some eighty-five Aravaipa Apache people who had put themselves under the protection of the military at a nearby fort, Camp Grant, caused national indignation, but was generally defended by the Arizona press—100 Americans, Mexicans and Papagos were indicted and tried for these murders and declared not guilty by a jury after less than a half hour's deliberation. A plenary representative of the President, sent to Arizona to take over Indian affairs after this incident, reported that "acts of inhuman treachery and cruelty" had made the Apaches "our implacable foes," after they had tried to be friends of the Americans in the beginning.

"How is it?" asked Cochise, chief of the Chiricahuas. "Why is it that the Apaches want to die—that they carry their lives on their finger nails?"

The Camp Grant massacre ended the war of Apache extermination—a war of almost ten years that had cost 1,000 American lives and more than forty million dollars and resulted in complete failure. The special report of the President's representative concluded that the country was no quieter nor the Apaches any nearer extermination than they were when it all began.

And so the policy of extermination was replaced by a policy of conciliation, while the frontier seethed with resentment. Fortunately, the command of the military department of Arizona was given in that same summer of 1871 to General George Crook. General Crook was an Indian fighter of skill and wisdom, and what was still more extraordinary, of an honesty as stubborn as one of his treasured pack mules. He would no more break his word to the leader of a pack of ragged Apaches than he would break his word to a field marshal of England. Fighting was his profession but people were his business. He realized that Apaches were not the hellhounds the frontier pictured them, and they were not the saintly martyrs pictured by the sentimental friends of the Red Man in the East. They were frightened people who were tremendously experienced at being the subjects of extermination, an experience that had made them the most polished masters of ruthless guerrilla fighting in the history of the United States.

Captain John G. Bourke, General Crook's adjutant for many years, became extremely well acquainted with Apaches, and wrote, "No Indian has more virtues and none has been more truly ferocious when aroused . . . For centuries he has been preeminent over the more peaceful nations about him for courage, skill, and daring in war; cunning in deceiving and evading his enemies; ferocity in attack when skillfully-planned ambuscades have led an unwary foe into his clutches; cruelty and brutality to captives; patient endurance and fortitude under the greatest privations . . . In peace he has commanded respect for keen-sighted intelligence, good fellowship, warmth of feeling for his friends, and impatience of wrong . . ."

The Apache could cover forty miles in a day on foot, shambling along in his sloppy legging-like moccasins, or could reel off seventy-five miles a day on horseback, caring nothing about running his horse into the ground since his remount station was the nearest ranch. He could live off the country, "hilarious and jovial" while a town-bred pursuer was perishing of hunger, thirst, and sunstroke. He could travel as invisibly as a ghost, appear or disappear as silently as a shadow. The soldier on his trail only knew of his presence when the lethal Apache bow or Winchester announced itself from a concealed and highly defendable position.

The dusty warrior, with a dash of color at the headband or in the Pima-like turban, was seldom seen, and if seen was seldom hit, and if hit was seldom knocked down to stay. Apaches were terribly hard to kill.

There being no solidarity among Apaches in general, Crook employed the warriors of conciliated bands to fight the bands that insisted on remaining hostile. Crook's Apache scouts became famous, and by the end of summer, 1874, all important hostile bands had been either conciliated or relentlessly rounded up, and were settled on reservations, peaceful, industrious, and reportedly happy. There was "almost a certainty," said the governor of Arizona in 1875, "that no general Indian war will ever occur again." This was the first phase of Crook's program. The second phase was not as easy. It consisted of protecting these peaceful Apaches from white troublemakers, well-meaning or otherwise.

General Crook said in 1879, "During the twenty-seven years of my experience with the Indian question I have never known a band of Indians to make peace with our government and then break it, or leave their reservation, without some ground of complaint; but until their complaints are examined and adjusted, they will constantly give annoyance and trouble."

The greatest cause of later trouble, among the Apaches, was

the arbitrary removal of bands from their homeland reservations to new reservations where they did not want to go. This was done by the Indian Bureau for reasons of operational efficiency, or to throw the business of an agency to some go-getting community that was pulling strings to get it, or for similar humanitarian motives. The second greatest cause of trouble was the activity of crooked "rings" that supplied supplies Indians never received, stole reservation land by shady manipulation, or practiced other such arts and crafts. Captain Bourke summed this up by saying that the wicked Indians labored under a delusion that a ration was enough food to keep the recipient from starving to death, while the agent issued supplies by throwing them through the rungs of a ladder—the Indians getting whatever stuck to the rungs, and the agent getting what fell to the ground. Finally, there were the seamy whiskey wagoners and petty thieves who were not averse to stirring the Indians up for a profit of two-bits.

General Crook again, on the subject of bad Indians: "I have never yet seen one so demoralized that he was not an example in honor and nobility compared to the wretches who plunder him of the little our government appropriates for him."

In New Mexico and Arizona these causes brought trouble from a number of Apache bands but most of all from the Chiricahuas, whose furious outbreaks of protest added considerable size to the Apache legend. The great Cochise died in peace on the Chiricahua reservation in the summer of 1874, but within eighteen months some of the Chiricahuas were rampaging into Sonora, killing innocent bystanders right and left along the way, to resist removal to another reservation.

For a fair share of the next ten years various Chiricahua groups, generally accompanied by some families of Mogollon, Mimbres, and Coyotero in-laws, were breaking loose to storm up and down the border country, performing ghostly raids and elusive campaigns that make the staid military reports read like fiction. Such leaders as Victorio and Geronimo (pronounced and in his day sometimes spelled Heronimo) entered the ranks of the West's top celebrities. Both these men were Mimbreños by birth; Victorio had been a lieutenant of Mangas Coloradas. After Victorio was killed by Mexican troops in 1880, a rheumatic old gentleman named Nana stepped up to take a turn stage center, and for a wild, incredible couple of months in 1881 led a handful of warriors, perhaps fifteen Chiricahuas, later joined by a couple of dozen Mescaleros, on the champion raid and running campaign of them all, fighting and winning a battle a week against 1,000 U.S. troops, Texas Rangers, armies of frantic civilians, and the military and police establishments of northern Mexico. Nana was some seventy or eighty years old at the time, and so stove up with aches and pains he had to walk with a cane. He liked to wear gold watch chains in his ears.

General Crook had been sent away to fight the Sioux in 1875, when Arizona was quiet and there was never again going to be an Indian war. He was brought back in 1882, and for four years patiently rounded up hostile Apaches and then patiently tried to pacify hostile elements on the home front, and then rounded up his Apaches again when they were prodded into another break. Geronimo came into the fore during this period and was given enormous publicity on both sides of the Border as part clown, part monster, part military genius; and has been given enormous publicity since as drunken simpleton and/or heroic freedom-fighter (from all of which biographers can take their choice).

There came a time when Crook's superiors had had enough of his patience and his insistence on honorable behavior, and replaced him with General Nelson A. Miles. When Apache scouts were able to talk Geronimo into surrendering again he and his band were packed off to Florida as prisoners, and for good measure Miles sent along Crook's old Apache scouts as prisoners too, and just to make sure he had everyone, sent along all or nearly all the other Chiricahuas he could lay hands on, including hundreds who had remained quietly on the reservation from the first.

This happened in 1886, and Crook was still waging a campaign in the halls of Congress to get his Apaches moved back west (at least as far as Oklahoma) when he died of a heart attack in 1890. A few months before his death he visited the largest group of exiled Chiricahuas, who had been temporarily settled at Mount Vernon Barracks, near Mobile, Alabama. They crowded around him, his old scouts and his ancient enemies—and a number were both—and there was quite a reunion, and this is as good a place as any other to declare a final, formal end of the Indian wars.

Old Geronimo was in the schoolroom at the time of General Crook's visit, threatening with a stick any children who misbehaved.

XVI
Reservations

From end to end of the two continents the American Indians lived, and they still do. Disease, conquest, mass executions, oppression, decay, and assimilation had by about the year 1900 reduced the number of Indians in the United States to perhaps some 250,000 or less (the census of 1900 returned slightly over 237,000), which would be only a small fraction, some estimates would say a fourth, some a tenth, some a twentieth, some a fortieth, of the estimated population in aboriginal times. From that low point the number of Indians has rather steadily in- creased, recently at a rate considerably faster than the increase of the general population. Latest census figures show a startling jump of more than fifty per cent in each of the last two decades, from some 343,000 in 1950 to nearly 792,000 in 1970. More than 500,000 of this total still live on reservations or other tribal lands, although from 1960 to 1970 the movement into urban areas (usually urban slums), a movement vigorously encouraged by the government, helped increase the number of urban Indians by 153 per cent, while rural Indian populations increased by only thirteen per cent. Besides the basic factor of a higher birth rate, this general population increase reflects an increased willingness, as the U. S. Census Bureau puts it, of persons to identify themselves as Indians. Even so some, possibly quite a few, Indian or part-Indian people are not listed as such in census reports or other government records; some estimates place this number at between 75,000 and 100,000.

The Eskimos, Aleuts, and Indians in Alaska are now estimated at more than 50,000. There may be as many as 500,000 Indians, Eskimos, and Métis in Canada; Canada's Indian Affairs Department has "relations" with something less than half that number, of which 160,000 or so live on reserves, as reservations are termed in Canada. Eskimos and Indians are still almost the only residents (apart from temporary residents such as oil-exploration crews who stay only long enough to extract something of value from the land) in vast reaches of the far northern country—of the total population of some 33,000 persons in Canada's North West Territories, which constitute more than a third of the country's entire land area, 25,000 are Inuit, Indians, and Métis, and Inuit communities make up the majority of Greenland's nearly 44,000 people.

But it is necessary to remember that all this area north of Mexico was peripheral to the central Indian world. Immense numbers of the people of that central Indian world still remain; many millions (some 30,000,000 would be a reasonable estimate) in Latin America are generally recognized as Indians, and regard themselves as such. Where the modern Indians of the United States equal less than one-half of one per cent of the total population, the present day Indians of Peru add up to forty-six per cent (by a 1968 estimate) of Peru's 13,000,000 people, more than half of Bolivia's 4,500,000, twenty-eight per cent (by a 1969 estimate) of Mexico's nearly 49,000,000. Many more millions who are to a lesser degree Indian in blood and heritage enhance the Indian character of various of the populations from Mexico southward; for example seventy per cent of Mexico's population is reckoned as mestizo—people of mixed European and Indian descent—in addition to the twenty-eight per cent identified as Indian. As these rather staggering figures make clear, Indians in the United States represent only a tiny portion, at the most one or two per cent, of all the Indian and part-Indian people of the hemisphere.

In some broad terms, Indian history throughout much of the rest of the New World paralleled the Indian story in the United States. The colonial structure of the 1700s—foreign rule by

European monarchs or Lords of Trade—in general provided a sort of shadow protection for Indians, if only as natural resources or Crown possessions. The egalitarian winds of the 1800s swept away this protection and left Indian groups and their remaining community holdings at the mercy of whatever bloc controlled local legislation.

Indian lands were broken up, Indians were changed into peons, whole peoples were quite ruthlessly exterminated—unlike the other Latin American countries just listed, such nations as Argentina and Chile (where some 700,000 descendants of the tough Araucanians still remain, on the edges of the general population of nearly ten million) and Uruguay (one per cent Indian, ten per cent mestizo) contain relatively few surviving Indians. Present day Brazil, accurately reflecting the replacement of vanished Indian populations with black slaves, reports eleven per cent Negroes, twenty-six per cent mulattos, and two per cent Indians in its total population of 93,000,000. Where Indians remained in enough strength wars of resistance were fought, sometimes for decades—as in the case of the Mayas in the Mexican state of Quintana Roo on the Yucatan peninsula, who fought a full-scale rebellion from 1847 to 1850, and continued resisting in some degree until the 1940s; in the early 1900s Mexican authorities shipped rebellious Yaquis south (in murderous five-day trips in locked boxcars) to be sold as slaves on the henequen plantations deserted by the rebellious Mayas. Efforts to seize Indian lands were now and then given up in the face of such tenacious opposition. And here and there, when an Indian struggle became hopeless, messiahs appeared. The talking cross of Chan Santa Cruz inspired the above-mentioned Mayas of Quintana Roo, and at the very time the dreamer and prophet Wovoka was originating the Ghost Dance that swept the western United States, in the late 1880s, a messiah was calling the Chiriguanos to arms in Bolivia, saying the guns of the soldiers would only spit water.

But in Latin America generally, Indian culture had mingled inextricably with European, and in regions of heavy Negro slavery with African. It had not so much resisted this mingling as it had retained, with remarkable persistence, certain Indian traits. In recent years there has been a growing recognition of Indian elements in the Latin American character, with a tendency to glorify Indian history and individual Indians, such as Juarez, who have been of moment in national history. This so-called Indianist feeling is strongest in Mexico, where it was a factor in the "Revolutionary" school of art that reached its climax with the great Mexican muralists of the 1930s, one of the few American art movements—up to that time—ever to be taken seriously by Europe.

"Indianism" has led to slightly revised policies toward the masses of pure Indians in some parts of Latin America, sometimes even in areas where caste distinctions still hold Indians to second-class status. A tendency toward genuine protection and encouragement of surviving Indians began to appear, sporadically, in various American countries in the first half of the twentieth century. Brazil founded in 1910 the Service for the Protection of the Indian, to bring some education, medicine, and the like to the many tribes of Amazonia; a good many members of the Service were sincere and dedicated people, indeed several lost their lives to prove it and to prove their respect for attributes of Indian culture which, as one director of the Service said, might have constituted "the strongest and most progressive race in the world, if they had been properly encouraged . . . by the first colonists." But scandals revealed in the 1960s that some officials of the Indian Protection Service itself had been involved in attacks on jungle Indians for the benefit of commercial interests who wanted to explore possible uses of Indian land. Brazil's Indian service was reformed and retitled the National Indian Foundation, but charges of widespread injustices, especially accompanying the building of Brazil's Trans-Amazon Highway and the "development" of lands and resources along its route, grew even more vociferous in the early 1970s. In fact, charges of anti-Indian violence on the part of governments serving commercial interests were heard increasingly over much of the hemisphere, from Canada to Colombia as well as Brazil, in the wake of growing nationalism and authoritarianism in many countries following World War II.

And yet during the same epoch the notion began to get around, albeit slowly and by no means steadily, that the Indian heritage might really contain values more subtle than those so far found in silver and gold and cheap labor. In the 1930s an inter-American group sponsored a study which demonstrated beyond doubt that the Indians all over the Americas were not a vanishing race but a rapidly growing race; this gave rise to the Inter-American Institute of the Indian organized in 1940 by nineteen American republics. Some of the results were a partial eradication of remnants of Indian slavery or forced labor; an occasional shot at bilingual education—encouraging learning and even literacy in an Indian as well as a European language; and an occasional inclination toward encouraging or sustaining the tribe or Indian community rather than shattering it. In Peru and Bolivia the ancient social structure of the ayllu owns and regulates the land in thousands of Indian villages or some predominantly Indian areas in cities, and in a few cases such a community has bought or built such neo-Inca contraptions as hydroelectric plants—perhaps in much the same manner as an ayllu of olden times participated in the building of a temple pyramid. Mexico began a program of restoring to at least some Indian and mestizo communities the community lands, the *ejidos*, that had been seized for great estates during the turbulent, greedy years of early independence in the nineteenth century.

Indianism as a symbol has had political potency all over the New World since the first of Mexico's revolutions—led, unsuccessfully, by a son of Hernando Cortes dressed in Indian costume—and such frolics as the Boston Tea Party. In the late 1960s political guerrillas in South America adopted the name Tupamaru or Tupamaro, from Tupac Amaru II, a descendant of the last of the Incas, executed by the Spanish authorities after a short-lived revolt in 1780, and the Tupamaru guerrillas were so successful in identifying with the memory of the Inca folk hero that merely publication of the name was made illegal in Uruguay. On the other hand the military junta in power in Peru also appropriated the name as a symbol of their established government, also with some (at least temporary) public-relations success.

In the United States repeated and rigorous attempts were made over many years to demolish tribal ties and structures. The ideal was to chew the Indian up in the social machine and assimilate him. The problem was complicated by many special aspects, among them the fact that most tribes still owned some property that various interested citizens never gave up trying to get—and, as shall be seen, haven't given up yet. A constant, overriding handicap was the depressing fact that any Indian program was subject to complete change at each change of political administration.

In the Indians' darkest hour—the couple of generations from the 1870s to the 1920s—there was, no doubt, much more silent suffering than will ever be related. On the spiritual side, religious activities were proscribed, the sun dance forbidden to the Plains Indians, Kwakiutl people sent to prison by Canadian authorities for participating in the social giveaway of a potlatch. Children were taught to feel shame and contempt for their "blanket Indian" parents and all their ways; life, in the case of many agency Indians, was made aimless and hopeless by the pervasive concentration-camp air. On the physical side, hunger was the big reality for those confined peoples who could only secure their dinners out of promised government subsistence. The Bureau of Indian Affairs labored for years under charges of crookedness that no amount of reform could seem to hush; President Grant even tried the expedient of appointing only church-nominated agents, who too often turned out to be mainly interested in proselytizing for their sects, and the heathen—especially the heathen—still went hungry.

A glimpse of the dark ages of reservation life comes from the report of an army surgeon in the early days of the Crow Creek, South Dakota, Agency: "Some time about the middle of the winter a large vat was constructed of cotton-wood lumber, about six feet square and six feet deep, in connection with the steam sawmill, with a pipe leading from the boiler into the vat. Into this vat was thrown beef, beef heads, entrails of beeves, some beans, flour and pork. I think there was put into the vat two barrels of flour each time, which was not oftener than once in twenty-four hours. This mass was then cooked by the steam from the boiler passing through the vat. When that was done, all the Indians were ordered to come there with their pails and get it . . . The Santees and Winnebagos were fed from this vat; some of the Indians refused to eat it, saying they could not eat it, it made them sick . . . The Indians reported several deaths from starvation. . . ."

Some individuals, particularly from dispersed or trans-planted eastern nations, made progress in coming to terms with the white world on the outside. The articles of surrender that Lee signed at Appomattox were penned by Grant's secretary, Brigadier General Eli Samuel Parker, a Seneca sachem (known among the Seneca as Doneihogawa, an official title meaning "keeper of the door") and grandson of the famous orator Red Jacket. Quite a few Sioux warriors found their way eased into the outside world via tours with Buffalo Bill's Wild West Show. One of the first to reach the scene of the Wounded Knee massacre was Dr. Charles Eastman, Santee Sioux graduate of Dartmouth and the Boston University medical school, then serving as government physician to the Pine Ridge, South Dakota, Agency; he described, quite dispassionately, the way young girls had knelt and covered their faces with their shawls so they would not see the troopers come up to shoot them.

Some organized tribal groups, such as the Cherokee, persisted with marvelous stubbornness, through Job's plagues of setbacks, in trying to reach full adjustment with the new scale of the world being built around them.

But the more typical adjustments were those of the thousands of dispirited people who merely killed time in the institutionalized slums of their reservations, becoming adept in the skills of wise old boys who have lived a long time in the orphanage. They learned how to wheedle and hoodwink the agency staff for the nickels and dimes in scraps of supplies that trickled down through the budget to their level, and how to give some point to a pointless existence by finding delight in unutterable trivia. And the friendly agents said in a fond way, "They're children." Unfriendly agents said, "Indolent, insolent, and uncivilizable," and often resigned. Friendly or unfriendly, the agents enjoyed an absolute rule: "They know no law but the will of the Agent," said an observer of the 1870s.

The Railroad Enabling Act of 1866 sliced some choice cuts off a number of reservations. This act gave to railroad builders alternate sections of public lands forty miles deep on either side of a projected right of way, as an inducement to railroad building. The forty-mile depth was later extended to fifty miles to offset losses from prior claims of white settlers, but the same thoughtfulness did not extend to the prior claims of Indians: for the purposes of the Act, reservations were considered public lands—a clear illegality in the face of numerous treaties—and unlucky Indian communities found themselves being ejected from tribal lands that had suddenly turned into railroad property.

Reservations, as previously noted, exist under the authority of treaties between groups of Indian people and the President of the United States, with ratification by the Senate, and thus, as numerous legal opinions have held, are under the authority of "the supreme law of the land"—arguments that Indian nations were not competent to serve as parties to a treaty were answered by several Supreme Court decisions holding that the "competency of the contracting parties to make a treaty is not a question into which courts can inquire as a condition precedent to regarding it as a law." Reservations were usually established as payment for huge land cessions and other tribal acts of cooperation, and usually confirmed the Indians in permanent and complete ownership of their reserved lands in the most explicit possible terms; as a rule the treaty commissioners felt they were making splendid bargains and as a rule they certainly were. Reservations are therefore neither prisons nor public lands (two widespread folk beliefs) but private property presumably held under the most secure of titles, more secure, technically, than the property held by most corporations, for example. Further, such treaties often stipulated additional payment to the Indians (for their land cessions and other cooperation) in the form of goods, tools, subsistence, annuities, services in providing education, roads, health care, and the like, and swore most solemnly to protect the Indians and all this property and these goods and services from any rapacious neighbors, including state and local governments. It is to effect this protection that the federal government holds trusteeship of Indian lands and services, and it is in this sense only that Indians are "wards" of the government.

After 1871, when the prevalence of scandal led to the end of treaty-making with Indian nations, reservations were established or enlarged or diminished, within limits, by executive order of the President. Reservation lands were still supposed to be inalienable, as the language of the agreements customarily stated. But later Congresses were under no obligation, of course, to keep the nation's promise, there being no power, at least not here below, to compel them to do so. The reservations began to look bigger and shinier every day, as land in the West picked up in value. And even friends of the Red Man had to admit that reservations fostered tribal unity, which was a bar, everyone said, to civilizing the savages.

Thus in 1887, after much strenuous politicking, the so-called Allotment Act became law, a rope trick designed to make all Indians and their problems disappear and place the broad reservations in the more appreciative hands of white owners. Under this law tribes were to surrender their reservations, fragments of which were to be allotted to individual Indians as small, family-sized farms—from 10 to 640 acres each. The immense reservation acreage left over was to be declared "surplus" and, after a token payment to the tribes involved, opened to white ownership.

Obviously the Allotment Act would break up the tribes and

change all Indians instantly into God-fearing, industrious small farmers indistinguishable from anybody else. In this belief many sincere Indian friends backed the measure, and even General Crook lent his considerable presence to the task of dragooning the Plains Tribes into going through the motions of accepting it. Since it would also give a massive shot in the arm to the land-office business, land speculation interests promoted the bill with an equal or even greater sincerity.

In this last objective the law succeeded beautifully. More than 100 reservations were allotted, principally on the plains, the Pacific coast, and in the Lakes states. Of the approximately 150 million acres owned by the Indians in 1880, most of it guaranteed by treaties made less than thirty or forty years before, over ninety million acres—an area roughly the size of Italy with a Switzerland or two thrown in—were extracted from the Indians' pocket. The process lost steam after some of the big plains reservations, the principal targets, were carved up and sold, but it has gone along in a desultory way ever since.

Indian Territory fell under the axe of the Allotment Act and became Oklahoma in 1907—Congress refused the name of Sequoyah, desired by the state's residents. The creation of the state brought to an end a hopeless effort by the exiled "Civilized Tribes" to keep the territory they had been promised would be theirs as long as water kept on running. "What about our people, who are, now, the legal owners?" wrote a Cherokee angrily in 1895. "Why the question is easy of answer. Crushed to earth under the hoofs of business gread, they would soon become a homeless throng, more scoffed at and abused than a Coxey's army." Pieces of the territory had been taken away at intervals ever since the arrival of the Civilized Tribes, for other groups of displaced Indians or for white settlement.

In its ostensible objective of civilizing Indians, the Allotment Act was a failure. If Indians were children just learning to walk, as *fin-de-siècle* unction expressed it, the Allotment Act helped this along by cutting their legs off at the knees. Allottees did not turn instantly into sturdy small farmers. It wouldn't have helped much if they had, in many cases, since even imported Russian peasants went gaunt trying to work small claims on the northern plains. Instead, by one means or another, allottees frequently lost their ragtag and bobtail patches of ground to white ownership, or leased the land for messes of pottage to larger operators. Some were thus utterly dispossessed, and congregated in junkyard squatter communities here and there, or piled in by wagonloads to "visit" with any relations who still had the wherewithal for a square meal of tough beef and fried bread. Hundreds of families collapsed into a permanent pauperdom. The Sioux centering in South Dakota were the hardest hit; their economic wreckage is evident yet.

The law provided that the government hold allotted land in trust for twenty-five years before making the allottee the outright owner by granting him a patent in fee simple. (The fee simple titles had the effect of putting the land on tax rolls—from which it had previously been exempt by treaty—and also made the land subject to alienation, that is, the Indian owner could sell it or otherwise lose possession of it.) As the pattern of allottee ruination came clear, the government adopted (in the 1920s) a policy of automatically renewing the trust periods. Much Indian land today is held under government trusteeship in this fashion; other reservation lands, often in desert or otherwise unproductive areas, have never been allotted. But the drastic reduction of reservations already accomplished had by the 1920s made Indian poverty chronic, and above all no room had been left for an expanding Indian population. When this totally unexpected event began to come to pass, overcrowding the reservations still further, poverty became widespread and acute.

A thorough government-sponsored survey carried out in the late 1920s stated in its opening sentence, "An overwhelming majority of the Indians are poor, even extremely poor, and they are not adjusted to the economic and social system of the dominant white civilization." The same study also found Indian health and education remarkably poor. Perhaps most important, it found that the battered Indians of the United States were very definitely a living race. Clearly the impatient and repressive policies of the Allotment Act era, designed to squeeze the vanishing American in his coffin and nail down the lid, had been in tragic error.

These policies were reversed in the Indian Reorganization Act of 1934, which put a stop to any more allotting of tribal lands, and tried to get back for the Indians any of the "surplus" reservation lands that had not yet been homesteaded. In keeping with the notions revolutionizing Indian affairs throughout the hemisphere at the time, this law endeavored to help the Indians get on their feet by encouraging group progress via a tribal approach.

A surprising amount of community spirit had survived the generations of attempts to break up the tribes. Not only did cohesive tribes and bands still exist, but a broader tendency toward pan-Indianism was becoming apparent, discernible in such items as the spread of the peyote religion. This cult, organized in 1918 under the name of the Native American Church, uses elements from various sources, including Christianity, and a vision-producing drug of ancient Mexican ancestry, peyote cactus buds; the church now has members in nearly all tribes, and represents the largest single Indian group in the United States today.

Government representatives went forth and talked with more than 250 tribes and bands, urging them to organize under the new Indian Reorganization Act with constitutions and charters of incorporation, and offering loan funds for constructive community purposes from a revolving credit program. Many Indian groups did organize; many refused. But with the help of the new law and its various accompanying agencies, tribe after tribe pulled itself up by its bootstraps toward a solid foundation for solvency or even prosperity, numbers of Indian families were restored to a life of some hope and independence, and for the first time in history Indian lands were increased, from about forty-seven million acres to about fifty million. The repayment record for loans from the revolving credit fund was excellent; twenty million dollars was eventually available, including a portion furnished by various organized Indian groups from their own trust funds. Native languages, crafts, ceremonies, and traditions were not only permitted but promoted, with some consequent reawakening of interest in what some Indians referred to as the old time religion. Venerable medicine men journeyed hundreds of miles in almost equally venerable cars or pickup trucks to teach the correct rituals to young people living in towns; factory workers came home from Detroit or San Francisco to take part in the Sun Dance or the Corn Dance.

By and large the people were still very poor, but communities here and there showed some definite material progress and a few made a considerable climb up from the slough of a century of despondency. The nations, those that were left, had been in a desperate struggle during that century merely to survive; clearly they still possessed a power to help themselves, if they were given an opportunity to use it.

The question of what constituted a proper opportunity,

though, remained debatable. Indian communities that rejected organization under the IRA feared the consequences of abandoning their purely Indian social and political structure to adopt a white man's model, with constitution, charter, council members elected in white-style political campaigns, and so on. Even some communities that accepted such organization did so with great reluctance, and over the objection of factions, sometimes consisting of a majority of the people, that, Indian-like, simply withdrew from any participation, rather than out-voting the "progressive" faction that favored the new organization.

Such was the case, for one example, with the Hopis, a voting majority of whom were persuaded to adopt the new form of organization. They were persuaded by Oliver La Farge, who had been persuaded to persuade them by John Collier, then (1936) Commissioner of Indian Affairs, both men honest, trustworthy, and immensely knowledgeable in Indian matters. After weeks spent visiting the Hopi towns and talking to the people, many of them old friends, La Farge wrote in his notes, "I still do not know if it is the right thing for these people to organize. I see a protection for them, I see a means of strengthening Hopi values, while opening the way for progress, for the more intelligent selection of the good things of each culture. But do I *know* that? No. I only think, and that as a white man, studying from the outside. What wreckage may not the alien structure cause?"

And at the end of three months, when it was apparent that his persuasion was going to succeed, he wrote in even greater doubt, "I really think I'd recommend that the whole matter be dropped for a generation." But it wasn't dropped, and the new superstructure, with its majority (of those voting) rule and its parliamentary pattern of tribal council politics, was uneasily erected upon the ancient "Hopi Way," an incredibly complex and delicate theocracy ruling with exquisite indirection in each of the ten theretofore completely sovereign Hopi villages.

World War II brought added pressures from the surrounding society when approximately 25,000 Indians (somewhat more than one-third of all able-bodied Indian men between eighteen and fifty) returned from service in the armed forces—and a long look at the outside world—full of new ideas for their families and communities; some had first learned English at this time, or a GI facsimile thereof.

But in 1950 the government's Indian policy was reversed

again. Efforts were made once more to reduce Indian land, and to weaken or break down the tribal societies. The revolving credit program ground to a virtual halt. Self-realization of Indian communities was no longer encouraged and aided, but obstructed. Indians were not urged to work together, but emphasis was placed on individual emigration to large cities to find wage work and, in a word, get lost. An intensive "termination" program was put into effect, with the idea of removing all federal protection and services from the various Indian tribes as rapidly as possible, thus bringing about, presumably, at long last, their dissolution. The objective was to get the federal government out of the Indian business.

This change of direction in Indian policy was the first ripple of the wave of political reaction in the early 1950s that took its name from right-wing extremist Senator Joseph McCarthy. The reaction as far as Indian policy was concerned persisted until the decline of "McCarthyism" in the late 1950s, when a gradual return to the previous policy of helpfulness to Indian communities took place. Said the principal government expert of the period on Indian legal affairs, the late Felix S. Cohen: "Like the miner's canary, the Indian marks the shifts from fresh air to poison gas in our political atmosphere; and our treatment of Indians, even more than our treatment of other minorities, reflects the rise and fall of our democratic faith."

Only a few tribes were terminated by specific acts of Congress—the most important being the Menominees of Wisconsin and the Klamaths of southern Oregon, both owners of rich stands of timber. One of the incidental results of the drive to remove essential services from the Bureau of Indian Affairs was the transferal of Indian health programs to the Public Health Service, which under an increased budget made some advance in the late 1950s in providing health services for Indians.

Another incidental result, in planning for the expected wholesale termination, was the establishment in 1947 of a special commission to clear up all unpaid Indian claims against unkept treaties, past acts of fraudulence, and the like. More than 800 claims were filed as a starter, of which in the first ten years 102 were decided, recovery being granted in twenty-one for amounts reduced from a total of a billion claimed to some thirteen million dollars paid; many more millions have been paid since. Anthropologists and historians who serve as expert witnesses in these cases prepare extremely detailed documents dealing with the history of the tribes involved; it is expected that these documents will ultimately provide the first thorough history of the Indians of the United States, a side-effect of the work of this court that may be of more lasting value than the money payments it grants.

Today in the 1970s most Indians are still very poor—by and large the most poverty-stricken group in the land. In general their health is not good, and the level of their education is low. They still own, as communities, a considerable hunk of property. The principal reason for the chronic poverty, though, is that the property is simply not sufficient to provide a living for their populations.

During the last hundred years, for one example, the lands and belongings of the Oglala Sioux have been stripped from them until the remnant now left cannot possibly support their community of more than 14,000, this even though the reservation they own, Pine Ridge in South Dakota, is still one of the largest in the country (1.5 million acres). This is a country of badlands and vast ranches: the productive land can provide a living for no more than a small fraction of the Oglala population, most of that in cattle-ranching. Only eight per cent of the reservation is suitable for dryland farming. There are very few other jobs of any kind within reach. And so, at a recent count (1958), some 955 persons had full-time jobs out of an "available labor force" of more than 3,000, with 607 others at work part time, including migrant farmhanding. One-third of the people had a family income, counting welfare and any other nickels and dimes from any source, of less than $999 per year; nearly one-half of the people were on some kind of welfare (average amount less than $25 per month per person); half of the people were still living in one- or two-room mud-caulked log houses and some hundreds in tents winter as well as summer; nine out of ten homes had no electricity, nineteen out of twenty no running water, with most householders transporting water a quarter-mile or more.

But the people will not break up their community and go away. During the vigorous "Indian Relocation" program carried out by the government over a ten-year period into the 1960s some one hundred Pine Ridge families a year were persuaded to emigrate—but over the same period the reservation population increased twenty-five per cent.

Pine Ridge is rather poorer than the Indian world as a whole—American space-age technology, for instance, has by now brought running water to almost half of all Indian reservation homes over the country as compared with the five per cent at Pine Ridge, and some others of the various services promised in treaties a hundred years ago have been better provided elsewhere than at Pine Ridge, but even so a somewhat similar picture is fairly common. The people want to stay together as members of living communities, but because of lack of productive land they don't have room—and because of hamstrung reservation development as well as the out-of-the-way location of most reservations there are not enough (are not any, in many cases) jobs handy.

In hard times, white Americans (or black or brown or yellow Americans for that matter) say "So long, it's been good to know you," and hit the road for brighter prospects otherwise. But red Americans are more inclined to cling through hell and high water to the life of their community, an overlife that is in a number of compelling ways more important to them than individual opportunity.

To a considerable extent, the people do persist in remaining together. Actual Indian communities continue (with marvelous stubbornness) to survive—some five to six hundred villages and reservations throughout the United States including Alaska —and some communities are at this writing even thriving, as communities. But the cost in individual distress is immense. Continuing Indian poverty springs in large part directly from this iron refusal to surrender and disperse and go get lost ("assimilated") in the white man's cities. And the insufficiency of lands and resources in these communities springs directly, of course, from the exorbitant seizure of land and resources that is the central fact of American Indian history over the last hundred and fifty years—the biggest gold mine in the world, for example, the Homestake in the Black Hills, was taken at gunpoint by means of the Sioux Wars of the 1870s (in direct contravention of the Sioux treaty of 1868) from the very people now dwelling in the impoverished barrens of Pine Ridge.

That these people will not depart even where their alien enclaves are rendered all but untenable, reduced to all but debris, entrains bitter consequences: they must be prepared to watch their infant children die at three times the national rate for the first year of life after coming home from the maternity clinic; a white child has a better chance of living to age forty-five than an Indian baby of living to its first birthday. They must be prepared, if they stay, to watch their surviving infant children sicken from the wild diarrhea that is related to malnutrition and the filth of poverty and apparently linked to permanent mental retardation. They must expect their growing children to contract the eye and ear infections that are all but unknown to the surrounding outside world and that so often lead to permanent disability. They commit their children, when grown, to staggering rates of alcoholism and, in some localities, suicide—"parents are lost in despair and do not dare to look their children in the eye," wrote an ethnologist long familiar with Fort Hall, Idaho, where a few years ago the suicide rate had run as high as ten times the national average and, for teenagers, had reached one hundred times the rate of the American world outside, and where sub-teen suicides had occurred as early as eight years of age.

The Indian world, the world of actual Indian communities, is under relentless siege still, as it has been ever since Europeans encountered it. The primary reason for this is, apparently, its basic alienness, that alienness rooted in its very foundations, which rest, still today, on a sense of community as against a foundation of individual competition, contention, acquisition, underlying the surrounding world. It is the alienness, so often mentioned in these pages, attuned to a harmony of human relationships rather than a harmony of commerce and industry, attuned to belonging rather than belongings. American Indians remain our one unhyphenated minority, their world so alien to us (so alien still, after all the generations of mortal embrace) that no one would say Indian-Americans any more than one would say Martian-Americans.

These continuing attacks on this alien world do not usually receive much recognition from the general public. Although in the 1960s and 1970s a growing awareness of Indian history brought numerous public comments deploring injustices committed toward Indians a hundred years ago, few persons—except the besieged themselves, the aliens, the Indians—seem to notice that the process is still in business, very much so. The chasm of alienness appears to be so deep that contemporary injustices are somehow rendered invisible within it.

One incident that did receive some public attention was the Kinzua dam, established on Seneca lands in western New York State in spite of the opposition of the Seneca people supported by a treaty dating from President Washington's administration confirming the lands in question as "the property of the Seneca Nation; and the United States will never claim the same, nor disturb the Seneca Nation . . . in the free use and enjoyment thereof. . . ." The small furor that brought some attention to this dispute may well have raised the price of the conscience money paid the Seneca Nation, but in the end the Corps of Engineers did get the land it wanted and the treaty was violated.

A typical sort of incident that did not succeed in gaining any public interest involved the little reservation of Soboba in southern California and the Metropolitan Water District of Los Angeles, an old hand at the legerdemain of private right and public wrong so prevalent in Indian affairs. In 1936 the Water District drove a tunnel through the mountains above Soboba and in doing so broke into the underground watercourse that gave the reservation its water supply. Soboba's three streams and two dozen artesian wells promptly dried up. Its couple of hundred residents, Cahuilla Indians, were left without water; a $200,000 hospital on the reservation, for the use of Indians in the surrounding region, fell into ruins; the people, those who tried to stay, had to haul water. Non-Indian ranchers in the vicinity received quick settlement of damages, but thirty-five years later the Indians were still trying to collect from the Metropolitan Water District, since grown into a huge complex of power, one of the ruling forces of California. The federal government, which, as trustee of the damaged lands, had to approve legal action, declined, for reasons of its own, to do so; a claim then brought against the government, following the establishment of the Indian Claims Commission, was still pending at the end of the 1960s.

There are quite a few such continued stories of modern-times Indian-fighting. Four tiny reservations (Pala, La Jolla, Rincon, and Pauma-Yuima) along the San Luis Rey River in southern California have been endeavoring since 1894 to bring some kind of action against a local water company that took their water, so they allege, without a by-your-leave. The Agua Caliente band of Cahuilla Indians at Palm Springs, California, the "Palm Springs" Indians, still have land holdings in that wealthy resort community and are therefore the richest Indians in the world, as everyone knows, or as everyone knew until 1967 when it was discovered they had been systematically short-changed, with the connivance of local and state courts and federal officials, for quite some while out of quite a lot of change. This particular instance revealed with considerable clarity that the Bureau of Indian Affairs, officially obligated to conserve and defend the rights and appurtenances of the Indian world, was not very well armed to withstand assaults from weighty politicians or influential local interests. The BIA has been still more vulnerable to sibling rivalry within its parent organization, the Department of the Interior, where it has long lived a stepchild's life in the secretariat of Public Land Management.

A classic sibling contest has been in progress for years at Pyramid Lake, Nevada, where the United States Bureau of Reclamation and sundry allies challenged the BIA for the waters of the Truckee River, which supply Pyramid Lake, which in turn is the highly valued property of the Northern Paiute Indian Tribe, but which may be removed from the Indians' possession by the simple expedient of drying it up.

No doubt it should go without saying that the officials and businessmen who launch these present-day attacks on Indian communities are seldom conscious of wrongdoing, any more than were the Indian despoilers of the 1820s. Certainly the many individuals high and low who put through the Kinzua project could not all have been conscious that they were outraging President Washington's—let alone their country's—word of honor. The engineers and the lawyers and the steel mill people (an important purpose of the Kinzua dam was "to slake the thirsty boilers of Pittsburgh steel mills," as one expert put it) and the politicians were for the most part just doing their jobs. It is difficult for officials of the busy workaday white world to take an Indian community seriously not only as a moral entity but even as a serious business enterprise. If Pyramid Lake were owned by an important public utility company rather than by an Indian community it is highly unlikely the surrounding business and bureaucratic world would be so united in conspiring to abduct it. The Pyramid Lake people charge that not only is their property being swiped for the ultimate benefit of white ranchers and the real estate speculators of nearby Reno, but that one of the principal projects designed to effect this end—the Reclamation Bureau's Newlands Project—is a resounding flop, for years at the bottom of the Bureau's Crop Production Report, highest in water cost, lowest in crop yield. Obviously the officials concerned are not overly concerned with weighing any such ultimates and absolutes, but are simply carrying out a local Bureau program initiated long ago. The Soboba people charge that the

Bureau of Indian Affairs has consistently refused to approve any settlement with the Metropolitan Water District until the Soboba community agrees to surrender its rights to certain tribal safeguards and government services, a "termination" agreement the BIA had long wished to force from the Soboba Cahuillas, and that the Soboba people had steadfastly refused. Certainly any officials endeavoring to wring this concession from the distressed community were disinterested, perhaps even uninterested, in the policy they were carrying out, a continuing action that was merely part of their job. The Palm Springs Indians were fleeced as an unfortunate side effect of a (presumably) most worthy operation, the development of Palm Springs, in which objective such greats as cinema stars and even the President of the United States were benevolently interested.

These examples could be multiplied, alas, many times over; and these particular examples are cited as representative rather than as particularly reprehensible—there are other examples considerably higher, alas, on any reprehensibility scale. The Army Corps of Engineers wrought infinitely more ruin upon the Arikara, Mandan, and Hidatsa people with the building of the Garrison dam on the upper Missouri in the 1950s than the Seneca suffered from Kinzua, for one random comparison.

Others of the present-day assaults on Indian communities are truly impressive in their ingenuity, as in the enormous powerplant complex being built in Navaho-Hopi country, taking advantage of the fact that Indian country has been "King's-X" as far as state or local restrictions against pollution are concerned—thus the first of these plants to become operative poured more pollution into the theretofore clear Southwestern sky than all the power plants in the Los Angeles area put together. Freedom from zoning regulations is a factor in the establishment of real estate subdivisions such as those in the works for the New Mexico pueblos of Cochiti and Tesuque—deals that will obliterate the respective Indian communities, say their opponents; charges have also been made that developers intend to secure free fire and police protection, and assistance with school financing, for their well-to-do suburbias from laws granting special services and financial assistance to residents of Indian reservations.

Techniques reminiscent of nineteenth-century treaty shenanigans are still in use, with manipulation of tribal councils taking the place of manipulation of treaty chiefs, Congress and the BIA obligingly bending promised protection of Indians into promotion of a more orthodox American dream, whether it be increased power supply for the twinkling lights of the Las Vegas Strip or water for new real estate developments in Los Angeles or the dream itself stepping straight out of the silver screen, Palm Springs. The traditional American way, catch-as-catch-can utilitarian, milks each resource for whatever it may provide and usually employs its biggest muscles in the service of the top dollar. Indian rights, in such fast company, are as a rule hopelessly overmatched. Now the fears Oliver La Farge felt thirty-five years ago for the unnatural tribal structure superimposed on the Hopi villages are all too concretely realized, with the Hopi tribal council, accused of acting for only a minority of the Hopi people, under fire, along with the Navaho tribal government, for the aforementioned power-plant project and an accompanying coal-mining operation, using destructive strip-mining methods, on the sacred mountain known as Black Mesa.

But these present actions are only minor, alas, compared to what the future appears to forebode. Aggressive attacks on Indian water rights, in many cases the last undeveloped water rights in the land and therefore quite literally priceless, are under way in region after region, mounted by powerful groups of investors allied with government agencies. The Four Corners Project, planned for the Navaho-Hopi country, includes a proposed model city that will cost a cool billion, along with marvelous plans for extracting all manner of wealth from the area, but has not yet included permission from, or even serious consultation with, the Indian people who happen to own the land. The North Central Power Project, getting under way at this writing, calls for the Bureau of Reclamation and thirty-five private utilities to strip-mine coal in northeastern Wyoming and burn it in power plants that will produce more electricity than that now being generated by England, West Germany, and Japan, giving out more nitrogen and sulfur dioxides than are now being produced by Los Angeles and New York combined, using an amount of water more than equal to half of New York City's annual water use, and reducing the flow of the Yellowstone River by more than seventy-five per cent. In Canada the James Bay Project, one of the biggest engineering works in history, is intended to install an enormous power and mining complex on Cree Indian lands in the remote, desolate, beautiful river and swamp country roundabout the heel of Hudson Bay. It will involve a land area

440 THE LAST AMERICANS

bigger than England and will bring shattering ecological effects, say environmentalists, to much of the north woods as well as to the Indians. The Cree people have gone to court against this development, but work on the project is getting under way regardless, a hint of the expected legal outcome.

Such matters as these occupy the attention of contemporary tribal Indians. Non-Indian Indian experts (one thing American Indians don't lack is Indian experts) are more likely to be concerned about education. It appears that Indians don't much cotton to regulation American education. School dropout rates are high. "Achievement" rates are low. Two schools of thought have developed around this problem: one believes we should reconstruct our Indian education to fit the Indian world; the other thinks we should keep hacking away at Indian children to make them fit our education.

It is impressive that after four centuries of force-fed misfit education so many Indians are still resisting. In 1966 some 10,000 to 16,000 (statistics differ) Indian children between the ages of eight and sixteen (thus somewhere around ten per cent of the total U.S. Indian school-age population of some 150,000) were out of school altogether. For some this was due to the fact that no schools were available, but for some (even though few Indian parents these days will admit it) it must be considered a deliberate withholding. The modern period in Indian statistics is neatly bracketed by the dates of 1891, when three Kiowa schoolboys froze to death trying to get home across blizzard-swept plains after running away from school, and 1967, when two Navaho students died in precisely the same way.

There is involved, it seems, a clash, a conflict so profound that it takes place in the soul's least conscious deeps. Our school system is naturally built to our own scale of values, "competitive, exploitative, oriented to acquisition and above all to individual success," in the words of an authority on Indian education in New Mexico, but these values are directly opposed to the gods of the Indian world, the customary Indian orientation being toward a sense of group endeavor rather than individual, toward accepting learning rather than competing for it. To the Indian child, therefore, our schools are likely to seem either silly or hostile, as he comes to realize they are teaching false values compared to the true values of home.

A number of recent studies have shown that the Indian family has usually presented to the schools a stable, well-adjusted, willing, quick-learning child, who has done splendidly at first and then at about the fourth or fifth grade has begun to regress, and by the time he has finished high school, if he does (sixty per cent drop out along the way), has in actuality acquired less than a tenth-grade education. Teachers galore have commented on the typical Indian child in kindergarten, so outgoing and happy and friendly, turning into the withdrawn, rather apprehensive child of later grades. Clearly he has approached the big outside world ready for a joyous embrace, and the big outside world has instead infected his spirit with the nightmare sickness of finding one's self out of kilter with a world one expected to love.

Worst of all, since the children have been danced into this invisible chasm of alienness without any idea that it is there, each child has been left feeling that his "failure" must mean there is something wrong with him personally. A 1966 government report much quoted by educators showed that twelfth-grade Indian students took bottom rank in answers to the question, "How bright do you think you are?"

Not surprisingly this misfit educational system long ago lost interest in its apathetic child victims; its "goals" tended more and more to benefit the system, not the students. Great prison-like boarding schools were established for easier administrative efficiency, better living conditions for the staff, convenience in using the visual-aid gadgets that to the administrative mind define "quality education."

In addition to the central misfit problem and of course related to it are various other handicaps real or apparent—language, for one. Classes are customarily in English, although two-thirds of the children know no English at all when they begin school. Well-to-do Americans think it an advantage for their children to have a bi-lingual education in French, but an Indian child is generally regarded as "disadvantaged" (by red and white alike) because he speaks Cherokee or Ojibwa or Tsimshian, this even though it is beginning to be recognized that Indian languages possess their own literatures, often literatures of beauty and sophistication, and their own great waiting worlds, as an authority on the Hopi language indicated several years ago in speculating that the abstract perceptions in some Indian languages may open the way to future new philosophies. Low esteem for their own language is revealed by Indians in a number of tacit ways, not the least interesting in the matter of family names, frequently rendered into derisory teamster-English by nineteenth century translators and yet retained as such by modern descendants rather than reverting to the original native form. A famous example of such mistranslation is the name of the Ojibwa leader known as Rocky Boy, which would have been better rendered Stone Child. The important Brulé Sioux family known among white Americans by the family name of He Dog is, in its Lakota form (always of course used at home in the Rosebud country), Sunkabloka; the well-known family name from the same region, Burning Breast, is a mistranslation of the Lakota Maku Eli; the family name of Walking Eagle is, in Lakota, Wambli Mani—any of these Lakota forms would presumably be quite acceptable in any ordinary American telephone directory, but are seldom or never used outside the home or the reservation; if the English version of the name becomes troublesome or embarrassing at school or in the army the bearer sometimes changes it to Thompson or Johnson or Bates, rarely even thinking, apparently, of using his own name in his own language.

Some motions toward bi-lingual education are being made—its great advantage is that speakers of an Indian language can learn to write and read their own language (several dozen Indian languages now possess written forms, usually based on scientifically designed alphabets) with greater ease than English-speaking children can learn to read and write English, notorious for its wild orthography. Literacy in one language then makes literacy in a second (English, in this case) far easier to acquire. But bi-lingual education for Indian pupils will need translations into the various Indian languages of grade-school textbooks dealing with social and natural sciences, history, mathematics, and so on, and not only Indian teachers (now rare—one to two per cent in predominantly Indian public schools, sixteen per cent in BIA schools) but especially teachers of the same tribal tongue as the pupils (now even rarer), all presenting considerable difficulties but all yielding plus-factors of such magnitude as to well repay, it is argued, the anticipated toils and troubles.

The number of Indian men and women in business and professional life, both outside the Indian world and within it, has increased a great deal in the past generation. Movement back and forth from the Indian to the white world has become immeasurably freer. Misfit though present Indian education may be, it can still train students in technical and professional skills. Indian parents see no way out of a poverty future for their children except to force them into the schools, and some Indian students do survive as tribal people while becoming doctors, lawyers, or Indian chiefs—many if not most native American leaders today are university-trained, although some of the ablest still sign their names with X's. Some students are left hopelessly deformed, and some are trapped by the alien gods and find themselves "assimilated." But most reject the education that is so foreign to their real world, a de facto rejection no less real because its existence is denied by everyone, Indians as well as experts; it is verified by the fact that the average Indian winds up with just five years of school.

Notions of reshaping Indian education in toto, to fit it a little less painfully to the Indian child, have gained some ground in official thinking. A reconstruction of Indian education around the fundamental structures of the Indian world might conceivably offer a vestibule to reconstruction (sorely needed) of education even in our mainstream world. But these hopes are left a good deal less likely by the current wholesale transferal of Indian students into public schools, which are of course generally more rigid than BIA schools in inflicting upon Indian children exactly the same education all other American children receive. The BIA boarding schools have come in for flaming criticism, from Indians as childrens' concentration camps and from right-wing white Americans alleging Indian schools slowed down "assimilation" by keeping Indian children fenced off from the melting pot, so in 1967 the government asked Indians what they thought of taking Indian children away from the Bureau of Indian Affairs and its segregated schools. Some younger Indians favored this but most tribal spokesmen protested vehemently, less out of love for the BIA schools than out of opposition to the goal of assimilation. The government thereupon went ahead and did so anyway but without saying so, and by 1970 more than two-thirds of all Indian pupils had been quietly transferred to public schools, where federal funds pay for them by the head, a switch that may be catastrophic, public schools being generally unprepared for Indian students and generally uninterested in any special preparation.

In spite of the long-standing criticism of BIA education, this removal of education from the BIA is suspiciously regarded by many Indians as another step toward dismemberment of the Bureau of Indian Affairs and thus toward "termination."

Termination (ominous ring) is truly a word of ill omen to

tribal Indians, its meaning being the termination of the responsibility of the federal government to protect and aid Indian
groups in the use of their (usually treaty) rights and possessions.
When this federal responsibility is abrogated, the Indian community thus "terminated" is more than likely to fall prey to
disintegration—few Indian communities are rich and strong
enough to survive on their own under state and local jurisdic-
tions armed with tax powers and hostile to the Indian community's way of life. The Menominee Nation, terminated at the end
of the 1950s and its lands transformed into Wisconsin's smallest
and poorest (if perhaps most scenic) county, seems already near
the end of a losing fight for life, unless the termination can be
reversed—a possibility now under consideration.

For many Indians such community disintegration is a fate
worse than death, but many Americans, in and out of
officialdom, have always pressed relentlessly for destruction of
these alien Indian communities. Foreign communities of all
sorts, from Amish to Orthodox Jewish, can be tolerated as long
as the people in them are properly earnest about toil, thrift, and
getting ahead; ethnic minorities can be sympathetically understood as long as all they want is a bigger slice of the American
pie. But the Indian communities don't much care for the pie at
all, and this is truly intolerable. This is (so the terminationists
feel) true un-Americanism.

The struggle between those anxious to "break up the tribes"
and the Indians who want to live as Indian communities has been
going on for a very long time, sometimes underground, sometimes in open view. This struggle underlies much of the action in
Indian affairs, even where it may not at first glance seem to be an
issue. Hamstringing the Bureau of Indian Affairs and other
government Indian agencies with red-tapism and fund shortages
is typical of this struggle; the more Indian criticism thus
provoked the better—it might even culminate in the abolition of
the agency which could produce (surprise!) termination.

There is no clear-cut political party-line division in termination. Nor does termination raise the question of Indians remaining "primitive" or becoming "modern." Indianness is not a
matter of handicrafts or beating drums but of the all-important
sense of community, which may well exist more genuinely in
overalls or business suits than in feathers and beads. It is the
community that is brought in question; it is only the tribal
community that lives under the constant menace of termination;

unassimilated urban Indians are already counted as captured (perhaps prematurely). But termination is aimed at reservation communities only, and turns on the issue of communal ownership, that is, of alienness. The menace is indeed real, and never entirely absent, even under the friendliest of climates (the native land claims settled in Alaska in the early 1970s on terms regarded as rather favorable for the native people also happened to include, as Indian and Eskimo groups beset by incorporation troubles are beginning to notice, the biggest termination coup in American history). Generally speaking, a covert plug for termination resides in political talk of "freeing" Indians from government interference and restrictions. (The program proposed at the end of 1972 for the reorganization of the BIA called for cutting the Bureau to one-third its size "to enable Indian tribes to assume more rapid control of their own affairs.") Any Indian community can free itself of restrictions, of reservation status, of the BIA, merely by dividing up its property among its members, i.e., by giving up its community life. What Indian communities have repeatedly requested is not the weakening and certainly not the destruction of the BIA but rather its redirection along lines designed to protect Indian communities from assault by hostile interests, instead of assisting commercial interests in the exploitation process, which has frequently been a major BIA role in the past.

The termination argument given widest circulation is as an economy measure, to take the Indians out of the federal budget and save some money even if it means violating all the remaining unviolated clauses in all our Indian treaties. In connection with this argument figures are often quoted of the high cost in federal funds and employees devoted to so few Indians (for 1968, $1179 per reservation Indian, and one federal Indian-business employee for every eighteen or nineteen Indians). However, this cost represents total cost of operation of the federally serviced reservations, that constitute, so to speak, a fifty-first shadow-state, larger in aggregate area than Nebraska or South Dakota and considerably larger in population than Nevada or Alaska, a shadow-state in which all services—such as roads, schools, police—are furnished either by the federal government or the tribal organizations themselves, combining all costs that in one of the other fifty states would be divided among town, city, county, state, and federal expenses. (In comparison, all governmental costs for the general population, federal and state and local costs combined, ran at the end of the 1960s $1353 per person, with one public employee for every seventeen or eighteen persons.) In any event the federal expense inevitably remains when Indian communities are terminated, although it may be more or less masked, as state and local governments demand increased federal aid in supporting the added costs the state and county and municipality have assumed.

Legislators considering Indian matters usually ask Indian opinion but also usually ignore it, very much as legislators have usually done for a hundred and fifty years. The so-called Indian Civil Rights amendment, tacked on the 1968 Civil Rights Bill, was very soon back in the shop for repairs that would embody recommendations a number of Indian witnesses had urged during six years of committee hearings. The subject is critically important to the communal Indian world. On one hand, civil rights represents a constant danger area in tribal life; group identity easily comes into conflict with individual liberties, and the more "successful," the more powerful the tribal administration, the greater the danger that authoritarianism may take over and run wild, as has happened on more than one reservation. On the other hand white government officials, chronically hostile to the whole idea of group identity and resolutely ignoring the quasi-religious nature of many Indian communities as well as all the other intra-community relationships that set such a group apart from the ordinary white municipality, would be not at all displeased to destroy the communal group in the name of civil rights, a splendid new weapon in the assimilation arsenal.

The one point on which most Indians and most experts seem to agree is that Indians should have more voice in their own affairs—especially in handling their own schools and their own money. Money earned by an Indian community from such sources as leases of land is customarily paid into the U. S. Treasury and then returned to the community via a maze of red tape, beribboned with controls. Funds appropriated to the Bureau of Indian Affairs for Indian benefit often travel a labyrinth wilder still. Everyone seems to agree on the need for a revision of the ungainly—indeed often stealthily hostile—regulations under which the BIA operates, but it should be repeated that an acceptable solution would not be the abolition or weakening of the BIA, which could mean termination. The BIA (or some sufficiently authoritative government agency in its place) is regarded by most communal Indians as absolutely essential as a trustee and protector of Indian rights and possessions—but it should be required to fulfill this function honestly, which as mentioned above would require a redirection of its policies and would also require giving it some added muscle, since the BIA has never yet been strong enough to fulfill this function even if it wanted to.

Indian control, or even supervisory participation, is also the most urgent need, it is argued, in reservation development. Colonialism dies hard—there is still a feeling in the business world that the lion's share of Indian resources, whether human, vegetable, or mineral, should of course go to the white raj. And on white terms, with dollar-profit to the investor as the absolute decision-maker. While most Indian leaders too give lip service to the pious aims of more money and better jobs, these are really only desirable on the Indian community's terms, with the far-reaching big wide world of the communal superlife as final decision-maker.

The most concrete Indian successes have usually been in group terms—tribal cattle herds, or the communal big business of recreation on some reservations. Or spectacularly in land: the financial renaissance within no more than ten years of the Cheyenne River Sioux in South Dakota (operating, among other things, a cattle business, sales pavilion, supermarket, and their own telephone company serving Indians and non-Indians in two counties) grew mainly from initial successes with a tribal land-consolidation program. The Tribal Land Enterprise agency of the Rosebud Sioux in South Dakota buys land at a rate reaching a quarter-million dollars a year, and the land-consolidation program of the Crows in Montana has reached a half-million dollars' worth a year.

But these occasional (often temporary) wins have barely made a dent in the massive Indian poverty. The much-publicized project of bringing industry to the reservations has made another (smaller) dent, offset by the fact that the main pitch to industry has been low capital cost and cheap labor and profitable evasion of certain regulatory controls, scarcely conducive on the whole to blue-chip deals. Obviously it will take more than dents to remedy reservation poverty—it would take a solid break-through in returning to the Indian communities sufficient land to live on. Land-consolidation programs financed by the Indians themselves cannot possibly fill the bill. As Indian spokesmen have pointed out for years, the nation simply needs to honor its given word in securing to the Indian communities a livable land base; nothing less will work.

The Navahos, with a fifteen-million-acre reservation and a population of more than 100,000, are the giants of the present-day Indian world in the United States. The still-numerous Cherokees of Oklahoma have no tribal organization other than a skeleton staff working for a "Principal Chief" (a businessman appointed to the post by President Truman, and regarded as sham by many Cherokees), although a number of full-blood communities in the backwoods manage to maintain, almost in secret, "one of the largest and most traditional tribes of American Indians." These people live in some of the most beautiful country in the land (they are, incidentally, some of the handsomest people in the land) under besieged conditions that make Pine Ridge look rosy; Senator Robert Kennedy, visiting the region in 1968, found ninety per cent of the Cherokee families of Adair County on welfare, ninety-nine per cent of the Choctaw families of McCurtain County on welfare, annual income—for those who could find work—averaging $700.

The 1970 census returned nearly 98,000 Indians for Oklahoma, including, besides Cherokees, large representations of Choctaws, Creeks, Chickasaws, Seminoles, Comanches, Kiowas, Pawnees, Potawatomis, Caddos, Poncas, Osages, Quapaws, Otoe-Missouris, Wyandottes, Sac and Foxes, Kickapoos, and smaller numbers from a couple of dozen or so other tribal affiliations. Many of these various people are more or less fully assimilated into the general population. The heaviest Indian population over the rest of the country is in Arizona, California (with many new Indian migrants to West Coast cities), New Mexico, North Carolina, Washington, South Dakota, New York, Montana, Minnesota, and Wisconsin.

Fighting men have come and gone but the people of peace, the Hopis, are still in their country, although a missionary stirred up a civil war among them some years ago over the occupation of their oldest town, Oraibi. They fought it out with a tug of war, and the losers moved. The peaceful Pimas are still along the Gila, as they have been for unnumbered thousands of years. They have been the intended victims of some extra-ingenious shady deals, due to those precious Gila waters, but they are still there. The great Spanish empire has long since vanished like castles in the air, but Zuñi, so easily conquered on that July day centuries ago, is still very real and very present.

The tourists who come by the many thousands to the Hopi towns, to Zuñi, and to the other Pueblo villages, find a value clear apart from the earnest sociological matters that have been the burden of these last pages. They find what may be one of the most important of all the American Indian's contributions—a sense of permanence, the sense of an infinite past that implies an infinite future. The thought is comforting, and one for which the world seems hungry. It is good to feel that the history of the American Indian, any more than the history of America, is not finished.

A Portfolio of American Indian Poetry

(For, perhaps more so than in the case of any other people, poetry sums up the essence of the history of Indian America.)

MAYA: *on wisdom, a fragment*

He never arrives who travels an evil road
and so the people
                    weigh their words
lest there be no end to lies

MAYA: *tarantula seizure, an incantation*

the red tarantula
tarantula blood
tarantula eruption
tarantula seizure

then on the seashore it enters into the water the tarantula-water all about the trees would burn

four days would rot the fish licking
the froth of the water
the white saliva of tarantula seizure

his throat crammed with red froth *he* falls on the baked plain

there would he fall there
spoiling with the obstruction in his throat
the whipped red water

the white saliva of tarantula seizure

cast it there into the red liquid
there he spoils the wooden man the stone man

there I grasp the bowl of my red genitals my white genitals
squeezed over the wooden man
the stone man

 thirteen are my hail waters with which I calm your force
 I am your mother I am your father

NAHUATL: *to an Aztec daughter*

Hear well O my daughter O my child
the earth is not a good place

It is not a place of joy it is not a place of contentment

It is merely said it is a place of joy
  a place of joy with fatigue
  a place of joy with pain
  so the old men went saying

In order that we may not go forever weeping
  in order that we may not die of sorrow
  our creator gave us laughter

sleep

sustenance

strength

force

and carnal knowledge

COCHITI: *Coyote sings for the Prairie Dogs*

Old Man Coyote had a little drum
he sat by the road
beating his drum and singing

> Look out now look out now
> Coyote is going to hit you hit you
> right on the back the back

All the prairie dogs came running

> Dear me Grandfather how
> beautifully you sing

> Sing again
> and we will dance

Coyote beat his drum again and
the prairie dogs made a circle and danced

> Look out now look out now
> Coyote is going to hit you hit you
> right on the back the back
> sang Old Man Coyote

All the prairie dogs stepped round and round in time

> Oh Grandfather sing it again
> it is such fun to dance to your song

and they danced and danced

> But let me sing
> cried Grandmother Coyote

> now let me sing a while

> No no
> said the prairie dogs
> you sing so nicely Grandfather
> you sing again

> No
> said Old Man Coyote
> I'd better not

> You see your grandmother is calling me

We know she is calling you
said the dancing prairie dogs
but please sing some more

You sing such a beautiful song

Sing it again and
maybe we can learn it

OSAGE: *benediction, a fragment*

I
as a person
make my abode in the days that are peaceful and calm.

When the little ones make of me their symbol
they also shall dwell
as a people
in the days that are peaceful and calm.

I have removed all signs of anger.

With me as a symbol they
shall be able to remove
even from the gods
all signs of anger.

Even from the god of daylight I have removed all anger and
      violence.

Truly from all the gods I have removed all anger.

When the little ones make of me their symbol
they shall enable themselves to remove all anger and violence
as they travel
as they travel
the path of life.

OSAGE: *corn planting song, from the Rite of Vigil*

Footprints I leave here are good and mysterious
Footprints I leave here while smoothing the ground

Footprints I leave making corn hills in rows
                              like stripes
                                        on the earth

Footprints I leave here are sacred and fertile
In footprints I leave here the corn starts to sprout
In footprints I leave here shoots sway in the wind
                              springing up
                                        from the earth

Footprints I leave when the cornstalks stand upright
Footprints I leave while the holy songs are sung
Footprints I leave picking ripe ears of corn
                              side by side
                                        from the earth

Footprints I leave taking corn in profusion
Footprints I leave bending down the tall stalks
Footprints I leave bringing joy to my house
                              to my home
                                        on this earth

Footprints I leave here are good and mysterious
Footprints I leave here are good and mysterious
Footprints left here now the sacred act is done
                                        on this earth

PAWNEE: *prayer from the Hako*

(The ceremony called by ethnologists the Hako is a five-day
observance of "prayer for children, in order that the tribe may
increase and be strong; and also that the people may have long
life, enjoy plenty, and be happy and at peace." The following
version of one of the opening prayers is based on a literal
translation made in 1900 by James R. Murie, then the principal
leader of the Skidi Pawnee, and on added explanation given by
the chief priest, the Ku'rahus, an elder of the Grand Pawnee,
a man named Tahirussawichi, some seventy years of age in
1900. The Ku'rahus told a very old story which "came with"
this very old song of prayer and which is in the minds of the
singers and hearers when the song is sung, thus evoking ideas
beyond the actual words, rather as "Hail Mary, full of grace,"

presents various ideas to informed Christians beyond the literal
meaning of "Hello pretty Mary.")

I

My children I do not know
if my singing (of the ancient songs)
if my prayers (in the ancient words)
can reach the holy power

II

My children
I now know
that my singing (of the ancient songs)
my prayers   (my recitations of the ancient words)
were heard and answered
for here
now you may see
my own child

IROQUOIS: *At the Wood's Edge—the welcoming ceremony
opening the ancient rites of the Condoling Council*

Your voice has come to me startling from the forest
                                                my children

You have come to me with troubled mind over all obstacles
                                                my children

Wherever you went you saw the footprints of our forefathers

You saw all but imperceptible the smoke
                        where they used to smoke the pipe together

Can then your mind be at ease when you are weeping on your
        way?

I give great thanks that you have arrived

For indeed all around us are difficulties

                                        thorny paths
                                        falling trees
                                        beasts in ambush

By any of these you might have perished
>
> my children

or by floods
> my children

or by an upraised war club in the dark

Or by invisible disease you might have died
> my children

Let us give thanks therefore great thanks
> that in safety you arrive through the forest

Our forefathers made the rule that here we are to kindle a fire

a fire of welcome and condolence here at the wood's edge

That here we are to comfort one another with the embrace of
condolence

That I shall then lead you by the hand to a place of honor.

MALECITE: *tale*

there was once a woman who admired a dog
the dog was handsome
she liked his face

that night the dog turned into a man
he became her husband

never tell anyone I used to be a dog
never mention it at all
he said to his wife

for a long time they lived together
she never thought of him as a dog
she never spoke of it

but one day she saw some dogs in the village
they were all chasing a bitch
everywhere here and there

so she asked her husband if he would like to be one of them
and instantly he said yes and turned back into a dog
and away he ran with the others

NATCHEZ: *Frog's wife*

There was a frog
  all day he swam around whooping
  he did nothing but swim around
  singing and whooping

His grandmother said
  you do nothing serious
  you will lose your wife
  she will be taken away

But Frog only sang
  and sprang into the river
  and swam all day
  singing and whooping

Sure enough he lost his wife
  people came and stole her
  they caught her
  they carried her away

His grandmother wailed and wept
  she said Wartfrog's wife
  his wife his wife

When Frog came home she said
  they stole her
  they caught her and took her
  I told you they would

Whaw said Frog
  am I angry
  whaw whaw whaw
  give me my leggings
  whaw whaw whaw
  my garters
  whaw whaw
  my belt

Dressed for war
  Frog went leaping
  grandmother following
  away they went

They followed the people
  who had taken Frog's wife
  they followed them leaping
  Frog fiercely whooping

They came to a big square
  a dancing ground
  there people were gathered
  ready to dance

That Wartfrog
  these people said
  what does he want here
  why is he coming here

So they grabbed him by an arm
  and threw him
  PLUP
  into a gully

And he fell down the hill
  BOKTS

Then they threw his grandmother
  PLUP
  in the same direction

And
  BOKTS
  she fell near him

For a little while
  Frog stayed right there
  and for a little while
  his grandmother stayed right there

Then they came to life
  and looked up
  and all around
  and poked up their heads

Then they went away
  then they went leaping away
  straight westward.

HAIDA: *cradle song*

Look, look, someone has fallen here
someone has fallen here
someone has fallen here

Where did you fall from,
           where?
Where did you fall from,
           where?

All the way from the
top of the salmon-berry bushes?

All the way from the
top of the salmon-berry bushes?

KIOWA: *a peyote poem by Monroe Tsa Toke*

The Peyote Man prays
to an unknown mystery
he has no name for it
                but life

The Peyote Man prays
to a great light
to the great light
to understand the light
                within himself

Postface:
The Last World

Archaeologists of some future race (maybe a race of dung beetles), searching through the layers of fused green glass to study our ancient vanished culture, will probably not be able to distinguish many American Indian remains among the mountains of our steel and plastic leavings. Materialistically, the Old American World of the Indians will be pretty well buried, has already been pretty well buried, by the concrete giantism of our New World.

Spiritually, it's something else. If the dung beetle archaeologists can work out a radiocarbon technique to measure spiritual presence the American Indian world will loom large among the relics.

The Indian world was and is essentially a world of the spirit. At night before going to bed a man of the northern plains stepped out of his lodge and shot an arrow high into the starry sky, by way of good night to the world, and at dawn when getting up a family in the golden Southwest cast a pinch of sacred cornmeal toward the sunrise by way of good morning. In making a cradleboard or a quiver the precise right furs and woods had to be used in the precise right way, Pueblo people "sang up the corn" in the precise right way, and on the high plains the Mandan Young Girls' Society sang to the rising moon, and if they sang in exactly the right way the moon fell in love with them and sang back. A number of religious doctrines held that the world had been destroyed several times before, by such catastrophes as flood or earthquake, and that the present last world would be destroyed by fire, a fate that could only be delayed by devout practice of the precisely right cycles of prayer. Birth and death, creation and eternity, and all events in between were accepted with the precise right gestures, the precise right rhythms, to maintain the living spirit of the world and the right way of living in it.

Europeans in their early meetings with American Indians marveled at this emphasis on living, at this spiritual, this intensely religious world, devoted to the religion of living the right way, in right relation with all forces and all things about them. Europeans infected this world of the spirit with pots and pans and axes and alcohol and war, but Europeans were infected in return by the silent spirit, infected to an extent undreamed-of in our orthodox histories.

Thomas Traherne, a St. John the Baptist for William Blake, wrote in the 1660s, "that Earth was better than Gold, and that Water was, every Drop of it, a Precious Jewel. And that these were Great and Living Treasures; and that all Riches whatsoever els was Dross in Comparison . . . The Sun is Glorious, A Man is a Beautifull Creature . . . The Stars Minister unto us, The World was made for you . . . But to say This Hous is yours, and these Lands are another Mans and this Bauble is a Jewel and this Gugaw a fine Thing . . . is deadly Barbarous and uncouth . . . becaus the Nature of the Thing contradicts your Words . . . By this you may see who are the Rude and Barbarous Indians. . . ."

The Indian world of the spirit, the faith in living and living in faith, answered no questions, offered no gurus. It was not "practical"; it was not "serious" in the European view. But even while the European invaders happily plundered it, the silent spirit touched them and opened their eyes to problems they never knew they had.

The Indian image of freedom and equality produced far-reaching effects on European thinking in the 1600s and 1700s— in 1721 the smash hit of the Paris stage (for one instance among many) was a play about an American Indian tourist in France, who attributes all the evils he sees there to property and money and especially to the monstrous inequality which makes the poor slaves of the rich, and says to his friend (a Frenchman) who had brought him on this trip, "Why, villain, have you brought me here from my country only in order to teach me that I am poor? I want to be a free man, nothing more. . . ."

The material Indian world, with its terrible fragility, was no match whatever for the European newcomer, bred on war and business. But the spiritual Indian world, even aside from its silent influence on the rest of the world Old and New, has been of incredible durability. Indian societies have vanished by the score in the last four hundred years but an astonishing number, considering the oceans of disaster through which they have voyaged, still remain.

The sense of community that is the central mystery of the Indian world is in direct opposition to the ancient European gods of work-as-a-virtue, and personal riches as the goal of life.

But this sense of community is a good deal more than an essence of nations. The essence seems to be rather in a sense of relationship, the relatedness by blood or spirit one to another, the sense of relation—via the community—to all time and all things in the visible and invisible world. The philosopher Scott Buchanan used to say that all the world is relations. The world is built of relations. Wisdom is an intuition of right relations. Magic is tricks with relations, especially with the relations of time. A powerful sense of relations, as in the American Indian sense of community, may actually create a different world in which one moves. Our cities today are notable as non-communities, thronged with non-related, that is to say alienated, people. The commonest psychiatric problem for modern urban man is precisely his agony of unrelatedness. The thing the modern world most lacks and most needs is precisely this sense of relationship, this sense of community.

And yet the Indian sense of community has been under constant attack for centuries, all over the hemisphere, by the new American nations, apparently because it is so fearfully alien to the European kingship and competition tradition, fearfully radical, truly revolutionary.

A preoccupation with spirit is of course treason to a materialist industrial state. How can such people make "useful" citizens? An angry Hamburger representing German business interests in the American Indian countries, Mexico, Guatemala, and so on, used to curse the Indian wantlessness, the money-wantlessness, the damned wantlessness as he said—in the German language the *verdammte Bedürfnislosigkeit*.

Our everyday world at this moment continues to be respectably fixed on the billboarded attitudes of Succeed! Want! New! but still the image of the Indian world, still though stripped to a skeleton spirit all but imperceptible, still faces its other way, still infecting the Succeed! Want! New! with Want not and ye shall have/Not eternal getting but eternal living. Who is to say the infection of the subtle Indian image, the still-lingering tradition of the subtle Indian spirit, is not still altering the world beneath our feet?

NOTES

INTRODUCTION

General works used for this chapter are Hodge, *Handbook*; Swanton, 1953; Kroeber, 1953; MacLeod; Driver and Massey; Driver; McNickle, 1949; Steward, *Handbook*; Wauchope, *Handbook*; *Jesuit Relations*; Lafitau; Morgan, 1871, 1877; Du Tertre; Rousseau, 1754; Chamberlain; Hallowell, 1957; Boas, 1938; Peter Martyr; Chinard, 1911, 1913; Atkinson, 1920, 1922;

and for page

1 James Bryce, *The American Commonwealth*, 2 vols., revised edition (New York, 1924), II, 891–892. Frederick Jackson Turner Papers at the Henry E. Huntington Library, San Marino, California (TU File Drawer no. 13). The quotation is from a handwritten draft for a summary of a half-term's work at Harvard on the history of the West. Ray Allen Billington, through whose kindness this quotation was provided, dates the draft at about 1921.

2 The DeVoto quotations are from his introduction to Joseph Kinsey Howard's *Strange Empire* (New York, 1942), viii and ix.
Francis Parkman, *La Salle and the Discovery of the Great West* (originally published in 1869, used here in the paperback edition, New York, 1953, with a foreword by John A. Hawgood), 136, 173, 178 and *n.*; and from the closing lines of his introduction to *The Jesuits in North America in the Seventeenth Century* (1867).

3 Kroeber, 1948, 763–764. Boas, 1938, 198. And see Robert H. Lowie, *Are We Civilized?* (New York, 1929).

4 The passage from Peter Martyr is summarized here as it appears in the first English translation, Richard Eden, *Peter Martyr the History of Travayle in the West and Easte Indies*, etc. (London, 1555). This edition adds, in the second book of the first Decade: "The inhabitants of these Islands have been ever too used to live at libertie, in play and pastyme, that they can hardly away with the yoke of servitude which they attempt to shake of by all meanes they maye."
Du Tertre is quoted from II, 356. On the following page the author adds, ". . . They have no other clothes than that with which nature has covered them. They have no police among them; they live, all, at liberty; they drink and eat when they are hungry or thirsty, they work and rest when they please; they have not a care . . . preferring rather to possess little than to purchase more at the cost of their contentment. . . ."
Pierre F. X. de Charlevoix, *Letters to the Dutchess of Lesdiguieres, Giving an Account of a Voyage to Canada and Travels Through that Country and Louisiana to the Gulf of Mexico* (London, 1763), 28.

5 Lafitau, I, 103–108, outlines the "Character of the Savages in General."
Rogers is quoted from Robert Rogers, *A Concise Account of North America* (London, 1765), 210.
Atkinson, 1920, 14.
Diderot is quoted from "Le Temple du Bonheur," date uncertain, Vol. VI, 439, *Oeuvres*.
Rousseau expresses his debt to Diderot in Book VIII of the *Confessions*.

6 John Florio's translation of Montaigne's *Essays*, 1603, is quoted, 106.
Columbus is quoted from his letter of February 15, 1493, in John Boyd Thacher, *Christopher Columbus, His Life, His Work, His Remains*, 3 vols. (New York, 1903), II.
Alexis de Tocqueville, *Democracy in America* (1839).
Morgan, 1876, 267.

7 On Morgan in the Marxist canon, see Leslie A. White, ed., *Lewis Henry Morgan, The Indian Journals* (Ann Arbor, Mich., 1959), 11, and *n.* 58, 202.
Marx is quoted by Friedrich Engels in the preface to the first edition (1884) of *The Origin of the Family, Private Property and the State, in the Light of the Researches of Lewis Henry Morgan*.

8 Mark Twain, *Roughing It* (New York, 1872), 154–158.
Hubert Howe Bancroft, *Native Races* (Vols. I to V of the *Works*, San Francisco, 1886–1890), I, 155.

9 William Bradford, *History of Plymouth Plantation, 1620–1647*, 2 vols. (Boston, 1912), is quoted from I, 202–203.

Sir Ferdinando Gorges, *Briefe Narration . . . etc.* (London, 1658), 3.
The Wappinger quotation is from "Notes by D. David Pietersz. de Vries" (Hoorn, 1655), in *Collections of the New York Historical Society*, 2d Series, Vol. III, Part 1 (New York, 1857).
Captain John Smith is quoted from *A True Relation of Virginia* (London, 1608) and from a petition of 1616 to Queen Anne on behalf of the Lady Pocahontas.

10 The quotation regarding Columbus is from Thacher, XXX *op. cit.*, II,
The Cartier incident is quoted from John Pinkerton, *A General Collection of the Best and Most Interesting Voyages and Travels in All Parts of the world*, 17 vols. (London, 1808–1814), III, 650.
The quotations from Alvar Nuñez Cabeza de Vaca are from F. W. Hodge and Theodore H. Lewis, eds., *Spanish Explorers in the Southern United States, 1528–1542* (New York, 1907), 56 and 54.
All the quotes from "early explorers" are from Parkman, *La Salle*, 141, 223, 298, and 194–195 and *n.* 194, in the edition previously cited, dealing with accounts of La Salle, Membré, and Hennepin.
Castañeda is quoted from Bolton, 1949, 246.
Captain Barlow is quoted in Irwin R. Blacker, ed., *Hakluyt's Voyages* (New York, 1965), 293.

11 Bolton, 1913, 308, lists correspondence re the two Vial expeditions.

12 The "numberless" Indian allies are mentioned by Hernando Cortes in his third letter to Charles V, 1521, quoted in Diaz, 410, 412.

13 Edmond Atkin is quoted from Jacobs, 1954, 40.

16 Sir William Johnson is quoted from MacLeod, 449.
Atkin from Jacobs, 1954, 38, 40.

17 Adolph F. A. Bandelier, "On the Art of War and Mode of Warfare of the Ancient Mexicans," in *Reports of the Peabody Museum, XX, Vol. II* (Cambridge, 1880), 99.

18 The Court of Claims opinion is in United States Indian Affairs, *Report of the Commissioner for 1895* (Washington, 1896), 427; see also 417–418.

21 Parkman is quoted from his introduction to *The Jesuits in North America*, xxvii.
Henry Marie Brackenridge, *Journal of a Voyage up the River Missouri . . . etc.* (Baltimore, 1816), reprinted as the first part of Vol. VI of Reuben Gold Thwaites, *Early Western Travels* (Cleveland, 1904), from which it is quoted here.
The quote on the Opatas is from the *Rudo Ensayo*, quoted in Spicer, 1962, 322.

22 The modern economist is quoted from Gerard Piel, *Consumers of Abundance*, pamphlet published by the Center for the Study of Democratic Institutions (Santa Barbara, California, 1961), 3.
Whorf is quoted from John B. Carroll, ed., *Language, Thought, and Reality: Selected Writings of Benjamin Lee Whorf* (New York, 1956).
The idea of the Indian civilization so firmly committed to its strange attitudes that it nourished its own conquerors and abetted its own conquest is expressed in the synopsis of a play on the fall of Mexico by the surrealist poet Antonin Artaud: "Potlatch of mighty hosts for their mighty guests," included in the American translation of Artaud's *The Theater and Its Double* (New York, 1968), 126–132.

23 Teilhard de Chardin is quoted from Sol Tax, ed., *An Appraisal of Anthropology Today* (Chicago, 1853), 44.

Chapter I

General works used for this chapter are Wormington, 1957; Kroeber, 1948 and 1953; Martin, Quimby, and Collier; Steward, *Handbook*; Driver and Massey; Bennett and Bird; Swanton, 1953; Willey, 1966 and 1971; Peterson; Vaillant, 1950; Wauchope, *Handbook*; Jennings and Norbeck, 1964; Spencer and Jennings, 1965; M. D. Coe, 1962 and 1966; Girard, 1962 and 1966; Morley and Brainerd; Thompson, 1927 and 1935; Hodge, *Handbook*; Spinden, 1928; Jennings, 1968;

and see for pages

25 T. D. Stewart, "A Physical Anthropologist's View of the Peopling of the New World" in *Southwestern Journal of Anthropology*, 16/3 (Autumn 1960), 259–273.
Lee Eldridge Huddleston, *Origins of the American Indians/European Concepts, 1492–1729*, No. 11 of Latin American Monographs, Institute of Latin American Studies, the University of Texas (Austin, 1967).

26 The quotation is from Carl Ortwin Sauer, *Land and Life?: A Selection from his Writings . . .*, edited by John Leighly (Berkeley, 1963), 239; the same selection, 231, remarks on the antiquity of the American Indian race.
Genetic uniformity of most American Indian groups as evidenced by blood type is discussed in T. Dale

Stewart's article cited above. William C. Boyd, *Genetics and the Races of Man* (Boston, 1950), classifies American Indians "genetically as a separate race, distinct even from the Asiatic mongoloids." Boyd also discusses blood-group evidence in an earlier article, "The Blood Groups and Types," in W. S. Laughlin, ed., *The Physical Anthropology of the American Indian* (New York, 1951), 127–137. This same volume contains Marshall T. Newman, "The Sequence of Indian Physical Types in South America," 69–97. For Middle American and South American evidence that somewhat complicates the issue, M. T. Newman, "A Trial Formulation Presenting Evidence from Physical Anthropology for Migrations from Mexico to South America," in *Migrations in New World Culture History*, R. H. Thompson, ed., Social Science Bulletin No. 27, University of Arizona (Tucson, 1958) 33–40.

27 For problems in Ice Age chronology, H. E. Suess, "Absolute Chronology of the Last Glaciation" in *Science*, 123/3192 (1956), 355–357; R. F. Flint, *Glacial and Pleistocene Geology* (New York, 1957); A. L. Bryan and Ruth Gruhn, "Problems Relating to the Neothermal Climatic Sequence," in *American Antiquity* 29/3 (1964); C. S. Chard, "New World Origins: A Reappraisal," in *Antiquity* 33/129 (London, 1959), 44–49; Hansjürgen Müller-Beck, "Paleohunters in America; Origins and Diffusions," in *Science*, 152 (1966) 34–36; Fred Wendorf, "Early Man in the New World: Problems of Migration," in *The American Naturalist* 100/912 (1966), 253–270.

28 The German geographer is Albrecht Penck, quoted in Carl O. Sauer, "A Geographic Sketch of Early Man in America" in *Geographical Review*, 34/4 (October 1944).

29 Australian migrations to South America were speculated upon by Paul Rivet in *Bulletin de la Société de Linguistique de Paris*, 26 (Paris, 1925).

30 The amateur archaeologist was "a now-famous pipeline worker, Keith Glasscock," who to "his everlasting credit" left his find undisturbed while the called upon experts from the Texas Memorial Museum and the University of Texas to assess it (Spencer and Jennings, pp. 20–21).

31 Edward P. Lanning and Thomas C. Patterson, "Early Man in South America" in *Scientific American*, 217/5 (November, 1967), provide some discussion of recent dating sequences to add to Willey, 1971.
Cynthia Irwin-Williams, "Comments on the Association of Archaeological Materials and Extinct Fauna in the Valsequillo Region, Puebla, Mexico," in *American Antiquity* 34/1 (1969) 82–83, deals with a bit of esoteric controversy that developed over the Valsequillo dates.

32 Investigation at the Calico site is summarized in Ruth D. Simpson, "Ice Age Archaeology in the Calicos," in *Pacific Coast Archaeological Society Quarterly* 5/4 (1969) 43–50. At this writing papers and abstracts have not yet been released on the Calico conference, but I have had the good fortune to see an unofficial and informal report prepared by Keith A. Dixon, a participant at the conference, for *The Informant*, 1/10 (December, 1970), journal of the Anthropology Club of California State University at Long Beach.
The Pima quotation is from J. William Lloyd, *Aw-aw-tam Indian Nights* (Westfield, N.J., 1911).
The recent study listing nineteen skeletal finds of reasonably certain antiquity is T. D. Stewart, *op. cit.* Fred Wendorf, Alex D. Krieger, and Claude C. Albritton and T. D. Stewart, *The Midland Discovery: A Report on the Pleistocene Human Remains from Midland, Texas* (Austin, Texas, 1955), and Fred Wendorf and Alex D. Krieger, "New Light on the Midland Discovery" in *American Antiquity* 23 (1959), 66–78, furnish results of dating tests which lead Stewart to conclude ". . . it seems still possible that the Midland skeleton may be as much as 20,000 years old." (Stewart, *op. cit.*, 260.)
No report has at this writing been published on "Yuha Man"—the mention here is from recent news items.

35 The archaeologist cited in a survey of Wisconsin artifacts is A. D. Krieger, in Sol Tax, et al., eds., *An Appraisal of Anthropology Today* (Chicago, 1953) p. 248.
G. K. Neumann, "Archaeology and Race in the American Indians," in J. B. Griffin, ed., *Archaeology of Eastern United States* (Chicago, 1952), 13–34, is one of several interesting studies speculating on the physical types of early Wisconsin man and possible survival into identifiable groups of historical American Indians.

36 E. W. Haury, "The Greater American Southwest," in *Courses Toward Urban Life*, R. J. Braidwood and G. R. Willey, eds. (New York, 1962), 106–131, outlines one possible route for the early diffusion of maize, squash, and beans northward.

38 The comparative notes in Stith Thompson's classic *Tales of The North American Indians* (Bloomington, Ind., 1929), 271–360, give some idea of the wealth of samenesses and differences in legends, hero stories, creation stories.
See also Judity Ullom, *Folklore of the North American Indians: An Annotated Bibliography*, Library of Congress (Washington, 1969).
Genetic samenesses and differences in look (i.e., stature, features) are discussed in T. D. Stewart and Marshall T. Newman, "An Historical Resumé of the Concept of Differences of Indian Types," in *American Anthropologist*, 53/1 (1951).

40   Sauer, 1963, 191, observes that the grasslands seem to have formed late, well within human time, and the "only explanation for the great savannas that meets all conditions is fire. . . ." This remains a controversial point, and Sauer reviews various of the arguments in the same selection, 216–221.
J. R. Caldwell, *Trend and Tradition in the Prehistory of the Eastern United States* (Menasha, Wis., 1958), develops in detail the concept of "primary forest efficiency." For the transition from Archaic to agriculture, see also G. R. Willey and Philip Phillips *Method and Theory in American Archaeology* (Chicago, 1958).

41   Paul C. Mangelsdorf, R. S. MacNeish, and W. C. Galinat, "Domestication of Corn," in *Science*, 143/3606 (1964); and Mangelsdorf, MacNeish, and G. R. Willey, "Origins of Agriculture in Mesoamerica," in Wauchope, *Handbook*, I, 427–445.
There are numerous interesting studies bearing on this subject; for example, Margaret A. Towle, *The Ethnobotany of Pre-Columbian Peru* (Viking Fund Publications in Anthropology, No. 30, 1961); Charles B. Heiser, Jr., "Cultivated Plants and Cultural Diffusion in Nuclear America," in *American Anthropologist*, 67/4 (1965), 930–949, concludes that there may have been two independent origins of agriculture in the Americas. Stuart Struever, "Implications of Vegetal Remains from an Illinois Hopewell Site," in *American Antiquity*, 27/4 (1962), 584–587, suspects some plants now thought of as wild weeds were very early domesticates—such as pigweed, lamb's-quarters, wild grape.
Carl O. Sauer discusses the early spread of cultivated plants over the entire world in *Agricultural Origins and Dispersals* (New York, 1952).
Herbert J. Spinden, "The Origin and Distribution of Agriculture in America," in *Proceedings of the International Congress of Americanists*, 19th Session (Washington, 1917), 269–276, postulated a connection between irrigation and the earliest motions toward agriculture, a notion that nowadays receives small support. But one example of irrigation practiced by a pre-agricultural people is described in Julian H. Steward, "Ethnography of the Owens Valley Paiute," in *University of California Publications in American Archaeology and Ethnology*, 33/3 (Berkeley, 1933), 233–250.

42   M. R. Harrington, *A Pinto Site at Little Lake, California*, Southwest Museum Papers No. 17 (Los Angeles, 1957), cited in Spencer and Jennings, p. 42, interprets evidence at the Stahl site in California as a series of post mold patterns indicating houses, dating from 2000 B.C. or earlier.
Philip Phillips, "The Role of Trans-Pacific Contacts in the Development of New World Pre-Columbian Civilizations," in Wauchope, *Handbook*, vol. IV (1966), 296–315, questions the "fertility goddess" identification of early figurines, some of which, as he points out, were made by nonagricultural people, and many of which offer only a crudely standardized female body but go to great pains with the head and hairdo.

43   Wigberto Jiménez Moreno, "El Enigma de los Olmecas" in *Cuadernos Americanos*, 1/5 (Mexico, 1942), 113–145, details a sequence of different peoples down through the centuries in the Olmec country.

44   Dating sequences of ancient Olmec centers are considered in M. D. Coe, R. Diehl, and M. Stuiver, "Olmec Civilization, Veracruz, Mexico: Dating of the San Lorenzo Phase" in *Science*, 155/1399–1401 (1967); and in Rainer Berger, John A. Graham, and Robert F. Heizer, *A Reconsideration of the Age of the La Venta Site*, Contributions of the University of California Archaeological Research Facility, No. 3 (Berkeley, August 1967). The latter paper disputes the "mother civilization" thesis: "As with that earlier great event . . . [agriculture] . . . we incline not to see the whole of Mesoamerican civilization as the creation of a single group of brilliant people . . ." (7)
Philip Drucker, Robert F. Heizer, and R. J. Squier, *Excavations at La Venta, Tabasco, 1955* (BAE Bulletin 170, Washington, D.C., 1959): "The greatest of the La Venta stelae (No. 3) weighs about 50 tons . . . [and] supports Stirling's proposal that the columns, altars, and stelae were rafted to the site. . . ."
Ancient Olmec achievements in jade and parallels with Chou Dunasty jade work are discussed in M. W. Stirling, "The Olmecs, Artists in Jade," in Samuel K. Lothrop, *et al.*, *Essays in Pre-Columbian Art and Architecture* (Cambridge, Mass., 1961).

47   Tozzer is the source of the quotation.
The quotations are from *ibid.*; from Adrian Recinos, *Popol Vuh: The Sacred Book of the Ancient Quiché Maya*, English version by Sylvanus G. Morley and Delia Goetz (Norman, Okla., 1950); and from Morley and Brainerd, 58.

48   Among many general studies that deal with conflicting views on Mayan political and social organization is J. E. S. Thompson, *The Rise and Fall of Maya Civilization* (Norman, Okla., 1954).
The glottochronology of Proto-Maya is described in Morris Swadesh, "Linguistic Overview," in Jennings and Norbeck, 527–558; and in Norman McQuown, "Los Origenes y la differenciación de Los Mayas segun se infiere de estudio comparativo de las lenguas Mayanas," in *Desarollo Cultural de Los Mayas*, Evon Z. Vogt and Z. Ruz, eds., Publicación Especial del Seminario de Cultura Maya (Mexico, 1964), 49–81.

49   The Tres Zapotes date, reported by M. W. Stirling, *An Initial Series from Tres Zapotes, Vera Cruz, Mexico*, Contributed Technical Papers, Mexican Archaeology Series, 1/1, National Geographic Society (Washington, D.C., 1940), is assessed in numerous studies, among them Willey (1966), 104. Robert Wauchope, in the introduction to *The Indian Background of Latin American History* (New York, 1970), remarks that it

remains a "moot point" in which direction the calendrical stimulation was traveling (8). This date was verified by the find of an additional fragment of the Tres Zapotes stela announced in news items of January 16, 1972. Linton Satterthwaite, "Calendrics of the Maya Lowlands" in Wauchope, *Handbook*, 3, mentions an argument advanced by some students that the La Venta Olmec "originated the Long Count with a Baktun 7 inauguration date . . ." (616). Alfonso Caso, "Calendrical Systems of Central Mexico," in *Ibid.*, vol. X, remarks that the basic calendar is found at various sites dating back to 600 B.C. and "at all these places the calendar appears as a completely established and organized system. . . ." (333).

Quotes re the Long Count correlation are from M. D. Coe (1966), 29; and from Girard (1966), 442. Willey (1966) states (136), "To date, the question is still in doubt."

50 The *tzolkin* is described in detail in Peterson and in many other works; and the calendrics of the Long Count, based on the *kin* (1 day), the *uinal* (20 days), the *tun* (360 days), the *katun* (7,200 days) and the *baktun* (144,000 days)—all except the *tun* successive multiples of twenty, are considered in detail in Herbert J. Spinden, *The Reduction of Mayan Dates*, Papers of the Peabody Museum of American Archaeology and Ethnology, 6/4 (Cambridge, Mass., 1924); and in J. E. S. Thompson, *Maya Chronology: The Correlation Question*, Contribution No. 14, Publication No. 456, Carnegie Institution of Washington (Washington, D.C., 1935).

Francisco López de Gómara, *La Historia General de las Indias* (1554), quotes Friar Thomas Ortizius, before the Council of the Indies, "They sacrificed to Venus, which they considered the most excellent of stars, a royal slave on the day . . . when they perceived it in the autumn. It continued visible for two hundred and sixty days. They believed that it was influential over destinies, and accordingly they practiced divination by signs, which they painted and allotted to these two hundred and sixty days."

Spinden, 1928, coined the apt term "civic centers."

51 Irmgard Groth Kimball, *Mayan Terracottas*, introduction by José Dane, explanatory notes by Rafael Orellano Tapia (New York, 1961), is an unusually fine picture book, giving an excellent view of the Maya people, particularly of the "later empire."

52 The quotations are from Recinos, *op. cit.*; and from Ralph L. Roys, *The Book of Chilam Balam of Chumayel* (Washington, 1933).

R. Wauchope, "Late Horizons of Maya Prehistory," in Wauchope, ed., *The Indian Background of Latin American History* (New York, 1970), cites (100) J. E. S. Thompson as to the post-classic resetting of stela fragments upside down.

NOTES for Chapter II

General works used in this chapter are Peterson; Bennett and Bird; Tozzer; Caso; Vaillant; Morley and Brainerd; Sahagun; Spinden, 1928; Roys; Makemson; Seler; Wolf, 1959; M. D. Coe, 1962; Kubler, 1962; Thompson, 1970; Wauchope, *Handbook*; Steward, *Handbook*; Willey, 1966 and 1971; Spencer and Jennings; Driver and Massey; Martin, Quimby, and Collier; Kroeber, 1948 and 1953; Garibay, 1954; Leon-Porilla, 1969; Prescott, *Peru;*

and for page

55 A C-14 date between 3,100 and 3,500 years ago for the twig deer is given in Douglas Schwartz, Arthur Lange, and Raymond de Saussure, "Split-Twig Figurines in the Grand Canyon," in *American Antiquity*, 23/3 (January, 1958).

56 For the Zapotecs and Mixtecs in Oaxaca see John Paddock, ed., *Ancient Oaxaca: Discoveries in Mexican Archaeology and History* (Stanford, 1966); and William T. Sanders, "The Central Mexican Symbiotic Region: A Study in Prehistoric Settlement Patterns," in Gordon R. Willey, ed., *Prehistoric Settlement Patterns in the New World* (New York, 1956).

60 The story of the Toltec emigration is summarized and quoted from Don Fernando d'Alva Ixtlilxochitl, *Histoire des Chichimèques*, in Vols. XII–XIII of H. Ternaux-Compans, ed., *Voyages, Relations et Mémoires Originaux pour servir a l'Histoire de la Découverte de l'Amérique* (Paris, 1840). The *Historia Chichimeca* also appears as Vol. II of Ixtlilxochitl's *Obras Historias* (Mexico, 1891–1892).

Teotihuacan's environmental problems, rather than invaders, are surveyed in Sherburne Friend Cook, "The Interrelation of Population, Food Supply, and Building in Pre-Conquest Central Mexico," in *American Antiquity*, 13 (1947–1949).

Kubler, 1962, expresses a minority opinion that Chichén Itzá might have influenced or even founded Tula, rather than the other way around.

61 The quotation is from Cottie A. Burland's postscript to the English edition of Vaillant (London, 1950).

Sahagun (Dibble-Anderson translation) is quoted, from Book II, the ceremonies.

62 Daniel G. Brinton, *Rig Veda Americanus* (Philadelphia, 1890), speaks of the philosophical, moralistic, and religious connotations of ball-game allusions in his notes to the very beautiful "Hymn for Fasting." A more complete version of this hymn is found in Sahaoon (Anderson and Dibble translation), Book II, p. 212.

For a description of the ball game and its paraphernalia, see Frans Blom, "The Maya Ball-Game Pok-ta-pok, called Tlachtli by the Aztec," in *Tulane University, Middle American Research Series*, No. 4 (New Orleans, 1932), 485–530; and Stephan F. de Borhegyi, "America's Ball Game," in *Natural History*, 69/1 (January 1960). A detailed relation of the Topiltzin Quetzalcoatsl story is in Wigberto Jiménez Moreno, "Sintesis de la Historia Pretolteca de Mesoamerica" in *Esplendor del Mexico Antiguo*, C. Cook de Leonard, Coordinator, Centro de Investigaciones Antropologicas de Mexico (Mexico, 1959), vol. II, 1019–1108. I have depended mainly on Peterson's summary, which draws on Ixtlilxochitl, *Obras Historicas*, cited above. The evolution of a later god is the subject of Robert C. Padden, *The Humming Bird and the Hawk: Conquest and Sovereignty in the Valley of Mexico, 1503–1541* (Columbus, O., 1967).

63 A contemporary picture of this seething period is the Mixtec picture-manuscript telling the story of Eight-Deer Tiger Claw, an eleventh-century conqueror in Oaxaca. See Zelia Nuttall, ed., *Codex Nuttall, Facsimile of an Ancient Mexican Codex*, Peabody Museum of American Archaeology and Ethnology, Harvard University (Cambridge, Mass., 1902), half of which is taken up by the story of Eight-Deer Tiger Claw. This codex, as the editor points out in her notes, was upon its discovery (in Florence in the 1860s) only the tenth pre-Columbian Mexican Codex to be found still surviving in the modern world. (The other nine being the Vatican; Borgian; Bologna, or Cospian; Féjévary, or Mayer; Laud; Bodleian; Selden; Becker/Colombino; and Vienna.) She also points out that the Codex Nuttall contains a great many representations of women in responsible positions, on an equality with men, and thus "fully corroborates the documentary records concerning the existence of gyneocracies . . ."—page 27, note 1, lists this documentary evidence as Zelia Nuttall, *The Fundamental Principles of Old and New World Civilizations; A Comparative Research Based on a Study of the Ancient Mexican Religious, Sociological, and Calendrical Systems*, Archaeological and Ethnological Papers of the Peabody Museum, Harvard University, vol. II (Cambridge, Mass., 1901), pp. 194 and 60.

65 *Gold Before Columbus*, catalogue of "A survey exhibition, 2300 years of the art of the goldsmith in ancient America," presented by the Los Angeles County Museum in association with the Science and History Alliance of the Museum and the Center of Latin American Studies at the University of California, Los Angeles, 1964, lists the early date for San Agostin metalwork from Colombia.

Dudley, T. Easby, Jr., "Fine Metalwork in Pre-Conquest Mexico," in S. K. Lothrop, ed., *Essays in Pre-Columbian Art and Archaeology* (Cambridge, Mass., 1961), is the author of the quotation re the "fabulous" Mixįec treasure from Tomb 7 at Monte Albán, as well as the source of the following comment about the core compounds in use in ancient Mexico.

66 Carl O. Sauer, *Agricultural Origins and Dispersals* (New York, 1952), discusses in detail the agricultural "frontier" between North and South America.

The quotations are from the catalogue *Gold Before Columbus*, cited above, and Philip Phillips, "The Role of Trans-Pacific Contacts in the Development of New World Pre-Columbian civilizations," in Wauchope, *Handbook*, vol. IV (1966), 311.

67 The *"pampa-isla"* ridged fields found in Colombia, Ecuador and Bolivia, some of the causeways totaling in length more than 1,000 miles, are the subject of recent study in J. J. Parsons and W. M. Denevan, "Pre-Columbian Ridged Fields," in *Scientific American*, 217/1 (July 1967).

68 Rafael Larco Hoyle, *Checan* (Geneva, 1965), finds that erotic representations appear in Peruvian art between 500 and 800 B.C. and reach fullest flower in the Florescent Era (the Classic Age) of A.D. 1–800, reaching "its highest expression . . . exactly when the arts and the sciences do" (52). Erotic pottery was placed in many tombs along with other funerary offerings—"The strange thing is that they are found not only in the tombs of adults but also in those of children" (44).

The same author's article on the Mochica in Steward, *Handbook*, suggests similarities in the Mochica lima-bean writing system to Mayan ideographs.

Junius B. Bird and Louisa Bellinger, *Catalogue Raisonné, Paracas Fabrics and Nazca Needlework*, The Textile Museum, Smithsonian Institution (Washington, 1954), discuss in detail these textiles.

See also Edward P. Lanning, *Peru Before the Incas* (Englewood Cliffs, N.J., 1967).

69 The Inca hymn is taken from Clement Markham's pioneer history, *The Incas of Peru* (London, 1910). The quotation is from page 43 of the 1893 two-volume edition of William H. Prescott, *History of the Conquest of Peru*, originally published in 1847.

70 Prescott mentions the work by John Ranking, *Historical Researches on the Conquest of Peru, Mexico, Bogota, Natchez, etc. in the Thirteenth Century by the Mongols, accompanied with Elephants* (London, 1827).

The Tartar inscription is from Kingsborough (cited below), an extract from F. H. Alexander von Humboldt's *Monuments de l'Amérique* quoting Peter Kalm in his *Voyage en Amérique* (done in English in two volumes as *Travels into North America*, London, 1772), stating that M. de Verandier found the stone in 1746 and several Jesuits assured Kalm they had held it in their hands, and the Chevalier de Beauharnois, then governor of Canada, had had it presented to M. de Maurepas in France—who could question such respectable names? Edward King, Viscount Kingsborough, *Antiquities of Mexico, etc.*, 7 vols. (London, 1831), is a truly magnificent work, with sumptuous reproductions of the picture-ideographs of the Codex Mendoza, a picture-manuscript painted by Aztec artists in 1541 at the behest of Viceroy Antonio de Mendoza. See especially, in connection with these various theories, Robert Wauchope's entertaining *Lost Tribes and Sunken Continents* (Chicago, 1962).

71 An early work in English on the subject of Indians as lost Israelites is Thomas Thoroughgood, *Jews in America, or Probabilities that those Indians are Judaical made more probable by some Additionals to the former Conjectures. An Accurate Discourse is premised of Mr. John Elliot (who first preached the Gospel to the Natives in their own Language) touching their Origination, and his Vindication of the Planters* (London, 1649–1660). The Rev. John Eliot wrote the author, "By reading your book . . . I thought, I saw some ground to conceive that some of the Ten Tribes might be scattered even thus far, into these parts of America. . . ." The great classifier of culture-trait distribution was Erland Nordenskiold, whose vols. VIII–IX of *Comparative Ethnographical Studies: Origin of the Indian Civilizations in South America* (Ethnographic Museum, Goteborg, 1931); and his "The American Indian as an Inventor" (originally published in London in 1929), reprinted in A. L. Kroeber and T. T. Waterman, *Source Books in Anthropology* (1931), relate most directly the points here mentioned.
The quotation is from Bancroft, *Native Races of the Pacific States*, I, 17, 18.
F. Ridley, "Transatlantic Contacts of Primitive Man," in *Pennsylvania Archaeology*, 30 46–57; and A. B. Kehoe, "A Hypothesis on the Origin of Northeastern American Pottery," in *Southwestern Journal of Anthropology*, 18 (1962), 20–29, deal with the possibility of pottery introduction from north Europe. Compare the interesting notes on early pottery-dating by A. L. Kroeber in *Current Anthropology*, 2/2 (April, 1961), 90, commenting on Munro S. Edmonson's "Neolithic Diffusion Rates" in the same journal.
J. B. Hutchinson, R. A. Silow, and S. G. Stephens, *Evolution of Gossypium* (London, 1947), proposed the Asiatic cotton-crossing, and P. C. Mangelsdorf and G. R. Willey, "Origins of Agriculture in Mesoamerica," in Wauchope, *Handbook*, vol. I (1964), 427–445, cast doubt on the proposal.
One of the more extreme of the better-known proponents of Asiatic origin for New World high culture is Robert von Heine-Geldern, whose "The Problem of Transpacific Influences in Mesoamerica," in Wauchope, *Handbook*, vol. IV (1966), 277–295, sums up his views.

72 B. J. Meggers, C. Evans, Jr., and E. Estrada, *Early Formative Period of Coastal Ecuador*, Smithsonian Contributions to Anthropology, vol. I (Washington, 1965);
Emilio Estrada and Betty J. Meggers, "A Complex of Traits of Probable Transpacific Origins on the Coast of Ecuador," in *American Anthropologist*, 63 (1961), 913–939; and B. J. Meggers and C. Evans, eds., *Aboriginal Cultural Development in Latin America: An Interpretative Review*, Smithsonian Miscellaneous Collections, 146, (Washington, 1963), cover the matter of possible Valdivia connections with Japanese Jomon ware, and possible results stemming from such connection. Compare the review of the latter work by Julian H. Steward, in *American Journal of Archaeology*, 68 (1964).
Gordon F. Ekholm, "Transpacific Contacts," in Jennings and Norbeck gives a broad and sympathetic review of the case for Asian influences.
Kroeber, 1948, 626 and 727–728, presents very well the older orthodox view on the problem of New World metallurgy; Willey, 1966, 22–23, acknowledges the seriousness and complexity of the question.
Dudley T. Easby, *op. cit.*, mentions the working of platinum (36) and remarks, "When and where metalworking began in the New World, how it developed, and the extent to which metals were extracted from ores must still be viewed as open questions. There is plenty of debate but very little of what, as a lawyer, I would call evidence." A more recent summing-up by the same author is "Early Metallurgy in the New World," in *Scientific American*, (April, 1966)
Kroeber, 1948: "On the basis of archaeology the accumulation of American culture, after its first primitive start, seems so consecutive and step-by-step a process as to leave a strong impression that it was overwhelmingly determined from within—metallurgy along with the rest of it" (561).

73 The quotation is from Philip Phillips, "The Role of Trans-Pacific Contacts in the Development of New World Pre-Columbian Civilizations," in Wauchope, *Handbook*, vol. IV (1966), 302—an excellent summary of the problem in its broader aspects.
Robert von Heine-Geldern, "The Origin of Ancient Civilizations and Toynbee's Thesis," in *Diogenes*, 13 (Chicago, 1956), 90–99, proposes ship sailings from the Chinese coastal states of Wu and Yueh in the eighth century B.C. to plant the Chavin culture in the central Andes and further traffic to stimulate the various other American cultures until 333 B.C., when the Dong-son folk of Vietnam took over the commerce. The Han Dynasty (202 B.C.–A.D. 220) then resumed Chinese voyages which ended with the fall of the Han, and

Cambodia, the theory continues, then took over the trans-Pacific sailings, possibly continuing them until the death of Jayavarman VII of Angkor, circa A.D. 1219. However, these theoretical voyages are not documented in the various written records of the Asian groups involved.
Possible resemblances in art motifs are analyzed in R. von Heine-Geldern with Gordon F. Ekholm, "Significant Parallels in the Symbolic Arts of Southern Asia and Middle America" in *Selected Papers of the XXIXth International Congress of Americanists*, vol. I (Chicago, 1951).
Philip Phillips, *loc. cit.*, discusses the nineteenth-century German theory of the universality of history and its place in the New World controversies.

74 Julian H. Steward, *Handbook*, summing up New World culture development in vol. V, gives a total of more than 100 native American crops and the very few plants of this inventory known to the pre-Columbian Old World.
Paul Rivet, *Les Origines de l'Homme Américain* (Montreal, 1943), reviews his theory of Australian journeys to South America via Antarctica, first presented in the *Bulletin de la Société de Linguistique de Paris*, 26/1-2 (Paris, 1925). Most other Americanists have cast a skeptical eye on these supposed journeys, which presumably would have entailed long water crossings.

75 An early list of Asian ships on the Northwest Coast is Charles Wolcott Brooks, "Reports of Japanese Vessels Wrecked in the North Pacific from the Earliest Records to the Present Time," in *Proceedings of the California Academy of Sciences*, vol. VI (1875).
Early Spanish trans-Pacific seafaring is recounted in Ione Stuessy Wright, "Early Spanish Voyages from America to the Far East," in *Greater America: Essays Presented to H. E. Bolton* (Berkeley, 1945).
Sauer, 1952, mentions the Araucanian chickens with the Silkie look.
Rongo-rongo origins are discussed at length in Thor Heyerdahl and Edwin N. Ferdon, Jr., eds., *Reports of the Norwegian Archaeological Expedition to Easter Island and the East Pacific in 1955-1956*, vol. II (New York, 1966).
An alleged resemblance that caused a stir in the 1920s and is still often found in lists of significant parallels was the claimed identity between the scales of panpipes in use in the Solomon Islands and in northwestern Brazil. R. H. Lowie, "American Culture History," in *American Anthropologist*, 41 (1940), 409-428, says of "Von Hornbostel's demonstration" re the identity of these panpipe scales that ". . . Von Hornbostel's student, Dr. Herzog, remained unconvinced; and my colleague [at the University of California] Professor Manfred Bukohzer, a first-rate musicologist, is quite negative in his reaction. . . ."

76 Some prehistoric Hopi houses in Arizona were equipped with small chimneys, an invention apparently born of the necessity for a draft to carry away the fumes of the local soft coal they evidently used for heat—Martin, Quimby, and Collier, 150.
Julian H. Steward, ed., *Handbook*, surveys some of the basic differences of New World societies in vol. V—the same essential differences are summarized in J. H. Steward and L. C. Faron, *Native Peoples of South America* (New York, 1959), 34-43.
Lewis Henry Morgan, with *Systems of Consanguinity and Affinity of the Human Family*, vol. XVII of the Smithsonian Contributions to Knowledge (Washington, 1871); and with *Ancient Society* (New York, 1877) introduced "one of the most basic and significant generalizations of ethnology, namely, that primitive society is organized upon the basis of kinship relations, whereas modern society is based upon property relations."—Leslie A. White, ed., *Lewis Henry Morgan, The Indian Journals* (Ann Arbor, Mich., 1959), 6.

77 Bennett and Bird, 201, use the City Builders designation.
For a detailed discussion of Andean cities: Gordon R. Willey, ed., *Prehistoric Settlement Patterns in the New World* (New York, 1956).
Kroeber (1948) says of bronze, ". . . an independent development that is almost certain . . ." instancing "first of all the isolated and restricted distribution of the South American bronze art . . ." (560).

79 John H. Rowe, "Inca Culture at the Spanish Conquest" in Steward, *Handbook*, vol. II, cites as the most valuable single source on Inca customs Father Bernabé Cobo, *Historia del Nuevo Mundo, etc.*, written about 1653, Marcos Jiménez de la Espada, ed., 4 vols. (Seville, 1890-1895).

80 Rafael Karsten indicates in his title a prevailing view of the Inca world, "A Totalitarian State of the Past: the Civilization of the Inca Empire in Ancient Peru," in *Proceedings* of the Helsingfors Societas Scientiarum Fennica Humanarum Letterarum, 16/1 (Helsinki, 1949).

81 The Maya quotation is from Roys, 1933.
Information, however, differs on the matter of the four directions in Inca religion. Garcilaso Inca de la Vega, *Comentarios reales de los Incas* (1609), learned from his uncle, Cusi Hualpa, that in the beginning the deity divided the world into four parts. . . .
Overseers ordered the farmers, in cultivating the Inca's lands, to "maintain a tidy appearance, sing and dance, and at the end shout 'Hailli,' our cry of victory," so said F. Huaman Poma, sixteenth-century Indian author of the *Nueva Cronica y Buen Gobierno* (Paris, 1936), and *Los Cronistas del Convento* (Paris, 1938), translated as the basis of Bertrand Flornoy's *L'Aventure Inca* (in English *The World of the Inca*, New York, 1956).

82 A detailed description of Jibaro *tsantsa* rites is in Rafael Karsten, *Blood Revenge, War, and Victory Feasts among the Jibaro Indians of Eastern Ecuador*, BAE Bulletin 79 (Washington, 1923).
A bad *ayahuasca* trip is vividly pictured in Dr. P. Reinburg, "Contribution á l'Etude des Boissons Toxiques des Indiens du Nord-ouest de l'Amazone, l'Ayahuásca—le Yajé—le Huánto. Etude Comparative Toxico-Physiologique d'Une Expérience Personelle" in *Journal de la Société des Américanistes de Paris*, n.s. 13 (Paris, 1921), 25–54, 197–216.

NOTES for Chapter III

General works used in this chapter are Peterson; Vaillant; 1922; Driver and Massey; Sahagun; Prescott, *Mexico*; Caso; Steward, *Handbook*; Bernal Diaz; Tozzer; Morley and Brainerd; Thacher; Morison; Wolf; Wauchope, *Handbook*; M. D. Coe, 1962; Willey, 1966, 1971; Kubler, 1962; Las Casas; Garibay, 1954; Leon-Portilla, 1969; Jennings and Norbeck; Seler; Bancroft;

and for page

84 The quotation is from Ixtlilxochitl, *Obras Historicas*, cited previously. A detailed archeaological look at Tula is given in Bertha P. Dutton, "Tula of the Toltecs" in *El Palacio*, 62/7–8 (Santa Fe, 1955), 195–251.

87 Sahagun is quoted, from Book X, Chapter 29.
Pedro Armillas, "Northern Mesoamerica," in Jennings and Norbeck, concludes that Tenochtitlán was a "protectorate" of Culhuacan, Tlatelolco of Azcapotzalco.

88 The verses quoted are adapted from a translation by Fanny Calderon for William H. Prescott and printed by him in a note to his *Conquest of Mexico*.
A great many detailed or specialized sources on the history of the Aztecs are listed and evaluated in Paul Radin, *The Sources and Authenticity of the History of the Ancient Mexicans* (Berkeley, 1920). Plus more recent syntheses, such as Wigberto Jiménez Moreno, "Sintesis de la Historia Precolonial del Valle de Mexico," in *Revista Mexicana de Estudios Antropologicos*, 14, part 1 (1954–1955), 219–236; and Robert H. Barlow, *The Extent of the Culhua Mexica* (Berkeley, 1949).
Early chronicles, mainly sixteenth- and seventeenth-century, in both Spanish and written Nahuatl (and picture-writing codices, a number of which have been published with translation and commentary), are of course the primary source for all this pre-Hispanic history, and of course all ultimately depend on original native accounts. An interesting recent study—Rodolfo van Zantwijk, "La Pas Azteca: la Ordenación del Mundo por los Mexicas," in *Estudios de Cultura Nahuatl*, Universidad Nacional de Mexico, vol. III (Mexico, 1962), 101–135—has found a (not surprising) anti-Aztec bias in most of these native accounts covering the period of Aztec hegemony: 1434–1520. One of the most important such accounts was written in 8 Annales and a Memorial by Domingo Francisco de San Anton Muñon Chimalpahin Quauhtlehuanitzin (1579–1660), a native of the town of Chalco, conquered by the Aztecs in 1465. His work is preserved in the Bibliothèque National de Paris (MS Mexicain No. 74), and various parts have been translated into French or Spanish or German—the 6th and 7th Relations into French in 1889, the 4th into Spanish in 1948, and parts of the 2d, 3d, 4th, 5th, and 6th into German in 1958 and 1960, for which last publication see Hasso von Winning, Reviews, in *American Antiquity*, 25/3 (1960), 437–438, and 27/1 (1961), 125–126.
Chimalpahin, like other early writers, Indian and Spanish, had sources available that have since disappeared, and hints of the contents of some of these lost sources can be found by a comparison with the known and still available sources Chimalpahin used, and listed in his final relation. Using this sort of detective work, Robert H. Barlow posited a "Cronica X" which may be brought to light, little by little, by further such painstaking comparisons.
A previous historian used by Chimalpahin, and one who could scarcely be accused of anti-Aztec bias, was Fernando de Alvarado Tezozomoc (b. ?1525), a grandson of Moctezuma, who wrote in Spanish the *Cronica Mexicana* (c. 1598), ed. by Manuel Orozco y Berra (Mexico, 1944), and in Nahuatl the *Cronica Mexicayotl* (1606), translated into Spanish by Adrian Leon (Mexico, 1949). Tezozmoc, with the sixteenth-century Spanish chronicler Diego Duran, wrote *Historia de las Indias de Nueva Espa a y Islas de Tierra Firme* (Mexico, 1951)—a manuscript copy in the Bancroft Library, Berkeley, California, was more convenient for my use—emphasizes the story of Tlacaelel, while Ixtlilxochitl, *op. cit.*, *Monarchia Indiana* (Madrid, 1723), are among other early chroniclers who regard him as only legendary. See Hasso von Winning, "Tlacaelel, Aztec General and Statesman," in *The Masterkey*, 38/2 (Southwest Museum, Los Angeles, 1964), 44–53.
Von Winning points out that the present trend in studying ancient Mexican history involves an emphasis on philosophical and religious thought as a key to the course of events, Garibay (1953–1954) and Leon-Portilla (1963) being good examples of such work.
Obviously both Tezozomoc and Duran used the same source, which was, as Alfredo Chavero showed in *Apuntes Viejos de Bibliografia Mexicana* (Mexico, 1903), the Codex Ramirez, published (Mexico, 1944), as *Relacion del Origen de los Indios que Habitan esta Nueva Espa a*. Bancroft, in his *The Early American*

Chroniclers (San Francisco, 1883)—his sources are in vol. XV of the *Works*, Chapters 3 and 4; vol. XVII, Chapters 1 and 2; for Native—aces, vol. I—says of Duran, "dangerously zealous priest in defending natives." I have made rather much in this text of the story of the old king Tezozomoc, both because it is a significant revelation of ancient Mexican political history and because it was a popular contemporary theme for poets and philosophers, such as Nezahualcoyotl, one of whose purported works, as adapted from Daniel G. Brinton, *Ancient Nahuatl Poetry* (Philadelphia, 1881), reads: "That great man that great conqueror Tezozomoc/(at the age of a hundred years)/his palaces and gardens surely so one thought/would last forever/ . . . Sad and impressive indeed to reflect on that great Tezozomoc. . . ."

89   The quoted description of Huitzilopochtli is from Sahagun, Book I.
The god's formal epithet is from a translation in Kingsborough, cited in the notes to the preceding chapter.

90   On the city of Tenochtitlan see also Jacques Soustelle, *La Vie Quotidienne des Aztéques à la Veille de la Conquete Espagnole* (Paris, 1955).
Chinampas past and present are the subject of Robert C. West and Pedro Armillas, "Las Chinampas de Mexico: Poecia y Realidad de los Jardines Flotantes," in *Cuadernos Americanos*, vol. IX (Mexico, 1950), 165–182.
William T. Sanders, "Pre-Conquest Settlement Patterns: Sources" in Robert Wauchope, ed., *The Indian Background of Latin American History* (New York, 1970)—an excerpt from Sanders, "The Central Mexican Symbiotic Region: A Study in Prehistoric Settlement Patterns," in Gordon R. Willey, ed., *Prehistoric Settlement Patterns in the New World* (New York, 1956)—remarks on the apparent existence of backyard chinampas in sixteenth-century colonial Mexico City, but concludes they would have had only a slight effect on the total community economy.
Sanders, although acknowledging that most sixteenth-century accounts give 60,000 houses for Tenochtitlan, maintains that this must be "a certain exaggeration" (88). He contends that the total population must have been approximately 60,000 persons, not 60,000 hearths, or families, and cites the Anonymous Conqueror, *Narrative of Some Things of New Spain and Great City of Temistitlan* (New York, 1917), as giving the population of the city at 60,000 persons. The Anonymous Conqueror was one of Cortes' soldiers (as yet unidentified—Bancroft suggests Francisco de Terrazas, majordomo for Cortes) whose account has come to us only in an Italian translation. It relates nothing of the events of the conquest and deals almost entirely with a description of the city of Mexico and its people, and is generally regarded as in the main reliable. This is, however, the only contemporary source to give a figure of 60,000 population—most of the others give a figure of 60,000 houses, with a resultant total population therefore estimated at between 200,000 and 400,000 persons.
A bit of evidence that might possibly apply to this controversy is found in a remark in the third of Cortes' *Letters* (one of the five letters Cortes wrote to the Emperor Charles V, known as the *Cartas de Relación*—the third letter was written from Coyoacan, May 15, 1522) mentioning looking out over the city from the summit of the great temple of Tlatelolco, and observing that the Spaniards were then in control of about seven-eighths of the city—and mentioning later that the large quarter the enemy still held "consisted of more than a thousand houses. . . ." Simple arithmetic projected from this figure would produce some 8,000 houses for the entire city, with a correspondingly low figure for the total population—that the quarter the enemy still held consisted of residences on a par with the rest of the city may, however, be disputed.
Alexander de Humboldt, *Political Essay on the Kingdom of New Spain, etc.* . . . translated from the original French by John Black, 2 vols. (New York, 1811) estimates (I, 51) from the fragments of ruined houses and the "recital of the first conquerors" a population for Tenochtitlán three times that of the Mexico City of his day—which was some 113,000 by the census of 1790. Humboldt remarks that the Abbé Clavigero—Francisco Javier Clavijero, *The History of Mexico, etc.* . . . (originally published in Italian, 1780; in English translation in London, 1787)—collected estimates of the city's aboriginal population varying from 60,000 to a million and a half.

91   The poem is from John H. Rowe's previously cited article in Steward, *Handbook*, vol. II. A later summation of Rowe's work is available in John H. Rowe and Dorothy Menzel, *Peruvian Archaeology: Selected Readings* (Palo Alto, California, 1967).

92   For the interesting theory re Tlaxcala's independence see von Winning, "Tlacaelel . . .," 40. Andres de Tapia says Moctezuma gave him the same explanation—quoted in the translator's commentary, page 122 of Bernal Diaz, edition of 1908, translated by A. P. Maudslay.

93   Old Wolf is quoted from Sahagun, Book II.
Ibid., the quotations.
The suggestion of a precipitation sacrifice surviving in the Volador is in John Barr Tompkins, "Codex Fernandez Leal," in *Pacific Art Review*, 1–2 (Summer 1942).

94   Another view has it that the stone of Tizoc was used as the gladiator's stone—see Peterson, 99.

95   The quotations are from Sahagun, Book XII; and from the "Lienzo de Tlaxcala" (which is to say the "record on painted cloth from Tlaxcala") in *Antiguedades Mexicanas* (Mexico, 1892), plates 66–175.

96   The lines quoted are from Columbus' first letter, written February 15, 1493, and sent from Portugal March 9, addressed to Luis de Santangel, Chancellor of the Royal Household of Aragon—the text is reprinted in Thacher, II, 18.

97   The first journal-quotation is from Ferdinand Columbus' biography of his father, written with the Journal before him, quoted in Morison, 300.
The second quotation is from Las Casas' abstract of the Journal, using here Columbus' exact words: Las Casas, *Historia*, vol. I, 204.
Sherburne Friend Cook and Woodrow Wilson Borah, authors of the most thorough and painstaking demographic studies made on the region, arrive in *Essays in Population History: Mexico and the Caribbean* (Berkeley, 1971), at the astounding figure of eight million for pre-Columbian Hispaniola. The few thousand "Indios" shown in censuses of 1514, 1516, 1520, etc., include Indians brought from other islands as servants and laborers. There may have been none at all of the original millions of people of Hispaniola (modern Santo Domingo and Haiti) left by 1520, one short generation after the first appearance of the people from heaven.

99   Quotations describing the smallpox are from Tozzer, *Landa*.
Ralph L. Roys, The Political Geography of the Yucatan Maya (Washington, 1957), calls the Mayapan rule a "joint government" (1).

100   Quotations from the start of the Cortes expedition are from Bernal Diaz.
Tozzer, *Landa*, is the source of the quotations concerning Malinal.

101   On population figures: Woodrow Wilson Borah and Sherburne Friend Cook, *The Aboriginal Population of Central Mexico on the Eve of the Spanish Conquest* (Berkeley, 1963).

102   The first Aztec treasures sent by Cortes to Europe were seen in Brussels on their arrival by Albrecht Dürer, who wrote of ". . . the things which have been brought to the king from the new land of gold: a sun all of gold a whole fathom broad and a moon all of silver of the same size, also two rooms full of the armor of the people there, and all manner of wondrous weapons of theirs, harness and darts, wonderful shields, strange clothing, bedspreads, and all kinds of wonderful objects of various uses . . . beautiful to behold . . . All the days of my life I have seen nothing that has gladdened by heart so much as these things, for I saw amongst them wonderful works of art. . . ." Wolfgang Stechow, *Duerer in America* (National Gallery, Washington, 1971).
Each day in the Mexican calendar possessed both a name and a number—the day count being composed of a series of twenty named days revolving through an endlessly repeated number series of one to thirteen. Children of the Nahua world were given the designation of the day of their birth as the first part of their name, e.g., the day Ce Acatl, or One Reed, as the first part of the name of Ce Acatl Topiltzin Quetzalcoatl; and years were named for the names of the days on which they began. Due to the meshing of the 260-day ceremonial calendar with the 365-day solar year, there were only four day names that could begin a year (called the "Year Bearers" by the Maya)—one of these names was Acatl, "Reed"—and as these names turned through thirteen numbers any particular combination of number and name would be repeated in a "Calendar Round" every fifty-two years. According to tradition, Quetzalcoatl disappeared in a year that began with the day Ce Acatl, saying he would return in another year of Ce Acatl; and it was in another year of Ce Acatl—an unknown number of fifty-two-year cycles later—that the Spaniards appeared.
Excellent simplified explanations of ancient Mexican calendrics are in Peterson, 180–201; and in Spinden (1922), 96–113.
The quoted words are from Bernal Diaz.
Prescott says Moron, whom he calls Moran, died the following day of his wounds (I, 383); Cortes, in his letters to the king (Hernando Cortes, *Five Letters*, translated by J. Bayard Morris, London, 1928; or a recent edition in Spanish, *Cartas de Relación de la Conquista de Mejico*, Mexico, 1946), acknowledges no fatalities. Bernal Diaz says that by the end of the Tlazcalan fighting "over forty-five of our soldiers had been killed in battle, or succumbed to disease and chills" (134).

103   The numbers of Tlaxcalan warriors is anybody's fantasy—Cortes says 150,000, Bernal Diaz 40,000. Francisco Lopez de Gomara, The History and Conquest of Mexico (1552), says 80,000—but tradition says it was due to indignation over Gomara's history, which overglorified Cortes, that Bernal Diaz wrote his account: Irving A. Leonard's *Introduction* to Bernal Diaz, xvi.
Antonio de Herrera, *Historia General de los Hechos de los Castellanos en las Islas i Tierra Firme del Mar Oceano* (1601), and Torquemada, who both made use of Bernal Diaz' manuscript, give the size of the Tlaxcalan armies as 30,000. Most later historians use the first published version of Bernal Diaz (Madrid, 1632), which was extensively altered by its editor, Fray Alonzo Remón, who "suppressed whole pages . . . interpolated others, garbled the facts, changed the names . . . increased or lessened the numbers, modified the style . . . moved thereto either by religious fervor and false patriotism, or by personal sympathy and vile literary taste," says Genaro Garcia in the *Introduction* to his correct edition of Bernal Diaz, published in English in five volumes in 1908 by the Hakluyt Society.
The total population of the Tlaxcalan region in 1568 was 165,000—Sherburne F. Cook and Woodrow Borah, *The Indian Population of Central Mexico 1531–1610*, Ibero-Americana: No. 44 (Berkeley, 1960), p. 67.

The red Flemish hat is mentioned by Bernal Diaz, 122 and 127; and the knightly scene of the mare's head presented on the point of a lance by Antonio de Solis, *Historia de la Conquista de Mexico*, 2 volumes (Madrid, 1783), I, 248.
Solis and most of the Spanish historians speak of the Tlaxcalan "Senate" and "Republic" and are followed in this by Prescott, but a note by Maudslay (Bernal Diaz, 122) gives a minority opinion: ". . . their form of government was much the same as that of other Nahua communities; but as they had achieved no foreign conquests, they were compelled to be self-supporting."
The Spaniards as "encantadores" are mentioned in Solis, *op. cit.*, 263.
The further quotations are from Bernal Diaz, 135.
Cortes gives his Cholula casualty figures in his *Five Letters*, cited above. Prescott, II, 39, sums up reports of 6,000 or more in most other accounts.

104 The remark re Cholula's factions is from Bernal Diaz, 179. The modern historian is Frans Blom

105 The quotation is from Cortes, *loc. cit.* For Juan Sedeño—Bernal Diaz, 39.
Malinal's 300 Tlaxcalan handmaidens is reported by Diego Muños Camargo, a native of Tlaxcala who wrote in the sixteenth century, frequently cited by Prescott from his manuscript, *Historia de Tlaxcala*, cited here in Prescott, I, 426.
Axayacatl's administration is usually dated 1469-1481. It was during his time that the famous "Aztec Calendar Stone" was carved.

106 Vaillant (251 seq.) says: "The downfall of the Aztecs cannot be explained in terms of European history, and the standard reasons give a false picture. Moctezuma, singled out by European authors as a weak and vacillating monarch, was a tribal leader devoid of the constitutional rights of a European sovereign. [For mass action he had to rely on the group decision of the clans comprising his tribe—234.] His empire is also a European creation, since it consisted, in reality, of communities sufficiently intimidated to pay tribute, but in no wise bound to Aztec governmental conventions. Warriors the Aztecs were, but not soldiers in the European sense. . . ."

707 The quotation is from Bernal Diaz, 309.
The Spanish sources generally report that Moctezuma was killed by his own people; the Indian version, as given for example to Sahagun (Book XII), was that the Spaniards killed Moctezuma and threw his body over the walls of their quarters. It seems unlikely they would have further straitened their straits by killing their hostage, but it is perhaps unlikely that if Moctezuma died of wounds—however inflicted—the Spaniards then in rage and frustration may well have thrown his body to the attacking Indians. See also Duran, *op. cit.*, Chapter LXXVI, 50.

108 Bernal Diaz, 293: ". . . and a very black affair it was for New Spain, for it was owing to him that the whole country was stricken and filled with it, from which there was great mortality. . . ."
Las Casas, *Historia*, III, Chapter CXXVIII, 270-271, describes the epidemic in Hispaniola, capping a generation of death and disaster: "I do not believe that 1000 souls can have escaped from this misery, out of the immensity of people our own eyes had once seen living in this island. . . ."
Bernal Diaz (352) mentions two faces flayed, the beards left on, offered on a temple altar—as well as four horse hides "with the hair on and the horse shoes. . . ."
The Florentine Codex (Sahagun, Book XII) pictures horse's heads included on the skull rack.

109 The quotations from Cortes are from the third of the *Five Letters*. His figures of Aztec losses would need to be enormously reduced (especially recalling the great previous losses from smallpox) to fit the 60,000 total Aztec population proposed in Sanders cited above, in note to page 130.
The streets of the city were (except for a few principal avenues) all of two lanes—one of hard earth like pavement, the other of water, "so that they can go out along the land or by water. . . ."—the Anonymous Conqueror, *op. cit.*
The quotation is from Vaillant, 254.
The poem is from Antonio Peñafiel, *MS Coleccion de Cantares Mexicanos*, National Library of Mexico, Folio 17; reprinted here from Caso.

110 Las Casas, *Historia*, mentions the common report that Solis was eaten, adding (III, Chapter LXXXIII, 105), that since no witnesses had lingered on the shore to watch, he wondered how they knew.

111 Alexander von Humboldt gives his estimate of the dollar value of the Inca's ransom, and other interesting calculations on New World wealth in *Essai Politique sur la Royaume de la Nouvelle Espagne*, 5 volumes (Paris, 1811), the reference taken here from Charles Howard Shinn, *Mining Camps: A Study in American Frontier Government* (New York, 1948), 47. Prescott, *Conquest of Peru*, I, 410-411 and *n.*, makes the amount nearer fifteen million.

NOTES for Chapter IV

General works used in this chapter are Prescott, *Mexico* and *Peru*; Vaillant; Martin, Quimby, and Collier; Swanton, 1953; Russell; Wormington; Hodge, *Handbook*; Kroeber, 1939 and 1948; Driver and Massey;

Hackett; McNickle; Steward, *Handbook*; Hammond and Rey, *Narratives*; Bolton, *Coronado*; Willey, 1966 and 1971; Driver, 1969; Oswalt; Sauer, 1971; Las Casas; Wauchope, *Handbook*; J. E. S. Thompson, 1970; Spicer, 1962; Bancroft; Bandelier; Roys, 1957; Parsons, 1939; Stevenson, 1904; Benedict, 1934 and 1936; Fenton, 1952; Shiels; Caso; Kurath;

and for page

114 Shiels, 13, *n.* 4: "Isabella . . alone had title to the Indies, having commissioned Columbus, guaranteed the contract, paid the royal contribution, issued orders for the voyage, and directed overseas development until her death in 1504."

Cortes was poor and in debt "although he had a good encomienda of Indians who were getting him a good return from his gold mines" and raised some money "secured on his Indians and estates." Bernal Diaz, 32–33. See Lesley Bird Simpson, *The Encomienda in New Spain* (Berkeley, 1929), and *Studies in the Administration of the Indians in New Spain* (Berkeley, 1934).

Las Casas recounts the Cuba story, its background, and its reduction, in II, 505–548 of his *Historia*.

115 The weapons of the Aztecs—in warfare the most successful people north of the Incas—were the *atlatl* or spear-thrower, sometimes double-barreled, which hurled with considerable force javelins with fire-hardened points; bows and arrows; slings; spears; and the *macana* or *maquahuitl*, often called by Bernal Diaz a broadsword, a flat blade of wood fitted along each edge with sharp bits of flint or obsidian. Thrown rocks and stones account for most of the casualties reported in the Mexican fighting, and, so says Bernal Diaz, 310, for the death of Moctezuma.

116 Leopold von Ranke, *The Ottoman and the Spanish Empires in the Sixteenth and Seventeenth Centuries* (original German edition, 1827; first English edition, London, 1843), is by some regarded as the first work using modern historical techniques. Ranke was to Europeans the foremost historian of his time, and a forerunner of the German vision of universal history mentioned previously in these notes. He was also the leading political conservative in the Prussian academia of his day, and was also the "Dryasdust" of Carlyle's *Frederick*: "The Prussian Dryasdust . . . He writes big books wanting in almost every quality. . . ."

118 It was to support a request for reward for their services that the Tlaxcalans prepared their famous picture history of the conquest, the *Lienzo de Tlaxcala*.

Bancroft, in *The Native Races* and in *The Conquest of Mexico*, presented the picture of an absolute Aztec monarchy, following in this the Spanish chroniclers. This view was attacked by Lewis Henry Morgan in *Montezuma's Dinner . . . etc.* (New York, 1876) (reprinted by the *Labor News*, New York, in 1950, with an Introduction by Eric Hass and reprinting a tribute by Friedrich Engels). Morgan depended chiefly on his researches among the Iroquois and other Indian groups in the area of the United States to dispute the concept of feudalism, aristocracy, kingship, and especially private ownership of real estate among the Aztecs. Bancroft responded with *The Early American Chroniclers* (San Francisco, 1883), citing the formidable list of his sources—sometimes with none too accurate comments, as when he describes Solis as the mainline source for Prescott, which is far from the case.

Adolph F. A. Bandelier published, in the meantime (1880), his three brilliant studies on the art of war, on the tenure and distribution of lands, and on the social organization and government of the ancient Mexicans. These studies supported Morgan's position. They were examined in detail and generally upheld by T. T. Waterman, *Bandelier's Contribution to Study of Ancient Mexican Social Organization*, University of California Publications in American Archaeology and Ethnology (Berkeley, 1916–1917).

More recent studies have emphasized the existence of inherited rank and military authoritarianism both among the Aztecs and the later Maya, who are presumed to reflect some Mexican ways; or have stressed the complexity of Indian governmental structures. These include such as the painstakingly detailed work by Roys, 1957, heavily depended upon by subsequent students. Similar points are emphasized in both Coe and Wolf in dealing with Mexico. A sample of a continuing rearguard action by what might be called the Old Liberals is John Collier's review of Wolf's *Sons of the Shaking Earth* in the *Saturday Review*, taking issue with what he terms "a bias toward totalitarian interpretation" in Wolf's thesis.

But by the 1960s the controversy had been turned into other lines by students who acknowledged the futility of trying to express Indian history in European terms and turned instead to analyses in the light of Indian thought and values. These include such as Seler and Vaillant and Caso, and the seminal works by Garibay and Leon-Portilla listed previously.

The recent authority quoted on the calpulli is Sanders in Wauchope, *Handbook*, vol. X, 14. The figure of sixty calpullec in Tenochtitlan, in contrast to Bandelier's twenty, is found on page 24.

Waterman, *loc. cit.*, mentions the Spaniards finding the same official bearing various titles.

119 The quotations are from Sahagun, Book VIII.

120 Caso, 117, describes religion "intervening" in all areas of life.

Tezozomoc, *op. cit.*, recounts Tlacaélel's role as Cihuacoatl—see von Winning, 1964, who remarks (50) on the "dual principle of life and the power that governs" thus symbolized by these two representatives (of the gods Quetzalcoatl-Cihuacoatl) who "functioned necessarily as a team, sharing equal powers. . . ." (51).

The idea of dualism in Indian government has been the subject of countless studies—see, for example, the important paper, dealing with areas far outside Mesoamerica, by William N. Fenton, "Factionalism in American Indian Society," in *Actes* du IVe Congrès International des Sciences Anthropologiques et Ethnologiques, II (Vienna, 1952), especially instructive in its reflections on the governments "inside the wall" and "outside the wall" at Taos Pueblo, New Mexico, in recent times. The "division of authority was complicated," as Roys (*loc. cit.*) remarked of the late Maya.

121 In colonial times several Aztec land claims were brought before the viceroy based on lands (or the proceeds therefrom) the claimants claimed were distributed by Tlacaélel, documented by a manuscript in picture-writing, the Codex Cozcatzin—see von Winning, 1964, 49.

Roys, 1957, finds "some evidence" that the hereditary aristocracy among the later Maya "all considered themselves to be descended from Mexican invaders (3)." He concludes that this class "had a preferred position in regard to the apportionment of land."

The tradition of the caciquedom and its perquisites remaining in a specific family is well documented in villages remote from the seats of broad political power—e.g., Sherburne Friend Cook, *Santa Maria Ixcatlan* (Berkeley, 1958), with its comments on the "Cacicazgo of Ixcatlan" in Appendix II, 73–75.

The classic study referred to is T. T. Waterman, *op. cit.*, who cites in corroboration a bristling array of early authorities.

122 The verse first quoted is from the song of Nezahualcoyotl referred to previously, 127. The quotation from the Tezcatlipoca sacrifice is from Sahagun, Book II, as adapted in my volume of American Indian poetry, *The Magic World* (New York, 1971).

The paraphrase of Boethius is drawn from C. S. Lewis, *The Discarded Image* (Cambridge University Press, 1964), 83.

The verses attributed to Virgil are from the *Copa Surisca*.

The Columbus quotation is from the first printed version of his letter to Luis de Santangel, cited previously.

Vallaint, 127, provides the quotation referring to individual liberty. The quotations on cooperative labor and cultural symbiosis are from William T. Sanders in Wauchope, *Handbook*, X, 16.

124 The obviously exaggerated figures of 20,000 to 80,000 sacrifices at one fell swoop are reported by Tezozomoc and Ixtlilxochitl and Duran, who all say 80,400; by Torquemada, in *Monarquia Indiana*, I, 186, as 72, 344; the *Codex Telleriano-Remensis*, translated by Paul Radin (Berkeley, 1920), gives 20,000; the commemoration stone seems to indicate 20,000, a figure accepted by Orozco y Berra, "Dedicación del Templo Mayor de Mexico," in *Anales Museo Nacional*, I, 61. Some say two files of victims, some four files, extending miles out along the causeways. Peterson, 101, settles for four files, each over three miles long, rather than a specific total. Prescott chooses an indeterminate number of files two miles long (I, 97). But Prescott does note an assertion by Las Casas that figures of this range are put forward as "the estimate of brigands, who wish to find an apology for their own atrocities" and that the total number of sacrifices yearly "was not above 50." (Quoted by Prescott from La Casas, *Oeuvres*, ed. Llorente, Paris, 1822, I, 365, 386.)

Sahagun reproduces a plan of the Tecpán, or temple enclosure, in Tenochtitlán (location of the Civic Center in modern Mexico City). This shows the twin temples on the great twin-topped pyramid, one temple dedicated to Tlaloc, the other to Huitzilopochtli, with twin altars, and even twin trails of blood staining the temple steps. It was at the dedication ceremonies for this great pyramid that the alleged multi–myriad sacrifices took place, and the concept of twin files of victims does seem to fit best with the picture of the twin altars at the twin temples as the focus of the action. There were, however, other temples within the Tecpán—Sahagun says a total of twenty-five—at which other sacrifices, presumably specialized, such as those at the temple of Xipe, could take place. A figure of 20,000 sacrifices for the great celebration of 1487 might be tolerable if all other temples in the city—better yet, all other temples in all the surrounding cities over the whole country—were assumed to be participating. For the ceremony as described in most accounts, though, the figure is clearly out of kilter with simple arithmetic.

Sherburne Friend Cook, "Human Sacrifice and Warfare as Factors in the Demography of Pre-Colonial Mexico," in *Human Biology*, 18/2 (May 1946), 81–102, makes an arithmetical calculation on the data, of the great sacrifice, allowing three minutes per sacrifice rather than the one minute I am willing to imagine (Dr. Cook being a professor of physiology). However, he opts for four lines of victims and four teams of priests, and also makes the assumption that the process was kept going day and night for four days—a total of ninety-six hours. This seems a highly questionable assumption, given the importance of offering the fresh-plucked hearts to the sun. Even with four files and around-the-clock operation, Cook's calculations can only produce 11,520 total victims. Applying his three-minute sacrificing time to my own calculations yields a grand total of 1,920, rather closer to 2,000 than 20,000.

In the same study, Cook offers interesting calculations based on the actual count of the skulls in Tenochtitlan's famous skull rack made by two of Cortes' soldiers—136,000 (Andres de Tapia, *Relación sobre la Conquista de Mexico*, ed. by J. Garcia Icazbalceta, Mexico, 1866, 583), with in addition two sizable "towers" made of skulls and bones. If the skulls in the rack were all collected in the years following the dedication of the great temple in 1487, they would indicate 4,250 sacrifices per year, including the large number, whatever it was, at the dedication (Cook, p 89). Or further guesses might be permissible: if kept since the last New Fire Ceremony (1507, fourteen years before), the average per year would be 9,785. Or, if kept for the approximate 200 years of Tenochtitlán's existence, the average would be some sixty-eight deaths per year.

125 Re the execution of Cuauhtémoc, a document recently found in the Archives of the Indies at Seville—a petition of 1612 from the then Chontal ruler for a pension because of his grandfather's services in 1525 in refusing Cuauhtémoc's invitation to join in a conspiracy against the Spanish invaders and, instead informing Cortes of their plan, seems to support Cortes' side of the story (Morley and Brainerd, 115). The marriage of Tecuichpo to Don Thoan Cano is mentioned by Cano in Appendix II, No. 11, Prescott, *Mexico*, III, 384, 391. *Ibid.*, 250, Marina's marriage. Tecuichpo lived to wed two other grandees of Spain.

126 The two lines quoted are from Tozzer, *Landa*; and from Maud W. Makemson, *The Book of the Jaguar Priest* (New York, 1951).

127 Sherburne Friend Cook and Lesley Bird Simpson, *The Population of Central Mexico in the Sixteenth Century* (Berkeley, 1948); S. F. Cook and Woodrow Wilson Borah, *The Indian Populations of Central Mexico, 1531–1610* (Berkeley, 1960); and Borah and Cook, *The Aboriginal Population of Central Mexico on the Eve of the Spanish Conquest* (Berkeley, 1963) are the recent and detailed Aztec population studies referred to.
The middle-of-the-road guesses of a few years ago reflect the figures of Angel Rosenblat, *La Población Indigena y el Mestizaje en América*, vol. I (Buenos Aires, 1954).
Population estimates revised upward by the work of Cook and Borah (who approach 100 million for the hemisphere) are favorably reviewed by Henry F. Dobyns, "Estimating Aboriginal American Population, an Appraisal of Techniques with a New Hemisphere Estimate," in *Current Anthropology* (October 1966), 395–449, who extends the projections of Cook and Borah to the area north of Mexico and obtains nearly ten million thereby. However, his base figure, taken from Rosenblat, is in gross error, as was pointed out by Harold Driver in comments to the Dobyns article in the same issue of *Current Anthropology*; correcting this base figure, the nadir of Indian population in the area of the United States, Driver thereby adjusts Dobyns' figure downward to some four million for aboriginal North America north of Mexico, which figure Driver finds acceptable. MacLeod, writing in 1927, estimated a north-of-Mexico population of three million, after careful study of early East Coast reports (MacLeod, 16).
A bit of information perhaps of some interest in estimating population in certain regions is found in Francis La Flesche, *A Dictionary of the Osage Language*, BAE Bulletin 109 (Washington, 1932), which includes a number of common sayings taken from a primer of 1834, phrases such as, "Who do you suppose instructs the birds how to build their nests . . .?" or "Wherever you are and whatever you do God sees you. . . ." Among these are, "There are not many men these days [1834] who can kill forty deer a season. . . ." and, "Formerly men killed two hundred deer apiece. . . ." Lewis and Clark gave the Osage some 1200 to 1300 warriors in the three bands (Great and Little Osage and the Arkansas band); Mooney, whose figures are now being revised drastically upward for the country as a whole, estimated total Osage population for 1780 as 6,200 (James Mooney, *The Aboriginal Population of America North of Mexico*, Smithsonian Miscellaneous Collections, 80:7, Washington, 1928), yielding a number of heads of family about equal to the Lewis and Clark estimate. At two hundred deer per season per man this would give a deer-kill of 240,000 to 260,000—compare the 200,000 deerskins shipped each year from Charleston in the 1730s (see notes for p. 350, Chapter IX, below). Upward revision of population estimates for the region—embracing large parts of Missouri and Arkansas—would presumably entail a proportionate enlargement of the deer-kill, if these reading-book phrases are to be taken seriously as conveying any real information.
The earliest Cochise stage, called Sulphur Springs, gives radio-carbon dates of about 7350 to 6270 B.C., seemingly a little late in the day for the mammoth bones on the scene, so perhaps "the mammoth lingered on in southern Arizona to a relatively late period"—Willey, 1966, p 58.

129 The quotation referring to the canals is from Schoolcraft.

130 The Pima description of a magician's house is from Russell, 356.
Ibid., 353, 356, 362, for the quotations here.
Russell's work on the Pima is noteworthy for its magnificent translations. For Papago ethnography, see Ruth Murray Underhill, *Social Organization of the Papago Indians* (New York, 1939) and *Papago Indian Religion* (New York, 1946).
It should be mentioned that some archaeologists argue an invasion and conquest from Mesoamerica, rather than gradual peaceful diffusion of the Mesoamerican elements among the Hohokam—see Willey, 1966, 235, 236, 237. The more generally accepted reconstruction stems mainly from such as H. S. Gladwin, *Excavations at Snaketown IV: Reviews and Conclusions* (Globe, Ariz., 1948); E. W. Haury, *et al.*, *The Stratigraphy and Archaeology of Ventana Cave, Arizona* (Albuquerque, 1950); and E. W. Haury, "The Greater American Southwest," in R. J. Braidwood and G. R. Willey, eds., *Courses Toward Urban Life* (New York, 1962), 106–131.

131 The quotation is from Irving Rouse in Steward, ed., *Handbook*, IV, 552.

132 The testimony of the early explorer is in Ruy Diaz de Guzmán, *La Argentina: Historia de las Provincias del Rio de la Plata . . .*, found in vol. IX of Anales de la Biblioteca Nacional (Buenos Aires, 1914) and cited by Metraux in Steward, ed., *Handbook*, III, 467. Reginalda de Lizarraga, in *Descripción . . . del Rio de la Plata . . .* in the Nueva Biblioteca de Autores Españoles, vol. XV (Madrid, 1909), 552, estimates that during the sixteenth century the Guarani (or Chiriguano) had eaten some 60,000 Chané. The Chané, also known as Chaná or Guaná, were also described by Ulrich Schmidel, the earliest source for the region (a soldier of fortune under Pedro de Mendoza and other explorers) as "peaceful farmers" who had been subjugated by the roving Mbaya (this was in another part of the forest) and—long before their discovery by the Spaniards—"reduced to a condition of vassalage. Each Guaná village was subordinate to a Mbayá band." Schmidel, *Viaje al Rio de la Plata (1534–1544)* (Buenos Aires, 1903), 252.

133 Kroeber (1948) mentions the mounting evidence that everyone's head seems to be getting rounder all the time (128). Willey (1966) speaks of the same trend, "possibly . . . of a general evolutionary nature" (15).
A recent study of the Anasazi is Jesse D. Jennings and Eric K. Reed, "The American Southwest: A Problem in Cultural Isolation," in *Seminars in Archaeology: 1955*, R. Wauchope, ed. (Salt Lake City, 1956).
The dates come from tree-ring dating as given in Martin, Quimby, and Collier, 48–49, who use the work of A. E. Douglass; and in Wormington, 1959, who in noting the last building date we have for Mesa Verde (1273) remarks that the great houses may have been occupied for some time thereafter, the final departure probably coming any time within the great drought period, 1276–1299 (86).
As in the case of Old Oraibi, where Dr. Douglass was not able to find a beam predating the years 1260–1344, which however does not necessarily mean there was no community there previously. "On the basis of pottery types, we can say that Oraibi was founded on Third Mesa in the mid-twelfth century . . . and Shungopovi on Second Mesa at least within the next hundred years . . . According to the traditions of Shungopovi and Oraibi, Shungopovi is slightly older than Oraibi. . . ." Florence Hawley Ellis, 61 of an unpublished manuscript analyzing Pueblo myths in relation to the comings and goings of peoples in the Southwest, prepared in conjunction with the Wetherill Mesa Archaeological Project carried out at Mesa Verde, Colorado, under the direction of Douglas Osborne, from 1959 to 1965.
In this same study Ellis reviews linguistic and other indications of Pueblo relationships that suggest the Anasazi ancestors of the Hopi began moving into the general Pueblo area perhaps some 2,000 years ago (60).

135 Various arrow releases are charted in Driver and Massey, 353–355, and Map 140, 354, based on Edward S. Morse, "Ancient and Modern Methods of Arrow-release" in *Bulletin of the Essex Institute*, 17 (Salem, 1885), 145–189; and A. L. Kroeber, "Arrow Release Distributions," in *University of California Publications in American Archaeology and Ethnology*, 23 (Berkeley, 1927), 283–296.
A theory emphasizing the weakness or unwieldiness of Pueblo social structure when applied to large communities is suggested in Mischa Titiev, *Old Oraibi: A Study of the Hopi Indians of the Third Mesa*, Papers of the Peabody Museum of American Archaeology and Ethnology, 22/1 (Cambridge, Mass., 1944). Pueblo organization has apparently never operated on a multi-town basis, with the exception of the period of the 1680 revolt (Willey, 1966, 218).

136 The quotation is from Schoolcraft.
The Puebloans resident for several generations among the Hohokam are given the name Salado by archaeologists—Willey, 1966, 228: ". . . there are signs that they actually moved into the same sites and communities with the Hohokam. The two societies, with their distinctive brands of Southwestern culture, lived side by side in apparent peace for more than a century."
Martin, Quimby, and Collier, 189: ". . . while living together, each group conserved its own way of life, each adopting little from the other . . . This is truly astonishing."
Some typical Pueblo recipes and foods are in Wilfred William Robbins, John Peabody Harrington, and Barbara Freire-Marreco, *Ethnobotany of the Tewa Indians*, BAE Bulletin 55 (Washington, 1916).

137 Reginald G. Fisher, "An Outline of Pueblo Government," in Donald B. Brand, ed., *So Live the Works of Men* (Albuquerque, 1939), 148: "In giving a picture of Pueblo government, the greater amount of attention must be directed to the priestly offices . . ."
The line quoted is from Robbins, Harrington, and Freire-Marreco, cited above, 83.

139 Carl O. Sauer, an expert both in geography and the people of northwestern Mexico, studies the question of Fray Marcos in *The Road to Cibola*, Ibero-Americana No. 3 (Berkeley, 1932), and in "The Discovery of New Mexico Reconsidered," in *New Mexico Historical Review*, 12/3 (July, 1937), 270–288; and in the same journal in "The Credibility of the Fray Marcos Account," 16/2, (April 1941). This same issue contains a note by Lansing B. Bloom, "Was Fray Marcos a Liar?" while in Volumes IX and X (1934 and 1935) another specialist is heard from, with Henry Raup Wagner, "Fray Marcos de Niza" and "A 'Fray Marcos de Niza' Note."
The quotations on this and the preceding page are found in Bolton, 1949.
Frederick Webb Hodge, *History of Hawikuh, New Mexico* (Los Angeles, 1937) gives a close look at Zuñi-Cibola.
The reported number of pueblos is found in Hammond and Rey, *Narratives*, which also reports eight plazas at Pecos rather than the five archaeologists accept.

140 The lines from Castañeda are found in F. W. Hodge, ed., "The Narrative of the Expedition of Coronado by Pedro de Castañeda" in *Spanish Explorers in the Southern United States*, 1528–1543 (New York, 1907).

141 A good many variations on tribal names are listen in Swanton, 1953; while Spicer, 1962, includes a list of equivalent tribal names from the Southwest.
The description of the lay brother left at Pecos is from the "Relación del Suceso," in Hammond and Rey, *Narratives*, 294; of the mission party to the plains from Juan de Jaramillo in the same volume, 306–307; and the picture of Do Campo arriving in New Spain is from Bolton, *Coronado*, 359.
There are shadowy reports of a third missionary; and a few Indians from Mexico also remained.

142 The 1581 expedition, led by Fray Agustin Rodriguez, is related in George Hammond and Agapito Rey, editors and translators, *Obregon's History of Sixteenth-century Explorations in Western America* (Los Angeles, 1928), 272 *et seq.* The unauthorized expedition of de Sosa is detailed in Dorothy Hull, "Castaño de Sosa's Expedition to New Mexico in 1590," in *Old Santa Fe*, 3/12 (October 1916), 307–332. The intrusions of further freebooters of the same period are in H. E. Bolton, *Spanish Exploration in the Southwest, 1542–1706* (New York, 1916), 201 *n.* and 218; and in Bancroft, *Arizona and New Mexico*, 108–109.

143 George P. Hammond and Agapito Rey, eds., *Don Juan de O ate, Colonizer of New Mexico, 1595–1628* (Albuquerque, 1953), consists of two volumes of documents with a brief introduction; the line quoted is from II, 850. The usual number of converts given in the reports is 400, but witnesses at Oñate's trial testified to fifty to eighty; theologians of the Council of the Indies were considering whether to abandon these converts or bring them forcibly to Mexico when came word of thousands of converts, and New Mexico was retained in the Spanish empire.

144 The prerevolutionary details are in France V. Scholes, "Civil Government and Society in New Mexico in the Seventeenth Century," in *New Mexico Historical Review*, 10 (April, 1935); "Troublous Times in New Mexico, 1659–1670," in the same journal, 12, 13, 15, 16 (1937, 1938, 1940, 1941); and *Church and State in New Mexico in the Seventeenth Century* (Cambridge, Mass., 1943).
Hackett is the source for the quotations, and the quoted words on the preceding page.

145 Robbins, Harrington, and Freire-Marreco, *op. cit.*, discuss (8) the shortage of classificatory names for plants among the Tewa.
Quotations are from De Vargas, *Journal of an expedition to the Moqui Provinces*, November 1692, MS RI 21 in the Ritch Collection, Henry E. Huntington Library, San Marino, California.

NOTES for Chapter V

General works used in this chapter are Steward, *Handbook*; Hodge, *Handbook*; Wauchope, *Handbook*; McLeod; McNickle; Hanke, 1949; Peter Martyr; Driver; Cook and Borah, 1960; Foster; Brebner; Bridges;

and for page

148 The forty years' wars of the neo-Inca are detailed in George Kubler, "The Quechua in the Colonial World" in Steward, *Handbook*, vol. II, 331–410; and "A Peruvian Chief of State: Manco Inca," in *Hispanic American Historical Review*, 24 (1944), 253–276.

149 Karsten, 1923, previously mentioned (in notes for Chapter II, 119), gives a full description of the ceremonies associated with the preparation of the "tsantsa," the trophy head, among the Jivaro.
Wars with the tough Araucanians furnish the theme of Alonso de Ercilla y Zuniga's epic poem, *Araucana* (1569–1590), of genuine historical interest (he was there) but unfortunately—having been praised by Cervantes and Voltaire—regarded by generations of Spanish schoolteachers as of high literary value and perforce taught to generations of long-suffering schoolchildren.

151 The 33,000 head of cattle are mentioned in Herbert E. Bolton and Thomas M. Marshall, *The Colonization of North America 1492–1783* (New York, 1920), 58.
The quotation is from Richard J. Morrissey, "The Northward Expansion of Cattle Ranching in New Spain, 1550–1600," in *Agricultural History*, 25/3 (1951), 120. Also see Philip W. Powell, *Soldiers, Indians, and Silver; The Northward Advance of New Spain 1550–1600* (Berkeley, 1952).

152 The Sierra Azul hasn't yet been found in Hopi country but appears in Don Carlos de Sigüenza y Gongora, *Mercurio Volante con la Noticia de la Recuperación de las Provincias del Nuevo Mexico . . . (An Account of the First Expedition of Don Diego de Vargas into New Mexico in 1692,)* first published 1693, translated and edited, with an introduction by Irving Albert Leonard (Los Angeles, 1932).
Also see José M. Espinosa, "Legend of Sierra Azul," in *New Mexico Historical Review*, 9/2 (April 1934), 113–159.

153 Robert Hale Shields, "The Enchanted City of the Caesars, Eldorado of Southern South America," in *Greater America, Essays Presented to H. E. Bolton* (Berkeley, 1945), introduces the Land of the Caesars; the same author's voluminous collection of Césarista material in the Bancroft Library, Berkeley, will furnish further information for those who may want to keep on looking.

One of the Chicoreans shanghaied to Santo Domingo later turned up in Europe and gave Peter Martyr, the first historian of the New World, his information on the people of the Floridas.

155 The Alvar Nuñez Cabeza de Vaca narrative, translated by Buckingham Smith, is in F. W. Hodge and Theordore H. Lewis, eds., *Explorers of the Southern United States 1528–1543* (New York, 1907); the same volume contains the narrative of the expedition of Hernando de Soto by the Gentleman of Elvas. A wealth of detail is in *Final Report of the U. S. De Soto Expedition Commission*, 76th Congress, 1st Session, House Document 71 (Washington, 1939). Attention should also be called to the work of semi-fiction based on the Alvar Nuñez story, *Interlinear to Cabeza de Vaca*, by the poet Haniel Long. Oviedo first recorded Alvar Nuñez Cabeza de Vaca's tale of the four castaways—Gonzalo Fernandex de Oviedo Valdes, *Historia General de las Indias*, published in part in the sixteenth century but not in a complete edition until 1851–1855, where the Nuñez story is told in Book XXXV, Chapters 1–7. Alvar Nuñez' own *Relación* was first published in Spain in 1542, with added material evidently filched by the publisher from early reports of the Coronado expedition, and remained a prized article of equipment for northering explorers for years to come.

156 Montaigne is quoted from Edward Dowden, *Michel de Montaigne* (Philadelphia, 1906), vol. III, 144. The last surviving Conquistador in 1589 was said to be Mancio Serra (who had received for his share of the loot the image of the sun from the Temple at Cuzco, and lost it instanter in a card game): Hanke, 1949

157 Brother Bernadino is quoted from Lewis Hanke, "Pope Paul III and the American Indian," in *Harvard Theological Review*, vol. XXX (1937), 65–102.
The quoted opponent of Las Casas is Fray Toribio de Benavente, called Motolinía, in his *Memorial* to Charles V (in *Colección de Documentos Ineditos, Relativos al Descubremiento, Conquista y Organización de las Antiguas Posesiones Espa oles de América y Oceania, sacados de los Archivos del Reino, y muy especialmente del de Indias*, 42 vols. (Madrid, 1864–1884), vol. VII, 262–263.) (A following series of the same title but ending in *Posesiones Espanoles de Ultramar* was issued in 25 vols. [Madrid, 1885–1932]. Ernst Schafer, *Indice de Documentos Inéditos de Indias*, 2 vols. [Madred, 1946–1947] is an index to both series.) The debate between Las Casas and Sepulveda is the subject of Lewis Hanke's fine study, *Aristotle and the American Indians* (New York, 1959; Bloomington, Indiana, 1970). The specific point of the debate is quoted from the 1970 (paperback) edition, page 41, and the quotations from Las Casas from pages 112 and 113. Spain's zenith of glory is from Américo Castro, *The Structure of Spanish History* (Princeton, 1954), 190.

159 Lewis Hanke, *The Spanish Struggle for Justice in the Conquest of America* (Philadelphia, 1949), discusses in detail the various laws regulating discovery and conquest, from the famous "Requirement" of 1513 onward. Also, for a general statement of Spain's Indian policy, see Philip W. Powell, *Tree of Hate* (New York, 1971).
Population figures are from the report of the official geographer, Lopez de Velasco, and quotations on the population decline are from Cook and Borah, 1960, 50. Cook and Borah (their documentary research "is a model of critical handling of materials"—Harold E. Driver, in *Current Anthropology*, 7/4 [October 1966], 430) working in the main from tribute rolls, give a probable decline in Mexico (exclusive of the Maya country and the northern frontier) from a possible twenty-five million on the eve of the Conquest to 16,871,408 in 1532; 1,891,267 in 1580; to a nadir of 1,069,255 in 1605 (Cook and Borah, 1960, Table 6, 48).
The gross estimates in my text here have been rounded out from 6,300,000 (Kroeber, 1939), and 71,243,000 to 89,053,000 in Henry F. Dobyns, "Estimating Aboriginal Indian Population, An Appraisal of Techniques with a New Hemisphere Estimate," in *Current Anthropology*, 7/4 (October 1966), 395–499. Driver, 1969, examines Dobyns' conclusions anew and, pointing out a gross error in a nadir figure for the United States area, cuts his estimate for that area by about half (63–65).
Albornoz is quoted from Hanke, 1970, 80.
To quote a contemporary source other than Las Casas, namely his bitter foe Motolinia: to count the dead in the ruined lands of the Caribbean was to count the drops of rain or the sand in the sea—and the bodies of those killed by "service" at Oaxaca literally covered the earth for a mile around, and the sky was dark with scavenging birds—from Hanke, 1970, 22, quoting Luis Nicolau d'Olwer, *Fray Toribio de Benavente*, 195 and 65.

160 Woodrow Wilson Borah, "Silk Cultures in Colonial Mexico," in *Greater America* (Berkeley, 1945): "The whole population of one town entered the conspiracy and between nightfall and dawn chopped down every mulberry tree within its limits. Eggs, silk houses, reeling apparatus, skilled workmen—all the preparation of years—became useless . . ." But the "greatest disaster which befell Mexican silk culture" was the rapid decline of the Indian population from European pestilences "to numbers inadequate to supply the needed labor." See also, for an excellent general study of the period, Charles Gibson, *The Aztecs Under Spanish Rule, A History of the Indians of the Valley of Mexico 1519–1810*.

161 Brebner, *The Explorers of North America*, furnishes the quotation.
The Spanish move into Florida is detailed in Woodbury Lowery, *Spanish Settlements within the Present Limits of the United States 1513–1561* (New York, 1911).

Clifford Merle Lewis and Albert J. Loomie, *The Spanish Mission in Virginia, 1570–1572* (Chapel Hill, 1953), give documents and translation.

162 Or even priests inciting Indians against other priests. Lesley Bird Simpson, *Many Mexicos* (New York, 1941), 83, 84: The Franciscan friars, complained the Dominican Archbishop Montifar in 1559, "were inciting the Indians to riot against the secular priests and driving them out of the villages."

163 Louis B. Wright, *Gold, Glory, and the Gospel* (New York, 1970), 273, "Modern economic historians do not agree that American bullion was the mainstay of Spain's finances; they point out that other commodities brought from the New World and the market for Spanish goods in her overseas colonies make a more substantial basis for prosperity in the Iberian peninsula. Raleigh also realized that Spanish trade to the New World was essential to that country's well being, and he thought English colonies in Guiana would help to 'impeach' that trade. . . ." But see, cited by Wright on the same page, Sir Walter Raleigh, *The Discoverie of the Large, Rich, Beautiful Empyre of Guiana, with a relation of the great and Golden Citie of Manoa (which the Spanyards call El Dorado . . . Performed in the yeare 1595* (London 1596), from the preface epistle "To the Reader": ". . . But if we now consider of the actions both of Charles the fifte, who had the Maydenhead of Peru, and the abundant treasures of Atabalipa, together with the affaires of the Spanish king now living, what territories he hath purchased, what he hath added to the actes of his predecessors, how many kingdoms he hath indangered, how many armies, garrisons, and navies, he hath and doth maintaine, the greate shippes with their artillery, and that no yere is less unfortunate but that many vessels, treasures, and people are devoured, and yet notwithstanding he beginneth againe like a storme to threaten shipwracke to us all, we shall find that these abilities rise not from the trades of sackes [sherry], and Civil [Seville] Oranges, nor from out else that either Spaine, Portugal, or any of his other provinces produce: It is his Indian Golde that indaungereth and disturbeth all the nations of Europe, it purchaseth intelligence, creepeth into Councels, and setteth bound loyalty at libertie, in the greatest Monarchies of Europe." Raleigh, who eventually lost his fortune and literally his head over Guiana anticipated in this same epistle to an earlier reader that that Empyre of Guiana "shall suffice to inable her Majesty, and the whole kingdome, with no lesse quantities of treasure, then the king of Spayne hath in all the Indies. . . ."
Spain's economic troubles are neatly outlined and put in European context in Will and Ariel Durant, *The Age of Reason Begins* (New York, 1961), from which have also been drawn the figures re Hawkins' slave-run of 1564 (31, 32).
R. B. Cunninghame Graham, *The Conquest of the River Plate* (London, 1924), is the source of the beautiful phrase on pampas streams. In the same work Cunninghame Graham notes that a name sometimes applied to the City of the Caesars, Trapalanda, is really the name of the "paradise of the wandering Indians of the Pampa, where, in the Milky Way, they hunted ostriches, whose feathers, floating through the sky, formed the Magellan Clouds" (261). Trapalanda as the City of the Caesars is eternal, says Cunninghame Graham, "and deserves to be so if only for the beauty of the name. . . ." (264).

NOTES for Chapter VI

General works used in this chapter are Le Page du Pratz; Swanton, 1946 and 1953; Hodge, *Handbook*; MacLeod; Martin, Quimby, and Collier; Kroeber, 1939; Driver and Massey; Underhill; Spencer and Jennings; Oswalt;

and for page

165 The question of Adena-Hopewell agriculture—or its absence—is a lively one, as Willey, 1966, 268; and Spencer and Jennings, 66, make clear.
Schoolcraft is the source of the 1790 quotation.

166 Paul Radin, in *The Story of the American Indian* (New York, 1927, 1934, 1944) pictured a sea route from Vera Cruz to the lower Mississippi (155), an idea perhaps now finding a little more support among the experts than formerly.
The quotation is from Spencer and Jennings, 71.

167 The erudite traveler quoting Ariosto was Baron Armand Lahontan, *New Voyages to North-America, etc. . . . Done into English. In Two Volumes.* (London, 1703), vol. I, 234.
The great battle with de Soto was in defense of a fortified village on the west bank of the Mobile River a few miles below the forks of the Tombigbee and Alabama (Swanton, 1953, 159). The Spaniards took the town with heavy losses on both sides—claiming 2,500 Indian casualties.

168 Swanton, *Myths and Tales of the Southeastern Indians*, BAE Bulletin 88 (Washington, 1929), tells the story of the heavenly canoe.

170 Herbert Landar, *The Tribes and Languages of North America: A Checklist* (Center for Applied Linguistics, Washington, D.C., 1972), gives "Nah-tchi" for the native pronunciation.

173 The quotations here and on pages 174 through 179 are all drawn from Le Page du Pratz.

The five dependable accounts are assessed in detail—Le Page du Pratz taking first place—in Swanton, 1946.

179 The English account is James Adair, *The History of the American Indians* (London, 1775; Johnson City, Tenn., 1930).

Charles Edward O'Neill, *Church and State in French Colonial Louisiana, Policy and Politics to 1732* (New Haven, 1966), gives the name as d'Echepare.

The five dependable accounts are assessed in detail—Le Page du Pratz taking first place—in Swanton, 1946.

NOTES for Chapter VII

General works used in this chapter are *Jesuit Relations*; Driver; Willey, 1966; Jacobs, 1972; Oswalt; Jenness; MacLeod; Swanton, 1953; Hodge, *Handbook*; Kroeber, 1939 and 1949; Driver and Massey; Martin, Quimby and Collier; Schoolcraft; Underhill; Sauer, 1971; Lafitau;

and for page

182 For the trickster god see a new edition of Paul Radin, *The Trickster, A Study in American Indian Mythology*, with Commentary by Karl Kerenyi and C. G. Jung and a new Introduction by Stanley Diamond (New York, 1972).

The Irish comparison is from William Wood, *New Englands Prospect, A True, Lively, and Experimentall Description of that part of America, commonly called New England; Discovering the State of that Countrie, Both as it Stands to our Newcome English Planters; and to the old Native Inhabitants . . .* (London, 1634).

183 The quotation is from Thomas Hariot, *Narrative of the First English Plantation of Virginia* (London, 1588 and 1590, reprint, 1893), quoted here from John Pinkerton, *A General Collection of the Best and Most Interesting Voyages and Travels in all parts of the World . . .*, 17 vols. (London, 1808–1814), vol. XII, 613.

Hariot was with a supply squadron sent out by Sir Walter Raleigh to the colony of Roanoke, founded the year before, and fated to vanish a year or two or three later.

The best known early look at the people of the middle Atlantic coast has recently been given a sumptuous new edition in Paul Hope Hulton and David Beors Quinn, *The American Drawings of John White, 1577–1590*, 2 vols. (London, 1964), vol. I being a catalogue raisonné and a study of the artist (whose granddaughter was Virginia Dare of the lost Roanoke colony), and vol. II, reproductions of the originals, pictures (as White stated in his autograph title) "of sondry things collected and counterfeited . . . in the voyage made by Sir Walter Raleigh knight, for the discovery of LA Virginea. In the 27th yeare of the most happie reigne of our Soveraigne lady Queene Elizabeth and in the yeare of ye Lorde God, 1585."

184 The quotations from Will Wood here and on page 259 are from his *New Englands Prospect*, mentioned above.

Thomas Morton is quoted from *The New English Canaan . . .* (1637).

For a number of recent discussions of Indian woodland "war" see the note to page 308, Chapter VIII, below. Sauer, 1971, remarks in general of early (sixteenth-century) war reports: "Occasionally an Indian tribe was said to be an enemy of another, but there was no record of serious hostility such as warring for possession of territory" (304).

186 Captain John Smith's map shows and names more than 160 of the nearly 200 Powhatan villages—John Smith, *Works*, ed. by Edward Arber (Birmingham, Eng., 1884).

187 William Strachey, *The Historie of Travaille into Virginia Britannia, Expressing the Cosmographie and Comodities of the Country, Together with the Manners and Customs of the People*, Hakluyt Society Publication, vol. VI (London, 1849).

The considerable public works of the Hopewell people—for example, mounds and enclosures evidently serving as religious centers for numbers of surrounding small villages, might seem to indicate some form of fairly involved social organization, the most reasonable supposition being a confederacy.

Martin, Quimby, and Collier, speculate (266) that the previous "Adena culture contained the seeds of city-state confederacy, a style of government found in later cultures in the Mississippi Valley," and (277) "surmise that the Hopewell Indians were bound together in a loose confederacy that extended from Kansas to New York and from the Gulf of Mexico to Wisconsin."

188 Captain John Smith is quoted, first, from MacLeod, 177–178; second from "A True Relation" written in 1608, reprinted in Lyon G. Tyler, *Narratives of Early Virginia, 1606–1625* (New York, 1907), 32–38.

Captain Smith had the bright idea of selling protection to the Indians by occupying their chief village on the excuse of defending it from the Siouan peoples of the piedmont (the reason for the village's defensive stockade), Powhatan paying tribute to the Englishmen for this. The package deal was to include sale of corn to the English at the price of an inch square of copper for a bushel. But this excellent offer "did those furies refuse," wrote Captain Smith. Said Powhatan: "I can revenge my own injuries" (*Proceedings*, in Arber, ed., *Works*).

189 Captain Smith is quoted from the dedication to his *Generall Historie of Virginia* (written 1616); an excerpt regarding Pocahontas is in Tyler, 1907, 326–327.
The John Rolfe letter is printed (correctly, previous printings being corrupt) in the *Virginia Magazine* for 1914.
The best of her hundred poets is Hart Crane, in whose American vision of *The Bridge* Pocahontas is the chiefest heroine; and the pretty cartwheeling picture from Strachey serves as her introduction in part II.
The most ambitious of her hundred failed novelists is (so far) the otherwise excellent David Garnett, with *Pocahontas or the Nonpareil of Virginia* (London, 1933). Philip Young, "The Mother of Us All: Pocahontas Reconsidered" in *Kenyon Review*, 24/3 (Summer, 1962), sums up what might be called the major lines of the Pocahontas literature.
Philip L. Barbour, *Pocahontas and Her World* (Boston, 1970), echoes contemporary anti-Indian prejudice—see the review by Wilbur R. Jacobs in *New York Historical Quarterly*, 55 (1971), 188–189. The same author's well-received biography of Captain Smith, tackling all the long-standing questions of Smith's veracity or lack of same, is Barbour, *The Three Worlds of Captain John Smith* (Boston, 1954).

190 Ben Jonson is quoted from *Staple of News* (1625).
MacLeod summarizes the background and origin of the colonizing joint-stock companies of North America, 131–143.
Peckham is quoted from William Warren Sweet, *The Story of Religion in America* (New York, 1939).
Sir Ferdinando Gorges, *America Painted to the Life, etc. . . .* (London, 1659).

191 The verses quoted are from Sir John Beaumont, "The Metamorphosis of Tobacco"—dedicated to Michael Drayton. Spenser, however, went even a little farther, calling it "our holy herb nicotian."
Tobacco drunkenness is quoted from Père du Creux, *History of Canada*, cited in Lafitau, vol. II, 113–142.

192 Algonquian terms for Englishmen are taken from James Hammond Trumbull, *Natick Dictionary*, BAE Bulletin 25 (Washington, 1903), page 183.
American Anthropologist, 9/1 (1907), a special issue on early Virginia, contains David I. Bushnell, "Virginia, from Early Records"; Charles C. Willoughby, "The Virginia Indians in the Seventeenth Century"; James Mooney, "The Powhatan Confederacy, Past and Present"; and other articles dealing with the period.
James Mooney, in Hodge, *Handbook*: "The Indians were generally friendly until driven to hostility by the exactions of the whites"—vol. I, 300.
See also David I. Bushnell, "The Native Tribes of Virginia," in *Virginia Magazine of History and Biography* for 1922; and Frank G. Speck, "Chapters of the Ethnology of the Powhatan Tribes of Virginia," in *Indian Notes and Monographs*, Museum of the American Indian, Heye Foundation (New York, 1928), vol. I, 227–335.

194 Opechancanough's knowledge of the Enclish civil war is discussed in MacLeod, 231, citing *A Perfect Description of Virginia . . . 1649* from the *Force Tracts*, vol. II.
Hodge, *Handbook*, vol. II, 139, advances the omen theory.
The quotation is from Andrew Burnaby, *Travels Through the Middle Settlements in North America* (London, 1775), 31–32, in this excerpt reprinted in Paul M. Angle, ed., *The American Reader* (New York, 1958), 55.

195 Recent studies of colonial attitudes toward Indians include Nancy Oestreich Lurie, "Indian Cultural Adjustment to European Civilization," in James Morton Smith, ed., *Seventeenth Century America, Essays in Colonial History* (Chapel Hill, 1959), 33–60; and Wilcomb E. Washburn, "The Moral and Legal Justification for Dispossession of the Indians" in the same volume, 15–32, this piece later expanded into a book, *Red Man's Land, White Man's Law* (New York, 1971). Also, Wilbur R. Jacobs, "British-Colonial Attitudes and Policies Toward the Indian in the American Colonies," in Howard Peckham and Charles Gibson, eds., *Attitudes of Colonial Powers toward the American Indian* (Salt Lake City, 1969), 81–107—this essay is also included in Jacobs, 1972.
The figures on the Tuscarora expeditions are from the article by J. N. B. Hewitt in Hodge, *Handbook*, vol. II, 845–846.

196 The tradition of the antiquity of the Nanticoke confederacy is quoted from the Maryland *Archives*, Proceedings of the Council for 1636–7, 503, by James Mooney and Cyrus Thomas in Hodge, *Handbook*, vol. II, 25.
A recent work on the Delaware migration record is *Walam Olum, or Red Score: The Migration Legend of the Lenni Lenape or Delaware Indians*, Indiana Historical Society (Indianapolis, 1954).
Daniel G. Brinton offered a translation of the Walam Olum in vol. V, *The Lenapé and Their Legends*, of his Library of Aboriginal American Literature, 6 vols. (Philadelphia, 1882–1885).

E. G. Squier, "Traditions of the Algonquins," in W. W. Beach, ed., *The Indian Miscellany: Containing Papers on the History, Antiquities, Arts, Languages, Religions, Traditions and Superstitions of the American Aborigines* (Albany, 1877), speaks of finding among the papers of C. S. Rafinesque—one of the more extraordinary of early nineteenth-century characters—a manuscript "entitled the Walum Olum (literally, painted sticks), or painted and engraved traditions of the Lenni-Lenape . . . This manuscript also embraces one hundred and eighty-four compound mnemonic symbols, each accompanied by a sentence or verse in the original language, of which a translation is given in English. The only explanation which we have concerning it, is contained in a foot note, in the hand of Rafinesque, in which he states that the manuscript and wooden originals were obtained in Indiana in 1822, and that they were for a long time inexplicable, 'until with a deep study of the Delaware, and the aid of Zeisberger's manuscript dictionary in the library of the Philosophical Society, a translation was affected.' This translation, it may here be remarked, so far as I have been able to test it, is a faithful one, and there is slight doubt that the original is what it professes to be, a genuine Indian record . . . The only additional information we have respecting it, is that it was 'obtained by the late Dr. Ward of Indiana, of the remnant of the Delawares on the White river.' "

Rafinesque himself—Constantine Samuel Rafinesque, author of *A Life of Travels and Researches in North American and the South of Europe, from 1802 till 1835* (Philadelphia, 1836)—is the subject of a poem by James Whaler, *Green River: a Poem for Rafinesque* (New York, 1931).

197   Notions of land ownership among the woodland Indians of the Northeast are analyzed in George S. Snyderman, "Concepts of Land Ownership Among the Iroquois and Their Neighbors," in William N. Fenton, ed., *Symposium on Local Diversity in Iroquois Culture*, BAE Bulletin 149 (Washington, 1951).

Nils Gustafson is quoted from Peter Kalm, *Travels into North America* (London, 1772), this excerpt quoted in Pinkerton's *Voyages* previously cited, vol XIII, 538.

The quotation is from John G. E. Heckewelder, *An Account of the History, Manners and Customs of the Indian Nations Who Once Inhabited Pennsylvania and the Neighboring States* (Philadelphia, 1819, reprint, 1876), quoted here from James Mooney in Hodge, *Handbook*, vol. II, 683.

198   Mooney in the same volume, I, 800, gives the traditional view of Manhattan island being held by a Wappinger group, citing Edward M. Ruttenber, *History of the Indian Tribes of Hudson's River; Their Origins, Manners, and Customs; Tribal and Subtribal Organizations; Wars, Treaties, etc.* (Albany, 1872), 77.

Swanton, 1953, 48–49, states, however, that the Canarsee occupied the south end of Manhattan island. Since Mahattan was apparently only used as a site for a few hunting and fishing villages the question of actual control is difficult to settle.

Peter Minuit's report of the purchase is in the Holland Documents, vol. I of E. B. O'Callaghan, ed., *Documents Relative to the History of the State of New York*, 15 vols. (New York, 1858–1887), and in O'Callaghan, *History of New Netherlands*, 2 vols. (New York, 1846–1848), vol. I, 103.

The market value of the Manhattan price is reckoned up in MacLeod, 194.

Dutch repurchase of lands (under Peter Stuyvesant's policy of Indian conciliation) is mentioned in Allen W. Trelease, "Dutch Treatment of the American Indian, with Particular Reference to New Netherland," in Peckham and Gibson, eds., *Attitudes of Colonial Powers toward the American Indian*, 55. Also see Allen W. Trelease, *Indian Affairs in Colonial New York: The Seventeenth Century* (Ithaca, N.Y., 1960).

The atrocity stories are from D. David Pieterszatz De Vries, "Notes . . . " (Hoorn, 1655), in *Collections of the New-York Historical Society*, 2d Series, vol. III, part I (New York, 1857); *Broad Advice to the New Netherlands*, a calumnious pamphlet, authorship sometimes attributed to Cornelis Meyn, 1649; Ruttenber, *op. cit.*, 108; MacLeod, 224–226; E. B. O'Callaghan, ed., *Documentary History of the State of New York*, 4 vols. (New York, 1849–1851), vol. IV, 105. The word "Swannekin" is from De Vries.

199   Quotations are from the "Report" in O'Callaghan, *History of New Netherlands*, Appendix E, quoted in MacLeod, 229–230.

For a detailed and more objective account of the causes of a later Indian "war" see *A Brief and True Narrative of the Hostile Conduct of the Barbarous Natives towards the Dutch Nation*. Translated by E. B. O'Callaghan (Albany, 1863), a petition of October 31, 1655, concerning an Indian attack with heavy loss to the Dutch in the Manhattans. The opinion of Director Stuyvesant, among the documents in the Appendix: "We concur in the general opinion that the Indians had, on their first Arrival, no other intention than to wage War against the Savages on the east End of Long Island . . . and that a culpable want of Vigilance, and a too hasty Rashness on the part of a few hot-headed Spirits, had diverted the Indians and been the cause of the dreadful Consequences and enormous Losses" (33). The Director with troops had been at the time on an expedition to "the South River of New Netherland, for the purpose of resenting the Affronts and Insults suffered from the Swedes."

The relative density of New England population rests on Kroeber, 1939, Table 8, 142.

Sir Ferdinando Gorges, *Briefe Narration* (London, 1658), tells of seizing upon Tasquantum, one of five natives from the vicinity of "a River on the Coast of America, called *Pemmaquid* . . . " Later, toward the year 1613, another English captain brought "unto me" a native of the island of "*Capawick*, a place seated to the southward of Cape Codd . . . " who had been taken with twenty-nine others to sell as slaves in Spain, "but being understood that they were *Americans,* and found to be unapt for their uses," the Spanish would not buy; this captive had therefore been brought to England and "shewed in *London* for a wonder. . . . "

200 The other and more usual Tisquantum story is told in Samuel Purchas, *Hakluytus Posthumus, or Purchas his Pilgims: Containing a History of the World in Sea Voyages and Land Voyages by Englishmen and Others* (London, 1625-1626; reprint, 1915); and is also related in the *Dictionary of American Biography. The description of the plague is quoted from Thomas Morton, op. cit.*
"These English . . . falling in with Cape Cod . . . tacked about to the southward for Hudson's river; but Jones, who was the master of the ship they came in, having been bribed by the Hollanders to carry them and land farther to the northward, instead of putting to sea entangled them among dangerous shoals, which made them willing to get ashore where they were, and give over the design upon Hudson's river. . . . " (Pinkerton's *Voyages,* vol. XII, 349).
The more customary story, as in Woodrow Wilson, *History of the American People* (1902), relates that "when at last . . . they sighted land, it turned out to be Cape Cod, not the Virgnia coast at all. The master of the ship had let his reckonings go wrong, was many leagues north of the landfall he had been instructed to make . . . and found himself, as he closed with the coast he had blindly come upon, involved in shoals from which he did not very well know how safely to extricate himself. . . . The immigrants had half a mind to make for Hudson's River, after all. But the season was late and stormy, and the captain surly and unwilling, and they determined to land where they were and make the best of what they had hit upon."
The cleared Indian fields (cleared by burning) are described by Will Wood, *op. cit.* Wrote a capable observer more than two centuries later, of Indian fields: "They regularly cleared extensive tracts for cultivation, and these were always level tracts where the soil was light—such as they could turn over with their crude hoes. Such was the land which they are known to have cultivated extensively in this town [Concord], as the Great Fields and the rear of Mr. Dennis's sandy plains. . . . " (Henry David Thoreau, *Journal,* vol. XIV [1860], 272).

201 Gorges is quoted from *Briefe Narration.*
The colony's historian quoted is William Bradford, *History of Plymouth Plantation, 1620-1647,* 2 vols. (Boston, 1912), vol. I, 202-203.

202 Morton is quoted from *New English Canaan,* previously cited, wherein he also remarks that the sale of liquor brings great benefits to the planters, as for it the "Salvages . . . will pawne their wits" but that in all his commerce he has "never proffered them any such thing."
The poetry is from William Morrell, *New England, or a Briefe Narration of the Ayre, Earth, Water, Fish, and Fowles of that CountrR . . . etc. in Latine and English Verse* (London, 1625). Morrell, an Episcopal clergyman armed with authority to superintend such churches as might be established in New England, came in 1623 under the protection of the son of Sir Ferdinando Gorges but in spite of the new land's delights went home after one year.
This was not the first Latin poem propagandizing for the New World among the Latinist English—Stephen Parmenias, a Hungarian with Sir Humphrey Gilbert in 1583, wrote "an elegant Latin poem about Newfoundland (and died at sea, with the admiral and nearly one hundred of the crew) that same year . . . "
The poem is in vol. IX of the *Collections of the Massachusetts Historical Society:* Lydia Sigourney, *Traits of the Aborigines of America* (Cambridge, Mass., 1822), *n.* 2 to line 45, Canto Second, 18-19.
The Puritan chronicler quoted is Captain Edward Johnson, *Wonder-Working Providence of Zion's Savior in New England* (1654; ed. by W. F. Poole, 1867).

204 The quotation is from Bradford, *op. cit.*

206 The colonies covertly fighting each other via their Indians is illustrated by the death of Miantonomo, executed by order of the Commissioners of the United Colonies of New England after a "disgraceful" trial in which theological bias against Roger Williams (a friend of Miantonomo's) "played some part"—Alexander F. Chamberlain in Hodge, *Handbook,* vol. I, 855, quoting John W. De Forest, *History of the Indians of Connecticut from the Earliest Known Period to 1850* (Hardford, 1851), 198.

207 The soldiers' doubt is quoted from G. E. Ellis, *King Philip's War* (1906), quoting the Ruggles Manuscript, 152, 155, cited in MacLeod, 239.
See also Anne K. Nelson, "King Philip's War and the Hubbard-Mather Rivalry," in *William and Mary Quarterly,* 27 (1970), 615-629.

208 Quotations are from Benjamin Trumbull, *Complete History of Connecticut from 1630 to 1764,* 2 vols. (New Haven, 1818); and Nathaniel Morton, *New England's Memorial or Zion's Savior* (1669; 5th ed., John Davis, ed., 1826), 353; and Davis' notes to same, Appendix, 454.

209 New England refugees working for La Salle on the Mississippi are mentioned in Francis Parkman, *La Salle* (1962 ed.), 214, 217.
Military expenses are from the calculation of MacLeod, 243.
The summary of damage is from Edward Everett, *An Address Delivered at Bloody Brook, in South Deerfield, September 30, 1835, in Commemoration of the Fall of the "Flower of Essex" at that Spot in King Philip's War,*

September 18, (O.S.) 1675, (Boston, 1835), 26 and 34: "It was not till the year 1759, till Quebec fell, that the settlements on Connecticut River were safe. . . . "
Philip's crippled hand (injured by the explosion of a pistol in former years) was given my Captain Thomas Church to "Alerman, the Indian who shot him, to show to such gentlemen as would bestow gratuities upon him; and accordingly he got many a penny for it"—Samuel Gardner Drake, *Biography and History of the Indians of North America, From Its First Discovery,* 11th edition (Boston, 1851). Drake adds that Captain Church ordered "his old Indian executioner" to behead and quarter the fallen Indian leader and the "executioner" made a speech over Philip's body before he struck with his hatchet, saying, "You have been a very great man, and have made many a man afraid of you; but so big as you be I will now chop your ass for you. . . ." Philip's body was left unburied, but having been quartered "was hung upon four trees, and there left as a monument to shocking barbarity" (227).
Cotton Mather, writing more than twenty years after Philip's head was placed on its Plymouth pole: "It was not long before the hand that now writes, upon a certain occasion, took off the jaw from the exposed skull of that *blasphemous leviathan.* . . . " *Magnalia Christi Americana: or, the Ecclesiastical History of New England, from its First Planting in the Year 1620, unto the Year of our LORD, 1698* . . . (London, 1702).
Douglas E. Leach, *Flintlock and Tomahawk, New England in King Philip's War* (New York, 1958), states that in "proportion to population the war inflicted greater casualties upon the people than any other war in our history." Wilcomb Washburn, reviewing this work in *Pennsylvania Magazine of History and Piography,* 82 (1958), argues that the English were the aggressors in the war, shed the first blood, attacked Narragansetts and Pennacooks and Connecticut Valley Indians without justification, and that the English only had military successes when they used more Indian allies than English troops. See also Leach, *The Northern Colonial Frontier, 1607–1763* (New York, 1966.)
A recent work defending Puritan policy is Alden T. Vaughan, *The New England Frontier, Puritans and Indians, 1620–1675* (Boston, 1965).
Theological quotations are from Morton, *New England's Memorial.*
Philip's wife and child and other Indians sold as slaves by the English and French to the West Indies could join there the 80,000 Irish captives shipped as chattel slaves by Cromwell and the survivors—if there were any—of the Highland Scots sold there after the battle of Worcester in 1651 (MacLeod, 170).

210 Frank G. Speck, *Family Hunting Territories and Social Life of Various Algonkian Bands of the Ottawa Valley,* Canada Geological Survey, Memoir 70 (Ottawa, 1915); and in *Beothuk and Micmac,* Indian Notes and Monographs, Museum of the American Indian, Heye Foundation (New York, 1922), where part II, 81 *et seq.,* is devoted to Micmac hunting territories discusses the question of the Algonquian family hunting territory, "which was first mentioned in this region by Le Clercq in 1691" (*n.,* 71)—Father Chretien Leclerq, *New Relation of Gaspesia, with the Customs and Religion of the Gaspesian Indians* (Paris, 1691; and in an English translation by William F. Ganong, The Champlain Society, Toronto, 1910).
The older traditional view of the Iroquoian people as an amalgamation of several peoples is expressed in Martin, Quimby, and Collier, 257–258. The Owasco culture, where remains offering some identity with historical Iroquoian first appear, is now dated as emerging in A.D. 500–700—Willey, 1966, fig. 5–3, 251, and 310. W. A. Ritchie, the standard reference, sums up his previous works in *The Archaeology of New York State* (New York, 1965); but see also his "Iroquois Archaeology and Settlement Patterns," in W. A. Ritchie and John Gulick, eds., *Symposium on Cherokee and Iroquois Culture,* BAE Bulletin 180 (Washington, 1961).

212 Captain Smith is quoted from Hodge, *Handbook,* vol. II, 653; Will Wood, *op. cit.;* the Cartier report is from Pinkerton's *Voyages,* vol. XII, 653, Cartier at the time being on the way to Hochelaga, since identified as an Iroquoian town; the enthusiastic French missionary was Le Jeune, of the *Jesuit Relations.*
Reports on the hardships of Indian life were by no means limited to the Iroquois—Father Francois de Crepieul, among the Montagnais from 1671 to 1697, gives a detailed picture of the squalor, filth, and privation attendant on "the Long and slow Martyrdom" of his years with the Indians:*Jesuit Relations,* Thwaites, ed., vol. XLV, Document 170.

213 The best early ethnography quoted is Lafitau, vol. I, 290.
The story of Aharihon is synopsized in A. F. C. Wallace, 1970, 31–33.

NOTES for Chapter VIII

General works used in this chapter are *Jesuit Relations;* Morgan, *League;* Jenness; Hunt; MacLeod; Kroeber, 1953; Swanton, 1953; Driver; Sir William Johnson; Peckham; Colden; Beauchamp; Wraxall; Lafitau; Schoolcraft; Jacobs, 1972; Fenton, ed.; Hale; Parker; A. F. C. Wallace, 1970; Hodge, *Handbook;* Charlevoix; Alvord; Billington;

and for page

219 The number of Iroquois captives burned by the Hurons in 1639 is from Hunt, 73, citing *Jesuit Relations,* Thwaites, ed., vol. XV, 185–187, and vol. XVII, 63–77.
A more common theory on the derivation of "Huron" relates it to "hure"—a boar's head or any striking head

of hair, supposedly from the Huron, and Iroquois, occasional style of roached hair—*Jesuit Relations*, Thwaites, ed., vol. XVI, 229–231.
Ibid., vol. XXII, 255, the quotation, which is from Father Barthelemy Vimont, his relation for 1642.
Huron population estimates are from Hunt, 40; *ibid.*, 188, *n.* 3, the double-talking French reports of Huron plague losses.
The quotation is from Hunt, 165, quoting Governor Dubois d'Avaugour to the Minister, August 4, 1663, in *New York Colonial Documents*, vol. IX, 13.

220 The number of Iroquois guns is from Hunt, 90, discussing larger estimates in Louise Phelps Kellogg, *The French Regime in Wisconsin and the Northwest* (Madison, 1925), 85.
An analysis of traditional motives in Iroquoian "war" is in A. F. C. Wallace, 1970, 44–48, emphasizing a number of functions other than economic—such as maintaining king-group equilibrium with accompanying emotional and social equilibrium, or maintaining security and fulfillment in the family setting. See also George S. Snyderman, "Behind the Tree of Peace: A Sociological Analysis of Iroquois Warfare," in *Pennsylvania Archaeologist*, 18 (1948), 38–43; and Wendell S. Haddock, "War Among the Northeastern Woodland Indians," in *American Anthropologist*, 49 (1947), 204–221.
Hunt, 20–22, makes a case for the first introduction of war, real war (in the Northeast at least), as an adjunct of European trade, reiterating Charles H. McIlwain in his introduction to Wraxall, as have a number of other writers on the subject.

221 Iroquois population figures are based on conclusions in Hunt, 66. Iroquois and Erie forces are as given by J. N. B. Hewitt in Hodge, *Handbook*, vol. I, 430–431. Hewitt also adopts the usual view that the Erie possess only bows and arrows although citing the Jesuit Relation of 1656 that speaks of one Erie palisade being lost because they ran short of powder. The accounts of the Jesuits speak of the Erie using poisoned arrows, unusual for the area, if true. Hunt follows Jesuit accounts that number Erie warriors at 2,000, and Iroquois effectives in the storming the principal town at 700; 101.
Interesting theories on the causes of the Erie–Iroquois war are reviewed by Hewitt, from the *Jesuit Relations* for 1655 to 1656, Chapter 11, a story of thirty Erie ambassadors at the Seneca capital, one accidentally killing a Seneca, the Seneca then massacring all but five of the ambassadors. Hunt (101) mentions a tradition that the war started over a Five Nations victory in an athletic contest, which of course could be related to the accidental death. In the view of most non-Indian historians, the presence of Huron troublemakers among the Erie seems more cogent.

222 The Iroquois a minority in their own towns is mentioned in the *Jesuit Relations* for 1656 and 1660. Thwaites, ed., vol. XLIII, 265, the Relation of 1656–1657, edited by Paul le Jeune: ". . . these victories cause almost as much loss to them as to their enemies, and they have depopulated their Villages to such an extent that they now contain more Foreigners than natives . . ."—the same passage adding that there were then seven different nations in Onondaga and eleven in Seneca. The Relation of 1659–1660 by Hierosome Lalemant (Thwaites, ed., vol. XLV, 207): ". . . difficulty in finding more than 1,200 pureblooded in all the Five Nations ". . ." and adding that the total population can only furnish 1,700 warriors.
William Hand Browne, Aubrey C. Land, *et al.*, eds., *Archives of Maryland*, 71 vols. to date (Baltimore, 1883 to date)—vol. III, *Proceedings of the Council of Maryland, 1636–1667*, discusses Maryland's efforts in trying to arrange the "matter of so great consequence"—a peace between the Susquehannas and Senecas (499, June 7, 1664).

223 *Ibid.*, vol. II, 378, Maryland's deal with the Iroquois, and abandonment of the Susquehanna (cited in MacLeod, 248).
Allen W. Trelease, "The Iroquois and the Western Fur Trade: A Problem in Interpretation," in *Mississippi Valley Historical Review*, 48/1 (June 1962), 32–51, argues convincingly against the "single cause" of the Iroquois wars as advanced by Hunt and by Macleod (282, 288) among others. Geographical determinism would surely have favored a Huron–Onondage–Susquehanna alliance; the geographical value of such an alliance, as described by Hunt, would have been enhanced by a vertical (north–south) barrier rather than by the horizontal (east–west) barrier of the Five Nations; and trade motives would surely have favored a grand Iroquoian alliance of all these nations—Neutrals, Petun, Huron, and Susquehanna—together with the Great League. The complex questions that produced other results, and that strengthened the extraordinary survival power of the League, can scarcely be summed up in one factor alone—an explanation that completely evades, for example, the simple question (which becomes enormously complex upon investigation) of why the Five Nations always won.
The orator quoted is Ondaaiondiont, Huron emissary to the Susquehanna in 1647, the words intended as propaganda and instead truly prophetic, two years before the fact (*Jesuit Relations*, Thwaites, ed., vol. XXXVIII, 67).
The quotation from Alcaeus is given in Thucydides' paraphrase, neater than the original which runs ". . . not houses . . . not walls of stone . . . neither narrow streets nor harbors a city make, but men . . ."

224 The French administrator quoted is Jean Talon in 1667, quoted in Hunt, 135.
Seventeenth-century Iroquois information rests mainly, besides the Jesuit Relations, on Edmund B. O'Callaghan, *et al.*, eds., *Documents Relative to the Colonial History of the State of New York*, 15 vols.

(Albany, 1853–1887). vol. XI (Albany, 1861) is a general index, in which Iroquois entries take up some dozen pages of the three dozen pages listing Indian matters—281–314. In addition, important information is found in Charlevoix; and in Emma H. Blair, ed. and trans. of the Nicolas Perrot Memoir in *The Indian Tribes of the Upper Mississippi Valley and Region of the Great Lakes*, 2 vols. (Cleveland, 1911–1912), vol. I, 25–275, and (Perrot's biography), vol. II, 249–257.
Big Mouth is quoted from Louis Armand, Baron de Lahontan, *New Voyages to North America*, ed. by Reuben Gold Thwaites, 2 vols. (Chicago, 1905), vol. I, 82, although the quotation here is altered in comparison with the original French edition, previously cited. Lahontan, also, is witness for the displeasure of the French governor (Lefebvre La Barre).
The Jesuit accolade is quoted in Hunt, 132, from *Jesuit Relations*, Thwaites, ed., vol. XLIV, 149.

225 The ennobled French frontiersman was Charles Le Moyne, called by the Iroquois The Partridge, father of the famous Iberville and Bienville.
The quoted picture of the Iroquois council is from Lafitau, vol. I, 478–480.
The tale of the thirty-six councilors returned from the galleys is told in Charlevoix, French edition, vol. I, Book XI, 509. Carolyn Thomas Foreman, *Indians Abroad* (Norman, Okla., 1943), 32, gives the number also as thirty-six, but other accounts say thirteen or say Frontenac brought back to France two years later (1689) thirteen survivors; Pierre Margry, ed., *Découvertes et Etablissements des Français dans l'Ouest et dans le Sud de l'Amérique Septentrionale*, 1614–1754, 6 vols. (Paris, 1877–1886), provides a list of twenty-one ordered released by the king.
The Iroquois visit to Queen Anne is related in detail in Foreman, cited above, 34–39.
The governor of New York (Governor Dongan) is quoted from MacLeod, Appendix VIII, p 556, citing O'Callaghan, *Documentary History*, vol. III, 593. *Ibid.*, the Albany Commissioners; and the Pennsylvania secretary, quoted from McIlwain's Introduction to Wraxall, xxxvi. The French missionary recording the same thing is the Jesuit historian Charlevoix, *Letters to the Dutchess of Lesdiguieres, Giving an Account of a Voyage to Canada and Travels Through That Country and Louisiana etc.* . . . (London, 1763), used here from the French edition, Tome III, 271, Letter XVIII, June 1721.
The recall of all French traders (or nearly all) from the forests ruined Nicolas Perrot, a bitter experience bitterly related in his Memoir edited by Emma H. Blair in her *Indian Tribes of the Upper Mississippi Valley* mentioned above. The order, promulgated in Paris May 26, 1696, reached the remote Canadian beaver country in 1698. While recognizing factors such as Iroquoian politics, Fénélon's influence on Madame de Maintenon is given the chief role by Clarence W. Alvord, *The Illinois Country 1673–1818*, vol. I of The Centennial History of Illinois (Springfield, Ill., 1920), 104–109.

226 The Iroquois quotation referring to the Tuscarora is quoted in Hodge, *Handbook*, vol. II, 845 from O'Callaghan, ed., *Documents Relative to the Colonial History . . . of New York*, vol. V, 376.
The predecessor to Mason's and Dixon's line is mentioned in Hodge, *Handbook*, vol. II, 847, agreed to at a meeting between the Five (just becoming Six) Nations and Governor Spotswood of Virginia at Albany, September 6 to 13, 1722.
Colden, I, 4 (from the 3d edition, London, 1755), pictures the old Mohawk sachem.
The Dutch pastor quoted is "Johannes Megapolensis, Jr.," *A Short Sketch of the Mohawk Indians in New Netherland* (1644; reprinted in the Collections of the New-York Historical Society, 2d Series, Vol. III, Part 1, New York, 1857; and in J. Franklin Jameson, ed., *Narratives of New Netherland*, 1609–1664, New York, 1909). The same point is made by Colden, "Their Great Men, both Sachems and Captains, are generally poorer than the common People, for they affect go give away and distribute all the Presents or Plunder they get in their Treaties or War, so as to leave nothing to themselves. If they should once be suspected of Selfishness, they would grow mean in the Opinion of their Country-men, and would consequently lose their Authority."—From the New York, 1727, edition, xvi.

227 Lafitau is quoted from the dedication to the Duc d'Orléans, "Epitre," vol. I, ii and iii; and from I, 71, 72. Again, Colden echoes the identical observation: "None of the greatest *Roman* Heroes have discovered a greater Love to their Country, or a greater Contempt of Death, than these People called Barbarians have done, when Liberty came in Competition . . ." and ". . . The *Five Nations* have such absolute Notions of Liberty, that they allow of no Kind of Superiority of one over another, and banish all Servitude from their Territories."—From the 3d edition, 1755, the Introductory Epistle to General Oglethorpe, v, and from 11.
The ritual quotation is adapted from "At the Wood's Edge," the welcoming ceremony opening the "Ancient Rites of the Condoling Council" in Horatio Hale, *The Iroquois Book of Rites* (Philadelphia, 1883).
Wraxall is full of French instigation of Iroquois wars with the "far nations" and other intrigue with the insidious objective of Iroquois destruction, e.g., 73, 229–230, and many more.
William N. Fenton, *The Iroquois in History*, a paper prepared for a symposium, Theory and Method in American Indian Ethnological and Ethnohistorical Research, August 7–14, 1967, under the auspices of the Wenner Gren Foundation, notes that "the French Jesuits at Oneida abetted the Iroquois to take up arms against the Indians of the Southeast, who lived at the back of the English colonies . . ." but finds it "difficult to explain these campaigns in other terms than the traditional drive for honors, scalps, and above all for captives" (31). In this same paper Fenton rejects the single-cause analysis of Iroquois history (21): "The

image of the Iroquois as 'economic man' or even as 'middleman' has never appealed to me as being at all consistent with his character or his culture" while nevertheless stressing as an important factor the Iroquois position as stated by a spokesman in 1735, "Trade and peace we take to be one thing" (19).

231   MacLeod, 248–251, relates the events leading up to Bacon's Rebellion, citing *Maryland Archives*, vol. II, 378, and index for 1675; and a letter of July 19, 1676, from an Episcopal clergyman in Maryland to the Archbishop of Canterbury, in *Proceedings of the Council of Maryland*, vol. IV, 133 following.
The Berkeley quotation is from vol. I of *Tracts and Other Papers Relating to the History of America*, collected by Peter Force (Washington, 1836, *et seq.*).
Woodrow Wilson is quoted from his *History of the American People* previously mentioned, vol. I, 269.
The customary account of Bacon's Rebellion as a struggle for liberty has been challenged by Wilcomb E. Washburn, *The Governor and the Rebel: A History of Bacon's Rebellion in Virginia* (Chapel Hill, 1957), which argues that Bacon was primarily interested in killing friendly Indians to obtain their land. Thomas J. Wertenbaker, *Give Me Liberty: The Struggle for Self-Government in Virginia* (Philadelphia, 1958), presents the customary view, disputed by Bernard Bailyn, "Politics and Social Structure in Colonial Virginia," in James M. Smith, ed., *Seventeenth-Century America* (Chapel Hill, 1959), who presents as a principal factor social competition of rival cliques, and rebutted by Wilcomb Washburn, "The Effects of Bacon's Rebellion on Government in England and Virginia" in *Contributions from the Musueum of History and Technology*, U. S. National Museum Bulletin 225 (Washington, 1962), 135–152, arguing that the thrust for self-government in Virginia came not from the rebellion but from the overreaction of the royal commission sent out to investigate. Warren M. Billings, "The Causes of Bacon's Rebellion: Some Suggestions," in *Virginia Magazine of History and Biography*, 78 (October 1970), 409–435, points out that none of the above have discerned, as court records for the fifteen years previous to the rebellion reveal, the conditions of worsening economy, failing power of the governor and consequent political unrest, all contributing to the events of 1676.

232   The Jeffersonian quotations are from his preface to *The Beginning, Progress, and Conclusion of Bacon's Rebellion in Virginia, in the Years 1675 and 1676* (Washington, printed by Peter Force, 1836, in *Force Tracts*, vol. I), first printed in Richmond, Virginia, *Enquirer*, of the 1st, 5th, and 8th September, 1804, from an exact copy of the original MS, "a copy made by Mr. Jefferson, then President of the United States."
Richard M. Dorson, ed., *Davy Crockett, American Comic Legend* (New York, 1939), is an anthology and survey of the "uniquely American figure that emerged from *The Sketches and Eccentricities of Col. David Crockett* in 1833 and the *Narrative of the Life of David Crockett* in 1834, and the series of Crockett almanacs published from 1835 to 1856."

233   The story of Sylvanus is from "A Narrative of the Captivity of Mrs. Johnson," in John Frost, ed., *Indian Battles, Captivities, and Adventures* (New York, 1856), 128–182.
Dutch scalp bounties were first tried out in 1641 by Governor Kieft (MacLeod, 223). Drake, *loc. cit.*, mentions that the Puritan soldiers who were in at King Philip's death were being paid (their only wages) thirty shillings for each enemy death or capture. MacLeod, 244, *n.* 1, mentions the scale of Massachusetts scalp bounties, and outlines, 400–402, the Pennsylvania scalp bounties of 1756 and following years.
The murder of the Susquehannas at Conestoga and the political background are the subject of a recent study by W. R. Jacobs, *The Paxton Riots and the Frontier Theory* (Chicago, 1967).
Bounty on Beothuk heads or scalps is mentioned in Jenness, 266; their extinction is described in Hodge, *Handbook*, vol. I, 142.

235   The quotations dealing with the Walking Purchase are from "Narrative of the Long Walk by John Watson, Father and Son, Communicated to the Historical Committee of the American Philosophical Society, Philadelphia, in 1822," reprinted from Hazard's *Register of Pennsylvania* (Philadelphia for October 9, 1830) in W. W. Beach, *The Indian Miscellany* (New York, 1877), 90–101. The account was written in 1815 by John Watson, Sr., a surveyor, from the testimony and extracts found in deeds and grants used in his work, with added notes provided by the son in 1822 from oral information given him in previous years by one of the three men who undertook, for pay (never received, by the way), to perform the Long Walk.
A. F. C. Wallace, *King of the Delawares: Teedyuscung 1700–1763* (Philadelphia, 1949), is the modern study cited—Chapter II, 18–19. This chapter summarizes a fuller account in P. A. W. Wallace, *Conrad Weiser, 1696–1760: Friend of Colonist and Mohawk* (Philadelphia, 1945), 95–99, who concludes by quoting a complacent letter from Thomas to John Penn telling of the Walk and John's pleased reply saying "you have got the Confirmation of the Delaware Indian's at an easy rate . . ." to which the author remarks, "The rate seemed less easy after Braddock's defeat" (99).

236   Canassatego's speech is quoted from Carl Van Doren and Julian P. Boyd, eds., *Indian Treaties Printed by Benjamin Franklin, 1736–1762; Their Literary, Historical, and Bibliographical Significance* (Philadelphia, 1938). See also Lawrence Counselman Wroth, "The Indian Treaty as Literature" in the *Yale Review*, 17 (July 1928), 749–766.
Further quotations referring to the Long Walk are also from the Watson Narrative mentioned above.

237   MacLeod, 399, lists the Braddock scalp bounties.

Braddock's scalp bounties were widely publicized in France as a sample of enemy atrocity, a vol. VIII of current events added by a French editor, "M. de Grace," to Samuel, Freiherr von Pufendorf, *Introduction a l'Histoire Moderne, Générale et Politique de l'Univers; ou l'on voit l'Origine, la Révolution et la Situation Presente des différents états de l'Europe, de l'Asie, de l'Afrique et de l'Amérique: Commencée par le Baron de Pufendorff* . . . (Paris, 1759), stating that this "action, as contrary to the laws of good politics as to those of justice, made so many enemies for England as there were Savages informed of a so foolhardy and cruel proclamation" (vol. VIII, 604).

Iroquois invitation of the English into the Ohio country brought violent French reaction and "the French and Indian War was on," argues A. F. C. Wallace, 1970, 113–114.

The quotation here referring to the Long Walk is also from the Watson Narrative.

238 Post's Journal, October 25, 1758–January 20, 1759, is in Thwaites, ed., *Early Western Travels*, 32 vols. (Cleveland, 1904–1907), vol. I, 234–295. The story of Tedyuskung and Post is synopsized in the article on Tedyuskung by George P. Donehoo in Hodge, *Handbook*, vol. II, 714–717, citing *Colonial Records of Pennsylvania*, vols. VI and VIII (Harrisburg, 1851–1853); *Pennsylvania Archives*, ed. by Samuel Hazard, 2d Series, vols. II and III (Harrisburg, 1875–1890); and *Frontier Forts . . . of Pennsylvania*, vol. I (Harrisburg, 1896).

Mary Carson Darlington, ed., *History of Colonel Henry Bouquet and the Western Frontiers of Pennsylvania 1747–1764* (Cleveland, 1920), lists the important Delaware leaders who were won over by Christian Post as Shingas, Killbuck, King Beaver, Delaware George, and Pisquetumen and says that since, as a result of Post's visit, the Indians refused to join the French in attacking Forbes on his march, the French, "knowing the fort was too dilapidated to stand an assault, burned it and left the country in barges for Venango and the lower Ohio" (121).

Tedyuskung's acceptance of a present of 400 pounds to drop charges against the Walking Purchase is stated as fact in Donehoo, *loc. cit.*, and in Joseph S. Walton, *Conrad Weiser and the Indian Policy of Colonial Pennsylvania* (Philadelphia, c. 1900), who cites *Colonial Records of Pennsylvania*, vol. VIII, 708; 739–740. A. F. C. Wallace, 1949, points out that matters of supposed bribes and treaties involving Tedyuskung are involved with the whole complex of Pennsylvania politics at the time, Tedyuskung operating as a front man for the Quakers in the basic political conflict between the Quaker faction and the proprietors, which is to say Colonials vs British (248).

John Bartram, *Observations on the Inhabitants . . . and Other Matters Worthy of Notice in . . . Travels from Pensilvania to Onondago, Oswego, and the Lake Ontario in Canada. . . .* (London, 1751), remarks on the used-up condition of the mighty Iroquois who "enjoy the character of being the most warlike people in North America . . now their numbers being very much diminished by constant wars . . . and perhaps a good deal partly by the spiritous liquors, and diseases the Europeans have brought among them . . . the prisoners they take . . . are [now] almost always accepted by the relations of a warrior slain in his place, and thus a boy of 15, is sometimes called father by men of 30 . . ." (78)

The quotation asking by what right one European power could give away Ottawa country to another European power is from Jacobs, 1972, 79, quoting George Croghan to Jeffery Amherst, April 30, 1763, *Bouquet Papers* om the Canadian Archives, Ottawa.

The exhortation of Neolin is from A. F. C. Wallace, 1970, p 118, quoting excerpts from the so-called Pontiac MS, a manuscript by an unknown author presumably based on information provided by French-Canadians who were present at Indian councils preceding the outbreak of Pontiac's war. The manuscript is the principal source material on events leading up to the war, and was used by Francis Parkman, *The Conspiracy of Pontiac and the Indian War after the Conquest of Canada* (Boston, 1898), and by Howard H. Peckham, *Pontiac and the Indian Uprising* (Princeton, 1947).

The Pontiac MS, now believed to be the work of Robert Navarre, is published in English, translated by R. Clyde Ford, in Milo M. Quaife, ed., *Journal of Pontiac's Conspiracy, 1763* (Chicago, 1958); and in both French and English in M. Agnes Burton, ed., *Journal of Pontiac's Conspiracy, 1763* (Detroit, 1912), published and with preface by Clarence Monroe Burton.

239 Alvord, *The Mississippi Valley in British Politics*, is the source of the quotation referring to land speculators: "Far more important than traders' tricks and British parsimony was the encroachment of the settlers on the Indians' hunting grounds. In this the land speculator was particularly guilty, for he carried into his bartering for Indian lands the low, cunning tricks of the traders" (vol. I, 186).

Amherst's suggestion of giving the Indians smallpox by means of infected blankets is mentioned in Jacobs, 1972, 81, citing Parkman, *Conspiracy of Pontiac*, vol. I, 173–174; and giving the reply to Amherst by his field commander from Pennsylvania Historical Survey, *The Papers of Col. Henry Bouquet* (Harrisburg, 1940–1943). A. T. Volwiler, ed., "William Trent's Journal at Fort Pitt, 1763, in *Mississippi Valley Historical Review*, 9/3 (December 1924), 390–413, quotes the Fort Pitt commander as noting that when two Indians appeared from the woods saying they were friends "we gave them two Blankets and an Handkerchief out of the Small Pox Hospital. I hope it will have the desired effect" (400).

239 A. T. Volwiler, *George Croghan and the Westward Movement, 1741–1782* (Cleveland, 1926), sums up the cost to the English of Pontiac's war, 164. Croghan, on his way to London with Sir William Johnson's plans for peace, shipwrecked on the coast of Normandy, losing everything but his papers ("I Traveld about

140 Miles in france Butt Never See So Much pride and poverty before") only arrived in London in February 1764, to find that Lord Hillsborough, the new president of the Board of Trade, had hastily drawn up and announced the Proclamation of October 7, 1763 ("Pontiac's uprising hastened the partial announcement of a western colonial policy by the imperial government . . ." [170]); and because of the necessity for haste, the Indian boundary line—beyond which no settlements were to be permitted—was not rationally marked out for surveying, but was located at the Appalachian divide where the Indians could easily identify it (171).

Alvord, *The Mississippi Valley in British Politics*, describes the haste with which Hillsborough was forced to prepare the Proclamation of 1763, "one of the most important state documents concerning America ever promulgated by the British government . . . Lord Shelburne's recommendation that a proclamation be prepared to quiet the fears of the Indians had lain on the table since the fifth of August, and during the intervening period more complete news of the successful uprising of the Indians had been received. Action must be taken at once" (198–199). The quotation referring to the boundary line ("To satisfy the Indians a conspicuous and tangible boundary must be announced . . .") is also from Alvord, this work, 202.

Jacobs, 1972, Chapter VIII, discusses at length the justification, or lack of same, for calling Pontiac's war a "conspiracy."

240 The frontier official quoted is Sir William Johnson, as quoted in MacLeod, 423, Johnson to the Board of Trade July 10, 1765.

241 Hendrick's supposed remark is quoted in Samuel Gardner Drake, *Biography and History . . .*, 11th edition (1851), 536.

Johnson's recruitment of brisk allies is quoted in William L. Stone, *Life of Joseph Brant—Thayendanegea, Including the Indian Wars of the American Revolution*, 2 vols. (New York, 1838), vol. I, 15.

242 The quotation attributed to Daniel Boone is found in "The Adventures of Daniel Boone," in Gilbert Imlay, *A Topographical Description of the Western Territory of North America* (London, 1797), 340.

The price paid by Judge Henderson is from Ray A. Billington, *Westward Expansion*, 3d edition (New York, 1967), who adds, "No one paid the slightest attention to the company; the immigrants reasoned that it had obtained possession illegally and they would do the same" (169–173).

The Overhill Cherokees (or the "Over-the-Hills and Valley Settlements") constituted one of the three principal divisions into which early traders usually divided the tribe: the Lower, Middle, and Upper or Mountain (or Overhill), each group with a distinctive dialect. The Overhill towns were in western North Carolina, eastern Tennessee, and upper Georgia.

Reuben Gold Thwaites and Louise P. Kellogg, eds., *Documentary History of Lord Dunmore's War, 1774* (Wisconsin Historical Society, 1905), contains in the Introduction the statement, "A study of contemporary documents will convince any fair-minded student of history that Lord Dunmore acted in this episode with disinterested discretion . . ." Frederick Jackson Turner's copy of this work, now in the Henry E. Huntington Library, San Marino, California, bears beside this statement a marginal note in Turner's hand: "Land spec—bdy question?"

243 The quotations are from Stone, *Life of Brant*, 1838 edition, from the introduction, vol. I, xv–xvi. *Ibid.*, vol. I, 256, the proclamation of Benedict Arnold; and Appendix VIII.

Thomas Campbell is quoted from *Gertrude of Wyoming* (1807); in later years Campbell wrote that his estimate of Brant had been in error.

Losses at Oriskany "were higher in proportion to men engaged than in any other battle of the war"—H. E. Bolton and T. M. Marshall, *The Colonization of North America* (New York, 1920), 496.

Cherry Valley and Wyoming statistics rest on the carefully researched account in A. F. C. Wallace, 1970, 137–140.

244 *Ibid.*, Sullivan's campaign in the Iroquois country, 141–144.

"Yankeys" is Joseph Brant's spelling—Wallace, 1970, 167, quoting Stone, *Life of Brant*, 1838 edition, vol. II, 275.

245 Ritual quotations are adapted from the "Ancient Rites of the Condoling Council," in Hale, previously cited.

NOTES for Chapter IX,

General works used in this chapter are Swanton, 1946 and 1952; Hodge, *Handbook*; Schoolcraft; McKenney and Hall; MacLeod; Abel, 1906; Grant Foreman, 1932 and 1934; Kroeber, 1953; Debo; Jacobs, 1954; U. S. Statutes at Large, vol. VII; Kappler; Bassett; Oswalt; De Rosier; M. E. Young; Cotterill, 1954;

and for page

246 Washington is quoted from a message to the Senate, August 22, 1789: J. C. Fitzpatrick, ed., *The Writings of George Washington* (Washington, D.C. 1939), XXX, 305.

The 1790 treaty with the Creeks became the subject of comment by Thomas Jefferson, in relation to its force of law, and in the classic legal analysis of the Constitution, "Story on the Constitution". See H. A. Washington, ed., *The Writings of Thomas Jefferson*, 107 vols., (Washington, 1854), 6, 557–560, and *n*., 505; and Joseph Story, *Commentaries on the Constitution of the United States*, 5th ed., edited by Melville M. Bigelow (Boston, 1905), 2 vols., 2, 609.

J. Leitch Wright, Jr., "Creek–American Treaty of 1790: Alexander McGillivray and the Diplomacy of the Old Southwest," in *Georgia Historical Quarterly*, 51/4 (December, 1967), 379–400, argues that due to the opposition of the Spanish and of dissident factions among the Creeks, the Treaty of 1790 was "never executed" (397) and "never went into effect . . ." (395) But note 43, 399 observes: "It is true that eventually the main provisions of the 1790 treaty . . . would take effect. But it was not until 1796 that it could be said these key objectives were gained."

The agent (actually Deputy Agent) was Major Caleb Swan, quoted from Schoolcraft, vol. V, 258.

247 Ibid., the quotations.

248 Yahou-Lakee is quoted from Peter Force, *Tracts and Other Papers Relating to the History of America* (Washington, 1836–1846), vol. VI.

The Long King from *ibid.*

The pretty line describing Savannah is quoted in Carolyn Thomas Foreman, *Indians Abroad* (Norman, Okla., 1943), 57.

Speculative statistics on the Florida missions are from J. R. Swanton, *The Early History of the Creek Indians and Their Neighbors*, BAE Bulletin 73 (Washington, 1924); W. Lowery, *The Spanish Settlements Within the Present Limits of the United States*, 2 vols (New York, 1901 and 1905), vol. II; MacLeod, 104–106.

249 Statistics on the 1704 raid are from Swanton, 1924, 123.

The point of Spanish law granting freedom to any foreign slave reaching Florida is from MacLeod, 107, citing *Recopilacion de Leyes de los Reinos de las Indias* . . ., 5th edition (Madrid, 1841), Ley 5, tit. 2, lib. 3, of A.D. 1550.

The number of Spanish soldiers for the whole "province of Apalatchee" is from MacLeod, 108.

John Walton Caughey, *McGillivray of the Creeks* (Norman, 1938), deals (pp. 337–339) with Spanish efforts to turn the Creeks against the Georgians and Americans in the fall of 1792, and with political intrigue among the Creeks "to get the Treaty of New York set aside" which, he says (p. 51), "did not get far . . ."

American State Papers, Indian Affairs, vol. IV (Washington, 1832), gives an indication of the success McGillivray was enjoying in finding one of his principal opponents (Bowles) blamed for violent disturbances in the Creek border country, in a letter (p. 269) from Governor Blount of Tennessee to General McGillivray, Knoxville, May 17, 1792: "Sir. I am already informed that the murders and horse stealings lately committed by the Creeks, may, in a great degree, be charged to the attention they paid to the pernicious counsels of Mr. Bowles. . . ."

250 Wrongs suffered by the Tuscarora, particularly enslavement of children, are set forth in their petition to Pennsylvania in 1710, *Pennsylvania Provincial Council, Minutes*, 16 vols. (Philadelphia and Harrisburg, 1852–1853), vol. II, 511; summarized in Hodge, *Handbook*, vol. II, 843–844; and in MacLeod, 297–299, 106–109.

The quotation is from John Lawson, *A New Voyage to Carolina; Containing the Exact Description and Natural History of that Country; Together with the Present State thereof, and a Journal of a Thousand Miles Travel thro' Several Nations of Indians* (London, 1709). Also see Lawson, *History of Carolina, etc.* . . . (London, 1714, reprinted, Raleigh, N.C., 1860)

252 The "great service" is mentioned by Swanton (1952), 99 and 103—the people driven away by the Shawnee are usually called the Westo, a group Swanton believes to have been a part of the Yuchi.

The lines quoted describing Charleston cargoes are from J. Pinkerton, *General Collection of Voyages and Travels, 758–1826*. 16 vols (London, 1808–1814), vol. XII, 345.

The quoted prospectus of 1717 is by Sir Robert Mountgomery, *A Discourse concerning the design'd Establishment of a New Colony to the South of Carolina, in the Most Delightful Country of the Universe*, in *Force Tracts*, vol. I.

Oglethorpe is quoted from *Force Tracts*, vol. VI, "The Colony of Georgia under Gen. James Oglethorpe, Feb. 1, 1733."

253 Jonathan Daniels, *The Devil's Backbone, The Story of the Natchez Trace* (New York, 1962), 23, takes seriously the importance of the Battle of Ackia, a claim made by James Adair, *The History of the American Indians* (London, 1775, reprint, Johnson City, Tenn., 1930).

254 Young Washington is quoted during the French and Indian War from a letter to Lieutenant-Governor Robert Dinwiddie of Virginia in September 1756, in Dinwiddie, *Official Records* . . . *1751–1758*, R. O. Brock, ed., (Richmond, Va., 1883–1884), vol. II, 669–671: "Those Indians who are coming should be shown all possible respect and the greatest care taken of them. It is a critical time, they are very humorsome, and their assistance very necessary. . . ."

Carolyn Thomas Foreman, *op. cit.*, tells of the Creek embassy to England and gives Tomochichi's speech, 56–63; see the same work, 44–55, for the previous visit of seven Cherokees under the aegis of Sir Alexander Cuming.

255 The eighteenth-century list of goods "proper for the savages" is from Armand L. de Lahontan, *New Voyages to North America*, 2 vols (London, 1703), quoted in Pinkerton, *Voyages*, vol. XIII.
Franklin is quoted from *Two Tracts: Information to those who would Remove to America, and, Remarks Concerning the Savages of North America* 3d edition (London, 1784). In this same pamphlet Dr. Franklin rather belies his modern reputation as the iron duke of the Puritan work ethic by saying of Indians, "Having few artificial wants, they have abundance of leisure for improvement by conversation. Our laborious manner of life compared with theirs, they esteem slavish and base; and the learning on which we value ourselves, they regard as frivolous and useless. . . ." and by adding, apparently with hearty approval, an account of Six Nations Iroquois in 1744 refusing an offer by Virginia to educate some of their youth and offering instead to educate a dozen of Virginia's sons "and make men of them" if the "Gentlemen of Virginia" are willing. Franklin's complex personality has been reassessed in a judicious recent work, Wilbur R. Jacobs, ed., *Benjamin Franklin: Statesman-Philosopher or Materialist?* (New York, 1972),
Remarks and quotations re the Chickasaw and the Choctaw horse are from Robert West Howard, *The Horse in America* (Chicago, 1965), 26–27 and 184, quoting *inter alia* David Ramsay, *History of South Carolina* (Charleston, 1809): "Before the year 1754 the best horses for the draft or saddle in Carolina were called the Chickasaw breed . . . handsome, active and hardy, but small; seldom exceeding thirteen and a half hands in height. The mares . . . when crossed with English blooded horses, produced colts of great beauty, strength and swiftness."

256 The excerpts of 1753 are from Wm L. McDowell, Jr., ed., *Colonial Records of South Carolina* (Columbia, S.C., 1958), Documents relating to Indian Affairs, May 21, 1750–August 7, 1754, Report of Ludwick Grant to Governor Glen, February 8, 1753.
Cf. David H. Corkran, *The Cherokee Frontier: Conflict and Survival, 1740–1762* (Norman, Okla., 1962), and *The Creek Frontier 1540–1782* (Norman, 1967); Grace Steele Woodward, *The Cherokees* (Norman, 1963).

257 Pushmataha is quoted (attributively, anyway) from Jonathan Daniels, *op. cit.*, 188. (Pushmataha's sister married a Frenchman—their daughter, a "high-up lady," Rebecca Cravat, married Louis LeFleur; one of the eleven children born to this union was Greenwood LeFleur, better known as Leflore.)
Cotterill, 1954: "Meigs characterized the Cherokee government as a mild aristocracy which because of the number of chiefs was really a democracy . . ." (205, citing I.O.R. Retired Classified Files, Agent Meigs to Secretary of War, Dec. 30, 1817).
Cotterill, 224, lists among the important half-blood ruling families the Colberts (Chickasaw), the Folsoms and LeFlores (Choctaw), McIntoshes, Taitts, and McGillivrays (Creek), and Rosses, Vanns, Hickses, Lowrys, and McCoys (Cherokee).
M. E. Young points out that among the Creeks McGillivray was the last principal half-blood leader: ". . . though the resident trader and planter remained a familiar figure among the Creeks, none after McGillivray rose to high office in the nation. Where half-blood town chiefs exercised more than local influence, they wielded it through fullblood chieftans" (35).
The quotation of the Creeks' key location is from *Colonial Records of South Carolina, loc. cit.*

258 Mary A. O'Callaghan, "An Indian Removal Policy in Spanish Louisiana," in *Greater America: Essays in Honor of Herbert Eugene Bolton* (Berkeley, 1945), 281–295, outlines Indian movements across the Mississippi after 1763.

259 Colonel Anthony Hutchins, one of the first grantees in the Natchez district, arrived in 1772 and built his house on the White Apple Mound: Jonathan Daniels, *op. cit.*, p 27.

260 Quotations referring to the Cherokees are from Lydia Sigourney, *op. cit.*, notes.
A Cherokee census in 1810, published in an English church magazine, the *Christian Observer*, 1 (November 1811), 723 (quoted in John B. Davis, cited below): "Of negro slaves they have 598. The number of their cattle is 19,600, of horses 6,100, of hogs 9,400, of sheep 1,037. They have now in actual use 13 grist mills, 3 saw-mills, 3 salt-petre works, and 1 powder mill. They have also 30 wagons, between 480 and 500 ploughs, 1600 spinning wheels, 467 looms, and 49 silversmiths."
Quotations are from Grant Foreman, *Sequoyah* (Norman, 1937). John B. Davis, "The Life and Work of Sequoyah" in *Chronicles of Oklahoma* vol. VIII, 149, also brings together the better known facts and guesses and offers a bibliography. The often-quoted presumption that Sequoya was the son of a white man (Nathaniel Gist is sometimes suggested as his supposed father) rests on nothing sound whatever in the way of evidence.

263 Jackson is quoted from *Daring Deeds of American Heroes*, anonymously authored (New York, 1860), 244.
Cotterill, 1954: "The Creek War was, in its beginning at least, a civil war, having its cause neither in Tecumseh's visit in 1811 nor in British seductions in 1812, but in a long-gathering dissatisfaction with the civilization program . . . officially countenanced by the tribal government" (177).
Menewa (Hothlepoya) is variously spelled in reports and works of the period.

265 Abel (1906), 241–259, gives a long cool and careful look at Jefferson's intentions and actions in respect to Indian removal; the idea of Indian colonies in Upper Louisiana is discussed in the same work, 270–275.

De Rosier speaks of Jefferson's ideas on Indian removal, his excuse of national security—and the fact that he did not alter his policy when the ostensible security emergency subsided—and the "even more odious aspect" of his recommended method for obtaining Indian lands, 25-28.
Francis Paul Prucha, S. J., "Andrew Jackson's Indian Policy: A Reassessment," in the *Journal of American History*, 56/3 (December 1969), outlines the "principles of security" involved in Jackson's "exultation" over Indian cessions of 1815, 527-529.

266   Lewis Cass is quoted from F. P. Prucha, *Lewis Cass and American Indian Policy* (Detroit, 1967), p 15.
Anti-removal sentiment was not uncommon in the thinking of would-be Indian civilizers who were more sincerely interested in the Indian's welfare than in his land, *e.g.*, *Thoughts on the State of the American Indians. By a Citizen of the United States.* (New York, 1794), a pamphlet signed "Lycurgus," which makes as one of its principal points: "Another cause which has had no inconsiderable influence in retarding the civilization of the Indians, is their removal from the neighbourhood of the whites into the interior and uncultivated part of the country" (p. 17). "Lycurgus," however, agrees most earnestly that "Another principle which contributes to form the basis of civil society, and which distinguishes social from savage manners, is the establishment and management of private property" (p. 30).
The Reverend Jedidiah Morse, speaking to a group of Ottawas in 1820, summed up criteria of "civilization" then current: "Your father the President, wishes Indians to partake with his white children in all the blessings which they enjoy . . . These blessings, Indians cannot enjoy, so long as they remain distinct, independent nations, each having its own government and laws, and language, and lands; while they remain ignorant of our language, of our religion, of our government and modes of life, while you live in the hunter state, dress as you now dress . . . Your father wishes you to . . . collect together . . . on some of your own good lands, of sufficient extent, and have these lands divided into townships and farms, as the lands of the white people are divided and each man to have a farm of his own, with a title which he can transmit to his posterity. . . ." Jedidiah Morse, *Report to the Secretary of War of the United States, on Indian Affairs, comprising a Narrative of a Tour Performed in the Summer of 1820, under a Commission from the President of the United States, for the Purpose of Ascertaining, for the Uses of the Government, the actual State of the Indian tribes in our Country*, (New Haven, 1822), appendix, 10-14.
The Reverend Morse explained that missionaries were to be sent among the Indians, and "All who accept them will be in the way to be saved, and raised in respectability and usefulness in life. Those who persist in rejecting them, must, according to all past experience, gradually waste away . . . *Civilization* or *ruin*, are now the only alternatives of Indians . . . Among the means for your civilization, in addition to what have been already mentioned, we will bring you the best, the only *effectual* means of making you truly happy—we will bring you our BIBLE, the best of all Books. . . ."
Reverend Morse made more or less the same speech to a number of Indian communities on his trip, hoping to persuade them to accept missionary teachers authorized by an act of 1819 appropriating $10,000 for the employment of such teachers. He pointed out in his Report that 200 million acres of "some of the best lands in our country have been purchased, after our manner, and at our own price, of the Indian tribes" and that these could be presumed to "yield to the government a net profit of more than FIVE HUNDRED MILLIONS OF DOLLARS!!" of which the actual existence of this first ten thousand dollar appropriation as an earnest was, said he, "animating in no common degree. . . ." (93-95).
Cotterill, 1954, remarks of missionary activity among the southern Indians following this appropriation, "Anyone cynically inclined would not fail to notice the great increase in missionary ardor after the President's decision to subsidize the missions. Three missions were established before 1820 [when the subsidy became available]; eighteen were added by 1826" (227).
Jackson is quoted from De Rosier, 60, citing a letter to John C. Calhoun, then Secretary of War, while preparing the ground for the huge Choctaw cession of 1820.
Prucha, 1969, accepts the *pro forma* excuse of Jackson and his advisers as the valid motive for removal. Most specialists in the subject, such as Cotterill, 1954, and De Rosier (both works based on meticulous research), reach opposite conclusions. Wilcomb Washburn, in "The Writing of American Indian History: A Status Report," in *Pacific Historical Review*, 40/3 (August 1971), 261-283, greets Father Prucha's thesis with "incredulity."
In an earlier article—Wilcomb Washburn, "Indian Removal Policy: Administrative, Historical, and Moral Criteria for Judging its Success or Failure" in *Ethnohistory*, 12/3 (Summer 1965), 274-278—Washburn gives as Prucha's fundamental moral assumptions that "white advance was inevitable and, ultimately, beneficial, and that Indians constituted a 'savage' and 'pagan' race who had to be conducted along the road to 'civilization' and 'Christianity.'" Washburn added that, "Neither assumption, in my opinion, is necessarily or completely valid." Father Prucha develops these assumptions in *American Indian Policy in the Formative Years: The Indian Trade and Intercourse Acts, 1790-1834*.
In a later work—F. P. Prucha, *The Sword of the Republic: The United States Army on the Frontier 1783-1846* (New York, 1969)—Father Prucha develops a further basic assumption, that "on the frontier the need for order was clear" (395). There is some similarity between this position and that of Joseph de Maistre, the leading anti-revolutionary reactionary in Europe during Napoleonic times, who adopted as his first principle

the necessity of order. (He wrote a panegyric on the executioner as the foundation of social order, arguing that all other matters, such as justice, must come later, no social action, just or otherwise, being possible without order.) The definition of "order" would seem to be complicated, though, by the fact that the "order" imposed by one faction might mean disorder for another faction—the "order" imposed, for example, by a dominant commercial faction of white society sometimes very definitely entailed disorder and disaster for the Indian nations. (The "order" imposed by the executioner, that is to say, brings a fatal disorder, obviously, to the victim.)

At the time of the Treaty of Dancing Rabbit Creek, the Choctaw removal treaty, in 1830, there were enrolled in the Choctaw nation 151 whites: De Rosier, 126. (There were also 521 black slaves held in the nation, principally of course by well-to-do half-bloods.)

Runaway blacks taken in by Indian communities had been a problem for neighboring white communities from the earliest times; escaped black slaves among the Seminoles constituted a substantial group and, perhaps, a substantial motive for the Seminole war on the part of their irate ex-owners.

In the early eighteenth century the Mohawks refused to surrender an indentured servant who had escaped to their country: "No, they answered, we never serve any Man so, who puts himself under our Protection . . ." but ". . . though we never will deliver him up, we are willing to pay the Value of the Servant to his Master." Colden, vol. I, 13.

Senator Reed is quoted from De Rosier, 91.

267   Paul Wallace Gates, *The Farmer's Age: Agriculture 1815–1860*, (New York, 1960), writes that pioneering in the new cotton areas of the Old Southwest ("rich planters with their scores of slaves clearing the forests, burning the canebrake") differed from the typical "frontier" image (140). He adds: ". . . the great profits in agriculture came not from tillage but from buying virgin land cheaply, improving and selling it while its fertility was still rich . . ." (143).

Frank L. Owsley, "The Pattern of Migration and Settlement on the Southern Frontier," in *Journal of Southern History*, 11 (May 1945), 146–177, finds that up until the annexation of Oregon the open land area in the South was twice as great as that of the North, while the white population was less than half (148–149). Owsley cites (149–150) a typical example of sales literature that heled form the typical frontier image: John M. Peck, *A New Guide for Emigrants to the West* (Boston, 1837): "First comes the pioneer, who provides for the subsistence of his family chiefly upon the natural growth . . . and the proceeds of hunting. His implements of agriculture are rude; chiefly of his own make, and his efforts directed mainly to a crop of corn and a 'truck patch.' . . ." This, oddly enough, might be a fairly accurate description of an average woodland Indian household.

Cotterill, *The Old South* (1936), speaking of the rush of immigration into inland Georgia: "Much more spectacular than the rush of settlers, however, was the rush of speculators. . . ." Corrupt governors granted to speculators almost thirty million acres in an area only ten million acres in extent, and seven million acres in the frontier county of Montgomery, which only totaled 400,000 acres.

Several studies have shown that the "yeoman planter" who owned few or no slaves did indeed make up a significant segment of the early population in the frontier South. However, Cotterill, 1936, uses slave-population statistics to state: "It is evident from the number of slaves that Mississippi Territory was a planting community from the beginning. . . ." (117). The cotton kingdom as a whole in 1820 was almost half-slave of its total non-Indian population of one million, and Mississippi, the farthest frontier, with 32,814 slaves out of a total population of 75,448, fully equalled the ratio of previously settled areas (126).

Says M. E. Young: "The picture of the 'actual settler' or the 'poor Indian' may be in considerable measure one of those images of small men which persist because large men can make use of them" (72).

Avery O. Craven, *Soil Exhaustion as a Factor in the Agricultural History of Virginia and Maryland, 1606–1860* (Urbana, Ill., 1926): ". . . exhausted and abandoned lands behind the advancing frontier were but a counterpart to the mineral waste and charred stumps in the train of the exploiter of mineral wealth or of virgin forest . . ." (22). ". . . the exhausted and eroded surfaces that appeared on all sides . . . the 'galled and butchered' lands. . . ." (90–91).

Owsley, *op. cit.*, quoting a letter of January 1817 from U. S. Senator Charles Tait of Georgia, who had sent his son "with a few Negroes" into Alabama public domain to select a future home for the family: ". . . a stream near at hand for a mill and machinery—a never failing spring at the foot of a hillock, on the summit of which a mansion house can be built in due time. . . ." (173).

De Rosier (107) quotes the need of Indian lands to "encourage immigration."

Ray Allen Billington, *Westward Expansion* (New York, 1949), sums up the situation: "The helpless Indians were now at the mercy of an unsympathetic president and ruthless state officers who vied with each other in making life miserable for the red men. . . ." (315).

Cotterill, 1954: "On two vital points they had remained unchanged and, it may be, unimproved. They had not accepted the white man's religion or his idea of holding land in severalty . . . In 1825 the Southern Indians were as strongly communistic as in 1775. . . . Tribal ownership permitted private utilization and private control but forbade private alienation . . . an occupant of land could transfer his holdings only with tribal consent . . . tribal ownership of land seemed to be the foundation of tribal unity; private ownership an evidence, if not a cause, of tribal disintegration" (230).

Ideological proselytizing for private property was not limited to the United States. In eighteenth-century Mexico, Bernardo de Galvez recommended that Indians be encouraged to "become greedy for the possession of land."—Lewis Hanke, "Indians and Spaniards in the New World: A Personal View" in Howard Peckham and Charles Gibson, eds., *Attitudes of Colonial Powers Toward the American Indian* (Salt Lake City, 1969), 11.

268 Lewis Cass is quoted in Prucha, 1967, 13.
Policy of the new United States toward the Scioto Land Company is weighed (and found wanting) in Abel, 1906, 265–267.
Andrew Jackson is quoted from Bassett, vol. III, 88.
Bassett sums up Jackson's character in his preface to vol. III: "He was nearly incapable of seeing any side of a question but that on which he had ranged himself. . . ." (xv).
James Parton's assessment of Jackson's weaknesses: "No man in this country has ever been subjected to such a torrent of applause, and few men have been less prepared to withstand it . . ." (vol. III, 639).
Cotterill, 1954, of Jackson as a treaty commissioner: ". . . supplemented open intimidation with wholesale hidden bribery . . ." (204). ". . . unscrupulous Indian baiter . . ." (202). ". . . plundering . . . grand larceny . . ." (165). ". . . provided commissioners could be found with the capacity for the necessary chicanery and intimidation. Fortunately, Andrew Jackson again became available . . ." (206). And see De Rosier, 63, 69.

269 Pushmataha and the Choctaws at New Orleans are dealt with in detail in De Rosier, 36; Cotterill, 1954, 183–184 and 190; Bassett, vol. II, 73–74. The legislative resolution of thanks—for help in the Creek War—and gifts is reprinted in *Chronicles of Oklahoma*, 6/4 (1928), 481–482. For the 1816 U.S. promise of everlasting friendship, De Rosier, 37.
Typical of the deceit put forward in Indian treaty negotiations: Jackson, in arguing for the cessions at Doak's Stand, stated there were five white settlers to every Indian in Mississippi and yet the settlers were living on one-third as much land. But the white population in 1820 was 42,800, as against some 25,000 or more Indians—numbering 23,400 even eight years later.

270 *Speeches on the Passage of the Bill for the Removal of the Indians, Delivered in the Congress of the United States, April and May, 1830* (Boston 1830), a collection of speeches opposed to the bill, states in the introduction, page vi, that states' rights was a chief issue; and adds that the advocates of the bill "placed no reliance upon argument" but "trusted only to the power of self-interest and party discipline" (viii). "The opposition to the bill was made in great earnestness, and with every mark of entire sincerity. There was no indication that the concern expressed for the national honor, and the dread of seeing a foul and indelible stain fixed upon the character of the country, were affected, or overstated." On the other hand, some of the bill's advocates "expressed a strong belief that the removal of the Indians would be for their benefit; but other boldly declared, that this was not *their* object . . ." (viii). The two foremost arguments advanced in favor of the bill, says the introduction, was that "it is very absurd to suppose that independent States will suffer their limits to be curtailed by tribes of savages . . . That [Georgia] . . . is determined to assert and maintain the rights of sovereign and independent States . . ." (vi) and ". . . acquisition of the lands . . ." (vii).
Some of the speeches on both sides may be seen in Thomas Hart Benton, ed., *Abridgment of the Debates of Congress, from 1789 to 1856*, vol. X (New York, 1859), in which the argument that removal "is demanded by the dictates of humanity" is bluntly answered by "Who urges this plea? They who covet the Indian lands . . ." (vol. X, 526).

271 Evasion by "obvious" and "overwhelming" fraud of Article 14 of the Treaty of Dancing Rabbit Creek (the Article permitting individual Choctaws to enroll as allottees and remain in their homeland) is detailed in De Rosier, 135–137.

272 The story of Emubby's murder is one of many related in Foreman, 1932.
The government spokesman (Secretary of War Eaton) guaranteeing the permanence of the new Indian territory is quoted in McKenney, *Memoirs*, vol. I, 254.
De Rosier quotes the Southern sentiments of dissent, 105–106, and the sentiment of ethnocentricity, 108. *Ibid.*, 114 and 125, for the bribes received by Greenwood LeFlore and other chiefs and captains.

273 Young, 28–29, quotes the hot-gospel motto.
De Rosier, 120–121, and *n.* 121, speaks of the barring of the missionaries from the treaty grounds.

274 The nation in mourning is quoted from Muriel H. Wright, "The Removal of the Choctaws to Indian Territory," in *Chronicles of Oklahoma*, 6/2 (1928), 103–128.

275 The incidents of removal rest mainly on Foreman, 1932, and the detailed account of Choctaw removal in De Rosier, 137 ff.
Foreman, 1932, p. 65, the wintry delays of Major F. W. Armstrong.
Washington Irving is quoted from his notes "for the Conspiracy of Neamathla," 1823, MS, Henry E. Huntington Library. His published sketch is found in *Wolfert's Roost and Other Papers* (New York, 1863).

276 Foreman, 1932, is found in *Wolfert's Roost and Other Papers* (New York, 1863).

277   *Ibid.*, is found in *Wolfert's Roost and Other Papers* (New York, 1863).
The quotation on Creek custom in land ownership is from D. W. Eakins, 1847, quoted in Schoolcraft, vol. I, p. 277.

278   The Creek quotation is from Foreman, 1932, 113.

279   The quotations are from Foreman, 108, *n.* 7; 134.
The Georgia Compact of 1802 called for the cession to the United States of all Georgia's claimed land west of the present Georgia boundary, on condition that the U.S. pay certain sums, validate certain previous grants, make compensation to various land companies involved in previous (occasionally fraudulent) speculations. One provision stated "That the United States shall, at their own expense, extinguish, for the use of Georgia, as early as the same can be peaceably obtained, on reasonable terms, the Indian title to the country of Talassee, to the lands left out by the line drawn with the Creeks, in the year one thousand seven hundred and ninety-eight, which had been previously granted by the State of Georgia, both which tracts had formally been yielded by the Indians; and to the lands within the forks of Oconee and Ocmulgee rivers; for which several objects the President of the United States has directed that a treaty should be immediately held with the Creeks; and that the United States shall, in the same manner, also extinguish the Indian title to all the other lands within the State of Georgia."—S. G. McLendon, *History of the Public Domain of Georgia* (Atlanta, 1924), p. 112.
This last phrase, with its curious air of an afterthought, is what caused the subsequent trouble in seeming to lend a color of legality to Georgia's efforts to drive all Indians from her borders. Since no Indian nations were signatories to the Compact, the question arises by what authority the United States thus agreed to dispose of their lands, especially since by previous treaties the U.S. had explicitly guaranteed protection of the Indian nations in the possession of their remaining lands. Thus this last clause would seem to be in clear and direct conflict with treaties such as the Treaty of New York with the Creeks in 1790, Article V of that treaty reading: "The United States solemnly guarantee to the Creek Nation, all their lands within the limits of the United States to the westward and southward of the boundary described in the preceding article" (Kappler, vol. II, 27).
Article II of this same Treaty of 1790 stipulated that the "Creek Nation will not hold any treaty with an individual State" (Kappler, vol. II, 25), thus specifically prohibiting state jurisdiction for the Creek nation, a jurisdiction, however, that both federal and state governments later imposed on the Creeks.
The Jackson quotations are from Thomas L. McKenney, *Memoirs* (1846), vol. I, 258–259; Parton, *Jackson*, vol. III, p. 283, quoting a toast delivered by President Jackson at the Jefferson Day Dinner of 1830; Bassett, vol. IV, 504, an extract from a letter to Martin Van Buren, December 23, 1832.

280   *Ibid.*, vol. IV, 498, for the Jackson quotation.
The newspaper quotation, from the Boston *Gazette*, is found in Parton, vol. III, 39.

281   The quotations are from Prucha, *Sword of the Republic*, and from Foreman, 1932, p. 153.

282   The Jackson administration's capital assurance is from McKenney, *Memoirs*, vol. I, 249. The further protestations of U. S. support and protection for the Cherokees are from *ibid.*, vol. I, 256.
George Washington is quoted from *ibid.*, vol. I, 130–131.
Henry Clay is quoted from Thurman Wilkins, *Cherokee Tragedy—The Story of the Ridge Family and the Decimation of a People* (New York, 1970), 256–257.

283   Quotations are from *ibid.*, 257; and from F. P. Prucha, *The Sword of the Republic*, 263–264.
National Archives, *List of Documents Concerning . . . Indian Treaties*, provides a summary of treaties between the United States and the Cherokee Nation from 1785 to 1835; a great deal of correspondence from the treaty commissioners, William Carroll and the Reverend John F. Schermerhorn; various drafts, instructions, and proclamations concerned with the treaty; and supplemental articles signed in March 1836. The Reverend Schermerhorn (McKenney in his *Memoirs* sarcastically underlines his title) was much in demand at the time as a treaty commissioner, having produced treaties in 1833 with the Western Cherokee and in 1832, 1834, and 1835 with the Potawatomi.
Public Statutes at Large, vol. VII, lists (p. 487) a supplemental article, Article 20, guaranteeing payment by the United States of all "unpaid just claims upon the Indians, without expense to them, out of the proper funds of the United States, for the settlement of which a cession or cessions of land has or have been heretofore made by the Indians, in Georgia. Provided the United States or the State of Georgia has derived benefit from the said cession or cessions of land without having made payment to the Indians therefore." This article was stricken out (p. 489) by the Senate. *Cf.* notes for p. 422, in Chapter XI, below.
General Jackson is quoted from Wilkins, *op cit.*, 254.
See also Morris L. Wardell, *A Political History of the Cherokee Nation 1838–1907* (Norman, 1938); Grace Steele Woodward, *The Cherokees* (Norman, 1963); and John Phillip Reid, *A Law of Blood: The Primitive Law of the Cherokee Nation* (New York, 1970).
One actual record of a vote between the pro-treaty Cherokee faction (the Ridge party) and the faction opposed to the treaty (the Ross party) is revealed in a letter to his children from Lewis Ross, brother of principal chief John Ross, March 1, 1837, first printed in *Nimrod, a Literary Review published in cooperation*

with the University of Tulsa, 16/2 (Tulsa, Okla., 1972), 16: "On the 15th of last month an election was held at New Echota by a notice from our agent, General N. Smith for the purpose of ascertaining what disposition the Cherokees wished to be made of monies due the Nation under former treaties. The notice was very short—only fifteen days. We rallied our friends and went down. The votes were taken. Ninety-seven votes were voted by Ridge Party for it to be paid for Ridges' Committee. Our members, those opposed to Ridge and his party, voted 1,269 strong directing the money to be paid into the hands of Mr. George Sowrey [sic—Lowrey was probably meant]—subject to the order of our committee and Council. There you see that Ridges' party are but a small faction of the nation, and yet have assumed the power and have sold our country from us, contrary to the known will of the Cherokee people."

284 The Superintendent, Thomas L. McKenney, is quoted from McKenney, *Memoirs*, vol. I, 272, and vol. II, 126.
Losses and costs of the Seminole War are totaled in Prucha, *Sword of the Republic*, 301.
General Thomas Sidney Jesup, in a report of June 10, 1837, quoted in E. C. McReynolds, *The Seminoles* (Norman, 1953): "If the war were carried on it must necessarily be one of extermination. We have, at no former period in our history, had to contend with so formidable an enemy. No Seminole proves false to his country, nor has a single instance ever occurred of a first rate warrior having surrendered."
The following month, July, 1837, Jesup urged that the U. S. should give up insisting on the removal of the Seminoles, "that to insist upon it would prolong a useless war without any hope of a satisfactory conclusion . . ." Secretary of War Joel Poinsett replied that the principles and motives were "not a question for the executive now to consider. The treaty has been ratified, and is the law of the land; and the constitutional duty of the president requires that he should cause it to be executed" (Prucha, *Sword of the Republic*, 290–291). Three months later, in October, Jesup instituted, with the capture of Osceola and his party, the program of treacherously taking captives under a flag of truce. The son of Philip, principal chief on the St. John's river, was captured when he came to St. Augustine in September or October 1837 under a flag of truce to consult his prisoner-father about the future policy of his people (Foreman, 1932, citing *Army and Navy Chronicle*, vol. V). The Cherokee delegation in Florida in November brought in a leading chief, Mikanopy, with eleven other chiefs and fifteen or twenty warriors, under a flag of truce to Fort Mellon, arriving December third—these people were all imprisoned by General Jesup at St. Augustine, calling forth the protest quoted from John Ross (*American State Papers*, "Military Affairs," vol. VII, 690; *New York Observer*, December 16, 1837, *et seq.*; Ross, writing to the Secretary of War, is quoted in *U. S. House Document 285*, 25th Congress, 2d Session). The young chief Wild Cat escaped and enflamed his people with news of such imprisonments; other prisoners were then moved to Fort Moultrie on Sullivan's Island, Charleston, where escape was impossible—these prisoners included Mikanopy, Coahadjo, Philip, Cloud (later a major in the Confederate Army and killed in the Civil War), 116 warriors, eighty-two women and children, and Osceola; later with 220 other prisoners they were moved to Fort Pike Barracks, New Orleans. "Osceola seems to be in great distress of mind," wrote the painter Catlin, after an interview, and Osceola died soon afterward. The war going badly, Jesup sent word to the Indians to come in for a conference (February 1838), after which the Indians agreed to assemble within ten days near Fort Jupiter to hear what the general might learn from communicating with the President. Jesup then captured 513 assembled Indians on March twenty-first and the two succeeding days (Foreman, 1932).
Colonel Hitchcock is quoted from *ibid.*, 378, *n.* 17.
See also Grant Foreman, ed., *A Traveler in Indian Territory, The Journal of Ethan Allen Hitchcock, late Major General in the United States Army* (Cedar Rapids, Iowa, 1930), foreword by John R. Swanton—who says, of the Great Removal: ". . . this undertaking seems to have been used as a means of the most cold-blooded systematic looting of public and tribal moneys and was accompanied by a cynical disregard for human suffering and the destruction of human life . . ." (7). Hitchcock was sent to Indian Territory in 1841 to investigate frauds connected with the Removal; Swanton remarks that his report was not made public and "its mysterious disappearance from all official files proves at one and the same time the honesty of the report and the dishonesty of the national administration of the period"—from the Foreword, 8.
Quotations are from Prucha, *Sword of the Republic*, 294 and 300.

286 Menewa is quoted from McKenney and Hall.

NOTES for Chapter X

General works most used in this chapter are Hanke, 1949; Peter Martyr; Curtis; Steward, *Handbook*; Rousseau; Morgan, *Ancient Society*; Hodge, *Handbook*; McKenney and Hall; Tozzer, *Landa*; MacLeod; *Jesuit Relations*; Swanton, 1953; Jackson, *Century of Dishonor*; Du Tertre; Chinard; Atkinson;

and for page

287 Columbian details are from John Boyd Thacher, *Christopher Columbus, His Life, His Work, His Remains*, 3 vols. (New York, 1903); and Samuel Eliot Morison, *Admiral of the Ocean Sea*, 2 vols. (Boston, 1942).

288 The quotation is from the Latin version of Columbus' letter to Gabriel Sanchez, Crown Treasurer, dated Lisbon, March 14, 1493, as reprinted in *Mémoires de la Sociéte d'Ethnographie*, 2d Série, Tome Premier (Paris, 1877).

289 The great debate between Las Casas and Sepulveda is the subject of Lewis Hanke, *Aristotle and the American Indians* (New York, 1959; Bloomington, 1970).

290 The recent theory on the origin of syphilis is stated in E. H. Hudson, "Treponematosis and Man's Social Evolution," in *American Anthropologist*, 67/4 (August 1965), 885–902.
Science News Letter, June 11, 1960, 384, reports the "friendly debate" on the origin of syphilis between Dr. T. Dale Stewart, curator of physical anthropology at the Smithsonian Institution, and Dr. Charles W. Goff, Yale University School of Medicine.
A typical example of the widespread supposition in the seventeenth century that syphilis was brought from America is in Alexander Ross, *The History of the World: The second part, in six books: being a continuation of the famous History of Sir Walter Raleigh, Knight: Beginning where he left; Viz. at the end of the Macedonian Kingdom, and deduced to these Later-Times . . .* (London, 1652), 503, speaking of Charles VIII at war with the Venetians and the Sfortians in 1494: "Charles indeed got the Victory; but shortly after lost all his booty, being carried away by the Mercenary Greeks, . . . so the French return home, having brought nothing with them but the Neapolitan disease, which the Spaniards conveyed thither from America. . . ."
The Maya quotation is from Maud W. Makemson, *The Book of the Jaguar Priest; a Translation of the Book of Chilam Balam of Tizimin, with Commentary* (New York, 1931).

291 The first (fragmentary) English translation of Peter Martyr is Richard Eden, *Peter Martyr the History of Travayle in the West and Easte Indies, etc.* (London, 1555).
Montaigne is quoted from John Florio's translation, 1603, in which "Of the Canniballes" appears in Chapter XXX, Book I.

292 Sir Sidney Lee mentions Sir Thomas More's South American sources, and numerous other early American influences, in sixteenth-century England, in "The American Indian in Elizabethan England" and "The Path to Jamestown," both in *Elizabethan and Other Essays* (Oxford, 1929); and in "The Call of the West: America and Elizabethan England," in *Scribners*, 41 (May 1907), 537–551—this last article emphasizing the Spanish contribution to later English action, especially scientific precision in navigation, mapmaking, and so on, mentioning specifically Drake's Portuguese pilot, Raleigh's long and profitable conversations with his sometime prisoners Don Antonio de Berro and Don Sarmiento de Gamboa, the "little army of Spanish grandees" who came to London in Prince Philip's nuptial retinue, some of them enriched by New World fortunes (one was Martin Cortes, born twenty-one years before in Mexico City), not to mention the ninety-seven chests of New World silver brought as a wedding gift in 1554.

293 Goethe is quoted from *Conversations with Eckermann* (January 18, 1827).
McNickle, 1949, discusses the place of Montaigne and Rousseau in what he calls "The Golden Myth" (118–123).

294 For Morgan to Engels to Marx, previously discussed in the notes to the introduction, see Leslie A. White, ed., *Lewis Henry Morgan, The Indian Journals* (Ann Arbor, 1959).

295 Quotations re Tamanend and the Tammany Society are from J. Mooney's article on Tammany in Hodge, *Handbook*, vol. II, 633–634.

296 Cotton Mather is quoted from Book VII, vol. 108, *Magnalia Christi Americana* (1702).
The quotation is from Clark Wissler, *Indians of the United States* (New York, 1940), 254, quoting from *Historical Account of Bouquet's Expedition against the Ohio Indians, in 1764* (Cincinatti, 1868), 80–81.

297 Jefferson is quoted from McKenney and Hall, and Landa from Tozzer, *Landa*.

299 *Indian Anecdotes and Barbarities . . . etc.* (Barre, Mass., 1837), 32 pages.
Bernard W. Sheehan, *Seeds of Extinction, Jeffersonian Philanthropy and the American Indian* (Chapel Hill, 1973), demonstrates that the concept of the Indians' "savage character" is by no means yet extinct: ". . . they inflicted on him the painful refinements of many centuries of savage violence" (186); ". . . Indians inflicted pain with much less misgiving than did civilized men" (198); ". . . cunning . . . frenzy of savage conflict and torture . . ." (211), *inter alia*.
Jung's observation is mentioned in A. Irving Hallowell, "The Impact of the Indian on American Culture" in *American Anthropologist*, 59/2 (April 1957).
The quotation is from Allan Nevins and Henry S. Commager, *A Short History of the United States* (New York, 1966).

300 The epic poem quoted is *Ma-Ka-Tai-Me-She-Kia-Kiak; or, Black Hawk, and Scenes in the West. A National Poem: in Six Cantos.* by Elbert H. Smith (New York, 1849).
The story of Petalesharo is from Thomas L. McKenney, *Memoirs* (New York, 1846), vol. II, 94–96.
For a recent study of the Pawnee world see Gene Weltfish, *The Lost Universe* (New York, 1965).
Francis Parkman is quoted from his prefatory note to *The Oregon Trail* (1849).

502   THE LAST AMERICANS

301   The description of Eleazar Williams is quoted in J. N. B. Hewitt's biographical sketch of Williams in Hodge, *Handbook*, vol. II, 955.
John Dunn Hunter, *Memoirs of a Captivity Among the Indians of North America* (1823), claimed to have been a white child captive brought up among the Osage, became a considerable and controversial celebrity with his efforts to organize the Red and White Republic of Fredonia. His veracity is still an open question, as witness a book new at this writing that undertakes to clear his name of long-standing charges of charlatanism, Richard Drinnon, *White Savage, The Case of John Dunn Hunter* (New York, 1972).
The Dutch pastor is again "Johannes Megapolensis, Jr.," cited in notes to Chapter VIII, 317. The Seneca sachem is Red Jacket, quoted in McKenney and Hall.
The Jesuit priest (Le Jeune) and the (probably) Algonkin priest are paraphrased from the *Jesuit Relations* as quoted in McNickle, 1949, 128.

302   The Mohawk Duke of Northumberland is quoted from W. L. Stone, *Life of Joseph Brant* (1838 edition), also cited for Chapter VIII.
Lydia Sigourney also quoted references to the magnificence of Indian oratory (in *Traits of the Aborigines of America*, (Cambridge, 1822, *n.* 34, line 530, Canto Third, p. 250): "Sansom, in his travels in Canada, remarks, 'when Father Charlevoix, a learned Jesuit, first assisted at an Indian council, he could not believe that the Jesuit, who acted as interpreter, was not imposing upon the audience the effusions of his own brilliant imagination . . . accustomed to the Orations of Massillon, and Bourdaloue . . . he confesses that he had never heard anything so interesting, as the extempore discourses of an Indian chief.'" Even those persons, she adds, who have heard Burke and Sheridan and Fox and Pitt "during the most splendid period of British oratory, have freely acknowledged that they never heard anything more impressive than an Indian speech."

304   "The Blue Juniata," by Marian Dix Sullivan (1850) is a fine example of false-flying folklore, antelopes not through forests going, and wild-roving Indian girls' tresses surely not wavy flowing, leastways not without the help of curling irons. The Indian created in the white man's image may be in some respects the most telling if not the unkindest nineteenth-century cut of all.

NOTES for Chapter XI

General works most used in this chapter are Abel, 1904 and 1906; Kappler, vol. II; Statutes at Large, vol. VII; American State Papers, Indian Affairs; Gates, 1954; Hodge, *Handbook*; Swanton, 1953; Kroeber, 1953;

and for page

305   The principal authority quoted is Annie Heloise Abel, 1906, 267.
James L. Clayton, "The Impact of Traders' Claims on the American Fur Trade," in David M. Ellis, ed., *The Frontier in American Development, Essays in Honor of Paul Wallace Gates* (Ithaca, 1966), 299–322, is the source for the total of traders' claims (303).

306   F. P. Prucha, *Lewis Cass and American Indian Policy* (Detroit, 1967) remarks (18) on the interest historians have taken in the special friendship between Cass and the American Fur Company.
P. W. Gates, Introduction to *The John Tipton Papers*, ed. by Nellie Armstrong Robertson and Dorothy Riker, 3 vols. (Indianapolis, 1942), gives the Richardville figures, pages 49 and 44.
The quotation referring to speculators obtaining hundreds of thousands of acres is from the foreword by Frederick Merk to Ellis, ed., *op. cit.*
The quotation referring to Tipton is from Gates, introduction to the *John Tipton Papers*, 49.
The recent study quoted on the prevalence of speculators is Leslie E. Decker, "The Great Speculation: An Interpretation of Mid-Continent Pioneering," in Ellis, ed., *op. cit.*, 379.

307   Abel, 1906, 266, speaks of the troubles stemming from the Scioto land grant and similar acts of statesmanship.
Ibid., the quotation on the Treaty of Greenville.
Analysis of Tecumseh's position rests on Abel, 1906, 269. The Cherokees attempted to establish an agreement among sixteen Indian nations, meeting at "Talequa" in the new Indian Territory in June 1843, that no nation would, without the consent of all, sell or cede "any part of their present Territory"—Thomas L. McKenney, *Memoirs* (1846), vol. II, 128.
The purported Tecumseh quotation is from Anonymous, *Daring Deeds of American Heroes, etc.* (New York, 1860), 108–109.

308   The story of Tecumseh discarding his uniform for buckskins is mentioned in the biographical sketch by James Mooney in Hodge, *Handbook*, vol. II, 714.

309   Quotations dealing with the Potawatomi are from Gates, Introduction to the *Tipton Papers*, 45.
Irving McKee, ed., *The Trail of Death, Letters of Benjamin Marie Petit*, Indiana Historical Society Publications, 14/1 (Indianapolis, 1941)—the letters of a priest who accompanied the Indiana Potawatomi on

their forced march into exile—quotes Lewis Cass while Secretary of War (1834) as objecting to any Potawatomis at all remaining in their homeland: ". . . they ought all speedily to go" (19). However, Commissary General Gibson, "upon whose department lay the responsibility of conducting an emigration," explained that the intention of the government was not to remove all the Indians to the West, "but rather to extinguish their nationality." Petit concludes that Gibson's statement reveals "either a lack of unity or a duplicity in the policy of the War Department" (21).

Petit, writing to his Bishop in 1838 of a Potawatomi delegation that had gone to Washington with a vain protest—"'I do not wish to speak of it,' said the President. 'Your names are on the treaty; your lands are lost,' said the Secretary of War. 'But here is one of the witnesses to the treaty who will show you how everything was a fraud.' 'I do not need to be shown, and we did not need your signatures: the great chiefs of the nation were entitled to sell your reserve.' . . ."

At a council held in Indiana to arrange the "emigration," a leading chief interrupted the interpreter, "seized the agent's hand, and said to him: 'Look here, Father; our lands belong to us. We shall keep them; we do not wish to talk to you any more.' This was taken as an insult to the President, and a report was made asking for authorization to use force if they refused to leave their lands. But there will be no occasion for this, as they have no idea of resistance" (81–82). A note, *n.* 14, pp. 81–82, quotes what may have been the complete speech giving this objection, made by the chief known as Menominee: "Members of the Council: The President does not know the truth. He, like me, has been imposed upon. He does now know that your treaty is a lie, and that I never signed it. He does not know that you made my young chiefs drunk and got their consent and pretended to get mine. He does not know that I have refused to sell my lands and still refuse. He would not by force drive me from my home, the graves of my tribe, and my children who have gone to the Great Spirit, nor allow you to tell me your braves will take me, tied like a dog, if he knew the truth. My brothers, the President is just, but he listens to the word of the young chiefs who have lied; and when he knows the truth he will leave me to my own. I have not sold my lands. I will not sell them. I have not signed any treaty, and will not sign any. I am not going to leave my lands, and I don't want to hear anything more about it."

For some later history of these Potawatomi—who in Kansas came to be called the "Mission Band"—see James A. Clifton, "Culture Change, Structural Stability and Factionalism in the Prairie Potawatomi Reservation Community," in *Midcontinent American Studies Journal*, 6/2 (Fall 1965), 101–123.

310 The Horace Greeley remark, from the *New York Tribune*, June 2 and 9, 1859, is quoted in Gates, 1954, 102.

311 The record number of statues to Sacagawea is mentioned in W. J. Ghent's biographical sketch of her in the *Dictionary of American Biography*.

NOTES for Chapter XII

General works most used in this chapter are Jenness; Birket-Smith, 1959; Holm, 1965; Driver, 1969; Boas, 1888; Wormington, 1957; Willey, 1966; Hodge, *Handbook*; Kroeber, 1953; Curtis; Bancroft;

and for page

314 Willey, 1966, 414, states that data are still too scarce for the archaeology of the Arctic and Subarctic to offer a formal chronological organization. But among a number of important recent studies are R. S. MacNeish, *Men Out of Asia, As Seen from the Northwest Yukon*, Anthropological Papers, University of Alaska, 7/2 (Fairbanks, 1959); the same author's *Investigations in the Southwest Yukon: Part II: Archaeological Excavation, Comparisons and Speculations*, Peabody Foundation for Archaeology Papers, 7/1 (Andover, Mass., 1964); C. S. Chard, *The Old World Roots: Review and Speculations*, Anthropological Papers, University of Alaska, 10/2 (Fairbanks, 1963); and J. L. Giddings, *The Archaeology of Cape Denbigh* (Providence, R.I., 1964).

315 Speculation on relationships between the Eskimo and other languages is from the intriguing article by W. Thalbitzer, "Possible Early Contacts Between Eskimo and Old World Languages," in Sol Tax, ed., *Indian Tribes of Aboriginal America: Selected Papers of the XXIXth Congress of Americanists* (Chicago, 1952).

317 Boas, 1888, gives several Central Eskimo traditions regarding the Tornit (634–636 and 640), although adding (n. page 616) that the stories were "curtailed, as some parts were considered inappropriate for this publication. The full text will be found in the *Verhandlungen der Berliner Gesellschaft für Anthropologie, Ethnologie and Urgeschichte*, Berlin 1888.

The quotation is from Knud Rasmussen, "Intellectual Culture of the Iglulik Eskimos," in *Report of the Fifth Thule Expedition*, Vol. VII (Copenhagen, 1929), 2.

Among others, Kaj Birket-Smith, in "The Caribou Eskimos" in *Report of the Fifth Thule Expedition*, vol. V, part 1 (Copenhagen, 1929), suggests the Tunit as probable bearers of the Thule culture.

319 The fragment of poetry is from Rasmussen, "Intellectual Culture of the Copper Eskimos," in *Report of the Fifth Thule Expedition*, vol. IX (Copenhagen, 1932).

320   The stellar names are from K. Birkiet-Smith in "The Caribou Eskimos," cited above. The quotation is from Rasmussen, ". . . Iglulik Eskimos," in vol. VII of the *Fifth Thule Report* (Copenhagen, 1929).

321   One of the best of many fine books picturing the high culture of the Northwest Coast is Audrey Hawthorn, *Art of the Kwakiutl Indians and Other Northwest Coast Tribes* (Vancouver and Seattle, 1967). See also the detailed work on totem poles, Marius Barbeau, *Totem Poles*, 2 vols., National Museum of Canada, Anthropological Series No. 30, Bulletin 119 (Ottawa, 1952). European contact is the subject of Wilson Duff, *The Indian History of British Columbia, Vol. I, The Impact of the White Man*, Victoria, B.C., Provincial Museum of Natural History and Anthropology, Anthropological Memoir No. 5 (Victoria, 1964). Two recent general surveys of the people of the Northwest Coast are Thomas R. McFeat, ed., *Indians of the North Pacific Coast* (Seattle, 1967); and Philip Drucker, *Cultures of the North Pacific Coast* (San Francisco, 1965).

322   Sir Edward Belcher, *Narrative of a Voyage Round the World . . . in Her Majesty's Ship Sulphur, During the Years 1836–1842*, 2 vols. (London, 1843). The American captive is quoted from John R. Jewitt, *A Narrative of the Adventures and Sufferings of John R. Jewitt, Only Survivor of the Crew of the Ship Boston, During a Captivity of Nearly Three Years Among the Savages of Nootka Sound* (Middletown, Conn., 1815). Bancroft, *History of the Northwest Coast*, II, 649, says: "In those days every chief worthy the name possessed from fifty to one hundred slaves, worth thirty blankets each, generally purchased from the natives of Queen Charlotte Island, the great slave mart of the Northwest Coast." Hodge, *Handbook*, II, 598, cites other authorities estimating the price of an adult slave as about $500 in blankets, the price of a child about $150, or fifty blankets.

323   The spirit story is found in Ruth Benedict, *Patterns of Culture* (New York, 1934).

324   *Ibid.*, for the potlatch quotations.

325   The quotation re the honorable nature of wealth is from Franz Boas, *The Ethnology of the Kwakiutl, Based on Data Collected by George Hunt*, 35th Annual BAE Report (Washington, 1921), 43–794, who gives an outline of a young man beginning his business career among the Kwakiutl: When the boy is about to take his third name, he borrows blankets from the other members of the tribe. He must repay these after a year, at 100 per cent interest. At the celebration of his new name, he distributes these blankets among his own people, who make it a point to repay him three times the number given them, when they have any occasion to distribute blankets at any public function—this is usually done within a month or so, so that he now has three times the number of blankets originally borrowed, two-thirds of which, though, he must still repay after the lapse of a year. He may continue loaning out these excess blankets among his friends so that at the close of the year he may own four times the original number borrowed. When the young man has a fair reserve of blankets he may take a share, along with an older and richer friend, in the purchase of one of the cheaper coppers, worth, say 500 blankets. The boy may contribute 200 as his share and receive possession of the copper, becoming a debtor to his partner for the 300 contributed by the latter. The young man then announces that he will sell the copper the following year but is willing to deliver it at once, at which the chief of a rival tribe may take the copper and pay a first installment of 100 blankets. The boy then promises a distribution of blankets for the following year and loans out the 100 blankets he has received, and the next year calls in all his outstanding debts and invites all the neighboring communities to a feast, to which his own tribe contributes food and fuel. At this feast, he *repays* to the chief who bought his copper the 100 blankets paid on account, together with another 100 as 100 per cent interest, upon which the purchaser pays the full price of 750 blankets for the copper" . . . In this manner the young man continues to loan and to distribute blankets, and thus is able, with due circumspection and foresight, to amass a fortune. . . ."

326   Ruth Benedict, *op. cit.*, (basing the passages on Boas, 1921, cited above), gives the Bear Dancing and Cannibal Dancing scenes. Oscar O. Winther, *The Great Northwest* (New York, 1947), states in his Chronology, under the date of 1796, speaking of the split in the North West Company: "The loser, however, was neither contestant, but rather the impartial Indian on whom, during a two-year period, no less than 195,000 gallons of liquor were expended by the rivals in pursuance of the fur trade."

327   Alexander Mackenzie, *Voyages from Montreal, on the river Saint Lawrence, through the continent of North America, to the Frozen and Pacific Oceans; in the Years 1789 and 1793* (London, 1801). The description of the Aleuts is found in Martin Sauer, *Account of a Geographical and Astronomical Expedition to the Northern Parts of Russia* (London, 1802).

328   A glimpse of the fur business at Sitka is in Washington Irving, *Astoria, or Anecdotes of an Enterprise beyond the Rocky Mountains*, edited by Edgely W. Todd (Norman, Okla., 1964), 466–467.

329   Samuel P. Johnston, ed., *Alaska Commercial Company, 1868–1940* (San Francisco, 1940), gives the number of stockholders in 1872.

The investigation of 1876 is found in *House Committee Reports*, 44th Congress, 1st Session, 623, 37.
Bancroft, *Alaska*: "At no period in the annals of Alaska were there so many Indian émeutes as during the few years of the [U.S.] military occupation; at no period were lust, theft, and drunkenness more prevalent among Indians and white persons alike. After the withdrawal of the troops in June 1877, disturbances among the natives became fewer in number and less serious in character, and it is probable that many lives would have been saved if no United States soldier had ever set foot in the territory." And quoting William S. Dodge to Vincent Colyer, special Indian commissioner, 1869: The soldiers made ". . . the Inhabitants of Sitka what Dante characterized Italy—'A grand house of ill fame'. . . ."
Charles Erskine Scott Wood, as a young army officer in Alaska in 1877, wrote in his journal (MS, Henry E. Huntington Library, San Marino, California): ". . . Phillipson's account of the 'old times' under the Russian government. 'They was the most 'appiest people I ever see . . .' Contrast now . . . Drunkenness, squalor. Debauchery, prostitution, stagnation, filth and all uncleanness. . . ."
The deaths of 1888 on St. Lawrence Island are from J. Arthur Lazell, *Alaskan Apostle, The Life Story of Sheldon Jackson* (New York, 1960).

330 Ibid., the quotation.

NOTES for Chapter XIII

General works used in this chapter are Kroeber, 1925, 1953; Bolton, 1913, 1930; Caughey, 1952; Curtis; Steward, 1938; Cook, 1943; Oswalt; Bancroft, *California* and *Oregon*; Hodge, *Handbook*; Swanton, 1952; Dunn;

and for pages

332 Quotations are from the record of the voyage written by Father Antonio de la Ascensión, first published in abridged form in Juan de Torquemada, *Monarchia Indiana* (1615), from which it was reprinted with some changes by Gonzales Barcia in 1723, and again reprinted by Miguel de Venegas, *Noticia de la California* (Madrid, 1757). The first English edition of Venegas (London, 1759) was used for *The Voyage of Sebastian Vizcaino to the Coast of California . . .*, foreword by Oscar Lewis (San Francisco, The Book Club of California, 1933).
For previous voyages to the Pacific Coast see Henry Raup Wagner, *Spanish Voyages to the Northwest Coast of America in the Sixteenth Century* (San Francisco, 1929).
Vizcaino is quoted from George Butler Griffin, ed., "Documents of the Sutro Collection," in *Publications of the Historical Society of Southern California*, part 1 (Los Angeles, 1891).

334 An anonymous correspondent (signing himself "Quis") published in the *Los Angeles Star*, August 27, 1859, an account of Owens Valley pre-agricultural irrigation. The account is reprinted in J. M. Guinn, ed., "Some Early History of Owens River Valley," in *Annual Publications of the Historical Society of Southern California*, 10/3 (Los Angeles, 1917), 41–47.
H. H. Bancroft, in vol. VII of the *History of California*, 486, speaks of the massacres of these Owens River people only a few years later, in 1862–1865, by newly arrived white miners and stock-raisers exasperated by the Indians—who being driven from their lands were forced to steal cattle for food. "The lesson," says Bancroft, "proved effective, especially so far as those that were killed were concerned."
Julian H. Steward, "Ethnography of the Owens Valley Paiute," in *University of California Publications in American Archaeology and Ethnology*, 33/3 (Berkeley, 1933), 233–250, provides a detailed reconstruction of this pre-agricultural irrigation.
Salvador Palma (Olleyquotequiche) is quoted from a letter to Viceroy Antonio Bucareli, November 11, 1776 (the letter was written by Anza from the Indian captain's dictation), printed in J. N. Bowman and R. F. Heizer, *Anza and the Northwest Frontier of New Spain*, Southwest Museum Papers, No. 20 (Los Angeles, 1967), 154.

335 The explorer was Anza, quoted in Robert Glass Cleland, *Wilderness to Empire* (New York, 1944).

336 Datura (*Datura Meteloides*) was used also as an element of the Chingichnich cult, described in the manuscript notes kept during Mission times by Father Geronimo Boscana—reprinted in J. P. Harrington, trans., *A New Original Version of Boscana's Historical Account of the San Juan Capistrano Indians of Southern California*, Smithsonian Miscellaneous Collections, 92/4 (Washington, 1934). The Chingichnich cult is usually supposed to have originated in or about the region of present-day Los Angeles, but L. J. Bean and K. S. Saubel, *Temalpakh, Cahuilla Indian Knowledge and Usage of Plants* (Banning, California, 1972), state, 65, that "recent studies carried out by Thomas Blackburn suggest that the cult may have originated with the Chumash."

337 The ironic commander was Gaspar de Portolá, quoted from Charles Edward Chapman, *A History of California: The Spanish Period* (New York, 1921), 227. Chapman's previous work, founded on study in the Archive of the Indies in Seville, *The Founding of Spanish California: The Northwestward Expansion of New Spain, 1687–1783* (New York, 1916), made the point that the supposed Russian menace was only an excuse for the colonization of California, the principal reason being the surge of vigor in the Spanish administrative renaissance, exemplified in this action by the *Visitador* José de Gálvez, who was quite literally mad with ambition. And so, said the weary Portolá, he has fortified Monterey "by a royal fortress . . . built of poles and earth" just in case the Russians, by some "extravagant fancy," should really covet this brushy, rocky, barren California.

338 Quotations are from Father Juan Caballeria y Collel, *History of the City of Santa Barbara California from its Discovery to our Own Days . . .*, trans. by Edmund Burke (Santa Barbara, Cal., 1902), 17–18.
The birth-rate figures at the missions are from Warren A. Beck and David A. Williams, *California, a History of the Golden State* (New York, 1972).
Maynard Geoger, O.F.M., *Mission Santa Barbara 1782–1965* (Santa Barbara, California, 1965), gives for Santa Barbara the total number of baptisms from 1786 to 1804 as 3,000, while for "the next fifty-five years only 1,771 baptisms were administered . . ." one factor being "the preponderance of deaths over births after about 1812 . . ." (31).
The basic authoritative picture of California Indians during mission times is Cook, 1943.

339 The artist quoted is Louis Choris, *Voyage Pittoresque Autour du Monde* (Paris, 1822).
The summary quotation is from Ray Allen Billington, *The Far Western Frontier* (New York, 1956), 7.

340 The Spanish quotation is from A. R. Rojas, *The Vaquero* (1964).
The British travel writer is George Frederick Augustus Ruxton, *Life in the Far West*, ed. by LeRoy R. Hafen (Norman, Okla., 1951).

342 Figures for California Indian populations are from the generally accepted authority in this field, Sherburne Friend Cook, who in 1964 estimated the aboriginal population as 275,000, or in the range from 250,000 to 300,000, adding that in his own opinion "the upper figure more closely represents the real value than the lower" (Sherburne F. Cook, *The Aboriginal Population of Upper California*, Actas y Memorias del XXXV Congreso Internacional de Americanistas, Mexico, 1962). Since that date, however, Dr. Cook has studied new data dealing with the population of the Sacramento Valley and Mission areas, and at present gives 325,000 as his reconsidered estimate (personal communication, May 1973).
The 1848 figure is from S. F. Cook, "The Destruction of the California Indian" in *California Monthly*, 79/3 (Berkeley, December 1958), 16.
H. H. Bancroft was the first of the "modern" historians to see the California Indian wars as illegitimate—see his *History of California*, vol. VII, 477.
S. F. Cook is quoted from his 1968 article in *California Monthly* cited above, 16.

342 *Ibid.* the news items, the first found in the *Red Bluff Beacon* for January 7, 1858; the second in the *Sacramento Union*, July 19, 1862.
The 1850 quotation is from William H. Ellison, "Indian Policy in California 1846–60" in *Mississippi Valley Historical Review*, 9/1 (1922); Don Benito Wilson is quoted from John W. Caughey, ed., *The Indians of Southern California in 1852, the B. D. Wilson Report and a Selection of Contemporary Comment* (San Marino, Calif., 1952).

343 The quotations are from Horace Bell, *Reminiscences of a Ranger* (Santa Barbara, California, 1927). The cave incident is quoted from T. T. Waterman, *The Yana Indians*, in University of California Publications in American Archaeology and Ethnology, 8/2 (1918), 35–102. The Yahi children killed in the cave were members of the band that included Ishi, himself then a child of eight or nine. Theodora Kroeber, *Ishi in Two Worlds* (Berkeley, 1961), tells in detail the story of attempted Yahi extermination, pp. 56–90. The government inspector was J. Ross Browne, speaking in bitter irony but expressing a common notion of the time, quoted in Caughey, 1952, xxxiii, from an article in *Harper's Magazine* in 1861 recounting an inspection tour in California in 1858.

344 See R. F. Heizer and A. B. Elsasser, *Original Accounts of the Lone Woman of San Nicolás Island*, University of California Archaeological Survey, No. 55 (Berkeley, 1961).
The best known first-hand account of the lost woman of San Nicolás is in George Nidever, *The Life and Adventures of a Pioneer in California since 1834*, ed. by W. H. Ellison (Berkeley, 1937).

346 Reuben Gold Thwaites, ed., *Original Journals of the Lewis and Clark Expedition* (Cleveland, 1904), has long been the basic Lewis and Clark document. Bernard DeVoto in *The Course of Empire* (Boston, 1962), feels however that Coues has "stood up much better" (613): this is Nicholas Biddle, *History of the Expedition under the Command of Captains Lewis and Clark* (1814), ed. by Elliott Coues (New York, 1893).
The expedition which colonized San Francisco was led by Juan Bautista de Anza—although some question has been raised in recent years of exactly what constituted "San Francisco" in which "colonizing" effort: see Bowman and Heizer, *op. cit.*; and Bolton, *Anza*.

347 Correspondence dealing with Vial's abortive efforts is listed in H. E. Bolton, *Guide to Materials for the History of the United States in the Principal Archives of Mexico* (Washington, 1913).
Vial's extraordinary career is the subject of Noel Loomis and A. P. Nasatir, *Pedro Vial and the Roads to Santa Fe* (Norman, Okla., 1967).

Francis D. Haines, *et al.*, *The Appaloosa Horse* (Lewiston, Idaho, 1951). Also see Francis D. Haines, "Nez Percé and Shoshoni Influence on Northwest History," in *Greater America* (Berkeley, 1945).

349 Literature on the overland Astorians is surveyed in William Brandon, "Wilson Price Hunt" in LeRoy R. Hafen, ed., *Mountain Men and the Fur Trade* (Glendale, Calif., 1967), VI, 185–206.
Compare, in connection with the Whitman massacre, *Senate Executive Document No. 37*, 41st Congress (Washington, 1903).

351 Figures on the Rogue River "War" are from Bancroft, *History of Oregon*. The Rogue River War, as a focus for the general malaise of the Indian service in the 1850s, is examined in detail in Stephen D. Beckham, *Requiem for a People: The Rogue Indians and the Frontiersmen* (Norman, Okla., 1971).

352 The exterminators' motto, and the squad records, are from Dunn; and from Bancroft, *Oregon*. *Ibid.*, the quotation.

355 Richard Dillon, *Burnt-Out Fires* (Englewood Cliffs, N.J., 1973), tells the story, admirably researched, of the heads of Captain Jack, John Schonchin, Boston Charly, and Black Jim finding their final resting place in our National Museum (335–336). The hangman's knots from the necks and Kintpuash and Schonchin John are in the Indian Museum at Fort Sutter, California (333).
See also Keith A. Murray, *The Modocs and Their War* (Norman, Okla., 1959).
Young Joseph, "An Indian's View of Indian Affairs" in *North American Review*, 128 (New York, 1879), 412–433, says (417) that his father, Old Joseph, refused to sign the June 1855 treaty. ("I will not sign your paper . . . you go where you please, so do I; you are not a child, I am no child; I can think for myself. No man can think for me. I have no other home than this. I will not give it up to any man. My people would have no home. Take away your paper. I will not touch it with my hand.") However, Joseph's attested mark appears on the treaty (Kappler, II, 705), third among the Nez Percé signers, after Lawyer and Looking Glass. The wording of Young Joseph's account would seem to apply better to a later treaty conference, since at the 1855 conference Old Joseph was not being asked to surrender his home country of Wallowa. Old Joseph's name is conspicuously absent from later agreements, even from the innocent agreement of October 1855 setting up buffalo-hunting rules to avoid collisions between the Nez Percé, Flathead, and Kutenai people west of the Rockies and the Blackfoot, Piegan, Blood, and Gros Ventre people east of the mountains, although Looking Glass and White Bird (of Joseph's band) are among the Nez Percé signers. Dun (633) says that Old Joseph's claim that he did not sign the treaty at all, though his name was affixed, evidently meant "that he never signed a treaty ceding his land, which is true." Old Joseph also refused any annuity goods from the 1855 treaty, saying, "If we take the pay, the white man will say he has bought our land also . . ."
A history of the Nez Percé written by a Nez Percé in 1880 also says:
"In 1855 a treaty was made between Nez Perce Nation and United States
Wal-la-mot-kin (Hair tied on forehead) or Old Joseph,
Hul-lal-ho-sot or (Lawyer),
were the two leading Chiefs of the Nez Perce Nation in 1855,
both of these two Chiefs consented to the treaty
and Nez Perce sold to the United states
part of their country.

"In 1863 another treaty was made
in which Lawyer and his people consented
but Joseph and his people refused to make the second treaty.

"from that time Joseph's people
were called None-treaty Nez Perce.

"The treaty Nez Perce number 1800
None-treaty numbered 1000."
Quoted from "History of Nez Perce Indians from 1805 up to the Present Time 1880 by James Reuben, Nez Perce Indian," in *The Magic World: American Indian Songs and Poems*, ed. by William Brandon (New York, 1971), 133–134, somewhat abridged from the original text by James Reuben deposited in the cornerstone of the Nez Percé and Ponca school on October 20, 1880, recovered when the schoolhouse was torn down and first printed in the *Chronicles of Oklahoma*, XII (September 1934). James Reuben, a nephew of Chief Joseph and son of Reuben, Lawyer's successor as chief of the Upper Nez Percé, was one of several Christian Nez Percé scouts who served from time to time with General O. O. Howard's forces against Chief Joseph's band and who ("with their white men's names!") were roundly hated by the other Nez Percé warriors if Yellow Wolf (in McWhorter, cited below) is typical. Nevertheless, James Reuben went to live in exile with Chief Joseph's surviving people in Indian Territory, where he occasionally acted as interpreter (although he was not the official agency interpreter). It seems likely the contents of his "History" would have been read to and approved by the rest of Joseph's community, including Joseph himself. (Mark H. Brown, cited below, quoting, p. 415, a war correspondent in the *San Francisco Chronicle*, October 10, 1877, in an interview with Chief Joseph: "I asked him [Joseph] if he bore any ill will toward James Reuben, a Nez Percé Indian who acted as a scout for us near Kamia, and he answered promptly, 'No; a war is a thing where there are two sides.' . . .")

356 Young Joseph is quoted from Dunn, 639.
An amendment to the 1863 treaty, signed August 13, 1868, by Lawyer, Timothy, and Jason, for the Nez Percés (not signed by Joseph), provided for those outside the reservation to remain on "the lands now occupied and improved by them, provided, that the land so occupied does not exceet twenty acres for each and every male person [21 years of age or head of a family] . . ." and shall be protected by the military in this occupation and also in the privilege of grazing their animals upon surrounding unoccupied lands (Kappler, II, 1024–1025). These restrictions, plus Young Joseph's observation ("An Indian's View of Indian Affairs," 422) that there was no good land left unoccupied on the reservation accounted for the Indians' supposition "that after they go to Lapwai reservation or one similar, they will be obliged to give up their horses, which constitute their main wealth, and that as a community they will cease to exist" (Dunn, 637).
In 1873 the Department of the Interior moved to declare the Wallowa Valley a reservation and pay the eighty-seven squatters there $67,860 for their improvements, but in 1875 Congress refused, sorely disappointing the squatters, "who had settled for the purpose of being bought out. If a man discover where a reservation is to be located, he cannot do better financially than locate upon it" (Dunn, 637). Dunn is inclined to blame local party politics for this Congressional refusal, particularly Governor Grover of Oregon who seemingly wanted to save some political face by the action; Dunn also blames missionaries, who were engaged in fighting the Dreamer religion that had many communicants in Joseph's band—"Father Wilbur . . . recommended that the Indians be 'brought within the Christianizing influences of the reservation' even if force were necessary to accomplish the removal" (Dunn, 640).
There was no pressure of white settlement in Wallowa Valley, said a military report of August, 1875 (Dunn, 632): "The population is less than it was a year ago. Since the valley was restored to settlement, three families have disposed of their improvements for a trifle, and moved away; nor do I believe any others have come in. Not a man has taken a claim in the valley since that time. One of the most enterprising, reliable, and best citizens in the settlement, has told me, within the past week, that he thought the people of the valley were disappointed to learn it was not to be taken for an Indian reservation; that he regretted it for one; that he should sell out at first opportunity, and settle in a more promising locality. This shows how the white people who reside here regard this valley. On the other hand the Indians love it." General Howard, in his report of September 1, 1875, supported this report, but even so Howard, serving on the Commission of 1876 to study and decide the matter, apparently voted, along with the other members of the Commission (D. H. Jerome, William Stickney, and A. C. Barstow) to drive Joseph's band out of this unwanted Wallowa Valley; Dunn blames this Commission directly for the resulting war, and points out that in his later public writings (his article in the *North American Review*, 129, 1879, and his book, *Nez Perce Joseph*, Boston, 1881) Howard does not mention his part in the Commission.

357 The quotation from Joseph is found in Young Joseph, "An Indian's View of Indian Affairs," 423. The C. E. S. Wood quotations are from his manuscript journal, 1877, in the Henry E. Huntington Library, San Marino, California.
A glimpse into the minds of white settlers who encouraged the Nez Percé war is found in Eugene E. Wilson, ed., *Hawks and Doves in the Nez Percé War of 1877—Personal Recollections of Eugene Tallmadge Wilson* (Helena, Mont., 1966), containing such lines as ". . . the Idaho boys . . . struggling against overwhelming odds and surrounded by whirling, yelling, painted fiends . . ." (7). The introduction states that the "volunteers . . . were defending their homes and families against what they believed to be villainous and marauding Indians. . . ."

358 The argument that Joseph played less than a leading role in the military successes of the Nez Percé during their flight was convincingly presented by Lucullus Virgil McWhorter, *Yellow Wolf: His own Story* (Caldwell, Idaho, 1940), 502–507. McWhorter quotes Curtis as the first to deny Joseph the role of war-chief and give more credit to Looking Glass (Curtis, VIII, 163–169), and maintains that the fact that there was no single military genius "adds to rather than detracts from" the "heroic stature" of the Nez Percé war, the campaign thus being "not the work of a single brilliant leader in arms, but the combined effort of the group." McWhorter's conclusion has been supported by various subsequent works including Merrill D. Beal, *"I will Fight No More Forever:" Chief Joseph and the Nez Percé War* (Seattle, 1963); Alvin M. Josephy, Jr., *The Nez Perce Indians and the Opening of the Northwest* (New Haven, 1965); and Mark H. Brown, *The Flight of the Nez Percé* (New York, 1967). Works published during Joseph's lifetime, including newspaper reports of the Nez Percé War, reports of the principal U. S. Army officers involved, and including the history by James Reuben cited above ("Joseph and his followers broke out/ and there was Nez Perce War bloody one/ nine great battles fought/ the last battle lasted five days/ which Joseph surrendered with his people/ 1000 Indians had went on the war path/ but when Joseph surrendered/ there was only 600"), generally accepted the notion of his overall leadership. See for example Mooney, 1896. Joseph himself seems rather to imply his leadership in newspaper interviews given after his surrender, but in his *North American Review* article he speaks usually of "we" and offers a number of insights into the problem of defining chieftainship, political as well as military—"It required a strong heart to stand up against such talk, but I urged my people to be quiet, and not to being a war" (423); "This plan [one apparently favored by Joseph] was voted down in the war council . . ." (424).

359 The quotations are from Dunn, 660.

360 General Nelson A. Miles, U. S. Army, "The Indian Problem" in *North American Review*, 128 (New York, 1879), says of "Our relations with the Indians . . . by treaties and trade . . ." that "we find the record of broken promises all the way from the Atlantic to the Pacific, while many of the fortunes of New York, Chicago, St. Louis, and San Francisco can be traced directly to Indian tradership" (306).
The Wood quotations are from a letter published in the *Oregon Inn-Side News* (Portland, November–December 1947).
It would be presumptuous to paraphrase C. E. S. Wood because of the quality of his writing rather than because of the authority of his facts; he told the story of Chief Joseph many times during his long life, with occasional disparity in the details bringing woe to researchers, as Mark H. Brown, *op. cit.*, bears witness.
Joseph was made a prisoner by Miles while engaged in talks under a flag of truce, held overnight, and only released because an American lieutenant had been seized by the Indians as a hostage to guarantee Joseph's safety. This incident, recounted by Joseph in the *North American Review* article previously cited, has been substantiated by testimony presented by McWhorter, *op cit.*, 489, from Wood and from the lieutenant held as hostage, and by Mark H. Brown, *op cit.*, who includes a letter from Miles to his wife saying he had had Joseph in his power but had had to give him up due to the lieutenant's presence in the Nez Percé camp. Brown concludes that the Nez Percé surrender, which came three days later only after the arrival of General Howard and his column, was delayed by theair of treachery proceeding from this little pas de deux.
Wood's information as to the fate of Joseph's lost daughter is in error; she was not sent to join him in Indian Territory but instead was brought up on the Lapwai Reservation, where eventually she married and had a family.
The famous surrender speech is usually quoted, somewhat differently, from *U. S. Secretary of War, Report, 1877*, 630–631.
James Reuben, *op. cit.*, concludes,
"Take it in the right light—
Nez Perce have been wrongly treated by the Government . . .
When this is opened and read may be understood
how the Indians have been treated by the Whiteman. . . ." (135)

NOTES for Chapter XIV

General works most used in this chapter are Dunn; Wildschut, 1960; Orchard, 1929; Lowie, 1935, and 1954; Grinnell, 1923 and 1956; Crook, 1946; Ewers, 1955 and 1968; Roe, 1955; Hyde, 1937, 1968; Kappler; Annual Reports of the Commissioner of Indian Affairs; Mooney, 1896; Neihardt, 1961; Hodge, *Handbook*; Swanton, 1953; Driver; Driver and Massey; Oswalt; Catlin, 1844; Wedel, 1959; Clark;

and for page

362 Peter Masten Dunne, "Pioneer Jesuit Missionaries on the Central Plateau of New Spain," in *Greater America* (Berkeley, 1945), mentions (164) the mounted Lagunero chieftain in 1594.
This same collection of essays also contains John James Johnson, "The Spanish Horse in Peru before 1550" dealing with the early introduction of horses into South America. And see Robert M. Denhardt, "The Chilean Horse," in *Agricultural History*, 24/3 (July 1950), 161–165; and in the same journal the same author's "The Horse in New Spain and the Borderlands," 25/4 (October 1951), 145–150.

363 Francis D. Haines, "How did the Indians Get Their Horses?" and "The Northward Spread of Horses Among the Plains Indians," in *American Anthropologist*, 40 (1938), 112–117 and 429–437; and see the same author's "Horses for Western Indians," in *The American West*, 3/2 (1966), 4–15, 92. Compare Roe, 1955; and Ewers, 1955.
Of considerable interest, besides where the horses came from, are matters of Indian tack, for which see Clark Wissler, *Riding Gear of the North American Indians*, Anthropological Papers, American Museum of Natural History, 17/Part I (New York, 1915); and the same author's "American Indian Saddles," in *American Museum Journal* (December 1916); also John C. Ewers, "The Indian Buffalo Hunter's Saddle" in *Western Horseman* (September 1949). Glenn R. Vernam, *Man on Horseback* (New York, 1964), discusses riding equipment of all times and places, including that of plains Indians.

364 The recollection of the first horse seen by Blackfeet people was recorded by David Thompson in 1787 from the reminiscence of an elderly Nahathaway (Cree) who had lived among the Piegans since childhood and was at that time thought to be some seventy-five to eighty years old. J. B. Tyrrell, ed., *David Thompson's Narrative* (Toronto, 1916), 330, 334.
Beadwork was of course by no means limited to the plains or to post-European times—Orchard, 1929, 20, estimates more than 16,500 beads in a dentalium-shell string, 41 1/2 feet long, from the Chumash of California. The same author's *The Technique of Porcupine-Quill Decoration Among the North American Indians*,

Contributions of the Museum of the American Indian, Heye Foundation, 4/1 (New York, 1916), points out (3–5) that bird quills were also used, particularly as edging.
Norman Feder, *Art of the Eastern Plains Indians* (Brooklyn, N.Y., 1964), is a catalogue of the Nathan Sturges Jarvis Collection gathered by Dr. Jarvis in the 1830s while he was an army surgeon at Fort Snelling, near present-day Minneapolis. The collection, now in the Brooklyn Museum, is extraordinarily well documented, and the exhaustive notes make this catalogue an excellent reference work on the use and manufacture of numerous workaday objects now beginning to be recognized as objects of art.

365 "There is a narrow ravine in Sarsi territory near Calgary, Canada, at the bottom of which have been found the bones of buffalo in such numbers that modern Sarsi Indians (1920) made a business of collecting and selling them for fertilizer." (Driver and Massey, 191.) In this same paragraph a statement is made that may be of some interest to the occasional controversy over the possible effect of hunting by man on the extinction of the horse in America: "Cliff-driving dates from paleolithic times in the Old World, where at Solutre it is estimated that 100,000 wild horses were killed in this manner." But it was in the Old World that horses survived.

367 Reginald and Gladys Laubin, *The Indian Tipi* (Norman, Okla., 1957; New York, 1971), is an authoritative work on the ubiquitous Indian lodging of the plains.

368 The Crows, vastly outnumbered by the Blackfeet and the Teton Dakota, were believed by early white observers to be facing extermination at the hands of these powerful invaders, the Blackfeet moving in from the north, the Dakota from the east.
Wildschut, 1960, citing Catlin writing in the 1830s and Edwin Thompson Denig, "Indian Tribes of the Upper Missouri, Edited with Notes and a Biographical Sketch by J. N. B. Hewitt," in the *46th Annual BAE Report* (Washington, 1930), writing in 1854 after twenty-one years in the country, describes the Crows as having for years been fighting "desperately for their lives against great odds . . ." (172).

372 As Waldo Wedel points out, in *An Introduction to Pawnee Archaeology*, BAE Bulletin 112 (Washington, 1936), 10–11, French fur traders and trappers were established perhaps as early as the middle of the seventeenth century among many tribes of the Missouri Valley, and the La Salle brothers mentioned in 1682 the Pawnee, living "more than 200 leagues to the west," and their neighbors the Kiowa "who sell them horses which they steal apparently from the Spaniards of New Mexico." But the Spaniards of New Mexico had of course been driven out, leaving their stock of all kinds behind in Indian hands, in the Pueblo revolt of 1680.
Detachments from La Salle's colony exploring in what is now southeastern Texas in the summer of 1686 found the towns of the Hasinai Confederacy rolling in Spanish loot (brought from the west in trade) and rich with Spanish horses—La Salle traded for several (Francis Parkman, *La Salle*, 298, 300). The presence of so many horses among the Hasinai certainly indicates some Indian commerce in horses considerably antedating 1680, for the Hasinai had surely not learned overnight the complex art of using and keeping horses.
Rumors and reports from westering Frenchmen were not infrequent on the Mississippi Valley frontier at the beginning of the eighteenth century—two French traders from Pimitoui (Peoria) accompanied a trading party of Illinois people to the Missouri and Osage in 1693 (Sister Mary Borgias Palm, *The Jesuit Missions of the Illinois Country, 1673–1763*, Cleveland, 1933, 24, citing *Archives Nationales des Colonies*, Paris, C¹³B, 7); reports from Louisiana in 1705 and 1706 speak of traders going "near" the Spanish frontier in New Mexico and stopping in an Indian village from which Spanish traders had just departed (Pierre Margry, *Mémoires et Documents* . . . (Paris, 1888), vol. VI, 181–182); *ibid.*, 183, a letter from Nicolas de La Salle, 1708, speaking of Canadian voyageurs who have traveled 300 to 400 leagues up the Missouri River; and *Ibid.*, 180, a letter from d'Iberville of 1703 speaking of twenty Canadians gone "to discover New Mexico."
Clarence W. Alvord, *The Illinois Country 1673–1818* (Springfield, 1920) states in summary that by 1710 French fur traders had traveled the Missouri as far as the Kansas, had visited the lead mines of Galena and Missouri, and soon afterward reached the forks of the Platte (141).
In the second and third decades of the eighteenth century French explorers Du Tisne and La Harpe worked their way part way across the plains, and Saint-Denis made two trips across Texas to the Spanish settlements of Mexico.
The expedition at the Mandan towns in 1739 was led by the Sieur de la Vérendrye—see the detailed account in Bernard DeVoto, *The Course of Empire* (Boston, 1952; paperback edition, 1962, with an Introduction by Wallace Stegner), 209–212.
The French lead miners and Santo Domingo blacks in the Missouri country are mentioned in Bolton and Marshall, *The Colonization of North America 1492–1783* (1920), 282.

373 Ann Woodbury Hafen, "Son of Bird Woman," in the *Denver Post*, July 21, 1946, tells the story of Baptiste Charbonneau.
The quotation is from LeRoy R. Hafen, "Fraeb's Last Fight" in *Colorado Magazine*, 7 (1930).

374 The quotation of a good price for barrel hoops is from the same Hafen article listed above.

376 Newspaper coverage of the great 1851 council is summarized in Burton S. Hill, "The Great Indian Treaty Council of 1851," in *Nebraska History*, 47 (March, 1966), 85–110.

377 Mari Sandoz, *Hostiles and Friendlies* (Lincoln, Nebraska, 1959), writes that the site of Conquering Bear's burial scaffold "later became part of our orchard on the Niobrara. In my childhood an occasional old Sioux used to come to dance a few solemn steps there, and then smoke a pipe in the evening sun. . . ."

379 General Crook is quoted from F. C. Lockwood, *The Apache Indians* (New York, 1938). Similar sentiments are quoted in James T. King, "A Better Way: General George Crook and the Ponca Indians" in *Nebraska History*, 50 (Fall 1969), 239–256, dealing with Crook's earlier career; and in the same author's "George Crook, Indian Fighter and Humanitarian," in *Arizona and the West*, 9 (Winter 1967), 333–348, dealing with Crook's later career.
The quotation on whiskey-sellers in Montana is from Dunn, 524.

380 A Sioux spokesman at the council of August, 1876, suggested putting the Indians on wheels, quoted in Dee Brown, *Bury My Heart at Wounded Knee* (New York, 1971), 285.
Dee Brown, *op. cit.*, quotes General Sheridan's remark in regard to buffalo hunters operating illegally on Indian land, "Let them kill, skin, and sell until the buffalo is exterminated, as it is the only way to bring lasting peace and allow civilization to advance" (254).
Frank Gilbert Roe, *The North American Buffalo: A Critical Study of the Species in Its Wild State* (Toronto, 1951), argues that while in earlier times Westerners had resented wasteful buffalo slaughter by visiting dudes, later opinions of Army men and Western congressmen brought a change of heart: Appendix H, "Buffalo, Indians, and Legislation," 804–816. He cites Colonel Richard I. Dodge as an example of Army men making "no secret of wanting the buffalo destroyed" (357–358, 477, 810).
On the other hand there were prominent westerners who continued to inveigh against the buffalo kill, the best known being himself a buffalo hunter, Charles (Buffalo) Jones, who with his own hands saved a few calves from the final rush of extinction: see Mayer and Roth, *The Buffalo Harvest* (cited below, note for 561, Chapter XV), 84–85.

381 Colonel Richard Irving Dodge, *Our Wild Indians: Thirty-three Years' Personal Experience Among the Red Men of the Great West* (Hartford, 1883), maintains that it was the breech-loading rifle and metallic cartridges that turned the plains Indian "into as magnificent a soldier as the world can show" (451).
Martin F. Schmitt and Dee Brown, *Fighting Indians of the West* (New York, 1948), quote Colonel Henry B. Carrington on the Red Cloud war: "There never was a more ill-considered impulse of the American people than that which forced the army into the Powder River and Big Horn countries in 1866, to serve the behests of irresponsible speculative emigration, regardless of the rights of tribes rightfully in possession."

382 Red Cloud is quoted from Underhill, 1953, 172.
George R. Stewart, "Travelers by Overland" in *The American West*, 5/4 (July 1968), 12, describes the Cherokee Trail through Colorado.

384 An immense literature is growing up around the Sand Creek massacre. Quotations and details are from Grinnell, 1956; Hyde, 1968; 38th Congress, *Senate Report No. 142*; 39th Congress, *Senate Report No. 156*; 39th Congress, *Senate Executive Document, No. 26*.
Stan Hoig, *The Sand Creek Massacre* (Norman, Okla., 1961), and Donald J. Berthrong, *The Southern Cheyennes* (Norman, 1963), contain full-scale studies of the event. Most recently, scholarship has turned more and more toward background analysis, e.g., Harry Kelsey, "Background to Sand Creek" in *Colorado Magazine*, 45 (Fall 1968), 279–300, which investigates the inept management of Indian affairs—entangled with Republican politics—that preceded the tragedy. Michael A. Sievers, "Sands of Sand Creek Historiography" in *Colorado Magazine*, 49 (Spring 1972), 116–142, concludes that the overall story of the massacre and its complex causation has not yet been written.
The quotation is from *Condition of the Indian Tribes: Report of the Joint Special Committee Under Joint Resolution of March 3, 1865* (Washington, 1867)—containing material also included in *Senate Report No. 156*, 39th Congress, listed above.
Grinnell, 1956, p. 138, quotes Kit Carson in testimony before the Joint Committee speaking of herder frequently blaming Indians for the result of their own negligence; and Bernice Blackwelder, *Great Westerner, The Story of Kit Carson* (Caldwell, Idaho, 1962), quotes Carson speaking of Chivington's troops: " . . . and you call them civilized men and the Indians savages . . ."

385 Roman Nose is quoted from Grinnell, 1956, 286. His war bonnet is described in Hyde, 1968, 307.

387 General Sheridan is quoted from Dunn, 534.
Confusion has sometimes plagued Sitting Bull's biographical record since, as pointed out by Mari Sandoz, "There Were Two Sitting Bulls," in *Blue Book Magazine*, 90/1 (November 1949), there were two prominent Lakota leaders of the same name in the same generation, the "other" Sitting Bull killed by Crows at the Cantonment on the Tongue in December 1876 after having participated in the attack on Julesburg, the Fetterman fight, and in two conferences (1870 and 1875) in Washington, D.C.

388 Lloyd Winter Chaser of the Rosebud Reservation, South Dakota, wrote in the Rosebud newspaper, *Eyapaha*, October 27, 1969, that his grandfather, who was at the Custer fight, heard men shouting, "Le anpetu kin ee" ("This is our day, let's go").

The literature on Custer would sink a battleship, which might not be a bad use for much of it. It seems to be turning more and more to periphera, as with the excellent article on the U.S. Army units of Indian scouts from their authorization by Congress in 1866 to their final close-out in 1914, with detailed attention to their work with Custer—John S. Gray, "Arikara Scouts with Custer" in *North Dakota History*, 35 (Spring 1968), 442–478; and to bizarrerie, as with Charles K. Hofling, "George Armstrong Custer: A Psychoanalytic Approach," in *Montana, the Magazine of Western History*, 21 (April 1971), 32–43, which explains that Custer was a natural-born loser, being an immature phallic narcissist. This article was answered by Edgar I. Stewart (author of *Custer's Luck*, Norman, 1955, a good study of the battle), in "A Psychoanalytical Approach to Custer: Some Reflections," in the same journal, July 1971, 74–77, arguing that Custer's defeat was due less to narcissism phallic or otherwise than to a lack of cooperation at a critical moment, he having used acceptable military tactics, no doubt much the same sort of tactics another general would have used in his place. The death toll of starved Montana Blackfeet in 1883 is from Mooney's article in Hodge, *Handbook*, II, 571.

389 The Big Ankle incident was obscure to newspaper readers and even to the military but was famous—and still is—to the Indian people of the vicinity. The uncle, and leader of the band attacked by the troops, was a man named Lame Deer. The action took place in early May 1877 on what was then called Muddy Creek and is now called Lame Deer Creek, near the present-day village of Lame Deer, Montana, central town of the Northern Cheyenne Indian Reservation. The scalps of the two men, the elder and the youth, were taken by White Bull, A Cheyenne then serving as an Army scout, who recounted the tale of their bitter bravery to George Bird Grinnell; Lame Deer's grave is on the hilltop above the site of the little battle. Grinnell, *The Fighting Cheyennes* (1915 edition), 373–382.
The *New York Herald* (for October 9, 1879) is quoted from Oliver Knight, *Following the Indian Wars* (Norman 1960), which deals with newspaper coverage of the plains wars, 289.
A great deal of excellent work has been done on the revivalist movements around the world similar to the Ghost Dance (often called "cargo cults" by anthropologists, referring to cargoes of good things expected to arrive on the day of messianic deliverance), ranging from Leslie Spier, *The Prophet Dance of the Northwest and Its Derivatives: The Source of the Ghost Dance* (Menasha, Wis., 1935), to Peter Worsley, *The Trumpet Shall Sound* (2d edition, New York, 1968).

NOTES for Chapter XV

General works most used in this chapter are Dunn; Russell; Bolton, 1913 and 1914; Coues, *Garcés*; Driver; Driver and Massey; Oswalt; Hodge, *Handbook*; Swanton, 1953; Kroeber, 1953; Hyde, 1959; Richardson; Calhoun, *Correspondence*; Kappler; Bourke, 1891; Crook; Grinnell, 1923 and 1956; Wedel; Catlin, 1844; Spicer, 1962; Nye, 1937; H. H. Jackson; Bancroft, *Arizona and New Mexico*, A. B. Thomas, 1935, 1940;

and for page

392 Fray Pedro is quoted from Bolton, 1913.

395 Grenville Goodwin, *American Anthropologist*, 37 (1935), 55–64, reckoned domesticates as furnishing 20 per cent to 25 per cent of the diet for Western Apaches.
Arthur L. Campa, "Piñon as an Economic and Social Factor" in *New Mexico Business Review*, 2 (October 1932), 144–147, describes the use of a wild food, piñon nuts, still very popular in the Southwest.

396 The high priority held by Indian politics in colonial calcuations in the eighteenth century is indicated by a remark in the preface to Bolton, *Athanase de Mezières*: "The history of the French and Spanish regimes in Texas and Louisiana is to a large extent the history of an Indian policy, in its various aspects . . ." (13, preface).

397 John P. Harrington, "Kiowa Memories of the Northland," in Donald D. Brand, ed., *So Live the Works of Men* (Albuquerque, 1939), 162–176, examines in detail place-name evidence of the Kiowa residence in the north.

398 W. P. Clark, *The Indian Sign Language* (Philadelphia, 1885), is one of the earliest and still the best compendium on the subject, and a good book on the old life of the plains people besides.

401 The outraged cleric was the Reverend Father Provincial, Fray Pedro Serrano, to the Most Excellent Señor Viceroy, the Marquis of Cruillas, in regard to the Custodia of New Mexico in the year 1761, published in C. W. Hackett, ed., *Historical Documents Relative to New Mexico etc. collected by A. F. and Fanny Bandelier* (Washington, 1937), 479–501, and listed in Bolton, *Guide*, 27, A. G. M. Historia. The lines in the text are quoted in L. R. Bailey, *Indian Slave Trade in the Southwest* (Los Angeles, 1966), 26. The report adds (487 in Hackett) that Indian slaves of both sexes, small and large, constitute "the richest treasure for the governors, who gorge themselves . . . while the rest eat the crumbs."
Bancroft, *Arizona and New Mexico*, 272–273, points out that this report is part of a lengthy and bitter quarrel between the friars and the governors, with flaming charges and countercharges from both sides. "The partisan bitterness and prejudice of the writers . . . indicate clearly enough that the accusations are too sweeping, and often grossly over-colored; yet enough of candor and honest evidence remains to justify the conclusion that

New Mexican affairs were in a sad plight, and that the pueblo Indians were little better than slaves."
The quotation of the late 1760s is from the journal of an official inspection tour of the frontier—Lawrence Kinnaird, ed., *The Frontiers of New Spain: Nicolas de Lafora's Description 1766-1768*, vol. XIII of the Quivira Society Publications (Berkeley, 1958), 94. Lafora's report states that sometimes the French come to the Comanche rancherias "and live there for years."

402 The 1821 party of traders was the Jacob Fowler–Hugh Glenn trading expedition, mentioned in Hyde, 1959, 208-209.
The model town experiment of the Jupes is told in detail in Alfred B. Thomas, "San Carlos: A Comanche Pueblo on the Arkansas River, 1787," in *Colorado Magazine*, 6/3 (1929).

403 Grace Jackson, *Cynthia Ann Parker* (San Antonio, Texas, 1959), says of Texas' most famous captive, after her "liberation"—"She would take a knife and hack her breast until it would bleed, then put the blood on some tobacco and burn it, and cry for her lost boys" (98).
Richardson is the source of the Comanche details.

404 The U. S. Army's destruction, by a force under the command of Colonel Ranald Mackenzie, of a reported 1,400 Kiowa horses and mules took place in Palo Duro Cañon on September 26, 1874.
Dale L. Morgan, *Jedediah Smith and the Opening of the West* (Indianapolis, 1953), brings together the various recountings of his death, 329-330, and Notes, 435-436. Maurice S. Sullivan, *The Travels of Jedediah Smith* (Santa Ana, California, 1934), reprints a letter of Austin Smith dated at Walnut Creek on the Arkansas, "300 Mile from Settlement," September 24, 1830, with a postscript saying "The Spanish traders say that the Indians succeeded in alarming his horse . . ." (155). Austin Smith had bought Jedediah's rifle and pistols from the Spanish traders he quotes; this letter speaks only of the death of one Indian, a "chief."

405 The tide of "irresistible settlement" is from a pronunciamento of 1847 by Texas politician David G. Burnet, found in Schoolcraft, vol. I, 240.
Texas, having been swept scrupulously clean of Indians, turned to tales such as Herman Lehmann's *The Last Captive* (originally published in 1899, with revised versions in 1927 and 1972, highly colored stories of the author's life as a naturalized captive among the Apaches and Comanches in the 1870s, and a wonderful evocation of the imitating Indian image in small-town Texas at the turn of the century.
The railroad land-grant totals are from Billington, Westward Expansion, 701.
Allan Nevins and Henry Steele Commager, *A Short History of the United States*, 5th edition (New York, 1966), quote (342), Robert Louis Stevenson on the transcontinental railroad: "When I think how the railroad has been pushed through this unwatered wilderness and haunt of savage tribes . . . how at each stage of the construction, roaring, impromptu cities, full of gold and lust and death, sprang up and then died away again; how in these uncouth places pigtailed Chinese pirates worked side by side with border ruffians and broken men from Europe . . . and then when I go on to remember that all this epical turmoil was conducted by gentlemen in frock coats and with a view to nothing more extraordinary than a fortune and a subsequent visit to Paris, it seems to me as if this railway were the one typical achievement of the age in which we live. . . ."

406 The Sheridan quotation rests only on the journalistic source in Edward S. Ellis, *Ellis's History of the United States, from the Discovery of America to the Present Time*, 6 vols. (St. Paul, 1899), which quotes (vol. IV, 1483) Charles Nordstrom: "It was the writer's good fortune to be present when General Sheridan gave utterance to that *bon mot* which has since become so celebrated. It was in January, 1869, in camp at old Fort Cobb . . . Old Toch-a-way . . .: 'Me, Toch-a-way; me good Injun.' A quizzical smile lit up the General's face as he set those standing by in a roar by saying: 'The only good Indians I ever saw were dead.'"
It is reasonably possible that the phrase was simply attached to a celebrity's name, in the traditional way of such things, and it seems at least reasonably possible that the story, as Ellis has it, is apocryphal. DeBenneville Randolph Keim went with Sheridan through the whole winter campaign of 1868-69 as a correspondent for the New York Herald and doesn't seem to have mentioned this celebrated *bon mot* (see Knight, *Following the Indian Wars*; and Sheridan, *Personal Memoirs*, vol. II, 346). Carl Coke Rister, *Border Command, General Phil Sheridan in the West* (Norman, Okla., 1944), while full of comments that could qualify, in spirit, does not repeat this particular remark; nor does Captain H. C. Greiner, *General Phil Sheridan as I Knew Him, Playmate—Comrade—Friend* (Chicago, 1908), although this volume makes a considerable effort to show us Sheridan's "Irish wit." Not even Robert J. Hendricks, *Innnnnnng Haaaaaaa! Savage Warfare, Southern Chivalry, Facts Stranger'n Fiction. The War to End the White Race—Soul of Philip Knit With Soul of David* (Salem, Ore., 1937)—which speaks of the Whitma massacre as "That frightful, merciless letting of innocent blood and unleashing of uncontrolled lusts by brutish, ungrateful savages . . ." and has much to say of Sheridan's greatness—not even this work credits Sheridan with authorship of the immortal phrase. It seems at least reasonably possible that the phrase, as the sentiment, was the invention of numberless small town newspaper editors, some, no doubt, long before Sheridan's time.
A good account of buffalo hunting by a buffalo hunter (or as they called themselves, a buffalo runner) is Frank H. Mayer and Charles B. Roth, *The Buffalo Harvest* (Denver, 1958).
Glenn Danford Bradley, *The Story of the Santa Fe* (Boston, 1920), 156, describes buffalo bones ". . . stacked up way above the tops of the box cars, and often there were not sufficient cars to move them. Dodge excelled

in bones, like she did in buffalo hides, for, there were ten times the number of carloads shipped out of Dodge, than out of any other town in the state, and that is saying a great deal for there was a vast amount shipped from every little town in western Kansas."
The tale of the army officer's bad practical joke is told in Paul I. Wellman, *The Indian Wars of the West* (New York, 1954).
White encroachment on Comanche and Kiowa reservations is recounted in William T. Hagan, "Kiowas, Comanches, and Cattlemen, 1867–1906: A Case Study of the Failure of U. S. Reservation Policy," in *Pacific Historical Review*, 40 (August 1971), 333–355.

407 Forrest D. Monahan, Jr., "Kiowa–Federal Relations in Kansas, 1865–1868," in *Chronicles of Oklahoma*, 49 (Winter 1971–1972), 477–491, demonstrates with archival evidence that the Kiowas made every effort to maintain peace with the United States.
The last years of warfare on the Southwestern plains are detailed in Wilbur S. Nye, *Plains Indian Raiders: The Final Phases of Warfare from the Arkansas to Red Rivers* (Norman, 1968).

408 The international art authority is the late Ananda K. Coomaraswamy, quoted in Father Berard Haile and Leland C. Wyman, *Beautyway: A Navaho Ceremonial* (New York, 1957), 155.
See, as samples of the many books in this field, Charles Amsden, *Navajo Weaving* (Santa Ana, California, 1934); and John Adair, *The Navajo and Pueblo Silversmiths* (Norman, 1944).
The Song of Talking God is taken from a translation in Robert W. Young, ed., *The Navajo Yearbook* (Window Rock, Ariz., 1961), 523.
Some of the earliest and still some of the finest translations of the beautiful Navajo religious literature were made by Washington Matthews, as in his *Navaho Myths, Prayers and Songs, with Texts and Translations*, University of California Publications in American Archaeology and Ethnology, 5/2 (Berkeley, 1907).
The mention of wit and merriment is from J. H. Beadle, *The Undeveloped West; or, Five Years in the Territories* (Philadelphia, c. 1873), quoted in Robert Young, ed., *op. cit.*, 546. Similar testimony is recorded a century later by a long-time Navajo-country resident, Bernice Eastman Johnston, in *Two Ways . . . in the Desert: A Study of Modern Navajo–Anglo Relations* (Pasadena, 1972).

409 Navajo relations with Spanish, Mexicans, and Americans have been summed up in a series of detailed studies by Frank D. Reeve, from "Navajo–Spanish Peace: 1720s–1770s" in *New Mexico Historical Review*, 34/1 (January 1959), to "Navaho Foreign Affairs, 1795–1846," in the same journal, 47 (July 1971), ed. by Eleanor B. Adams and John L. Kessell.
The New Mexico resident of the 1860s was Dr. Louis Kennon, quoted in Young, *op. cit.*, 542. The same witness, writing in 1865, estimated the number of Navajo slaves in the Territory as "five to six thousand" (Young, 543).
Ibid., 544, the quotation from Kit Carson.

410 Narbona is quoted from Calhoun, *Correspondence*, report of October 1, 1849.
Ibid., the account of Narbona's death.
The young army officer commenting on the handsome artillery was J. H. Simpson, *Journal of a Military Reconnaissance from Santa Fe, New Mexico, to the Navajo Country, etc.* (Philadelphia, 1852), reporting under date of August 31, 1849.
The experienced officer commenting on Fort Defiance was John G. Bourke, "Bourke on the Southwest" in *New Mexico Historical Review*, 11/1 (1936), 81, entry for April 25, 1881.

411 Lawrence C. Kelly, *Navajo Roundup: Select Correspondence of Kit Carson's Expedition against the Navajo, 1863–1865* (Boulder, Colo., 1971), presents Carson as a humanitarian, forcing the Navajos to surrender by destroying crops and thus avoiding pitched battles, and endeavoring to see that the captured Navajo people are well treated.
Some instances of aggression against the Apaches down through the generations are detailed in Helen Hunt Jackson (1965 edition), 333–336.

412 See the estimate, in the note to page 565 above, of Dr. Louis Kennon of New Mexico in 1865 that Navajo slaves alone numbered "five to six thousand." Dunn, 372, quotes the official estimate of 2,000.
Benjamin M. Read, *Illustrated History of New Mexico* (Santa Fe, 1895, 1912) says, 60, "Indian captives were bought and sold, one or more serving in each family of the wealthier class. This slavery existed by mere popular sufferance and not by law." He adds, however, "It was abolished by the president's emancipation proclamation of 1865, and orders issued in consequence of that measure."

413 The Apache spokesman is quoted in Dunn, 723.

414 Bourke in "Bourke on the Southwest" in *New Mexico Historical Review*, 9 (1934), 159, quotes T. E. Farish, *History of Arizona*, vol. II, 32–33, claiming that the "stupidity and ignorance" of the lieutenant who "violated his own flag of truce . . . probably cost five thousand American lives and the destruction of hundreds of thousands of dollars worth of property."

415 Nine thousand Navajo and Apache prisoners at Fort Sumner went hungry as a result of one of

General Carleton's many official feuds—detailed in Edmund J. Danziger, Jr., "The Steck–Carleton Controversy in Civil War New Mexico" in *Southwestern Historical Quarterly*, 74 (October 1970), 189–203.
Bourke in "Bourke on the Southwest" in *New Mexico Historical Review*, 3 (1928), 165, quotes the *Prescott Miner* which "in the autumn of 1871 published a list of Apache murders and atrocities occurring between March, 1864, and the fall of 1871. Three hundred and one pioneers had been murdered, two of whom were known to have been burned alive; fifty-three were wounded and crippled for life, and five carried into captivity."

416 The plenary representative of the President was Vincent Colyer, whose findings are included in the *Report of the Secretary of the Interior* for 1871, quoted in Dunn, 724.
Cochise is also quoted in Dunn, *loc. cit.*

417 Bourke is quoted from *An Apache Campaign in the Sierra Madre*, a new edition, with an Introduction by J. Frank Dobie (New York, 1958), 18.
Bourke's considerable learning and sharp eye are perhaps most evident in his "The Medicine-men of the Apache" in the *Ninth Annual BAE Report* (Washington, 1892).

418 Crook is quoted from Dunn; Bourke from *An Apache Campaign*, 20.
But the civilian Indian agents are defended in a recent article, William E. Unrau, "The Civilian as Indian Agent: Villain or Victim," in *Western History Quarterly*, 3 (October 1972), 405–420.

419 Odie B. Faulk, *The Geronimo Campaign* (New York, 1969), is based on the Arizona Pioneers Historical Society's Gatewood Collection (material assembled by the man who went into Geronimo's camp to persuade him to surrender to Miles), and is strongly favorable to Crook and critical of Miles.

NOTES for Chapter XVI

General works most used in this chapter are Collier; McNickle, 1949; Washburn, 1971; Cohen, *et al.*, 1958; H. H. Jackson; *The Annals*, 1957; Brophy and Aberle; Royce, *Indian Land Cessions*; Veeder, 1969; U. S. Congress, *Indian Relations*, 1959; U. S. Senate, *Hearings . . . on Indian Affairs*, 1929–1934; U. S. Senate, *Hearings . . . on Indian Education*, 1969; U. S. Senate, *Hearings . . . on Constitutional Rights of the American Indian*;

and for page

421 The U. S. Census Bureau is quoted from a news release of December 14, 1972.

422 Nelson Reed, *The Caste War of Yucatan* (Palo Alto, California, 1964), is a perceptive history of the long Yucatecan rebellion.
Stuart Chase, in *Mexico: A Study of Two Americas* (New York, 1931), writes, 118: "One of the most heart-rending odysseys I know is the march of the Yaqui Indians from the haciendas of Yucatan back across all Mexico to their beloved mountains. They had been sold into slavery at sixty-five dollars a head; they had been chained, whipped, branded, in a low, hot land utterly alien to their peaks and precipices. They broke their chains and left that land, passing over one of the most dangerous and God-forsaken swamp areas on earth. The survivors had tramped and fought for 2,000 miles when they reached their villages in Sonora." The commanding role of the great landowner in Mexico is illustrated by figures from the tax rolls of 1821, 3,406 landowners in "a territory of 4,800,000 square leagues . . ."—J. B. Eyriés and Malte-Brun, eds., *Nouvelles Annales des Voyages . . . etc.* Tome X (Paris, 1821).

423 Colonel Candido Mariano de Silva Redondo, organizer in 1910 of Brazil's Service for the Protection of the Indian, is quoted from Collier, 177.
Alleged outrages against Indians of Brazil and Colombia have been widely reported in the world press, including "The World Looks at Brazil" in *Atlas*, 18/1 (January 1970), extracting reports from the *London Times*; *Der Spiegel* of Hamburg; and *Jeune Afrique* of Tunis. Numbers of such reports have been summed up from time to time in the Indian newspaper, *Akwesasne Notes*, published since December 1968, under the editorship of Jerry Gambill (Rarihokwaits), at Rooseveltown, N.Y.
The study demonstrating that Indians were a rapidly growing race all over the hemisphere was prepared under the leadership of the late Dr. Ernest Huber, of Johns Hopkins, and presented at the Third International Eugenics Congress: Collier, 173.

424 An interesting offshoot of Indian community development in South America—quasi-tribal squatter organizations in urban areas—is discussed in William Mangin, "Squatter Settlements," in *Scientific American*, 217/4 (October 1967).
Lesley Bird Simpson, *Many Mexicos* (New York, 1941), analyzes the deep-lying troubles resulting from the long tradition of "latifundismo" (vast estates and accompanying peonage).

425 The quotation is from Dunn.
Efforts to remake the first American in the later American's image brought forth one of "the shortest and most effective formal speeches in history," quoted in Oliver La Farge, *A Pictorial History of the American Indian* (New York, 1956): "An Indian Bureau official was sent out to persuade the Shoshones to take up farming. After he had made his speech, the ordinary men and lesser chiefs had their say pro and con. Then Washakie rose to summarize. Summoning up what little English he knew, he said, 'God damn a potato!'"

426 The quotation from the 1870s is found in Pliny E. Goddard, *Life and Culture of the Hupa*, University of California Publications in American Archaeology and Ethnology, 1/1 (Berkeley, 1903).

427 The Library of Congress published (Washington, 1920) a *List of References on the Treaty-making Power*, quoting among others Samuel T. Spear, "Congress and the Treaty Power," in the *Albany Law Journal*, 22 (August 14, 1880), 126–129: "That every treaty made by the President of the United States with the consent and approval of the Senate, is, *ipso facto*, a supreme law of the land." The same author in a following issue of the same journal (September 11, 1880), 206–210, demonstrates explicitly that this judicial notice extends to treaties with the Indian tribes, quoting, among numerous references, Taney in two decisions on competency, from which the quotation in my text is extracted—C. J. Taney, in Doe *v*. Braden, 16 How., 635; Fellows *v*. Blacksmith, 19 How., 366.
Typical of the stubborn resistance to such clearcut legal opinion and the devious reasoning to get around it was that expressed by Julius H. Seelye, President of Amherst College, in (ironically) his introduction to the first edition of Helen Hunt Jackson's *A Century of Dishonor*: "A difficulty arises in the cases—of which there are many—where treaties have been made by the Government . . . with different Indian tribes, wherein the two parties have agreed to certain definitely named stipulations. Such treaties have proceeded upon the false view—false in principle, and equally false in fact—that an Indian tribe, roaming in the wilderness and living by hunting and plunder, is a nation. In order to be a nation, there must be a people with a code of laws which they practise, and a government which they maintain . . . These Indian tribes are not a nation, and nothing either in their history or their condition could properly invest them with a treaty-making power . . . And yet when exigencies have seemed to require, we have treated them as nations, and have pledged our own national faith in solemn convenant with them. It were the baldest truism to say that this faith and covenant should be fulfilled. Of course it should be fulfilled. It is to our own unspeakable disgrace that we have so often failed therein. But it becomes us wisely and honestly to inquire whether the spirit of these agreements might not be falsified by their letter, and whether, in order to give the Indian his real rights, it may not be necessary to set aside prerogatives to which he might technically and formally lay claim. . . ."
The unhappy authoress, answering (26–27) her eminent introducer: "It is also said, with unanswerable irrelevancy, by some who seek to defend or palliate the United States Government's continuous violation of its treaties with the Indians, that it was, in the first place, absurd to make treaties with them at all, to consider them in any sense as treaty-making powers or nations. The logic of this assertion, made as a justification for the breaking of several hundred treaties, concluded at different times during the last hundred years, and broken as fast as concluded, seems almost equal to that of the celebrated defence in the case of the kettle, which was cracked when it was lent, whole when returned, and in fact, was never borrowed at all. It would be a waste of words to reason with minds that can see in this position any shelter for the United States Government against the accusation of perfidy in its treaty relations with the Indians. . . ."
Professor Seelye, writing the above-mentioned introduction in 1880, states fairly well the attitude among good Christian Americans that brought the Allotment Act into being seven years later. Speaking of efforts already made toward civilizing the savages: "But the Indian would not work, and preferred his wigwam, and skins, and raw flesh, and filth to the cleanliness and conveniences of a civilized home . . ." and he adds that this great civilizing labor "will not be easily nor rapidly done; but all our policy should be shaped toward the gradual loosening of the tribal bond, and the gradual absorption of the Indian families among the masses of our people . . . Very difficult questions demanding very careful treatment arise in reference to just this point . . . They may need a long training before they are wise enough to manage rightfully what is nevertheless rightfully their own. This training, to which their property might fairly contribute means, should assiduously be given in established schools with required attendance. If the results thus indicated shall gradually come to pass, the property now owned by the tribes should be ultimately divided and held in severalty by the individual members of the tribes . . . the Indian himself should, as soon as may be, feel both the incentives and the restraints which an individual ownership of property is fitted to excite. . . ."
And again the unfortunate authoress replies (340–342, at the conclusion of her book): "To assume that it would be easy, or by any one sudden stroke of legislative policy possible, to undo the mischief and hurt of the long past, set the Indian policy of the country right for the future . . . is the blunder of a hasty and uninformed judgment. . . . However great perplexity and difficulty there may be in the details of any and every plan possible for doing at this late day anything like justice to the Indian, however hard it may be for good statesmen and good men to agree upon the things that ought to be done, there certainly is, or ought to be, no perplexity whatever, no difficulty whatever, in agreeing upon certain things that ought not to be done, and which must cease to be done before the first steps can be taken toward righting the wrongs, curing the ills, and wiping out the disgrace to us of the present condition of our Indians. . . . Cheating, robbing, breaking

promises—these three are clearly things which must cease to be done. One more thing, also, and that is the refusal of the protection of the law to the Indian's rights of property, of life, liberty, and the pursuit of happiness.' ..."

428 The quotation is from a report to S. H. Mayes, Cherokee principal chief, from a Cherokee delegation in Washington (S. W. Gray, Roach Young, J. F. Thompson) in 1895, quoted in Angie Debo, *Still the Waters Run.*

429 The government-sponsored survey quoted is Lewis Meriam and Associates, *Problem of Indian Administration* (Baltimore, 1928). Usually called the Meriam Report, the survey was carried out by a private organization at the invitation of the Department of the Interior. The major emphasis of its findings was on the need for education.
The Meriam Report showed what conditions were in the Indian world of the 1920s, but the people themselves are seen in the eleven fat volumes of U. S. Senate, *Hearings . . . on Indian Affairs,* 1929–1934: poignant reading indeed for present-day Indian readers, here are, in hearings held all over the land, their parents and grandparents at what may have been the bottom point in Indian history—everything from Oklahoma oil scandals and brutal Indian-country politics to John Collier, characterized as "a notorious Indian agitator, who is presently trying to destroy . . . the Indian Service" (vol. II, 1542), in the words of a politician's attack on the idealistic reformer who became Commissioner of Indian Affairs under Franklin D. Roosevelt. The hearings furnished information for the writing of the Indian Reorganization Act, one of the authors of the Act being Senator Burton K. Wheeler, a member of the subcommittee conducting the hearings (another principal architect of the IRA was Felix Cohen, using as a foundation his *Powers of Indian Tribes,* published in 1934—see McNickle, *Indian Man,* [cited below, in the Note to p. 595], 167).

430 See Weston La Barre, *The Peyote Cult* (New Haven, 1938); and J. S. Slotkin, *The Peyote Religion* (Glencoe, Ill., 1956).
The Native American Church, incorporated in Oklahoma in 1918, became a national organization in 1944 as the Native American Church of the United States, and in 1955, to include Canada, became the Native American Church of North America.
A pamphlet, *Peyotism and New Mexico* (Santa Fe, 1960—no author listed, but copyright in the name of C. Burton Dustin, Farmington, N.M.), discusses several studies of the peyote conflict at Taos Pueblo in the 1930s (Elsie Clews Parsons, *Taos Pueblo,* Menash, Wis., 1936; H. D. Lasswell, "Collective Autism as a Consequence of Culture Contact," in *Zeitschrift für Sozialforschung,* vol. IV, 1935) to reach the conclusion that "Pan-Indianism usually manifests itself, in the final stages of progressive acculturation, just before complete assimilation takes place. It functions as a final attempt to preserve aboriginal cultural patterns through a sense of intertribal unity" (14).

431 Oliver La Farge is quoted from D'Arcy McNickle, *Indian Man: A Life of Oliver La Farge* (Bloomington, Ind., 1971), 111.
A unique Indian adventure in World War II was that of the "Code-talkers"—a Marine Corps group of Navajos who used the language in radio communication, assertedly "the only unbroken code in military history." See C. Gregory Crampton, ed., *They Talked Navajo/diné bi-zaad choz'-iid: The United States Marine Corps Navajo Code Talkers of World War II,* Duke Indian Oral History Project, University of Utah (Salt Lake City, 1971).

432 The quotation is from Felix S. Cohen, "The Erosion of Indian Rights," in *The Yale Law Journal,* 42/3 (February 1953), 348.
An excellent study evaluating "what the Collier program has produced in the years since 1933" is Henry F. Dobyns, "Therapeutic Experience of Responsible Democracy," in *Midcontinent American Studies Journal,* 6/2 (Fall 1965), 171–186.

433 Announced for publication in 1973, on microfiche with printed indexes, are *The Decisions of the Indian Claims Commission* (New York, 1973); and *The Expert Testimony Before the Indian Claims Commission* (New York, 1973). The latter of these two immense works contains over 100,000 pages of historical, anthropological, geographic, and economic studies dealing with Indian matters.
Pine Ridge statistics are from figures released by the Aberdeen Area Office of the Bureau of Indian Affairs, June 30, 1968, and by the Oglala Sioux tribal office, January 16, 1969; a pamphlet, *Oglala Sioux "Our Resource Direction,"* prepared for a conference on Economic Development at Pine Ridge, May 27 and 28, 1969; a booklet, *Oglala Sioux,* prepared by the Reservation Program Office, Pine Ridge, January, 1969; a presentation, *Industrial Facts/Pine Ridge, South Dakota,* issued by Community Development Department, Consumers Power District, Columbus, Nebraska, February 1968; and a folder on Community Development prepared by John Kirk in 1968 and issued by the tribal office of the Oglala Sioux.

434 The Secretary of the Interior, in a statement issued in June, 1973, listed 488,000 persons "serviced" by the BIA in 478 tribes and groups; seventeen tribes and groups totaling 2,493 persons serviced by state governments; fifty-two tribes and groups totaling 63,866 persons not officially recognized by either federal or state agencies.

435   Recent statistics at this writing (news item, Washington *Post*, December 14, 1972) show steadily improving conditions in Indian health generally–life expectancy at birth rose from sixty years to sixty-four between 1950 and 1970 (that for whites rose from sixty-nine to seventy-one); infant death rate was halved between 1955 and 1970, but infant mortality was still forty per cent higher than for all Americans (in 1955 it was 140 per cent); in the same fifteen years (1955 to 1970) death rate from influenza and pneumonia dropped by 45 per cent, from gastro-intestinal disorders by 56 per cent, from TB by 79 per cent, although the TB death rate for Indians still is 3.8 times that for all Americans.

The quotation is from a superb study of modern reservation life, Sven Liljeblad, "Some Observations on the Fort Hall Indian Reservation," in U. S. Senate, *Hearings . . . on Indian Education*, vol. V, 2299.

See also, for some telling glimpses of postwar reservation life, John Stands in Timber and Margot Liberty (with the assistance of Robert M. Utley), *Cheyenne Memories* (New Haven, Conn., 1967).

436   The scandal concerning misuse of the resources of the Agua Caliente (Palm Springs) Indians was broken by George Ringwald of the Riverside, California, *Press-Enterprise*, who won a Pulitzer in 1968 for his work. A booklet, *The Agua Caliente Indians and Their Guardians*, n.d., including articles and editorials from the series, was subsequently published by the *Press-Enterprise*.

Ed Ainsworth, *Golden Checkerboard* (Palm Desert, California, 1965), foreword by Justice Tom C. Clark of the United States Supreme Court, was a puff-piece for Palm Springs' handling of its Indian affairs and had the bad luck to appear almost on the eve of the exposure of Palm Springs' Indian graft. The book was withdrawn shortly after publication and is now very rare—it contains, inadvertently, valuable insights into the Indian situation in the Palm Springs area.

437   The expert quoted is William N. Fenton, "From Longhouse to Ranch-type House: The Second Housing Revolution of the Seneca Nation," in Elisabeth Tooker, ed., *Proceedings of the 1965 Conference on Iroquois Research: Iroquois Culture, History, and Prehistory* (Albany 1967), 7.

438   Arthur E. Morgan, *Dams and Other Disasters* (Porter Sargent, 1971), discusses the Garrison dam amongst kindred catastrophes.

439   Current literature on the Four Corners pollution problem is sizable and still growing. A recent work emphasizing the fact that the intrusive pollution is not a crime against Indians only but against us all is Suzanne Gordon, *Black Mesa: The Angel of Death* (New York, 1973).

William H. Veeder, 1969, is a comprehensive statement of current problems concerning Indian water. Veeder, one of the country's foremost experts in the esoteric matter of water law, charges "innumerable violations of the surface and ground water rights of the Indians . . ." an "outrageous circumstance"—particularly outrageous since the government is supposedly the protector of Indian resources, and yet, says the Veeder report, Indian communities have been handicapped in defending their possessions by "the lack of legal assistance or outright opposition within the government and without. . . ." (518).

440   The New Mexico authority quoted is Anne M. Smith—see especially her *Indian Education in New Mexico*, Institute for Social Research and Development (University of New Mexico, 1968), 1.

Two papers much quoted in reference to Indian education are Bruce Gaarder, "Education of American Indian Children," an address given at the conference of the Southwest Council of Foreign Language Teachers at El Paso, Texas., in 1967; and the "Coleman Report"—James S. Coleman, *et al.*, *Equality and Educational Opportunity*, United States Office of Health, Education, and Welfare (Washington, 1966).

441   The authority on the Hopi language referred to was the late Benjamin Lee Whorf, see his *Language, Thought, and Reality: Selected Writings . . .*, ed. by John B. Carroll (New York, 1956).

442   Lakota is the language spoken by the Teton Dakota; Nakota the dialect of the Yankton and Assiniboin; Dakota that of the Santee.

The Lakota names are courtesy of personal communication from Clyde D. Dollar, August 7, 1969, then tribal historian for the Rosebud Sioux, with information from Joe Marshall of the Rosebud Reservation.

Grinnell, *The Cheyenne Indians*, vol. I, 107–108, mentions that Northern Cheyenne names were translated and entered in a tribal census in 1887, and that "distortions in translation led to a ruling in 1902 that native language names could be retained unless too long or awkward to spell. By that time, however, the translations with their often ludicrous character were almost everywhere in general use. . . ."

443   Suggestions for a basic reconstruction of Indian education runs through much of the five volumes of testimony and the Report of the Special Subcommittee of the U. S. Senate holding *Hearings . . . on Indian Education*.

Results of a survey of Indian groups regarding a proposal to change Indian education programs from the BIA to the Department of Health, Education, and Welfare are described on page 253, part 1, of these *Hearings*. In the same volume, page 20, Dr. Robert A. Roessel, founder of the Rough Rock Demonstration School and Many Farms Community College in the Navajo country, discusses the "termination" influence in Indian thinking concerning education, an "area of concern" which, in his words, "permeates and contaminates all aspects of Indian education. . . ." Said Dr. Roessel: "Indian people look at almost everything as a move toward or away from State control and a loss of their Federal relationship. This thinking colors Indian action on each and every program."

444 Nancy Oestreich Lurie, "Menominee Termination" in *The Indian Historian*, 4/4 (Winter 1971), 31–46, deals at some depth with Menominee problems following termination.

446 The Senate Committee *Hearings . . . on Constitutional Rights of the American Indian* took as a starting point the basic tenet that Indian tribes in the United States are, in Chief Justice John Marshall's words of 1832, "distinct, independent political communities." A tribe's powers of self-government are therefore not conferred by Congress or the states but may be limited by treaties or applicable State and Federal law. *Summary Report* (Washington, 1966), 1.

Peyotism in New Mexico, cited in the note to page 593 above, relates in some detail the acts of tribal officials in combating the "Peyote Boys" in Taos Pueblo, 10–15, and on the Navajo Reservation, 16–24.

Charges of repressive tribal government were given considerable publicity as a factor in the occupation of Wounded Knee, S.D., by Indian activists and sympathetic non-Indian allies in 1973.

John Stands in Timber, *et al., op. cit.*, mentions the problem of "White Man's Chief" central to tribal difficulties in dealing with whites from the first appearance of Europeans: "There was always confusion between the white people and the Indians on the matter of chiefs. The government always wanted one man who could speak for the tribe, as its leader, and among the Cheyennes there was no such man . . . And the white people grew impatient with this, and tried to set up chiefs of their own in various tribes . . ." (54).

448 The quotation referring to the present-day traditional Cherokee communities is from Albert L. Warhaftig and Robert K. Thomas, "Renaissance and Repression: The Oklahoma Cherokee" in *Trans-action*, 6/4 (February 1969), 42.

News from some of these Cherokee communities has been published in both English and Cherokee in *The Cherokee Report* (Tahlequah, Oklahoma, 1968–1972), by the Original Cherokee Community Organization.

Veeder, 1969, mentions (518) a recent attempt on those Pima waters.

J. A. Jones, "Historic Record Errs; Indians Forced to Fight for Rights," in *The Indian Historian*, 3/1 (Winter 1970), deals briefly with the history of various raids on Pima water over the last century.

NOTES for a Portfolio of American Indian Poetry

General works used in making these selections are Brinton; Spinden, 1933; Densmore, 1926; Garibay, 1954; Sahagun; Brandon, 1971; Leon-Portilla; Kluckhohn, 1945;

and for page

450 The Maya fragment is adapted in collaboration with Dorothy Bones from Maud Makemson, *The Book of the Jaguar Priest* (New York, 1931).

The Mayan incantation is adapted in collaboration with Marcia Kaufman from Ralph Roys, *Ritual of the Bacabs, Mayan Medical Incantations* (Norman, Okla., 1965).

451 The Nahuatl lines are adapted in collaboration with Betty Lou Frost from Sahagun, Book VI, *Rhetoric and Philosophy.*

452 The Cochiti recital is adapted from Ruth Benedict, *Tales of the Cochiti Indians*, BAE Bulletin 98 (Washington, 1931); a note, page 144, says: "Every baby so high knows that story. . . . It is said that the story never tells that Coyote killed the prairie dogs."

453 The Osage benediction is adapted from Francis La Flesche, *A Dictionary of the Osage Language*, BAE Bulletin 109 (Washington, 1932).

The Osage planting song is adapted from a set of songs belonging to the Tho'xe gens of the Osage, songs turning particularly on the woman's final act of planting, tamping down the seeded corn hill with the sacred and fertile imprint of her foot; from Francis La Flesche, "The Osage Tribe: Rite of Vigil," and "The Osage Tribe; Rite of the Chiefs; Sayings of the Ancient Men," in the *39th* and *36th Annual BAE Reports* (Washington, 1925 and 1921).

454 The Pawnee prayer is adapted from Alice C. Fletcher, "The Hako: A Pawnee Ceremony," in the *22d Annual BAE Report* (Washington, 1904).

455 The Iroquois ceremony is adapted from Horatio Hale, *The Iroquois Book of Rites* (Philadelphia, 1883).

456 The Malecite tale is reprinted from William Brandon, ed., *The Magic World* (New York, 1971). Copyright © 1971 by William Brandon. Adapted from Frank G. Speck, "Malecite Tales," in *Journal of American Folk-Lore*, 30 (1917).

457 The Natchez story is adapted from a tale in John R. Swanton, *Myths and Tales of the Southeastern Indians*, BAE Bulletin 88 (Washington, 1929).

459 The Haida lullaby is adapted from John R. Swanton, *Haida Songs*, vol. III of Publications of the American Ethnological Society (Leyden, 1912).
The peyote poem is reprinted from Willaim Brandon, ed., *The Magic World* (New York, 1971). Copyright © 1971 by William Brandon. Adapted from Willard Rhodes, *Music of the American Indian: Kiowa*, Library of Congress, Archives of American Folksong, circa 1955, quoting the description of a "peyote painting" by Monroe Tsa Toke, Kiowa artist, d. 1937.

NOTES for Postface: The Last World

for page

461 Traherne is quoted from Anne Ridler, ed., *Thomas Traherne: Poems, Centuries and Three Thanksgivings* (London 1966); the quotation is from the Third Century of Meditation, 269.

461 The Paris stage hit of 1721 was a comedy by Louis François de Drevetière Delisle, *L'Arlequin Sauvage*.

PRONUNCIATION GUIDE

Ahuitzotl	Ah-weet-zottl
Atahualpa	Atta-wall-pa
Axayacatl	Ah-shah-ya-cattl
Ayllu	Ail-yo
Ce Acatl	Say Ah-cattl
Chichimeca	Chee-chee-may-ka
Cihuacoatl	See-wah-ko-attl
Cuauhtemoc	Kwow-tay-mok
Culhuacan	Cool-wah-cahn
Hopi	Hoe-pee
Huascar	Wass-car
Hueytlatoani	Way-tlah-toe-ah-nee
Huitzilhuitl	Weet-seel-weetl
Huitzilopochtli	Weet-see-lo-poasht-li
Ixtlilxochitl	Eesht-leel-sho-cheetl
Jicarilla	Heeka-reeya
Nez Perce	Nezz-purse
Nezahualcoyotl	Nezza-wall-kee-oatle
Oaxaca	Wah-hock-ah
Papago	Poppa-go
Piegan	Pay-gann
Pima	Pee-ma
Pueblo	Pwebb-low
Quetzalcoatl	Kayt-zal-coe-attl
Tangaxoan	Tahn-gah-sho-ahn
Tenochtitlán	Ten-oash-teet-lahn
Tlacatecuhtli	Tlah-kah-tay-coot-lee
Tlazolteotl	Tlah-zol-tay-ottl
Xicotencatl	Shee-ko-ten-cattl
Xipe	Sheepay
Xiu	Shee-oo
Xochimilco	Sho-chee-meel-coe
Xochitl	Sho-cheetl

Bibliography

Abel, Annie Heloise
"Indian Reservations in Kansas and the Extinguishment of Their Title," in *Kansas State Historical Society, Transactions*, Vol. VIII (Topeka, 1904)

"The History of Events Resulting in Indian Consolidations West of the Mississippi," in *Annual Report of the American Historical Association for the Year 1906*, Vol. I (Washington, 1908)
This is the most important work on the subject of Indian Removal, by the best American historian to work specifically in American Indian history. Her work is sometimes (quite unaccountably) neglected by younger historians writing today.

Alvord, Clarence W.
The Mississippi Valley in British Politics: A Study of the Trade, Land Speculation, and Experiments in Imperialism Culminating in the American Revolution, 2 vols. (Cleveland, 1917)
An essential study of matters much involved in eighteenth-century Indian history. An able later study in the same area is Thomas P. Abernethy, *Western Lands and the American Revolution* (New York, 1937).

"American Indians and American Life," in *The Annals of the American Academy of Political and Social Science*, III, (Philadelphia, 1957)
Containing several articles of key importance, by Oliver La Farge (on termination), Nancy Oestreich Lurie, Ruth Underhill (on religion), D'Arcy McNickle, and others.

American Indian Oral History
The Duke Collection, Western History Center, University of Utah, Vol. I (Salt Lake City, 1968)
Principally taped interviews made circa 1966–1967. Vol. I contains over 200 entries, nearly 3000 pages of typescript.

American Indian Research Project
Oyate Iyechinka Woglakapi: An Oral History Collection, 4 vols., University of South Dakota (Vermillion, 1970–1973)

American State Papers, Documents, Legislative and Executive, 38 vols. (Washington, 1832–1861). Class III, 2 vols., covers Indian Affairs from the 1st to the 19th Congress, 1789–1827

Atkinson, Geoffroy
The Extraordinary Voyage in French Literature before 1700 (New York, 1920)

The Extraordinary Voyage in French Literature from 1700 to 1720 (Paris, 1922)

These works, and Chinard, listed also in this bibliography, are basic to assessing the influence of the American Indian world on European thought and literature.

Bancroft, Hubert Howe
Works, 39 vols. (San Francisco, 1886–1890)
Native Races make up Vols. I to V, published originally 1875–1876. The total of the *Works* present, in Allan Nevins' words, a "tremendous edifice" of Western history, covering Central America, Mexico, Texas, Arizona, New Mexico, California (7 vols., the heart of the matter), Nevada, Colorado, Wyoming, Northwest Coast, Oregon, Washington, Idaho, Montana, British Columbia, Alaska, and various special aspects. Wrote Bernard DeVoto in 1945: "I cannot imagine anyone's writing about the history of the West without constantly referring to Bancroft."

Bandelier, Adolph F. A.
"On the Art of War and Mode of Warfare of the Ancient Mexicans," in *Reports of the Peabody Museum*, Vol. II, 1876–1879 (Cambridge, Mass., 1880), 95–162

"On the Tenure and Distribution of Lands Among the Ancient Mexicans, and the Customs with Respect to Inheritance," *ibid.*, 385–449

"On the Social Organization and Mode of Government of the Ancient Mexicans," *ibid.*, 557–699

And see T. T. Waterman, *Bandelier's Contribution* ...., cited in the Notes (note to p. 118, Chapter IV).

Bassett, John Spencer, ed.
Correspondence of Andrew Jackson, 7 vols. (Washington, 1928–1929), Vols. II, III, and IV cover the Indian Removal period.

Benedict, Ruth
Patterns of Culture (New York, 1934)

Zuñi Mythology, 2 vols., Columbia University Contributions to Anthropology, Vol. XXI (New York, 1936)
Samples of the fine work done by an anthropologist who was really a poet.

Bennett, Wendell C., and Junius B. Bird
Andean Culture History (New York, 1949)

Billington, Ray Allen
Westward Expansion, 3d edition (New York, 1967)
Basic, comprehensive, the standard work on the American frontier.

Birket-Smith, Kaj
The Eskimos, translated from the Danish by W. E. Calvert, edited by C. Daryll Forde, revised edition (London, 1959)

Boas, Franz
"The Central Eskimo," in the *6th Annual BAE Report* (Washington, 1888), 409–675.

Race, Language, and Culture (New York, 1940)
Containing the famous "after-dinner" talk of 1911 (pp. 324–330) that influenced a long generation of anthropological thought.

Bolton, Herbert Eugene
Guide to Materials for the History of the United States in the Principal Archives of Mexico (Washington, 1913)

Athanase de Mezières and the Louisiana–Texas Frontier 1768–1780, 2 vols. (Cleveland, 1914)
Original documents from foreign archives illustrating Spain in the American West.

Coronado, Knight of Pueblo and Plains (New York, 1949)

Bolton, Herbert Eugene, ed.
Anza's California Expeditions, 5 vols. (Berkeley, 1930)

Borah, Woodrow Wilson, and Sherburne Friend Cook
The Aboriginal Population of Central Mexico on the Even of the Spanish Conquest (Berkeley, 1963)

Bourke, John G.
On the Border with Crook (New York, 1891)

Brandon, William, ed.
The Magic World: American Indian Songs and Poems (New York, 1971)
A selection meant to illustrate the literature as literature.

Brebner, John Bartlett
Explorers of North America (New York, 1933)
An excellent overview: you can't tell the explorers, or the explored, without a program.

Bridges, Esteban Lucas
Uttermost Part of the Earth (London, c. 1948; New York, 1950)
Life in Tierra del Fuego to 1910, by a son of a British missionary, born in the country in 1874. The one indispensable book on the Yahgan, the Ona, and their world; and incidentally a splendid glimpse of the British empire from its outermost fringe.

Brinton, Daniel G.
Library of American Aboriginal Literature, 8 vols., including *The Maya Chronicles*; Horatio Hale, *The*

Iroquois Book of Rites; The Comedy-Ballet of Gueguence; Creek Migration Legend; The Lenape and Their Legends; The Annals of the Cakchiquels; Ancient Nahuatl Poetry; Rig Veda Americanus: Sacred Songs of the Ancient Mexicans (Philadelphia, 1882–1890)
> Old but still fine translations, the most important being Horatio Hale's *Iroquois Book of Rites; Ancient Nahuatl Poetry*; and the *Rig Veda Americanus*. The *Comedy-Ballet of Gueguence* is a play from colonial Nicaragua in mixed Spanish and Nahuatl; the Cakchiquel collection is from the Cakchiquel Maya of the Guatemalan highlands. Modern philologists correct Brinton rather severely here and there, but this is no reason for throwing out the whole Brinton "Library"—any more than we would junk the King James version of the Bible on similar grounds.

Brophy, William A., and Sophie D. Aberle
The Indian, America's Unfinished Business. Commission on the Rights, Liberties, and Responsibilities of the American Indian (Norman, Okla., 1966)
> Good background on current problems.

Bureau of American Ethnology, Smithsonian Institution
Annual Reports, 1–48 (Washington, 1881–1933); *Bulletins,* 1 to date (Washington, 1887 to date); *Introductions,* 1–4 (Washington, 1877–1880); *Miscellaneous Publications,* 1–12 (Washington, 1880–1944); *Contributions to North American Ethnology,* Vols. I–IX (Washington, 1877–1893)
> A number of these BAE Reports and Bulletins have been listed separately, but the general BAE index, available in most university libraries, should be consulted in connection with any particular area of study.

Calhoun, James S.
Official Correspondence while Indian Agent at Santa Fe and Superintendent of Indian Affairs in New Mexico, edited by Annie Heloise Abel (Washington, 1915)
> Indian New Mexico, 1849–1851.

Caso, Alfonso
The Aztecs, People of the Sun, translated by Lowell Dunham, illustrated by Miguel Covarrubias (Norman, 1958)
> Something of a landmark study by this writer is "The Religion of the Aztecs," in *Revista Mexicana de Estudios Antropologicos,* 3/1 (Mexico, 1937).

Catlin, George
Letters and Notes on the Manners and Customs and Conditions of the North American Indians, 2 vols. (New York and London, 1844)

Caughey, John Walton, ed.
The Indians of Southern California in 1852, the Benjamin D. Wilson Report and a Selection of Contemporary Comment (San Marino, California, 1952)

Chamberlain, Alexander Francis
"The Contributions of the American Indian to Civilization," in *Proceedings of the American Antiquarian Society* (1905)
> A seminal article, much borrowed from by later writers dealing with Indian influence on modern American culture.

Charlevoix, Pierre F. X. de
Histoire et Description Générale de la Nouvelle France, avec le Journal Historique d'un Voyage fait par Ordre du Roi dans L'Amérique Septentrionnale . . . , 3 vols. (Paris, 1744) English translation by John Gilmary Shea (New York, 1866–1872)
> The first volume covers the period from 1523 to 1690; the second 1684–1690 to 1736; the third, entitled *Lettres . . . adressé a Madame la Duchesse de Lesdiguières . . .* deals with 1720–1722.

Chinard, Gilbert
L'Exotisme Américain dans la Littérature Française au XVIe Siècle . . . (Paris, 1911)

L'Amérique et le Rêve Exotique dans la Littérature Française au XVIIe et au XVIIIe Siècle (Paris, 1913)

Coe, Michael D.
Mexico, Ancient Peoples and Places, No. 29 (Aylesworth and Slough, England, 1962)

The Maya (New York, 1966)

Cohen, Felix S.
   Federal Indian Law (Washington, 1940); the latest edition, revised and updated through 1956 (Wash-ington, 1958)
      A basic reference; many students prefer the earlier edition, prepared by Cohen himself, even though some of its points are now superseded.

Colden, Cadwallader
   The History of the Five Indian Nations of Canada Which are Dependent on the Province of New York in America . . . (New York, 1727, and various later editions; the title listed here is that of the third edition, 2 vols., London, 1755) . . . *and are the Barrier Between the English and French in the part of the World. With Particular Accounts of their Religion, Manners, Customs, etc. . . . In which are Shown, the Great Advantage of Their trade and alliance to the British nation, and the intrigues and attempts of the French to engage them from us; a subject nearly concerning all our american plantations, and highly meriting the attention of the British nation at this junction.*
      A third part of this history, covering the period from 1707 to 1720, is printed for the first time in *The Letters and Papers of Cadwallader Colden* (New York, 1937), Vol. IX, pp. 359–434.

Collier, John
   Indians of the Americas, The Long Hope (New York, 1947)
      An optimistic survey by Franklin D. Roosevelt's Commissioner of Indian Affairs.

Cook, Sherburne Friend
   The Conflict Between the California Indian and White Civilization (Berkeley, 1943)

Cook, Sherburne Friend and Woodrow Wilson Borah
   The Indian Population of Central Mexico, 1531–1610 (Berkeley, 1960)
      And see listing under Borah.

Cotterill, Robert S.
   The Southern Indians: The Story of the Civilized Tribes Before Removal (Norman, 1954)

Coues, Elliott, ed.
   On the Trail of a Spanish Pioneer, The Diary and Itinerary of Francisco Garces, 1775–1776, 2 vols. (New York, 1900)
      A new translation of this journal has been published recently by John Galvin, *A Record of Travels in Arizona and California, 1775–1776* (San Francisco, 1963).

Crook, George
   Autobiography, edited by Martin F. Schmitt (Norman, 1946)

Curtis, Edward S.
   The North American Indian, 15 vols. (New York, 1907–1930)
      The great collection of photographs. Vols. I, II, and XII deal with the Southwest; III, IV, V, and VI with the Plains; VII, VIII, and IX with the Northwest; X and XI with the Northwest Coast; XIII, XIV, and XV with California.

Debo, Angie
   And Still the Waters Run (Princeton, 1940)
      History of the people of the Southeast from Removal to the 1930s.

Densmore, Frances
   The American Indians and Their Music (New York, 1926)
      A general view by the principal collector of native North American music in modern times.

De Rosier, Arthur H.
   The Removal of the Choctaw Indians (Knoxville, Tenn., 1970)
      Splendidly researched, superlative.

Diaz del Castillo, Bernal
   The Discovery and Conquest of Mexico 1517–1521, edited by Genaro Garcia, translated with an introduction and notes by A. P. Maudslay and with an introduction to the American edition by Irving A. Leonard (New York, 1956)
      One of the all-time great adventure stories—and an unequaled look at Aztec Mexico. This edition is available also in paper.

Dockstader, Frederick J.
Indian Art in America: The Arts and Crafts of the North American Indian (Greenwich, Conn., and New York, 1961)

Indian Art in Middle America (New York, 1964)

These are still the best general surveys on American Indian art. (An early work treating American Indian art as art was Oliver La Farge and John Sloan, *Introduction to American Indian Art*, 2 vols., written as a catalogue for the Exposition of Indian Tribal Arts in New York, 1931-1932.)

Driver, Harold E.
Indians of North America, 2d edition (Chicago, 1969)
The best general anthropological survey.

Driver, Harold E., and William C. Massey
Comparative Studies of North American Indians, Transactions of the American Philosophical Society, N.S., 47, Part 2 (Philadelphia, 1957)
Comprehensive, a basic reference.

Dunn, Jacob Piatt
Massacres of the Mountains, A History of the Indian Wars of the Far West (New York, 1886)
The basic reference for its subject; best for the background of most of the military actions considered, with a few exceptions—such as Sand Creek—Reverend Chivington being a personal friend of the author's.

Du Tertre, Jean-Baptiste
Historie General des Isles de S. Christophe, de la Guadeloupe, de la Martinique et autres dans l'Amérique . . . (Paris, 1654)

Historie General des Antille, habités par les Français, divisée en deux tomes et enrichée de cartes et de figures (Paris, 1667; Vols. III and IV were added in 1671)

A picture of the native people of the Caribbean in the seventeenth century, much borrowed from by later authors, among others by Rousseau.

Eggan, Fred, ed.
Social Anthropology of North American Tribes, ed edition, with an introduction by Robert Redfield (Chicago, 1955)
A symposium on system and society among American Indians.

Ewers, John C.
Indian Life on the Upper Missouri (Norman, 1968)

Feder, Norman
American Indian Art (New York, 1971)
A sumptuous picture book but short on text—of which the same author's *Art of the Eastern Plains Indians*, cited in the Notes (note to page 364, Chapter XIV) is such a fine example.

Fenton, William N.
"Factionalism in American Indian Society," from *Actes du IVe CongrèsInternational des Sciences Anthropologiques et Ethnologiques*, Vol. II (Vienna, 1952)
A paper of great interest in political theory.

American Indian and White Relations to 1830, including a bibliography prepared by L. H. Butterfield, Wilcomb E. Washburn, and William N. Fenton (Chapel Hill, 1957)

"The Iroquois in History," a paper prepared for a symposium, "Theory and Method in American Indian Ethnological and Ethnohistorical Research," August 7-14, 1967, under auspices of the Wenner-Gren Foundation.

Foreman, Grant
Indian Removal, The Emigration of the Five Civilized Tribes of Indians (Norman, 1932)

The Five Civilized Tribes (Norman, 1934)
An introductory note by John R. Swanton remarks, "This work and its predecessors are permanent monuments to the virtues and the strivings, the successes and the failures, of the Indian and supply a

record of contacts between Indians and whites with which it will be well for a member of the latter race to make himself familiar even though it contains all too much that he cannot contemplate with racial pride."

Foster, George M.
   Culture and Conquest: America's Spanish Heritage. Viking Fund Publications in Anthropology, No. 27 (New York, 1956)

Garibay K., Angel Maria
   Historia de la Literatura Nahuatl, 2 vols. (Mexico, 1953–1954)
   This work, apparently still untranslated into English, is essential to any serious study of the literature of the Valley of Mexico.

Gates, Paul Wallace
   Fifty Million Acres: Conflicts Over Kansas Land Policy, 1854–1890 (Ithaca, N.Y., 1954; New York, 1966)

Girard, Rafael
   Los Mayas Eternos (Mexico, 1962)

   Los Mayas, Su Civilización—Su Historia—Sus Vinculaciónes Continentales (Mexico, 1966)

Grinnell, George Bird
   The Cheyenne Indians: Their History and Ways of Life, 2 vols. (New Haven, 1923)

   The Fighting Cheyennes (New York, 1915; Norman, 1956)
   War stories, told by the Indian participants.

Hackett, Charles W.
   Revolt of the Pueblo Indians of New Mexico and Otermin's Attempted Reconquest 1680–1682 (Albuquerque, 1942)

Hale, Horatio
   The Iroquois Book of Rites, edited by William N. Fenton (Toronto, 1963)
   Especially instructive to compare with the listing under Brinton.

Hallowell, A. Irving
   "The Impact of the Indian on American Culture," in *The American Anthropologist,* 59/2 (April 1957)

Hammond, George P., and Agapito Rey, editors and translators
   Narratives of the Coronado Expedition 1540–1542 (Albuquerque, 1940)

   Don Juan de O ate, Colonizer of New Mexico 1595–1628, 2 vols. (Albuquerque, 1953)

   Fascinating eye-witness accounts, rich with color and detail, of Southwestern Indians in the sixteenth and seventeenth centuries.

Hanke, Lewis
   The Spanish Struggle for Justice in the Conquest of America (Philadelphia, 1949)

Hodge, Frederick Webb, ed.
   Handbook of American Indians North of Mexico, BAE Bulletin 30, 2 vols. (Washington, 1907–1910; reprinted, New York, 1959)
   A basic reference still, although a new vastly expanded multi-volume edition is on the way.

Holm, Bill
   Northwest Coast Indian Art (Seattle, 1965)
   ". . . the best informed presentday scholar on Kwakiutl ceremonialism"—Audrey Hawthorn, 1967.

Hunt, George T.
   The Wars of the Iroquois, A Study in Intertribal Trade Relations (Madison, Wis., 1940, 1960)

Hyde, George E.
   Red Cloud's Folk; a History of the Oglala Sioux Indians (Norman, 1937)

   Indians of the High Plains from the Prehistoric Period to the Coming of the Europeans (Norman, 1959)

   Life of George Bent; Written from His Letters, edited by Savoie Lottinville (Norman, 1968)

Jackson, Helen Hunt
A Century of Dishonor, A Sketch of the United States Government's Dealings With Some of the Indian Tribes . . . *Preface by H. B. Whipple, Bishop of Minnesota; Introduction by Julius H. Seelye, President of Amherst College. Appendix of XIV items, concluding with An Account of the Numbers, Location, and Social and Industrial Condition of each Important Tribe and Band of Indians within the United States* . . . (New York, 1881, and various subsequent editions; the edition of 1885, published in Boston, contained one additional appendix item, *Report on the Condition and Needs of the Mission Indians of California*, a special report made to the Commissioner of Indian Affairs in 1883 by Helen Hunt Jackson and Abbot Kinney)
For generations this book has been regarded by most American historians as exaggerated and biased. This is, alas, not so.

Jacobs, Wilbur R.
Dispossessing the American Indian (New York, 1972)
Essays dealing with the especially consequential Indian history of Colonial times.

Jacobs, Wilbur R., ed.
Indians of the Southern Colonial Frontier, The Edmond Atkin Report and Plan of 1755 (Columbia, S. C., 1954)

Jenness, Diamond
The Indians of Canada, National Museum of Canada, Bulletin 65, Anthropological Series No. 15, 5th edition (Ottawa, 1960)

Jennings, Jesse D.
Prehistory of North America (New York, 1968)

Jennings, Jesse D., and Edward Norbeck, eds.
Prehistoric Man in the New World (Chicago, 1964)
Papers by Heizer, Reed, Wedel, Wauchope, *et al.*

The Jesuit Relations and Allied Documents, Travel and Explorations of the Jesuit Missionaries in New France 1610–1791, edited by Reuben Gold Thwaites, 73 vols. (Cleveland, 1896–1901)
The introduction states that the *Relations* proper begin with Le Jeune (1632) and follow with forty volumes, all published in Paris, until 1673; a number of later volumes appeared irregularly; private Jesuit journals for 1645–1668 were published in Quebec in 1871; a few Jesuit letters from America appeared in the *Lettres Edifiantes et Curieuses écrité des Missions Etrangères*, 1702–1776. Edna Kenton edited *The Jesuit Relations: Selections* (1925); and *The Indians of North America* (1927), 2 volumes extracted from the *Relations*.

Johnson, Sir William
The Papers of .Sir William Johnson, edited by James Sullivan, *et al.* Prepared for Publication by the Division of Archives and History (Albany, The University of the State of New York, 1921, 1965), 14 vols.

Kappler, Charles J.
Indian Affairs: Laws and Treaties, 3 vols. (Washington, 1904), Vol. II, Treaties.
Kappler was clerk to the Senate Committee on Indian Affairs when he compiled this work. Beginning with the first treaty with the Delawares in 1778, it contains all the treaties and agreements between the Indian tribes and the United States up to the date of compilation.

Kluckhohn, Clyde
"The Personal Document in Anthropological Science," in Gottschalk, *The Use of Personal Documents* (New York, 1945)
Published by the Social Science Research Council, this article contains a list of personal accounts, mainly autobiographies, by American Indians as related to amanuenses, mainly white anthropologists, although a few are personal accounts written by the narrator himself, as the autobiography of Charles A. Eastman. But the best known of these accounts—*Black Elk Speaks; Chief Longlance Buffalo Child; Crashing Thunder*, and the like—are usually written by someone else, and their value, sometimes a very high value indeed, is consequently at the mercy of the amanuensis. It should also be noted that most of these accounts are nineteenth century, in feeling if not in origin. Therefore the considerable influence such accounts exercise on the general public throws the resulting conception of Indian history and literature out of balance.

Kluckhohn, Clyde, and Dorothy Leighton
The Navaho (Boston, 1946; revised edition, New York, 1962)

Kroeber, A. L.
Handbook of the Indians of California, BAE Bulletin 78 (Washington, 1925)
The basic reference for the region.

Anthropology, 2d edition (New York, 1948)

Cultural and Natural Areas of Native North America, University of California Publications in American Archaeology and Ethnology, Vol. XXXVIII (Berkeley, 1939, 1953)

Kubler, George
The Art and Architecture of Ancient America (Baltimore, 1962)

Kurath, Gertrude Prokosch, and Samuel Marti
Dances of Anahuac: The Choreography and Music of Precortesian Dances, Viking Publication No. 39 (1964)
Philosophy, narrative, ideas, ideals, drawn from a study of sculptures and inscriptions as well as from manuscripts and picture-writing.

Lafitau, Joseph François
Moeurs des Sauvages Amériquains, Comparées aux Moeurs des Premiers Temps, 2 vols. (Paris, 1724)

Las Casas, Bartolomé de
Historia de las Indias, edición de Agustin Millares Carlo y estudio preliminar de Lewis Hanke, 3 vols. (Mexico and Buenos Aires, 1951)
The introduction by Professor Hanke runs some seventy-seven pages and is a full account of Las Casas' work. It contains the judgment of his contemporaries and of modern historians—wildly varying then and now—and sums up with the assessment of Las Casas the historian as correct in his broad historical views although frequently in error in facts and details. Various of Las Casas' purely polemical writings, his *Tears of the Indies*, for example, have been translated many times over, but his *History*—one of the most important of early documents, regardless of its controversial points—has yet to be done into English.

Leon-Portilla, Miguel
Pre-Columbian Literatures of Mexico, translated from Spanish by Grace Lobanov and the author (Norman, 1969)
Recent English translations, excellent.

Le Page du Pratz, Antoine S.
Histoire de la Louisiane, 3 vols. (Paris, 1758; London, 1763, 1774)
Along with his superior reporting of events in Natchez, Le Page du Pratz included fanciful geographical information purportedly obtained from Indian travelers, which with some writers has unfortunately placed a cloud over the accuracy of all his work—see Bernard DeVoto, *The Course of Empire* (New York, 1952), pp. 66–68.

Lowie, Robert H.
The Indians of the Plains (New York, 1954)

The Crow Indians (New York, 1956)

MacLeod, William Christie
The American Indian Frontier (New York, 1928)
Multitudes of little errors, but for me a cornerstone work in Indian history, solid in most of its ideas and interpretations and ahead of its time in several.

McKenney, Thomas L., and James Hall
History of the Indian Tribes of North America, 3 vols. (Philadelphia, 1838–1844; and various succeeding editions)
Famous for its portraits of Indian leaders.

McNickle, D'Arcy
They Came Here First, the Epic of the American Indian (Philadelphia, 1949)
Still fine, sound, thoughtful.

Margry, Pierre
Découvertes et Etablissements des Français dans l'ouest et dans le sud de l'Amérique Septentrionale, 1614–1754, 6 vols. (Paris, 1876–1886). Vol. VI, dealing with explorations of the Mississippi and "discovery" of the Rocky Mountains, bears the covering dates 1679–1754.

Martin, Paul S., George I. Quimby, and Donald Collier
Indians Before Columbus, Twenty Thousand Years of North American History Revealed by Archeology
(Chicago, 1947)
An old standard, still very useful.

Mooney, James
"The Ghost Dance Religion and the Sioux Outbreak of 1890," in the *14th Annual BAE Report*, Part 2
(Washington, 1896), 641–1110.
An abridged edition of this famous piece of grand reportage, edited and with an introduction by Anthony F. C. Wallace, has been recently published (Chicago, 1965).

Morgan, Lewis Henry
Systems of Consanguinity and Affinity of the Human Family, Smithsonian Contributions to Knowledge, Vol. XVII (Washington, 1871)

Ancient Society or Researches in the Lines of Human Progress from Savagery Through Barbarism to Civilization (New York, 1877)

Morley, Sylvanus Griswold, and George W. Brainerd
The Ancient Maya, revised 3d edition (Stanford, 1956)

Murdock, George P.
Ethnographic Bibliography of North America, 3d edition, Human Relations Area Files (New Haven, 1960)

National Archives
List of Documents Concerning the Negotiation of Ratified Indian Treaties, 1801–1869, compiled by John H. Martin (Washington, 1949)

Records of the Bureau of Indian Affairs, Record Group 75 (Washington, 1968)
Containing among other things Letters Received and Letters Sent 1800–1823 by the Secretary of War regarding Indian Affairs; Letters Received 1806–1824 and Letters Sent 1807–1823 by the Superintendent of Indian Trade; Special Files of the Office of Indian Affairs, 1807–1904; Letters Received by the Office of Indian Affairs; "Records of Superintendencies of Indian Affairs," including: Michigan, 1814–1851; New Mexico, 1849–1880; Oregon, 1848–1873; Southern, no date; Washington, 1853–1874.

List of National Archives Microfilm Publications (Washington, 1968)
"Since 1940 the National Archives has been microfilming, as a form of publication, selected groups of our Nation's records that have high research value"—from the introduction, page xi. The National Archives' total holdings in 1968 (holdings of all kinds) amounted to about 900,000 cubic feet.

Newberry Library (Chicago)
Dictionary Catalog of the Edward E. Ayer Collection of Americana and American Indians, 8 vols. (Boston, 1961)
Listing of 90,000 items including material on all Indian tribes of the Americas.

Nye, Wilbur S.
Carbine and Lance; The Story of Old Fort Sill (Norman, 1937)
A good example of a voluminous and often historically valuable literature.

Orchard, William C.
Beads and Beadwork of the American Indians, Museum of the American Indian, Heye Foundation (New York, 1929)
Listed here because of its thoroughness and depth, specialized though it be, and as an example of the high quality of these MAIHF publications—a quality sustained through the years (as indicated by a more recent example, Harold L. Peterson, *American Indian Tomahawks*, with an appendix, particularly informative and interesting, on the frontier blacksmith shop, by Milford G. Chandler, MAIHF Contributions, Vol. XIX [New York, 1965]).

Oswalt, Wendell H.
   This Land Was Theirs: A Study of the North American Indian (New York, 1966)
      A fine, perhaps the best, view of the reality of the Indian world, obtained by treating in considerable detail certain groups as representative of larger areas—Chipewyan, Beothuk, and Kuskowagamiut in the North; Tlingit on the Northwest Coast; Fox in the upper Middle West; Pawnee in the Mississippi Valley; Iroquois in the Northeast; Natchez in the Southeast; Hopi in the Southwest; Cahuilla in California.

Parker, Arthur C.
   The Code of Handsome Lake, the Seneca Prophet. New York State Museum Bulletin 163 (Albany, 1913)
      More useful is William N. Fenton, ed., *Parker on the Iroquois: Iroquois Uses of Maize and Other Food Plants; the Code of Handsome Lake, the Seneca Prophet; the Constitution of the Five Nations,* New York State Study Series, Vol. II (Syracuse, 1968).

Parsons, Elsie Clews
   Pueblo Indian Religion, 2 vols. (Chicago, 1939)

Peckham, Howard H.
   Pontiac and the Indian Uprising (Princeton, 1947)

Peterson, Frederick
   Ancient Mexico, An Introduction to the Pre-Hispanic Cultures (New York, 1959)

Pietro Martire d'Anghiera (Peter Martyr)
   De Orbe Novo Decades: The Eight Decades of Peter Martyr d'Anghiera, translated from the Latin with notes and introduction by Francis Augustus McNutt, 2 vols. (New York, 1912)
      Peter Martyr published this work in separate parts, as reports on the New World, from 1511 to 1525; the first English edition, 1587, was dedicated to Sir Walter Raleigh and honored the Queen with the name "Virginia" on its accompanying map. There have been a number of good Spanish editions, the most recent edited by Edmundo O'Gorman (Mexico, 1964); Sauer (1971) prefers the Spanish translation by Joaquin Torres Asensio (Madrid, 1892; Buenos Aires, 1944).

Prescott, William Hickling
   History of the Conquest of Mexico (1843, and various subsequent editions); and *History of the Conquest of Peru* (1847)

Princeton University Library
   American Indian Periodicals in the Princeton University Library (Princeton, N. J., 1970)

The Public Statutes at Large of the United States of America, from the Organization of the Government in 1789 to March, 1931 . . ., 46 vols. (Boston and Washington, 1846–1931)
      Vol. VII (Boston, 1846), edited by Richard Peters, deals with treaties between the United States and the Indian tribes, differing from Kappler, Vol. II, in that changes in the treaties during the process through ratification are shown.

Radin, Paul
   The Trickster: A Study in American Indian Mythology, with Commentaries by Karl Kerenyi and C. G. Jung, introduction by Stanley Diamond (New York, 1973, a new edition in paper)
      The commentaries view the ubiquitous trickster god as an outlet for wild and ribald satire on "the onerous obligations of social order, religion, and ritual."

Richardson, Rupert N.
   The Comanche Barrier to South Plains Settlement (Glendale, 1933)

Roe, Frank Gilbert
   The Indian and the Horse (Norman, 1955)

Rousseau, Jean Jacques
   Discours sur l'Origine et les Fondements de l'Inégalité parmi les Hommes (1755 and numerous later editions)
      Notes to this discourse are included in Vol. II of *Oeuvres* (Amsterdam, 1769).

Royce, Charles C.
   "Indian Land Cessions in the United States," in the *18th Annual BAE Report,* Part 2, introduction by Cyrus Thomas (Washington, 1899), 521–997, with 67 pages of maps

Roys, Ralph L.
The Book of Chilam Balam of Chumayel (Washington, 1933)
Fragments of Mayan literature, compiled in 1782 by Juan José Hoil, a Maya priest. Roys has translated a number of other Chilam Balam collections, among his many authoritative writings on the area.

Russell, Frank
"The Pima Indians," extract from the *26th Annual BAE Report* (Washington, 1908)

Sahagun, Fray Bernardino de
General History of the Things of New Spain (the Florentine Codex), translated by Charles E. Dibble and Arthur J. O. Anderson. In 13 parts, no. 14 of the Monographs of the School of American Research and the Museum of New Mexico (Santa Fe, N. M., 1950 ff.)
The basic work of Aztec—and neighboring—literature, in a magnificent parallel translation with the Nahuatl. The volumes treat of I, the gods; II, the ceremonies; III, origins of the gods; IV, soothsayers; V, omens; VI, rhetoric and moral philosophy; VII, sun, moon, stars, years; VIII, kings; IX, merchants; X, the people; XI, earthly things; and XII, the Spanish conquest.
There are a number of fine Spanish translations for comparison, among them the five-volume edition with an introduction by Wigberto Jiménez Moreno (Mexico, 1938); and the four-volume edition edited by Angel Maria Garibay K. (Mexico, 1956).

Sapir, Edward
Edward Sapir: Culture, Language and Personality, ed. by David G. *Mandelbaum* (Berkeley, 1964)

Sauer, Carl Ortwin
Land and Life, edited by John Leighly (Berkeley, 1963)
A selection from his writings, the latest of which—and one of the most interesting—is *Sixteenth Century North America, The Land and the People as Seen by the Europeans* (Berkeley, 1971).

Schoolcraft, Henry Rowe
Historical and Statistical Information, Respecting the History, Condition and Prospects of the Indian Tribes of the United States, 6 vols. (Philadelphia, 1851–1857)

Shiels, W. Eugene
King and Church, The Rise and Fall of the Patronato Real (Chicago, 1961)
Matters of some moment to early colonial Indian history.

Speeches on the Passage of the Bill for the Removal of the Indians, Delivered in the Congress of the United States, April and May, 1830 (Boston, 1830)
Published by anti-Removal forces. Compare speeches of the period in Thomas H. Benton, *Abridgement of the Debates of Congress from 1789 to 1856 . . .*, 16 vols. (New York, 1857–1861), of which Vols. X (1828–1830) and XI (1830–1832) cover the period of debate over Removal.

Spencer, Robert F.
The North Alaskan Eskimo, BAE Bulletin 171 (Washington, 1959)

Spencer, Robert F., Jesse D. Jennings, *et al.*
The Native Americans, Prehistory and Ethnology of the North American Indians (New York, 1965)

Spicer, Edward H.
Cycles of Conquest, Indians of the Southwest 1533–1960 (Tucson, Arizona, 1962)

Spinden, Herbert J.
The Reduction of Mayan Dates, Papers of the Peabody Museum of American Archaeology and Ethnology, Harvard University, Vol. VI, No. 4 (Cambridge, Mass., 1924)

Ancient Civilizations of Mexico and Central America, American Museum of Natural History Handbook Series, No. 3, 3d edition (New York, 1928)

Stevenson, Matilda Coxe
"The Zuñi Indians: Their Mythology, Esoteric Fraternities, and Ceremonies," in the *23rd Annual BAE Report* (Washington, 1904), 3–608.

Steward, Julian Haynes, ed.
Handbook of South American Indians, BAE Bulletin 143, 7 vols. (Washington, 1946–1959)
The basic reference for South America. The original plan to publish four volumes dealing with four

principal culture areas was expanded to six volumes plus an index published as Vol. VII. Vol. I deals with the so-called marginal groups of Tierra del Fuego, Patagonia, the Pampas and Gran Chaco, and eastern Brazil; II, the great Andean civilizations; III, people of the tropical forests and adjacent savannah country; IV, the circum-Caribbean peoples; V is devoted largely to comparative ethnology; VI to physical anthropology and linguistics.·

Swanton, John R.
The Indians of the Southeastern United States, BAE Bulletin 137 (Washington, 1946)

The Indian Tribes of North America, BAE Bulletin 145 (Washington, 1953)
The basic reference for location, past and present, of the native peoples of the United States and Canada, and with a listing of the tribes of Mexico and Central America. Constantly useful, although the source of the information given is not usually indicated, raising occasional problems.

Thomas, Alfred Barnaby
After Coronado, 1696–1722 (Norman, 1935)

The Plains Indians and New Mexico, 1751–1778; a Collection of Documents Illustrative of the History of the Eastern Frontier of New Mexico (Albuquerque, 1940)

Thompson, J. Eric S.
Maya Archaeologist (Norman, 1963)
One of the great figures in Mayan studies, writing of field work—illustrated with drawings by Jean Charlot, a French artist associated with the Mexican muralists and author of one of the best books on this movement, *The Mexican Mural Renaissance* (New Haven, 1963).

Maya History and Religion (Norman, 1970)
A collection of pieces not always entirely cohesive, but summing up an immense body of important work.

Tozzer, Alfred M.
Landa's Relación de las Cosas de Yucatan, Papers of the Peabody Museum of American Archaeology and Ethnology, Vol. XVIII (Cambridge, Mass., 1941)

Underhill, Ruth Murray
Red Man's America, revised edition (Chicago, 1971)
Solid information on the native peoples of the United States area, by a veteran ethnologist.

United States Bureau of Indian Affairs
Annual Reports of the Commissioner of Indian Affairs to the Secretary of the Interior, 60 vols., title varies (Washington, 1839–1925)

United States Department of the Interior
Biographical and Historical Index of American Indians and Persons Involved in Indian Affairs, 8 vols. (Boston, 1966)
Arranged by subject.

United States Congress
Present Relations of the Federal Government to the American Indian, Committee Documents and Information Relating to . . . the Bureau of Indian Affairs . . . Indian Claims . . . State Expenditures for Indian Welfare and the History of Welfare Activities on Each Reservation, Indian Voting, Tribal Assets and Liabilities, Attorney Services Available to Indian Tribes, Organizations Interested in Indian Affairs. 85th Congress, 2d Session, House Committee Print No. 38, Printed for the use of the Committee on Interior and Insular Affairs (Washington, 1959)

United States Senate
Constitutional Rights of the American Indian, Summary Report of Hearings and Investigations by the Subcommittee on Constitutional Rights of the Committee on the Judiciary, U. S. Senate, 88th Congress, 2d Session, and 89th Congress, 2d Session (Washington, 1964 and 1966)

Indian Education, Hearings before the Special Subcommittee on Indian Education of the Committee on Labor and Public Welfare, U. S. Senate, 90th Congress, 1st and 2d Sessions, 5 vols. and a Summary Report (Washington, 1969)

Vaillant, George C.
The Aztecs of Mexico: Origin, Rise, and Fall of the Aztec Nation (New York, 1944; revised edition in paper, 1950; revised edition annotated by Suzannah B. Vaillant, 1962)

Veeder, William H.
"Federal Encroachment on Indian Water Rights and the Impairment of Reservation Development," in *Toward Economic Development for Native American Communities, a Compendium of Papers Submitted to the Subcommittee on Economy in Government of the Joint Economic Committee*, 91st Congress, 1st Session (Washington, 1969), Vol. II, Part 2
    An authoritative document on urgent current problems.

Wallace, Anthony F. C.
The Death and Rebirth of the Seneca (New York, 1970)
Ethnohistory at its best.

Washburn, Wilcomb E.
Red Man's Land/White Man's Law: A Study of the Past and Present Status of the American Indian (New York, 1971)

Wauchope, Robert, general ed.
Handbook of Middle American Indians, Vols. I–XI (Austin, Tex., 1964–1971)
    A basic reference for the region, similar in scope to the Handbook of South American Indians, with perhaps more emphasis, the matter of Vols. II, III, and IV, on archaeological problems.

Wedel, Waldo R.
An Introduction to Kansas Archaeology, BAE Bulletin 174 (Washington, 1959)
    See also, among his numerous other works, *Prehistoric Man on the Great Plains* (Norman, 1961)

Wildschut, William
Crow Indian Medicine Bundles, edited by John C. Ewers, MAIHF (New York, 1960)
    A splendid work, by two first-rate specialists, much broader than the narrow subject might seem to indicate.

Willey, Gordon R.
An Introduction to American Archaeology, 2 vols. (Englewood Cliffs, N. J., 1966 and 1971)
    Vol. I, North and Middle America; II, South America.

Wolf, Eric R.
Sons of the Shaking Earth (Chicago, 1959)

Wormington, Hannah Marie
Ancient Man in North America, Denver Museum of Natural History Popular Series No. 4, 4th edition (Denver, 1957)

Wraxall, Peter
An Abridgement of the Indian Affairs . . . Transacted in the Colony of New York from the Year 1678 to the Year 1751, edited by Charles H. McIlwain (Cambridge, Mass., 1915)
    An interesting collection of primary historical materials for the years covered, and also noteworthy for the introduction by C. H. McIlwain, which George T. Hunt once wrote of as the "best historical writing yet done (1940) on the Iroquois."

Wyman, Leland C., and Clyde Kluckhohn
Navaho Classification of Their Songs and Ceremonials, Memoirs of the American Anthropological Association, No. 50 (1938)

Young, Mary Elizabeth
Redskins, Ruffleshirts, and Rednecks, Indian Allotments in Alabama and Mississippi, 1830–1860 (Norman, 1961)
    Beautifully researched, a basic book for the subject.

Index